William Edward Hartpole Lecky

A History of England in the Eighteenth Century

Volume VII.

William Edward Hartpole Lecky

A History of England in the Eighteenth Century
Volume VII.

ISBN/EAN: 9783742846617

Manufactured in Europe, USA, Canada, Australia, Japa

Cover: Foto ©ninafisch / pixelio.de

Manufactured and distributed by brebook publishing software (www.brebook.com)

William Edward Hartpole Lecky

A History of England in the Eighteenth Century

A
HISTORY OF ENGLAND

IN THE

EIGHTEENTH CENTURY

BY

WILLIAM EDWARD HARTPOLE LECKY

VOLUME VII.

SECOND EDITION

LONDON
LONGMANS, GREEN, AND CO.
1890

PRINTED BY
SPOTTISWOODE AND CO., NEW-STREET SQUARE
LONDON

PREFACE
TO THE
SEVENTH AND EIGHTH VOLUMES.

I STATED in my last volume that the outbreak of the great French War in 1793 appeared to me the best and most natural termination of a History of England in the eighteenth century, and that it was not my intention to carry the English portion of my narrative beyond this limit. For the Irish portion, however, a different limit must be assigned, and in order to give it any completeness or unity, it is necessary to describe the rebellion of 1798, the legislative Union of 1800, and the defeat or abandonment of the great measures of Catholic conciliation which Pitt had intended to be the immediate sequel of the Union. I had hoped to do this in the compass of a single moderate volume, but a more careful examination has convinced me that, in order to do justice to this eventful period of Irish history, it is necessary to treat it on a larger scale. It is a period which has been very imperfectly written, and usually under the influence of the most furious partisanship. There is hardly a page of it which is not darkened by the most violently contradictory statements. It is marked by obscure agrarian and social changes, by sudden, and sometimes very perplexing, alterations in the popular sentiment, which can only be elucidated and proved by copious illustration. It is also a period of great crimes and of great horrors, and the task of tracing their true causes, and measuring with accuracy and impartiality the different degrees of provocation, aggravation, palliation, and comparative guilt, is an extremely difficult one.

In order to accomplish it with any success, it is necessary

to bring together a much larger array of original evidence, drawn from the opposite camps, than would be required in dealing with a history of which the outlines, at least, were well established and generally admitted. This is especially necessary, as our judgments must be, in a great degree, formed from manuscript materials which are not easily accessible, and as many of these manuscripts are the letters of men who, though they have all the authority of eyewitnesses, often wrote under the influence of panic or strong party passion. It is only by collecting and comparing many letters, written by men of different opinions and scattered over wide areas, that it is possible to form a true estimate of the condition of the country, and to pronounce with real confidence between opposing statements. Such a method of inquiry tends greatly to lengthen a book and to impair its symmetry and its artistic charm; but in the particular period with which I am now concerned, it is, I believe, the one method of arriving at truth; it brings the reader in direct contact with the original materials of Irish history, and it enables him to draw his own conclusions very independently of the historian.

In these, as in the preceding volumes, I have made much use of the correspondence between the English and Irish Governments that exists in the Record Office in London, and I have derived some side-lights from the papers in the French Foreign Office, which have been kindly opened to my inspection. Several other manuscript sources have been of use to me. By far the most important is a vast collection of papers in Dublin Castle, ranging from 1795 to 1805, which, through the kindness of Sir Bernard Burke, I have been enabled to spend many weeks in exploring. For more than sixty years these papers were deposited in two very large cases in the Birmingham Tower, carefully fastened down with the Government seal, and with the inscription, 'Secret and confidential; not to be opened.' They remained in this state until after the passing of the Records (Ireland) Act, in 1867, when it was thought desirable to open these cases, and to classify their contents. The work occupied some years, but it was at last accomplished, and the whole collection is now excellently arranged, in no less than sixty-eight boxes. A great proportion of it is of little or no historical value, but it contains, among other things, numerous letters from informers, written during the progress of the United Irish conspiracy, and during and after the rebellion, and also a large and exceedingly interesting series of letters from magistrates and Government officials in different parts of Ireland, describing in detail the state of the country. These letters have the same kind of value as the *cahiers*, describing the state of France on the eve of the Revolution, from which, since the days of Tocqueville, the best French historians have derived some of their most valuable materials. Occasionally, too, amid this great mass of serious, formal, and depressing documents, there may be found others of a very different character, which were seized among the papers of the conspirators, and which have sometimes a strangely pathetic interest. There are love-letters and rude poems; passionate expressions of youthful friendships; note-books in which eager scholars described their studies or recorded their passing thoughts; day-dreams of young and ardent natures, too often destined to end in exile or the gallows.

Another source from which I have derived much information has been the Pelham Papers, which have recently been deposited in the British Museum. Pelham was Irish Secretary from March 1795 to November 1798. His long and frequent visits to England while he was in office, made his correspondence unusually copious; and when he ceased to be Irish Secretary he still continued to correspond with leading persons in Ireland. The British Museum also possesses an interesting series of letters written by Percy, Bishop of Dromore—the well-known author of the 'Reliques of Ancient English Poetry'—to his wife, during the rebellion, and during the debates on the Union.

It remains for me to express my gratitude for some private collections of papers which have been opened to me. Lady Bunbury has kindly placed in my hands a very interesting correspondence of Lady Louisa Conolly and her friends; and Lord Colchester, the whole correspondence of Abbot, who was Chief Secretary to the Lord Lieutenant during the Administration of Addington. To Lady Louisa Fortescue I am indebted for permission to read the correspondence of Lord Grenville at

Dropmore, and to Lord George Hamilton for some curious papers describing the different interests and connections in the Irish Parliament.

It will be objected, that the addition of two long volumes to the large amount of Irish history already contained in this book has completely destroyed the proportion of my work. It must, however, be remembered, that the present volumes form in reality a supplementary history, dealing with Irish affairs during eight eventful years which are not comprised in my English narrative. The sketch of Irish history which has been given in the preceding volumes would be imperfect and, perhaps, even misleading, if it were not continued to the close of the Irish Parliament and to the resignation of Pitt, in March 1801. But if the fiercely contested events of those last years are related at all, it is very desirable that they should be related in a manner that may, if possible, raise them above the distorting atmosphere of party strife, and place the reader in a position to judge them in all their aspects. There is a method of dealing with historical facts which has been happily compared to that of a child with his box of letters, who picks out and arranges those letters, and those only, which will spell the words on which he has previously determined, leaving all others untouched. In Irish history this method has been abundantly practised, and among the many crimes and errors that have been committed by all parties, it is not difficult to select on either side the materials of a very effective party narrative. I have endeavoured to write this History in a different spirit. Perhaps another generation may be more capable than the present one, of judging how far I have succeeded.

LONDON: *July* 1890.

CONTENTS

OF

THE SEVENTH VOLUME.

CHAPTER XXVI.

	PAGE
Contrast between the sentiments of Parliament and of the country in 1793	1
Irish overtures to France—Mission of Oswald	2
Preparations for rebellion	3
Leading United Irishmen chiefly Protestants	4
Changes in the Catholic body.—Rise of a Catholic seditious party	5
McKenna on the state of Ireland	6
Character, objects, and proceedings of the Dublin Committee	8
Exile of Tandy.—Imprisonment of Rowan	9
The arming of the people discussed in the Dublin Committee	10
First results of the Relief Act of 1793	10

Defenderism

Its early history and growth	11
Strengthened by the Militia Act	14
Its purely Catholic character	16
Opinion of Westmorland.—Report of the Lords Committee	17
At first distinct from and hostile to the United Irish movement	19
Attempts of United Irishmen to suppress religious dissension	19
Defenderism at first not political.—French influence	20
Popular sympathy for France	21
The country more peaceful.—FitzGibbon made Viscount	21
Quiet of Ireland in 1794.—Grattan supports the war	22
Protest of Parsons	24
Proposed commercial treaty.—Ponsonby's Reform Bill.—Attitude of Grattan	25
Close of the Session.—Reports of an informer	26
Mission of Jackson	27
His arrest	28
Escape of Rowan—Growth of disloyalty	29
Decline of the influence of Grattan	31

The Fitzwilliam Episode

	PAGE
Whig secession in 1794	32
Ministerial changes—the direction of Ireland	33
Fitzwilliam designated as future Viceroy	35
Rising hopes of the Catholics	36
Fitzwilliam communicates with Thomas Grenville and Grattan	37
Grattan refuses office.—Negotiations in England	38
The time of the appointment of Fitzwilliam and the extent of his powers disputed	40
Opinion of Burke	45
Probable motives of Pitt	48
Dispute settled.—Appointment of Fitzwilliam.—His instructions	50
The Catholics determine to bring forward their claims	52
Fitzwilliam desires to yield—proposes a yeomanry	54
Announces his intention to accept the Catholic Bill	56
Dismissal of Hamilton and Cooke	57
And of Beresford	58
Anger of the Castle Party	60
Alarming state of Europe.—Parliament meets	62
Grattan moves the Address	63
Recognition of Irish prosperity	64
Extraordinary supplies voted.—Fitzwilliam urges the necessity of Emancipation	65
Strength of the Irish opinion in favour of it	68
Conduct of the English Ministers—Progress of the dispute	70
Last remonstrance of Fitzwilliam	75
Fitzwilliam ordered to stop the Catholic Bill	78
Review of his conduct about it	79
His recall.—Inquiry into its motives	80
Fitzgibbon argues that the King could not assent to Emancipation	84
Memorandum of the King against it	85
Memorandum of the Ministers	86
Memorandum of Fitzgibbon	88
Alarm in Ireland when the recall was announced	90
Speech of Parsons	91
Parliament votes its thanks to Fitzwilliam	93
Camden appointed Lord Lieutenant, and Pelham Secretary	93
State of the country.—Great Catholic meeting in Dublin	94
Departure of Fitzwilliam	96
Effects of his recall	97

CHAPTER XXVII.

Camden arrives March 31, 1795.—Riot in Dublin	99
Replies of Grattan to addresses	100
English Ministers stimulate the anti-Catholic feeling	101
Instructions to Camden	101
Portland on Fitzgibbon's letters to the King	103
Pitt's forebodings.—Letter of Windham	104
Dangerous state of the country	105
Meeting of Parliament (April 13).—Speech of Grattan	105
Debate on the second reading of the Catholic Bill	108

	PAGE
Defeated by 155 to 84.—Effect on Irish history	115
Fitzgibbon made Earl of Clare	116

Maynooth

Foreign education of the priesthood	117
Views of Hutchinson and Burke	118
Project of a Catholic college connected with Dublin University	119
Petition of the Catholic bishops in 1794	120
Correspondence of Burke and Grattan on the subject	120
Wolfe Tone's prediction of the effect of home education on the priests	121
Character of the Irish priests before Maynooth	122
Improvement under George III.—Patronage exercised by laymen	124
Government of the Church	124
Decline of clerical influence	125
Foundation and object of Maynooth	126
Magee's evidence relating to it	127
Petition of Catholics against its sectarian character	128
Burke's dislike to the Maynooth scheme	129
His letter shown to the Government	131
Letter of Burke on the Jacobin tendencies appearing among the Catholics	132
Confidential letter of the Duke of Richmond advocating an Union	134
Trial and suicide of William Jackson	136
Wolfe Tone sails for America	137
Leonard McNally—his career and treason	138
His picture of the state of Irish opinion	143
Reconstruction of United Irish Society—its organisation	144
A conference of the parliamentary Opposition	145
Rapid spread of Defenderism—its character and effects	146
Lawrence O'Connor	151

Agrarian system of Ireland

Tenure of land after the revolution.—The Timber Acts	152
The middleman	153
Causes that aggravated the competition for land in Ireland	155
Between the completion of the Penal Code and the accession of George III. the changes chiefly economical	157
After that date powerful political causes come into play	157
The Irish rental	158
Rapid rise in rents.—Canting	160
Subdivision of land—its causes	163
Modern parallels	165
Extreme poverty in parts of Ireland	167
Influence of landlords—its history and decline	169
The deportation of suspected Defenders	172

Rise of Orangism

Disputes of Peep of Day Boys and Defenders	174
Jackson's charity	174
Mutilation of Berkeley and his wife	176

	PAGE
The battle of the Diamond (Sept. 21)	177
Foundation and objects of the Orange Society—its precursors	177
Early celebrations of the revolution	178
Persecution of Catholics in Ulster—resolutions and letters of northern magistrates	179
Growth of religious animosity	187
The Ulster refugees in Connaught	188
Agrarian aspects of the Orange disturbances	191
Summary of their extent	192
They counteracted the United Irish policy of combining Catholics and Presbyterians	192
But contributed largely to the disaffection of the Catholics	193
Camden's judgment of them—the pretended Orange oath of extermination	194
Use made of Orangism by the United Irishmen	195

Parliamentary proceedings—Spring of 1796

Indemnity Act.—Demand for free trade with England	195
Insurrection Act	196
Attitude of Grattan	197
New Orange disturbances	199
Crimes connected with the United Irish and Defender movements	201
Intelligence of an intended invasion	201
Spread of disaffection among the Catholics	202

Parliamentary proceedings, Oct. and Nov. 1796

Suspension of the Habeas Corpus Act.—Speech of Grattan	203
Catholic Emancipation introduced for the last time in the Irish Parliament	205
Other measures of the session	206
Extreme anarchy in the country	206
Different classes concerned in it	208
Letters of McCarry	209
Francis Higgins	210
Enrolment of the yeomanry—their character	213
Potato diggings in Ulster	215
Alarming state of a great part of Ireland	216
Political assassinations	222
Junction of United Irishmen and Defenders	223
O'Connor, Emmet, and McNevin join the society—its military organisation	224
Letter of O'Connor to Fox	225
Organisation and strength of the United Irishmen	226
English and Irish Governments differ about the Insurrection Act	227
State of Ulster at the end of 1796	228

Influence of foreign affairs on Ireland

Condition of Europe	229
Failure of Lord Malmesbury's negotiation at Paris	231

	PAGE
Proceedings of Wolfe Tone in America	231
Undertakes a mission to France.—Report of De la Croix	233
Tone's memoir to the French Government	234
Mission of Fitzgerald and O'Connor to Hamburg	236
Arrival of Tone in France—his journals	238
Character of Tone's patriotism	241
His representations of the prospects of invasion	242
The Irish in the British navy	246
Mission of O'Shea to Ireland	249
French desire that rebellion should precede invasion	250
Hoche's expedition	252
Small number of naturalised Irishmen in it.—Later history of the Irish Brigade	253
French expedition sails Dec. 15	255
Arrives at Bantry Bay	256
Preparations to meet it	258
The great storm	259
Departure of the fleet	263
Conduct of the people	266
Concluding remarks	270

CHAPTER XXVIII.

Superficial character of much Irish disloyalty	272
Probability that Ireland would for a time have been lost if Hoche had landed	273
Increased loyalty.—Dr. Hamilton	274
Meeting of Parliament (Jan. 16).—First debates	275
Absentee tax proposed and rejected	277
Bank of Ireland suspends cash payments	278

Disturbances in the North

Their general character	278
State of Donegal and Roscommon	279
Tyrone and Donegal—Murder of Hamilton	280
Derry	281
Armagh.—Letters of McNally	282
Grattan's proposed volunteers	284
Lake ordered to disarm the North	285
His proclamation	286
Opposition of Grattan	288
Fox, with Grattan's assent, brings the state of Ireland before the British Parliament	289
The necessity of conciliating the Catholics urged	291
Determination of the Government to refuse.—The King's message to Camden	293
Ireland considered in a state of rebellion.—Seizure of arms	294
Dean Warburton's letters from Armagh	295
Letters from other parts of Ulster	296
Military force in Ireland.—Difficulties of disarming	299

	PAGE
Situation and sentiments of the yeomanry	301
Military outrages inevitable	302
The Ancient Britons near Newry	303
Other military outrages.—Lord Moira's speech	305
Rebels sent to the fleet	307
Transformation of Orangism.—It becomes the chief counterpoise to the United Irishmen	308
Lake on the methods that should be employed in Ulster	310
Correspondence of General Knox with Pelham	311
Dissatisfaction of the Government with the Ulster gentry	318
Attitude and wishes of the gentry	319
Addresses in favour of reform	320
Possibility that reform might have prevented rebellion	321
The Irish Government consider that it would be useless	322
Their estimate of the parties in Ireland	323
Their opposition to Catholic emancipation—Ponsonby's reform resolutions	324
Grattan's last speech on reform	325
His secession from Parliament.—Debates no longer published at length	328
Grattan's conduct and position in 1797	329
He acknowledges the failure of parliamentary government in Ireland	330
Disaffection among the troops.—Orangemen, Archbishop Troy and other priests suspected	331
Arrest of O'Connor &c.—The 'Northern Star' stopped.—Newell's information	332
Alleged complicity of the United Irishmen with assassination	333
The Union Star.—Cox's confessions	336
Improvement in Ulster.—Proclamation of May 17—many captures	338
Command of Ireland and Viceroyalty offered to Lord Cornwallis	339
Refused on account of his views on the Catholic question.—Offer repeated	340
Revival of Orange outrages	340
Flight of the Catholics	341

The Disarming

Lord Blayney's severities—events in Westmeath	343
At Multifarnham and Charleville	344
State of Tyrone and Dungarvan &c.	345
Evidence of increase of the religious hatreds in the North	347
Green and Orange badges—Religious riots	348
Distrust of the militia.—Success of the disarming in Ulster	349
The September Assizes	350
The case of William Orr	352
Examination of the degree of responsibility of the Government in producing the rebellion	361
Spread of sedition to Catholic Ireland—its first centres	364

fluences that acted on the Catholic masses

Catholic emancipation and parliamentary reform had little part	365
The tithe question	365

THE SEVENTH VOLUME.

	PAGE
The question of rent	366
The revived sentiment of nationality	367
Comparison between 1641 and 1797.—Prophecies of Columkill	368
Fear of Orange massacres.—The pretended Orange oath	369
Defenderism in the King's County	370
Carlow, Kilkenny, Kildare, Wexford, and Wicklow tainted	371
Political opposition of Kildare gentry	372
Pollock's report of the condition of the central counties	373
Illustrations of the panic about the Orangemen	373
Troubles near Dublin.—State of Tipperary	374
Cork and Bandon	375
Mallow.—Reports about the Methodists	376
Appalling spread of crime	377
Connaught less tainted than the other provinces—Sligo—Ennis—Mayo	379
General state of Ireland	380
New hope of foreign assistance—Mission of Lewins	381
Dutch fleet in the Texel—Mission of Jagerhorn	383
Mission and memoir of McNevin	384

Negotiations at Lille

Vicissitudes of the war in 1796, 1797	386
Preliminaries of Loeben	387
Pitt offers to negotiate.—The plenipotentiaries at Lille	387
Pitt's ardent desire for peace	388
Majority of the Directory hostile to peace.—Their demands	390
Secret understanding between Lord Malmesbury and Maret	390
Double object of Pitt	392
Peace signed between Portugal and France.—Indignation of Grenville	393
Possibility of corrupting the Directors	394
Revolution of 18 fructidor	394
Lord Malmesbury ordered (September 16) to quit France	395
Lingering hopes of peace dispelled	396
Proofs that Irish interests had no real place in French diplomacy	397
Parallel from the history of the Irish Brigade	398
Death of Burke	398
Renewed French negotiations in Ireland. Channels of information of the Government	399

Disaffection in the Fleet

Mutiny at Spithead	403
Mutiny of the Nore	404
Its suppression.—The 'Hermione'	405
Restoration of the tone of the navy. The British sailor	406
The Dutch fleet in the Texel	407
Long-continued adverse winds	408
Reports received from Ireland	409
Probable effects of the invasion.—Postponement of the expedition	410
Battle of Camperdown	411

CONTENTS OF THE SEVENTH VOLUME.

	PAGE
Death of Hoche. Indifference of Buonaparte to Irish affairs	412
Dissolution of the Irish Parliament	412
Honours conferred.—The Kenmare peerage	413
Election of the last Irish Parliament	416
Grattan's 'Letter to the Citizens of Dublin'	416
State of Ireland at the end of 1797.—Pelham's estimate	421
Clare's estimate of the situation.—Expectations of invasion	422
Alarming reports from McNally	423
Establishment of 'The Press'	424
Abercromby made Commander-in-Chief	425
His estimate of the state of Ireland	426
Attempts to restore discipline and legality	428
The general orders, February 26, 1798	430
Cabal against Abercromby	432
His resignation and letters	433
His expedition through Leinster and Munster.—Martial law	436
Lake made Commander-in-Chief	438
Abercromby on the prospects of Ireland	439
Concession to Catholics refused.—Higgins pleads their cause	439
Letter from the Bishop of Derry	440
Meeting of Parliament, January 9.—Speech of Parsons	442
Acts of military violence	443
The Opposition.—Plunket	445
The absentee tax	447
Calm in Ulster	448
Anarchy and growing sedition in the other provinces	449
Letters of Beresford	452
Change of sentiment among the gentry	453
Knox's correspondence with Bell	454
Rapid growth of religious animosity	455
The Spring Assizes, 1798	456
The trials at Maryborough	458
No resolution yet taken in England about the introduction of an Union Bill	459
English ministerial policy towards Ireland—favourable to the Catholics	460
Close connection between England and Rome.—Lord Hood's fleet &c.	461
Burke desires diplomatic connection with the Vatican	461
Hippisley and Erskine	462
Signs of friendly feeling between the Vatican and the Court of St. James	463
Views of Camden	464
Conclusion	465

HISTORY OF ENGLAND

IN

THE EIGHTEENTH CENTURY.

CHAPTER XXVI.

IN the concluding chapter of the last volume I noticed the remarkable contrast which was presented between the attitude of the Irish Parliament in the spring and summer of 1793 and the general condition of the country. In Parliament the Government, at the outbreak of the great French war, was supported with an almost absolute unanimity. Grattan had declared in the strongest terms that it was both the duty and the interest of Ireland to give England an unequivocal support, and all the important measures of this memorable session for the purpose of maintaining the war, of repressing sedition and insurrection, and of relieving the Catholics from their disabilities, were either carried without a division or by overwhelming majorities. But in the meantime, throughout the country, sedition and anarchy were rapidly spreading. Demonstrations in favour of France and in opposition to the war were constantly multiplying. An extremely seditious press had arisen, and Paine's writings were profusely distributed. Clubs of United Irishmen were formed in numerous counties, and were actively engaged in democratic and revolutionary propagandism. The Defender movement was assuming a new character and a new importance, and efforts were made in the towns to enroll national guards modelled after those of France.

The relations between discontented Irishmen and French agents were becoming very frequent, and from this time Irish affairs began to occupy a prominent place in the archives of the French Ministry of Foreign Affairs. There is reason to believe that one at least of the Catholic delegates who came to London in December 1792 to present to the King the petition of the Catholic Convention had on that occasion a secret interview with Chauvelin, who does not, however, appear to have given much encouragement.[1] Nearly at the same time Lord Edward Fitzgerald came to Paris on a visit to Paine, and he is said to have assured him that if the French could enable 4,000 volunteers to subsist in Ireland for a few months, a revolution could be effected. Lebrun, who was then Minister for Foreign Affairs, was so much impressed with the statement that he resolved to send another secret agent to Ireland, and selected, at the recommendation of Paine, an American named Oswald, who had volunteered in the French service and had risen to be colonel of artillery. Oswald passed over to Scotland, and at last succeeded, with much difficulty, in reaching Ireland in June. He had received instructions from the French Minister to enter into communications with disaffected Irishmen, and to offer men and money if an insurrection could be made, but his report to the French Government was not altogether encouraging. He had found, he said, both in Scotland and Ireland the people in great confusion through the numerous bankruptcies, the interruption of commerce, and the dismissal of workmen, occasioned by the war, but he thought there was at present little to be expected from Ireland. The people were discontented and agitated, but the volunteers had been successfully suppressed, and Oswald saw no immediate prospect of active insurrection.[2]

The Gunpowder Act and the proclamation against volunteering had been imperatively needed to check a most formidable

---

[1] The authority for this statement is a letter from Reinhard to De la Croix, 29 floréal, an iv (May 18, 1796), French Foreign Office. Reinhard says Lord Edward Fitzgerald reminded him of certain communications which the deputies from Ireland, sent to make 'réclamations' to the English Government in December 1792, had with Chauvelin, and adds that Chauvelin had not received them with all the interest the importance of the matter demanded. This negotiation, I imagine, is alluded to in a disjointed fragment of Wolfe Tone's journal, written in March 1793. After referring to the deputation to England &c. he writes: 'Motives of Catholic leaders; not corruption. Some negotiations carried on by one of them in London unknown to the others. The others probably unwilling to risk their estates.' (Tone's *Life*, i. 108, Washington edition.)

[2] See the papers of Oswald, June and July 1793, French Foreign Office. See, too, McNevin's *Pieces of Irish History*, p. 71.

scheme for arming, under the guise of volunteers, the great body of the republican and disaffected party in Ireland, and placing them under leaders of their own opinions. An incendiary address, urging the volunteers to arm, and to make Catholic emancipation and the extension of the elective franchise to the whole body of the people their leading objects, had been issued by the United Irishmen in December 1792.[1] In the following February delegates from thirty-five volunteer companies, representing more than 2,000 men, had assembled at Antrim and agreed on a scheme for a general arming of volunteers throughout the kingdom, for the appointment of committees and officers to direct them, and for the accumulation of military stores; and they had issued a significant circular to all the volunteers of the country, recommending them not to publish any resolutions.[2] In a report drawn up in the following month by the House of Lords it was stated that prayers for the success of the French arms had been offered up at Belfast from the pulpit, in the presence of military associations which had been newly raised in that town; that bodies of men composed mostly of the lowest classes of the people, and armed and disciplined under officers chosen by themselves, had been enrolled in different parts of the North; that great supplies of arms and gunpowder had been collected and were collecting at Belfast and Newry; that constant efforts were made to seduce the soldiery and obtain military men to discipline the new levies; that at Belfast bodies of men were drilled and exercised almost every night for several hours by candlelight. The declared object of these military bodies, the report said, was to procure a reform of Parliament, but there was an obvious intention to overawe the Parliament and the Government, and hopes were held out of assistance by a French descent upon Ireland.[3] The establishment in Dublin of national guards closely imitated from those in France has been already mentioned, and the formation of similar bodies was contemplated at Belfast, Derry, and Galway. In Dublin their suppression was not effected without some difficulty; it was found necessary to call out the troops, and the condition of Ulster in the spring of

---

[1] Madden's *United Irishmen,* i. 234–237.
[2] Tone's *Life,* i. 268.
[3] Report from the Secret Committee of the House of Lords, 1793. See Tone's comments on the report, i. 108.

1793 was so serious that the Government strongly urged the necessity of sending reinforcements to that province.[1]

The great majority of the more conspicuous United Irishmen at this period, as well as in the subsequent periods of the movement, were nominally either Presbyterians or members of the Established Church, though a large proportion of them were indifferent to theological doctrines. Tone, Butler, Emmet, Hamilton Rowan, Napper Tandy, Arthur O'Connor, Lord Edward Fitzgerald, Bond, Russell, Drennan, Neilson, and the two Sheares were all Protestants, and Belfast and other parts of Presbyterian Ulster were the special centres of Irish republicanism. On this point the Government despatches and the writings of the United Irishmen were perfectly agreed. The Test Act and the disabilities relating to marriage which especially affected the Presbyterians, and the commercial restrictions which were peculiarly felt by a section of the population that was essentially commercial, had, it is true, of late years been abolished, but the resentments they had produced had not passed away. The republican religion of the northern Presbyterians gave them some bias towards republican government, and their sympathy with the New England Puritans in their contest against England had been passionate and avowed. They had scarcely any part among the landed gentry of Ireland, and were therefore less sensible than other Protestants of the necessity of connection with England for the security of their property, while they were more keenly sensible than any other class to the evils of the existing system of government. They claimed to outnumber the members of the Established Church,[2] but under the existing system of monopoly they had scarcely any political power, and scarcely any share in the patronage of the Crown. An intelligent, educated, energetic middle-class community naturally resented such a system of exclusion and monopoly far

---

[1] Westmorland to Dundas, March 29, 1793.

[2] Wolfe Tone pretended that the Protestant Dissenters were twice as numerous as the members of the Established Church (Tone's *Life*, i. 277, 278), but this must have been an enormous exaggeration. In the census of 1834 the former were computed at 664,164, and the latter at 852,064. Mr. Killen, however, gives some reason for believing that the Episcopalians were then overrated and the Presbyterians underrated; and he even claims a slight superiority of numbers for the Presbyterians. (Continuation of Reid's *History of the Irish Presbyterians*, iii. 576–579. See, too, Lewis's *Irish Disturbances*, pp. 342–344.)

more keenly than a poor, dependent, and perfectly ignorant Catholic peasantry, and they especially detested the legal obligation of paying tithes to an Episcopalian Church. The growth of religious scepticism or indifference in the intelligent town populations had at the same time prepared the way for the reception of the doctrines of the French Revolution, and for that alliance with the Catholics which the United Irishmen preached as the first condition of obtaining a democratic reform. We have seen the powerful assistance which the northern Protestants had given to the Catholic cause in the latter stages of its struggle, and their strenuous support of the democratic party in the Catholic body, and it is an undoubted and most remarkable fact that almost the whole guiding influence of the seditious movement in 1793 was Protestant or Deistical, while the Catholic gentry, the Catholic prelates, and, as far as can now be judged, the bulk of the Catholic priesthood were strongly opposed to it.

The power of the priesthood, however, in Ireland, as in all other countries, had been diminished by the influences that led to the French Revolution. The Catholic gentry were too small a body to exercise much authority, and their weight had been in the last months steadily declining, partly through the growth of a great Catholic trading interest in the towns, and partly through the secession of Lord Kenmare and his followers from the committee, and the triumph of the democratic party in that body. It is probable, too, that the prediction of Parsons was verified, and that the Relief Act of 1793 still further weakened them. As they could be neither members of Parliament, sheriffs, nor sub-sheriffs, they could not assume their natural place as the leaders of the great political power which the new Act had suddenly called into existence. It is incontestable that a party had arisen among the Catholics which was in full sympathy with the United Irishmen, not only in their desire for Catholic emancipation and parliamentary reform, but also in the spirit that animated them, and in the ulterior objects which were gradually dawning on their minds. We have seen that the aims and wishes of Wolfe Tone had been from the beginning directed to a complete separation of Ireland from England,[1] and he tells

[1] See vol. vi. p. 467.

us that he had privately communicated his genuine political sentiments without any reserve to John Keogh and Richard McCormick, the two men who, after the secession of Lord Kenmare and of his party, were most powerful in the Catholic Committee. It was observed by a Government informer in 1793 that Keogh was a most regular attendant at the meetings of the committee of the United Irishmen in Dublin. Tone notices that almost from the first formation of the United Irish Society 'the Catholics flocked in, in crowds,' and he had no more doubts than Duigenan or Clare about the future sedition of the Catholic democracy. 'I well knew,' he wrote, 'that however it might be disguised or suppressed, there existed in the breast of every Irish Catholic an inextinguishable abhorrence of the English name and power.'[1]

Early in 1793, and before the Catholic Relief Bill had been carried, a pamphlet appeared from the pen of Theobald McKenna, who was one of the most prominent literary representatives of the Catholic party of Lord Kenmare, which has much interest as expressing their sentiments. It was called 'An Essay on Parliamentary Reform and the Evils likely to ensue from a Republican Constitution in Ireland,' and it is a solemn protest against the revolutionary and republican tenets which Wolfe Tone and the other United Irishmen were diffusing through Ireland. It was true indeed, he admitted, that a parliamentary reform was much needed in Ireland, and its nature and limits were not difficult to ascertain. The first and most essential defect of the Irish Legislature was the exclusion of Catholics from political power. The next was the practical exclusion of merchants, which left the trading interest destitute of its natural influence and weight. To these two causes most of the real evils of the Irish parliamentary system may be traced. Corruption was the natural result of the narrowness of the constituencies, and 'in many counties a great proportion of the men of property were disfranchised under pretext of religion.' The relation of classes was injuriously affected by the same cause, for 'when the gentry feel not any necessity to court the favour of their inferiors, they are deficient in offices of protection and tenderness.' The 'barbarous feudal notion' that still lingered in Ireland, 'that the

---

[1] Tone's *Memoirs*, i. 52, 55, 63.

mercantile is less honourable than other occupations,' was due to the fact that a House of Commons, which was full of lawyers, scarcely contained a single merchant.

At the same time McKenna urged that the Revolution of France should act rather as a warning than an example, and that the dangers of the age sprang rather from democratic than monarchical excess. He dwells on the peril of weakening the Crown; of endangering the connection with England; of throwing the political guidance of the country into the hands of conventions and military associations; of sacrificing the distinctive merits of constitutional government in the pursuit of an impossible equality. 'It matters little,' he said, 'how men are appointed to seats in Parliament provided they be eminent and deserving persons, selected from the different professions of importance. This, in fact, and not the parcelling of the country into districts of nominally equal importance, is a fair and impartial representation.' He denied in the most emphatic terms that Ireland was on the whole an ill-governed country, and that its people were in the deplorable condition represented by Wolfe Tone. 'We are indeed,' he said, ' peculiarly well circumstanced in Ireland. We have the advantages of a limited monarchy without incurring anything near the degree of expense which in other countries is annexed to the maintenance of royalty.' 'The taxes of Ireland even compared with its means are lower than those of any other country.' 'No class of men or branch of manufacture languishes in this country under national imposts. These fall on the superfluities, not on the necessaries of life, and a reduction of them would not augment the poor man's comfort.' 'If the connection were dissolved, or if we adhered so loosely to England that she should learn to consider us a separate nation, the expense of a distinct Government would amount to much more than our present revenue.' The county cess for the maintenance of the roads is often scandalously or unnecessarily extravagant, but at least there is no compulsory labour as in France. 'The bounties on tillage have advanced prosperity in Ireland.' 'The moneyed interest is rising rapidly.'

On one point, however, McKenna fully agreed with Tone. It was that the French Revolution had entirely changed the character of Irish politics. 'The first and greatest of all revolutions,' he says, 'has been produced among us, without the aid of plan or project. The public spirit of the Catholics has been excited. The controversy on the French Revolution extended more universally in Ireland than any other literary discussion. The public mind was prepared by the diffusion of general principles.'

The United Irish movement in the North was chiefly directed by a secret committee which sat at Belfast, and which had established a small sub-committee of correspondence for the purpose of entering into communications with sympathisers in other parts of Ireland. In Dublin there was another committee, which met at fortnightly and sometimes weekly intervals. The Government had secured one of its members, whose subscription to the society was paid, and who received from time to time remittances in money from the Castle, and in return forwarded anonymous reports of the proceedings of every meeting.[1] The society as yet differed very little from the democratic clubs that had long existed in Great Britain. Several of its members were undoubtedly speculative republicans. All of them were advocates of a measure of very democratic reform, warm admirers of the French Revolution, and strong opponents of the war, and they were bound together by a resolution which stated that the weight of English influence was the master evil in the Government of Ireland, and that it could only be resisted by a cordial union of Irishmen of all religious persuasions. But their real and final object at this time was parliamentary reform on a democratic and unsectarian basis, though some of them were from the first convinced that this could only be obtained by separation, while others believed that it would be attained, like the Constitution of 1782, by a menace of force. This had been the object of the attempted organisation of the National Guards, and two sentences of Flood were often quoted among the United Irishmen: 'When have you negotiated,' he had once said, 'that you have not been deceived? When have you demanded, that you have not succeeded?'

About forty or fifty members were usually present at the

[1] He was a Dublin silk merchant, and can be identified by a letter from Cooke to Nepean, May 26, 1794, in the Record Office. His reports will be found in the 'Secret and Confidential Correspondence' in the Irish State Paper Office.

meetings of the Dublin Committee. The chief business was electing new members, corresponding with societies in England and Scotland, drawing up addresses which were chiefly written by Dr. Drennan, elaborating a plan of parliamentary reform which Irishmen of all classes were exhorted to hang up in their houses or cabins. The quarrel of Napper Tandy with the House of Commons had made 'undefined parliamentary privilege' a leading grievance, and when the House of Lords in the spring of 1793 established a committee of secrecy for investigating the disturbances in some counties, and when this committee assumed the power of compelling attendance and enforcing answers upon oath to interrogatories tending to criminate the person examined, the United Irishmen issued a paper contending that it had exceeded its legal power. The House of Lords promptly took up the matter, and Simon Butler, the chairman, and Oliver Bond, the secretary of the society, who signed the paper, were imprisoned by their order for six months and fined 500*l.* each. The fines were paid by the society.[1]

Two other important members of the society about this time passed for a short period from the scene. Napper Tandy, the most indefatigable of the agitators in Ireland, being threatened with prosecutions for libel and for having taken the Defender oath, sought safety on the Continent, and soon after Hamilton Rowan was prosecuted for seditious libel on account of an address to the volunteers. He was defended by Curran in one of the most eloquent speeches ever delivered at the bar, but was found guilty and sentenced to two years' imprisonment and to a fine of 500*l.*

As we have already seen, the United Irishmen were as yet bound by no oath, and the pledge which every member took was a very innocent document, merely binding him to use all his abilities and influence 'to obtain an impartial and adequate representation of the Irish nation in Parliament,' and as a means to that end to promote a brotherhood of affection among Irishmen of all religious persuasions. In April 1792, however, a proposal was made to abolish this pledge, 'as it is found by experience that it prevents a number of very warm friends to a

---

[1] Madden's *United Irishmen,* i. 248-253; McNevin's *Pieces of Irish History,* pp. 49, 50.

reform from joining us; but,' adds the Government agent, 'I shall oppose it, as we have no business with any of your lukewarm fellows who may hesitate at going as great lengths as ourselves. If the test should be abolished, the members will increase amazingly. Therefore resist it.'[1]

The first openly seditious movement appears to have come from a branch society at Lisburn, which applied to the parent society in the first days of 1793 for assistance to purchase arms and ammunition. The Dublin Committee, after a discussion, resolved 'that it was impossible to comply with their request.' 'In the course of a debate on the above measure,' writes the informer, 'it was strongly urged that it would be highly improper for the society to arm other bodies of men without first adopting the measure themselves; and as their sole intent of first forming themselves into a society was for the purpose of obtaining a full representation of the people in Parliament, that great object should be obtained *if possible* without recourse to arms. Councillor Emmett agreed in the propriety of the resolution, but hoped the society would reserve to itself the expediency of resorting to arms if necessity required the measure.' It was proposed at the same time to get rid of the buttons and cockades, as they kept many from joining. 'I shall oppose the alteration,' wrote the informer, 'for a very substantial reason, which I can explain if necessary to my friends.'[2] In the summer 'a gentleman waited on Mr. Grattan by the desire of Messrs. Butler and Bond, with a petition to the House of Commons from them, and praying him to present it, which he declined, declaring at the same time that he did not approve of the conduct of the United Irishmen in many instances.'[3]

The materials for writing the secret history of the United Irishmen are very ample, but there were important movements at this time among the Catholics which are much less easy to describe, for the evidence relating to them is at once scanty, conflicting, and prejudiced. I have mentioned the probable effect of the Relief Act of 1793 on the influence of the loyal Catholic gentry. As far as can now be judged, the Protestant

---

[1] April 13, 1792 (Irish State Paper Office).
[2] January 4, 1793.
[3] May 31, 1793.

gentry were ready to carry out the Act with liberality, and it is remarkable that in this very year, out of the twenty-three grand jurors returned by the high sheriff for the county of Dublin, no less than twelve were Catholics,[1] but the clause enabling corporations to elect Catholics was in many, probably in most cases, defeated by the municipal, class or trade jealousy of the existing members.[2] The Corporation of Dublin continued, as it had long been, violently anti-Catholic; and as the Government exercised an overwhelming influence in that body, the Government bore, in the eyes of the public, a great part of the blame. The Catholic prelates, however, seemed more than satisfied, and they all, to the great indignation of the United Irishmen, joined in an address to the Lord Lieutenant, expressing unbounded loyalty and unqualified gratitude.[3] Munster, most of Connaught, and a great part of Leinster were very free from political troubles; but several counties of Ulster, and some adjoining parts of Leinster and Connaught, were the scenes of most serious disturbances which amounted to little less than civil war.

As we have already seen, the quarrel between the Defenders and the Peep of Day Boys appears to have been at first of the nature of a faction fight, originating in 1784 or 1785 in the hatred which had long subsisted between the poorer Catholics and the poorer Presbyterians in the county of Armagh, and it principally took the form of the plunder of arms, and the wrecking of Catholic chapels and houses. The name taken by the Catholics implies that the Protestants were the aggressors, and the stress of evidence favours the conclusion that in the northern counties this was the case,[4] but many atrocious crimes were perpetrated on each side, and many lives were lost. The disturbances rose and fell during several years. For a time they

---

[1] *Anthologia Hibernica*, i. 323.
[2] A few curious particulars of what took place in Dublin will be found in the *Anthologia Hibernica*, ii. 74, 75, 316. The 'Corporation of Cutlers, Painters, Stainers, and Stationers, or Guild of St. Luke,' in 1793 unanimously admitted nine Catholics to their freedom. The Guild of Merchants rejected the petition of some Catholics for admission and adjourned the others. The 'Corporation of Shoemakers' acted in the same way. The 'Corporation of Apothecaries' admitted some Catholics.
[3] McNevin, p. 61.
[4] See McNevin, p. 52; Wolfe Tone's *Memoirs*, i. 174. Musgrave, who has devoted a good deal of attention to the matter, says it began with a quarrel between two individuals in the county of Armagh in 1784, and speedily expanded, first into a faction fight, and then into a religious war.

appear to have been suppressed by the volunteers,[1] but in 1791 and 1792 they broke out again on a much larger scale in the counties of Tyrone, Down, Louth, Meath, Cavan, and Monaghan. There were frequent combats of large bodies of armed men, numerous outrages, rumours of intended massacres of Catholics by Presbyterians and of Presbyterians by Catholics, threatening letters which showed by clear internal evidence that they were the work of very ignorant men. In the county of Louth the Catholics appear to have been the chief offenders, for it is stated that in the spring assizes of 1793 at Dundalk twenty-one Defenders were sentenced to death and thirty-seven to transportation and imprisonment, while thirteen trials for murder were postponed.[2] In the county of Meath, also, which was during several months in a condition of utter social anarchy, it is admitted by the best Catholic authority that the Catholics were the aggressors.[3] The disturbances broke out near the end of 1792, in a part of the county adjoining the county of Cavan, where there were large settlements of Presbyterians, between whom and the Catholics there had long subsisted a traditional animosity. At first the Catholics plundered the Protestants of their arms with impunity, but soon a large body of well-armed Presbyterians, or, as they were still commonly called, 'Scotch,' came from the county of Cavan, accompanied by some resident gentry, and turned the scale. There were pitched battles in broad daylight; soldiers were called out and many persons were shot. The Presbyterians were accused of having 'overrun the country, pillaged, plundered, and burned without requiring any mark of guilt but religion.' Magistrates were alternately charged with apathy, connivance, timidity, and violent oppression. There was great difficulty in obtaining legal evidence, and two or three informers were murdered.

For six or eight months Defender outrages continued in this county almost uncontrolled, and it was noticed that every kind of crime was perpetrated under the name. It was found that the most efficient means of suppressing the Defenders was the for-

---

[1] McNevin's *Pieces of Irish History,* p. 46.
[2] Musgrave's *Rebellions in Ireland* (2nd edition), p. 63.
[3] *Candid Account of the Disturbances in the County of Meath in 1792, 1793, and 1794, by a County Meath Freeholder* (Dublin, 1794). This pamphlet, which is evidently written by a well-informed and moderate Catholic, is the fullest account I know of the Defender movement at this period.

mation of a secret committee of gentlemen—one of whom was a Catholic—who bound themselves not to disclose the names of informers. At last the gang was broken up and several members turned approvers. A clergyman named Butler appears to have shown admirable courage, judgment, and skill in his capacity as magistrate, and it was said to have been chiefly due to him that in a few months Defenderism scarcely appeared on the western side of the Boyne and Blackwater. In October 1793 he was shot dead near the palace of the Bishop of Meath at Ardbrackan. Two or three leading Catholic shopkeepers of Navan were arrested on suspicion of being concerned in a popish conspiracy for murdering him, and one of them, of the name of Fay, was put on his trial. He had been secretary of a Catholic meeting at Trim in the preceding year, and appears to have been exceedingly respected by his coreligionists. They alleged that his detention was very harsh and his trial very unfair, and it is at least certain that the evidence against him completely broke down, and that with the full assent of the judge he was honourably acquitted by a Protestant jury. Large rewards had been offered for informers, and it appears that some perjured evidence was brought against respectable Catholics. One informer was actually transported for perjury, and several prisoners were acquitted.[1] In the county of Meath it was noticed with much indignation that while the juries had previously consisted chiefly of Catholics, they were now almost wholly Protestants; but those who have any real knowledge of Irish life will probably hesitate to pronounce that such an exclusion under such circumstances was in the interests of public justice unnecessary.

Lord Bellamont at this time showed great activity both in Cavan and Meath, but in general the great proprietors were absentees, and the difficult and dangerous duty of suppressing the disturbances was thrown chiefly on the smaller Protestant gentry. The motives that were at work in convulsing the country were evidently of many kinds. There was an extreme

---

[1] Grattan's *Life*, iv. 159. A report of Fay's trial was published in Dublin in 1794. There was only a single witness for the prosecution, and he was a man of infamous character, and was contradicted on oath as to several parts of his evidence. I do not, however, see any evidence of unfairness on the part of Judge Downes, who tried the case, and he certainly summed up strongly for an acquittal

chronic lawlessness which a spark could at any moment ignite. There was some religious animosity and a great deal of race hatred, for the Scotch Presbyterians and the Irish Catholics were still like separate nations. The late measure of enfranchisement had aroused wild hopes and expectations on one side, exaggerated fears and resentments on the other, and the new position acquired by Catholic forty-shilling freeholders was likely to affect to a considerable degree the competition for land. There was also much keen and real distress, for the year 1793 was eminently a 'hard year,' and great numbers of labourers were out of employment. Defenderism soon ceased to be either a league for mutual protection or a mere system of religious riot. It assumed the usual Irish form of a secret and permanent organisation, held together by oaths, moving under a hidden direction, attracting to itself all kinds of criminals, and making itself the organ of all kinds of discontent. It became to a great extent a new White Boy movement, aiming specially at the reduction and abolition of tithes and the redress of agrarian grievances, and in this form it passed rapidly into counties where the poorer population were exclusively Catholic, and where there was little or no religious animosity. It was also early noticed that it was accompanied by nightly meetings for the purposes of drill, and by a profuse distribution of incendiary papers.

Another element of disturbance of a different nature broke out about the same time. The creation of a militia was intended by the Government to be a great measure of pacification; but the new system of compulsory enlistment, which was wholly unnecessary in a country where voluntary recruits were always most easily obtained, was fiercely resented and resisted. Truly or falsely it was generally believed that in the American war the Irish Government had shamefully broken faith with a regiment nicknamed the Green Linnets, which had been enlisted on the understanding that it was not to serve out of Ireland, and which had notwithstanding been transported to America. A report was now spread, and readily believed, that they meant to act with still greater perfidy towards the new militia. It was said that they wished to expatriate or banish those who had signed the declarations originated by the Catholic Committee, and that they were accordingly forcing them into the militia in order to send them to Botany Bay. The officers of the new force were all Protestants, while the privates were Catholics, and there was a growing belief that the Ministers were hostile to the Catholics and had not forgiven their recent agitation. The attitude of the grand juries, and the speeches of Foster, and still more of Fitzgibbon, had created suspicions which were industriously fanned, and which passed swiftly and silently from cabin to cabin. In nearly every county there was resistance, and in some it was very formidable. At Athboy, in the county of Meath, 1,000 men took arms. They searched the country houses for guns, and resisted the soldiers so effectually that the result was a drawn battle in which several men were killed. An attack was made on the town of Wexford in order to rescue some prisoners. The expense of soldiers billeted among the people, the fines exacted when the Act was not obeyed, the severe punishment of rioters, many of whom besides long periods of imprisonment were publicly and severely whipped, and the acts of violence and injustice which were tolerably certain to be occasionally perpetrated by soldiers and perhaps by magistrates in a society so convulsed and disorganised, all added to the discontent. In three or four months, it is true, the military riots were allayed by a measure encouraging voluntary enlistments and making some provision for the families of those who were drawn by lot, but they contributed largely to the growing disaffection and to swell the ranks of the Defenders.[1]

There are numerous letters about these disturbances among the Government papers, but in reading them we must remember the great difficulty Irish magistrates have always had in penetrating the secret motives and intentions of the Catholic population, and the strong fear which actuated many who had bitterly opposed the recent Relief Acts. In Sligo and Roscommon it was reported that 'almost the whole of the lower orders of Roman Catholics are in a state of insurrection' about the Militia Act; and although by the prompt and energetic action of the magistrates in those counties the movement was soon checked, it was spreading to Mayo, and it had become 'obvious that under one pretext or another the minds of

---

[1] McNevin; *Candid Account of the Disturbances in the County of Meath,* p. 60; Gordon, *History of Ireland,* ii. 335, 336.

the lower classes of Roman Catholics have become unfortunately formed to a readiness for insurrection.'[1] One officer 'would be tempted to attribute the source of these disorders to the Roman Catholics, for the oath of the insurgents chiefly runs to be true to the Catholic cause, if he did not know that some Protestants were among the most daring depredators.' 'The decent Catholics in Sligo,' wrote a magistrate from that county, 'have joined the Protestants,' and sixteen insurgents have been taken. The beginning of the trouble was the Militia Act, but the hopes raised by the Popery Act, he thinks, had much to say to it. The people hoped 'that not only religious equality but one of property would be produced. They now find this to be a dream, and they are determined to effect by force that equality of property they vainly hoped for.' 'However, the militia is the pretext,' wrote a magistrate from Enniskillen; 'not one Protestant is concerned in Leitrim, and prisoners have been heard to say that not one Protestant should be alive in a month.' In the county of Wexford the oath bound the Defenders 'to cut down their own clergy to a certain rate of parish dues, not to take tithes from tithe proctors, nor pay more than sixpence per acre for tillage, to be true to each other, not to divulge who has administered the oath,' and 'all smiths and carpenters are sworn not to work for any man who had not taken the oath.' Some of the rioters said they would return peaceably to their homes if they were sure that they would not be kidnapped and forced into the militia. Some were sworn to be true to the Catholic cause, and to pay no rent for three months. Many pikes were found among the Defenders, and on several occasions they encountered the soldiers. Rumours were flying about the country of an impending insurrection, of a massacre of Protestants, of a division of property, of an abolition of rents and taxes, of a secret alliance with the French, who were coming over to sweep away the tithes and free the people from every grievance. In the May of 1794 about seventy persons were killed in a single conflict at Ballina.[2]

To the Irish Government it must have been extremely mor-

[1] Westmorland to Dundas, May 25, 29, 1793.
[2] See Westmorland to Dundas, March 29, and very numerous letters on the subject in May, June, and July. See, too, the *Beresford Correspondence*, ii. 35.

tifying to contrast the condition of Ireland during the spring and summer of 1793 with her condition during the wars of George II. and even during the American war, when it had been found both possible and easy to send the whole Irish army, except about 5,000 men, to fight the battles of England. Westmorland attributed the evil mainly to the republicans of Belfast and Dublin; to 'the levelling principles of the French Revolution;' to associations connected with the United Irishmen which were propagating sedition with unceasing activity in various parts of Ireland; and to 'the agitation of the Catholic question, which was so managed as to throw the lower orders of that persuasion into a state of fermentation.' He mentions that at a time when the condition of Ulster made it most necessary to send additional troops to that province, he had been prevented from doing so 'by the breaking out of an insurrection of the lower Catholics in the county of Louth, who, being privately instigated by the leaders of seditious associations in Dublin and the North, proceeded to plunder the houses of Protestants of their arms.' 'Their meetings,' he continued, ' and their attacks were by night; they arrayed themselves under different captains, enlisted all the lower Catholics, imposed an oath of secrecy, and endeavoured to learn the use of arms. Their expeditions were so secret for some time as to elude the military. . . . The disorders spread through the counties of Louth, Meath, Dublin, Cavan, Monaghan, and Armagh. All the Protestants were driven into the towns; no gentleman could be in security without a guard in his house, and whenever their attacks were successful the arms were carried off.'[1]

In a discussion on the subject in the House of Lords in the February of 1793, Lord Clonmel stated his belief that French emissaries were already active among the Defenders, and a Secret Committee which was appointed by the House of Lords to investigate the subject, and which is said to have consisted mainly of very anti-Catholic members, threw some suspicion on the Catholic Committee in Dublin. 'The people at this time called Defenders,' the report said, 'are very different from those who originally assumed that appellation, and are all, as far as the committee could discover, of the Roman Catholic persuasion;

[1] Westmorland to Dundas, March 29, 1793.

in general poor, ignorant, labouring men, sworn to secrecy and impressed with an opinion that they are assisting the Catholic cause; in other respects, they do not appear to have any distinct, particular object in view, but they talk of being relieved from hearth money, tithes, county cesses, and of lowering their rents. . . . They assembled mostly in the night, and forced into the houses of Protestants and took from them their arms. . . . At first they took nothing but arms, but afterwards they plundered the houses of everything they could find.' The committee acknowledged that they had no reason to believe that the body of the Roman Catholics in Ireland in any way promoted or countenanced the movement, but they mentioned as suspicious circumstances the regularity and system with which the outrages were committed, the large sums of money that were collected by the authority of the Catholic Committee in the chapels in all parts of the kingdom, and especially the fact that a conspicuous member of the Catholic Committee had made inquiries into the trials of the Defenders, and had employed an agent and counsel to act for several persons who were accused of that offence.[1]

There does not, however, appear to me to be any evidence that French emissaries were in connection with the Defenders during the year 1793. The charges against the Catholic Committee were at once and indignantly repudiated. It was shown that the avowed and legitimate objects of the committee fully accounted for the chapel collections; that the committee, instead of promoting, had made earnest efforts to allay a religious animosity which was directly opposed to the alliance with Protestants they were endeavouring to establish, and that if they had undertaken to support in the law courts a Catholic whom they believed to have been unjustly accused, they had abandoned their intention when further inquiry led them to believe that they had been deceived.[2]

The Defender movement is extremely important in Irish history, for it appears to have been mainly through this channel that the great mass of the poorer Roman Catholics passed into the ranks of disaffection. It was ultimately connected with and

[1] This report is reprinted in the appendix to the Report of the Committee of Secrecy, in 1798.
[2] McNevin's *Pieces of Irish History*, pp. 52, 53. See, too, the Catholic address in January 1793 (Grattan's *Life*, iv. 133).

absorbed in the United Irish movement, and it formed one of the chief Catholic elements in the rebellion of 1798. The parallel between what was then taking place in Ireland and what we have ourselves witnessed is very striking. There were two movements which were at first completely distinct. One was purely political, and was directed by educated men, influenced by political theories and aiming at political ends. The other was a popular movement which speedily became agrarian, and was to a great extent directed against the owners of property. These two movements at last combined, and the result was the most bloody rebellion in modern Irish history.

They were, however, in their origin not only distinct but violently antagonistic.[1] It was the main object of the United Irishmen to put an end to the dissension between Catholics and Protestants, and especially to unite the Presbyterians and the Catholics in the closest alliance, for the purpose of breaking the influence of England in Irish politics, and obtaining a democratic and unsectarian measure of parliamentary reform. This was the very purpose for which their society had been constituted, and they had met with great success in the large towns of the North, and especially among the Dissenting ministers. Nothing could be more disconcerting to their plans than a new and violent outburst of religious animosity in the country districts. Wolfe Tone declared that it was 'certainly fomented by the aristocrats of this country,'[2] and he himself, in conjunction with Neilson, Keogh, and Leonard McNally, went on a mission to the county of Down for the purpose of putting an end to the quarrel, and of directing the energies of both parties into the cause of the United Irishmen. He found the soil to a considerable extent prepared for his seed. In one place there had been a meeting of eighteen Dissenting ministers from different parts of Ulster, who were all of them well disposed towards Catholic liberty. At Ballinahinch a United Irishman named McClokey had laboured so effectually, that a corps of volunteers which had been

---

[1] 'My theory of Irish politics,' wrote Wolfe Tone, 'is comprised in these words. I trace all the miseries of Ireland . . . to the blasting influence of England. How is that influence maintained? By perpetuating the spirit of internal dissension grounded on religious distinctions. How, then, is it to be obviated? By a cordial union of all the people.' (*Memoirs*, i. 285.)

[2] Ibid. i. 171.

originally raised on Peep of Day principles had chosen him as their lieutenant, and the Catholics now lent the Protestants arms for their exercises and came to see them on their parade. At Newry the delegates induced a large party of Catholics, who had been bickering, to meet them at the inn, where Keogh preached peace and union, and advised them to direct their animosities against the common enemy, the monopolists of the country, and the whole company rose with enthusiasm and shook hands, promising to bury all past feuds in oblivion. At Rosstrevor a number of Catholics and Protestants were brought together at a public dinner, and a Dissenting minister pronounced the benediction, and the toasts of the United Irishmen were received with enthusiasm.[1] Napper Tandy made similar efforts to turn the Defender movement into the United Irish channel, and he appears to have actually taken the Defender oath in order to penetrate into the secrets of the organisation. The Government discovered the fact, and this, as we have seen, was one cause of his flight to the Continent.[2]

As far as can now be ascertained, however, there was as yet scarcely any political element in the religious riots of the North, or in the outrages that were perpetrated in other parts of Ireland. The rioters belonged almost exclusively to classes sunk in the deepest ignorance and poverty, and a village schoolmaster of Naas, who was hanged in 1796, is said to have been the only educated person who is known to have been identified with them.[3] At the same time it was not difficult to predict that illegal organisations at war with the Government, in the existing condition of Ireland and of Europe, would ultimately become political. The contagion of the great centres of agitation established at Dublin and Belfast; the influence of the 'Northern Star;' the writings of Paine, which were disseminated at an extremely low price, and the proclamations of the 'United Irishmen' inviting the co-operation of the Catholics, were sure to affect an anarchical population suffering under some grievances and much poverty. Besides this, rumours of French invasion were already spreading, and the connection between France and Ireland was so close that any agitation in the greater country produced a

---

[1] *Memoirs,* i. 169–177.   [2] Madden's *United Irishmen,* i. 115; iv. 15.
[3] Ibid. i. 115.

responsive pulse in the smaller one. Among educated men, and especially among those of the middle class, the French Revolution had been from the beginning a subject of the keenest interest and discussion, but the interest was not restricted to them. The ideas of an English peasant seldom extended beyond his county town, and the continental world was to him almost as unknown as the world beyond the grave. But tens of thousands of young Irishmen had passed from the wretched cabins of the South and West to the great armies of the Continent. From almost every village, from almost every family of Catholic Ireland, one or more members had gone forth, and visions of sunny lands beyond the sea, where the Catholic was not looked upon as a slave, and where Irish talent and ambition found a welcome and a home, continually floated before the imaginations of the people. The letters of the Irish exiles, the active smuggling trade which was carried on around the Irish coast, the foreign education of the innumerable priests and monks who moved among the poor, kept up the connection, and it was strengthened by the strong natural affinity of character between the Irish and the French. Names of great battles where Irish soldiers had borne an honoured part under a foreign flag were remembered with pride, and vague and distorted images of the events that were happening in France—of the abolition of tithes, of the revolution in landed property, of the offer of French assistance to all suffering nations—soon began to penetrate to the cottier's cabin, and to mingle with the cottier's dreams.

For the present, however, the danger seemed averted, and in the latter part of 1793 the militia riots appear to have wholly ceased, while the disturbances of the Defenders had greatly diminished. In July, Hobart wrote to England that the country was in so alarming a state that he was quite unable to conjecture whether a rebellion would not break out in every corner of the kingdom.[1] In August he pronounced the country almost quiet, and he was already preparing to send a powerful reinforcement of Irish troops to the war.[2] Ten promotions in the Irish peerage were made as the reward of services during the past session, and among the promoted peers was Fitzgibbon, the Chancellor, who now became a viscount. Westmorland had

[1] Hobart to Nepean, July 21, 1793.　　[2] Ibid. August 17, 1793.

spoken in the strongest terms of the value of his services, and had especially insisted on the sacrifice he had made in voting for the Catholic Relief Bill in spite of his conviction of its dangers,[1] but the promotion at this critical time of a man who was justly regarded as the most formidable enemy of the Catholics was, in my judgment, a great political mistake. Before the Parliament met for the session of 1794, Hobart himself had been created a peer and had resigned his office in Ireland.

The quiet continued with little intermission during 1794. Emmet, who had the best means of information, confessed that a great inaction on the question of reform had at this time fallen upon the nation.[2] It was partly due to the defeats, and partly to the excesses, of the French, and partly also to the great measures of the last session, and to the political attitude of Grattan. While on all occasions maintaining with the most fervid eloquence the cause of nationality and the cause of Catholic emancipation, it was his strongest conviction that the true interests of England and Ireland were inseparable, and that no greater calamity could befall the lesser country than the growth of the spirit of disloyalty to the connection. He hated French ideas almost as cordially as Burke, and on the question of the French war it soon became apparent that he had completely separated from Fox. In the session of 1793 this was rather gathered from his tone than expressly asserted, but in speaking on the address in the January of 1794 his language was entirely unambiguous. He had always, he said, maintained that Ireland should improve its constitution, correct its abuses, and assimilate it as nearly as possible to that of Great Britain, but that 'this general plan of conduct should be pursued by Ireland, with a fixed, steady, and unalterable resolution to stand or fall with Great Britain. Whenever Great Britain, therefore,' he continued, 'should be clearly involved in war, it is my idea that Ireland should grant her a decided and unequivocal support, except that war should be carried on against her own liberty.'[3]

[1] Westmorland to Nepean, March 21, 1793.
[2] McNevin's *Pieces of Irish History*, pp. 66–69.
[3] Grattan's *Life*, iv. 145. The report in the Parliamentary Debates is exceedingly abridged. The new secretary, Douglas, in reporting the speech to England, said that Grattan said 'that the errors of the Government in this kingdom had been in a great degree corrected by laws of the last session; that he deemed other measures of reform, and particularly

The speech was not pleasing to all Grattan's friends, and it was a profound disappointment to the United Irishmen. 'Politics do not go on well, I think,' wrote Lord Edward Fitzgerald. 'The leaders of Opposition are all afraid of the people and distrusted by them. . . . Grattan's speech last night on the address was very bad, and the worst doctrine ever laid down, viz. that this country is bound, right or wrong, without inquiry to support England in any war she may undertake.'[1] The Government view of it was clearly shown in a very confidential letter which was written shortly after, by Cooke. 'You are doubtless extremely pleased,' he said, 'in England with the conduct of the Irish Parliament. I now write just to put you in mind of the measures which passed in the last session. They were the seed, you are now reaping the fruits. If the Place Bill, the Pension Bill, and the Treasury Board had not been granted, Mr. Grattan could not with honour have supported. . . . What would have been the effect of a strong parliamentary Opposition which could add the discontent of the moderate to the plots of the factious, is easy to be conjectured. But now the support of the moderate, conjoined to the force of Government, is able to extinguish sedition. . . . Much credit is due to Mr. Grattan. He told Sir J. Parnell last year privately, that if the concessions in agitation were granted, he would no longer give any vexatious opposition. He has more than made good his word, for he has given decided support. Previous to the opening of the session, it was known from his private conversation in the country that he would support the war, but I believe he did not fully communicate to the members acting with him in opposition, the decided part he intended to take.' His speech, in the opinion of Cooke, spread consternation among his own followers, but its result was that the address was carried without dissent or amendment. 'What use,' continues Cooke, 'are we to make of this conjuncture? My best opinion is that Grattan is the most important character in Ireland, and that

a proper reform of Parliament, to be necessary, and trusted that the servants of the Crown would concur in them; that he did not, however, mean to propose such measures as matters of stipulation, but should give his unconditional support to the assistance of Great Britain engaged in a war with our natural enemy, France, without questioning the merits or conduct of that war.' (Douglas to Nepean, Jan. 21, 1794.)

[1] Moore's *Life of Lord Edward Fitzgerald*, i. 234, 235.

attaching him to Mr. Pitt's Government would be essential. This is difficult. He is very high-minded and resentful, and suspicious. He is, however, very steady and honourable, and will act up to his professions. He has great sway over the public mind, and he must play such a part as not to lose his authority. He wants not, perhaps would not take, situation; he would stipulate for measures. If any compliment were shown him, he would like it immediately from Mr. Pitt. In the uncertainty of events his conduct here might be decisive, and therefore he should be early thought of. Government is strong in numbers. They want not aristocratical addition. They want the chief of the people. . . . The lower classes are, however, still indisposed in many parts, and there is an active French party which we are endeavouring to watch.'[1]

Although the authority of Grattan for a time quelled all opposition to the war, an indirect protest was a few days later made by Sir Lawrence Parsons. This very able man had been a devoted friend, follower, and admirer of Flood, and if the Government was rightly informed he was far from friendly to Grattan. He moved an address asking that copies of all the treaties and conventions which had been laid before the British Parliament should be laid before the Parliament of Ireland, and he appears to have supported his motion on the ground that it was the right and duty of the Irish Parliament to discuss the cause and conduct of the war. Grattan, however, strongly and eloquently opposed him. The right of the Irish Parliament to call for treaties, he said, was universally admitted, but to exercise that right at this critical moment would be to tell France that Ireland had not made up her mind on the war. It would check military efforts and chill the military spirit at a time when the promptest energy was supremely necessary, and it would give a new vitality to the French party in the country. Only nine members voted for the address, while one hundred and twenty-eight opposed it.[2]

There were only two other subjects of considerable importance discussed in Parliament during this year. Grattan again brought forward his motion asserting the necessity of establishing a

---

[1] Cooke to Nepean, Feb. 7, 1794.
[2] The Parliamentary Debates (xiv. 16) do not report the speeches, but Cooke notices the debate (to Nepean, Feb. 7), and Grattan's speech is given in his *Collected Speeches*, iii. 119–122.

definite and final commercial understanding between the two countries on the basis of perfect reciprocity, the manufactures of Ireland being received in the ports of Great Britain on the same terms on which the manufactures of Great Britain were received in the ports of Ireland. His speech on the subject was strongly hostile to protecting duties on either side, and his views of commercial policy appear to have been not less enlightened than those of Pitt. The proposition was received on the part of the Government with a profusion of compliments, but with an earnest plea for delay, and it was accordingly at their desire withdrawn. We shall see that, a few years later, one of the ministerial arguments employed for the Union was that no such commercial arrangement existed.[1]

The other important measure of the session was Ponsonby's Reform Bill. It was substantially the same as that of last year, its principal features being the addition of a third member to each of the thirty-two counties, and to the cities of Dublin and Cork, and the opening of the boroughs by extending the right of voting in them to all 10*l.* freeholders in a specified section of the adjoining country. There was little more to be said about the anomalies of the Irish parliamentary system, but it had been recently shown by a detailed statement, that out of the 300 members of the House of Commons 124 were actually nominated by 52 peers, and 64 by 36 commoners, while 13 others were said to owe their return in a great measure to the influence of single families.[2] The debate on the subject was very able, and the transcendent importance of meeting the democratic and revolutionary spirit by removing indefensible abuses, and placing the representation on a broad and safe basis, was strongly urged. Grattan, Jephson, and Parsons spoke with admirable force upon this theme, but the first at the same time repudiated emphatically the democratic Reform Bill of the United Irishmen, and exposed the dangers of the theory of personal representation with a strength of reasoning and language which Burke

---

[1] *Irish Parl. Deb.* xiv. 48-53. Grattan's *Speeches*, iii. 122-127.

[2] *Anthologia Hibernica*, ii. 268-71. In a pamphlet published in 1797 there is a slightly different analysis of the representation. According to this account, forty-one temporal peers returned 112 members; four spiritual peers 8; private persons 96; thirty-two counties 64; three cities 10; four boroughs 6; potwalloping boroughs 4. (*An Appeal to the Understanding of Englishmen on the State of Ireland.* London, 1797.)

himself could hardly have surpassed. The principal argument on the other side was the danger of reform in time of revolution, and the fate of the moderate reformers in France. The Government resisted the Bill, and it was rejected by 142 votes to 44.[1]

In justifying the reintroduction of a Bill which had been rejected in the preceding year Ponsonby said, 'There was one capital objection which then existed against the measure, but which is now done away. The country was then in a state of disturbance, it is now in perfect tranquillity.'[2] This assertion is fully corroborated by a private letter from Parnell, the Chancellor of the Exchequer, to Lord Hobart. He speaks emphatically of the great tranquillity of Irish politics. 'Nothing but some mistaken principles of politics can now disturb us. We have got a loan of near 1,400,000$l.$, and new taxes necessarily affecting the bulk of the people without murmur, and there is no appearance at present of the revival of the sedition which lately prevailed.'[3] The short and peaceful session was terminated on March 25.

The proceedings of the United Irishmen in the early part of the year, as they were reported by the Government informer, were not very important. The usual attendance at the Dublin meetings seems to have sunk to thirty or thirty-four. A suspicion had spread that Government spies were abroad, and the informer describes a curious scene which took place at a meeting on the last day of January. After some ordinary business had been transacted, 'Mr. Nelson said that though a stranger in town and almost so to every member of the society, except in sympathy of sentiments, he boldly declared that he had the strongest assurances that there were traitors in the society, who constantly conveyed whatever passed in it within a few hours after, nay a few moments, to the Castle; and in order at this very solemn crisis to guard against the effect of treason, he would recommend the society to appoint a committee of twelve, to be called the Committee of Public Welfare, with powers to transact all the business of the society. . . . Mr. Simon Butler declared that he wished the hall to be uncovered, and all the people of Dublin, of all Ireland, to be present at their debates,

---

[1] *Parl. Debates*, xiv. 62-108.   [2] Ibid. p. 62.
[3] Parnell to Lord Hobart, March 1794.

as he knew of nothing having been agitated but what was perfectly constitutional. . . . Nothing material,' continued the informer, 'will be attempted but through the committee proposed by Nelson, and you may depend on it that such a one, self-elected, now exists. If you have any idea of the cause of those suspicions, for God's sake let me know. . . . I will see you towards evening at eight o'clock.' A fortnight later the same subject of traitors in the camp was brought forward by John Sheares, who proposed a dissolution of the society, and a new ballot. He afterwards consented to withdraw his proposal, and Butler again asserted that all their proceedings were perfectly legal. There was evidently great distrust and much discouragement in the party, and when Grattan made his attack on their reform scheme, both Sheares and Emmet considered the incident a fortunate one, as the parliamentary notice had 'rescued the society from that state of insignificance into which it had lately fallen.'[1] A reply was issued by the society which commented in very bitter terms on the conduct of Grattan and of the Opposition.

The measures of the United Irishmen, however, were not all so innocuous. The events of the last session had fully convinced them that no party in Parliament was in the least likely to accept their scheme of universal suffrage and equal electoral districts, while the triumphant march of the French arms made French assistance continually more probable. In the spring of 1794 a new and important overture was made to them. The agent chosen by the French Committee of Public Safety was an Anglican clergyman named William Jackson, who had once been a popular preacher in London, had afterwards been employed by the notorious Duchess of Kingston in her quarrel with Foote, and had attained an infamous notoriety as the chief instigator of a groundless and atrocious charge against that dramatist.[2] After these transactions Jackson had long lived in France, where he professed strong revolutionary sentiments, and he undertook to ascertain what support might be expected from the English democratic party in the event of an invasion. Finding the result of his inquiry in England very discouraging,

---

[1] February 1, 15, 22; March 8, 1794 (I.S.P.O.).

[2] See Cooke's *Life of Foote*, i. 200-231.

he determined to proceed to Ireland, and he confided his mission and his intention to an attorney named Cockayne, with whom he had long been on terms of friendship, and who, like himself, had been in the service of the Duchess of Kingston. Cockayne at once betrayed him, and by the direction of the Government pretended to enter into his scheme, and accompanied him to Dublin. Cockayne had formed a professional friendship with Leonard McNally, a Dublin barrister, who was much mixed in the proceedings of the United Irishmen, and at the table of McNally the two travellers met several of the leaders of the party, who received them cordially and spoke freely of their hopes. They obtained without difficulty access to Hamilton Rowan, who was still in prison and who threw himself heartily into the French designs, and a representation of the state of Ireland, written by Wolfe Tone, but copied by Rowan, was given to Jackson to be presented to the French Government. Jackson was delighted with it, and desired Tone himself to go to France to lay his views before the Committee of Public Safety. Tone at first accepted, but afterwards refused, and Jackson did not encourage the proposal of Rowan that Dr. Reynolds, another leading member of the party, should undertake the charge. In the meantime, through the instrumentality of Cockayne, the representation of Tone fell into the hands of the Government, and on April 24, 1794, Jackson was thrown into prison on a charge of treason. The perfidy of Cockayne was still unsuspected.

A whole year elapsed before Jackson was tried, and the Government for some time doubted what course they would pursue. There was a chance that Jackson might turn king's evidence against the leading conspirators, but even in that case the evidence against them seemed very slender, so it was determined to prosecute Jackson.[1] The knowledge of his arrest

[1] 'The Attorney-General is afraid if Drennan is caught that we have not a tittle of evidence against him, and as little against Tone, for you observe Cockayne, whose evidence will be taken *cum grano*, will not speak positively to the different conversations of these persons, but only caught the substance by hints and accidental words. I cannot agree in thinking it wise to save Jackson and punish the others. Jackson is sure to be convicted; with him we should very likely fail in punishing either of the other two. With how bad an appearance of evidence (Cockayne and Jackson, hardly a corroborating circumstance), we should go into court. Not a person in court but would attribute the whole scheme to a snare, and

spread much alarm among the United Irishmen. Tone indeed remained to brave the consequences, and no prosecution against him was instituted, but Reynolds fled to America, and Rowan, who had hitherto taken a very prominent part among the United Irishmen, contrived on May 1 to escape from prison and make his way to France. Unlike most of those who were engaged in the conspiracy, he was a gentleman of fortune and position. He was foolish and impulsive, but also brave, honourable, chivalrous, energetic, and charitable, a man of great physical strength and beauty, always ready to meet any opponent with his pistol, and to throw himself headlong into adventures. A proclamation was at once issued and widely disseminated offering a reward of 1,000l. from the Government and of 500l. from the City for his capture, but a friend named Sweetman procured a small fishing boat manned by three poor sailors to take him to France. The sailors had not been informed of the service for which they were engaged, but before they started on their long and perilous journey one of them drew from his pocket the Government proclamation and asked if this was Mr. Rowan they were carrying to France. 'Yes,' said Sweetman, 'and here he is.' 'By God,' was the reply, 'we will land him safely;' and turning to Rowan he said, 'Our boat is small, but God watches over those who, like you, have the blessings of the poor.'[1] They kept their word, and placed him on shore near Brest. A few days after his flight, the Government, acting on the information of their habitual informer, seized the room where the United Irishmen met, took possession of their papers, and for a time broke up the organisation.

A more marked tone of disloyalty was now manifestly spreading through the country. A large proportion of the Belfast party had long been theoretical republicans, but they always declared that they would have been content with a democratic parliamentary reform. The attitude of the Government and of the Parliament during the last session convinced them that it would be easier to obtain a republic than a reform under the existing Government; that without foreign aid they

---

the Government would be sadly disgraced.' (Westmorland to Dundas, May 12, 1794.) Cockayne had previously been tried for perjury, but acquitted.

[1] Rowan's *Autobiography*. Letter of H. Rowan to the Committee of Public Safety, 10 vendémiaire, an iii. (Oct. 1, 1794), F.F.O.

could never effectually resist the coalition between the English Government and the Irish aristocracy, and that their chance of obtaining such aid was now very considerable. They had at the same time begun to argue, as Adams and his colleagues had argued in the beginning of the American troubles, that the French would only assist them in a struggle for independence. The reform of the Irish Parliament could be no object to France. The establishment of an independent Irish republic would be a great triumph of French policy. With the vast dissemination of seditious or republican literature the area of discontent was enlarging, and it was spreading more and more among the Catholics. The signs, indeed, were not yet clear and unequivocal, and some months were still to elapse before they became so; but it was impossible that the new doctrines of political equality, of the indefeasible right of majorities to govern, of the iniquity of tithes and other religious endowments should not have their influence upon men who would gain so greatly by their triumph. The gentry and the higher clergy reflected very faithfully the Catholic conservatism of Europe; but the tradesmen and merchants, who were so active in the towns, were of a different type. Some of the most important members of the Catholic Committee were unquestionably seditious, and, in spite of the very earnest remonstrance of Grattan, the committee retained Wolfe Tone as its secretary. Colonel Blaquiere in the session of 1794 startled and scandalised the House of Commons by declaring his belief that 'there was not a man among them who, in case of commotion, could find fifty followers on his estate perfectly attached to the Constitution.' 'What,' he continued, 'had the poor to defend? Was it because their landlord now and then gave them a dinner, or treated them civilly when he met them, that they should be attached to him?'[1] He believed that half the nation, or more than half, were attached to the French. His words were drowned in indignant denials. In no country, it was said, were the landlords less oppressive than in Ireland; but an uneasy feeling was abroad, and although outrages and riots appear to have somewhat diminished, those who knew the country best believed that the Defender system was advancing with a rapid though stealthy

[1] *Irish Parl. Deb.* xiv. 37.

progress. Our best evidence seems to show that it was not yet connected with the United Irish movement, and that it aimed chiefly at Whiteboy objects, but a political element was beginning very perceptibly to mingle with it. The idea was spreading that the redress of all grievances would be effected by a French invasion, and that in the event of such an invasion it was the duty of the Defenders to assist it. Oaths pledging them to do so were in some districts largely taken, and in others the project was well understood.[1] That it had not taken as much hold upon the people as was sometimes thought, is proved by the most decisive of all arguments, by their actual conduct when an invasion took place; but there were at least signs that what was to be feared among the poorest Catholic population was not merely turbulence and lawlessness, but also a positive hostility to the connection.

The influence of Grattan also had been fatally weakened. His position was at this time one of the most difficult that can fall to the lot of any statesman, and he was maintaining it with admirable courage and skill. At a time when the enthusiasm for the French Revolution was at its height, when French ideas and theories of reform were making numerous proselytes among the adventurous and enthusiastic, he was steadily opposing the stream, preaching at once the duty of a close connection with England and the Whig theory of the Constitution. But unlike those who occupied a corresponding position in England, Grattan continued to be a zealous and consistent reformer, contending that without the abolition of political distinctions on account of religion and a temperate reform of Parliament there could be no security in Ireland. In one aspect of his policy he resembled Burke; in the other he resembled Fox. It was inevitable under these circumstances that his position should have been somewhat isolated. The coalesced interests opposed to all reform detested him as the most formidable enemy to their monopolies, and much of the enthusiasm which had in old days supported him was passing into new channels. His loyalty to the connection, his support of the war, his inflexible opposition to the United Ireland scheme of radical and democratic reform, had alienated the class

---

[1] See the interesting sketch of Defenderism in 1793, by Emmet. (McNevin's *Pieces of Irish History*, p. 71.)

of mind which naturally bends with the dominant enthusiasm of the time. With the better class of Catholics he had, it is true, still great authority, and his influence was perhaps even greater with his own class—with the great body of Protestant gentlemen of moderate fortune who were unconnected with the chief borough owners, and who, though they were very inadequately represented in Parliament, comprised perhaps the largest part of the patriotism, the intelligence, and the energy of Ireland.

It seemed, however, for a time as if his policy and his power were about to rise higher than ever. In July 1794 the long-pending secession from the Whig party in England took place, and the Duke of Portland, Lord Fitzwilliam, Lord Spencer, and Windham joined the Government. By this change, at a time when the aspect of affairs on the Continent was peculiarly menacing, parties in England were virtually united in support of the war, and opposition sank into complete insignificance; but if the adhesion of the Whig leaders gave Pitt a great accession of strength, it also brought with it some embarrassments. The section of the Whig party which joined him was so important that it was entitled to claim a large share both of patronage and power, but Pitt was scarcely less autocratic in his cabinet than his father and Walpole, and Dundas appears to have been the only minister to whose judgment he greatly deferred. With a prime minister of this character it might easily be foreseen that the introduction into the Cabinet of politicians of great rank, great parliamentary following, great pretensions and very moderate abilities, drawn from the opposite party, was likely to lead to difficulties. The negotiations that preceded and immediately followed the coalition were carried on almost entirely by conversations, and when this is the case it will nearly always be found that misunderstandings arise even among men of the most indisputable honour. The general drift of propositions is remembered, but qualifications and limitations by which they had been guarded are neglected or underrated. Something is tacitly assumed on one side which the other side had not meant to concede, and men who starting from opposite points are anxious to come to an agreement, will often half unconsciously omit, attenuate, or evade topics of difference. Add to this that the Whig leaders never professed to have abandoned any of their old views of domestic policy, though they undertook to support the war; that the King, though glad to break up the Whig party, still looked on all who had supported that party with suspicion and aversion, and that a great portion of Pitt's own followers, as Burke truly said, 'considered Mr. Pitt's enlarging his bottom as an interloping on their monopoly,'[1] and it will be easily understood that there were abundant elements of disagreement.

These considerations will not appear irrelevant when we attempt to thread our way through the perplexed and contradictory evidence relating to the viceroyalty of Lord Fitzwilliam. When the coalition was formed in July, the third Secretaryship of State, which had been abolished in 1782, was revived. Lord Grenville was now Secretary of State for Foreign Affairs, Dundas for War and the Colonies, and Portland for the Home Department, which comprised Ireland as well as Great Britain. It is a significant fact that at the very outset of the coalition a grave misunderstanding arose between Dundas and Portland about the limits of their respective provinces,[2] but it is at least certain that Ireland lay within the department of Portland; it is equally certain that it was agreed, or believed by the Whig leaders to have been agreed, that Portland was to have the chief direction of Irish politics, that Lord Westmorland was to be replaced by a Lord Lieutenant belonging to the Whig party, and that some change of system favourable to the Catholics was to be effected. It is true, indeed, that Pelham, who was Chief Secretary in Ireland in the administration that succeeded that of Lord Fitzwilliam, asserted in the Irish House of Commons that the Duke of Portland had coalesced with Pitt 'unconditionally,' 'without any stipulation whatever,'[3] but the evidence in contradiction to this assertion appears to me overwhelming. On July 27, at a time when no dispute had yet arisen, Lord Auckland, who hated the Portland party, sent the following account to Beresford of the secret history of the coalition. 'If Mr. Pitt felt that the calamities of the times required this change (for such it is) in his administration, there was nothing more to be said. I can

---

[1] See a very remarkable letter in Windham's *Diary*, p. 326.
[2] Stanhope's *Life of Pitt*, ii. 252–255.
[3] *Irish Parl. Deb.* xv. 184, 190.

freely confide to you my persuasion, that he has made a bad move on his political chess-board. I believe that Dundas was the only person of his old friends materially consulted on the occasion. He will find that he has destroyed the weight of a party which was material to be preserved, and which will now become at least insignificant, and he will also find that he has gained nothing in point of talents and efficiency; and lastly, that he is in a decided minority in his own Cabinet. I understood that when this coalition was formed, Ireland was offered to the Portland party together with the other offices, which were accepted; and I have heard (which I mention in great confidence) that an apology was made to Lord Camden, to whom Ireland had before been destined. Lord Spencer and the Duke of Devonshire and Lord Fitzwilliam having declined the viceroyalty, it may possibly remain for the present in Lord Westmorland, but that tenure cannot be, I think, long, and in short it is under the Duke of Portland's department.'[1]

It may be said that Auckland, though in intimate connection with the leading statesmen of the Tory party, had no official knowledge of what had occurred, but the evidence of those who had the most incontestable means of knowing is equally decisive. Ponsonby, who had the most intimate private and official relations with Lord Fitzwilliam, declared in Parliament that the 'coalition would never have taken place had not his Grace received ample authority to reform the abuses which he knew existed in the Government.'[2] Grattan, as his son reports, stated that the words of the Duke of Portland to him on the subject were: 'I have taken office, and I have done so because I knew there was to be an entire change of system.'[3] Burke assured Windham that, from a conversation with Portland shortly after the coalition, he gathered that, rightly or wrongly, he 'considered without a doubt that the administration of Ireland was left wholly to him, and without any other reserves than what are supposed in every wise and sober servant of the Crown;'[4] and Fitzwilliam himself, who took a leading part through the whole negotiation, has left a most emphatic statement to the same effect. 'When the Duke of Portland,' he wrote, 'and his friends

---

[1] *Beresford Correspondence* (privately printed), ii. 37, 38.
[2] *Irish Parl. Deb.* xv. 184.
[3] Grattan's *Life*, iv. 193.
[4] Windham's *Diary*, p. 322.

were to be enticed into a coalition with Mr. Pitt's administration, it was necessary to hold out such lures as would make the coalition palatable, or even possible, for them to accede to. If the general management and superintendence of Ireland had not been offered to his Grace, that coalition would never have taken place. The sentiments that he had entertained and the language he had held so publicly for many years back on the subject, rendered it a point that could not be dispensed with. Accordingly it was offered from the beginning of the negotiation, as was also the Home Department of Secretary of State.'[1]

When the coalition took place, Fitzwilliam was appointed President of the Council; but as there appears to have been a difficulty in finding a Whig Lord Lieutenant, in fulfilment of the arrangement that has been indicated, Fitzwilliam, after long hesitation and with great reluctance, consented to accept the post. It was stipulated that Lord Westmorland must first be provided for, but subject to this condition the nomination was fully accepted by Pitt. It was settled, at least as early as August 11,[2] and the arrangement seems to me quite inexplicable, except on the supposition that some real change of policy was contemplated, and that Irish affairs were in a very special sense under the direction of the Whig section of the Cabinet. Lord Fitzwilliam had scarcely a month before accepted a Cabinet office in England. He had no wish to go to Ireland, and Lord Westmorland never appears to have intimated any intention of resigning. If it was intended to make no change in the system of governing Ireland, the whole proceeding is unintelligible.

---

[1] *Second Letter to Lord Carlisle*, pp. 25, 26. Grattan, in one of his speeches on the subject, said: 'It has been said that the reform of abuses in Ireland formed no part of the ground of the coalition. I do not pretend to say what did form that ground, but I do say that one quarter of the Cabinet did assert that a principal inducement to his acceptance of office was a reform in the abuses of the Irish Government. . . . One great motive to the acceptance of office was stated to be very extensive powers in Ireland.' (*Irish Parl. Deb.* xv. 191.) Lord Holland says that the Duke of Portland distinctly encouraged these hopes. '"At least we have secured the Catholics," said he to some English friends; and he did not scruple to affirm to Mr. Grattan that his chief object in taking office was to secure the objects which the Irish Whigs had pursued, and a large share of the patronage and power in Ireland to their party. Nearly thus did Lord Fitzwilliam understand it.' (*Mems. of the Whig Party,* i. 74.)

[2] See Buckingham's *Courts and Cabinets of George III.* ii. 281.

Independently of all negotiations, the mere fact of the accession of a great portion of the Whig party to office had a powerful and an immediate effect in Ireland. Portland had been Lord Lieutenant when the independence of the Irish Parliament had been conceded in 1782; he was known to be in favour of Catholic emancipation, and Grattan had long regarded him with an admiration which he would scarcely have felt if he had had the advantage of perusing his confidential despatches. Fitzwilliam was extremely popular in Ireland from his large property, his decided advocacy of the Catholics, and his close friendship with Grattan. Ponsonby, who had publicly committed himself to the admission of Catholics to Parliament, and to a moderate parliamentary reform, and Grattan, who was the most powerful advocate of both measures, had long been in closer connection and correspondence with the party which had joined the Government than with any other section of English politicians. They were essentially Whigs, and it was inevitable that their influence and their policy should appear to have gained by the coalition of the Whig leaders with the Government. Nor did there seem any reason for believing that the completion of the Act of 1793 would be distasteful to the other section of the Cabinet. The policy of admitting the Catholics to political power was the policy of Pitt. It had been steadily advocated by his Government. The opposition which restricted or delayed the measure did not come from England, or from the Irish Parliament, or, to any considerable extent, from the Irish Protestants, but from a small junto of high officials in Ireland under the guidance of Fitzgibbon. Irish public opinion was now in so dangerous and critical a condition that it would be in the highest degree calamitous to raise hopes and then refuse to fulfil them, and the simple fact of the accession of the Duke of Portland and Lord Fitzwilliam to power at once brought the Catholic question again to the forefront. 'I have the best grounds for believing,' Lord Fitzwilliam afterwards wrote, 'that on the day of the Duke of Portland's kissing hands, it was determined to bring it [the Catholic question] forward this session. All the old friends with whom he had acted when he was here as Lord Lieutenant, and whom, it was concluded, he would again call to his councils on taking to himself the government, of which there was at that time a general expectation, were known from their public declarations and from their proceedings in Parliament to intend a full and complete emancipation; his own opinions were universally believed to coincide with his Irish friends', as to my knowledge they certainly did. Immediate measures were therefore taken by the Catholics preparatory to the expected change of administration here.'[1]

The first proceeding of Lord Fitzwilliam, after he had consented to be the future Lord Lieutenant, is very significant, and shows decisively how fully his position was recognised by Pitt's section of the Cabinet. As early as August 11 he wrote to Thomas Grenville, who was then in a diplomatic capacity at Vienna, offering him the post of Chief Secretary in his coming administration. Thomas Grenville was brother of Lord Grenville, the Secretary for Foreign Affairs and one of the most important colleagues of Pitt before the coalition had taken place. It must also be noticed that he had been offered and had refused this office in 1782, when the Duke of Portland had been made Lord Lieutenant.[2] Thomas Grenville would have greatly preferred an English post, but he was very anxious to leave the Continent; and after consultation with his brother, and with the full assent of his brother, he accepted the office, expressing, however, at the same time his hope that if an English office became vacant, Portland would not forget his claims.[3]

Not quite a fortnight after he had written to Thomas Grenville, Lord Fitzwilliam wrote to Grattan. He stated that, though he was not yet appointed to succeed Lord Westmorland, there was certainly 'great probability of that event taking place very soon;' that he intended to pursue the same system as the Duke of Portland had pursued when he was Lord Lieutenant; that his main object would be 'to purify, as far as circumstances and prudence will permit, the principles of government, in the hopes of thereby restoring it to that tone and spirit which so happily prevailed formerly,' but that he despaired of succeeding in this attempt unless he obtained the support of distinguished Irishmen. 'It is, sir, to you,' he added, 'and your friends the Ponsonbys, that I look for assistance. . . . Without the hope,

---

[1] *First Letter to Lord Carlisle*, p. 16.
[2] Buckingham's *Courts and Cabinets*, ii. 299   [3] Ibid. pp. 277, 300.

which I am vain enough to entertain, of that assistance, I should decline engaging in so hopeless a task as the government of Ireland. It is that assistance which I am, therefore, now soliciting. I know well the honourable, the useful, the important support Government has received at your hands on many critical occasions and at different periods; but except during the momentary administration of the Duke of Portland, I believe it has so happened that you never have approached the Castle in confidence and avowed friendship; great obstacles have always stood in the way. Should these obstacles be removed, I trust that distance will no longer be necessary, and that I may entertain a hope of seeing you form with the Castle that sort of intimate, direct, and avowed connection as will render support doubly efficacious.' In a postscript he added: 'I beg not to be quoted as having announced myself in the character of a Lord Lieutenant elect; my name not having yet been mentioned to the King, on account of his absence at Weymouth.'[1]

Grattan, however, persisted in the resolution which he had early formed that he would not take office under the Crown, and would content himself with giving an independent support. He appears to have considered that he had pledged himself to such a course when he accepted a grant from Parliament, and he probably thought that in the very difficult position he had assumed as at once the head of the reform party in Parliament and one of the chief opponents of the republican party in Ulster, it was essential to his authority that his disinterestedness should be beyond possible suspicion. At the same time he could not neglect the invitation of Lord Fitzwilliam. Early in September he went over to London to consult with the leading statesmen. The two Ponsonby brothers, Sir John Parnell the Irish Chancellor of the Exchequer, and some other Irish politicians were there, and they had conferences not only with the Portland section of the Cabinet, but also with Pitt and with the Grenvilles. As far as can now be gathered, Grattan does not appear to have at all desired the removal of all who held office under Lord Westmorland's administration. With Sir John Parnell, at least, he was on terms of the most intimate friendship, and he insisted, in opposition to some of his own friends, that Parnell

[1] Grattan's *Life*, iv. 173. (The letter was written August 23, 1794).

should continue in office, but he seems to have represented that if any serious advance was to be made in the direction either of parliamentary reform or of Catholic emancipation, it would be necessary to remove some prominent officials, and especially the Chancellor, Lord Fitzgibbon. These men had been the most persistent and vehement opponents of all changes in those directions. They had defeated the efforts of the English Government in 1792, and in 1793 Fitzgibbon had done his utmost to destroy the conciliatory effect of the Relief Bill by a speech fraught with the bitterest invective against the Catholics. He had asserted, with a cynical boldness that no other politician had approached, the propriety of governing Ireland by corruption, and he was at the head of a small group who were virtually controlling the Executive and using all their power for the maintenance of monopolies and abuses.

The particulars of the interviews in England are very imperfectly preserved. Grattan noticed that the Grenvilles and Ponsonbys seemed cold and hostile to each other, and, although Pitt treated all parties with courtesy, some disquieting sentences fell from him. When Parnell spoke with congratulation of the union that was being accomplished between the Protestants and the Catholics, Pitt answered, ' Very true, sir; but the question is, whose will they be?' 'What does Ireland want?' he said on another occasion to Grattan; 'she has already got much.'[1] At the same time, for some weeks neither Portland nor Fitzwilliam, nor any member of their party, appears to have had the smallest doubt that the contemplated arrangements would be effected. The details, however, were still in the stage of confidential negotiation, and it is a singular fact that no communication on the subject from the responsible minister, appears as yet to have been made to the Irish Government. In a letter written on September 5 to Auckland, Lord Sheffield mentions an interview which he had had with Douglas, the Chief Secretary of Lord Westmorland, and adds: ' It is curious that he seems to know nothing of the appointment of Lord Fitzwilliam to the viceroyalty of Ireland.'[2]

It appears to me evident from these statements, that there

---

[1] Grattan's *Life*, iv. 174–177. 237. Compare Buckingham's *Courts and Cabinets*, ii. 313.
[2] *Auckland Correspondence*, iii.

had been much less frankness, fullness, and precision than there ought to have been in the discussion of Irish affairs. The system of government to be pursued had not been clearly defined or settled, nor had the limits of the powers of the new minister been formally ascertained. On the other hand, the department of Ireland had been definitely placed under the direction of Portland, who was at the head of the Whig section of the Cabinet. Fitzwilliam as the representative of that section had been offered and had accepted the viceroyalty. Although the post was not yet vacant, he was actually engaged, with the full knowledge of Pitt, in framing the outline of his Government, and the ministerial Whigs had, as it seems to me, ample reason to conclude that Pitt was prepared to place the general direction of Irish affairs in their hands, and to assent to the system of policy which they notoriously advocated. The negotiation with Ponsonby and Grattan was carried on with perfect openness, and it could have but one significance. It must have meant that the Government was inclined to look with favour on moderate parliamentary reform, and on the admission of the Catholics into the Irish Parliament, or at least upon one of these measures. It was impossible that the steps which had been taken could be disclosed without raising in Ireland hopes which it would be most dangerous to disappoint.

In the letters of Lord Grenville we may trace the first signs of the dissension which soon became so formidable. On September 15 he wrote to Thomas Grenville: 'I am afraid there is less discretion on that subject [Ireland] than there should be. The intended successor of Lord Westmorland is talked of more openly than I think useful at a time when there is yet no arrangement made for his quitting his station. But, what is worse than that, ideas are going about, and are much encouraged in Dublin, of *new systems* there, and of changes of men and measures. Whatever it may be prudent to *do* in that respect, I know that you will agree with me, that till the time comes when that question is to be considered with a view to acting upon it immediately, the less *said* about it the better.'[1]

Twelve days later, in a letter to Lord Buckingham, he complains

---

[1] Buckingham's *Courts and Cabinets*, ii. 302.

that Buckingham had too readily believed vague reports about the Government of Ireland. 'I know of no such measure as you say we have adopted. I have never varied in my opinion as to the impolicy of the conduct held in Ireland during the time of Lord Rockingham's administration, nor do I believe that anyone is disposed to repeat that conduct now. . . . I certainly have not, for one, consented, as you express it, to surrender Ireland to the Duke of Portland and Lord Fitzwilliam, under the Government of Mr. Ponsonby.' At the same time he does not see why the Government should feel any particular interest in the existing system in Ireland, and he added some enigmatical words which probably pointed to a great change in the constitutional relation of the two countries, that was already in the minds of the Ministers. 'It has long appeared to me, and, I believe, to you also, that to make the connection with Ireland permanently useful to Great Britain, that connection must be strengthened by a systematic plan of measures, well considered and steadily pursued. Whether the present moment, or any other moment that is in near prospect, would be favourable to such a plan, is another and a more difficult question, but I am sure that every year that is lost increases the hazard of our situation as with respect to Ireland. . . . I cannot conceive what other interest you or I have, or ought to have, on that subject except that Ireland should be so managed, if possible, as not to be an additional difficulty in our way, when so many others are likely to occur.'[1]

It was not, however, till about the middle of October that the storm burst. The Duke of Portland urged the immediate appointment of Fitzwilliam as a thing already arranged, and explanations speedily ensued, which disclosed an entirely unexpected amount of disagreement, and for more than a fortnight made it probable that the coalition would fall to pieces.

The evidence concerning this quarrel is not very abundant or very consistent, but the chief points at issue may, I think, be ascertained with tolerable clearness. Pitt did not dispute that Lord Fitzwilliam had been duly designated as the future Lord Lieutenant of Ireland, but he maintained that Portland and Fitzwilliam had exceeded their powers when they communicated

---

[1] Buckingham's *Courts and Cabinets*, ii. 305, 306.

with the Ponsonbys and other persons in Ireland, on the understanding that a change of administration was immediately to take place, and especially when they intimated that Fitzgibbon was to be removed, and that a change in the system of government in Ireland was to be made. 'I am fully determined,' he wrote to Dundas, ' that I will not give way either to Lord Westmorland's recall without a proper situation for him here, or to Lord Fitzgibbon's removal on any terms.' 'I am confirmed,' he wrote to Windham, 'in the impossibility either of consenting to the Chancellor's removal, or of leaving either him or any of the supporters of Government exposed to the risk of the new system.' 'Besides the impossibility of sacrificing any supporters of Government or exposing them to the risk of a new system, I ought to add that the very idea of a new system (as far as I understand what is meant by that term), and especially one formed without previous communication or concert with the rest of the King's servants here, or with the friends of Government in Ireland, is in itself what I feel it utterly impossible to accede to.' In a memorandum which he appears to have drawn up for his own use during the discussion, he expresses his opinion that the best solution of the difficulty would be that Lord Fitzwilliam should not go to Ireland, but that it was impossible, if satisfaction were given on other points, to put a negative on his going. The change of administration in Ireland, however, could only be permitted on four conditions. First, all idea of a new system of measures or of new principles of government in Ireland, as well as of any separate and exclusive right to conduct the department of Ireland differently from any other in the King's service, must be disclaimed and relinquished; second, complete security must be given that Lord Fitzgibbon and all the supporters of Government shall not be displaced on the change, nor while they continue to act fairly in support of such a system as shall be approved in England; third, a seat in the Cabinet, and also a great Court office, must be found for Lord Westmorland; and fourth, an adequate provision must be made for Douglas, the present Chief Secretary.[1]

The dispute on both sides was extremely angry. The transfer of the chief management of Ireland to the Whig section

[1] Stanhope's *Life of Pitt*, ii. 283, 289-291.

of the Cabinet had, it was said, been one of the main conditions of the coalition; the selection from that section of a future Lord Lieutenant had been one of its first results, and it could never have been intended—though Pitt now evidently desired it—that the actual change should be postponed to a distant and indefinite future. The offer of the Chief Secretaryship to the brother of Lord Grenville, and the interviews of Pitt with Ponsonby and with Grattan, furnished on this point conclusive arguments. It had, it is true, been stipulated that Westmorland was to receive another office before Lord Fitzwilliam was appointed, but it was understood that Pitt would at once make it his business to create a vacancy, and it could not be seriously contended that he was unable to do so. The Duke of Portland, as a former Lord Lieutenant of Ireland, had his own political connections in that country, and it had been very naturally assumed that when Ireland was again placed under his direction, those connections would be again entrusted with a great part of the administration; in other words, that a change of power and patronage would take place, in some degree resembling that which follows a change of ministry in England. Grattan, it is true, who acted during the whole of this crisis with an admirable temper and moderation, appears to have cared very little what men were in office, but some of the other leaders of his party placed no control upon their indignation. They accused Pitt of having duped them, of having obtained their alliance on false pretences. The management of Ireland, they said, had been expressly offered to them, and offered without reservation. The right of appointing to offices in Ireland naturally belonged to the Lord Lieutenant and Secretary of State for the Home Department, and it was fully within their province to pension off a secretary or even a chancellor. From the fact that the new ministers had a well-known Irish policy and a well-known set of Irish connections, it plainly followed that when they were entrusted with power, that policy and those connections would be in the ascendant, and they asserted that it had been clearly intimated at the time of the junction that a change of system must take place. To offer the management of Ireland was perfectly nugatory, if the Secretary of State and the Lord Lieutenant were divested of their natural right of appointing or removing officials. Pitt, it was said, had allowed his new colleagues to go on week after week till they had so committed themselves that they could not recede without dishonour, and he had then withheld from them the powers of which they had every reason to believe themselves possessed. The question was not a mere question of men. Serious reforms in Ireland would never be accomplished if the chief posts of influence and power were in the hands of their opponents, and a viceroyalty was likely to be little more than a prolonged humiliation if there was no cordiality between the head and his subordinates.

The substantial justice of these complaints appears to me incontestable. On the other side it was denied that any change of system such as was described had been contemplated or promised at the time of the coalition, or that the new Ministers had any right to displace the old and faithful servants of the Crown. The Whigs were accused of treating the government of Ireland as a mere departmental question which might be determined without the consent or even the knowledge of the remainder of the Cabinet. 'The system of introducing English party into Ireland,' wrote Grenville, 'the principle of connecting changes of Government here with the removal of persons high in office there, . . . is so utterly irreconcilable with any view that I have of the state of that country, that I should be inexcusable if I could make myself a party to such a measure, and in this opinion Pitt entirely concurs.' If 'a new system of men and measures' had been intended before the junction, it ought surely to have been stated then; if it had only been conceived since that event, it ought to have been communicated to the Cabinet 'before any pledge or assurance was given to individuals who might be concerned in it' in Ireland. The removal of Lord Fitzgibbon was completely inadmissible. Lord Grenville asserted—what it is utterly incredible that any man who knew Ireland can have believed—that 'the only ground on which the Ponsonbys can desire the Chancellor's removal is the conduct he held during the Regency,' and that it would be therefore dishonourable and degrading for those who had been ministers during that contest to permit it. The question was treated on this side, as merely a question of patronage. 'The Portland set,' said Lord Auckland, 'are absorbed in the old and sleepy game of patronage, in the pursuit of which they are at this instant risking the convulsion of Ireland.'[1]

Burke was at this time removed from active politics, and overwhelmed with grief, on account of the very recent death of his son; but Windham, who was the most devoted of all his disciples, was one of the recent adherents to the Ministry, and the old statesman tore himself from his private sorrow to write some admirable letters on the crisis that was pending. He viewed it with profound grief, but also with much impartiality. To Pitt he was under great recent obligation, and he looked upon him as the one man who could resist the invasions of Jacobinism. To the Whig leaders who had taken part in the secession he was attached by many years of private friendship and political cooperation; their junction with Pitt had been the realisation of his most ardent wish, and he at the same time followed Irish politics with a greater interest and knowledge than any other statesman in England. He considered the dispute that had arisen, a calamity of the first magnitude. There were politicians, no doubt, who would tell Pitt that 'the disgracing his colleagues would be to him a signal triumph,' 'a splendid mark of his power and superiority,' but such politicians were very short-sighted. Pitt could have gone on without a junction with the Whigs, but his Ministry, which was of such transcendent importance to Europe, could hardly long survive a new disruption; yet Burke did not see how Portland and Fitzwilliam could remain in office without utterly discrediting their characters. What were the exact terms of the arrangement between the Whig leaders and Pitt on the subject of Ireland, he did not pretend to say. All he knew was that Portland and Fitzwilliam considered without a doubt that the administration of Ireland was left wholly to them, and 'proceeded as if there was no controversy whatever on the subject;' that Fitzwilliam 'hesitated a long time whether he should take the station;' that when he agreed to it, he thought he had done a real service to the Ministry, and that, anticipating no difficulties from his colleagues, he 'invited several persons to converse with him in all the confidence with which men ought to open themselves to a

[1] *Auckland Papers*, iii. 253; Buckingham's *Courts and Cabinets*, ii. 312–316.

person of honour, who though not actually, was virtually in office.' It was not in accordance with strict prudence, or 'with an entire decorum with regard to the other Cabinet Ministers, to go so far into detail as has been done, until all the circumstances of the appointment were settled in a more distinct and specific manner than they had been.' The Whig leaders undoubtedly 'thought that a very large discretion was committed to them,' but they must have been strangely mistaken, for 'it seems Mr. Pitt had no thought at all of a change in the Irish Government, or, if he had, it was dependent on Lord Westmorland's sense of the fitness of some other office to accommodate him on his resignation. . . . These are some of the mischiefs which arise from a want of clear explanation on the first digestion of any political system.'

The great question was whether Lord Fitzwilliam could honourably consent either to continue in his present office, abandoning his claims to the viceroyalty, or to accept the viceroyalty on the terms on which it was now offered to him? 'With infinite sorrow'—'with sorrow inexpressible,' Burke concluded that both courses were impossible. 'He has consulted with many people from Ireland of all descriptions as if he were virtually Lord Lieutenant. The Duke of Portland has acted upon that supposition as a fundamental part of his arrangement. Lord Fitzwilliam cannot shrink into his shell again, without being thought a light man, in whom no person can place any confidence. If, on the other hand, he takes the sword not only without power, but with a direct negative put upon his power, he is a Lord Lieutenant disgraced and degraded.' He must resign, and those who entered into the Ministry with him must accompany him.

Englishmen with little knowledge of Ireland, considered the question a mere personal one, and asked why Fitzgibbon might not continue Chancellor while Fitzwilliam was Viceroy. 'After what has passed, the true question is, which of the two is to govern Ireland.' No position can be more helpless or degrading than that of a Lord Lieutenant who is not effectually supported by the English Minister, who is surrounded by subordinates opposed to him, and is liable to be thwarted at every turn by the parties in Ireland. If this is the position intended for Lord Fitzwilliam, a worse choice could not have been made, and it would have been far better to keep Lord Westmorland in Ireland. 'It is not to know Ireland to say that what is called Opposition is what will give trouble to a real viceroy. His embarrassments are upon the part of those who ought to be the supports of English Government, but who have formed themselves into a cabal to destroy the King's authority, and to divide the country as a spoil amongst one another. *Non regnum sed magnum latrocinium*—the motto ought to be put under the harp.'

'Ireland,' he continued, ' is no longer an obscure dependency of this kingdom. What is done there, vitally affects the whole system of Europe. . . . It will be a strong digue to keep out Jacobinism, or a broken bank to let it in. . . . By the meditated and systematic corruption . . . of some, and the headlong violence and tyrannical spirit of others, totally destitute of wisdom, and the more incurably so as not being destitute of some flashy parts,[1] it is brought into a very perilous situation.' If the junto who were governing it were not speedily checked, Burke clearly predicted that a calamity was inevitable which might involve the ruin of the Empire. 'There is a set of men in Ireland who . . . by their innumerable corruptions, frauds, oppressions, and follies were opening a back door for Jacobinism to rush in. . . . As surely as you and I exist, so surely this will be the consequence of their persisting in their system.'[2]

In reviewing this whole controversy, it appears to me evident that the Whig leaders had just reason to complain of the conduct of Pitt—that they had real grounds for believing that powers had been promised them, which were afterwards withdrawn or denied. It seems as if Pitt had either failed to realise the full import of the concessions he had made, or else had changed his mind, and desired to withdraw from a position which was disadvantageous to him. The secret motives that governed him, must always be a matter of conjecture. What motives were likely to be attributed to him, Burke very clearly stated. The Whig leaders had been warned before they made the alliance, that it was not in the character of Pitt to give them

---

[1] An evident portrait of Fitzgibbon. [2] Windham's *Diary*, pp. 321-333.

any real confidence or any real share of power—that he would accept their alliance, but on the first difference, when they had broken with their friends and original connections, and had lost all credit with the independent part of the country, and all power of formidable opposition, would turn them out as objects of universal scorn and derision.

It is not, however, necessary, or, I believe, just, to attribute such calculations to Pitt. Like most English statesmen, he had a very slight and superficial knowledge of Irish affairs, which depended upon conditions of character and circumstances wholly unlike those with which he was familiar, and from the moment the contemplated change was announced, a constant stream of the most alarming letters, which were evidently intended to be laid before him, poured over from the high officials in Ireland. If the proposed changes were effected, it was said, Ireland would pass completely into the hands of the Duke of Portland, and the Government in England would never be able to take it out of them again. The Ponsonbys were already boasting that they were the masters of the country. The whole of the highly artificial system by which the Irish Government was kept in permanent subjection to the English Executive would be broken. Popular questions would acquire a momentum that it would be henceforth impossible to withstand. Those men who had for years made it their policy to resist the popular wishes, and to act on all occasions as the exclusive servants of the English Government, would consider themselves betrayed, and would either sink into complete impotence, or enlist under new banners. The main object of Pitt's Irish policy was to keep the country at once quiet and subservient, and he was most anxious that no new field of domestic embarrassment should be opened at a time when the condition of the Continent and the prospects of the war were so alarming. He was full of doubt about the dispositions and future tendencies of the Irish people. He could give Irish affairs but a small share of his attention, and he was told that if he carried out the arrangement that was proposed, they would pass wholly and for ever beyond his control. The demand for the removal of Fitzgibbon must, also, have been peculiarly unpalatable to him. It was quite true that the part which this able man had taken both on the question of Reform and on the question of the Catholics had made his removal a matter of the first political importance or necessity if a policy of conciliation was to be pursued, and in this consideration the path of duty was, I think, clearly indicated. But, on the other hand, Fitzgibbon in 1788, almost alone among prominent Irish politicians, and at the imminent risk of the ruin of his career, had supported Pitt on the Regency question, and had supported him against the very men who now asked for his removal. We have seen, from the letter of Lord Grenville, that it was already pretended that the part taken by Fitzgibbon in the Regency debates was the real reason of the demand. It was quite in the character of Pitt that the dread of such an imputation or misconstruction should have weighed with him more heavily than the great political issues that were at stake.

It is possible that another consideration may have entered into his calculations. We have seen that the project of a legislative union was already in his mind as the ultimate solution of Irish politics, and that it had been warmly encouraged by Lord Westmorland. Fitzgibbon, next to Castlereagh, was the Irishman who did most to carry it; and although there is, I believe, no absolute proof that he at this time knew the designs of the Government, it is, at least, highly probable. Westmorland confided in him more than in any other Irish politician. Fitzgibbon had always strongly maintained the necessity of keeping the whole machinery of Irish politics in complete and permanent subordination to the English Executive; and he has himself stated, that ever since the Relief Act of 1793 he had looked forward to a legislative union, and had uniformly pressed its urgent necessity on the English Ministers.[1] The astronomer can detect the attracting or disturbing presence of an invisible planet by the aberrations of the bodies that are in sight, and Irish writers have long believed that the secret design of an union was the cause and the explanation of much that appears mysterious in the proceedings of Pitt. We shall find, I think, some confirmation hereafter of the suspicion. It is, at least, certain, that if the Irish representative system had been reformed, the chances of carrying such a measure would have been enormously diminished. Pitt may not have believed those who told him, with perfect truth,

[1] *Auckland Correspondence*, iv. 8; Clare's *Speech on the Union*, p. 3.

that if that system were not reformed, a rebellion would in a short time become inevitable.

The quarrel between Pitt and his new allies lasted for some weeks, but it was finally composed by an imperfect and unsatisfactory compromise. The recall of Lord Westmorland was hastened; he was transferred to the position of Mastership of the Horse, and Lord Fitzwilliam was appointed to succeed him. Thomas Grenville declined the office of Chief Secretary, and it was conferred upon Lord Milton. It was agreed that Fitzgibbon should remain Chancellor, and that no general change should be made in the Irish administration. It is extraordinary and most inexcusable that, after the experience he had just had, Lord Fitzwilliam did not insist on the exact terms of his powers being clearly defined, and defined in writing, but so it was. He, at least, fully believed that he was authorised to remove some men in whom he could not place confidence, though probably not without compensation. We shall see that this power was afterwards disputed.

Apart from questions of patronage, the great pressing question was that of the admission of Catholics to Parliament, and on this question the line indicated to Lord Fitzwilliam was tolerably clear. He was instructed not to bring it forward as a Government measure, and if possible to prevent its agitation, and to obtain its postponement till the peace. At the same time, Pitt announced himself in principle favourable to the measure, and if, contrary to the wishes of the Government, Lord Fitzwilliam found it so pressed that it could not be evaded, he was authorised to accept and to support it.

It may be advisable to give the exact words of some of the chief persons concerned in the question, as a controversy subsequently arose upon it. 'I was decidedly of opinion,' Lord Fitzwilliam afterwards wrote, 'that not only sound policy, but justice, required, on the part of Great Britain, that the work which was left imperfect in 1793 ought to be completed, and the Catholics relieved from every remaining disqualification. In this opinion the Duke of Portland uniformly concurred with me; and when this question came under discussion previous to my departure for Ireland, I found the Cabinet, with Mr. Pitt at their head, strongly impressed with the same conviction. Had I found it otherwise, I never would have undertaken the government. I at first proposed that if the additional indulgences should be offered from the Throne, the very best effects would be secured; . . . but to this proposal objections were stated, that appeared of sufficient weight to induce the adoption of another plan. I consented not to bring the question forward on the part of Government, but rather to endeavour to keep back until a period of more general tranquillity, when so many material objects might not press upon the Government; but as the principle we agreed on, and the necessity of its being brought into full effect, was universally allowed, it was at the same time resolved, that if the Catholics should appear determined to stir the business, and to bring it before Parliament, I was to give it a handsome support on the part of Government.'[1]

This statement of fact has never been disputed, though after the quarrel, which is to be described, the Government accentuated somewhat more strongly than Lord Fitzwilliam had done, the undoubted fact that they had desired that the question should, if possible, be adjourned. 'As to the Catholic question,' wrote Portland, 'it was understood that Lord Fitzwilliam was to exert his endeavours to prevent its being agitated at all.'[2]

Lord Fitzwilliam arrived in Ireland on January 4, 1795; but before his arrival, the agitation for Catholic emancipation had fully begun. The knowledge that statesmen who were avowedly favourable to it were in power, and the belief, that was rapidly spread, that they had full authority to carry the measure, had very naturally an instantaneous effect. The Catholic Committee, which had fallen into a somewhat dormant state, at once became

---

[1] *Letter to Lord Carlisle,* pp. 3, 4. In a debate in 1799, speaking of his administration, Fitzwilliam said: 'Yielding to the argument of not wishing to entangle Government in difficulties upon the subject at that period, I admit that, under orders, clearly understood by me, not to give rise to or bring forward the question of Catholic emancipation on the part of Government, I assumed the government of Ireland. But, in yielding to this argument, I entered my protest against resisting the question, if it should be brought forward from any other quarter; and I made most distinct declarations, that, in case of its being so brought forward, it should receive my full support. With these declarations, I assumed the government of Ireland. This I state upon my honour.' (*Parl. Hist.* xxxiv. 672.) In perfect harmony with this statement were the words, describing his intentions on the Catholic question, used by Pitt to Grattan, which the latter at once wrote down, and which were published by his son: 'Not to bring it forward as a Government measure, but, if Government were pressed, to yield to it.' (Grattan's *Life,* iv. 177.)

[2] Secret Instructions to Lord Camden, March 26, 1795.

active, and in December 1794 it was resolved that in the ensuing session an application should be made to Parliament, praying for a total repeal of the penal and restrictive laws affecting the Catholics of Ireland, that this address should be entrusted for presentation to Grattan, that the Catholics all over Ireland should be recommended to petition for the measure, and that an address should be presented to Lord Fitzwilliam on his arrival. 'I was no sooner landed,' he afterwards wrote, 'and informed of the real state of things here, than I found that this question would force itself upon my *immediate* consideration.'[1]

There was an interval of not quite three weeks before the meeting of Parliament, and Fitzwilliam employed it in endeavouring to obtain full information on the subject, and in reporting the result of his inquiries to the Duke of Portland. On January 8 he wrote: 'I tremble about the Roman Catholics. I mean, about keeping them quiet for the session, because I find the question already in agitation, and a committee appointed to bring forward a petition for the repeal of the penal and restrictive laws. I will immediately use what efforts I can to stop the progress of it, and bring them back to a confidence in the good intentions of Government, and, relying on that, to defer for the present agitating the question.' Lord Shannon agreed in thinking it ought to be postponed, and if it is brought on, 'I think,' said Fitzwilliam, 'he will be against it, more, I see, for the sake of consistency, than from any fear of mischief arising from its being granted; and, indeed, he expressed very explicitly an opinion, that if its stop could not be negotiated on grounds of temporary expediency, it ought not to be resisted by Government.'[2]

The Lord Lieutenant had no means of acting on the Catholic Committee, but he hoped to put off the question by availing himself of the influence of the leading Catholic gentry. In a letter of the 15th, after describing the successful efforts that were being made to enlist soldiers for the war, both among the Catholics and the Protestants, and the loyal addresses he had received, both from the Dissenters and from the Catholics of Dublin, he adds: 'Towards the latter, the Catholics, I have endeavoured to keep clear of any engagement whatever, though

[1] Plowden, ii. 468–470. Fitzwilliam's *Letter to Lord Carlisle*, p. 4.
[2] Fitzwilliam to Portland, Jan. 8, 1795.

there is nothing in my answer that they can construe into a rejection of what they are *all* looking forward to, the repeal of the remaining penal and restrictive laws. I say all, because I mean not only the Dublin Committee, but the seceders—that is, the noblemen and gentlemen of landed property.' He had sounded Lord Kenmare and Lord Fingall, and found them both moderate and anxious to avoid embarrassing the Government, but they both looked forward to the removal of all disabilities. Lord Fingall especially dwelt on the impossibility of abandoning the hope. 'I conversed with him,' said the Lord Lieutenant, 'upon the general state of those of his persuasion; how completely the great mass were already in possession of equal rights with their fellow-subjects, and upon that ground with what justice we might expect perfect loyalty and attachment on the part of the general mass. He admitted the justice of our expectation, but observed that the reason of the thing did not decide the multitude; that what it was they probably did not know and did not inquire, but they did know that something remained undone for those of their persuasion, and that if there was disaffection to be found among that class (which he admitted, and which not one man of any sort or description hesitates to admit), he conceived this to be the ground of it.'[1]

The very serious condition of the country impressed itself more and more upon the Lord Lieutenant, and he clearly saw that without considerable and permanent remedies, there was everything to be feared. 'Not a day,' he said, 'has passed since my arrival, without intelligence received of violence committed in West Meath, Meath, Longford, and Cavan.' He found the whole texture of government miserably weak; scarcely any real responsibility among officials; half a dozen governors sometimes presiding over a single county; magistrates invariably appointed by private favour. In many parts of the country general officers were employed as civil magistrates, and this system, though it approached closely to martial law, was by no means inexpedient, as the soldiery were often 'the only magistracy in real authority,' and the only power who could repress the Defenders. They could, however, give no permanent protection. 'An outrage is committed. Government sends a

[1] Fitzwilliam to Portland, Jan. 15, 1795.

military force to animate the magistrates; they act under that protection; the outrage is put an end to; all appears submission; the military retire, and the house, life, or family of the magistrate instantly pays the penalty of his activity.'[1] The Defender outrages were not political, but they derived much of their importance from a feeling of sullen and bitter discontent, which had spread through the Catholic population—a discontent which Fitzwilliam was more and more convinced could only be effectually met by the abolition of all religious disqualifications. He had not been more than ten days in the country, before he expressed his judgment and decision on that point. 'I shall not do my duty,' he wrote, 'if I do not distinctly state it as my opinion, that not to grant *cheerfully* on the part of Government all the Catholics wish, will not only be exceedingly impolitic, but perhaps dangerous. The disaffection among the lower orders is universally admitted (though the violences now committed from time to time are not the violences arising from disaffection or political causes, but merely the outrages of banditti, fostered, however, under that pretended cause). Though the higher orders are certainly firmly attached, and to be relied upon, and perhaps the wealthy of the second class hardly less so, because they are fearful for their property, yet the latter, at least, have certainly shown no forwardness to check these outrages and to reconcile the affections of the lowest, which is to be imputed, and can be imputed, to no other cause than that there is something left behind that rankles in their bosoms. They conceive, as they express themselves, that they are marked people, but this done away, . . . I feel confident of their zealous and hearty support in the worst of exigencies.'[2]

If the disabilities were removed, a measure might be carried out, which Fitzwilliam was convinced—and on this point the Chancellor fully agreed with him—would be the only possible remedy for the chronic but spasmodic outbreaks of violence which had become so formidable. It was the creation of 'an armed constabulary composed of the better orders of the

---

[1] Fitzwilliam to Portland, Jan. 10, 15, 31, 1795. The Bishop of Cloyne, in a letter to Lord Westmorland, mentions the astonishment and alarm of Lord Fitzwilliam on learning that Defenders were drilling every night in the county of Meath. (*Westmorland Correspondence*, I.S.P.O.)

[2] Fitzwilliam to Portland, Jan. 15, 1795.

people, of those who have an interest in the authority of the law.' Hitherto the police system in Ireland had been utterly inefficient, and when Whiteboys or other depredators became formidable, either the military were called in, or the country gentlemen associated themselves together, raised volunteers among their tenantry, hunted down the banditti, and dealt in a very summary manner with those who fell into their hands.[1] The Peace Preservation Act of 1787 had empowered the Lord Lieutenant to appoint a chief constable in each barony, and the grand juries to appoint sixteen Protestant sub-constables in each of the same districts, to pay them, in addition to fixed salaries, threepence a mile for the conveyance of each prisoner whom they apprehended, from the place of arrest to the county gaol, and to give the same sum to any Protestant who assisted them in this duty. The Act was permissive, and many counties failed to adopt it. A few new regulations about the 'baronial constables' were made by an Act of 1792. These men wore no uniform, were under no regular supervision or discipline, and followed their usual occupations when they were not called out for public duty. They were manifestly inadequate to the task of preserving the peace of the country, in a time of widespread and organised lawlessness.[2] One of the first necessities of Ireland was a large and disciplined constabulary, which could habitually discharge the duties that were now thrown upon soldiers or upon volunteers. 'But of what description of men,' asked Fitzwilliam, 'must this constabulary be composed?' 'Of the first tenants, that is, the middle man between the landlord and the tenant. Who are they, and what are they? In three provinces all Catholics. Shall we wait till they have arms in their hands, and then grant them their requests; or shall we begin by making them content, and then confide in them?'

That the Catholics would some day obtain what they desired, he considered indisputable; but by deferring the concessions, Ireland was exposed to the risk that, in the event of invasion, the mass of the people would be found disaffected. He then sums up his views, and states his intentions in language which

[1] See vol. iv. p. 342. See, too, an example of these associations in Lord Cloncurry's *Personal Recollections*, p. 23.

[2] 27 Geo. III. c. 40; 32 Geo. III c. 16. Curtis's *Hist. of the Royal Irish Constabulary*, pp. 2, 3.

it was impossible to misunderstand. 'All this,' he writes, 'I submit to your consideration; no time is to be lost; the business will presently be at hand, and the first step I take is of infinite importance (pray do not delay to talk with Pitt on the subject). If I receive no very peremptory directions to the contrary, I shall acquiesce with a good grace, in order to avoid the manifest ill effect of a doubt, or the appearance of hesitation, for in my opinion even the appearance of hesitation may be mischievous to a degree beyond all calculation. Two evils it would inevitably produce, the loss to Government of the confidence and affection of the Catholics, and the giving rise to a Protestant cabal, which will be a certain consequence. On the other hand, a cheerful acquiescence on the part of Government will keep that down perhaps altogether; for in truth the great body of the Protestants feel the necessity, and indeed propriety, of the measure, and the opposition to it, being among a very few, never can have the semblance of being formidable but inasmuch as Government appears to waver. Convinced as we all are of the necessity as well as fitness of the measure taking place at no distant period, to attempt to defer it, is to incur the certain inconvenience of rendering the Catholics useless at least, if not dangerous, of making them unwilling to act for external defence, unsafe to have committed to their hands the means of restoring law, order, and tranquillity, which can only be restored by the means of a strong police, universally established under the mask of a yeomanry cavalry, about which, as I stated before, there is not to be found a second opinion, provided the relief to the Catholics precedes it; but the one done and the other established, I should feel a great load off my mind. I should look forward to great security from an external enemy, to much good order within.'[1]

In a letter written a few weeks later, he recurred in very emphatic terms to the growing disaffection of the lower classes in the country districts, and warned the Government to be under no illusions on the subject. 'A shameful want of protection for the lower orders of the people, a partial and harsh measure of law, together with a variety of oppressions, have alienated them from the Government, and rendered them indifferent to the interests

[1] Fitzwilliam to Portland, Jan. 15, 1795.

of their country. That full and ample extent of right and privilege lately granted to this class of subjects, has failed to reconcile their affections. . . . No man acquainted with the circumstances of this country, if he speaks frankly and honestly, can give any other than this account, that the whole body of the lowest orders of the people are, at the time of my writing, and have been long, in rebellion; that is, if oaths and engagements entered into for the purpose of destroying the Government, and of assisting any foreign invaders, may be said to be a state of rebellion.' The want of arms and leaders, and the disappointment of the hopes of foreign assistance, alone prevented a rebellion.[1]

In addition to his inquiries into the Catholic question, Fitzwilliam, before the meeting of Parliament, either made or proposed a few changes in the administration. William Ponsonby was recommended for the post of Secretary of State. Sackville Hamilton, and Cooke, who were in subordinate but very confidential positions, were at once removed. 'Neither I nor my Chief Secretary,' wrote Fitzwilliam, 'with whom they were in hourly intercourse, felt inclined to give them that confidence, or to suffer the business of their respective offices to be conducted on the system which we found had been lately introduced there;' and he complained of Cooke, that 'his tone and style rendered his approach to a superior not to be supported.' Hamilton was one of the oldest servants of the Crown in Ireland, and he had been Under Secretary for about twenty-five years. He appears to have acquiesced in his dismissal, and to have been contented with the compensation that was promised to him; but Cooke, who was Secretary for War, complained bitterly that a pension of 1,200*l*. a year, which was bestowed on him, was a wholly inadequate reward for his services, and he at once carried his complaint to England. He was an able man, who bore a very important and confidential part in the Irish politics of the last years of the century, and was distinguished for his hostility to Catholic emancipation in the Irish Parliament, for his support of the harshest measures that preceded and immediately followed the rebellion, and for his powerful advocacy of the Union. Fitzwilliam also proposed to the English Govern-

---

[1] Fitzwilliam to Pitt, Feb. 14, 1795. In a letter to Portland on the 13th, he mentions the general expectation of a coming rebellion.

ment that Wolfe and Toler, the Attorney and Solicitor General, should be removed, and replaced by George Ponsonby and Curran, who were greatly their superiors in debating talent, and who were also in harmony with the new administration. In case the arrangement was carried out, ample provision was to be made for the removed law officers, and the promotion of George Ponsonby appears to have been recommended by the Duke of Portland.[1]

The change, however, which was really important from its consequences, was the removal of John Beresford, who held the not very prominent office of Commissioner of the Revenue. Beresford was one of the most distinguished examples of a class of politicians who were a peculiar and characteristic product of the Irish political system. He belonged to a family which, though entirely undistinguished in Parliament and in responsible statesmanship, had secured so large a proportion of the minor offices in administration, had employed its patronage so exclusively for the purpose of building up a family influence, and had formed in this manner so extensive a system of political connections and alliances, that it had become one of the most powerful controlling and directing influences in the Government of Ireland. In a curious and valuable paper drawn up for or by Lord Abercorn in 1791, called an 'Analysis of the Irish Parliament,' in that year, the party which was called the Beresford party is reckoned at only eight members, but it is added that the Chancellor, the Attorney-General, and Cooke were allied with it. John Beresford, the writer says, was the First Commissioner, with an official house and a salary of 2,000l. a year, and he had obtained the office of Taster of Wines, with a salary of 1,000l. a year, for his own life and that of his eldest son. His son Marcus—an active and useful member of the House—was first counsel to the commissioner, with a salary of 2,000l. His second son, John Claudius, had a very lucrative office in

[1] Fitzwilliam to Portland, Jan. 8, 15, 1795; Fitzwilliam's *Letter to Lord Carlisle.* The case of the removed officials will be found in the letters of Cooke to Buckingham. (*Courts and Cabinets,* ii. 329–333.) Several particulars relating to these changes will be found in a memorandum on what passed between the Ministers and Lord Fitzwilliam, before the departure of the latter for Ireland, which is among the Pelham papers. It is there stated that the Ministers thought the position of Secretary of State ought to be combined with that of Chief Secretary, and another position found for W. Ponsonby, and also that Fitzwilliam had not mentioned his intention of promoting Curran.

the revenue. His son-in-law would probably be provided for in the first law arrangement. William Beresford was Bishop of Ossory, he looked for the highest Church preferment, and he was married to the Chancellor's sister. The son of the Bishop was member for the episcopal borough. The Chancellor had a large following, and the Attorney-General sat in the House of Commons with his son and his nephew. Lord Waterford had the patronage of the counties of Waterford and Derry. 'This party,' it was added, ' undoubtedly govern the kingdom.' 'Lord Waterford is said to stand remarkably well with the King, and to have had a constant connection with England, with the persons who had the ear of the Minister, such as Mr. Robinson, Mr. Rose, &c.'[1]

The influence was steadily growing. A few years after the viceroyalty of Lord Fitzwilliam, it was said that at least a fourth of all the places in the island were filled with dependants or connections of the Beresfords,[2] and during Fitzwilliam's time the influence of John Beresford was, or was believed to be, so overwhelming, that he was called the King of Ireland.[3] He was politically closely allied with the Chancellor, who was bitterly and notoriously hostile to Fitzwilliam and his policy, and among his correspondents and supporters in England were Auckland, and the last two viceroys, Buckingham and Westmorland. From the first announcement of Lord Fitzwilliam's appointment, Beresford had written of it to England with undisguised hostility and apprehension, and he and his family were strenuously opposed to the Catholic policy of the Government. It was not in the character of Fitzwilliam to brook this rivalry. He said that his confidential servants must be men in whom he could confide ; that it was essential to the consequence and dignity of the English Government, that family cabals for monopolising

---

[1] I am indebted for my knowledge of this curious paper to the kindness of its possessor, Lord George Hamilton.

[2] Wakefield's *Ireland*, ii. 384.

[3] Beresford himself, in relating his interview with Daly, who came to inform him of the intention of the Government to remove him, reports that Daly said : ' No Lord Lieutenant could exist with my power ; that I had made a Lord Chancellor, a Chief Justice of the King's Bench, an Attorney-General, nearly a Primate, and certainly a Commander-in-Chief ; that I was at the head of the revenue, and had the law, the army, the revenue, and a great deal of the Church, in my possession ; and he said expressly that I was considered the King of Ireland.' (*Beresford Correspondence*, ii. 51.)

the Government should be broken up; and that the Government, and Government patronage, in all its branches, should be in the hands of the representative of the Sovereign. One of his first acts after his arrival in Ireland was the dismissal of Beresford. He acted in this matter hastily, curtly, and probably injudiciously, and without waiting for any act of overt opposition; but Beresford was granted for life his entire official salary, and he received an assurance that none of the other members of his family would be removed. 'They were still left,' wrote Fitzwilliam, 'in the full enjoyment of more emoluments than ever were accumulated in any country upon any one family.'[1]

Fitzwilliam believed that this proceeding was within his undoubted powers; and if he had ever any doubts on the subject, they had been removed by an interview with Pitt which took place before his departure for Ireland. He expressly states, that he then told Pitt that it might be necessary for him to remove Beresford, and that Pitt had made no objection.[2] The veracity of Fitzwilliam is beyond dispute, but there was probably on this, as on other points, a misunderstanding. In a memorandum relating to these proceedings which is among the Pelham papers, and which is known to have been corrected by Pitt himself, the following passage occurs: 'It appears that Lord F. conceives himself to have stated to Mr. Pitt, in their first conversation on the subject of Ireland, that he was apprehensive Mr. Beresford must be removed, and that Mr. Pitt made no objection in reply to this. Mr. Pitt has no recollection of anything having been said to him which conveyed to his mind the impression that Mr. Beresford's removal from his office was intended.' Beresford, on his side, wrote letter after letter to his friends in England, describing himself as an injured and persecuted man; he appealed passionately to Pitt to support him, and he went over to England to lay his complaint before the Ministers.[3]

The hatred with which Fitzwilliam was regarded by the old permanent officials can hardly be exaggerated. The Bishop of Cloyne gave Lord Westmorland a curious account of the dinners at the Castle. They were, he said, 'miracles of stupidity.' 'As half the company tremble for their places, and

---

[1] *Letter to Lord Carlisle.*   [2] Ibid.   [3] *Beresford Correspondence*, vol. ii.

have been for so many years hostile to the other half, not a word is spoken, and Lord F. never speaks himself.' On one occasion, the Bishop says, a long silence was broken by the Speaker, who suddenly called for a bumper 'to the immortal memory of King William, who delivered us from popery.' Cooke wrote to Lord Westmorland constant accounts of the proceedings of the Lord Lieutenant, which were probably laid before Ministers in England, and which give a vivid picture of the consternation and indignation that prevailed. The Ponsonbys, he said, were now all-powerful, and boasted that the kingdom was in their hands. Everything was managed by the Lord Lieutenant, Lord Milton, the two Ponsonbys, Grattan, and Yelverton. The Ponsonbys will now secure their old friends, gain many new ones, and make government impracticable in any form not connected with them. Lord Fitzwilliam is laying 'the crown at the feet of Ned Byrne [of the Catholic Committee], by offering him full powers on the three conditions of supporting the war, which the committee have hitherto opposed; of opposing parliamentary reform, to which they are pledged; and of supporting the peace of the country, which they have notoriously disturbed these four years.' 'The universal idea is, that what is proposed must inevitably lead to union or separation.' 'Mr. Pitt seems to have tied all the old friends of Government to the stake, for Lord Fitzwilliam to flog.' 'Mr. Pitt's character depends upon his support of Mr. Beresford.' The dismissal of Beresford is 'one of the sorest wounds English Government could receive.' 'Whatever Government shall take place in England, it must in Ireland crouch to Grattan and the Ponsonbys. They have at length defeated the Crown. They have rooted up all confidence in the Crown, and all confidence in any minister deriving from the Crown.' For himself, he says, after twenty-five years of service, and after all his fidelity to Mr. Pitt, he had lost 1,300*l.* a year 'by this new system of coalition and cordiality.'[1]

While these things were happening in Ireland, the political horizon of Europe was rapidly darkening. The close of 1794 saw the great coalition against France, torn by division and

[1] Bishop of Cloyne to Westmorland, Jan. 12, 1795; Cooke to Westmorland, Jan. 9, 15, 18, 23, 26; Feb. 2, 1795 (*Westmorland Papers*).

treachery, and almost hopelessly shattered by repeated defeats. The Belgic provinces, which had been recovered by the Austrians in 1793, were once more completely French. The Austrians and the Prussians were in full retreat. The French flag floated over every town on the left bank of the Rhine, except Mayence and Luxemburg; the cloud of invasion was manifestly impending over Holland, and it was the belief of the most sagacious judges in England, that if the Dutch ports, shipping, and magazines fell into French hands, an invasion of the British Isles would almost certainly follow. 'There is a gloom over this country,' wrote Auckland in November, 'such as I cannot describe. It is a mixture of rage at the triumphs of the Jacobins, of mortification at our own disgraces, of extreme indignation and horror at the infatuated turpitude of some of the allied Powers, of grief and alarm at the ruin which is coming upon Holland and upon the whole European continent, and all this with . . . the doubt whether we can prosecute the war, and the doubt whether it is possible to make any step towards peace.' In England this acute judge did not believe that the spirit of Jacobinism had made much way, but in parts of Scotland it already prevailed, and in Ireland there was a restlessness and a disaffection which a French invasion would assuredly kindle into a blaze. 'The attachment of the country at large to Government,' he added, 'is naturally weakened by the long course of calamities which has baffled and disappointed all the measures of Government. . . . The horror which justly belongs to the wickedness and atrocities of the French Convention, insensibly loses itself in admiration of the French successes, and in a forced acknowledgment of the perseverance, courage, and conduct of the French armies.'[1] In the first weeks of 1795 the dreaded catastrophe arrived. On January 11 the French troops crossed the Waal, and within a fortnight the Prince of Orange had been compelled to fly for refuge to England; the Dutch fleet, which was frozen in the Texel, was captured, and all resistance to the French arms in Holland had ceased.

It was under these gloomy circumstances that the Irish Parliament met on January 22, 1795. The ports and fleets of Holland being now in the hands of the French, Fitzwilliam wrote that he expected a speedy invasion, and he added that

[1] *Auckland Correspondence*, iii. 261, 271, 272.

the prospect of the defence depended mainly on the attitude of the Catholics.[1] The speech from the throne spoke with unusual solemnity of 'the present awful situation of affairs,' and urged upon the Parliament to make the most strenuous efforts to meet the great and pressing danger. These efforts, the speech observed, would be facilitated by the encouraging fact that even 'during the existence of such a war as the present, the public revenue, together with the commerce of the kingdom, has kept up, and has even been augmented,' and that 'the great staple manufacture of this kingdom has increased beyond the most sanguine expectations.' In accordance with the wishes of the English Cabinet, nothing was said on the Catholic question, but a hope was expressed that the 'united strength and zeal of every description of subjects' would be elicited, and the Lord Lieutenant expressed his own 'cordial affection to the whole of Ireland.' Parliament was at the same time invited to consider the state of education, with the object of establishing some extended system which might confer its benefits on 'the several descriptions of men which compose his Majesty's faithful subjects in Ireland.'

The address was moved by Grattan. In a long and eloquent speech he reiterated his doctrine that the Irish Parliament should abstain from entering into any investigation of the causes of the war, and should accept the simple fact that England was engaged in it, as a sufficient reason for supporting her. He painted in vivid colours the dangers that menaced Europe from French ambition, the impotence of continental Europe, which could oppose nothing to the revolutionary spirit but 'a chaos of forms without force,' the ruin that would fall upon Ireland if England succumbed, the darkening cloud of invasion that was gathering rapidly upon the horizon. 'You know enough,' he said, 'of the levels of Europe to foresee that that inundation of barbarity and infidelity, that dissolution of government, and that sea of arms, if it swells over the Continent, must visit our coast.' The French party in Ireland he believed to be still 'contemptible and inconsiderable;' but if Parliament showed any hesitation or division, it might become formidable. The King, he said, by his recommendation to 'national harmony,'

[1] Fitzwilliam to Portland, Jan. 23, 1795.

'touched with the sceptre those troubled waters which had long shattered the weary bark of your country, under her various and false pilots, for ages of insane persecution and impious theology.' It was 'a pious and profound recommendation,' 'the olive descending from the throne.' Let Parliament act on the lines which were indicated to it. The present was eminently a time for 'the union of all the property of the country in support of the laws, and all the talents in support of the property, with measures to redress and to unite.'[1]

Scarcely a discordant voice was heard. Duquerry and Lord Edward Fitzgerald alone ventured to say something in favour of peace and of the French;[2] but they found no support, and the loyal addresses to the King and Lord Fitzwilliam were carried with enthusiasm. Perhaps the most remarkable feature in these addresses is their emphatic testimony to the substantial and growing prosperity of the country, even in time of war. After promising to make adequate provision for the war, the Commons continued: 'We learn with the greatest satisfaction that the present state of the commerce and revenue of the kingdom will much facilitate our efforts in making that provision, and do most gratefully acknowledge that an increasing commerce and a rising revenue during the existence of such a war as we are now engaged in, are advantages which, under the Divine Providence, we owe to the care and vigilance of our Sovereign. . . We view with peculiar joy the increase of our great staple manufacture, an increase commensurate with our efforts, but exceeding our most sanguine expectations.'[3]

The loyalty of the Parliament did not expend itself in empty

---

[1] *Irish Parl. Deb.* xv. 4–11.
[2] Lord Milton to J. King, Jan. 22, 1795.
[3] *Irish Parl. Deb.* xv. 17, 18. In presenting the money bills the Speaker said: 'It is owing to the unexampled prosperity and growing resources of the nation that they [the Commons] now offer to his Majesty, without laying much additional burthen on the people, or lessening those bounties and pecuniary encouragements under which trade and manufactures have increased and are increasing; and the same causes have allowed them amidst these liberal supplies to gratify his Majesty's paternal benevolence and their own anxious feelings by relieving all the poorer classes from the tax of hearth money.' (Ibid. p. 155.) In the course of the debates Mr. Cuffe said: 'What was the state of Ireland at this moment? A state of unexampled prosperity. The landlord gets his rent to the hour. The tenant finds money for the produce of his land the moment he brings it to market, and the manufacturer finds employment and payment to his satisfaction. Ireland has the constitution of England, without its debt.' (Ibid. p. 168; see, too, p. 182.)

words. It at once made greater provisions than any previous Parliament in Ireland had ever done for carrying on the war The combined force of regulars and militia was raised to a little more than 40,000 men, and a vote of 200,000*l.*, moved by Grattan, for the British navy, was speedily carried. For this last vote the only precedent was that of 1782, when a vote of half that amount had been proposed by Grattan, as a testimony of gratitude and loyalty after the concession of independence. It was in vain that Sir Lawrence Parsons urged, in an impressive speech, that the House should accompany its grant with a stipulation for the equalisation of duties and the reform of Parliament. The grant was carried, Fitzwilliam wrote, 'without a thought of stipulation,' 'all subjects of bargain between the countries as to this point being kept out of sight.'[1] Whatever doubt there might be about the feeling of the country, there could, at least, be none about the loyalty of the Protestant Parliament, or about the popularity of the administration of Lord Fitzwilliam.

We must now follow the confidential letters of Fitzwilliam. The Catholic question was rapidly coming to a climax. On January 28, he again recurred to his plan of a yeomanry cavalry, as being the most effectual means of suppressing local disturbances, but he added that it would be prudent to adjourn the measure for the present, 'for should the Catholic question fail, we must think twice before we put arms into the hands of men newly irritated.' He was, however, more and more confident that there was no serious obstacle to be encountered in the Irish Parliament, or from the Irish Protestants, to the complete and immediate settlement of that question. 'I have little doubt,' he says, 'the Catholic business will be carried easily.' In a conversation with the Chancellor, 'I stated distinctly to him that, now that the question was in agitation, I should not hesitate to give my full support.' The objections of Fitzgibbon were undiminished: he 'entered fully and earnestly, but with perfect temper, on the subject, . . . but he concluded by saying, that if it was my intention to give support to the petition, there was no doubt of its being easily carried.' Fitzwilliam was confirmed in this opinion by an address which he had just received, from the pre-eminently Protestant Corporation of London-

[1] Fitzwilliam to Portland, Jan. 31; *Irish Parl. Deb.* xv. 77, 78.

derry, expressing their wish 'to see all Ireland united in one interest.'[1]

On February 10, he again wrote confidentially and very fully on the subject: the Catholic Committee were determined to bring on the question at once, and Fitzwilliam found that Lord Kenmare, and the other Catholic gentry who had seceded from the committee, were fully resolved to support it, and fully convinced that it was necessary to the security of the country that it should be speedily settled. 'This subject, therefore,' continued Fitzwilliam, 'is now before the public unavoidably in public discussion, and ought to be finally and conclusively settled.' 'Any distinction or difference [between the religions] that is suffered to exist, will not be simply the cause of disaffection and jealousy to the Catholics, but it will continue to be, what is much more mischievous, a cloak to the machinations of a very different nature of the factious and designing. If equality of rights between the Protestants and Catholics is dangerous, all the danger is already incurred by the Act of '93. . . . The body of the lower orders of the people in this country is, in three provinces out of four, composed altogether of Catholics, whilst, on the other hand, in the higher orders you find none but Protestants. The number of Catholics of this description is beneath calculation. To the class, therefore, in which Catholicism prevails, perfect equality is already granted. It remains now to consider whether the symbol of it shall be granted to or withheld from that class in which, to a moral certainty, they never can receive but the shadow. They are not capable of the reality on account of the circumstances I have just mentioned. It is therefore my earnest recommendation, that this point may no longer be a subject of eager contention and animosity, but that the peace, tranquillity, and harmony of the country may now be sealed and secured for ever. . . . We have occasion enough for having unanimity among the higher orders. We cannot depend upon

---

[1] Fitzwilliam to Portland, Jan. 28, 1795. Cooke, who was strongly opposed to the measure, wrote about this time: 'Lord Shannon has declared against the attempt to give anything to the Catholics. I believe Lord Hillsborough has done the same. The Speaker holds his own language; but I never saw an instance that Government could not carry a single measure, if there was no general opposition, and of that I see no probability.' (Cooke to Westmorland, Jan. 23, 1795, *Westmorland Papers*.)

the affection and attachment of the lower. The whole united strength of the higher may be necessary to control and keep the lower in order. . . . We must unite the higher orders in our common cause. The time I believe propitious to the purpose; not a single petition against it to the House of Commons from any Protestant body, though the subject has already been six weeks in agitation. Individuals who dislike it, and who perhaps, from a desire of maintaining a line of consistency, may say a feeble word against it, I believe have no intention to defeat it, and this opinion they decidedly entertain, that if anything is to be done, the business should be completed, and the question closed for ever. . . . The Catholics having put the business into the hands of Grattan, I have desired him not to proceed in it before his plan has been first laid before the Cabinet in London, and his Majesty's pleasure taken on it. His plan is a short and simple one: a general repeal of all restrictive and disqualifying laws; and that done, a complete change in the oath of disqualification. . . . The great reason is, that the people may be made one people, one Christian people, binding themselves in one common cause by one civil oath. . . . It is upon the large principle of leaving not a point of distinction in rights and capacities between Protestants and Catholics, that I propose, as I do, that no reserve should be made, not even of the highest offices of the State, not even the seals nor the bench. To make the reserve, would be to leave a bone of contention. It would be leaving a splinter in the wound that would, . . . to a certainty, sooner or later, break out again. It would mar the great object of laying the question to rest for ever. It would frustrate that great desideratum at this critical juncture, unanimity and harmony among all the higher orders of the kingdom. Should any melancholy event happen, should we see an enemy landed upon our shore, the safety of the kingdom depends upon that, and upon that only; such is the insubordination of the lower orders, such their disaffection, that nothing will control them, nothing retain them in their duty and allegiance, but the unanimity, harmony, and joint efforts of the better orders. . . . I trust you will endeavour to impress his Majesty with the extent of the mischief that may arise, that probably will, by any attempt on my part, as acting in his Government, to oppose or circumscribe the measure of favour to the Catholics.'[1]

Two days later he wrote: 'I despatched a messenger with my letter of the night before last, in hopes of obtaining an immediate answer to it, and an approbation of granting an equal participation of rights to Catholics, to *the full extent* of what is proposed. Nothing short of it will produce the desirable end of a perfect harmony and a hearty unanimity in the general cause. I press it the more, because I feel that it is not simply expedient but *necessary*, and it is further necessary that a most gracious and unequivocal support should be given on the part of Government, for two forcible reasons: first, that the measure may meet with no opposition, for nothing but the appearance of backwardness and reserve on the part of Government will raise an opposition; and the next is, that Government may recover the confidence and affection of the Catholics. . . . I think myself fully authorised to decide for myself on the subject, but still, considering the extent proposed, I am desirous to have the mode considered in England in the present stage, while I hope it is still within my reach to have it limited and modified before the Bill itself is introduced, and before the plan is yet known to the Catholics themselves. Leave for bringing in the Bill is moved to-day.'[2]

The condition of the country was at this time very remarkable. The Catholics all over Ireland were evidently thoroughly aroused, and their hopes were raised almost to the point of certainty. For some days a perpetual stream of petitions for relief had been pouring in from every quarter, and, although they were perfectly loyal and respectful in their tone, they clearly showed that a complete removal of religious disabilities must be carried if Catholic loyalty was to be retained. Above half a million of signatures are said to have been appended to the petitions for complete emancipation of the Catholics, which lay upon the table of the House of Commons.[3]

All classes of Catholics—the committee and the seceders, the Tories and the democrats—were on this question united, and never since 1782 had an expression of national will so

[1] Fitzwilliam to Portland, Feb. 10, 1795.
[2] Ibid. Feb. 12, 1795.
[3] This is the statement of Dr. Hussey (*Burke's Correspondence*, iv. 277).

genuine, so strong, and so unequivocal, been brought to the threshold of Parliament. On the other hand, the Protestants of Ireland as a body were perfectly ready to concede what was asked. An aristocratic faction, very powerful from its borough influence, disliked the measure as threatening their monopoly, but it was plain that they would not resist the determination of the Government. A furious sectarian spirit raged among the farmers and labourers in some counties of the North, but it found scarcely any echo in political life. The great mass of the Protestants were plainly convinced that the time had come for completing the Act of 1793. That Act had given the Catholic body the substance of power, but had left the badge of degradation and inferiority unremoved. It had granted power to the most ignorant, most turbulent, and most easily disaffected, and it had confirmed the incapacities of a loyal and conservative gentry, whose influence over the lower classes of the community it was vitally important to maintain. The Protestant gentry of Ireland had many faults, but they were at this time remarkably free from religious bigotry,[1] and, unlike the English Ministers, they at least knew Ireland. They saw that the United Irishmen were successfully using the Catholic question as a lever for uprooting the masses from their old allegiance; that, under the influence of the democratic spirit, which the French Revolution had engendered, the ascendency of property, rank, and intelligence, was strained and weakened; that multitudes of ignorant and turbulent men were drifting away from their old moorings, and were beginning to follow new and dangerous leaders; that classes which had hitherto at worst been only lawless and riotous, were rapidly becoming steadily and systematically disaffected. The evil could only be met by at once depriving the agitator of his most formidable weapon, by

---

[1] I have collected much evidence of this in former volumes. I may add one passage from Sir Richard Musgrave, which will appear singularly curious when it is remembered that the writer represented the extreme anti-Catholic spirit produced by the rebellion of 1798, and that he apparently approves of what he relates. 'The Roman Catholics of a parish frequently solicit Protestant gentlemen for ground to build chapels on, and I never heard of the request being refused; and in many cases they built them at their own expense. Whenever a popish chapel is to be built by subscription, the Protestants never fail, when solicited, to contribute largely to it.' (Musgrave's *Rebellions in Ireland*, 2nd edition, 1801 p. 635.)

conferring political power on men who were tolerably certain not to misuse it, by uniting the upper ranks of all denominations in support of the Constitution. There were doubtless many who wished that the Catholic question had never been raised, but such regrets were now very idle. A revolution of power had been made in 1793. A revolution of opinion, which was much more formidable, had followed or accompanied it. The Catholics had become keenly sensible of their rights, their degradation, and their power. It remained for the Government to decide between a policy of concession, and a policy of resistance, which, in the excited state of Ireland, was almost certain to lead to bloodshed.

The former policy would have encountered no serious difficulty in Ireland. As we have already seen, the Chancellor, who was the ablest of all its opponents, admitted that it could easily be carried. When Grattan moved for leave to introduce the Bill into Parliament, Duigenan and Ogle were the sole opponents, and there was, as yet, not a single petition to Parliament, not a single address to the Lord Lieutenant, on the part of any Protestant body, against it.[1] There may be endless controversy about the effects that would have followed Catholic emancipation in 1795, and about the propriety of the conduct of Lord Fitzwilliam. One fact, however, is as certain as anything in Irish history—that if the Catholic question was not settled in 1795, rather than in 1829, it is the English Government, and the English Government alone, that was responsible for the delay.

It is necessary, in order to understand the sequel, to follow closely the dates of the correspondence, and on the most charitable supposition they certainly disclose, on the part of the English Ministers, a neglect of duty which is simply astounding. We have seen that, as early as January 8, Fitzwilliam had warned Portland that the Catholic question was in full agitation in the country, and that he found it would be impossible to prevent it from being introduced in the ensuing session of Parliament. We have seen that, on January 15, he had informed Portland that

---

[1] 'Not a petition to the House of Commons, not an address to me, has yet come up against it [the Catholic Bill], on the part of any Protestant body; but, on the contrary, the fair construction of some of their addresses has been an approbation of the measure. I hope this favourable opportunity of making the people of Ireland one people, may not be lost.'. (Fitzwilliam to Portland, Feb. 13, 1795.)

the Catholic question had, in his opinion, become one of the most urgent and vital importance, that it was impossible to defer its solution without extreme danger to the country, that it would inevitably be one of the first measures introduced in the session of Parliament which was to open within a week, and that, if he did not receive peremptory instructions to the contrary, he would acquiesce in the Catholic claims. The English Government were thus fully apprised of the situation, of the opinion, of the Lord Lieutenant, of the course which he meant to pursue, and of the supreme importance of an immediate decision. Yet for weeks they left him without the faintest clue to their opinion, or the smallest indication that they disapproved of his conduct or his intentions. On January 13, Portland acknowledged Fitzwilliam's letter of the 8th. He informed him that the King consented to the peerage for Wolfe, but he made absolutely no reference to the Catholic question. Fitzwilliam's letter of the 15th must have arrived in London on the 17th or 18th. It might have been supposed that Portland would not have lost a day in consulting with Pitt, and in sending instructions that might have arrived before the opening of the Irish Parliament, which was fixed for the 22nd. Yet after Fitzwilliam's letter of the 15th had been received, two, if not three, letters arrived in Dublin from the Secretary of State, without a word of instruction on the Catholic question, or the slightest intimation that Fitzwilliam had been acting upon it without sufficient caution and discretion.

The natural, and, it seems to me, the inevitable, inference drawn by Fitzwilliam from this strange silence, was that the Government did not dispute his judgment, or intend to interfere with his policy. It was only on February 8 and 9, when Parliament had been sitting for nearly three weeks, when the extraordinary supplies had been voted, when the Catholic hopes were excited to the highest point, and when petitions for emancipation were pouring in from every part of Ireland, that a discordant note was struck. On the 9th, Pitt wrote to Fitzwilliam, expostulating with him on the dismissal of Beresford, and on the negotiations with Wolfe and Toler. The letter contained no allusion to the Catholic question, and it concluded with an apology for withdrawing his attention 'from the many important considerations of a different nature, to which all our minds ought to be directed.' By the same mail a letter arrived from Portland, dated on the preceding day, in which, for the first time, he expressed an opinion on the question which during a whole month had been pressed upon him by the Lord Lieutenant, as of the most vital and the most urgent consequence. He cautioned Fitzwilliam not to commit himself by 'engagements,' or even by 'encouraging language,' to giving his countenance to the immediate adoption of the measure. The deferring it, he added, would be 'the means of doing a greater service to the British Empire than it has been capable of receiving since the Revolution, or, at least, *since the Union*.'[1]

Fitzwilliam was greatly and not unnaturally irritated by these letters. In his reply to Pitt, after describing in a few words the extremely dangerous and disaffected state of the country, he expressed his surprise at the objections that were made to the dismissal of Beresford. Before leaving for Ireland, he said, he had told Pitt that he feared he must take that step, and Pitt had made no objection. He found that the influence of Beresford was so great as seriously to injure the Government if thrown against it, and it was quite necessary for him at this critical time to have subordinates on whom he could rely. As Beresford retained his full salary, and received an assurance that his family and connections should not be removed from 'any of their innumerable offices,' there was no hardship. Pitt must choose between him and Beresford. If English Ministers did not mean to support the King's representative in Ireland, the sooner they recalled him, the better.[2]

To Portland he wrote, lamenting in bitter terms that, while the urgency of the Catholic question appeared to those who were on the spot to increase from hour to hour, it appeared to English Ministers, who were at a distance, to grow less and less, and that he was now for the first time pressed to defer it to some future occasion. He positively refused to attempt it. 'All I have to add,' he wrote, 'is, that I will not be the person

---

[1] These two letters are not in the Record Office, and that of Portland, I believe, has never been printed. The substance and extracts, however, are given by Fitzwilliam in his *Second Letter to Lord Carlisle*. Lord Stanhope has printed Pitt's letter in his *Miscellanies*.

[2] Fitzwilliam to Pitt, Feb. 14, 1795.

so to put it off on the part of Government. I will not be the person who, I verily believe, would by doing so raise a flame in the country that nothing short of arms would be able to keep down.'[1]

In a second letter to Portland, marked 'secret and confidential,' he again justified his conduct towards Beresford, and he took a false step, which afterwards led him into much trouble. In addition, he said, to the dangerous power of Beresford, and the impossibility of relying on him, there was another reason which justified his dismissal. His conduct in the sale of a public lease under Lord Westmorland's administration had left a serious imputation on his character, and extraordinary measures had been taken to baffle inquiry. It was in order to prevent this inquiry, he said, that Westmorland had brought the last session of Parliament to a sudden, unexpected, and premature close. The transaction has never been clearly elucidated, certainly never established, and it was wholly unnecessary, for the justification of Fitzwilliam, to refer to it.[2]

These letters from Fitzwilliam crossed two from Portland, which were both written on the 16th. The first, though marked 'private,' was intended to be shown if necessary. The second was for Lord Fitzwilliam alone. In the first letter the Lord

---

[1] Fitzwilliam to Portland, Feb. 14. Writing soon afterwards to Carlisle, Fitzwilliam said: 'As to resisting altogether, I should have belied my own conviction, and betrayed my situation, if I did not represent, as I have repeatedly done, that it would not only defeat every hope I had formed for the general security and defence of the country, but be attended with a certainty of the most alarming and fatal consequences. Of this (as I have already observed to you), every day presented me with additional indisputable proofs. The alarm that has been universally spread by the rumour of the measures being to be resisted, the language of every person with whom I converse, even of the boldest of its former opposers, the resolutions and addresses from the City, echoed already from the cities of Cork, Londonderry, and the county of Kildare, and actually adopted through every part of the kingdom, the debates of these last days in the House of Commons—all these must prove to you, that my representations were at least nothing short of the truth.' (*Letter to Lord Carlisle*, p. 20.

[2] Fitzwilliam to Portland, Feb. 13, 1795. In his published letter to Lord Carlisle, Fitzwilliam, speaking of Beresford, said: 'I decided at once not to cloud the dawn of my administration by leaving, in such power and authority, so much imputed malversation.' In consequence of these words, a duel was arranged between Fitzwilliam and Beresford; but the combatants were interrupted on the field, and Fitzwilliam then made an apology. (*Beresford Correspondence*, ii. 111-120.) Fitzwilliam declared, in one of his letters to Portland, that there had been much scandalous jobbing in reversions in the last weeks of Lord Westmorland's administration.

Lieutenant is instructed to send a fuller enumeration of the arguments against, as well as in favour of, Catholic concession, and also the various estimates of the probable strength of the Catholics in the Irish House of Commons in case they were emancipated. Portland hopes that Fitzwilliam will act 'very deliberately' on the Catholic question, and he doubts the necessity for the proposed yeomanry cavalry, now that the Irish Parliament had voted a force of soldiers and militia amounting to no less than 40,000 men. He feared much the ultimate consequences of yielding. The last great concessions to the Catholics had not stopped demands, and was it likely that those now contemplated would be more efficacious? He hoped that the establishment of Catholic seminaries might do some good, and also that a provision 'might be made for their parochial clergy, by which they would in some degree be removed from the state of dependence in which they are kept by even the lowest orders of their parishioners, and that rank of the people would be proportionately relieved at the same time from some part of the burden of maintaining their clergy.' In this way, he trusted that all classes might be disposed to rely with confidence on the good intentions of the Government towards them.[1]

This letter evidently foreshadowed a course of policy altogether different from that which was contemplated in Ireland. In his second letter, which was long and elaborate, Portland entered in detail into his reasons for opposing the whole policy of Catholic emancipation. They are almost identical with those which had been urged a few years before by Lord Westmorland. The chief argument in favour of the Catholics was their superiority of numbers, but this argument was only too likely to overthrow both the parliamentary system and the ecclesiastical establishment now existing in Ireland. The most striking feature in the constitution of the Irish House of Commons, was the great number of boroughs in which the right of election was vested in not more than twelve electors. These boroughs secured the Protestant ascendency; but was it in accordance with common sense and with human nature to suppose that, if the Catholics were admitted to Parliament on the plea of numbers, they would not use all their efforts to overthrow these

[1] Portland to Fitzwilliam, Feb. 16, 1795.

oligarchical monopolies? With what better confidence could statesmen hope that the present Protestant establishment would be preserved? In every country the established religion must be that which is professed by those who are in possession of the civil government, and 'all the declarations, all the assurances, all the obligations and oaths that ever were or can be devised,' will fail to save a Protestant establishment if the dominant power in the civil government is transferred to Catholics. Then follows a passage which is peculiarly significant. 'I want to preserve the Protestant establishment in Church and State, and am willing and desirous to give the Catholics every right and every benefit which good subjects are entitled to, but I wish not to attempt it until I can be sure that the present establishment in Church and State are unquestionably secured, and that the participation to which I would admit the Catholics would be as little likely to be called in question.' The proposed yeomanry cavalry, being chiefly Catholic, would place the real power of the country in the hands of the enemies of the Church, and the tithe system, which was already disliked by so many Protestants, was not likely long to survive the admission of Catholics to the Legislature. 'In the attack on it,' indeed, 'there is but too much reason to apprehend the countenance and co-operation of one, at least, of our most able and best friends.'[1]

It was evident that the Government was completely opposed to the measure which the Irish Catholics, with great reason, had believed to be almost certainly attained. Fitzwilliam perceived it plainly, but in one more long and earnest despatch he attempted to avert the calamity which he foresaw. Rightly or wrongly, the inference which he drew from the last despatch, and from a passage which I have cited from the letter of the 8th, was that the English Government desired to delay the measure, in hopes of obtaining that legislative union [2] which had

---

[1] Portland to Fitzwilliam, Feb. 16, 1795. The last sentence, no doubt, alludes to Grattan.

[2] In his *Second Letter to Carlisle*, Fitzwilliam quoted the passage from Portland's confidential letter of the 8th, for which he was much blamed. He afterwards said (*Beresford Correspondence*, ii. 113), that his letters to Carlisle were printed without his knowledge or consent. Pelham, commenting upon the quotation, wrote to Portland: 'The construction that is put by many people (though falsely, in my opinion), is, that the intention of his Majesty's Ministers was to keep the question of the Catholics alive and in suspense until a peace, and that then it was to be employed as the means of forming an union between

undoubtedly been for a long time in their minds, and which Westmorland had assured them could only be accomplished by maintaining the division between Protestants and Catholics. 'I am at a loss,' he wrote, 'to conjecture what those benefits are which, it is expected, will accrue to the British Empire by deferring the consideration of this question. . . . Can it be in the contemplation of any man, that a state of disturbance or rebellion here will tend to the desirable end (which, I think, I discover to be alluded to in your letter) of an union between the two kingdoms? Doubtless the end is most desirable, and perhaps the safety of the two kingdoms may finally depend upon its attainment; but are the means risked such as are justifiable, or such as any man would wish to risk in hope of attaining the end? Through such a medium I look for an union, I am ready to grant, but it is not the union of Ireland with Great Britain, but with France. . . . But supposing the object may be thought attainable in the end by such means, still, it must be allowed to be at a distance, and must be admitted not to be a moral certainty. Who, then, will advise to be hunting after a distant and contingent good, at the evident and admitted price of a certain and immediate evil?'

He then proceeds to examine one by one the arguments against emancipation. It was said that it would lead to a Catholic ascendency, dangerous to property and to the whole constitution of the country. But what additional danger is to be apprehended from the admission of the higher orders, who in

the two countries. Whether the quotation was made with a view of sounding an alarm upon that subject, I will not pretend to say, but it is suspected by those who are unfriendly to Lord Fitzwilliam. . . . Hearing the subject discussed in society, I thought it right to mention it to the Lord Chancellor, who was convinced that great use would be made of it in Parliament, and seemed, I think, to entertain some suspicion of that being the real design of the British Cabinet. I did not think it necessary to discuss that point with him further than to say, that I was convinced your Grace never intended to convey that idea; and that I was ready to say, that I never would be concerned in an administration in Ireland that would attempt it. . . . He thought it would be very proper, in some general words, to express a determination "to support the Constitution as established in 1782, and still further assimilated to that of Great Britain by Acts that have since passed." These were the Chancellor's own words, which, I think, convey the idea of his Majesty's Ministers, that the Catholics should not be admitted to any share of legislative authority, and refute the notion of any sinister attempt to force an union.' (Pelham to Portland, March 30, 1795.) There is, as far as I know, no evidence that Portland, either in public or private, disclaimed the meaning which had been attached to his words.

number and property must always be insignificant compared with the Protestants? If there is danger of this kind, it springs from the admission to power of the class which is at once numerous and ignorant, turbulent and poor, but that class is already admitted. 'Those to whom anything remains to be granted, have the same evils to dread from the misuse of those rights, and from the subversion of law and establishment as the Protestants. . . . I go further, and I say that should an union with Great Britain be necessary for Ireland in order that property may be preserved, they will call as loudly for it, and act as zealously towards its attainment, as the Protestants.' The only danger to be feared from the upper classes of Catholics is, that, if they are thrown into a state of disappointment, discontent, and irritation, they may possibly be induced to act more under the influence of passion than of enlightened self-interest.

The next argument is the danger to the Protestant Church. 'Its property, as well as the property of every other corporation, is fenced and guarded by the same laws that preserve the property, and the same opinions that preserve all settlements, and I venture to say that things never will be ripe for the subversion of the one till they are ripe for the subversion of the other. . . . Oaths and obligations enforced by law, and resting all their efficiency upon the respect for law, are the only security you can have either for property, the Protestant establishment, or the Protestant succession, and if ever they fall, they will fall together.'

'The third point is, I suppose, the jealousy and dissent of the Protestant body. From this quarter I do not see how any danger is to arise, and, forming my judgment upon the conversation of those I have talked with, and upon every other appearance, just as little, or indeed no difficulty to the question. I hear no expression of alarm. I receive no remonstrance from the Protestant corporate bodies, I perceive no stir among them; no preparations made to resist and defeat it by parliamentary or other petitions, though the subject has now been two whole months fairly in agitation. On the contrary, in the addresses presented to me from Protestant corporations, particularly from Londonderry and Waterford, very different sentiments from those of jealousy and dissent are expressed. They mark approbation of the principle, and do not hesitate to declare that it is called for by the exigencies of the times, and anticipate the happiest consequences from its being carried into effect. But I desire not to be understood to convey that the approbation of the Protestants goes to the length that no individuals are to be found who still retain their ancient prejudices and old jealousies, but only that they are not sufficient in numbers to create the least difficulty about carrying the measure into effect.'

'I feel that I have personal weight and influence enough to carry it through without difficulty; and carrying it through, I am confident of uniting cordially in the defence of the country all its weight, property, and influence, if I may be allowed to except a certain description of Protestants whose views will never permit them to unite with the friends of a system that has such a share of monarchy and aristocracy in its composition as ours has. Of the real and hearty support of all other descriptions, I feel myself confident.'[1]

The appeal was a weighty one, but Fitzwilliam himself can have scarcely believed that it could be successful, and before it was written the decision of the Ministers had been taken. In a tone which completely broke the private and political friendship that had long subsisted between them, Portland wrote to Fitzwilliam expressing his astonishment that, with the full assent of the Government, leave had been given by Parliament to introduce a Catholic Relief Bill. The Cabinet unanimously agreed that the matter must not be pressed on so quickly; that the arguments of both sides must be sent to England; that they could give no assent till the draft of the Bill was laid before them. They were astonished that the Lord Lieutenant should have suffered a Bill of such magnitude to receive the countenance of Parliament, when it had not even been laid before the Cabinet of England. He had never been authorised to commit himself so far, and it was the earnest wish of Ministers that the question should be deferred to the peace. 'In the plainest and most direct terms,' Fitzwilliam was now ordered to take the most effectual means in his power to prevent any further proceedings being taken on the Bill before the House, till the King's pleasure was signified.[2]

[1] Fitzwilliam to Portland, Feb. 20, 1795.
[2] Portland to Fitzwilliam, Feb. 18, 1795.

This letter has a plausible sound, and to those who have not followed the course of events with the necessary minuteness, the charge of having unduly pressed on the question, and committed the Government, may appear established. After the best consideration, however, I can give, I can see no other course which Fitzwilliam could have adopted. The agitation had acquired formidable dimensions before he arrived in Ireland. He lost no time in informing the Government most fully of its pressing character, and as early as January 15 he clearly told them that he would exercise the discretion which he had received when he was appointed, and would accede to the Catholic demands, unless he received peremptory instructions to the contrary. The Government sent him no such instructions, though the Catholic movement was acquiring almost hourly additional strength: they pronounced no hostile opinion, when they had been emphatically told that, in the judgment of those who were responsible for the government of Ireland, the rejection or postponement of the measure would probably throw the country into a flame of rebellion; they never proposed that the meeting of Parliament, which was appointed for January 22, should be deferred, and they suffered Fitzwilliam to meet that Parliament under the full impression that his representations of the state of the country had been accepted by the Cabinet. When Parliament met, it was totally impossible that the introduction of the Catholic question could have been prevented. The country was thrilling with the most passionate excitement on the subject. Even if Grattan had consented to relinquish it for the session, there were many members who were desirous of introducing it,[1] and in that case, as Lord Fitzwilliam truly said, 'the measure might come into hands with which neither he nor the King's Ministers had any connection, which would leave the Government only the disagreeable part of altering or modifying, if any alteration or modification had been thought necessary by the British Government, depriving his Majesty thereby of the whole grace and effect of what was done.'[2] The only possible way in which Fitzwilliam could have prevented the Bill coming before the House of Commons, would have been by openly opposing the

---
[1] *Letter to Lord Carlisle,* p. 18.
[2] See his protest in the House of Lords (Grattan's *Life,* iv. 206, 207).

leave to introduce it, and in that case he would have thrown himself into violent opposition to the whole current of excited Catholic feeling, would have precipitated the very evils of which he had warned the Government, and would have acted in direct contradiction, not only to his own sentiments, but to the instructions which he had received when he was appointed.

Under these circumstances, he had adopted the most judicious course in putting himself in connection with Grattan, who was not in office, who had been entrusted with the petition of the Catholic Committee, but who at the same time was in the close confidence of his administration, and anxious to do all that was in his power to smoothe its path. As we have seen, Grattan consented to postpone introducing the measure till its leading provisions had been sent to England. As early as February 10, the Cabinet had been fully apprised of them, as well as of the opinion of the Irish Parliament upon them, in order that the English Government should be able to limit and modify the Bill if it appeared to them too unrestricted. When leave was given to introduce it, its terms were kept back from Parliament and from the Catholics until the opinion of the Cabinet had been received upon it, and they had not yet been communicated when the censure of the Cabinet arrived. If the measure was not sufficiently discussed, this was entirely the fault of the English Ministers, who had so strangely neglected it during the whole interval before Parliament met, and during the first fortnight of its session. If, with the usual ignorance of their class, they understood Ireland so little as to imagine that the question was one which might safely be indefinitely postponed, they had only themselves to blame, for nothing could be clearer or more emphatic than the warning they had received. The censure, therefore, which they sent to Fitzwilliam on February 18, appears to me perfectly unmerited. The next day the Cabinet agreed to recall Fitzwilliam, and on the 23rd he was directed to appoint lords justices to conduct the government till the arrival of his successor.

After all that has been written on the subject, a considerable obscurity still hangs over the real motives that induced the English Government to take a step which, they were repeatedly assured, must bring down upon Ireland a train of calamities of the most appalling description. The final opinion of Fitzwilliam, which was strongly shared by the Ponsonbys and by Grattan, was that the Catholic question had in reality nothing to say to their decision. The question they considered was merely one of family influence. The great social and political weight of the Beresfords, supported by Westmorland, Buckingham, and Auckland in England, and by Fitzgibbon in Ireland, was strained to the utmost against the Ponsonbys, and the influence they brought to bear was such that, although Pitt was believed by Fitzwilliam to have acquiesced in the removal of Beresford when it was first proposed, he now determined at all hazards to resist it.

'Let my friends no longer suffer the Catholic question to be mentioned,' wrote Fitzwilliam, 'as entering in the most distant degree into the causes of my recall. . . . Had Mr. Beresford never been dismissed, . . . I should have remained.'[1] 'In my opinion,' said George Ponsonby, 'the Catholic question had no more to do with the recall of Lord Fitzwilliam than Lord MacCartney's embassy to China. Lord Fitzwilliam was to be recalled, and this was considered the most popular pretext for the measure.'[2] The Ministers, said Grattan, 'excited a domestic fever at the hazard of the general interest, for no object, or for an object too despicable or too criminal to be mentioned.'[3]

The arguments in support of this grave charge are very strong. The fact that, before Fitzwilliam went to Ireland, both Pitt and Portland professed themselves in principle favourable to Catholic emancipation; the discretion they had given to Fitzwilliam to support the measure if he believed it to be necessary; the complete silence with which week after week they received his representations that it could not be deferred, and that he intended, unless he received directions to the contrary, to accept it; the manner in which he was permitted to meet a Parliament, which must necessarily have been mainly occupied with this very question, without any instructions to oppose or to discountenance it—all these things form a chain of evidence which it is difficult, if not impossible, to resist. In the letters of Portland, the Catholic question is given the first place, and it is probable that it had a real if not the chief influence over his

---

[1] *Second Letter to Lord Carlisle,* p. 22.
[2] *Irish Parl. Deb.* xv. 173.
[3] Ibid. 192.

mind; but the earliest intimation Fitzwilliam received that English Ministers were discontented with him, was a private letter, written on February 2, by Windham to Lord Milton, stating that Pitt was displeased at the removal of Beresford, though the Duke of Portland appears not yet to have been aware of that fact.[1] Pitt is said to have described the dismissal as 'an open breach of a most solemn promise.'[2] His letter to Fitzwilliam of the 9th was wholly occupied with the Beresford question, and the negotiations relating to Wolfe and Toler; and when Fitzwilliam in his reply said that Pitt must choose between Beresford and his Lord Lieutenant, Pitt accepted the challenge on that issue. In a letter of February 21, he stated, it is true, that he concurred with the general desire of the Cabinet, that Grattan's Bill should not be allowed to make any further progress, and that the Cabinet 'should receive and consider the information which they thought it their duty to call for;' but he places the dismissal of Lord Fitzwilliam mainly upon the ground of the removal of former supporters of the Government, which he stated himself bound to resist, 'from a regard to the King's service and to his own honour.'[3] The Chancellor, Lord Loughborough, wrote to Grattan concerning the trouble that had arisen, and this letter does not contain a word about the Catholics, but is exclusively occupied with the dismissal of Beresford.[4]

'A certain family cabal,' wrote Burke, 'are in the sole possession of the ear of Government.'[5] Pitt was surrounded by followers who hated his new Whig allies. He was himself, directly or indirectly, in constant intercourse with the leading supporters of monopoly in Ireland, and with the last two Lords Lieutenant, both of whom were violently hostile to Lord Fitzwilliam and his system. It is not difficult to understand the kind of arguments that may have influenced him. Fitzgibbon had been his most powerful and unflinching Irish supporter

---

[1] *Second Letter to Lord Carlisle*, p. 12.
[2] Stanhope's *Life of Pitt*, ii. p. 301; *Second Letter to Lord Carlisle*, p. 23.
[3] *Letter to Lord Carlisle*.
[4] Grattan's *Life*, iv. 197, 198.
[5] Ibid. p. 202. Just after Lord Fitzwilliam's recall, Pelham, the secretary of his successor, wrote to Portland about the unpopularity of the Beresfords. He said: 'If any sacrifices are necessary (which, you know, I never admit à priori in politics), Pitt must submit to Beresford's removal. I am sorry to say ... that Pitt seems more animated about men on this occasion than he ought to be; I am by no means satisfied with his conduct about Beresford, when I met him at his house with Lord Camden. I very much wished to have seen Lord Grenville upon that subject before I left London.' (Pelham to Portland, March 22, 1795.)

during the evil days of the Regency debates. Beresford had taken a considerable, if not a prominent, part in framing the commercial propositions of 1785. Cooke had been appointed to his present office by the brother of Pitt's favourite colleague, Lord Grenville. Hamilton had served for nearly fifty years in the Government of Ireland. The powers possessed by Lord Fitzwilliam when he went to Ireland were only described by word of mouth, through the intervention of the Duke of Portland, and grave misunderstandings had arisen. It was clearly understood, indeed, on both sides, that Fitzgibbon was not to be removed, and that there was not to be any complete change of men, though room was to be made for the introduction of the Ponsonbys into the Government; but Fitzwilliam contended that he had full power of pensioning off officials in confidential positions who were notoriously in opposition to his policy and his appointment, and that such a power was absolutely indispensable to the efficiency of his administration. He urged that it was possessed and exercised, in their respective departments in England, by the other members of the Whig party who joined the administration, though in England it was far less necessary than in Ireland, and he declared that he had obtained in England the tacit assent of Pitt to the probable necessity of the removal of Beresford.

Pitt, on the other hand, understood that no important change of men or measures was to be effected without previous communication with the English Cabinet, and that no old servants of the Crown were to be removed contrary to their wish, unless they had entered into a course of insubordination or opposition to the Government. But Fitzwilliam had not been more than two days in Ireland when he removed Beresford, peremptorily and curtly, and it seemed probable that the changes which were proposed or effected would amount to a most serious displacement of power in the permanent administration of Ireland. Appeals were made to Pitt, by men who had great weight with his party, 'to hold up a shield for the shelter of persons who had merited the favour of the last Lord Lieutenant by their services, and on whose conduct no blame or censure had been attached;'[1]

---

[1] The very active part which Buckingham (who was Lord Grenville's brother), Westmorland, and Auckland took at this crisis, the con-

and they were accompanied by the most alarming pictures of the dangerous fermentation which the measures of Lord Fitzwilliam were producing in Ireland.

Other political motives, which I have already indicated, very probably blended in his mind with these considerations. He was told that if the Ponsonbys, who were usually connected with the Whigs, obtained a real ascendency in Ireland, the whole department of Irish influence and patronage would pass into Whig hands. He may have believed that the easiest and safest way of governing Ireland was through that system of family monopoly which enabled the Government to count at all times, and amid all political changes, upon a subservient majority in the House of Commons. He shared the prevailing sentiment in England, that in the agonies of a revolutionary war, all great political changes should be as far as possible avoided or postponed, and he may have foreseen that if Grattan and Ponsonby carried the promised reforms, and gave a comparatively popular character to the Parliament of Ireland, the whole system of its past government would be infallibly destroyed, and the chances of obtaining a legislative union indefinitely diminished.

These were probably leading motives in producing the recall, but I do not think that the Catholic question was as completely foreign to it as the viceroy supposed. As far as 'the Irish clique' were concerned, it is probable that Burke did not greatly misjudge them when he wrote that their one object was 'to derive security to their own jobbish power. This is the first and the last in the piece. The Catholic question is a mere pretence.'[1] They employed it most skilfully for their purpose, and Fitzgibbon deserves to be remembered in history as probably the first very considerable man who maintained the doctrine that the King would violate the coronation oath, the Act of Settlement, and the Act of Union with Scotland, if he consented to a measure allowing the Catholic electors to send Catholic representatives into Parliament.[2] Even the English Chancellor, he

---

stant letters of Beresford, Cooke, and Fitzgibbon against the administration of Lord Fitzwilliam, and the great jealousy with which the old Tories looked upon their Whig allies, will be evident to anyone who compares Buckingham's *Courts and Cabinets of George III.* vol. ii.; the *Auckland*

Correspondence; the *Beresford Correspondence*; Stanhope's *Life of Pitt*; and the *Westmorland* (or, as it is now called, *Fane*) *Correspondence* in the I.S.P.O.

[1] Grattan's *Life*, iv. 204.
[2] I have noticed (vol. iii. pp. 498, 499) how the doctrine that the Scotch

wrote, would 'stake his head' if he affixed the great seal of England to such a measure.¹ No more extravagant doctrine has ever been maintained by a responsible statesman, but it fell upon a soil which was prepared for its reception, and it has had a great and most fatal influence on English history.

Even before Fitzgibbon had written to this effect, the King had declared his emphatic hostility to Catholic emancipation, and drawn up an elaborate memorandum in opposition to it. It was dated on February 6, and in it the King mentioned that it was only on the preceding day that he heard, to his great astonishment, that Fitzwilliam had proposed a total and immediate change of the system of government which had been followed in Ireland since the Revolution. The admission of Catholics to sit in Parliament, and the formation in Ireland of a yeomanry which would be essentially Catholic, were measures which, in the opinion of the King, could not fail, sooner or later, to separate the two kingdoms, or lead England into a line of conduct which it was the very object of the English Revolution and of the Act of Settlement to prevent. Such a measure, the King continued, was beyond the decision of a cabinet of ministers; even if they favoured it, 'it would be highly dangerous, without previous concert with the leading men of every order in the State, to send any encouragement to the Lord Lieutenant on this subject; and if received with the same suspicion I do (sic), I am certain it

Union and the coronation oath precluded the King from assenting to any law modifying the ecclesiastical establishments, appeared in the English Parliament in 1772. In the *Westmorland Papers* there is an argument, drawn up by the Archbishop of Cashel, against the abolition of the remaining restrictions on Catholics, based on the same grounds. It is undated, but was probably written during Lord Westmorland's struggle with the English Cabinet about the measures in favour of the Catholics then contemplated, for it states that, 'It is notorious that at least nineteen-twentieths of the Protestants of Ireland are utterly averse from the Popery Bill now in agitation,' which could hardly have been said by the most violent partisan, and certainly not with the faintest colour of plausibility, in 1795.

¹ See two remarkable letters in the *Beresford Correspondence*, ii. 70–76. He says: 'The only Acts which now affect Irish papists are the Act of Supremacy and Uniformity, the Test Act, and the Bill of Rights. The King cannot give his assent to a repeal of any of these without a direct breach of his coronation oath. ... Whenever Mr. Grattan brings in his Bill—and it is printed—I mean to send it over to England, with comments in reference to British statutes which certainly bind the King upon this subject. In their Bill for establishing papist colleges, they will find the same difficulties, if they do not take more precautions than they are capable of.' It will be observed in these letters, that Fitzgibbon suggests no doubt whatever, that the Irish Parliament would carry the Bills.

wrote, would 'stake his head' if he affixed the great seal of England to such a measure.¹ No more extravagant doctrine has ever been maintained by a responsible statesman, but it fell upon a soil which was prepared for its reception, and it has had a great and most fatal influence on English history.

Even before Fitzgibbon had written to this effect, the King had declared his emphatic hostility to Catholic emancipation, and drawn up an elaborate memorandum in opposition to it. It was dated on February 6, and in it the King mentioned that it was only on the preceding day that he heard, to his great astonishment, that Fitzwilliam had proposed a total and immediate change of the system of government which had been followed in Ireland since the Revolution. The admission of Catholics to sit in Parliament, and the formation in Ireland of a yeomanry which would be essentially Catholic, were measures which, in the opinion of the King, could not fail, sooner or later, to separate the two kingdoms, or lead England into a line of conduct which it was the very object of the English Revolution and of the Act of Settlement to prevent. Such a measure, the King continued, was beyond the decision of a cabinet of ministers; even if they favoured it, 'it would be highly dangerous, without previous concert with the leading men of every order in the State, to send any encouragement to the Lord Lieutenant on this subject; and if received with the same suspicion I do (*sic*), I am certain it

---

Union and the coronation oath precluded the King from assenting to any law modifying the ecclesiastical establishments, appeared in the English Parliament in 1772. In the *Westmorland Papers* there is an argument, drawn up by the Archbishop of Cashel, against the abolition of the remaining restrictions on Catholics, based on the same grounds. It is undated, but was probably written during Lord Westmorland's struggle with the English Cabinet about the measures in favour of the Catholics then contemplated, for it states that, 'It is notorious that at least nineteen-twentieths of the Protestants of Ireland are utterly averse from the Popery Bill now in agitation,' which could hardly have been said by the most violent partisan, and certainly not with the faintest colour of plausibility. in 1795.

¹ See two remarkable letters in the *Beresford Correspondence*, ii. 70–76. He says: 'The only Acts which now affect Irish papists are the Act of Supremacy and Uniformity, the Test Act, and the Bill of Rights. The King cannot give his assent to a repeal of any of these without a direct breach of his coronation oath. . . . Whenever Mr. Grattan brings in his Bill—and it is printed—I mean to send it over to England, with comments in reference to British statutes which certainly bind the King upon this subject. In their Bill for establishing papist colleges, they will find the same difficulties, if they do not take more precautions than they are capable of.' It will be observed in these letters, that Fitzgibbon suggests no doubt whatever, that the Irish Parliament would carry the Bills.

would be safer even to change the new administration in Ireland, if its continuance depends on the success of this proposal, than to prolong its existence on grounds that must sooner or later ruin one, if not both kingdoms.'[1]

It is obvious what a formidable obstacle the attitude of the King threw into the way of Fitzwilliam; and while the King was in this state of mind, Fitzgibbon's views about the coronation oath were communicated to him by Lord Westmorland.[2] He readily embraced them, and he ever after employed them as the best reason or pretext for resistance.

I have referred to a memorandum giving the case of the Ministers, which was drawn up by Grenville, corrected by Pitt, and afterwards sent for their approval to the other members of the Cabinet. It describes the course of the transaction much as I have told it, but with some further details relating to the disputes about patronage. It mentions that when the coalition had been formed in England in July 1794, the government of Ireland was destined for Lord Fitzwilliam as soon as a sufficient post could be found for Lord Westmorland; that the intention had been prematurely divulged, and a notion got abroad that an entire change of the system of Irish government, both as to men and measures, was contemplated, and that this suspicion was much confirmed when it was found that Fitzwilliam intended to remove Fitzgibbon. It adds, that explanations took place in which it was clearly settled that Fitzgibbon should not be removed, and an explicit assurance was given by Fitzwilliam, 'that he had not in view the establishment of any new system in Ireland, but that he was desirous of strengthening his Government by the accession of Mr. Ponsonby and his friends, and the support of Mr. Grattan.' Shortly before the departure of Fitzwilliam, a Cabinet meeting was held at Pitt's house to discuss doubtful or disputed points. In addition to Fitzwilliam and Pitt, Portland, Spencer, Grenville, and Windham were present. They discussed at great length many questions of patronage—the appointment of a Primate, and of a Provost for Trinity

---

[1] Stanhope's *Life of Pitt*, ii. 304; appendix, xxiii–xxv.
[2] *Auckland Correspondence*, iii. 303. We shall have additional evidence of this communication in the next chapter. Westmorland, in the debates on May 8, adopted precisely the argument of Fitzgibbon against Catholic emancipation. (*Parl. Hist.* xxxi. 1511.)

College, the posts to be given to the two Ponsonbys, the provision to be made for Wolfe and Toler, who were not to be removed unless such places were provided for them as there was just reason to believe they would have accepted under Westmorland. These points were easily settled, but more division arose upon the contention of Fitzwilliam that some of the new offices, especially in the revenue board which had been established by Lord Buckinghamshire and which had been so often and so severely condemned by Grattan, should be abolished. Pitt and Grenville said, 'that they considered themselves parties to the measures of Lord Buckinghamshire in Ireland, and could not on that account, independently of other considerations, concur in any measure which would appear to reflect on him.' Fitzwilliam disowned any intention of making such a reflection, but he still thought that the revenue board ought to be remodelled and reduced. In discussing the question, however, they soon found that none of them understood the details, and it was finally determined that it must be adjourned till the arrival of Fitzwilliam in Ireland, and 'that after his explicit disavowal of all intention to introduce a new system, or to countenance imputations on the former Government, his colleagues would willingly leave it to him to consider the subject . . . desiring only that before any such measure was adopted, they might have an opportunity of deliberating upon it.' 'Nothing,' the memorandum continues, 'was intimated in this conversation of any idea of removing Mr. Beresford, nor was even his name mentioned by Lord Fitzwilliam, although the different means which might be adopted for lessening the number of the commissioners of the revenue board formed a part of what he stated on the subject of those boards.'

After discussion of these and of some less important points, the conversation passed to measures, and the conclusions may be stated in the words of the memorandum. 'It was understood that on all important subjects Lord F. should transmit all the information he could collect, with his opinion, to the King's servants here, and that he should do nothing to commit the King's Government in such cases without fresh instructions from hence. It is also distinctly recollected by some of the persons present, that the Catholic question was particularly mentioned, though not discussed at much length; that no decided sentiment was expressed by anyone as to the line which it might be right ultimately to adopt; but that the same general principles before stated were considered as applying to this as well as to the other questions of importance, and that a strong opinion was stated that Lord Fitzwilliam should if possible prevent the agitation of the question at all during the present session.'[1]

This appears to have been the last conversation which took place between Fitzwilliam and the Ministers before the former departed for Ireland. The memorandum corroborates in all essential points the evidence that has been already adduced, and it seems to me rather to strengthen the view, that the Catholic question had, in the minds of the Ministers at least, only a secondary part in the recall of Lord Fitzwilliam, though it is probable that the opposition of the King to that measure weighed considerably in the balance. Among the Pelham papers of this date, there is a very elaborate legal argument to prove that Catholic emancipation was essentially inconsistent with the Constitution and the coronation oath. It was evidently drawn up by a lawyer, and is probably a copy of a paper submitted by Fitzgibbon to the King. After a full and interesting historical survey of the chief English and Irish statutes relating to the connection between Church and State, both before and after the Revolution, and an argument to prove that the Catholics, though freely admitted to the Irish Parliament before the Restoration, were excluded by the Act of Supremacy from the Parliament which sat from 1661 to 1666, the writer proceeds to argue that the legislation of the Revolution, and the clause in the Act of Union with Scotland providing that the Act of Uniformity, and all other Acts of Parliament then in force for the establishment and preservation of the Church of England, 'shall remain and be in full force for ever,' made Catholic emancipation a question beyond the competence of the Legislature to carry. 'It appears,' he writes, 'that the crown having been conferred at the Revolution under the express compact of maintaining a Protestant religion

---

[1] This memorandum is dated March 1795. A copy with a statement of its origin is in the *Grenville MSS.* There is another copy in the *Pelham MSS.* In one of Pelham's first letters from Ireland he says the recall of Lord Fitzwilliam was a fortunate event, for 'the notion of forming a popular administration had given such an encouragement to democracy, and so unhinged all the common machinery of government, that I really believe the business of Parliament would have stopped.' (Pelham to Windham, May 17, 1795.)

and Government, and the Irish Parliament having recognised that principle, a Bill to endanger the Protestant Government and religion could not, consistently with the Revolution, be entertained in the Irish Parliament, and that the King could not, consistently with the Declaration of Rights, his coronation oath, and the Act of Union, order the great seal to be put to such an Act, unless his Majesty should be thereto authorised by a special Act of Parliament. The Roman Catholic petitions demand the repeal of all penal and restrictive laws whatsoever. If this were agreed to, it would go to the repeal of the Act of Supremacy and Uniformity. It would go to the acknowledgment of the papal jurisdiction, and would be, in fact, a reconciliation with the Church of Rome, to which the King could not agree consistently with the tenure of his crown. . . . It is my opinion that an Act of Parliament to capacitate any person to sit in either House of Parliament without making and subscribing the 'Declaration against Popery,' and 'taking the oaths of allegiance and supremacy,' would be a direct violation of the Constitution as established at the Revolution, and a breach of the solemn contract then made between the King and the people, which contract every king and queen swears to preserve inviolate at his or her coronation, and which oath, I am of opinion, renders it the indispensable duty of such king to refuse his assent to any such Bill, should it pass through the two Houses of Parliament.'[1]

[1] Memorandum as to the Catholic claim to sit in Parliament, April 3, 1795; *Pelham MSS.* ('Miscellaneous Irish Papers'). This memorandum contains some curious information about the Act which was introduced by Yelverton, Grattan, and Fitzgibbon, immediately after the question of independence had been raised in 1782, in order to allay the doubts of those who feared that Irish titles to property derived under English Acts of Parliament, might be affected by the repudiation of the right of England to legislate for Ireland. 'The framers of this Bill merely proposed to quiet Irish titles, but Lord Auckland, then Chief Secretary, signified to them privately, that he could not answer for the Bill being returned from Great Britain, unless they should insert in it clauses for confirming such statutes as went to the connection of the two kingdoms; and the 3rd of William III. [the Act which excluded Catholics from the Irish Parliament] was particularly mentioned at the time. Accordingly, after much reluctance, the Bill was extended in its provisions, and the following proviso was introduced: "And whereas a similarity of laws, manners, and customs must naturally conduce to strengthen and perpetuate that affection and harmony which do, and at all times ought to subsist between the people of Great Britain and Ireland"—and then the Bill enacts, that all such clauses and provisions contained in any statutes made in England as relate to the taking any oath or oaths, or making or subscribing any declaration or affirmation in this kingdom &c. shall be accepted, used, and executed in this kingdom according to the present tenor of the same respectively.' The whole of this memorandum (which is too long for me to quote in full) is well worthy of study.

When the news arrived that the English Government had determined to recall Lord Fitzwilliam, and to dash to the ground the hopes which the Catholics had been given every reason to entertain, those who knew Ireland best foresaw nothing but ruin. Fitzwilliam himself predicted that the English Ministers must face 'almost the certainty of driving this kingdom into rebellion.'[1] Forbes, who was one of the most acute members of the Irish Parliament, wrote to a private friend: 'It is reported that Pitt intends to overturn the Irish Cabinet by rejecting Catholic claims. Should he pursue that line, ... it will end in the total alienation of Ireland.'[2] The ablest English-speaking Catholic bishop of the time was Dr. Hussey, who was largely employed by the Government in negotiations with the Irish Catholics, and who was a constant correspondent of Burke. At the end of January, when the Catholic question seemed certain to triumph under the auspices of the English Government, he wrote to Burke, that he found the loyal spirit of the Irish Catholics so strongly roused, that he believed that there were not five of them in the kingdom worth 10*l.* who would not spill their blood to resist a French invasion. Three weeks later, when doubts about the policy of the Government had begun to circulate, he wrote very solemnly that the question of this Emancipation Bill involved another very awful one—whether the Cabinet 'mean to retain Ireland, or to abdicate it to a French Government, or to a revolutionary system of its own invention.' When the decision was taken, he wrote in absolute consternation: 'The disastrous news of Earl Fitzwilliam's recall is come, and Ireland is now on the brink of civil war.'[3] From a wholly different point on the political compass, Charlemont, who had been so firm and steady an opponent of the concession of political power to the Catholics, pronounced that in the existing state of Ireland the recall of Lord Fitzwilliam was 'utterly ruinous,' and he predicted that by next Christmas the mass of the people would probably be in the hands of the United Irishmen.[4]

The remarkable memoir on the history of the United Irishmen which was drawn up in 1798 by O'Connor, McNevin, and Emmet, fully confirms the judgment of Charlemont. 'Whatever

[1] *Letter to Lord Carlisle.*
[2] Grattan's *Life,* iv. 197.
[3] Burke's *Correspondence,* iv. 268, 278, 282.
[4] Hardy's *Life of Charlemont,* ii. 347, 348.

progress,' they say, ' this united system had made among the Presbyterians of the North, it had, as we apprehend, made but little way among the Catholics throughout the kingdom, until after the recall of Earl Fitzwilliam.'[1]

It may not be out of place to add here the opinion of a great English statesman on the transaction. 'As to the Catholic Bill,' wrote Fox, ' it is not only right in principle, but, after all that was given to the Catholics two years ago, it seems little short of madness to dispute (and at such a time as this) about the very little which remains to be given them. To suppose it possible that, now they are electors, they will long submit to be ineligible to Parliament, appears to me to be absurd beyond measure, but common sense seems to be totally lost out of the councils of this devoted country.'[2]

Never at any other period of Irish history had the recall of a Lord Lieutenant struck such consternation through the country. In Parliament, Sir Lawrence Parsons made himself the chief mouthpiece of the prevailing feeling. We have seen that, when the supplies were voted, this very able man had warned the Parliament, with a sagacity which the event only too fully justified, against excessive confidence in the English Cabinet, and had vainly tried to induce them to unite their grants with stipulations for redress of grievances. He had not forgotten that, only ten years before, large additional supplies were voted by the Parliament of Ireland, in response to the offer of the English Minister to grant free trade between England and Ireland, and that, after those supplies had been granted, the commercial propositions were so mutilated that they were ultimately abandoned. On February 26 he rose to ask if the prevailing rumours of the recall of Fitzwilliam, and of the withdrawal of the concessions to the Catholics, were well founded. ' If those measures,' he said,' were now to be relinquished which gentlemen had promised with so much confidence to the country, and on the faith of which the House had been called on to vote the enormous sum of one million seven hundred thousand pounds, he must consider this country as brought to the most awful and alarming crisis she had ever known in any period of her history.'[3] On

---

[1] *Castlereagh Correspondence*, i. 356.
[2] Fox's *Correspondence*, iii. 100, 101. [3] *Irish Parl. Deb.* xv. 133, 134.

March 2, when the news was confirmed, he took the extreme step of moving a short supply Bill, prefacing his motion by a speech of great violence. 'The state of the kingdom,' he said, 'was most alarming. The people, under the auspices of their old friends, had been taught to expect measures which he feared would be shortly resisted. . . . The first he believed to be the Catholic Bill, and if a resistance to any one measure more than another was likely to promote dreadful consequences, it was this. He said nothing as to the original propriety of the measure, but this much he would say, that if the Irish Administration had countenanced the Catholics in this expectation without the concurrence of the British Cabinet, they had much to answer for. On the other hand, if the British Cabinet had held out an assent and had afterwards retracted—if the demon of darkness should come from the infernal regions upon earth and throw a firebrand amongst the people, he could not do more to promote mischief. The hopes of the public were raised, and in one instant they were blasted. If the House did not resent that insult to the nation and to themselves, they would in his mind be most contemptible; for although a majority of the people might submit to have their rights withheld, they would never submit to be mocked in so barefaced a manner. The case was not as formerly, when all the Parliament of Ireland was against the Catholics, and to back them the force of England. Now, although the claim of the Catholics was well known and understood, not one petition controverting it had been presented from Protestants in any part of Ireland. No remonstrance appeared, no county meeting had been held. What was to be inferred from all this, but that the sentiments of the Protestants were for the emancipation of the Catholics? . . . Was the British Minister to control all the interest, talents, and inclinations of this country? He protested to God that, in all the history he had read, he had never met with a parallel of such ominous infatuation as that by which he appeared to be led. Let him persevere, and you must increase your army to myriads; every man must have five or six dragoons in his house. . . . The House had voted additional taxes in the present session to the amount of 250,000*l*. . . . This was a charge of 6,000*l*. a year upon every county in Ireland, over and above all other taxes. Such a sum would never have been voted, without a dissenting voice, in support of a calamitous war, if Ireland had not been deceived either here or in the British Cabinet; he was inclined to suspect the latter.'[1]

The proposal of a short money Bill was, however, easily defeated, and Grattan concurred with Lord Milton in persuading Conolly to withdraw a resolution protesting against the prorogation of Parliament before the grievance complained of was redressed. The House contented itself with voting unanimously, that the viceroy had merited the thanks of the House and the confidence of the people. When Lord Fitzwilliam had left Ireland, there were debates on his recall both in the English and Irish Parliaments, but the Government refused all detailed explanations, and entrenched themselves behind the undoubted prerogative of the King to recall his representatives. In a long protest which was placed on the books of the House of Lords by Fitzwilliam and Lord Ponsonby, the chief facts of the case were clearly stated, and Fitzwilliam once more gave his emphatic testimony to the condition of Irish opinion on the Catholic question. 'He found the relief,' he said, 'to be ardently desired by the Catholics, to be asked for by very many Protestants, and to be cheerfully acquiesced in by almost all.'[2]

Lord Camden was appointed successor to Fitzwilliam, with Mr. Pelham as Secretary. Pelham had already held this position during Temple's short administration in 1783 and 1784. His health was now much broken, but he resumed the office at the urgent request of Portland, and with the warm approbation of Fitzgibbon.[3]

---

[1] *Irish Parl. Deb.* xv. 137-141. So Fitzwilliam wrote: 'I have had the good fortune not only to obtain larger and more considerable supplies ... than were ever before granted in this kingdom; but I must and shall have the additional boast of laying at the feet of his Majesty, on the part of his zealous and faithful subjects of Ireland, a most munificent aid for the general defence of his empire—an aid large beyond any example. I have the pride further to say, that all this has been effected, in its progress thus far, with a degree of harmony, cordiality, and unanimity scarcely ever before experienced, and never under circumstances similar to those in which I found the country.' (Fitzwilliam to Portland, Feb. 28, 1795.) It was 'no proof of wisdom nor generosity,' wrote Grattan, 'when this country came forward, cordial and confident, with the offering of her treasure and blood, and resolute to stand or fall with the British nation, ... to select that moment to dash away her affection ... and to plant a dagger in her heart.' (Grattan's *Life*, iv. 220.)

[2] *Parl. Hist.* xxxi. 1527.

[3] When the report that the Secretaryship had been offered to Pelham, arrived in Ireland, Fitzgibbon wrote to him: 'If such an application is made to you, for God's sake do not form your opinion of the state of this country from newspaper exaggera-

The interval between the announcement of the recall and the arrival of Camden was a very anxious one. A great meeting of the Catholics, summoned by the Catholic Committee, was held in Dublin, to petition the King that Parliament should not be prorogued till the Catholic question had been settled, and a petition for the continuance of Fitzwilliam in office was taken by delegates to London. Meetings of Protestant freeholders and freemen of Dublin, and of the merchants and traders, with a governor of the Bank of Ireland at their head, were held for the same purpose, and they expressed their entire concurrence in the removal of religious disabilities. Kildare, Wexford, Antrim, Londonderry, and other counties followed the example, while addresses from numerous counties and corporations, and from the students of Trinity College, were presented to Fitzwilliam and Grattan.[1]

The delegates sent on the part of the Catholics to London, to petition the King to continue Lord Fitzwilliam in office, were graciously received, but obtained no answer; and shortly after their return, the Catholic Committee convened another great and very important meeting. Its resolutions expressed the regret of the Catholics at the removal of Lord Fitzwilliam, 'contrary to the unanimous wish of the whole people;' their consolation 'in contemplating the rising spirit of harmony and co-operation among all sects and descriptions of Irishmen, so rapidly accelerated by that event;' their earnest wish that the Catholics of Ireland should 'cultivate by all possible means the friendship and affection of their Protestant brethren,' and their desire that Grattan should reintroduce the Catholic Bill in the next session of Parliament. The two memorable passages I have already cited from the letters of the English Minister, pointing, as was universally believed, to the desire of Government to postpone the Catholic question, with the object of effecting a legislative union, were then read, and this great and representative Catholic

---

tion. Believe me, that firmness and moderation on the part of English Government will very soon re-establish tranquillity in Ireland; and I do not know a man who could come here that would be so likely to succeed in composing the country as you. Be assured that, if you will come to us, you will have an opportunity of doing essential service to both countries, and acquiring a solid and permanent political character.' (Fitzgibbon to Pelham, March 12, 1795, *Pelham MSS.*)

[1] Grattan's *Life*, iv. 215-224; McNevin's *Pieces of Irish History*, pp. 92-95; Plowden, ii. 503, 504.

meeting proceeded to pass, without a single dissentient voice, the following resolutions: 'That we are sincerely and unalterably attached to the rights, liberties, and independence of our native country; and we pledge ourselves collectively and individually to resist even our own emancipation, if proposed to be conceded upon the ignominious terms of an acquiescence in the fatal measure of an union with the sister kingdom. That, while we make this undisguised declaration of our sentiments, in order to satisfy the public mind, we are of opinion that a measure so full of violence and ruin will never be hazarded; convinced as we are that no set of men will arrogate to themselves a power which is contrary to the ends and purposes of all government—a power to surrender the liberties of their country, and to seal the slavery of future generations.'[1]

The publication of the letters to Lord Carlisle, and especially of the confidential passage from Portland's despatch referred to in the foregoing resolutions, undoubtedly added largely to the dangerous excitement, and it is not, I think, possible to justify it. The mind of the Lord Lieutenant was evidently in a state of morbid irritation, which was probably greatly aggravated by the fact that he had received no support from his Whig colleagues in the Ministry; and though he disclaimed the publication, these letters appear to have been widely distributed with his sanction.[2] A singularly curious letter, written on the day of his departure, to Westmorland by the Chancellor, shows vividly the indignation this publication had produced, and at the same time casts some light on the meaning of the Duke of Portland's words. After describing the departure of the Lord Lieutenant, Fitzgibbon proceeds: 'So much malignity and folly and falsehood, and such notorious violation of public trust and private faith, never have been exhibited by any man to whom the management of a great kingdom was committed, as this infatuated man has manifested in these letters to his friend, Lord Carlisle. In one of these, your lordship will see, he has published a very serious and important passage in a private and confidential despatch, as he candidly states it to be, which he had received from the Duke of Portland—a passage intimating broadly his opinion, that if the

---

[1] Seward's *Collectanea Politica*, iii. 133-135.
[2] *Beresford Correspondence*, ii. 88, 89, 118.

Catholic claims could be postponed for consideration till there should be a peace, they might induce the Protestants of Ireland to consent to an union with the Parliament of England. I do most strongly suspect that this idea was drawn out from the Duke of Portland, by Lord Fitzwilliam's representation of a conversation which I had with him upon the subject of his popish projects, in which I stated to him distinctly my opinion that an union with the Parliament of England was the only measure which could give Great Britain a chance of preserving this country as a member of the Empire. I told him, however, that till Great Britain was at peace, and we had a strong army in Ireland, it would be impossible to carry such a measure, however necessary it might be. He told me, more than a month since, that he had reported my opinions on this subject to the British Government.[1]

The signs of disaffection were so menacing, that Fitzwilliam, who desired immediately to leave Ireland, was obliged, at the urgent request of the leading members of the Irish Government, to postpone his departure for a fortnight, as it was represented to him that the country would not be safe in the weak hands of the lords justices, till his successor arrived.[2] He at first peremptorily refused to adjourn the Parliament; but Fitzgibbon declared that unless such an adjournment took place, he would not be responsible for twenty-four hours, for the government of Ireland.[3] The twenty-fifth of March, when he sailed for England, was one of the saddest days ever known in Ireland. The shops of Dublin were shut. All business was suspended. Signs of mourning were exhibited on every side. The coach of the Lord Lieutenant was drawn by some of the most respectable citizens to the waterside, and the shadow of coming calamity cast its gloom upon every countenance. It was indeed but too well justified. From that time the spirit of sullen and virulent disloyalty overspread the land, 'creeping,' in the words of Grattan, 'like the mist at the heels of the countryman.'

[1] Fitzgibbon to Westmorland, March 25, 1795 (I.S.P.O.).
[2] Fitzwilliam to Portland, March 7; Fitzgibbon to Westmorland, March 7, 1795. Fitzgibbon says that he himself, with the Primate and the Speaker, told Fitzwilliam that the state of the country was too dangerous for him to leave it till his successor arrived. On receiving a written opinion from Fitzgibbon to that effect, he consented to delay his departure.
[3] Fitzgibbon to Westmorland, March 25, 1795. The Speaker, the Primate, and Pelham (who had just arrived) supported Fitzgibbon, and the Parliament was accordingly adjourned to April 13.

It has been strongly maintained by some modern English writers, that the importance of the recall of Lord Fitzwilliam in Irish history has been greatly overrated. That some exaggeration mingled with the first excited judgments on the subject, is no doubt true, and something of it may have passed into later history. Long before the arrival of Lord Fitzwilliam, some of the most active members of the Catholic Committee were in full sympathy with Wolfe Tone, and in large districts of Ireland the Defender movement had drawn great bodies of the Catholic peasantry into an armed organisation, aiming at Whiteboy objects, but already looking forward to French assistance and invasion as the means of attaining them. No one can read the letters of Westmorland, and especially of Fitzwilliam, without perceiving that the condition of Ireland was very serious, and that the danger would have been extreme if a French army had succeeded in establishing itself firmly on the soil, and had promised the abolition of tithes and the subversion of the existing system of landed property. Lawlessness, ignorance, extreme poverty, and a complete separation in character and sentiment of the Catholic tenantry in a great part of Ireland from the owners of the soil, were evils on which Catholic emancipation could have had little direct influence, though national education, and, still more, a commutation of tithes, might have done much to mitigate them. Under any circumstances, the condition of Ireland in the last years of the eighteenth century must have been exceedingly dangerous. Nothing disorganises and demoralises a country in which there are great internal elements of disorder, so certainly as a constant menace of invasion, prolonged through many years; and the situation was enormously aggravated by the fact, that the probable invaders were the soldiers of a great and contagious Revolution, whose first object was to set the poor against the rich, to sweep away established churches, and to destroy the whole existing distribution of property and power. Ireland was full of sympathisers with this Revolution, and no moderate reform would have contented them. Whether the introduction of a few Catholic gentry into the Legislature, and the moral effect of the abolition of religious disabilities, would have enabled Ireland successfully to meet the storm, is a question which may be easily asked, but which no wise man will confidently answer.

It appears to me, however, undoubtedly true, that the chances were immensely diminished by the recall of Lord Fitzwilliam. Great classes who were as yet very slightly disaffected, now passed rapidly into republicanism, and Catholic opinion, which had been raised to the highest point of excited hope, experienced a complete, a sudden, and a most dangerous revulsion. The recall of Fitzwilliam may be justly regarded as a fatal turning point in Irish history. For at least fifteen years before it occurred, the country, in spite of many abuses and disturbances, had been steadily and incontestably improving. Religious animosities appeared to have almost died away. Material prosperity was advancing with an unprecedented rapidity. The Constitution in many important respects had been ameliorated, and the lines of religious disabilities were fast disappearing from the statute book. The contagion of the French Revolution had produced dangerous organisations in the North, and a vague restlessness through the other provinces, but up to this time it does not appear to have seriously affected the great body of Catholics, and Burke was probably warranted when, in estimating the advantages which England possessed in her struggle with France, he gave a prominent place to the loyalty, the power, and the opulence of Ireland.[1] With the removal of the few remaining religious disabilities, a settlement of tithes, and a moderate reform of Parliament, it seemed still probable that Ireland, under the guidance of her resident gentry, might have contributed at least as much as Scotland to the prosperity of the Empire. But from the day when Pitt recalled Lord Fitzwilliam, the course of her history was changed. Intense and growing hatred of England, revived religious and class animosities, a savage rebellion savagely repressed, a legislative union prematurely and corruptly carried, mark the closing years of the eighteenth century, and after ninety years of direct British government, the condition of Ireland is universally recognised as the chief scandal and the chief weakness of the Empire.

[1] *First Letter on a Regicide Peace.*

CHAPTER XXVII.

LORD CAMDEN arrived in Ireland on March 31, 1795. His Chief Secretary, Pelham, had been already there for some days, and the state of the country was so evidently dangerous, that there were great fears for the safety of the viceroy on his entry into Dublin. In consequence, it is said, of secret information furnished by Francis Higgins, the proprietor of the 'Freeman's Journal,' the arrangements for the entry were at the last moment changed, and it was deemed a matter of no small congratulation that the procession passed almost unmolested through the streets. When Lord Fitzgibbon and the Primate were returning from the Castle, their carriages were attacked by a furious mob, and the Chancellor, who was especially obnoxious to the popular party, was wounded by a stone, which struck him upon the forehead. The riot rapidly spread. The mob attacked the custom-house, and the houses of the Chancellor, the Primate, the Speaker, and Beresford. It was found necessary to call out the soldiers, and two men were killed.

It was an ill-omened beginning of a disastrous viceroyalty. On the day when Grattan, who was regarded as the mouthpiece of the Government of Lord Fitzwilliam, obtained leave to bring in a Bill for Catholic emancipation, the loyalty of the Catholic population seemed to rise higher than it had ever risen since the Revolution, and it was believed that the policy of religious disqualification was for ever at an end. On the day when the English Government disavowed the acts of its Irish representatives, recalled Lord Fitzwilliam, and again brought to the helm the most violent opponents of the Catholics, a cloud seemed to fall on the spirit of the nation which has never been removed. Just before the arrival of Camden, Pelham wrote to England that he had received very alarming accounts of the proceedings of the

Catholic Committee. A select and secret committee, consisting of a very few, and entrusted with a larger power, was forming, and they were to be bound by an oath of secrecy and perseverance. 'It is said,' he continued, 'that upon a closer investigation of their strength and influence upon the recall of Lord Fitzwilliam, they [the Catholic Committee] are led to despair of anything effectual without the assistance of the French, and it is seriously in their contemplation to send an embassy to Paris, if the Catholic question should be lost in the Irish Parliament.'[1]

The replies of Grattan to the numerous addresses presented to him were eagerly scanned. They were marked by a great deal of that strained and exaggerated mannerism of expression which was habitual to him, and they speak in no doubtful tones of his indignation at what had occurred; but they were, at the same time, in substance eminently moderate, and evidently intended to maintain the Catholics in their allegiance. Their true policy, he told them, was to maintain strictly their union with Protestants, and to press on their claims steadily within the lines of the Constitution. 'Your emancipation will pass,' he said, 'rely on it, your emancipation must pass; it may be death to one viceroy; it will be the peace-offering of another, and the laurel may be torn from the dead brow of one governor to be craftily converted into the olive for his successor.' If, however, the old 'taskmasters' and the old system of government were restored, he predicted that they would 'extinguish this country.' He asserted that the public measures of the late administration, and especially that which was now disputed, had been stipulated and agreed to, and he pledged himself to bring in the Emancipation Bill of which he had given notice. Language was employed, which excited much alarm among the English Ministers, about the independence of the Irish Cabinet as a body responsible directly to the King, and not a mere subordinate department of the English Ministry.

It had been one of the great misfortunes of the English Government that, during a considerable period of its history, it had been either compelled or persuaded to adopt as its method of managing Ireland, the worst of all expedients, that of endea-

[1] Pelham to Portland, March 30, 1795.

vouring to inflame the animosities and deepen the divisions between the Protestants and Catholics. This was the policy of Cromwell, and it was the policy which was systematically pursued for a long period after the Revolution. The exclusion of Catholics by an English Act from the Irish Parliament; the lament of Bishop Burnet that the division of Whig and Tory was beginning to appear in a country where the sole divisions had hitherto been those between Protestants and Papists;[1] the habitual employment by the governors of Ireland, in the early years of the eighteenth century, of the terms 'common enemy' and 'domestic enemies' when speaking of the Roman Catholics, clearly indicate a policy which was steadily carried out. For a long time, as we have already seen, this spirit had almost wholly passed away. The relations of the English Government to the Irish Catholics had become very friendly. The penal laws had for the most part fallen into desuetude before they had been formally abolished, and the influence of English Ministers had been usually exerted in favour of the Catholics. The declarations of the grand juries in 1792 against the admission of the Catholics to political power had, no doubt, been chiefly inspired by men who were high in office in Ireland, but this was at a time when the Irish Administration on this very question was endeavouring to defeat the tolerant views of the English Cabinet. On the accession of Lord Camden, however, a great and most pernicious change took place. The English Cabinet had determined to resist the emancipation of the Catholics, contrary to the dominant sentiments of the Irish Protestants, and it therefore directed its Irish representatives to endeavour to kindle an anti-Catholic feeling in Ireland, and exert its enormous influence to organise an Irish party of resistance.

The secret instructions to Lord Camden clearly indicate this intention. The policy, the Duke of Portland said, which Lord Fitzwilliam ought to have pursued, was to have prevented if possible the Catholic question from being agitated at all, and if this proved impossible, to have collected the opinions of all parties, on the subject, for the information of the Ministers, and to have awaited their decision before committing himself in any way upon it. 'Although the business is far from being in the

[1] Burnet's *History of his own Times*, ii. 360.

same state, the outline which I have to mark out for your lordship's conduct must be the same, as nearly as circumstances will admit.' The agitation of the question cannot now be prevented, but the Lord Lieutenant must endeavour to convince the most important persons, that the contemplated concessions must be either subversive of the Protestant establishment, or else wholly insignificant. He must do his utmost to rally the Protestant interest against the concessions. He must hold a firm and decided language of hostility to them, but he must also tell the Protestants that, without their concurrence, the Government cannot effectually resist; that, with their concurrence, the Government 'will be ready to make every exertion they can desire, to prevent the admission of Catholics to seats in the Legislature.'

Such instructions, in the existing state of Ireland, meant nothing less than a revival of the old religious warfare. They meant that, while the United Irishmen were seeking to obliterate the distinction between Protestant and Catholic, the English Government, in order to perpetuate a system of proscription, were endeavouring to make that distinction indelible, and to stimulate and manipulate Protestant jealousies. The extreme centralisation of Irish administration had placed most posts of influence and power in a few easily managed hands, and the whole machinery was to be worked in hostility to the Catholics. If Lord Camden was convinced that resistance would be dangerous or ineffectual, he must even then abstain from taking any step in favour of concession till he had received explicit instructions from England, and he must not suffer anyone connected with his Government to bring forward or to countenance any measure which had not been expressly sanctioned.

While, however, the Lord Lieutenant was directed to place himself at the head of the Protestant interest, and to adopt a policy of open, energetic, and uncompromising resistance to Catholic emancipation, he was also, as far as it could be done consistently with this course, to conciliate the Catholics, and for this purpose Portland suggested measures which had been already mentioned to Lord Fitzwilliam. These measures were, the establishment of seminaries for the education of priests, and a provision for the parochial clergy, by which they might be relieved from their present state of dependence, and their parishioners from a portion of the burden to which they were subject. 'If beside these,' wrote the English Minister, 'any mode should occur to your lordship, by which the education of the lower ranks of the Catholics could be facilitated, so as to put them in that respect on a par with their Protestant brethren, your lordship may be sure of the fullest countenance and support of the Government.'

On the constitutional question, he speaks with no faltering accents. 'A notion has arisen within these few years, and has latterly but too generally prevailed, of the propriety of the existence of an Irish Cabinet. I therefore think it necessary to protest, and caution your lordship against it, in the strongest and most explicit terms, for to me it appears unconstitutional in the highest degree, and directly subversive of English government, and of the unity of the British Empire.' It would annihilate the responsibility of the Lord Lieutenant to the English Government, and would 'more immediately tend to the separation of the two countries, and the introduction of anarchy into Ireland, than any other means that could be devised.'[1]

In the confidential correspondence of Pelham, there are three letters, written at this time, which throw a considerable though casual light upon the feelings, motives, and divisions of the principal actors in this obscure period of political history. The first tells very plainly its own tale, and it is a tale of deep significance in Irish history. 'I cannot but inform you,' wrote Portland, 'for the purpose of putting you upon your guard, that we have learnt from the most unquestionable authority, that a correspondence has been carried on, or at least letters have been written by Lord Fitzgibbon to the King (to whom they have been delivered by Lord Westmorland), with a view, and with more effect than could be wished, to prejudice his mind and *to alarm his conscience* against the concession to the Catholics. I don't know how *your friend* Pitt feels this, but if this is to be the practice, no Government can go on in Ireland, and I believe there are not two opinions in the *greatest part* of the Cabinet respecting it.'[2]

[1] Portland to Camden, March 26, 1795 (secret). The words in italics are underlined in the original.
[2] Portland to Pelham, March 21,

A second letter seems to me clearly to show, that Pitt was full of grave doubts and forebodings about the policy he was pursuing. Portland mentions, that he had been present at a meeting at Lord Grenville's, 'for the purpose of finally settling the minutes of the conversation which passed at Mr. Pitt's some time previous to Lord Fitzwilliam's departure.' 'I found Mr. Pitt and Mr. W.' [Windham], he says, 'full of apprehensions, and gloom. I communicated to them *both* your letters, revived their spirits, and created in them both a degree of confidence which I think even Pitt was much further from feeling at my entering the room, than I have almost ever observed upon any former occasion. He caught with some sort of avidity at the opinion expressed by the Chancellor and Speaker on the subject of the Catholic question, but soon abandoned it, on its being observed that some allowance was to be made in the weight of their opinions, for the known prejudices of the persons by whom they were given.' In the same letter the duke adds, that he had heard from Ireland, 'that the idea of Grattan's being sacrificed and made a scapegoat has been very generally and industriously circulated,' and he adds somewhat ambiguously, 'after what you tell me, I see Grattan is *not less an Irishman* than the rest of his countrymen.'[1]

A third letter shows the anxiety of at least one of the ablest members of the Cabinet to minimise, as much as possible, the effects of the change of Government in Ireland, and to prevent it from assuming, either in reality or in appearance, the character of a complete change of system. The writer was Windham. 'It is my earnest hope,' he wrote, 'that you will still be able to preserve a good intelligence with Grattan, and to satisfy him that both in respect to men and measures, except in the single point of an immediate and unlimited concession to the Catholics, Lord Camden's Government will be such as he will not feel it necessary to be in opposition to. You will then, I think, be of opinion that it is a debt due in justice to Grattan, not to suffer the consequences of his fairness and real regard for the public welfare to operate to his disadvantage, nor pass in the eyes of the world as a want of power, rather than as a want of will, to do mischief. I say this, because in the minds of some of

[1] Portland to Pelham, March 28, 1795.

our friends on this side of the water, justice is not done to him in that respect, nor sufficient credit given him—at least, as I have sometimes thought—for that forbearance which he manifested during all the latter period of Lord Westmorland's administration. Few public men have, to my mind, given such an honourable proof of their willingness to sacrifice even their immediate political consequence—the last sacrifice that such men are in general willing to make—to the general interests of the country. . . . A steady hand held by Lord Camden between the two parties, with a turn even of the scale in favour of those newly ejected . . . joined to a pure and upright system of government, will, I am persuaded, disarm the hostile dispositions that may be at present felt, and place Mr. Grattan in a situation in which at worst he may think it sufficient to preserve a sort of armed truce. For my own part, I cannot bear the thought of being on any other terms with him, than those of confidence and co-operation in the great cause to which he has shown himself so truly attached. . . . I should be sorry to have him suppose that anything that has passed, or anything that I am persuaded can pass, can . . . make me otherwise than ambitious of his friendship and good opinion.'[1]

It was decided that Parliament should meet without any speech from the throne, and that no explanation should be given of the passage from the confidential despatch cited by Fitzwilliam, which was generally interpreted as pointing to an union. The silence maintained by Portland on this subject, in private as well as in public, is a strong presumption that this interpretation was a correct one, and it is difficult on any other supposition to find any sufficient explanation for his conduct towards the Catholics and towards Fitzwilliam. Two or three passages from the first letters of Camden and Pelham, show that they were aware of the danger of the task they had undertaken, though they had great hopes of surmounting it. 'The quiet of the country depends upon the exertions of the friends of the established Government, backed by a strong military force.' 'I confess, I am more alarmed at the general want of attachment to Government, than at any consequences that may arise from any violent or bigoted attachment to religious opinions.' 'All will

[1] Windham to Pelham, April 21, 1795.

be quiet if there is no invasion, and if troops are immediately sent.' But reinforcements must on no account be delayed. Government could easily obtain enough parliamentary support to secure the rejection of the Catholic Bill, and the better Catholics have no wish to embarrass the administration. The danger lies chiefly in 'the correspondences which persons of another description have established throughout the whole country. These persons are connected with, and directed by, the Society of United Irishmen, who, to promote their own views, have chosen that Catholic emancipation (as it is termed by them) should become the watchword of their party.'[1]

Parliament met on April 13. The customary congratulatory address to the Lord Lieutenant passed without a division, though Grattan expressed his personal dissent, speaking, as Lord Camden noticed, 'moderately and civilly, and with great temper.' On the 21st, however, he moved for a Committee on the State of the Nation, and a debate ensued, in which the whole question of the recall of Lord Fitzwilliam was discussed. Grattan professed himself unable to fathom the real motives of that measure, but he asserted that the removal of certain officials, and the acceptance of Catholic emancipation, which were the reasons alleged, had both been clearly stipulated before the Government was formed. Portland had formally declared to those whose support in Ireland he solicited, that he had 'accepted office principally with a view to reform the abuses in the Government of Ireland, that the system of that Government was execrable, so execrable as to threaten not only Ireland with the greatest misfortune, but ultimately the Empire,' and that he would have himself gone over, if he had not persuaded Lord Fitzwilliam to accept the chief post in the Government of Ireland with the object of reforming its manifold abuses. Portland had assured his supporters, that he had obtained 'extraordinary power' with reference to Ireland. He had consulted members of the Irish Opposition, touching his arrangements of men and measures. He had sanctioned 'those principal removals which are supposed to have occasioned the recall of the deputy. An explanation and limitation of his powers did, indeed, afterwards take place, but no such limitation or explanation as to defeat either the

[1] Camden to Portland, April 6, 7; Pelham to Portland, April 6, 1795.

stipulated measures or the stipulated removals, one only excepted,[1] which never took place.'

As to the Catholic question, Grattan and his friends had repeatedly declared that they never would support a Government that would resist Catholic emancipation, though they had acquiesced in the decision of the Cabinet that the Bill should not be introduced by Ministers. Their support of the administration had been the result of 'a precise engagement,' that 'if the Catholics insisted to carry forward their Bill, Government would give it a handsome support.' 'Not to bring it forward as a Government measure, but if Government were pressed, to yield it'—these, Grattan afterwards said, were the very words of Pitt when speaking to him on the Catholic Bill.[2]

He enumerated several measures of reform which had been intended by the administration of Fitzwilliam, some of which had actually been introduced. They comprised a simplification and completion of Lord Westmorland's measure for relieving the poorest classes from the hearth tax, an attempt to diminish drunkenness by increasing the duties on spirits and removing those on beer, a plan of education, a more equal trade between England and Ireland, a reform in the system of the Dublin police, a more stringent regulation of the public expenditure. The United Irishmen remarked with some bitterness that parliamentary reform had no place in this catalogue,[3] and it is evident that no power had as yet been given to concede it, but it was almost certain soon to follow Catholic emancipation. The Ministers refused all detailed explanations, alleging that the King had an undoubted right to recall a Lord Lieutenant, and that the Lord Lieutenant and his Secretary act under written instructions from the Cabinet. In his reply, Grattan, while admitting that there must be a close correspondence between the executives in England and Ireland, denied that the viceroy's function was simply to obey orders, and to be the agent of the English Cabinet. He was the representative of the King, and not of the Ministry. It was becoming the custom to establish in Ireland 'a monarchy of clerks, a government carried on by post, and under the dominion of spies,' 'a system where

[1] Fitzgibbon.
[2] Grattan's *Life*, iv. 177.
[3] McNevin's *Pieces of Irish History*, p. 97.

the clerks dominated, and their betters obeyed.' 'The Cabinet had heard appeals against the Lord Lieutenant from the persons removed, and tried unsummoned, on the testimony of partial witnesses, the representative of the King.' This was at least one cause of the recent recall. 'It is a matter of melancholy reflection, to consider how little the Cabinet knows of anything relating to Ireland. Ireland is a subject it considers with a lazy contumely, and picks up here and there, by accident or design, interested and erroneous intelligence.'

The statements of Grattan about the terms on which the Irish Whigs had agreed to support the administration of Lord Fitzwilliam, were fully confirmed by the two Ponsonbys. The concluding speech of Grattan had such an effect, that the galleries burst into uncontrollable applause, and the House was cleared, but it had no appreciable influence upon the vote, and his motion was rejected by 158 to 48.[1]

The second reading of the Catholic Bill came on for discussion on May 4, and the debate which ensued lasted during the entire night, and only terminated at ten o'clock on the morning of the 5th. It shows with a painful vividness the character of the Irish House of Commons—a body which contained a group of statesmen who in ability, patriotism, and knowledge would have done honour to any legislature, but also a body in which eloquence and argument dashed uselessly and impotently against a great purchased majority. 'In 1792,' said Parsons, 'a majority decided against giving any further privileges to the Catholics. In 1793 the same majority passed the Catholic Bill. At the beginning of this session, everyone believed that a majority would have voted for this Bill. Everyone believes that a majority will vote against it now, and should the English Ministers in the next session wish it to pass, who does not believe that a majority will vote for it? Besides, if the English Ministry should be changed, an event perhaps not very remote, this Bill would be immediately adopted.' The absolute necessity of completing, by a final abolition of disqualifications, the legislation of 1774, 1778, 1782, 1792, and 1793, was abundantly shown. It was argued, once more, that as certainly as the concession of landed property in 1778 and 1782 led to the concession of the suffrage

[1] *Parl. Deb.* xv. 165–192.

which is attached to this kind of property, so certainly the right of voting must lead to the right of sitting in the House; that, for the sake of excluding from political power a few highly educated, able, and loyal men, distinguished beyond all others for their hatred to revolution and attachment to hereditary monarchy, the Government were rapidly throwing the bulk of the Catholics into the arms of a revolutionary democracy; that the policy of relaxation had already gone so far, that the remaining disqualifications were impotent to restrain, and only powerful to irritate and to insult. Catholics were already admitted to the bar, but they could not be King's counsel or judges. They were admitted in the army even to the command of regiments, but they might not rise to the rank of general. They were admitted to the subordinate revenue offices, but not to the higher office of commissioner. They were given the right of voting for members of Parliament, but they could not be members of Parliament themselves. They were allowed to become a great power in the State, but they were still treated as separate, hostile, and inferior. And these disqualifications were maintained in a time of revolution and of war, when the army, the navy, and the militia were crowded with Catholics, and when England was in close alliance with the most Catholic Powers of the Continent.

The fatal consequences that would inevitably follow the rejection of the Bill, were most clearly seen. The policy of the statesmen of the Revolution, argued George Knox, in an admirable speech, was from their own point of view perfectly consistent. Believing it necessary to keep the Catholics in a condition of impotence, they very prudently deprived them of education and property; and they established by such means an undisturbed Protestant ascendency, but 'sank this country below the political horizon, in order that they might exclusively possess its eminences.' For good or for ill, that policy has been irrevocably abandoned. The Irish Parliament justly thought that 'we could not be a powerful, prosperous, and happy people, if three-fourths of us were ignorant and beggars.' It 'opened the gates of knowledge and opulence,' and by doing so, it created in Ireland 'unexampled and rapidly increasing prosperity,' and 'discovered with what usury protected and enfranchised industry repays its obligations.' But politically this enfranchisement was an act of infatuation or madness, unless it is carried further.

'The great body of the people is Catholic. Much of the real, and no small share of the personal, property of the country is in Catholic hands. The lower class, ignorant and turbulent, are fit instruments in the hands of irritated and unsubdued ambition. In a few years, if trade increases, the Catholics must possess almost a monopoly of the personal wealth of the kingdom, a control, therefore, over the numerous class of manufacturers and mechanics—a description of people the most prone to turbulence. . . . If we drive the rich Catholic from the Legislature and from our own society, we force him to attach himself to the needy and disaffected. We oblige him, if pride and ambition have their usual operation, to breed and nourish discontent, and keep alive a religious quarrel.' It is impossible that the question can rest there. 'Take, then, your choice; re-enact your penal laws, risk a rebellion, a separation, or an Union, or pass this Bill; for the hour is nearly arrived when we must decide. The hour is already come when we ought to decide. . . . There are objections to it not to be overlooked; but the dangers which would follow its rejection are inevitable and tremendous, being rooted in the very nature of men and of society, and those to which its reception exposes us are doubtful, distant, and avertible. . . . Let us not delay that entire political union on which without doors all ranks are now agreed. . . . If we continue to exclude and irritate the Catholic, we can have no real security against the subversion of property and religion, but an unconditional submission to Great Britain, and a resignation of the crown of Ireland into the hands of the British Parliament. But if we adopt the measure now, we shall gradually liberalise the Catholic gentry; they will see how much their property, their liberty, and their lives depend upon the Constitution; how much that Constitution depends upon our connection with Great Britain, and how much that connection rests on the uniformity of the State religion.'

'We shall admit the Catholic,' he continued. 'I foresee it well. But we shall withhold that admission so long, that at length we shall give without generosity what will be received without gratitude; we shall yield, not to reason, but to clamour; what ought to be the result of wisdom and reflection, will be the work of panic and precipitation; and that day which shall record the last triumph of the Constitution will be to us a day of humiliation and disgrace.'

George Ponsonby, who had been designated by Fitzwilliam for the post of Attorney-General, and whom Fitzwilliam had pronounced to be the ablest debater after Grattan in the House of Commons, reminded the House with great bitterness that the fluctuation of the Government was no new thing, and that it had been already abundantly shown in 1792 and 1793. 'We have seen,' he said, 'an administration encourage the Protestant against the Catholic pretensions. We have seen the same administration excite the claims of those same Catholics, and ultimately we have seen that very administration, after having alternately encouraged each party against the other, pass a Bill in favour of those Catholics, in opposition to the sentiments of the Protestants, which that administration had excited.' He entirely disbelieved that the last change was due to any conscientious scruples, or to any fear of danger from Catholic members of Parliament. The Catholic question was made use of, he believed, either to colour the recall of Lord Fitzwilliam, or to keep the country weak by keeping it divided. The argument from the coronation oath, which had suddenly risen to an extraordinary prominence, he treated with the contempt of a sound constitutional lawyer. The oath was enacted before the laws were passed which this Bill would repeal. It did not bind the King to refuse his assent to laws that might be enacted, but merely to execute those laws which were, or should be enacted, to preserve the Protestant religion. 'Could any gentleman seriously believe that this oath tied up the King in his legislative capacity? It would be a strange constitution, indeed, which could be guilty of such an absurdity. Unquestionably, it was in his executive capacity only that this oath restrained him. No men were ever so preposterous as to think of binding up one branch of the legislature, by oath, to all futurity.'

One of the most remarkable speeches in this debate was delivered by Arthur O'Connor. Like Emmet, McNevin, and Fitzgerald, he had not yet joined the United Irishmen;[1] but he was already at heart a rebel; his speech is in a different key from the others that have been quoted, and it shows clearly both the

[1] *Castlereagh Correspondence*, i. 309, 359.

influence of the new French ideas, and the process by which so many were now passing rapidly into rebellion. A great part of it consisted of rhetorical but powerful descriptions of the abuses which had made Irish representation the monopoly of a few families; of the steady evanescence throughout Europe of clerical influence and intolerant restrictions; of the effects of the exaggerated and ill-portioned endowments of the Established Church, in diverting clergymen from parochial duties, and turning them, to the great injury not only of religion, but of morals, into mere men of fashion and pleasure. 'It is no longer a secret,' he said, 'that the men who oppose the abolition of religious distinctions in our civil and military concerns, when the general voice of the nation has concurred in so wise, so just, and so politic a measure, are the men who usurp the whole political power of the country, and who have converted the whole representation of Ireland into a family patrimony.' But if the people of this country are convinced that the Constitution of 1782, which they so highly prized, 'has been destroyed by the bribery of a British Minister, and the unexampled venality of an Irish Parliament;' if they are convinced 'that, instead of reciprocal advantage, nothing is to be reaped from their connection with England but supremacy and aggrandisement on the one side, and a costly venality, injury, insult, degradation, and poverty on the other,' is it not inevitable that they will begin to seek for foreign alliances against the connection? This, said O'Connor, is the true lesson to be learned from the mission of Jackson, and from the papers that were found in his possession. The time is past, and past for ever, when public opinion would torpidly acquiesce in political monopolies and religious disqualifications. 'Do not imagine that the mind of your countrymen has been stationary, while that of all Europe has been rapidly progressive; for you must be blind not to perceive that the whole European mind has undergone a revolution, neither confined to this nor that country, but as general as the great causes which have given it birth, and still continue to feed its growth.' For Ireland, he believed, issues of the most momentous and far-reaching kind depended on the decision of the House. 'You, none of you, can be ignorant that the British Minister has designs, in procrastinating this question, to procure advantages for his own country, at the expense of yours, greater than she was capable of receiving 'since the Revolution, at least, since the Union.' And so strongly impressed is this on the public mind, that you, who shall on this night vote for the rejection of the Bill, will appear in the eyes of the Irish nation, not only as men voting, in obedience to the British Minister, against the voice of the people, but as men voting for an union with England, by which this country is to be everlastingly reduced to the state of an abject province.'

It is a very remarkable fact, that the Government speakers never attempted to deny the repeated assertion of the Opposition, that Protestant opinion was in favour of emancipation, nor did they endeavour to dispel the suspicion, which was spreading fatally and rapidly, that the Government were steering their bark through corruption, through revived religious animosities, through almost certain rebellion, towards a legislative union. Grattan skilfully availed himself of the resolution of the Catholic Committee, declaring that they would rather forego their emancipation than purchase it at the price of a legislative union, as an additional argument in favour of the former. 'The Roman Catholic,' he said, 'far from being dangerous, has borne his testimony in favour of the institution of the Irish Parliament, for he has resolved to relinquish his emancipation rather than purchase his capacities by an union. He has said, let the Catholic be free, but if his freedom is to be bought by the extinction of the Irish Parliament, we waive the privilege, and pray for the Parliament.'

The speech of Grattan was on the whole hopeful, more hopeful than wisdom could justify. He accused the administration of having begun a religious war in 1792, but he maintained that they had wholly failed to produce any serious division in Ireland. 'The Protestants of a number of the counties, of all the great cities, and all the mercantile interests,' have petitioned in favour of the Catholics. With the single exception of the Corporation of Dublin, there had been no application against them. Nothing prevents their success but the influence of the Government. 'Catholic emancipation ceases to be a question between the Irish Protestant and Catholic, and is now a question between the Ministers of another country and the people of Ireland.' It was a cheering sign, though perhaps not so important as Grattan represented it, that on the recall of Lord Fitzwilliam the students of Trinity College had presented an address in favour of emancipation. 'These young men,' said Grattan, 'in a few years must determine this question.' 'They will soon sit on these seats blended with Catholics, while we, blended with Catholics, shall repose in the dust.'

No one, I think, can read this debate without acknowledging that the immense preponderance of argument and ability was on the side of emancipation. Duigenan and some of the other genuine opponents of the Catholics restated their old arguments, but the Government case was entrusted to Toler, the Solicitor-General. He was one of those officials whom Fitzwilliam had desired to replace; and having been long known as a selfish, violent, and unprincipled advocate, he was made Chief Justice of the Common Pleas, was created Lord Norbury, and has left a most scandalous judicial reputation behind him. He placed the Government opposition to the admission of Catholics to Parliament, on the highest possible grounds. It would violate the fundamental principles of the Constitution as established by the Revolution. It would be contrary to the coronation oath by which the King held his throne, to the Bill of Rights, to the compact on which the connection of the two countries depended. The Roman Catholic was asking that the Constitution should be changed. 'He has no right to demand it, nor have the Crown and Parliament, who are but trustees for its preservation, a right to alienate what has been confided to them as a trust.'[1] In other words, the Catholics, at a time when the most cautious and conciliatory policy was imperatively required, were told on high Government authority that their disqualifications were permanent and indelible, essential to the connection of their country with England, essential to the maintenance of the monarchical constitution under which they lived. The independent voices in Parliament, and the voices of the Protestants beyond its walls, had spoken in no

---

[1] Marcus Beresford, in a letter to his father describing this debate, says: 'Toler spoke for above two hours, and left the question without an attempt to argue it, but concluded with a vehement assertion, that the Bill could not be carried without the repeal of the Bill of Rights, the breach of the coronation oath, and of the compact between the two countries.' (*Beresford Correspondence*, ii. 109.)

dubious terms; but the majority in the House of Commons, who a few months before had been perfectly ready to carry the Bill, were now equally ready to reject it, and it was thrown out by 155 votes to 84.[1]

From this time the Catholic question lost most of its prominence in the Irish Parliament, and from this time there is scarcely a page of Irish history on which a good man can look with pleasure. Anarchy and bloodshed, religious and class warfare, great measures almost wholly failing to produce their expected results, disaffection widening and deepening as grievances were removed, public opinion more and more degraded and demoralised, political life turned more and more into a trade in which the vilest men are exalted—these are the chief elements in the miserable story which the historian of modern Ireland is called upon to relate. It is impossible to say, with just confidence, whether this train of calamities could have been averted if all religious disqualifications had been removed in 1793 or 1795. The Protestants then undoubtedly desired it. Political agitation was almost unknown. The indispensable ascendency of property and loyalty was still unbroken; the relations of classes and creeds, which were hopelessly convulsed by the rebellion of 1798, and by the long agitation that followed it, were not yet essentially unsound, and more than a century had passed since Ireland had witnessed the clash of arms. In my own judgment, little permanent good could have been effected unless a moderate parliamentary reform and a commutation of tithes had been added to the abolition of religious distinctions; but with these measures, Ireland would probably have weathered the revolutionary storm. But though the chapter of what might have been, lies beyond human sagacity, the actual train of cause and effect is sufficiently evident, and it is not too much to say, that the undecided and contradictory policy of these critical years was a leading cause of the rebellion of 1798, and of the fatal consequences that flowed from it.

One more step remained to be taken, in order fully to impress the Catholics with the sentiments of the Government. It was

---

[1] See the full report of this long and most remarkable debate, from which I have only room to select a few passages. (*Irish Parl. Deb.* xv. 208-361.)

again to single out for conspicuous favour the man who was known to be their ablest and most implacable enemy. There is no reason to doubt that Fitzgibbon was perfectly honest in his opposition to the Catholics, and he unquestionably often proved himself a very useful servant of the English Government, but few judgments are more absurd than those which have represented him as a type of disinterested or self-sacrificing statesmanship. He had a great income, which he spent with the lavish profusion so characteristic of the Irish gentry,[1] and though wholly free from the taint of personal corruption, he was keenly ambitious. His rise, during the last few years, had been surprisingly fast. He had been made Chancellor and peer in 1789, chiefly as a reward for his services on the Regency question. Lord Westmorland had given him a reversion of 2,300*l.* a year for two lives.[2] Almost immediately after his mischievous attack upon the Catholics in 1793, he had been made a viscount; and having borne a leading part in the recall of Lord Fitzwilliam, he was now made Earl of Clare. Camden, in recommending him for the promotion, dwelt upon his services to the Government, and upon the attack which had been made on him, but he based his recommendation chiefly on the necessity of supporting and consolidating the anti-Catholic party. Yelverton, he said, who had been always on the side of the Catholics, had just been made a peer, and it was therefore peculiarly advisable to promote Fitzgibbon, who had strongly opposed them. No measure would do more to encourage those Protestants who were opposed to emancipation. They found it difficult to believe that the Government were in earnest. This would do much to convince them. Lord Fitzgibbon, Camden said, had previously asked for advancement in the peerage, but 'begged to leave the time entirely to my convenience.'[3]

---

[1] In the *Westmorland Correspondence* there are melancholy letters, written when Clare was dying, and immediately after his death, by Lady Clare, asking for some Government provision. Lord Clare, she says, by the will of his father could only settle on her a small provision out of his hereditary property. 'He certainly had a great income, but he lived up to and above it, and has not left more money than will pay his debts.' (Lady Clare to Westmorland Jan. 26, Feb. 8, 27, March 1, 1802.) Lord Redesdale, in a letter in 1802, recommending for some a·sistance, a first cousin of Lord Clare who was left completely destitute, expressed his regret 'that, with all the advantages possessed by the late Lord Clare, so many of his family should be in a state to sue for the public bounty.' (I.S.P.O.)

[2] *Parl. Hist.* xxxi. 1512.

[3] Camden to Portland, May 4, 1795.

The significance of the promotion, indeed, could not be overlooked. The Catholics and Reformers of Ireland were once more taught, that the man in whom the Government placed the greatest confidence, was the politician who had justified, with scarcely a qualification, the whole penal code, who had contended that it was a fatal error to admit any class of Catholics to any share of political power, who had at the same time shown himself the most powerful enemy of every attempt to reform the Parliament, to diminish corruption, and to abolish or mitigate the tithe grievances.

Portland, as we have seen, had instructed Camden to conciliate the Catholics, as far as was compatible with the main lines of his policy. The recommendation, under the circumstances, seemed little less than derisory; but Camden was ready to act upon it, and the measure which was taken with this object was the foundation of an ecclesiastical seminary at Maynooth.

During the greater part of the century, the ecclesiastical education of the Catholic priesthood was carried on, contrary to law, but without any serious attempt at molestation, in continental colleges and seminaries, and in many of these, foundations for their support had been established, either by private liberality or by the munificence of foreign sovereigns. It appears from a return made to Parliament in 1808, 'of the state of the establishments on the Continent for the education of Irish Catholic secular clergymen previous to the French Revolution,' that at the time when the Revolution broke out, there were 478 Irish ecclesiastical students on the Continent, of whom 348 were in France, and the remainder at Louvain, Antwerp, Salamanca, Rome, and Lisbon. They had received the rudiments of education in Ireland, and the greater number had been ordained before they were sent abroad to complete their studies, so that they were usually able to contribute to their own support, by officiating in petty chaplaincies, and discharging for small gratuities other offices of religion. The expense of their journey to the Continent was commonly defrayed by the Catholic gentry, and sometimes by collections in the chapels of their districts.

The deficiency, the hardships, and the dangers of this mode of education, had for some time attracted the attention of patriotic Irishmen. I have quoted in a former volume the very remarkable speech which was made on the subject in 1782 by Hely Hutchinson, in the Irish House of Commons. Hutchinson censured in the strongest manner the existing laws about Catholic education, but he equally insisted on the danger of establishing separate popish colleges. It was a matter, he maintained, of the very first political importance that the Catholics, and especially the Catholic priesthood, should receive the best possible education at home, and that they should not be educated altogether apart from their fellow-countrymen. He desired that their higher education should be carried on at the University of Dublin; that diocesan schools should be established at public expense, in which Catholics might receive gratuitously an education to prepare them for the university; that a grant should be made for the establishment of sizarships, and other premiums for the special benefit of their poor students; and that they should have a divinity professor of their own creed, to educate them in their own theology. In secular education, he would establish no distinction. 'I would have them,' he said, 'go into examinations, and make no distinction between them and the Protestants, but such as merit might claim.'[1]

Burke, in the same year, wrote a letter to Lord Kenmare, in which he dwelt, from a different point of view, on the same subject. Seven years before, when visiting Paris, he had paid special attention to the college which existed in that city for the education of Irish priests, and he had been struck with its efficiency. The very worst part of the penal code, he truly said, was that relating to education, for while the Catholics were deprived of the means of education at home, they were forbidden to seek education abroad. Burke, however, strongly dissented from that portion of the scheme of Hutchinson, which related to the education of the priesthood. It was impossible, he urged, that men who were intended for a life of celibacy, and for the delicate and dangerous duties of the confessional, could be properly educated in common with lay students, and in a Protestant university. History and reason abundantly showed that the Catholic priesthood might become an intolerable nuisance to a country, if they had not been formed to their pro-

[1] Vol. iv. pp. 530, 531; *Irish Parl. Deb.* i. 309, 310.

fession by an altogether special and separate system of discipline and education, and the establishment of such a system, in separate seminaries, had been the most valuable moral result of the Council of Trent. Burke considered it a great grievance that no such seminaries existed in Ireland, but until they were established, he wished the present system of education on the Continent, to be fully legalised. Men in power, he hoped, would at last learn 'to consider the good order, decorum, virtue, and morality of every description of men among them, ... of more importance to religion and to the State, than all the polemical matter which has been agitated among men, from the beginning of the world to this hour.'[1]

In the twelve years that followed, most of the more serious grievances of the Irish lay Catholics relating to education were removed. Their admission to degrees in Dublin University carried out one great part of the policy of Hutchinson, and although no provision had been made for the education of the priesthood in Ireland, it seemed as if a compromise between the views of Burke and of Hutchinson might, with no great difficulty, have been devised. A project, as we have seen, was much discussed of establishing a Catholic college in connection with Dublin University, and it might have secured for the ecclesiastical students the discipline and the professional education of a seminary, without withdrawing them altogether from the lectures and examinations of the university.[2] The singular liberality which, at this time, prevailed among the authorities of Dublin University, and the great moderation of the Irish prelates, made some such scheme appear very feasible, and it would be difficult to exaggerate the benefit, both moral and political, which Ireland might have derived from a priesthood imbued with the best liberal education of their time, and associated in some measure with the most cultivated and enlightened of their countrymen.

The French Revolution and the war of 1793 forced the

---

[1] Letter to a peer of Ireland on the penal laws. (Burke's *Works*, vi. 280-289.)

[2] See vol. vi. pp. 451, 452. A pamphlet called *Considerations upon the Establishment of an University in Ireland for Educating Roman Catholics*, advocating a purely Catholic university for both lay and clerical students, was published in Dublin in 1784. It contains an interesting account of the scanty education of the existing priests, and of the evils that resulted from their illiteracy.

question into sudden ripeness, by making the foreign education of ecclesiastical students impossible. In the beginning of 1794, the Catholic bishops presented a memorial to Lord Westmorland, stating that 400 students were constantly maintained and educated in France for the ministry of the Roman Catholic religion in Ireland; that in the troubles which had broken out in France, these seminaries had been abolished and their revenues confiscated, and that there was great danger that students educated in that country would be exposed to the 'contagion of sedition and infidelity,' and would introduce ' a licentious philosophy' into Ireland. They argued that an education at Dublin University, however well adapted for an ambitious laity, was not suited to men who ' were restricted to the humble walk of a subordinary ministry.' Certain branches of learning must be taught the priesthood, which were not included in the university course. Even in Catholic countries, candidates for holy orders received the most important part of their education in seminaries distinct from the public universities. A great proportion of the students for orders were too poor to bear the expense of education at the university, and of a constant residence in Dublin; 'and although the liberality of the present heads of the university might induce them to receive persons on the foundation, yet neither could a sufficient number be thus accommodated, nor would it prove grateful to the feelings of the parties.' Under these circumstances, the prelates petitioned for a royal licence, to endow ecclesiastical seminaries in Ireland under ecclesiastical superiors of their own communion.[1]

In the September of the same year, Burke wrote to Grattan urging his own opinion and that of his son, that if provision was not made for the instruction of ecclesiastical students in Ireland, 'barbarism and Jacobinism will almost certainly enter, by the breach made by the atheistic faction in France in the destruction of the Irish seminaries in that kingdom.'[2] Grattan fully concurred in this view. 'It is absolutely necessary,' he wrote, ' to allow the Catholic clergy a Catholic education at home. If they can't have a Catholic education at home, they can have none at all, or none which is not dangerous. I don't think any

[1] Plowden, ii. 446-448; *Castlereagh Correspondence*, iii. 72-75.
[2] Grattan's *Life*, iv. 155.

time should be lost; too much time has been lost already, both with regard to their education and Irish education in general; for which great funds of public, royal, and private donations have been granted and eaten. There is not one great public school in Ireland; and yet the funds are great, but sunk in the person of the Master. . . . At the time when our Government were assuming public ignorance as an argument against Catholic emancipation, there lay before them a report of a committee with authentic evidence of this misapplication, in which they persisted to connive. . . . Such subjects are now peculiarly interesting, when the fortunes of the world are in the scale, and the intellectual order in some danger of kicking the beam.'[1] In Lord Fitzwilliam's speech from the throne, new measures for Catholic education were promised. Seventeen Catholic bishops met to consider the subject in Dublin, and Dr. Hussey came over from England to consult with them, but nothing had been finally arranged when the viceroy was recalled.[2]

It is worthy of notice, that while Burke, and other statesmen, saw in the home education of the Irish priesthood the best means of securing them from the contagion of democracy and sedition, Wolfe Tone, with an incomparably juster forecast, advocated the same measure for exactly opposite reasons. He invariably represented the Catholic clergy of his time as men who were essentially Tory in their principles; who were in natural alliance with the aristocracy of their creed, and who were a most formidable obstacle to the seditious and anti-English movement it was his object to foment. 'This country never will be well,' he wrote, 'until the Catholics are educated at home, and their clergy elective. Now is a good time, because France will not receive their students, and the Catholics are afraid of the Revolution.' He feared that the higher clergy would not be favourable to the change, and rejoiced, from his own point of view, that the breaking up of the seminaries in France obliged them to consent. 'In this light,' he wrote, 'as in ten thousand others, the Revolution was of infinite service to Ireland. . . . This education business appears to me of infinite importance for a thousand reasons.'[3]

---

[1] Burke's *Correspondence*, iv. 245.
[2] Ibid. pp. 267, 282, 283.
[3] Wolfe Tone's *Memoirs*, i. 173, 195.

On the recall of Lord Fitzwilliam, Dr. Hussey, at the earnest request of the Duke of Portland, remained in Ireland to assist in elaborating the plan,[1] and although there was some divergence about the details, and especially about the degree to which it was to be placed under Catholic episcopal authority, the scheme itself was very generally welcomed. The war and the destruction of French seminaries made some change plainly necessary, and even in normal times it was a great hardship that the members of a very poor Church should be unable to educate their clergy in their own country. At the same time the evil was not without mitigations, and no subsequent generations of Irish priests have left so good a reputation as the better class of those who were educated in the seminaries of France, Italy, and Flanders, or at the Irish college at Salamanca.[2] They grew up at a time when Catholicism throughout Europe was unusually temperate, and they brought with them a foreign culture and a foreign grace, which did much to embellish Irish life. Their earlier prejudices were corrected and mitigated by foreign travel. They had sometimes mixed with a society far more cultivated than an Irish Protestant country clergyman was likely to meet, and they came to their ministry at a mature age, and with a real and varied knowledge of the world. If they produced little or nothing of lasting value in theology or literature, they had at least the manners and feelings of cultivated gentlemen, and a high sense of clerical decorum; they had no sympathy with insurrection, turbulence, or crime, and they were saved by their position from the chief vices and temptations of their class upon the Continent. The leaders of a poor and unendowed Church, which was appealing to the principles of religious liberty in order to obtain political enfranchisement, were not likely to profess the maxims of persecutors or to live the lives of epicureans.

This type of priest might be frequently met with in Ireland in the last years of the eighteenth century, and in the first quarter of the nineteenth century, and its disappearance has been an irreparable loss to Irish society. 'Mild, amiable, cultivated,

---

[1] Burke's *Correspondence*, iv. 297.
[2] The prominence of Salamanca as a place for the education of Irish priests, is curiously shown by the fact that between 1808 and 1816 no less than six priests, educated there, were made bishops in Ireland. See that very interesting work, *The Life of Mary Aikenhead*, by S. A. (2nd edit.), p. 143.

learned, and polite,' wrote one who knew them well, ' uniting the meek spirit of the Christian pastor to the winning gentleness of the polished man of the world, these men were welcome guests at the tables of the Protestant gentry. . . . In their own communion they lent their influence to soothe the asperities of the time, and they brought their knowledge of mankind and of their own and foreign nations, to enforce their lessons of patience, fortitude, and forbearance.'[1]

It is probable that such priests were most common in the latter half of the century, when religious persecution had practically ended. In its earlier years, when the penal laws were in force, and when the Catholic community was very poor and very much oppressed, a different type predominated, and it continued in the later years of the century, among the poor curates and mendicant monks, coexisting with the type I have described. Boys, springing from the very humblest peasant class, learnt their letters and a little Latin at a hedge school, and then travelled through Ireland as mendicant scholars till they had obtained the means of going to France, where by the performance of servile duties and by the assistance of some old endowments they obtained their education for the priesthood. They usually returned to Ireland with a slight tincture of scholastic and controversial theology, a large store of extravagant legends, all the zeal of an impassioned missionary, and most of the tastes, passions, and prejudices of an ignorant peasant.[2] They formed the democratic, and certainly not the least important, element in the Irish Catholic Church. Their fanaticism, their credulity, their coarse, violent, and grotesque sermons, their frequent pretensions to thaumaturgic powers, their complete sympathy with the ideas and feelings of the peasantry, gave them an influence often much greater than that of the learned and polished ecclesiastic, and neither their prejudices nor their interests inclined them to the side of the law. Men of this description are often mentioned as implicated both in agrarian and in revolutionary disturbances, though there is, I think, no good evidence

---

[1] See a vivid description of these priests, and of the difference between them and the generation formed by Maynooth, in O'Driscoll's *Views of Ireland* (1823), ii. 112–115.

[2] Newenham's *View of the Circumstances of Ireland*, pp. 179–181. That charming tale of Carleton, *The Poor Scholar*, throws a faithful light on this aspect and period of Irish life.

that any class of priests in the eighteenth century were guilty of the systematic encouragement of crime, which has been charged, on very serious authority, against not a few of their successors.[1]

It is not surprising that the type of priests in Ireland should have greatly improved in the early years of George III. The growing wealth of the Catholic community attracted men of a somewhat higher class to the priesthood, and provided better means of education and subsistence, and in settled times, and under the influence of religious liberty, the enforcement of ecclesiastical discipline became more easy. The Catholic gentry were also now a more considerable body, and it was a common thing for a Catholic landlord, when he found the son of a deserving tenant desirous of entering the priesthood, to defray the expenses of his outfit and of his journey to the Continent, and afterwards, by his influence with the bishop, to obtain for him some desirable professional situation. Much real though unrecognised patronage was thus exercised by the leading Catholic laymen, and kindly relations of friendship and gratitude grew up, which greatly softened and elevated the tone of Irish life. One of the first and most evident results of the establishment of Maynooth, was to weaken or destroy these relations.[2]

The Church was governed by four archbishops and twenty-two bishops, appointed by the cardinals of the Congregation De Propaganda Fide, subject to the approval of the Pope, but nearly

---

[1] See the very remarkable statement of Lord Clarendon (Nov. 26, 1847), which was sent to Rome, and the accompanying letter of Lord Palmerston to Lord Minto. Lord Palmerston did not hesitate to say: 'You may safely go further than Clarendon has chosen to do, and you may confidently assure the papal authorities, that at present in Ireland misconduct is the rule, and good conduct the exception, in the Catholic priests; that they in a multitude of cases are the open, and fearless, and shameless instigators to disorder, to violence and murder, and every week the better conducted, who are by constitution of human nature the most quiet and timid, are being scared by their fellow-priests, as well as by their flocks, from a perseverance in any efforts to give good counsel, and to restrain violence and crime. ... I really believe there never has been in modern times, in any country professing to be civilised and Christian, nor anywhere out of the central regions of Africa, such a state of crime as now exists in Ireland. There is evidently a deliberate and extensive conspiracy among the priests and the peasantry, to kill off or drive away all the proprietors of land, to prevent and deter any of their agents from collecting rent, and thus practically to transfer the land of the country from the landowner to the tenant.' (Ashley's *Life of Lord Palmerston*, ii. 49–53.)

[2] See the evidence of Archbishop Magee before a parliamentary committee in 1825, p. 785.

always selected from among a few names that were sent to Rome by the clergy of the diocese and by the bishops of the province. Old and infirm bishops were accustomed to choose coadjutors, who were almost invariably, on their recommendation, appointed their successors. The bishop usually held the best parish in his diocese, and in addition to the revenue derived from this source, he received a small sum, varying from a crown to a guinea, for every marriage licence, and a yearly tribute, varying from two to ten guineas, from each parish priest. The parish priests were appointed solely by the bishops, but after a certain tenure of office, they could not, except under extreme circumstances, be dispossessed. They were paid by Easter and Christmas dues, by fees at weddings, christenings, and generally at the visitation of the sick, and by masses, which were usually charged at the rate of two shillings each. In some parts of the country, tributes of hay, oats, and fish were given to the priest instead of money dues, and his turf was cut, his corn reaped, and his meadow mowed gratuitously. The curate had usually a third part of the general receipts of the parish.[1]

The clergy formed a well-organised and, to a great extent, a self-governed body, but it seems certain that their influence over their people had much diminished during the period between the accession of George III. and the rebellion of 1798. This was largely due to causes that affected Ireland in common with all Europe, and had led a great proportion of the best intellects of the day to believe that clerical influence, as a serious element in human affairs, could scarcely survive the eighteenth century. The lowering of the theological temperature, the spread of free-thinking tenets, the contempt for superstition in all its forms, the growing tendency to value religions on account of their common morality, and not on account of their distinctive dogmas, was felt in Ireland as it was felt elsewhere, and it was pronounced, on good Roman Catholic authority, that the relaxation of the popery laws had greatly weakened the hold of the priests over their people. In another class, and in another way, the Whiteboy convulsions of 1786 had a similar effect,[2] and the

---

[1] See a detailed and valuable account of the organisation and position of the clergy, in a letter from a priest of the diocese of Cork to Newenham (written in 1806). (Newenham's *View of the Circumstances of Ireland*, append. 39–42.)

[2] Ibid. The account which

spirit of the new political movement which had arisen among the Catholics was essentially unclerical. We have had much evidence in the course of this work how erroneously some of the most eminent statesmen and thinkers of the eighteenth century forecast the religious future, but those who judge mainly by the event will probably greatly underrate their sagacity. Among the changes of history there are some which are due to causes so powerful, so widespread, and so deep-rooted, that they could not have been averted or even greatly modified, but there are many which were clearly preventible, and which may be largely traced to accidental circumstances, and especially to political blunders. Had the inevitable changes in France at the close of the eighteenth century been effected in a peaceable and orderly manner, and by a well-organised Government, Europe might have been spared the great reaction which was the consequence of the horrible crimes that disgraced the French Revolution, and of the long and sanguinary wars that followed it. In Ireland the revival of ecclesiastical influence was largely due to events which were certainly not inevitable—to the rebellion of 1798, which rekindled all the passions of religious war; to the legislative union, which diverted a great part of the energies of the community from national to sectarian channels; to the agitation of O'Connell, which united the democracy of Ireland, under the guidance of their priests, in a fierce struggle for that Catholic emancipation, which the Parliament of the gentry of Ireland had been perfectly ready to grant in 1793 and in 1795.

A Catholic college on a small scale had been established at Carlow in 1793, and it counted among its professors some French refugee priests.[1] It was intended, however, for the education of laymen, and the College of Maynooth was the first Irish establishment since the Revolution for the education of the priesthood. Though instituted primarily for the education of that body, there was, at first, some question of including Catho-

---

Newenham's correspondent gives of the decline of ecclesiastical influence, is corroborated by several passages in Wolfe Tone's diary and autobiography, and by several statements in the Irish debates. It is curious to observe that as late as 1806, Alexander Knox, one of the most earnest and profound religious writers of his time, wrote to Hannah More: 'I have little doubt that a time will come when the Roman Catholic clergy of Ireland will, in a body, propose to conform to our Church.' (Knox's *Remains*, iii. 188.)

[1] Brenan's *Ecclesiastical History of Ireland*, ii. 321.

lic lay students in the establishment, and although, apparently, through the influence of Archbishop Troy, this project was dropped,[1] no further restriction was introduced into the Bill than that the college was to be 'for the better education of persons professing the popish or Roman Catholic religion.' Its government was placed in the hands of a body of trustees, to which the Chancellor and the three other chief judges officially belonged, but which consisted mainly of the Catholic bishops, who, however, were elected as individuals, and not as enjoying any titular rank or dignity. They were empowered to purchase lands to the annual value of 1,000*l.*, and to receive private subscriptions and donations without limit, for the purposes of the college. There was, at first, no Government endowment for the education of the students, but an immediate parliamentary grant of 8,000*l.* was voted to purchase a house and other necessary buildings for their accommodation. Dr. Hussey was appointed President.[2]

Hely Hutchinson, who had so clearly foreseen, and so powerfully stated, the danger of establishing in Ireland separate sectarian colleges, was no longer on the stage. He had died in September 1794, and the nation thus lost, in a most critical moment, the wisest and ablest advocate of liberal education. The discussion on the Maynooth Bill in the Irish Parliament is not reported, and I cannot tell whether any speaker dwelt upon the great evil of dissociating Irish clerical education from the education of the university. A very able man, who was then a fellow of Trinity College, and afterwards Archbishop of Dublin, in evidence which he gave before the House of Lords in 1825, has mentioned the strong objections which he and others outside Parliament had expressed to the scheme, and the pressure they put upon the members of the university to oppose it. 'The disadvantages,' he said, 'of the contracted and monastic plan, which a separate college for Roman Catholic priests would require, were strongly contrasted, in my mind, with the advantages which would redound both to the character of the Roman Catholic clergy itself, and to society at large, from the

---

[1] See on this subject the statements of Lord Kilwarden and of Lord Clare. (*Cornwallis Correspondence*, iii. 368, 369, 371, 372.)

[2] Camden to Portland, April 14, 1795; Pelham to Portland, April 24; 35 Geo. III. c. 21. (*Cornwallis Correspondence*, iii. 371, 372.)

mixture of the two denominations, Protestant and Roman Catholic, in the same university. At that time, Roman Catholic students abounded in Trinity College, and there was nothing of the hostility between the two religious descriptions that has since unhappily prevailed. It seemed, then, most desirable to bring the two classes together within the same seminary, and for this, great facility was afforded, there being nothing in the regulations of our university that could throw impediments in the way. . . . It appeared to me and others at that day, that under these circumstances an arrangement might be formed, whereby the Roman Catholic students might have every benefit of a liberal university education, and, at the same time, be provided, through some distinct scheme of religious institution of their own formation, with the instruction peculiarly requisite for their future profession, the heads of the university being at all times ready to offer facilities for such a plan.'[1]

The most remarkable fact, however, connected with the discussion, that has come down to us, is a Catholic petition, which was presented by Grattan, protesting against two parts of the scheme. The first objection of the petitioners was to the power which was given to the trustees to regulate the studies and make all appointments in the college. The end of education, they said, is 'the full and free development of human faculties, and the formation of a virtuous character,' and it should, therefore, be as little shackled as possible by any external restraint. They desired that both admission into the college, and all professorships and posts of dignity in it, should be thrown open to examination, and should thus be made the rewards of superior merit, without any possibility of jobbing. They cited the public examinations for fellowships and sizarships in Trinity College as examples, and they earnestly asked that a similar system should be introduced into their own Catholic college. The second objection is still more remarkable. It was to the clauses which provided that the college should be exclusively Roman Catholic —that no Protestant should be admitted among its students or among its teachers. Such an exclusion was pronounced by the Catholic petitioners to be 'highly inexpedient, inasmuch as it

---

[1] See the evidence of Archbishop Magee in 1825 before the Committee on the State of Ireland, p. 786.

tends to perpetuate that line of separation between his Majesty's subjects of different religions, which the petitioners do humbly conceive it is the interest of the country to obliterate; and the petitioners submit that, if the youth of both religions were instructed together in those branches of classical education which are the same for all, their peculiar tenets would, in all probability, be no hindrance hereafter to a friendly and liberal intercourse through life.' 'Having,' they added, 'in common with the rest of their brethren, the Catholics of Ireland, received, as one of the most important and acceptable benefits bestowed on them by his Majesty and the Legislature, the permission of having their youth educated along with the Protestant youth of the kingdom in the University of Dublin, and experience having fully demonstrated the wisdom and utility of that permission, they see with deep concern the principle of separation and exclusion, they hoped removed for ever, now likely to be revived and re-enacted.'[1]

We can hardly have a more striking proof of the change that has passed over the spirit of Irish Catholicism than is furnished by this petition, and if its recommendations had been carried out, the Irish priesthood might have been a very different body from what it has become. On wholly dissimilar grounds, Burke also looked on the new foundation with distrust. The strong bias in favour of sacerdotalism, which broadly distinguishes him from Grattan, appears to me to have often deflected his judgment, and I cannot regard the remarkable letters which he wrote to Dr. Hussey, who was now negotiating on the side of the Catholic priesthood, as evincing real prescience or wisdom. Burke was extremely anxious that Catholic colleges should be established, but he would have gladly placed them altogether under priestly control. The prelates, he said, should accept, from any Government, money for the establishment of such colleges; they should consent that accounts of the expenditure should be annually laid before a committee of the House of Commons, to prevent all suspicion of jobbing. But they should resist every other interference, and decline any offer which reserved to the members of the Irish Government a power of direction or control over clerical education. 'I would much

[1] *Irish Parl. Deb.* xv. 201–203.

rather trust,' he wrote, 'to God's good providence and the contributions of your own people, for the education of your clergy, than to put into the hands of your known, avowed, and implacable enemies—into the hands of those who make it their merit and their boast, that they are your enemies—the very fountains of your morals and your religion. . . . The scheme of these colleges, as you well know, did not originate from them. But they will endeavour to pervert the benevolence and liberality of others into an instrument for their own evil purposes. Be well assured that they never did, and that they never will, consent to give one shilling of money for any other purposes than to do you mischief. If you consent to put your clerical education, or any other part of your education, under their direction or control, then you will have sold your religion for their money. There will be an end, not only of the Catholic religion, but of all religion, all morality, all law, and all order, in that unhappy kingdom.'

He begs his correspondent, not to be misled by childish discussions about the rights of states and governments to control education. The real question, he said—and in this respect, his words were profoundly true, and have a much wider application than he gave to them—is, who are the men who would exercise this power. 'Know the men you have to deal with, in their concretes, and then you will judge what trust you are to put in them, when they are presented to you, in their abstract.' Such men as the Archbishop of Cashel, or Cooke, or Duigenan, or the Speaker, or, above all, Fitzgibbon—'you best know whether they are your friends or your enemies.'[1]

With these sentiments, it is not surprising that Burke should have been displeased with the Maynooth Bill. 'I hear,' he wrote, 'and am extremely alarmed at hearing, that the Chancellor and the chiefs of the benches are amongst your trustees. If this be the case, so as to give them the power of intermeddling, I must fairly say, that I consider, not only all the benefit of the institution to be wholly lost, but that a more mischievous project never was set on foot. I should much sooner make your college according to the first act of Parliament, as a subordinate department to our Protestant University—absurd as I always

---

[1] Burke's *Correspondence*, iv. 295-306.

thought that plan to be—than make you the instrument, or instruments, of the jobbing system. I am sure that the constant meddling of the bishops and clergy with the Castle, and of the Castle with them, will infallibly set them ill with their own body. All the weight which hitherto the clergy have had in keeping the people quiet, will be wholly lost.'

In the same letter, Burke, while expressing his regret at the Jacobinical tone which had appeared in the Catholic lay committee, protested against its dissolution, on the ground that the Catholics, without a complete organisation, would be unable to contend with their enemies. He strongly advocated a project, which had been formed, for making, with the assistance of their clergy, a religious census, in order to show their great numerical superiority; and he quoted, with approbation, a saying of Lord Fitzwilliam, that 'the depression of the Catholics is not the persecution of a sect, but tyranny over a people.' He concluded his letter, by desiring that some books, which had been left by his deceased son, should be presented as a memorial, either to the new Catholic college, or to that of Carlow.[1]

This letter appears to have been shown about in Catholic circles, and it came to the knowledge of one of the agents of the Government, who took a copy and sent it to the Castle. Pelham was at that time in England, but Cooke transmitted to him this copy with injunctions of profound secrecy, and as a document of the highest importance. 'If it be true,' he said, 'that the author has been the chief, if not sole, mover of all the measures with respect to the Irish Catholics, his real creed, principles, and object can no longer be misunderstood,' and he declared that the letter showed clearly that the design of Burke, and of his Irish followers, was to bring about a revolution in Ireland, and to make Ireland a popish country. In truth, however, this letter, though naturally exceedingly displeasing to the knot of men who had just obtained the recall of Lord Fitzwilliam, contained absolutely nothing which was not in full accordance with the well-known opinions of Burke, and Pelham wrote back to his alarmed correspondent, that he had already seen it, as it had been shown to him by Dr. Hussey.[2] Burke's

---

[1] Burke's *Correspondence*, iv. 320-323.

[2] Cooke to Pelham, October 6 (most secret), 23, 1795.

extreme distrust of Fitzgibbon and several other leading members of the Irish administration, had long been expressed, and he believed—as it appears to me very erroneously—that a system of separate clerical education which was wholly under ecclesiastical influence, would prove an antidote to the Jacobin spirit, which he saw rising among the Irish Catholics.

In another letter, written at this time, he expressed fully to Dr. Hussey the alarm with which he saw Catholic Ireland, or at least the lay leaders of Catholic Ireland, drifting into disaffection. 'I do not like,' he wrote, 'the style of the meeting at Francis Street.[1] The tone was wholly Jacobinical. . . . The language of the day went plainly to a separation of the two kingdoms. God forbid that anything like it should ever happen. They would both be ruined by it; but Ireland would suffer most and first. . . . It is a foolish language, adopted from the United Irishmen, that their grievances originate from England. . . . It is an ascendency which some of their own factions have obtained here, that has hurt the Catholics with this Government. It is not as an English Government, that Ministers act in that manner, but as assisting a party in Ireland. When they talk of dissolving themselves as a Catholic body, and mixing their grievances with those of their country, all I have to say is, that they lose their own importance as a body, by this amalgamation, and they sink real matters of complaint in those which are factious and imaginary. For, in the name of God, what grievances has Ireland as Ireland, to complain of, with regard to Great Britain; unless the protection of the most powerful country upon earth—giving all her privileges, without exception, in common to Ireland, and reserving to herself only the painful pre-eminence of tenfold burthens—be a matter of complaint? The subject, as a subject, is as free in Ireland as he is in England. As a member of the Empire, an Irishman has every privilege of a natural-born Englishman. . . . No monopoly is established against him anywhere. The great staple manufacture of Ireland . . . is privileged in a manner that has no example. The provision trade is the same. Nor does Ireland, on her part, take a single article from England, but what she has with more advantage than she

---

[1] The assembly of Catholics on April 9, at which the resolutions about the Union were carried.

could have it from any nation upon earth. I say nothing of the immense advantage she derives from the use of the English capital. . . . The tenor of the speeches in Francis Street, attacking the idea of an incorporating union between the two kingdoms, expressed principles that went the full length of a separation, and of a dissolution of that union which arises from their being under the same crown. . . . Ireland *constitutionally* is independent; *politically* she can never be so. It is a struggle against nature. She must be protected, and there is no protection to be found for her, but either from France or England.'

He proceeded to dilate upon the ruin which would befall Ireland if she placed herself under the dependence of France; the danger of the new Irish Jacobins, 'who, without any regard to religion, club all kinds of discontents together, in order to produce all kinds of disorders;' the madness and wickedness of Catholics who ally themselves with a power which is the inveterate enemy of all religions, but especially of Catholicism, and he warned the Catholic leaders that some of their members were entering on a course which would deprive them of their oldest and most trusted allies. 'Catholics, as things now stand, have all the splendid abilities, and much of the independent property, in Parliament, in their favour, and every Protestant (I believe, with very few exceptions) who is really a Christian. Should they alienate these men from their cause, their choice is amongst those who indeed may have ability, but not wisdom or temper in proportion, and whose very ability is not equal, either in strength or exercise, to that which they lose. They will have to choose men of desperate property, or of no property, and men of no religious and no moral principle.'

There is much more in this letter which deserves quotation, but my extracts have already extended too far. One sentence, however, with which Burke concluded his survey of Irish politics, must not be omitted. 'If Grattan, by whom I wish the Catholics to be wholly advised, thinks differently from me, I wish the whole unsaid.'[1]

It is interesting to compare this letter of Burke with a very

---

[1] Burke's *Correspondence*, iv. 308-317. This letter was written May 18, 1795.

confidential and very elaborate letter, which was written nearly at the same time by the Duke of Richmond to his sister, Lady Louisa Conolly, for the purpose of being laid before her husband, who was one of the most important members of the Irish House of Commons. This letter discloses very clearly another order of ideas about Ireland, which was certainly influencing the minds of some prominent English statesmen, and it is especially curious, as the writer had himself been at one time a parliamentary reformer of the most extreme democratic type. The duke expressed his deep conviction that the existing bond between the two countries was utterly precarious, and could not possibly be permanent, and that the full admission of the Catholics to political power in the independent Parliament of a country in which they are the great majority, must lead, in time, to their ascendency, to the ruin of the Protestants, to the ruin of the British Empire. Its first consequence, he said, would be the downfall of the Protestant establishment. The next would be the ruin of the landlords, for the Protestant ownership of land, which had been established by the Act of Settlement, the confiscations and the penal laws could not long survive a political revolution. The ascendant Catholics would then, very naturally, claim a Catholic king and government, which would mean separation from Great Britain, and separation would inevitably pass into hostility. All these calamities seemed impending in the near future, and the only possible way of averting them, was the speedy enactment of a legislative union of the two countries. Under such an union, the Catholics would 'only become a partial majority of a part of the Empire, and their claims must give way to the superior ones of the majority of the whole. . . . The whole argument and justice of the case, which was before in their favour, becomes against them, and the Protestant king, religion, and government may be maintained in Ireland.'

It may be said that the Catholics, perceiving this, will always resist an union, 'and that they will be joined by the Protestants, in opposing a measure so unpopular in Ireland, by which all parties will lose so much of their consequence. . . . But let the Protestants choose. It is, in my opinion, the only alternative they have, to carry such a measure, or to submit to the evils I have foretold, which will come on with rapid steps, and if they delay it, there will soon be no longer the Government that can do it. They had better, therefore, make this use of their power, while they yet have it, to secure, by one bold measure, their property and future consequence.' 'But,' continues the duke, 'I think the Catholics, too, might in the present moment be got to concur in the plan, by bribing them high. . . . Bribed they must be, as after all it is clear that an union is the deathblow of their vast hopes, which they will only give up for some certain present and considerable advantage, and Great Britain cannot be too liberal in its terms of union with Ireland, as England was with Scotland, for although the lesser nation should gain many preferences and peculiar benefits, the larger obtains that great security, which overbalances every little distinction that can be granted.'

A passage follows which some readers will regard as very significant. 'If there should be such opposition and resistance to this measure in Ireland, as to occasion a civil war, even that extremity, provided the Protestant interest of Ireland is hearty with us in the cause, would, in my opinion, be better, now that it can be fought on advantageous terms for such an object, than to let it arise a few years hence, inevitably as I think it must, on grounds we cannot maintain.' The question, however, though it is one of deep importance to the future of the British Empire, is primarily a question for the Irish Protestants. 'England may subsist without Ireland, but the Protestant interest in Ireland can be preserved, in my opinion, by no means but an union.'

'If Conolly,' continues the duke, 'should see this business in the light that I do, I would advise him to say nothing about it to Mr. Grattan, but to confer privately upon it with the Chancellor of Ireland, Lord Fitzgibbon, who will be best able to say what can or ought to be done to unite the Protestant interest for an union. Then the Chancellor might come over here, and talk to Mr. Pitt about it. Possibly our Government here, might have the weakness to be afraid of undertaking the only plan that can save Ireland, and preserve the connection. . . . If it fails of success, there will be at least this comfort, that one has done what one could.'[1]

On April 23, the long-deferred trial of William Jackson for high treason took place. He was defended by Curran and by several other counsel, and among them by Leonard McNally, at whose table he had met the leaders of the United Irishmen. The evidence of Cockayne, corroborated by the documents that had been seized, was conclusive, and after a trial which appears to have been perfectly fair, the prisoner was found guilty, but recommended to mercy. He had during his long imprisonment rejected a promising chance of escape, and appears to have been very weary of his wasted and discreditable life. He was brought up to receive judgment on the 30th. The spectators were struck with his ghastly pallor, with the convulsive twitches of his countenance, and with the perspiration that rose from him almost like a steam, but his arms were crossed and his features set with a desperate resolution. When asked why sentence should not be pronounced, he bowed silently and pointed to his counsel, who raised a technical objection and argued it at length. Before the discussion had terminated, Jackson fell down in the agonies of death. He had received that morning, apparently from the hand of his wife, a dose of arsenic, and he died in the dock. It is said that, as he entered the court, he had whispered with mournful triumph to one of his counsel, the dying words of Pierre, in Otway's 'Venice Preserved,' 'We have deceived the Senate.' Perhaps a truer picture of his last feelings may be gathered from some verses, copied in his handwriting, which were found upon him and produced at the inquest. 'Turn Thee unto me, and have mercy upon me; for I am desolate and afflicted. The troubles of my heart are enlarged: O bring Thou me out of my distresses. Look upon mine affliction and my pain, and forgive me all my sins. Consider mine enemies; for they are many; and they hate me with cruel violence. O keep my soul, and deliver me: let me not be ashamed; for I put my trust in Thee.'

The career of Jackson was not one to excite sympathy or enthusiasm, but his trial had the important effect of convincing

---

[1] The Duke of Richmond to Lady L. Conolly, June 27, 1795. This letter is among the papers of Lady Bunbury.

the Irish people, that the French Government was seriously attending to their affairs, and that a speedy invasion was very probable, and it also produced some considerable changes among the United Irishmen. Wolfe Tone, though he had founded the society, had lately quarrelled with its leaders, had devoted himself almost exclusively to the Catholic question, and had not attended a meeting or taken part in the concerns of the United Irishmen since May 1793.[1] He was now deeply compromised, for though he had refused the mission to France, his intercourse with Jackson was known, and his representation of the state of Ireland was in the hands of the Government. He did not, however, believe that there was any sufficient evidence to endanger his life, and the law officers were of the same opinion. He was a popular man, and the large circle of his friends included several who differed widely from his politics; among others, Marcus Beresford, the son of the all-powerful John Beresford. Through the kindly intervention of the Beresfords, and with the assent of the Attorney-General, Wolfe Tone made a compact with the Government. He acknowledged that he had held conversations of a very criminal nature with Jackson; he drew up in writing a minute account of all that had passed between Jackson, Rowan, and himself, and he agreed to leave Ireland, provided that he was not himself brought to trial, that he was not called as a witness, and that his confession was not made use of against either Rowan or Jackson, or to the prejudice of any other person mentioned, except for the purpose of preventing a renewal of treasonable practices. In May 1795 he sailed for Philadelphia, where he not long after met Napper Tandy and Hamilton Rowan.[2]

A less known but more important result of the arrest of Jackson, remains to be told. Hitherto the information which the Government had obtained about the proceedings of the United Irishmen, had been of a very slight and superficial character, but they now obtained the services of a man who had a real knowledge of the inner mechanism of the agitation, and whose

---

[1] Wolfe Tone's *Memoirs*, i. 121.

[2] Tone's own account of the transaction (*Memoirs*, i. 114–121), must be compared with the *Beresford Correspondence*, ii. 24–34. Beresford considered it a great object to get Tone out of the country. Tone's confession appears to have been ultimately given to Lord Clare.

letters form one of the best pictures of the events that are to be related. Leonard McNally had been for some time the most conspicuous lawyer connected with the movement. He was born in Dublin in 1752, and, in addition to his legal career, he mixed much both in literature and politics. He practised for a short time at the English bar. He edited a newspaper called the 'Public Ledger.' He published several plays and comic operas, some of which were very successful, and he attained considerable practice at the Irish bar,[1] though he was not quite in the first rank, and though some cloud of suspicion and discredit seems to have always hung over his reputation. Nature had not dealt kindly with him, and there was much in his appearance and manner that provoked ridicule and contempt. Sir Jonah Barrington had quarrelled with him, and his accuracy in narrative can never be trusted, but he had a keen eye for personal characteristics, and his picture of McNally seems confirmed by other evidence. He described him as 'a good-natured, hospitable, talented, and dirty fellow,' with a fine eye, but a grotesque figure nearly as broad as it was long, with legs of unequal length, a face that no washing could clean, a great deal of middling intellect, a shrill, full, good bar voice, great quickness at cross-examination, and sufficient adroitness in defence. He had, however, higher qualities than this sketch would imply—a singularly wise, just, and luminous judgment in politics, a genuine humanity of disposition and generosity of impulse, which never wholly deserted him in the midst of a base and treacherous career.

He appears to have been one of the many men who have been impelled by an eager intellectual temperament into situations of danger, which their nervous organisation was quite unfit to endure, and there is, I think, no reason to doubt that for many years he was sincerely attached to the popular cause. He wrote a pamphlet on the claims of Ireland, as early as 1782. He was counsel for Napper Tandy in his quarrel with the House of

---

[1] In a letter to the Government in 1805, asking for one of the places created by a new Police Bill, McNally said that he had then been twenty-nine years at the bar; that for sixteen years he had been in constant practice in the courts of criminal jurisdiction in Ireland, and that he had been employed for the defendant in almost every important trial in Ireland since 1790. He had published a successful book on 'the law of evidence,' and had written, but not yet published, another on 'the laws for preserving the peace.' (July 4, 1805, I.S.P.O.)

Commons. He was an original member of the United Irish Society, and when Barrington in 1793 made some imputation on that society, McNally challenged him, and was severely wounded in the duel. Shut out from all Crown patronage and greatly injured in his practice at the bar, by the imputation of disloyalty and by the disfavour of those in authority, McNally lost much more by his politics than he ever gained from the Government, and he was a trusted member of the National party. Like most of the first United Irishmen, he, however, probably only aimed at parliamentary reform; and he saw with dismay, that the movement to which he had committed himself, and which was at first perfectly legal, was sweeping on rapidly to revolution. In a letter, written in May 1794, the informer who has already been cited, mentions the great and evident terror shown by McNally at the meetings of the committee when matters began to assume a treasonable tone. There is, I believe, no ground for the suspicion, that, when with his accustomed hospitality he received Jackson and Cockayne at his table, and introduced them to the leaders of the movement, he was acting as a Government agent. Much treason, however, appears to have been talked on the occasion, and when the timid and nervous lawyer learnt that it had been all overheard, and noted down by a spy, he perceived that he was in the power of the Government, and he resolved to save himself from ruin by betraying the cause.

His first service was a peculiarly shocking one. Jackson, shortly before his death, had found an opportunity of writing four short letters, recommending his wife and child, and a child who was still unborn, to two or three friends, and to the care of the French nation, and he also drew up a will, leaving all he possessed to his wife, and entrusting McNally with the protection of her interests. He wrote at the bottom of it, 'Signed and sealed in presence of my dearest friend, whose heart and principles ought to recommend him as a worthy citizen—Leonard McNally.' These precious documents he entrusted, when dying, to his friend, and about three weeks after the death of Jackson, McNally placed them in the hands of the Irish Government.

A few days later, Camden sent a copy of them to England, with a 'most secret and confidential letter.' 'The paper which accompanies this,' he said, 'was delivered to Counsellor McNally, from whom Government received it. There is so much evidence against this person, that he is (I am informed) completely in the power of Government. Your Grace will observe, that the care of Mrs. Jackson is recommended by her husband to the National Convention, and that Mr. McNally is desired to assist her by every means in his power to procure her assistance from them. It has occurred to me, that an excuse might be made for Mr. McNally's being allowed to enter France for the purpose of attending to this woman's fortunes, that he should go through London, and in case your Grace should wish to employ him, I would inform you when and where he will be found.'[1]

Portland replied that he was perfectly ready to make use of the services of McNally in France, if Camden thought that he might safely be trusted, but he suggested that this was very doubtful. The control which Government possessed over him depended entirely upon the conclusive evidence of treason they had against him. Would that control continue in a foreign country? Camden, on reflection, agreed that it would not be safe to try the experiment. McNally, however, he was convinced, would be very useful at home.[2]

Of this, indeed, there could be little doubt. As confidential lawyer of the United Irishmen, he had opportunities of information of the rarest kind. It is certain that he sometimes communicated to the Government the line of defence contemplated by his clients, and other information which he can only have received in professional confidence, and briefs annotated by his hand, will be found among the Government papers at Dublin. He was also able, in a manner which was not less base, to furnish the Government with early and most authentic evidence about conspiracies which were forming in France. James Tandy, son of Napper Tandy, had been a brave and distinguished officer in the service of the East India Company, and although he had been a United Irishman in the beginning of the movement, he appears

---

[1] Camden to Portland, May 20, 1795 (Record Office). At the bottom of the copy sent by Camden is written, 'True copies from the originals delivered to me, May 14, 1795, by J. W.' J. W. is the signature under which McNally invariably wrote to the Government. I am unable to say what had happened to him between Jackson's death (April 30) and May 14, whether fresh evidence had been brought against him, and under what circumstances he was induced to surrender the papers of Jackson.

[2] Portland to Camden, May 22; Camden to Portland, May 26, 1795.

to have been very unlike his father both in character and opinions. McNally was his intimate friend, and by his means saw nearly every letter that arrived from Napper Tandy, and some of those which came from Rowan and Reynolds. The substance of these letters was regularly transmitted to the Government, and they sometimes contained information of much value. Besides this, as a lawyer in considerable practice, constantly going on circuit, and acquainted with the leaders of sedition, McNally had excellent opportunities of knowing the state of the country, and was able to give very valuable warnings about the prevailing dispositions.

Few men would have been thought less capable of long-continued deception than this good-humoured, brilliant, and mercurial lawyer; and in times when public feeling ran fiercely against all who were suspected of disloyalty, he was the most constant, and apparently the most devoted, defender of the United Irishmen. Curran, after a friendship of forty-three years, spoke of his 'uncompromising and romantic fidelity,' and Curran's son has left an emphatic testimony to his 'many endearing traits.' Yet all this time he was in constant secret correspondence with the Government, and there are, I believe, not less than 150 of his letters in the Castle of Dublin. He received strangely little for his services. Though an excellent lawyer, and a man of much undoubted ability, he was overwhelmed with debts, which were largely due to his supposed politics.[1] In letter after letter he describes himself as reduced to utter destitution; but from time to time he obtained from the Government some small subsidy, which extricated him from his immediate difficulties. It was doled out, however, with a most tardy, penurious, and uncertain hand.[2] At last, his crowning

---

[1] In one of his letters to the Government he writes: 'Why will not —— answer my request? I am in deep distress for money. He can inform you of my services. I had no resource but in the assistance of my friends. Everything professional is lost on account of my politics.' (Jan. 9, 1797.) In recommending McNally for a pension, Cooke (if he was the writer of the paper in the Cornwallis papers) adds: 'He was not much trusted in the rebellion, and I believe has been faithful.' (*Cornwallis Correspondence*, iii. 320.)

[2] The smallness of his subsidies is very remarkable. In one letter he says: 'P. [Pollock] assured me some considerable time ago that the L. Lnt. had promised me 200*l.* a year for the life of myself and children, yet I still remain without having this business settled.' (J. W., Sept. 3, 1796.) Shortly after, Pollock writes that J. W. should have some money for Cork. A guinea a week had been stipulated. 'He has not got anything for the last twenty weeks.' (J. Pollock, July 9, 1796.)

reward arrived in the form of a secret pension of 300*l.* a year, which was disclosed after his death. Had his politics from the beginning been of a different type, his professional talents would probably have raised him to the bench.

The interest, the singularity, and the melancholy of his career will certainly be enhanced by reading his letters. Written for the most part in great haste, without regular beginning or ending, but in the most beautiful of handwritings and in the tersest and happiest English, they reveal with great fidelity a strangely composite character, in which the virtues of impulse seemed all to live, though the virtues of principle had wholly gone. Though his revelations were very important, it was evidently his object to baffle plots without injuring individuals, and he retained all the good nature and native kindness of his disposition. He retained also, to a very remarkable degree, the calmness and independence of a most excellent judgment, a rare discrimination in judging the characters of men and the changing aspects of events. From no other quarter did the Government obtain so many useful warnings, and if the advice of McNally had been more frequently listened to, some of the worst consequences of the rebellion might have been avoided.

The country was now passing, with a portentous rapidity, into a condition of hopeless moral and political disorganisation, and disaffection was spreading through all classes. The memorial of Wolfe Tone, which had been brought in evidence against Jackson, and which was presented to the French Government in the beginning of 1796, described it as completely ripe for revolution. The Protestants of the Established Church alone, he said, supported England, and they only comprised about 450,000 of the population. The Protestant Dissenters, whom he believed to be twice as numerous, and who formed the most intelligent portion of the middle class, were almost all republicans. Republican ideas had spread widely among the Catholic leaders; and the bulk of the Catholic peasantry, 'who had been trained from their infancy in an hereditary hatred and abhorrence of the English name,' and were in a condition of the most abject misery, had almost all passed into the organisation of the Defenders. The picture seemed an exaggerated one, but McNally assured the Government that it was 'justly conceived and accurately written.' 'The whole body of the peasantry,' McNally said, 'would join the French in case of an invasion, or rise in a mass against the existing Government if any men of condition were to come forward as their leaders; and in either of these events,' it was very doubtful whether the militia or even the regular army could be fully depended on.

'The sufferings of the common people,' he continued, 'from high rents and low wages, from oppressions of their landlords, their sub-tenants, the agents of absentees, and tithes, are not now the only causes of disaffection to Government, and hatred to England; for though these have long kept the Irish peasant in the most abject state of slavery and indigence, yet another cause, more dangerous, pervades them all, and is also indeed almost universal among the middle ranks, by whom I mean the upper classes of artists and mechanics in the cities, and farmers in the country. This cause is an attachment to French principles in politics and religion lately imbibed, and an ardent desire for a republican Government. Rest assured these principles, and this desire to subvert the existing Government of the country, are more strongly rooted, and more zealously pursued by the Roman Catholics, than even by their teachers and newly acquired allies, the Dissenters. A contempt for the clergy universally prevails. Deism is daily superseding bigotry, and every man who can read, or who can hear and understand what is read to him, begins in religion as in politics to think for himself.' This is shown, not only by the language of the peasants, and by the rapid spread of Defenderism, but also by the contempt with which Archbishop Troy's address against the Defenders was generally received, though it was read publicly by the priests from the altars. 'This address, which, a few years ago, would have operated with the terrors of thunder on an Irish congregation of Catholics, is now scoffed at in the chapels, and reprobated in private. . . . So sudden a revolution in the Catholic mind is easily accounted for. I impute it to the press. The publication of political disquisitions, and resolutions by the societies of United Irishmen of Belfast and Dublin, written to the passions and feelings of the multitude, affected them with electrical celerity. These papers prepared the way for Paine's politics and theology. Several thousand copies of his various writings were printed at Belfast and Cork, and distributed gratis. . . . I am assured, and I believe it to be true, that in the county of Cork, Paine's works are read by the boys at almost every school, and that in most houses they now supply the place of the Psalter and Prayer Book.'[1]

The United Irishmen, whose meetings had been forcibly suppressed in 1794, reconstructed their society, in 1795, on a new basis, and it now became distinctly republican and treasonable. An oath of secrecy and fidelity was substituted for the old test, and great precautions were taken to extend and perfect its organisation. The inferior societies, which had at first consisted of thirty-six, were now composed of only twelve members each, and an elaborate hierarchy of superior directing committees was created. There were lower baronial committees, upper baronial committees, district and county committees, and provincial directories, each being formed of delegates from the inferior bodies; and at the head of the whole there was a general executive directory of five members, elected by ballot from the provincial directories, sitting in Dublin, and entrusted with the government of the whole conspiracy. The oath bound the members to form a bond of affection between Irishmen of every opinion, and to endeavour to obtain a 'full representation of all the people.' This phrase was substituted for 'an equal representation of the people in Parliament,' which was used in the original test, and the suppression of all mention of Parliament was not without its significance. In order to preserve secrecy, the names of the members of the supreme directory were only communicated to a single member of each provincial directory, and orders were transmitted from committee to committee by a secretary appointed in each. Emissaries were sent out, and much seditious literature disseminated, to propagate the system. A subscription of one shilling a month was paid by every member. Nightly drilling took place in many districts; arms were collected, and the prospect of a French invasion was kept continually in view. According to the Government information, there were sixteen societies in Belfast, a vast number in the counties of

[1] J. W., Sept. 12, 1795 (Irish State Paper Office). In order to shorten my references, I may mention that all the letters of McNally referred to in the following pages are in the collection of private and confidential correspondence in Dublin.

Antrim, Down, Derry, Armagh, and Dublin, and between two and three thousand in all Ireland. At Cork, the Government was informed, there were, in 1795, about 600 United Irishmen—'shopkeepers, merchants' clerks, one or two physicians, farmers residing in all parts of the county, and very young men who attend for the pleasure of debate. . . . They are mostly Protestant. The mayor and sheriffs are suspected of being friendly to them.'[1]

Contempt for the Irish Parliament, and distrust of constitutional agitation, were rapidly spreading. In the beginning of September, Grattan, Ponsonby, Curran, and one or two other leaders of the parliamentary Opposition, had a very private conference with the principal members of the democratic party among the Dissenters and the Catholics, which (probably through the medium of McNally) was speedily reported to the Government. Several of the leading Dissenters were there, and six Catholics, including Keogh and Byrne. Grattan spoke to them of the dangerous state of the country, the spread of Defenderism, and the necessity of forming a plan of action for the next session of Parliament, and he suggested an aggregate meeting of all classes, and an address to the King. The project was received with much coolness, and Grattan soon saw that he would receive no support. He can hardly have been ignorant of the hopes and sympathies of some of those who were before him, and his language to them—even as it appears through the untrustworthy medium of a secret Government report—seems to me, to have been very honourable to him, and excellently calculated to influence the kind of men he was addressing. He said he would not persevere in the plan which he had prepared, since it found so little favour, but he also said, 'every exertion should be made to put an end to the spirit of insurrection, and to resist invasion, as the French would merely treat Ireland in a manner most calculated to weaken England; that they would halloo the lower class against the higher, and make the whole country a scene of massacre; that in a year or two, it would be given up by the French again, to Great Britain, and that the convulsion would be the ruin of the country.' 'My reporter,'

[1] *First Digest of the Reports on the United Irishmen and Defenders* (Record Office).

writes Cooke to Pelham, 'had the whole from a leading man of the Catholics who was present. They consider it as a plunge of Grattan's, who they think in a cleft stick. You will be cautious of mentioning how this information comes to you.'[1]

Much more serious than the United Irish movement, was the rapid spread of Defenderism among the Catholic peasantry. It radiated in the first instance from the county of Armagh, and grew out of the local quarrel between Protestants and Catholics, but, as we have already seen, it almost immediately lost in most places its first character, and became a revived Whiteboy system, with the very serious difference, that a strong political element now mingled with it, through the belief that a French invasion was the most probable method by which its different objects might be attained. Numerous letters in the Government correspondence, show the terrible rapidity and simultaneity with which it broke out in many counties, the various forms of outrage that were perpetrated, the manner in which all agrarian and ecclesiastical grievances were drawn into the system, and the utter demoralisation that it produced. 'One of the first acts of violence,' said Lord Camden, 'and of system, was to put all the smiths into requisition, compelling them to make pikes and spears, some new, and others out of old scythes.' Parties went about plundering gentlemen's houses of arms, and their information was so good, that it was evident that they were in correspondence with the servants. There were instances of servants quitting their master with tears, saying that they would be murdered if they remained. In many parts of Leitrim, Sligo, Galway, Longford, and Mayo, depredations were taking place in the early summer of 1795. In Roscommon, the great graziers were 'so afraid of their cattle being houghed and killed, that they yielded to the demands of the people, by agreeing to raise their wages and lower the rent of the potato ground.' 'Both these measures,' writes Camden, 'were very just and necessary in themselves, but very improper and impolitic, forced, as they were, by intimidation,' and the concession naturally gave an immense encouragement to the rioters. 'In Galway,' it was noticed, 'there was not an equal pretence for discontent, the rent of the potato ground being lower, though the wages were higher,'

[1] Cooke to Pelham, Sept. 3, 1795. (*Pelham MSS.*)

and the disturbances there, were for a time at least, quelled when the adjournment of Parliament enabled the principal gentlemen of the county to return to their estates. The usual Irish type, of an agrarian code contrary to the law of the land and enforced by outrages, was very apparent. The rioters 'summoned people to appear before Captain Stout, the nickname for their leaders, and settled differences about wages and rent by a jury, and imposed fines.' 'I fear,' wrote the Lord Lieutenant, 'there is too general an expectation among the common people, of some good that they are to derive from fraternity, and they have lately assumed the name of brothers, and they are encouraged with the hope of being what they call up, or getting uppermost, which is totally unconnected with any religious sentiment, except so far as it serves as a pretext for influencing them at particular times.'[1]

The circle of disorder in a few weeks spread over Meath, West Meath, and Kildare. Emissaries, it was said, 'swear the lower Roman Catholics to secrecy, and to the French when they land,' and there were nightly meetings, and constant robberies of firearms. In most of the counties in Ireland the better sort of people showed but little energy, and there were many large districts without a single important resident gentleman. Very much, therefore, was thrown on the Central Government, who were obliged, as far as they could, to create 'an artificial, if they cannot establish a natural, civilisation.' 'The greatest pains appear to be taken to infuse a spirit of discontent through all the lower orders of people;' and although the disturbances were not likely to be seriously dangerous unless an invasion took place, they made it impossible to withdraw the troops. From the North it was reported, that Defender lodges were everywhere multiplying, the principal one being at Armagh. There was an active correspondence kept up, but never through the post office. Everywhere the Defenders were administering unlawful oaths and seizing arms. They were accustomed to burn the turf and root up the potatoes of those who refused to be sworn, cut down plantations for pike handles, dig up meadows, level banks, hough cattle, rob or set fire to houses, ravish or murder. In eight months there were 147 acts of murder, robbery, or rape,

[1] Camden to Portland, May 28, 1795.

in the single county of Longford. All the Protestants for forty miles round Carrick-on-Shannon were disarmed. Bodies of Defenders numbering 2,000 or 3,000 appeared in arms, and no less than thirteen counties in the course of this year were infected. There were notices put up threatening all who paid tithes or taxes, or let potato grounds for more than four guineas an acre. There were attempts to regulate the price of land and lower priests' dues. According to one proclamation, labour was to be paid one shilling a day for half the year, and tenpence a day for the other half, and though tithes might be paid to the clergymen, they might not, under pain of death and destruction of goods, be paid to tithe proctors or tithe farmers.[1]

The Government were very anxious to ascertain whether there was any connection between the United Irishmen and the Defenders; but after several hesitations of opinion, Camden at this time acknowledged himself unable to discover any clear proof of such connection. A careful digest was made of the evidence relating to both societies, and a comparison was sent over to England of their plans and objects. Personal representation, Camden said, was an aim peculiar to the United Irishmen. Using signs and catechisms was peculiar to the Defenders; and abolishing taxes and Church cess, lowering the priests' fees, lowering the prices of land, of potatoes, and of meal, raising the price of labour, equalising property, and restoring popery, were Defender objects, of which there was no trace among the United Irishmen. The characteristics or objects common to both were fraternising, numbering their committees, naming delegates, providing by all means pikes and guns, seducing the military, abolishing tithes and royalties, separating the two kingdoms, expecting assistance from France, looking forward to a general rising.

The outrages came and went, and sometimes almost disappeared in some of the infected counties, but then again broke out in neighbouring districts. On the whole, in the latter part of the year they appear to have perceptibly diminished, but they were still very serious, and wherever they had appeared, they left behind them sedition and demoralisation. 'It is difficult,' wrote Camden, 'to overcome the impression, so general in

[1] June and July letters.

the kingdom, of its inhabitants considering it a conquered country, and the jealousy of the English can only be lessened by the greatest attention to the interests of the lower ranks, who in many parts of the kingdom are grievously neglected.' He suggested that the old power once exercised by English justices at quarter sessions, of proportioning the price of labour to that of food, might be of great use in Ireland.[1]

At a trial of some militiamen for having leagued themselves with the Defenders, it came out in evidence that many had taken the Defender oath, simply because they then obtained a certificate which enabled them to travel throughout the kingdom free of expense, being lodged and provided with food gratuitously by their colleagues. 'To establish a solemn league,' wrote one informant, 'with gradations and authority, seems to be their first object; ... and this league is confined to Roman Catholics, and directed in the most violent degree against the whole body of Protestants, ... whose extirpation they confess to be resolved.' 'By their extreme ferocity, of which there are too many horrid instances, they have established such an ascendency over the lower orders of people, that Government has never been able to obtain an entire scheme of intelligence.' Labourers were prevented from working except at rates established by Defenders. Petty juries could not be relied on in Defender cases. Arms were never refused, except by some of the gentry. The Protestants in many of the disturbed parts were wholly disarmed. No traces had yet been found of any French correspondence, but the whole movement was evidently preparatory to a rising in case of French invasion. A great desire was shown to seduce the military and militia, but both had on the whole been very loyal. At Enniskillen, however, nine soldiers of the South Cork Militia had been found guilty of Defenderism, and there were a few other cases. No one with any stake in the country seemed involved in the movement, and the proclamations

---

[1] Camden to Portland, Sept. 25, 1795. 'Defenderism,' wrote Cooke at this time, 'puzzles me more and more; but it certainly grows more alarming daily, as the effect of executions seems to be at an end, and there is an enthusiasm defying punishment. The secret committee of gentlemen in West Meath have this day recommended the taking up and sending off, as sailors, the suspected, as the only way left to act. The late punishments of informers has struck such terror, that they cannot hope for legal conviction.' (Cooke to Pelham, Sept. 12, 1795.)

were evidently the work of very illiterate men. 'Alehouse keepers, artisans, low schoolmasters, and perhaps a few middling farmers, seem to be the leaders in the country and in the provincial towns, and inferior Roman Catholic priests its principal instigators.' In Dublin, Defenderism had taken great hold of the weavers in the Liberties, and generally of the lower mechanics. Many attempts had been made to tamper with the soldiers, and many deserters were concealed in the Liberties, and supplied with money and employment as weavers.

No direct communication, said the same writer, has been discovered between the Defenders and the United Irishmen. The latter are simply acting on the principles of pure French democracy, while the former are actuated by a great variety of motives. The successors of a class of people who had never been much attached either to the Government or to the landed proprietors, they had now caught the contagion of the seditious doctrines of the time, while religious animosities, and impatience of political restrictions, intensified their discontent. Under these circumstances, the soil was fully prepared for an explosion, and a provincial dispute between the Presbyterians and papists proved sufficient to annihilate any little regard for good order that remained.[1]

The tension of anxiety in some parts of Ireland was intolerable, and it continued unabated for several years. Country gentlemen and respectable farmers found life impossible without a military guard, while among the lower classes conspiracy in many districts was universal, though it is probable that most of the conspirators took the Defender oath merely in order to save themselves from depredation. The whole framework of society, and all the moral principles on which it rests, seemed giving way. Habits of systematic opposition to the law were growing up; outrages, sometimes of horrible cruelty, were looked upon merely as incidents of war, and savage animosities were forming. It is difficult, in a tranquil and well-organised community, adequately to realise the strain of such a state of society on the nerves and characters even of the most courageous men. Isolated, or almost isolated, in the midst of an alien population, not knowing whom they could trust, or how far the conspiracies

[1] *Second Digest of Letters relating to Defenderism.*

around them extended, with perpetual rumours of invasion, rebellion, and intended massacre floating around them, the Irish country gentlemen were supported by none of the fierce excitement which nerves the soldier in the hour of battle. McNally mentions the acquittal, in Londonderry, by a jury of wealthy men, of several persons charged with Defenderism, against the evidence and a strong charge by the judge. The judge ordered the sheriff to post up the jurors' names in the court house, as of persons unfit to serve in future. The sheriff obeyed, and several of the jurors determined to bring actions against him for libelling them.[1]

In Kildare, which had hitherto been a very peaceable and prosperous county, with a large resident gentry, the Defender movement almost assumed the dimensions of a rebellion, and it was noticed that some of the magistrates against whom the popular feeling ran most furiously, were Catholics.[2] The magistrates in this county appear to have acted with great energy, and Lawrence O'Connor, a Naas schoolmaster, was, with some others, found guilty of administering an oath to be true to the French. He appears to have been leader of the movement. Desperate attempts were made by several hundred armed men to rescue him. Vengeance was vowed against all who were concerned in his arrest, and one magistrate was three times fired at, and severely wounded. The law, however, was carried out, and O'Connor was hanged. He was evidently a genuine enthusiast, and after his condemnation he made a speech to the court, which is very interesting as explaining the motives that inspired him. There appears to have been nothing in it either of politics or of religion. He dwelt exclusively on the miseries and grievances of the poor—landholders refusing land for cottages, rack rents, land jobbers, potato plots let for six guineas an acre. In the course of his speech, there was an incident which could hardly, at such a moment, have occurred out of Ireland. Judge Finucane interrupted the prisoner by saying, that he at least 'had always let his lands to cottagers, and not to men who relet them to rack renters, by which his tenants prospered.' 'God bless your lordship for that!' exclaimed O'Connor; 'you will yet feel the benefit of it; but you must allow there are

[1] J. W. to Pelham, Sept. 17, 1795.   [2] Plowden, ii. 537.

few rich men like yourself in the country.' McNally, who was engaged in the defence, relates that O'Connor, after his condemnation, was offered a provision for his family if he would make discoveries. He answered, 'He who feeds the young ravens in the valley, will provide for them.'[1]

One of the most enduring effects of these disturbances was the diminution of the influence of the gentry over their tenantry. I have in former chapters described at some length the agrarian circumstances of Ireland, and it is constantly necessary, even at the risk of wearisome repetition, to keep these circumstances before our eyes, and to watch their obscure and often most perplexing changes, when relating political events. As we have already seen, the actual owner of the soil, in Ireland, rarely made or directly paid for improvements, but he threw the task of making them upon large tenants, who on this condition received great tracts at very low rents, on leases for lives, sometimes renewable for ever on the payment of a small fine at the fall of each life,[2] but more frequently extending over fifty, sixty, seventy, or even eighty years. This system of land tenure grew out of the social and political conditions of the country at a time when the population was exceedingly scanty, and whatever may have been its disadvantages, it was at least not in any sense inequitable. After the first few years, the contract was exceedingly lucrative to the farmer, and an undisturbed enjoyment for perhaps half a century, amply compensated him for his original outlay. By a remarkable series of laws known as 'the Timber Acts,' the Irish Parliament endeavoured to encourage planting, by giving tenants for life, or for years, a partial or abso-

---

[1] J. W. to Pelham, Sept. 17, 1795. An interesting account of this trial will be found in Walker's *Hibernian Magazine* for November 1795. The judges appear, as far as I can form an opinion, to have tried the case both fairly and mercifully. In the *Pelham Correspondence* there is a letter from the Castle giving some further particulars. 'O'Connor was executed yesterday at Naas. He was extremely penitent, acknowledged the veracity of the witnesses against him, and the justice of his sentence. The Roman Catholic clergy refused to attend him at the time of his execution, or to administer the Sacraments to him. His carcase is buried in the courtyard of the gaol, and his head is to be set up upon a pole in the front of the building.' (S. Hamilton, Sept. 8, 1795.)

[2] At the time of the Devon Commission, it was estimated that one-seventh of Ireland was held under this tenure, and there were complaints that landlords, who found the rent paid to them absurdly below the value of the land, frequently availed themselves of the negligence of tenants or of technical flaws to break these contracts. (*Digest of Evidence on Occupation of Land*, i. 232, 233.)

lute property in the trees they planted. The first of these Acts entitled them to one-third, and the second to one-half, of these trees. A third gave them the entire property in them, provided they were publicly registered, and it enabled them to cut them down at the expiration of the lease or at the maturity of the timber, unless the landlord or reversioner elected to purchase them at a price settled by a jury of freeholders at the sessions. A fourth Act still further extended the power of the tenant, enabling him to cut down, sell, and dispose of the trees he had planted, if duly registered, at any period during the term of the lease.[1]

It was under this system that most of the improvements in Ireland appear to have been made,[2] and if the first tenants had continued to occupy and to cultivate the soil, Ireland would have had one of the most flourishing tenantries in Europe. In some cases this actually happened. The great grazing farmers, whose condition contrasted so strongly with that of the small tenants, were probably often original tenants. Under any circumstances, however, it would be a rare thing, amid the many vicissitudes of life, for an original tenant and his descendants to remain attached to the same farm for seventy or eighty years; and it was almost inevitable, when the demand for land had increased, and when the long leaseholder found a great margin between his profits and his rent, that he should have proceeded to sub-let. If he was a man of an inferior stamp, he did so in order to become the idle, sporting, dissipated, and worthless squireen so graphically described in the pages of Young. If he was a man of energy and ambition, he probably took the same course, for he obtained a

[1] 8 Geo. I. c. 8; 9 Geo. II. c. 7; 5 Geo. III. c. 17; 23 & 24 Geo. III. c. 39.

[2] Another method was thus described by a very competent authority. 'Lord Redesdale, once Lord Chancellor in Ireland, states that leases with covenant of perpetual renewal arose in Ireland, instead of fee farms, in consequence of persons purchasing improvable estates, without having money to carry on their improvements, and then procuring it in this manner: they paid, for example, 15,000*l*. for an estate, and conveyed it to another in fee simple for 10,000*l*., taking a lease of the whole, with covenant for perpetual renewal, at a rent equal to the interest of the 10,000*l*.' (Ferguson and Vance's *Report on the Tenure and Improvement of Land in Ireland*, 1851, p. 8.) It is probable that, in the early part of the eighteenth century, the improvements were almost always made by the leaseholders. In Arthur Young's time, there were evidently many very enterprising and improving landlords. In modern times the drainage works have been in general chiefly paid for by the landlord, and a considerable proportion of other improvements are often made jointly by landlord and tenant.

considerable profit rent from his sub-tenant, and was thus enabled, with the advantage of a secure, independent income, to enter into the paths of trade or professional life. A very competent writer in 1787 has noticed that it was chiefly these large leaseholders who 'formed that middle race of men from which the bar, the pulpit, and the public offices are supplied with their most distinguished ornaments.'[1]

Sometimes too, but especially in the later years of the century, the great leaseholder was put over an estate which was already subdivided into numerous small tenancies, in order to act as the managing agent, and to secure without trouble a fixed and steady though moderate income to the landlord, instead of a larger but fluctuating income collected with difficulty from small tenants. Sometimes he was a land jobber, who made it his business to take large tracts of land at a low rent, subdividing them, and letting them to small tenants at a great profit; and very often he was a consequence of the embarrassments of the landlord.[2] It was a common thing for an owner who desired to raise at once a large sum of

---

[1] *Considerations on the Present Disturbances in Munster*, by Dominick Trant (1787). Settlements in Ireland, says the same writer, 'almost always leave the possessor of the estate a power of leasing for three lives or thirty-one years; the farmer taking a lease for lives (as was always the case among Protestant farmers, and is now the general usage since the late relaxation of the popery laws), chooses them among the healthiest of his own children or those of his neighbour.'

[2] Whitley Stokes described the middleman as made 'necessary by the indolence of the landlord, who will not be at the trouble of judging for himself of the character and responsibility of his tenants, nor of keeping small accounts. He is a most expensive agent, as his profit generally amounts to 7s. in the 1l.' (*Projects for re-establishing Internal Peace in Ireland*, by Whitley Stokes, 1799, p. 6.) Archbishop Magee, in his funeral sermon on Lord Clare, eulogised him for having always refused to surrender the peasants on his estate to the middleman, who 'views the cultivator like the clod he tills, but as a subject of profitable traffic,' and who 'constitutes one of the most perniciously operating causes of the wretchedness' of the poor. (Magee's *Works*, ii. 389.) 'This most pernicious system of middlemen,' says another well-informed writer, 'originated in the idleness and poverty of the Irish gentry. A gentleman involved in extravagance, and unable to provide for his immediate wants, would often let a portion of his estate on a long lease at a rent as small as three, four, or five shillings an acre, on condition of receiving a sum of money at the moment. The immediate lessee, either too proud or too lazy to cultivate this land himself, would let it on lease to another at a profit rent of ten or fifteen shillings an acre; and the next lessee would dispose of it at an advanced rent to a third person, until at last the most ignorant and indigent of the people became the occupiers and cultivators of that land, which, in the hands of an English yeoman, would have produced double the quantity of what it was in their power to make it yield.' (Bell's *Description of the Peasantry of Ireland between* 1780–1790 [1804], p. 37.)

money, to offer as an equivalent a long lease at a very low rent, or to reduce the rent of an existing leaseholder. A great proportion of the low perpetuity rents which are so common in Ireland, may be traced in this way to the necessities of a spendthrift heir. From one or other of these causes it resulted, that by far the greater part of Ireland was let by the landowner at long leases, and at rents so low that sub-letting was almost universally profitable, and the controlling power and management passed out of the hands of the owners, into the hands of men of a much lower social type.[1] But below the landlord and below the first tenant, land was again and again sub-let, and in these lower grades the competition became so fierce, the system of 'canting,' or putting up farms to auction without any regard to the old tenants, was so general, that rents were forced up to the highest point, and the cottier who held a little plot of potato ground from the farmer, and worked out his rent by labour, was one of the most miserable of mankind.

This economical condition was by no means peculiar to Ireland. We have already seen it in Scotland, and it may probably be found in the early agricultural history of many countries, but the special circumstances of Ireland had contributed to aggravate it. The old legislative destruction of manufactures, and the depressing influence of certain portions of the penal code, had thrown too many for subsistence on the soil, taken away some of the chief spurs to industry, and produced moral effects which con-

---

[1] Miss Edgeworth, in her very instructive sketch of the farming system at the close of the eighteenth century, says: 'There was a continual struggle between landlord and tenant upon the question of long and short leases.... The offer of immediate high rent, or of *fines to be paid down* directly, tempted the landlord's extravagance, or supplied his present necessities at the expense of his future interests; and though aware that the value of improvable land must rise, or that he was letting it under its actual value, yet if the landlord was not resident on his estate, and if he merely wanted to get his rents without trouble, he was easily tempted to this imprudence. Many have let for 99 years, and others, according to a form common in Ireland, for three lives renewable for ever, paying a small fine on the insertion of a new life, at the failure of each. These leases, in course of years, have been found extremely disadvantageous to the landlord, the property having risen so much in value that the original rent was absurdly disproportioned. . . . My father, in the course of his life, saw the end of two leases of 99 years. . . . In these and all cases where long leases had been granted, he did not find that the land had been improved by the tenants, or that they felt any gratitude for what had been originally desired and granted as a favour. On the contrary, long possession had made the occupier almost forget that he was a tenant, and consider his being forced to surrender the land at the expiration of the lease as a great hardship.' (*Memoirs of R. L. Edgeworth*, ii. 21–23.)

tinued long after the laws that created them were repealed. Absenteeism not only drew away a large proportion of Irish rents to England or to Dublin; it also produced or rendered possible many infamous abuses in the management of property. The tithe system, and especially the exemption of graziers, was exceedingly unfair to the poor, who were compelled to support the clergy of two religions, and the county cess, which was levied by the grand juries, and chiefly paid by the occupying tenants, was often scandalously excessive and scandalously misapplied.[1] It is admitted, indeed, on all hands that Irish roads were exceedingly good, but many of the contracts for making them appear to have been grossly corrupt. Not unfrequently, it is said, grand jurors got for their own tenants contracts for making or repairing portions of road at twice the proper price, and the tenants were thus enabled to pay off, out of public money, arrears of rent.[2] Parliamentary taxation, on the other hand, was very light, and after the repeal of the penal laws the Irish Parliament, as we have seen, showed no disposition to throw the burden unduly on the unrepresented classes. The hearth tax was the only direct tax paid by the poor, and in the latter years of the century about two millions of persons appear to have been exempted from paying it.[3] A very low standard of comfort, extreme and barbarous ignorance, the early and improvident marriages which naturally accompany these conditions, and the gregarious and domestic habits which made multitudes cling desperately to one small spot, often of miserable soil, were the real root of the evil, and great moral changes were necessary before it could be removed.

The agrarian changes which took place after the completion of the penal code, and before the accession of George III., con-

---

[1] In a very able pamphlet, called *Lachrymæ Hibernicæ, or the Grievances of the Peasantry of Ireland*, published in 1822 by Ensor (the author of a remarkable book on moral philosophy), it is said that about that date, 'in many parishes the grand jury cess exceeds the whole amount of the money collected for tithes, in the proportion of three to one, sometimes more. This is the case, with few, if any, exceptions, in the province of Connaught.' (P. 16.) See, too, O'Driscoll's *Views of Ireland* (1823), ii. 394–396.

[2] See the description of the system in Miss Edgeworth's *Absentee* (ch. x.), and in the *Life* of her father (ii. 31, 32).

[3] 'Of these millions [the Catholic population of Ireland], it is a known fact that two millions one hundred thousand are, by the late Hearth Money Act, excused, on account of poverty, from paying a tax of about fourpence a year each to the State.' (Mr. R. Johnson, *Irish Parl. Deb.* xv. 278.) According to Mullala (*View of Irish Affairs*, ii. 202, 203), about a million and a half were exempted.

sisted chiefly of violent fluctuations in the proportion between arable and pasture land, resulting from fluctuations in the price of cattle. Since the accession of George III. powerful political influences had come into play. Such were the Octennial Act, making it a more pressing interest for landlords to multiply the voters upon their estates; the legislation of 1778, enabling Catholics to take leases for lives, instead of being restricted to leases for thirty-one years; the legislation of 1782, bringing Catholic purchasers into the land market, and the corn bounties, which, in conjunction with the English demand for corn, greatly raised the value of land, and made Ireland an essentially arable country. The Dublin Society laboured with zeal and intelligence, during the greater part of the century, to correct the extreme ignorance of agriculture that generally prevailed among the farmers; and I have mentioned the desire which Arthur Young noticed, and so warmly praised, among the more improving landlords and in the more prosperous parts of the country, to put an end to the system of middlemen when leases fell in, and to bring the occupying tenant into immediate relations with his landlord. This was a great advantage to the landlord, and in general a still greater advantage to the tenant, who usually found the farmer of his own race and creed immeasurably more oppressive than the Protestant gentleman; but, as I have already hinted, it had political and social effects which were not so good. Removing a connecting link between the highest and lowest classes, it brought two classes into direct juxtaposition who were deeply separated by religion, by race, and by bitter memories of old confiscations. It also altered in some degree the character of the management of land, placing it much more than formerly in the hands of bailiffs and 'drivers,' who had no direct interest in the soil.[1] It must be added, too, that a great

---

[1] The arguments in favour of middlemen are stated powerfully, but with, I think, an undue leaning towards the middlemen, in the *Lachrymae Hibernicae* (p. 23). Writing in 1822, the author describes the middlemen as having 'nearly disappeared.' There is an excellent account of the different classes of middlemen, in Ferguson and Vance's *Report on the Tenure and Improvement of Land in Ireland* (1851). These writers, after speaking of the extortionate rents exacted from the under-tenant, say, what is, I believe, indisputably true: 'These rents were higher, were sooner called for, and more rigidly exacted, in proportion as the middleman descended in the scale of society, and approximated to the degree of the peasant.' (P. 184.) On the other hand, the middlemen often took their rents in produce or labour, and this system was not unpopular in Ireland.

wave of extravagance had lately passed over the gentry, both of the first and second degrees. The sudden rise in the value of land which followed the American war and the corn bounties; the substitution of annual for biennial sessions of Parliament, which led to an increased residence in Dublin; and also the more extravagant hospitality which became the fashion during the administration, and through the example, of the Duke of Rutland, are said to have been the chief causes. The volunteer movement, which obliged many country gentlemen to raise large loans upon their land, added seriously to the encumbrances of property; and when the war broke out, great changes occurred. A very competent writer has expressed his belief, that in the twenty or thirty years from 1790, more land was sold under decrees, than during the preceding eighty years.[1]

This was certainly by no means an unmixed evil, and in many cases it was the large leaseholders who became the owners. A very large part of the present smaller landowners of Ireland are probably the descendants of tenants, who originally held their land under leases, and at last obtained possession of it subject to the payment of a small head rent. Two other closely connected agrarian changes, however, of a much more doubtful character, took place at the same time—a raising of rent perhaps more rapid and general than in any other period of Irish history, and a great subdivision of farms.

Of the first fact there can be no doubt, but it is an extremely difficult, if not an impossible thing, to measure with accuracy its amount and its consequences. Looking broadly over Irish agrarian history for the last two centuries, it may, I think, be confidently asserted that it has not been the general custom of the real owners of Irish land to ask the full market, or competitive, rent from their tenants. This custom has prevailed, and does prevail, over a great part of the continent of Europe, and in Ireland it has prevailed to a terrific extent, in the relations of the middlemen and the farmers with their sub-tenants and cottiers, but the rent paid by the tenant to the landlord has usually been governed by other principles. This is the conclusion which must, I think, be forced upon everyone who reads

---

[1] See a very able pamphlet, called *A Detail of Facts relating to Ireland for the last Forty Years* (Dublin, 1822), p. 62.

the account of Arthur Young in the eighteenth century,[1] and it is the conclusion to which the best contemporary investigators have also arrived.[2] It does not rest merely on the testimony of isolated and, perhaps, prejudiced observers. As I have already urged, it is proved beyond all reasonable doubt by the fact that, for more than a century, the immediate tenant almost invariably sub-let his tenancy at an enhanced rent, and that the same process was continued two or three deep; and also by the fact that, wherever it has been the custom to allow the tenant to sell his right to occupy his farm on the terms agreed on with his landlord, this sale of tenant-right has become a constant and lucrative transaction. In our own day we have seen a number of valuable legal rights, which, a few years ago, incontestably belonged to the landlord, transferred without compensation by English legislation to the tenant, with the result, that an estate which, in the eyes of the law, was the sole property of the nominal owner, and which, in innumerable cases, had been recently sold to him by the Government itself, under a parliamentary title, has become, both in law and in fact, a joint property of landlord and tenant. I do not here dilate upon the essentially confiscatory character of this legislation. I refer to it only because it has been mainly justified on the ground that the rights of tenants, which recent legislation has established, had, for many generations, been generally recognised by custom, though entirely without the sanction of the law. We can hardly have a more striking illustration of the blindness and

---

[1] I have examined this subject more fully (iv. 315–317). In Dean Tucker's tract on *Union or Separation*, which was written in 1785, but published by Dr. Clarke in 1799, there is an interesting note on the agrarian system in Ireland. The writer notices (pp. 11, 12) that the rents received in Ireland by the owners in fee, are 'extremely low and moderate,' but that the rents paid by the actual cultivators are much higher than in England. He says: 'The great tracts of land that are given in lease, and divided by the lessee, to be subdivided by other lessees, until the cottager is crushed by the number of those he has to support above him, is a sore and crying evil.'

[2] Thus the Bessborough Commission in 1881 summed up the results of a careful examination into this point. 'Though the amount of rent was always at the discretion of the landlord, and the tenant had, in reality, no voice in regulating what he had to pay, nevertheless it was unusual to exact what in England would have been considered as a full or fair commercial rent. Such a rent over many of the larger estates, the owners of which were resident, and took an interest in the welfare of their tenants, it has never been the custom to demand. The example has been largely followed, and is, to the present day, rather the rule than the exception in Ireland.' (*Report*, p. 3.)

the dishonesty that party spirit can produce, than the fact that, the very politicians who have contended that such rights should be transferred by law, on the ground of immemorial usage, have also, in many instances, described the men on whose properties such rights had for generations existed without legal sanction, as a class of rapacious and extortionate tyrants.

These facts are, indeed, quite compatible with great and general faults of negligence on the part of the landlord class, with many instances of casual oppression, and with much defect of sympathy between the landlord and tenant, but they are not compatible with a state of society in which the relations between these two classes are generally regulated on the principles of strict competition. There have been, however, short periods in Irish history which were, in this respect, exceptional, and in which the sharp competition that existed in the lower stages of the Irish land markets extended to the direct relations between landlord and tenant, and there is reason to believe that the last fifteen years of the eighteenth century formed such a period. The corn bounties and the war prices had raised suddenly and immensely the profits of farming, and the landlords were becoming acutely sensible of how large a proportion of the profits of their estates had been intercepted by middlemen. A traveller mentions one case—which was probably by no means extraordinary—of a single large middleman, who derived a revenue of not less than 4,000$l.$ a year from the difference between the rent which he paid to the owner of the soil and the rent which he exacted from his sub-tenants.[1] It appeared from an inquiry instituted in 1799, that cottiers paid in rent to the farmers on an average three times as much, and sometimes four times as much, as the farmer paid for the same quantity of land to the landlord;[2] and as the old leases fell in, the pernicious system of canting, which had long flourished in the lower strata of the agrarian community, began to extend widely to the dealings of landlords with their tenants.

It is stated, indeed, by some considerable authorities, to have been at this time extremely general. Thus, when the Catholics complained, in 1793, that without the suffrage they were at a

---

[1] Hoare's *Tour in Ireland*, p. 308.
[2] Whitley Stokes's *Observations on the Population and Resources of Ireland* (1821), pp. 25–27.

disadvantage as farmers, because Protestant landlords naturally gave the preference, in the competition for farms, to those who could support them at the elections, Duigenan answered: 'It was now the almost universal mode of letting land in Ireland, for the landlord to advertise his lands at the expiration of a lease, to be let to the best and highest bidder, and to let them accordingly, without considering the religion of the tenant, but merely his solvency and the price he offers.'[1] 'There is hardly an estate,' said Ogle a few years earlier, 'which is not let to the highest penny, and much above its value.'[2] This may refer mainly to the dealings of middlemen with sub-tenants; but Crumpe, who published his 'Essay on the best Means of Employing the People' in 1793, strongly maintained, in opposition to Arthur Young, that 'the proportionate rent' derived by the landlord was higher in Ireland than in England. It is true, he said, that the middlemen 'are the class from which the poor principally experience that oppression to which, we have asserted, they are still subject,' but he described the system pursued by the landlords when leases fell in, as wholly different from that in England. 'When a lease is expired, in place of such an amicable adjustment [as takes place in England], the lands are advertised to be let to the highest bidder; the proposals of each are kept secret, and by this unfair species of auction, a promise of exorbitant rent is obtained, very frequently to the exclusion of the former occupier, who is considered as having no stronger claim to them than the most perfect stranger, unless he exceed him in the amount of the proposed rent.'[3]

Several other almost equally emphatic statements may be collected, especially from the speeches and writings of those who endeavoured to defend the tithe system in Ireland, and who usually made it their object to prove that rent rather than tithe was the great burden on the poor. That these statements were

[1] *Irish Parl. Deb.* xiii. 114.
[2] Ibid. vi. 435.
[3] Crumpe's *Essay*, pp. 232–235. The reader may find some more information on the subject, and a very strong statement of the extent to which 'canting' prevailed, in a pamphlet called *Reflections on the best Means of securing Tranquillity, submitted to the Country Gentlemen,* by P. Winter, Esq. (Dublin, 1796.) As early as 1731, Dobbs stated that, 'Agents, particularly of those noblemen or gentlemen who reside in England, or at a distance from their estates, who have been empowered to treat with tenants and give leases, to ingratiate themselves with their employers ... have, in some places, taken proposals sealed up, under a promise to divulge none of the names but that of the person who offered most, whose proposal was to be accepted.' (Dobbs *On Irish Trade,* part ii. p. 79.)

far too general, appears to me evident. The great part which leaseholders played in the management of estates, gave them enormous advantages in bargaining for renewals with a negligent landlord class. The records, traditions, and customs of most Irish estates, and the judgment of the most careful investigators, will, I believe, show that a long continuance of the same families as tenants on the same estates [1] has been at least as characteristic of Ireland as of England; and the fact, which appears universally admitted, that agriculture in all its gradations was steadily improving in the last decades of the century, proves that though rents had risen rapidly, they had not reached a point which is incompatible with prosperity.[2] Much of the change probably took place only in the upper tenancies, and left the condition of the occupiers of the soil unaltered; and it must be added that, within certain limits, the raising of rent was not merely consistent with, but powerfully productive of, increased agrarian prosperity. Arthur Young—who considered the rental of Ireland in his time abnormally low—is but

[1] See, e.g., the remarks of Dr. Sigerson (a writer who is violently prejudiced against the landlord class), on the confidence of the tenants on some large estates, 'in a good old modus—namely, that their land would never be given to another tenant [on the expiration of their lease], so long as they were able and willing to pay a reasonable raised rent.' (Sigerson's *Hist. of Land Tenures in Ireland*, pp. 296, 297.) See, too, Miss Edgeworth's account of her father's policy in renewing leases. (*Life of R. L. Edgeworth*, ii. 15, 16.)

[2] Newenham, in his *View of the Circumstances of Ireland*, published in 1809, says: 'About thirty years ago, when Mr. Young travelled through Ireland, the average price of day labour was 6½d. It now appears, by the statistical surveys of sixteen counties, by parochial returns from three others, and by information from different parts of the rest, to be 10½d. So that in thirty years it has risen about two-thirds, which is infinitely more than it had risen in any former period of equal extent.... Since the year 1782, the rent of land, which, a short time before that year, had begun to fall in many places, has been much more than doubled in all parts of Ireland one with another, more than trebled in many.... If Mr. Young ... was grounded in computing the rental of Ireland at six millions in 1778, there can be no hesitation in stating it as upwards of fifteen millions at present, exclusive of the ground rent of the houses in the different towns.... Since the year 1789, the imports have more than doubled; the exports also, if the real value be taken, have more than doubled.' (Pp. 230–234.) Crumpe, while maintaining that the rental of Ireland was unduly high, acknowledges at the same time that, 'The situation of the peasant has, since the pacification of the kingdom, but more especially since the settlement of its constitution in 1782, been daily improving.' (*Essay on the Employment of the Poor*, p. 201.) Miss Edgeworth's father, writing about 1808, and resuming his experience of Ireland since 1769, says: 'Since the time of which I write, the people of Ireland have improved more than any other people in Europe.' (*Life of R. L. Edgeworth*, i. 229) See, too, his daughter's testimony (ii. 1, 2); and the facts I have myself collected, vol. vi. pp. 437, 438.

one of many observers, who noticed how little the system of long leases at very low rents contributed to the prosperity of the country and the comfort of the tenants. It was remarked that it was precisely on estates so situated that there was most subdivision and least improvement, the most slovenly cultivation, and the lowest standard of comfort, and that they often presented in these respects a striking contrast to adjoining estates let at reasonable rents and for terms of twenty-one years.[1] It must be added also, that the period we are considering was not a period of great evictions, dissociating an agricultural population from the soil. When pasture-land was gaining on tillage, a great displacement of population necessarily occurred. But with the strong impetus towards tillage in the closing years of the eighteenth century, the tendency was reversed, and there was therefore as yet no want of farms for industrious farmers.

The process of subdivision, and the rapid increase of population which accompanied it, had begun, and the most powerful motives, moral, economical, and political, were hastening the change. The priests, partly from considerations of morality, and partly from obvious considerations of self-interest, have always encouraged early marriages; and the strong domestic feeling, which is one of the most amiable characteristics of the Irish peasants, has always led the Irish farmer to desire to settle his children on detached portions of his farm. The increase of tillage, through the English demand for corn, through the corn bounties, and through the high prices that followed the war, made it for the advantage of the landlords to take the course which was incontestably the most popular, and place no restraint

---

[1] This is very emphatically stated in Ferguson and Vance's *Report on the Relation of Landlord and Tenant in Ireland* (1851), p. 62. I may add two authorities who will not be suspected of any landlord prejudice. Wolfe Tone writes in his diary: 'A farm at a smart rent always better cultivated than one at a low rent—probable enough.' (Tone's *Memoirs*, i. 148.) Theobald McKenna, in his Essay on Parliamentary Reform, which was published in 1793, says: 'In several parts of Ireland the rents have been tripled, nay quadrupled, within forty years past. And this was not so much the effect as the cause of national prosperity, for the great wealth of a country may frequently lie dormant, if the inhabitants, residing listlessly upon the surface, will not exert themselves to investigate its resources. Before the above-mentioned period, when rent was very low and other taxes little known, half the year was lavished in carousing. But so soon as labour became compulsory, fortunes have been raised both for the tenantry and landlords, and the civilisation of the country has advanced materially.' (McKenna's *Political Essays*, p. 187.)

upon subdivision. The bias of the law was in the same direction. It was still the prevailing belief, that a rapidly multiplying population was the first condition of national prosperity. Clauses in leases forbidding sub-letting under penalties, were looked upon as tyrannical, and contrary to the public interest. The law courts frequently decided against their validity; the difficulty of obtaining formal legal proof of sub-letting was very great, and it was found almost impossible to induce juries to find verdicts enforcing the penal covenants.[1]

Whitley Stokes, who decidedly favoured the movement of subdivision, and whose tracts throw much light upon this period of agrarian history, gives an illustration of the process which was going on. 'A gentleman in the county of Cork,' he says, 'made a fortune by purchasing or renting large tracts of land, and setting it in as small portions as the people wished. He informed me in the year 1798 that he had eighty tenants, who paid each 12*l.* or less for their entire rent, and he found that they paid more regularly than those who had larger farms,[2] and he thought this was generally the case in the county of Cork. . . . It very seldom happened in his neighbourhood that the immediate occupiers of the land broke; they who did were oftener farmers who paid from 50*l.* to 100*l.* a year, than those who paid 12*l.* or under.' Stokes insists much on the value of small farms in preventing mendicancy, and he adds some remarks which, coming from an excellent man of science, whose sympathies were strongly popular, and who actually joined the United Irishmen through the purest motives of philanthropy, throw an instructive light on the ideas of the time. He considered that the gentry erred rather by repressing than by encouraging sub-letting, and that the system of middlemen was highly advantageous to the country. 'If we could prove,' he says, 'to the satisfaction of impartial persons, that further subdivision of land is valuable to the working people of Ireland, and that they are willing to pay largely for the advantage, it is not to be wondered at, that the landlords should be slow to adopt

---

[1] See the remarks of Mr. H. Jephson, *Notes on Irish Questions*, p. 25. It was not till after the war, that this policy was reversed. See, too, Ferguson and Vance's *Report*, pp. 178-189.

[2] Arthur Young had noticed that the smaller farmers were 'the best pay' on the estates, 'the intermediate gentleman tenants the worst.' (*Tour in Ireland*, ii. 99.)

such a plan. They dread with reason the dealing with great numbers of the lower class of people. The attempt is painful, hazardous. It is not every gentleman who is fit for it. Fortunes have been made by this process, but the difficulties will not be encountered by those who have inherited property, and have been reared in refinement or indulgence. This state of things produces the middleman. The middleman is necessary to Ireland, as the shopkeeper is necessary to London. The London consumer cannot deal conveniently with the merchant, nor the Irish small farmer with the nobleman or gentleman who possesses a large estate. . . . If you impede the appointment of middlemen, there will be fewer small farms, and higher prices will be given for them. . . . So far from discouraging middlemen, I would venture to recommend again, as I did twenty-one years ago, that a company should be formed for purchasing estates as they came to market, and subdividing them.'[1]

The Act of 1793, granting votes to Catholic forty-shilling freeholders, gave an additional impulse to the movement of subdivision, by making it the interest of each landlord to multiply the votes that he could command. By many writers, indeed, this Act has been represented as the main cause, but this view is a gross and manifest exaggeration.[2] When the tenant class were anxious to subdivide, and when the landlord class had strong economical reasons for allowing them to do so, the result could hardly have been doubtful, and political motives can have only slightly accelerated it. Land jobbers multiplied in the last years of the century, because the trade had become very profitable; leaseholders subdivided because it was their plain interest to do so, and in similar circumstances similar evils will inevitably appear. It is not necessary to look to remote or barbarous countries for a parallel. In the last few years, parliamentary inquiries have disclosed exactly the same evils, springing from the same cause, in great districts of London and of our provincial towns. We find there, all the leading features of the Irish

---

[1] Stokes's *Observations on the Population and Resources of Ireland* (1822), pp. 29–31. Edgeworth seems to have been one of the few landlords who set his face against subdivision, by inserting in all his leases, and stringently enforcing, 'alienation fines.' (*Memoirs*, ii. 17, 18.)

[2] I have seen it stated, that the subdivision of farms was nowhere greater than on glebe and other Church lands, where political motives can hardly have applied.

agrarian system at the close of the eighteenth century: landlords who have let their land for a long period, and have thus lost all power of management and control; leaseholders who, as the pressure of population becomes more intense, find it their interest to subdivide their holdings into minute fractions; a whole race of speculators in poor men's dwellings; rents forced by the competition of the very poor to an enormous height; an excessive congestion of population; an utter neglect of the conditions of comfort and health. In Paris, under land laws very different from those of England, precisely similar signs have appeared. An excellent observer, who has lately described the condition of the overcrowded workmen's quarters there, writes: 'The wretched houses they contain, are generally constructed by a speculator of a low order, who has taken the land at a long lease, and built, in the most economical and defective manner, cabins of wood and plaster, which he lets at exorbitant prices—140 or 200 francs a year for a room. He obtains from his speculation 20 to 25 per cent., which assures him a little fortune at the expiration of his lease, especially if he has also carried on the trade of spirit dealer. . . . It is curious to observe the analogy between these Paris quarters and the pestilential courts in London, where a principal tenant, who also makes 20 to 25 per cent. by the transaction, and who holds his houses under a very long lease, extorts enormous rents from wretched sub-tenants.'[1]

It is not less curious, I think, or less instructive, to trace the analogy of these things with the excessive subdivision of land, the rapid rise of rents, and the multiplication of a pauper tenantry in Ireland in the closing years of the eighteenth century. The change was still far from its maturity, and the effects were as yet very various. Farmers who held their farms under leases made before the corn bounties and the war, made rapid fortunes. The high price of farm produce, increased wages, and the general alteration of all the conditions of agriculture, opened out many paths of wealth to skill, enterprise, cunning, and industry; but the great majority of the Irish farmers had none of these qualities, and the sudden rise in rents and prices, and the displace-

---

[1] Much evidence on this subject is collected by M. Raffalovich in his very valuable little work, Le Logement de l'Ouvrier. See especially pp. 97, 138, 139, 269, 270.

ment of old tenants by others who offered larger rents, contributed much to swell the agrarian discontent which found its expression in the Defender outrages. At the basis of the Irish agrarian system there was still a great mass of abject poverty, and it is by no means certain that it had diminished. The price of labour had indeed risen considerably, but not in all parts of the island, and there had been a considerable and general rise in the price both of oatmeal and potatoes, the two principal articles of the food of the labourer.[1] The pictures of the misery and the oppression of the cottiers and migratory labourers, which I have extracted from writings twenty or thirty years earlier, might all be paralleled in the period we are considering; and if the area of prosperity was enlarged, reckless marriages, and the consequent rapid increase of population, were then, as always, most conspicuous among the most wretched, the most ignorant, and the most improvident. It was still true that, at the beginning of every autumn, the roads were crowded with barefooted and half-naked mountaineers, who were travelling on foot 150 or 200 miles, to work for the harvest in England, where they commonly fell into the hands of contractors known as 'spalpeen brokers,' who distributed them among the farmers, intercepted a substantial part of their scanty wages, and imposed on them an amount of labour which few West Indian planters would have exacted from their negroes.[2] It was still true, that it was a common thing for large farmers, whose land included barren mountain tracts, to place cottiers on these lands in order to reclaim them, and to turn them adrift as soon as by hard labour they had made them productive.[3] It was still true, that cottiers were often obliged to work out the extravagant rents

---

[1] See the report of a committee to inquire into the state of the labouring poor, appointed by the Whig Club in 1796. (Grattan's *Life*, iv. 246-248.) Whitley Stokes was of opinion that, though the price of labour had nominally risen, it had not done so in proportion to the cost of provisions. The landlord and the farmer, he said, were doing well, through the increase of the value of land and farm produce, but not the cottier. (*Projects for re-establishing Internal Peace in Ireland.* Dublin, 1799.)

[2] See Bell's *Description of the Condition and Manners of the Peasantry of Ireland between* 1780 *and* 1790 (London, 1804), pp. 10-12—a book of great and painful interest—and also the report of the Whig Club on the state of the labouring poor. (Grattan's *Life*, iv. 246-248.)

[3] Bell's *Description*, p. 7. In that remarkable book, *Uncle Pat's Cabin*, by Upton, which is one of the truest and most vivid pictures of the present condition of the Irish labourer, exactly the same grievance is described as still existing.

that were charged for their potato plots, at the rate of fourpence and fivepence a day; that their sole food, in many districts, was potatoes mixed with the milk that remained when the butter had been made; that during part of the year they were often reduced to potatoes and water; and that even potatoes could not always be counted on.

In one of the tracts of Whitley Stokes, there is a terrible picture of the condition of the poorest Irishmen, at a time which has been considered the most prosperous in Irish history. 'Generally,' he wrote, 'the cottier has but an acre. Sometimes, I know it from personal inquiry, in situations remote from any town, he pays three guineas a year for a house whose first cost was certainly not five, and a rood of ground. In some places the cottier pays four times the rent of the farmer, and in one place where this happened, the cottiers were so distressed, that they could afford themselves but one meal a day, and that consisted of potatoes and of butter milk, for which they paid a penny a quart, and they could never afford to procure themselves turf; and that place was the hill of Oulart,' the spot in Wexford where the most formidable portion of the rebellion of 1798 took its rise. In many places, the same writer tells us, the poor were exposed to a variety of diseases, and especially to putrid diseases, from the poorness of their diet or the exclusive use of the potato. 'In Kerry,' he says, 'they live so low, that I am assured by a medical man, that the addition of any small quantity of butter to their potatoes, is used as a cordial when they are ill, with evident advantage.'[1]

This mass of extreme and chronic poverty was now beginning to surge with wild and indefinite hopes, and busy missionaries were actively fanning the flame. As outrages multiplied, the landlord had every inducement to leave his estate, and the system of tenure existing in Ireland made his absence peculiarly

---

[1] Whitley Stokes's *Projects for reestablishing Internal Peace in Ireland*, p. 9. 'One of the principal causes of the rebellion, though not hitherto mentioned by any person, is the extraordinary increase in the population of Ireland, which has furnished an opportunity to greedy jobbers in land to raise the price of small farms infinitely beyond their real value. This has brought distress, poverty, and disaffection on the wretched peasantry, who are under an absolute necessity (from their total want of all other means of existence), to promise whatever rent their immediate landlord shall fix upon their hovel or little farm.' (R. Griffith to Pelham, July 31, 1798. *Pelham MSS.*)

easy. Since the world began, no large class of men have ever discharged efficiently, dangerous, distasteful, and laborious functions, if they had no inducement to do so except the highest sense of duty, and this was rapidly coming to be the position of the landlord, whose lot was cast in the midst of the anarchy of Defenderism. It was not a natural thing that a landlord should have great power, when his land was placed beyond his control by the system of long leases, and the authority which Irish landlords had for so many years exercised under this system, was to a great degree artificial. Among the many contradictions and anomalies of Irish life, nothing is more curious than the strong feudal attachment and reverence that frequently grew up between the resident Protestant landlord and his Catholic tenantry, in spite of all differences of race and creed and traditions. It is a fact which is attested by everything we know of Irish life in the eighteenth century, and it subsisted side by side with the Whiteboy outrages, with vivid memories of the old confiscations, and with many other indications of war against property. The country gentleman had many qualities, not all of them very estimable, that were eminently popular among the people—a lavish hospitality, keen sporting tastes, great courage in duels, a careless, thriftless, good-natured ostentation, a tone of absolute authority and command, mixing curiously with extreme familiarity, in dealing with inferiors; a great knowledge of their character, and a great consideration for their customs and prejudices. In the management of his property there was a combination of negligence and indulgence, which has always been peculiarly popular in Ireland. His kitchen was open to all comers from his estate; he seldom or never interfered when his tenants wished to settle their children on a portion of his land, or insisted on much punctuality of payment, and he laid great stress on hereditary attachment to his family. The pride of family and of county influence was nowhere stronger than in Ireland, and it was fully shared by the humblest dependant.

The feudal spirit was clearly reflected in the customs and contracts of land; clauses were constantly inserted in leases, obliging tenants to furnish their landlords with horses or labour for several days in the year, or with tributes of poultry, turkeys, or geese; there were sometimes clauses, which fully coincided with the political ethics of the Irish tenant, obliging the leaseholder to vote always with his landlord; there was the curious custom of 'sealing money'—a perquisite given to the squire's wife by the tenant on the sealing of their leases.[1] The penal code concentrated immense magisterial and administrative powers in the hands of the landlord class, and formed a tradition which long survived the laws, while the middlemen diverted from them much of the unpopularity which in times of distress might have attached to them. The landlord was the arbiter of innumerable disputes; he often exercised his influence as magistrate to protect his tenants who were in difficulties through faction fights or illicit distilling, and they in their turn were always ready to keep the bailiff from his door. There was on neither side much regard for law, but the landlord usually maintained both his authority and his popularity.

A governing type was developed in the class, which was very remote from modern English ideas, but which was well adapted to the conditions under which they lived. The admirable picture which Miss Edgeworth has drawn in 'Ormond,' of the relations between King Corney and his people, will enable the reader to understand it. The Irish landlords were able, without the assistance of any armed constabulary, to keep the country quiet during the greater part of the eighteenth century, even in times of war, when it was almost denuded of troops. They again and again suppressed Whiteboy disturbances, by parties raised among their own tenantry; and when they placed themselves at the head of the volunteer movement, the nation followed them with enthusiasm. A class who were capable of these things may have had many faults, but they can have been neither impotent nor unpopular.

I have already quoted the well-known description, which Arthur Young gave in 1779, of the absolute authority exercised at that time by a Protestant landlord over his Catholic tenantry.

---

[1] Miss Edgeworth describes most of these customs in *Castle Rackrent*. See, too, the very curious and instructive pictures of Irish country life, in her continuation of the life of her father, and also in *Ormond* and the *Absentee*. A gentleman informed me, only a few years ago, that he found the clause relating to votes in one of his old leases. Maxwell's *Wild Sports of the West* belongs to a somewhat later period, but it illustrates, I believe very truly, the kind of feeling that often prevailed between the gentry and their tenants.

'The power and influence of a resident landlord,' he said in another place, ' is so great in Ireland, that whatever system he adopts, be it well or ill imagined, he is much more able to introduce or accomplish it, than Englishmen can well have an idea of.'[1] But under the influence of the Defender movement, this state of things in many districts was rapidly changing. How great an alteration had taken place in fifteen years, is clearly shown by the diagnosis which Camden sent to England of the causes of Irish disturbances. 'From the nature of the tenures they grant,' he writes, 'the gentry who inhabit this kingdom have not the weight they might otherwise have in the country. From the uncultivated state of considerable parts of the kingdom, the landlords are induced to give leases for years under the terms of houses being built and improvements made upon the land. This mode puts the tenant out of the power of the landlord, and he considers himself as possessing such a right in the land, and for so long a term, as to make him extremely indifferent to the good opinion of his lord; and in proportion as feudal notions have been dissipated, the rights of man have been promulgated, and these independent tenants have opportunities enough of being informed of the little influence which their landlords have over them. These persons having seen that, in times of danger, England has been induced to give way to the threatening appearances in this country, they are encouraged by the possibility of their being again able to carry their favourite notions by a perseverance in tumult and outrage, which they conceive will weary instead of exasperate the more quiet parts of the kingdom.'[2]

These last words might have been written in our own day, and they illustrate curiously the persistence of the same morbid influences in Irish affairs. The state of the country required strong remedies, remedies beyond the law as it was administered in England. Nothing can be more fatuous than to suppose, that it is possible to govern a disaffected country on exactly the same principles or by the same methods as a loyal country; that organised crime, taking a form nearly akin to rebellion, and supported by the sympathies of a great portion of the population, can be mastered by a machinery which is intended only

[1] Young's *Tour*, ii. 105.   [2] Camden to Portland, Sept. 25, 1795.

to deal with the isolated instances of individual depravity. It was perfectly reasonable, too, and perfectly in accordance with the best English precedents, that new outbursts of crime should be encountered by special laws of unusual severity. Such had been in England the 'Stabbing Act,' attributed to the frequent quarrels between English and Scotch at the court of James I.; the Coventry Act of Charles II. against maiming and disfiguring the person; the 'Waltham Black Act' of George I., intended to repress the cruelties and depredations of the Hampshire poachers. Legislation of this kind has been frequent in Ireland, and it may be abundantly justified. At the same time, it was the first duty of the Government, in combating the spirit of illegality, to be itself legal, and no more fatal blow could be given to the cause of order, than for those who were charged with supporting it, to defy the restraints of the law. This was what actually happened in Ireland. Lord Carhampton was charged with the pacification of Connaught, and under his direction the magistrates took a great number of those whom they suspected of being Defenders, and without sentence, without trial, without even a colour of legality, they sent them to serve in the King's fleet—a tender sailing along the coast to receive them.[1]

The measure was as completely illegal as the proceedings of the Defenders themselves, and it must not be confounded with an ordinary press. It was not professional sailors, but for the most part agricultural labourers, many of whom had never even seen the sea, who were suddenly torn from their families and

[1] Plowden, ii. 537, 538; Grattan's *Life*, iv. 240; McNevin's *Pieces of Irish History*, p. 112. Lord Camden says: 'A measure which, I am afraid, is not very defensible, and to which I have taken the utmost care not to give either my own individual consent or that of Government, has contributed very much to alarm these persons [the Defenders]. The magistrates in several districts, not finding that the regular mode of endeavouring to convict these offenders had the effect which was expected, have, in cases where they were convinced of the guilt of the person, sent them on board the tender, and entered them for the King's service. I am afraid some of the magistrates have been incautious enough, not to carry on this measure so secretly as to have escaped the notice of the public. . . . It has certainly, however, done much to quiet the country, and I shall of course take care to protect these gentlemen as far as I am enabled with propriety to do so.' (Camden to Portland, Nov. 6, 1795.) In another letter he speaks of 'the proceeding of the magistrates in sending *acquitted* Defenders to sea;' and adds: 'Lord Carhampton, whom I sent during the last year into the province of Connaught, found it necessary to act in some instances in a summary manner, and certainly did not confine himself to the strict rules of law.' (Ibid. Jan. 22, 1796.) See, too, the letter I have quoted, p. 149.

their homes, and sent to the war-ships, to pestilential climates, and to a great naval war. To such men the fate was more terrible than death, and if the measure produced for a time the tranquillity of consternation, it left behind it the seeds of the most enduring and vindictive animosity. It has been stated, that more than one thousand persons were thus illegally transported. In general the victims and their friends were too poor and helpless to seek legal redress, but in a few cases writs of Habeas Corpus were applied for and granted, when the Government interposed, and induced Parliament to pass an Act of indemnity stopping the prosecutions, and legalising all that had been done. Thus, in the words of Grattan, 'the poor were stricken out of the protection of the law, and the rich out of its penalties.'[1]

In the meantime, another and most formidable and persistent element of disturbance was growing up in the North. The year 1795 is very memorable in Irish history, as the year of the formation of the Orange Society, and the beginning of the most serious disturbances in the county of Armagh.

It is with a feeling of unfeigned diffidence that I enter upon this branch of my narrative. Our authentic materials are so scanty, and so steeped in party and sectarian animosity, that a writer who has done his utmost to clear his mind from prejudice, and bring together with impartiality the conflicting statements of partisans, will still, if he is a wise man, always doubt whether he has succeeded in painting with perfect fidelity the delicate gradations of provocation, palliation, and guilt. The old popular feud between the lower ranks of papists and Presbyterians in the northern counties is easy to understand, and it is not less easy

---

[1] 36 Geo. III. c. 6. Writing to Pelham, Camden says: 'The country is much quieter, and I believe Lord Carhampton's *doctrine* has done a great deal of good, although he has carried it on rather too publicly. I understand he will certainly have actions brought against him for his conduct in Roscommon; and I think it probable that this measure is so notorious, that it will be a subject for parliamentary inquiry, and that a Bill of indemnity may be necessary to cover the magistrates, who have exerted themselves so zealously and yet so indiscreetly.' (Camden to Pelham, Oct. 30, 1795.) In a pamphlet, which had a great circulation, defending Lord Carhampton's treatment of the Defenders, it is said: 'If it please your Excellency to permit them to go to war with us, and will permit us only to go to law with them, it will not require the second sight of a Scotchman to foretell the issue.' (*Considerations of the Situation to which Ireland is reduced by the Government of Lord Camden*, 6th edit. 1798.)

to see how the recent course of Irish politics had increased it. A class which had enjoyed and gloried in uncontested ascendency, found this ascendency passing from its hands. A class which had formerly been in subjection, was elated by new privileges, and looked forward to a complete abolition of political disabilities. Catholic and Protestant tenants came into a new competition, and the demeanour of Catholics towards Protestants was sensibly changed. There were boasts in taverns and at fairs, that the Protestants would speedily be swept away from the land and the descendants of the old proprietors restored, and it was soon known that Catholics all over the country were forming themselves into committees or societies, and were electing representatives for a great Catholic convention at Dublin. The riots and outrages of the Peep of Day Boys and Defenders had embittered the feeling on both sides. In spite of the strenuous efforts of some of the principal gentry of the county, and especially of Lord Charlemont and Mr. Richardson, and in spite, too, of the hanging or public flogging of several culprits of both creeds, these riots had continued at short intervals for ten years before the Orange Society was established.[1]

Members of one or other creed were attacked and insulted as they went to their places of worship. There were fights on the high roads, at fairs, wakes, markets, and country sports, and there were occasionally crimes of a much deeper dye. At a place called Forkhill, near Dundalk, a gentleman named Jackson, who died in 1787, left a considerable property for the purpose of educating a number of children of the Established Church as weavers or in other trades; providing them with looms when their education was finished, and settling them upon the estate. No displacement of old tenants was contemplated, but some park and waste land was colonised with industrious Protestants; and the terms of the will directed, that when vacancies occurred, the pupils in Jackson's schools should be settled in small holdings in preference to other claimants. The object was to plant a nucleus of industry and order in the midst of a savage, bigoted, idle, and

[1] Vol. vi. p. 450. Many curious particulars about these riots, and the means taken to suppress them, will be found in a manuscript, *Historical View of Orangism*, in the Stowe MSS. in the Irish Academy. See, too, a pamphlet, bitterly hostile to the Government, but written with considerable knowledge, called, *A View of the present State of Ireland, and of the Disturbances in that Country*. (London, 1797.)

entirely lawless population, who seem to have been allowed for many years to live and to multiply, without any kind of interference, guidance, or control.

Among the trustees of the charity was a very intelligent and liberal-minded clergyman named Hudson, who was an intimate friend, and a frequent correspondent, of Lord Charlemont. In an interesting letter, written at the end of 1789, he describes how he was endeavouring to introduce some decent manufacturers into this wild district, and what formidable obstacles he encountered. 'I hope,' he adds, 'to make our savages happy against their will, by establishing trade and industry among them.' He noticed 'how many traces of savage life' still remained in the population; 'the same laziness and improvidence, the same unrelenting ferocity in their combats, the same love of intoxication, the same hereditary animosities, handed down from generation to generation. Add to this, that they are all related to each other, and I believe there are not at this moment ten families in the parish which are not related to every other in it. ... It unfortunately happened that this estate was for thirty-five years possessed by the most indolent man on earth. He kept more than half of it waste during that time, on which they, in fact, subsisted. The idea of its being let, set them mad. A report has been industriously spread, that several of the old tenants had been dispossessed, and that this gave rise to a combination here. I do most solemnly assure your lordship, that in no one instance has even an acre been taken from any man. ... They were not only continued in their old possession with some addition, but an abatement of rent to the amount of 117*l*. was to have been made them at the very time they broke out, and some hundreds of arrears were actually forgiven. All would not do. They found some Protestants had taken land, whom they determined to drive out. They therefore assembled the Defenders from all parts of the country, and struck such horror that none of those Protestants but half a dozen ever appeared here afterwards.'[1]

The school, however, still went on and flourished, and at last, in the beginning of 1791, a long series of outrages culmi-

---

[1] Charlemont MSS. (Irish Academy). See, too, the report of the Endowed Schools Commissioners for Ireland (1858), iii. 460, and the Irish statute, 29 Geo. III. c. 3. Jackson's charity is still flourishing, and celebrated its centenary in 1888.

nated in one of those ghastly crimes which make men's blood boil in their veins. A very excellent Protestant schoolmaster named Berkeley was the most successful of the teachers. Hudson notices that, though he was only paid by the trustees for teaching sixty scholars, he had for six months been teaching upwards of a hundred without any additional charge. At last one evening a party of forty or fifty men entered his house. They stabbed him in several places. They cut out his tongue, and they cut off several of his fingers. They mangled his wife in the same way and in other ways also, and they then proceeded to mutilate hideously a boy of thirteen. No other reason was assigned, except that Berkeley was a prominent member of the new colony which had been planted in the district. The party plundered the house, and they then marched triumphantly along the road with lighted torches. The feeling of the neighbourhood was indisputably with them. Only one of the culprits was brought to justice; he would give no evidence against his accomplices, and he went to the gallows attended by his priest, and maintaining, it is said, all the demeanour of a martyr.[1]

Outrages, however, were by no means confined to one side, and the violent alternation of hope and despondency that followed the appointment and the recall of Lord Fitzwilliam, the constant rumours of rebellion and invasion, and the great extension of the Defender movement through Ireland, contributed to aggravate the situation. In the county of Armagh the Protestants were decidedly in the ascendant, but there was a considerable minority of Catholics, who were generally Defenders, and there were numerous collisions between the two parties.

[1] See, for the particulars of this crime, a letter of Hudson to Francis Dobbs (Jan. 29, 1791), in the Charlemont MSS., as well as some later letters from Hudson, and from a gentleman named Prentice, to Charlemont. See, too, the documents on the subject collected by Musgrave. (*Rebellions in Ireland*, pp. 59–63.) Colonel Verner related all the circumstances of this crime, before the Parliamentary Committee on the Orange Society, in 1835. (*Report*, quest. 30.) He says, Berkeley asked those who were torturing him, whether he had ever injured them. They said not; 'but this was the beginning of what all his sort might expect.' Colonel Verner says that this crime, and especially this declaration, chiefly produced the hostility to the Catholics in the North. He acknowledges, however, that the Peep of Day Boys had previously existed. During the disturbances of 1798, Dean Warburton wrote urging the expediency of arresting two priests of infamous character, and he mentioned that one of them had been parish priest at Forkhill, and was removed by his bishop, as he was supposed to have been concerned in the outrage on the schoolmaster there. (Dean Warburton to Cooke, May 29, 1798. I.S.P.O.)

THE ORANGE SOCIETY.

In September 1795 riots broke out in this county, which continued for some days, but at length the parish priest on the one side, and a gentleman named Atkinson on the other, succeeded in so far appeasing the quarrel that the combatants formally agreed to a truce, and were about to retire to their homes, when a new party of Defenders, who had marched from the adjoining counties to the assistance of their brethren, appeared upon the scene, and on September 21 they attacked the Protestants at a place called the Diamond. The Catholics on this occasion were certainly the aggressors, and they appear to have considerably outnumbered their antagonists, but the Protestants were better posted, better armed, and better organised. A serious conflict ensued, and the Catholics were completely defeated, leaving a large number—probably twenty or thirty—dead upon the field.[1]

It was on the evening of the day on which the battle of the Diamond was fought, that the Orange Society was formed. It was at first a league of mutual defence, binding its members to maintain the laws and the peace of the country, and also the Protestant Constitution. No Catholic was to be admitted into the society, and the members were bound by oath not to reveal its secrets. The doctrine of Fitzgibbon, that the King, by assenting to Catholic emancipation, would invalidate his title to the throne, was remarkably reflected in the oath of the Orangemen, which bound them to defend the King and his heirs 'so long as he or they support the Protestant ascendency.'[2] The society took its name from William of Orange, the conqueror of the Catholics, and it agreed to celebrate annually the battle of the Boyne.

In this respect there was nothing in it particularly novel. Protestant associations, for the purpose of commemorating the events and maintaining the principles of the Revolution, had long been known. Such a society had been founded at Exeter immediately after the Revolution. Such a society, under the name of 'The Old Revolution Club,' had long existed

---

[1] See, for the particulars of the battle of the Diamond, the *Parliamentary Report* of 1835 on the Orange Association, questions 80–84, 8937–8955. See, too, McNevin's *Pieces of Irish History*, pp. 114, 115; Plowden, ii. 539. The evidence collected in the *Parliamentary Report* referred to, furnishes the fullest particulars about the history of Orangism.

[2] The conditional oath of allegiance was exchanged, about 1821, for the ordinary oath, and that was abolished in 1825.

in Scotland.[1] In Ireland, too, the Revolution of 1688 was so closely connected with the disposition of property and power, that it naturally assumed a transcendent importance, and the commemorations which are commonly associated with the Orange Society were in truth of a much earlier date. The twelfth of July—which by a confusion between the old and new styles was regarded as the anniversary of both the battle of the Boyne and the battle of Aghrim[2]—and the relief of Londonderry were annually commemorated in Ireland long before the Orange Society existed. From the time of the Revolution till the beginning of the nineteenth century, November 4, which was the birthday of William III., was celebrated in Dublin with the greatest pomp. The Lord Lieutenant held a court, and followed by the Chancellor, the judges, the lord mayor, and a long train of the nobility and gentry, he paraded in state round the statue of William III. in College Green. At the drawing-room the ladies appeared decorated with orange ribbons,[3] and orange cockades were worn by the soldiers. These commemorations were universally recognised as mere manifestations of loyalty to the Constitution and the dynasty, and were fully countenanced by men who were very friendly to the Catholics. The volunteers, who did so much to bridge the chasm between the two sects, held some of their chief assemblies around the statue of William III. Every year, during the great period of the volunteer movement, they met there on the birthday of William, decorated with orange lilies and orange cockades; and the 'Boyne Water' was played, and a *feu de joie* was fired in honour of the occasion. Wolfe Tone has noticed, as a most significant fact, that in 1792, for the first time since the institution of the volunteers, this ceremony was objected to, and omitted. It was on the occasion of the commemoration of July 12, that the Ulster volunteers

---

[1] On the English and Scotch societies, see *Orangism, its Origin, Constitution, and Objects*, by Richard Lilburn (1866). The Orange Society at first called itself, 'The Boyne Society, commonly called Orangemen.' See Cupple's *Principles of the Orange Association*, pp. 19, 20.

[2] The battle of the Boyne was fought on July 1, old style, which corresponds to July 12, new style. The battle of Aghrim was fought July 12, old style.

[3] This was the occasion of Lord Chesterfield's well-known lines to Miss Ambrose:

'Say, lovely traitor, where's the jest
Of wearing orange in your breast;
While that breast, upheaving, shows
The whiteness of the rebel rose?'

assembled at Belfast, presented their famous address to Lord Charlemont in favour of the admission of Catholics to the suffrage.[1]

A very different spirit, however, animated the early Orangemen. The upper classes at first generally held aloof from the society; for a considerable time it appears to have been almost confined to the Protestant peasantry of Ulster, and the title of Orangeman was probably assumed by numbers who had never joined the organisation, who were simply Peep of Day Boys taking a new name, and whose conduct was certainly not such as those who instituted the society had intended.[2]

A terrible persecution of the Catholics immediately followed. The animosities between the lower orders of the two religions, which had long been little bridled, burst out afresh, and after the battle of the Diamond, the Protestant rabble of the county of Armagh, and of part of the adjoining counties, determined by continuous outrages to drive the Catholics from the country. Their cabins were placarded, or, as it was termed, 'papered,' with the words, 'To hell or Connaught,' and if the occupants did not at once abandon them, they were attacked at night by an armed mob. The webs and looms of the poor Catholic weavers were cut and destroyed. Every article of furniture was shattered or burnt. The houses were often set on fire, and the inmates were driven homeless into the world. The rioters met with scarcely any resistance or disturbance. Twelve or fourteen houses were sometimes wrecked in a single night. Several Catholic chapels were burnt, and the persecution, which began in the county of Armagh, soon extended over a wide area in the counties of Tyrone, Down, Antrim, and Derry.[3]

---

[1] Compare Gilbert's *History of Dublin*, iii. 40-53; Tone's *Memoirs*, i. 203; Grattan's *Life*, iii. 228; and an article in the *Quarterly Review*, Dec. 1849, on the Orange Society.

[2] The later Orangemen have been extremely anxious to disclaim all connection with the outrages of 1795 and 1796, which they attribute wholly to the Peep of Day Boys. See the evidence of the Orange leaders before the Parliamentary Committee of 1835, and also Mortimer O'Sullivan's *Case of the Protestants of Ireland*, pp. 173–176. It seems clear that the society was originally founded with a defensive object. On the other hand, the depredators called themselves, and were called by others, Orangemen, and the Peep of Day Boys rapidly merged into Orangemen, and ceased to exist as a separate body. See the evidence of Mr. Christie in the *Parl. Rep.* on the Orange Society, quest. 5575-5578. We shall have further evidence on this matter as we proceed.

[3] *Parl. Rep.* Orange Society, quest. 5567-5600.

On December 28, about three months after the battle of the Diamond, the Earl of Gosford, who was governor of the county of Armagh, and a large number of magistrates of great property and influence, met at Armagh to consider the state of the country. With a single exception, they were all Protestants, and among them were three clergymen of the Established Church, who were afterwards raised to the bench.[1] The opening speech of Lord Gosford has often been quoted, and it furnishes the clearest and most decisive evidence of the magnitude of the persecution. 'It is no secret,' he said, 'that a persecution, accompanied with all the circumstances of ferocious cruelty which have in all ages distinguished that dreadful calamity, is now raging in this county. Neither age, nor even acknowledged innocence as to the late disturbances, is sufficient to excite mercy, much less afford protection. The only crime which the wretched objects of this merciless persecution are charged with, is a crime of easy proof. It is simply a profession of the Roman Catholic faith. A lawless banditti have constituted themselves judges of this species of delinquency, and the sentence they pronounced is equally concise and terrible; it is nothing less than a confiscation of all property, and immediate banishment. It would be extremely painful, and surely unnecessary, to detail the horrors that attended the execution of so wide and tremendous a proscription, that certainly exceeds, in the comparative number of those it consigns to ruin and misery, every example that ancient and modern history can afford. For where have we heard, or in what history of human cruelties have we read, of more than half the inhabitants of a populous country deprived at one blow of the means, as well as of the fruits, of their industry, and driven, in the midst of an inclement winter, to seek a shelter for themselves and their helpless families where chance may guide them? This is no exaggerated picture of the horrid scenes now acting in this county. . . . These horrors are now acting, and acting with impunity. The spirit of impartial justice (without which law is nothing better than tyranny) has for a time disappeared in this county, and the supineness of the magis-

---

[1] One of them was Mr. Warburton, Rector of Lough Gilly, afterwards Dean of Armagh, and Bishop of Cloyne, a man who was certainly one of the very ablest magistrates in Ireland. See *Parl. Rep.* 1835, quest. 3251–3277.

tracy of this county is a topic of conversation in every corner of the kingdom.'

This terrible picture appears to have been fully acquiesced in by the assembled gentlemen. Resolutions were unanimously carried, to the effect that the Roman Catholic inhabitants of the county of Armagh were 'grievously oppressed by lawless persons unknown, who attack and plunder their houses by night, unless they immediately abandon their lands and habitations.' A committee was at once formed, and several measures were taken to repress the disturbances.[1]

It is not to be supposed that the law was silent about such crimes. One of the Whiteboy Acts had already made them capital, and directed the grand juries to grant compensation to the victims.[2] It was said in Parliament, in October 1796, that a considerable number of Catholics had obtained compensation, but it was also said, and apparently with great truth, that these were only a small fraction of the sufferers. The law had the defect of leaving a large option to the grand juries; it seems certain that in some districts, and especially in the earlier stage of the outrages, these showed themselves shamefully apathetic, and the Government were very generally accused of conniving at their apathy.[3] In spite of the resolutions of Lord Gosford

---

[1] Lord Gosford's speech, and the resolutions of the magistrates, will be found in the *Parl. Rep.* of 1835, and have been printed by Plowden (appendix, xcix), and many other writers. When sending the resolutions to Pelham, Gosford wrote: 'Of late no night passes that houses are not destroyed, and scarce a week that some dreadful murders are not committed. Nothing can exceed the animosity between Protestants and Catholics at this moment in this county.... When I came here in the month of October, I found the country in a state of extreme disorder, and that of a nature peculiar to itself. The Protestant and Catholic inhabitants were inflamed to the highest pitch of animosity; but the former were greatly superior in strength, and made no scruple of declaring, both by words and actions that could not be misunderstood, a fixed intention to exterminate their opponents.'(I.S.P.O.)

[2] 15 & 16 Geo. III. c. 21.

[3] See the remarkable extracts on this subject from the speeches of Parsons, Grattan, and others, in Plowden, ii. 553–557. In the *Pelham Correspondence* there is a letter from General Dalrymple, dated from near Armagh, 'Aug. 8,' and probably written in 1796. He said: 'The effects of the want of energy at the last assizes have been most severely felt, and total inaction on the part of the magistrates, and despondency on the part of the Catholics, has followed. Many of them are preparing for flight the moment their little harvests are brought in.... Their houses are placarded, and their fears excessive. All this I have stated many times to the Government, but no answer have I received. At this moment almost all are absent, and business sleeps. The Catholics conceive the fault to be mine, and that I am partial, and attached to their enemy, supposing me to possess powers not in me.... Laws exist, but their explanation and execution are in the hands of those who approve not of them.'

and his brother magistrates, the outrages continued with little abatement through a great part of the following year. As might have been expected, there were widely differing estimates of the number of the victims. According to some reports, which were no doubt grossly exaggerated, no less than 1,400 families, or about 7,000 persons, were driven out of the county of Armagh alone. Another, and much more probable account, spoke of 700 families, while a certain party among the gentry did their utmost to minimise the persecutions.

The most conspicuous document of this latter kind with which I am acquainted, is an elaborate and interesting paper, 'On the Disturbances in the County of Armagh,' by Mr. Alexander of Boragh, dated November 1796. This gentleman dwells strongly on the evident and menacing change of demeanour which had been displayed by the Catholics, on the great spread of Defenderism among them, on the conspiracies and outrages of the Northern Defenders in previous years, on the undoubted fact that the Catholics were the aggressors in the battle of the Diamond. If it had not been, he said, for the Orangemen, and for the issue of that battle, the county of Armagh, with some neighbouring counties, would have been practically under the dominion and the terrorism of committees of Defenders and United Irishmen. He admits that barbarities had been perpetrated by the Protestants, who, for a considerable time after the battle of the Diamond, destroyed the habitations of the Defenders, and would not suffer them to return to their neighbourhood or cultivate their land. He admits also, that some of the gentlemen of the county had shown great indolence and supineness, partly from 'a real desire that the Defenders should be banished from the country, as a set of men hostile to its peace.' The outrages, however, had, he said, been grossly exaggerated, and he believed that the number of families driven from the county of Armagh was less than 200, that the stories of rapes and mutilations perpetrated by Protestants were wholly untrue, and that, exclusive of those who fell in the battle of the Diamond, only about six lives had been lost. Some of the fugitives had been able to return, and many had not fled on account of acts of violence directed personally against themselves. The panic had extended to districts where there had been no actual violence, and prophecies (which needed no supernatural illumination) of great calamities impending over the Catholics, had been widely circulated and readily believed. He adds that, 'not a family left the country without disposing of such tenures as they had of their lands, to the highest advantage.' 'The Orangemen,' he continued, 'are almost entirely composed of members of the Established Church, attached to the established Government of this kingdom, and its connection with England, . . . and all they have of late done, has originated from those attachments,' and from the jealousies very justly produced by the associations and conspiracies, the language and the conduct of the Defenders. Such men must be prevented from committing outrage, but they must not be treated as disloyal conspirators. The worst acts had been done by 'an armed peasantry, undisciplined and unofficered,' by a small gang of 'boys and idle journeyman weavers,' and 'the name of Orangemen has been frequently assumed by a plundering banditti, composed of all religious denominations, whose sole object was robbery.'[1]

Even in this picture, the colours are sufficiently dark, but the authority of Alexander certainly cannot compete with that of Lord Gosford and the magistrates who assembled at Armagh, and the correspondence in the possession of the Government appears to me, to do little or nothing to attenuate the picture. It was in the beginning of 1796, that Camden first informed the English Government that the Protestants, in the county of Armagh, 'finding themselves the most numerous, have been induced to commit acts of the greatest outrage and barbarity against their Catholic neighbours;' and he adds very significantly, 'this circumstance has been owing to the magistrates of that county having imbibed the prejudices which belong to it, and having been swayed by their predilections in the discharge of their duty.'[2] At the Armagh Assizes which were held at the end of March 1796, Wolfe, the Attorney-General, was present. He appears on this, as on all other occasions, to have discharged his duties with ability, impartiality, and humanity, and the information which was sent to the Govern-

---

[1] I.S.P.O. I may here mention, that nearly all the magistrates' letters and other local reports quoted in the following pages, are in Dublin Castle
[2] Camden to Portland, Jan. 22, 1796.

ment was on the whole encouraging. 'The witnesses of both parties and religions,' wrote a prominent gentleman, 'have, in giving their testimony against each other, displayed a candour and a temperate honesty that bespeak dispositions the most favourable to future peace. Congratulations on that circumstance, and on the fortunate selection of the petty juries, are in the mouths of all parties.' Both Protestants and Catholics sat on the juries, and two Defenders and two Orangemen were capitally convicted. One whole day was occupied in examining the petitions of men whose property had been destroyed by the Protestant banditti. One hundred and fifty persons proved themselves entitled, under the Statute of Compensation, to damages, and rather more than 2,000*l.* was distributed among them. At the same time, Wolfe was sorry to learn that the outrages continued even during the assizes, and that, a few days before he wrote, several houses had been 'papered and pulled down,' near Lurgan.[1]

In the county of Down, the evil seemed extending. 'The wreckers,' wrote a magistrate from that county in June, 'are again at work. Last night . . . they wrecked and destroyed eight houses, used the people with great cruelty, and stole a large quantity of yarn. These fellows disgrace the revered name of Orange by taking it to themselves, and I can safely affirm that getting possession of arms is not their only object, as they have wrecked all and robbed most of the houses they went into. . . . My list of houses burned or wrecked since Armagh Assizes, in this county, amounts to fifty-eight, and I dare say some I have not heard of.'[2]

Another magistrate, writing from Waringstown in the same county, urged that a distinction must be drawn between the Orangemen, who were simply a loyal body enlisted for self-defence, and the depredators who had assumed the name. 2,500 or 3,000 Orangemen, with many flags and emblems of loyalty, had lately marched through the town. Their conduct was perfectly regular and sober, and they declared themselves 'ready to turn out upon all occasions to assist the civil power.' At the same time depredations of the Armagh type occasionally took place, and 'six or eight people of this neighbourhood, whose houses

---

[1] The Right Hon. J. Corry to Pelham, April 1, 3; Wolfe to Pelham, April 1, 5, 1796.
[2] J. Waddell, June 14, 20, 1796.

had been destroyed, got presentments for about 600*l*. to be levied off the parish.' 'I have not a doubt,' wrote this magistrate, 'of Defenderism and that hellish system of United Ireland spreading rapidly through this country. . . . Within these eight days a general terror prevails amongst the Protestants in this neighbourhood that their throats are to be cut by the papists, aided by the militia, and they now seem to place their salvation on the Orangemen solely. . . . I lament as much as you can, the emigrations that the wrecking of the Roman Catholic houses has occasioned. They will naturally carry with them the strongest resentment for the injuries they have sustained, into a country where their religion preponderates, and retaliation will and must be the consequence. As to the loyalty of the Roman Catholics, I differ from you in opinion. They never can forget that they have been the proprietors of this country, wrested from them and withheld by the strong arm of power. . . . Sorry am I to say, that the establishment of a militia has turned out a most unfortunate measure. . . . They have in general by their behaviour, wherever they have been quartered, disgusted the people beyond measure, and by their actions and declarations have given the strongest proofs of disloyalty.'[1]

In July two Orangemen were capitally convicted at Armagh Assizes. Several others, a magistrate reported, were acquitted, though there was the clearest evidence against them, and in spite of the charges of the judges.[2] 'On the whole,' wrote Lord Gosford about this time, 'this county in all appearance is, in my opinion, in rather a quiet state, and growing more so since the last assizes.' At the same time he adds: 'The people here, I fear, wait for a favourable opportunity to revive the spirit of religious quarrel. . . . On the borders of this county, in the county of Down, outrages, I fear, are getting to an alarming height.' Great Orange meetings with scarfs and banners were held on July 12, and the Orangemen professed themselves very loyal to the Crown.[3]

'As to the Orangemen,' wrote a very efficient magistrate at Dungannon, 'we have rather a difficult card to play; they

---

[1] H. Waring to Cooke, July 23, 1796.
[2] J. Kemmis (Armagh), July 24,
[3] Lord Gosford, July 10, 1796.

must not be entirely discountenanced—on the contrary, we must in a certain degree uphold them, for with all their licentiousness, on them must we rely for the preservation of our lives and properties should critical times occur. We do not suffer them to parade, but at the same time applaud them for their loyal professions.'[1]

In September a dreadful tragedy is stated to have taken place near Lord Gosford's residence, and eighteen Catholics, tenants of Lord Charlemont's, were said to have been attacked in the night and killed. I can find no further particulars of this affair, which was probably greatly exaggerated, but the correspondent of the Under Secretary who mentions it, states that the supineness with which it was treated by the Government was much blamed.[2]

Rightly or wrongly, it was believed that the Government wished to interfere as little as possible with the outrages in Armagh. Curran introduced the subject in the House of Commons on more than one occasion, and he tried in vain to induce the Ministers to consent to a special inquiry into them. He stated that not fewer than 1,400 families had been driven from their homes; that this system went on in broad daylight, and that the existing law was quite inadequate to remedy the evil. Like Grattan, he believed that nothing short of a compulsory compensation would be sufficient. The debate had a special interest from a speech of Mr. Verner, who represented the extreme Protestant party among the Ulster gentry. He said that the number of the expelled had been enormously exaggerated; that the Orangemen were a very loyal body, and that the outrages they had no doubt committed, had been committed under great provocation. The Catholics in 1795 had systematically attempted to deprive the Protestants of their arms. They had assembled together, in their own language, 'to destroy man, woman, and child of them;' they had treacherously attacked them in the battle of the Diamond, and they had been beaten in open fight. Many, he said, who fled, had been active in the Defender disturbances; and others had gone with the idea of getting cheap land in the West. 'These persons sold the interests of their farms

---

[1] Thos. Knox, Aug. 13, 1796.
[2] Edward Boyle to Cooke, Sept. 6, 14, 1796.

at a high price, and emigrated to the West at the instance of persons who had large tracts of waste land, and employed agents to invite people to take farms from them.' Armagh was now quite quiet.[1]

Some remarks of Pelham, which tended to minimise the importance of these outrages, produced a letter from Lord Moira which gives some very precise and important information. 'The newspapers,' he wrote, 'mention you as having said in your speech on the first day of the session, that the violence suffered by his Majesty's Catholic subjects in the county of Armagh had been much exaggerated. Lest false information should have been designedly given to you upon so serious a point, I cannot but feel it incumbent to assure you, sir, . . . that the outrages have gone to a much greater extent than I ever heard stated in Dublin, and the persecution is even now continuing with unabated activity. I have a detached estate bordering upon the county of Armagh, which, though in an inferior degree, has felt the effects of that licentious barbarity. Upon reading your speech, I deemed it advisable to procure an authenticated account of the number of my tenantry who have been driven within the last year from only four townlands within the parish of Tullylish. I have the honour to inclose a list of ninety-one persons who have been expelled in that manner from their possessions, and I have to add, that most of them have had their little property either destroyed or taken; many of them have been cruelly wounded. . . . The place where this has happened is in the heart of the linen manufactories, and is one of the most industrious parts of Ireland.'[2]

The manner in which religious animosity was fast creating a new line of cleavage, and running counter to the schemes of the United Irish party, is curiously shown in a letter from a gentleman at Omagh. He mentions that after Divine service, he had been addressing a meeting of nearly 2,000 Presbyterians on the necessity of forming volunteer corps, in order to resist the French, and also 'the Belfast principle.' The strongest spirit of loyalty, he says, prevailed among them: 'hatred of the Roman Catholics is very great, so much so that should one be

---

[1] *Irish Parl. Deb.* xvii. 147–154. This debate was on Oct. 26 and Nov. 7, 1796.

[2] Lord Moira to Pelham, Oct. 19, 1796.

admitted in any corps, they declared they never would join with them, as a spirit of Defenderism and revenge exists in that body against administration. This violent change has been wrought within the year—a change fraught with the best consequences to our King and Constitution.'[1]

We must now pass to evidence derived from another quarter. The great majority of the Ulster refugees took refuge in Connaught, and Lord Altamount was one of the largest proprietors and one of the most active magistrates in that province. In July 1796, he wrote to the Under Secretary at the Castle. 'The emigration from the northern counties to these parts still continues, and I consider it the more alarming because the extent of it does not seem to be understood, nor the causes to have been sufficiently investigated by Government. . . . I can see most clearly, that the causes and the consequences are highly dangerous to the peace and safety of the kingdom. Plunder, religious prejudices, and a wish for disturbance from disaffection to the State, appear to me to have been the groundwork of the persecution that has been raised against the Catholics. The result has been, that many of the well-affected, many of the industrious, and all of the timid, have fled from the danger that hung over them, and taken refuge where the numbers of their own persuasion gave them more confidence and security. That ill-intentioned persons have mixed with them, I think more than probable; and that they may themselves be ultimately led to disturb those parts in which they have neither interest, connection, nor property, I think much to be apprehended. All the unhappy sufferers that I have seen, have been in various ways deprived of the principal part of their subsistence; and though, from the cheapness of provisions here, they have been able to hold out in tolerable comfort hitherto, with the little means they brought with them, these must soon be exhausted . . . and the desire for revenge may follow.' Emissaries, Lord Altamount believes, had already come, from other parts of the kingdom, to incite the refugees, and he strongly suspected some men who were carrying crucifixes and pretending to be prophets. Then follows an extremely significant and important paragraph. 'There is another matter to which I must call your atten-

[1] Mr. Buchanan, Sept. 19, 1796.

tion, and it is of the most serious importance. You may perhaps receive it with some doubts, because, though I advance it as a *positive fact that I know*,[1] I cannot commit to paper my authority, nor must I be quoted for it myself. An idea has gone abroad, that the persecutions in the North have been fomented by Government, and however diabolical and absurd such a measure would be for any purpose of politics, it has gained belief, and has disaffected a great body of the Catholics of every rank throughout the kingdom.'[2]

A few months after this letter, Denis Browne, the brother of Lord Altamount, sent the Government a list of the fugitives who were on Lord Altamount's estate, and especially in the neighbourhood of Castlebar. He described them as very unwilling to give information, 'from suspicion of the motive of inquiry, natural enough in their aggrieved and distressed situation.' 'You may be assured,' he continued, 'that though the list I send you of names in this part of Mayo amounts to 950, yet that it is short of the numbers about here. . . . It is certainly of the greatest consequence to the well-being of this country, the Government should be informed accurately of the circumstances of a matter so new and alarming as this strange and cruel persecution. . . . Be assured that no circumstance that has happened in Ireland for a hundred years past, has gone so decidedly to separate the mind of this country from the Government. . . . The emigration from the North continues; every day families arrive here with the wreck of their properties.'[3]

'I am assured,' wrote Lord Altamount a few days later, 'and I have no reason to doubt the truth of it, that near 4,000 of those unhappy fugitives have sought shelter in the county of Mayo, and a number that I cannot take on me to compute, in other parts of the province of Connaught. All of them that have come within my reach have conducted themselves peaceably, or very generally so, and I have the most positive assurances from the priests, that intimation will be given if any ill intentions should be found among them; . . . but nevertheless I cannot but recommend that every additional precaution should be used, having in consideration the cruel injuries they allege

---

[1] Underlined in the original.
[2] Lord Altamount to Cooke, July 27, 1796.
[3] Denis Browne, Nov. 5, 1796.

themselves to have received, and the suspicious quarter from whence they have come.'[1]

Another centre of the refugees was the little town, or, as it then was, village, of Ballina, in the county of Mayo, and a magistrate named Cuffe, who lived in the neighbourhood, went over there to inquire into the circumstances. 'About sixty men,' he says, 'as nearly as I could guess, attended, and I must own the account they gave of themselves and their sufferings was most melancholy, and affected me much. I examined them very particularly, and received from every one of them the fairest and most satisfactory answers. They told me the place from whence they came, the landlords under whom they had lived, and such as had leases stated the nature of their interests, and named the persons to whom they had sold, and the sums they had received. They all produced certificates of their good conduct, and referred me besides to gentlemen of the country from whence they came, for their characters. In short, they have satisfied me most clearly, that they are all of them honest and industrious men. All of them I have yet seen are of the Roman Catholic religion, and almost all from the county of Armagh.' It did not appear to Mr. Cuffe that the fugitives at Ballina were in any degree disloyal, or had taken any seditious oath, and he found them quite ready to take the oath of allegiance, but in the mountainous districts of Mayo there were said to be Northerners of a different description.[2]

A month later, and after a fuller inquiry, he sent the Government a complete list of the refugees at Ballina, with what appears to me to be a very candid and temperate estimate of the causes of their exile. 'These people,' he writes, 'are all of the Roman Catholic religion, and almost all of them weavers. . . . I found them all decent, well-behaved men, and much more intelligent than the natives of the place. . . . Four of them had

---

[1] Lord Altamount, Nov. 27, 1796. In the *Dublin Evening Post*, Aug. 27, 1796, it is stated that a single gentleman (Col. Martin, of the county of Galway) has given asylum to more than 1,000 souls on his own estate, all peaceable, inoffensive, and living by the labour of their hands.' I cannot find any statistics about the exiles in the South. In a letter from the county Kerry, it is said: 'The account given by Mr. Frizell of the four men taken up at Tralee is exactly the truth. They were innocent, ignorant people, whose fears made them leave this country for fear of being destroyed by the Presbyterians. I believe they had not the smallest idea of doing any mischief.' (John Miller (Moneymore), Dec. 17, 1796.)

[2] James Cuffe to Pelham, Nov. 25, 1796.

been plundered, and as many more had been "noticed" (*sic*). The others honestly owned to me that they had not been injured or persecuted, but had left their country of their own free will. As far as I can judge from what they told, the cause of their emigration, in general, was that the Peep of Day Boys (with whom they, under the name of Defenders, have been in a constant state of warfare for above thirty years) have lately become too powerful for them, and they therefore thought they would be happier in any other county. Many of them owned to me candidly, that they had been in fault in the beginning, and they all agreed that if the gentlemen of their country had been as attentive to the police of it as I was to that of my country, they might have remained at home unmolested. . . . Upon the whole, the result of my inquiry was, that none of them appeared to have fled from justice, very few from persecution, and the bulk of them because their antagonists, the Peep of Day Boys, are become too powerful, and likely to worst them at fairs and other places where they meet them.'[1]

The flight of the Catholics from some districts was sufficiently considerable to affect seriously the agrarian condition. A Catholic historian asserts that, some months after the disturbances broke out, it was found that when a farm was to be let, the number of bidders was so reduced, that not much more than half the former rent could be obtained, and he malevolently ascribes to this fact the strong resolutions of the magistrates under the presidency of Lord Gosford.[2] The insinuation is probably unfounded, but it is, I believe, perfectly true that in these, as in most Irish disturbances, the agrarian element had a considerable part. The Catholics and the Presbyterians in the North, had long confronted each other as two distinct and dissimilar nations, and the low standard of comfort which accompanied the inferior civilisation of the Catholics, enabling them to offer higher rents than the Protestants, gave them an advantage in the competition for farms. There had been, as I have already noticed, in certain districts, a great displacement of the Protestant by the Catholic element owing to this cause, and although it was not the

---

[1] James Cuffe to Pelham, Dec. 22, 1796.
[2] Hay's *Insurrection of the County Wexford*, p. 39 (edit. 1803). A similar assertion is made in O'Driscoll's *Views of Ireland*, ii. 152, 153.

immediate and direct motive of the disturbances, it no doubt intensified the animosity which difference of religion, difference of race, and great difference of civilisation had already produced.

The reader is now in possession of evidence which, although of a somewhat fragmentary description, is sufficient to enable him to form his own judgment of the Orange disturbances in Ulster. It is plain, I think, that these disturbances, considered as a whole, cannot be regarded as unprovoked. They were a continuation or revival of the war between the Peep of Day Boys and the Defenders, which had raged fiercely in Ulster for many years before the Orange Society was founded. The Defender movement had long ceased to be a mere league for self-defence. It was distinctly treasonable, for it was intended to assist and provoke a French invasion; it was accompanied by numerous and horrible outrages, and in 1795 it had spread over twelve counties, or more than a third part of Ireland. It is also true that in the battle of the Diamond, which was the immediate cause of the Orange outbreak, the Catholics were the aggressors. It is, I think, no less evident that the Protestant retaliation soon assumed the form and dimensions of a most serious religious persecution; that through violence, or through fear of violence, multitudes of industrious and inoffensive men were compelled to abandon their homes, driven from the trades by which they lived, despoiled of almost all they possessed, and obliged to seek refuge in remote Catholic districts. It is probably no exaggeration to say, that the exiles may be numbered by thousands, and it is impossible to resist the conclusion that some of the magistrates shamefully tolerated or connived at the outrages. Nothing of this kind had occurred in Ireland since the days of Cromwell, and the consternation, the panic, the wildly exaggerated rumours it produced, exercised an enormous influence on Irish politics.

In the first place, the fierce revival of religious animosity was a fatal obstacle to that co-operation of Protestants and Catholics for the purposes of revolution, which it was the object of the United Irishmen to produce. The revolutionary movement in its earlier stages existed mainly among the Protestants of the North, and in 1795 nothing would have appeared more improbable than that the rebellion should have been chiefly Catholic, and chiefly confined to Leinster. The course which it ultimately took was largely due to the distrust which the events in the North had sown between Protestants and Catholics, and which was afterwards intensified by the crimes in Wexford. On the other hand, the religious animosities which were thus engendered left an enduring root of bitterness in Irish life, and the disloyalty of the Catholic masses advanced with gigantic strides. Up to the period of the recall of Lord Fitzwilliam, though there was great positive lawlessness, and almost complete alienation of sympathy from the Government, there appears to have been, in these masses, but little active political disaffection. After that period, a change passed over their spirit; but although the Defenders looked forward to a French invasion, as likely to redress their tithe and agrarian grievances, the political element in their combinations was still a subordinate one. The numerous poor peasants who were dragged from their homes, and sent without trial to serve in the King's fleet, produced a new and fiercer spirit of resentment, which the outrages in Armagh raised to fever heat. The plundered fugitives from the North, as they recounted their wrongs among the Catholic peasantry of Connaught and Munster, preached rebellion more powerfully than any other missionaries, and it was soon believed, in the words of a Catholic historian, 'that about five thousand (some say seven thousand) Catholics had been forced or burned out of the county of Armagh, and that the ferocious banditti who had expelled them, had been encouraged, connived at, countenanced, instigated, or protected by the Government.'[1] In this belief, the United Irishmen at last found an effectual means of arousing the Catholics, and it was industriously diffused from one end of Ireland to the other.

Whatever may have been the case with some of the subordinate members of the Government, it is certainly not true that Lord Camden looked upon these outrages with any other feeling than horror and dread, and one of his letters, written in August 1796, shows how clearly he foresaw their effects. The Government had by this time, he hoped, stopped the outrages in Armagh, but not, he says, before 'a multitude of families fled

[1] Plowden, ii. 563.

from the country, and were obliged to resort for new settlements to other parts of the kingdom, where they related their sufferings, and, I fear, have excited a spirit of revenge among their Catholic brethren. The Committee of Belfast, which had been long engaged in forming democratic societies and clubs upon the principles of the French Revolution, took advantage of this ill conduct of the Dissenters in Armagh, to form a junction with the societies of Defenders in the western and midland counties, and to revive their committees. . . . I am concerned to add, that their endeavours have been attended with much success. . . . Their conduct is cautious, and they are never guilty of outrage, so that the part of the country whence most danger is to be apprehended, is apparently most quiet and peaceable.' They boast of their success in seducing the military, and these boasts 'are too well grounded, especially among the militia men, who are Catholics, and whose feelings may have been irritated by the ill behaviour of the Dissenters and Orangemen in Armagh. . . . Emissaries have been among them [the Catholics], to influence them against the Dissenters of Armagh, to instil into their minds that the persecution of the Catholics is protected by Government. . . . The party of Dissenters called Orangemen keep up a system of terror at least, if not of outrage, in Armagh, and have begun to carry their vexation of the Catholics into the county of Down. Some of them were recently apprehended by a spirited magistrate, but on prosecution at the late assizes, the Catholics, on whose examinations they had been taken up, through terror or other causes, prevaricated on trial, and the offenders escaped.' These outrages, though 'not aimed immediately at Government, are perhaps more dangerous than even direct conspiracies, as they justly irritate the Catholics, and give a pretence for the disaffected to act upon.'[1]

The terror inspired by the Orangemen was extreme. As the Armagh depredators had taken that name, their outrages were naturally regarded as the deliberate acts of the society, which was said now to be intended for the extermination of the Catholics, and to have embodied this object in its secret oath. Of this charge no evidence has been adduced. The society in its first conception was essentially defensive, and at a later period,

[1] Camden to Portland, Aug. 6, 1796.

when many respectable country gentlemen joined it, they solemnly declared that no such oath had ever been taken by its members. But the false report had struck too deep a root to be eradicated, and the United Irishmen very skilfully put themselves forward as the champions of the oppressed. Catholic fugitives were sheltered and protected by Presbyterian families in Down and Antrim, and prosecutions were carried on, though with little or no success, by the United Irish Committee in Ulster against the rioters, and even against conniving magistrates.[1] It was sworn that some of these latter had actually refused to take the examinations of aggrieved Catholics, and had themselves threatened them with banishment.[2] 'To the Armagh persecution,' wrote the United Irish leaders, in the memoir which they afterwards drew up in prison, for the Government, 'is the union of Irishmen most exceedingly indebted. The persons and properties of the wretched Catholics of that county, were exposed to the merciless attacks of an Orange faction, which was certainly, in many instances, uncontrolled by the justices of the peace, and claimed to be in all supported by the Government. . . . Wherever the Orange system was introduced, particularly in Catholic counties, it was uniformly observed that the numbers of United Irishmen increased most astonishingly.'[3]

The parliamentary proceedings in the spring and in the winter of 1796 did little to improve the situation. The reports for this year are much more imperfect and fragmentary than those for previous years, but, as far as can be judged, the strength of the Government and the violence of the Opposition had both greatly increased. The short session, which began on January 21, and ended on April 15, 1796, was mainly occupied with the Act of indemnity for such persons as had in the preceding half-year exceeded their legal powers in the preservation of the public peace, and with the Insurrection Act, but Grattan also brought forward, as an amendment to the address, a resolution demanding free trade between Great Britain and Ireland, on the basis of equalisation of duties. He was defeated in one

---

[1] McNevin's *Pieces of Irish History*, p. 117.
[2] Seward's *Collectanea Politica*, iii. 168.
[3] McNevin, p. 178.

division by 122 to 14, and in another division by 82 to 16. In his speech on the address, he adopted the tone of violent opposition, and enumerated, in a bitter retrospect, the chief grievances of several successive years—the sale of peerages under Lord Buckinghamshire; the efforts of conspicuous members of the Westmorland Government in 1792, to excite a spirit of hostility to the Catholics; the violation during several months, by Lord Westmorland, of the law which expressly ordered that an effective force of 12,000 men should be retained in Ireland; the conduct of the same viceroy, in creating fourteen new places tenable by members of Parliament, and in granting no less than thirteen reversions; the fact that some of the most valuable of these reversions were granted after his successor had actually been appointed; and finally, the crowning grievance and perfidy of the recall of Lord Fitzwilliam.

The power of the Government was, however, perfectly unbroken, and its chief measures were carried almost without divisions. The Act of indemnity was justified chiefly by English precedents. Such an Act had been carried by the English Parliament in the first year of William III., after the Jacobite rebellions of 1715 and 1745, and after the Gordon riots in 1780, and the Irish Act now passed with apparently no further formal opposition than a motion of Grattan, that the judges should first be summoned to give information to the House.[1]

The Insurrection Act, that accompanied it, is one of the most severe and comprehensive in Irish history, and it was preceded and justified by some resolutions, describing the extremely dangerous and anarchical condition of some parts of the country. The Attorney-General mentioned that in three counties in Connaught, the Defenders in open day had attacked the King's troops, that on one occasion forty or fifty of the Defenders fell, and that the operation of the ordinary law was, in many places, almost paralysed by intimidation, and especially by the frequent murder of witnesses. The Act made it death to administer, transportation for life voluntarily to take, a seditious

---

[1] Grattan condensed the arguments against it with great power, in a petition which he drew up for the Whig Club. Musgrave states (p. 145) that the measure was violently opposed by the minority. See, too, Grattan's *Speeches*, iii. 204-208.

oath. It compelled the production of all arms for registration, changed in several important respects the criminal procedure, and enabled the Lord Lieutenant and Council, upon a memorial from the magistrates, to proclaim particular districts as in a state of disturbance. In proclaimed districts, the inhabitants were forbidden to be out of their houses from one hour after sunset until sunrise, and justices of the peace were empowered to search all houses during the prohibited hours, to ascertain whether the inmates were abroad, or whether arms were concealed. They might also demand the surrender even of registered arms, and there were stringent clauses against 'tumultuous assemblies' by daytime, against meetings by night in public-houses, against men and women who sold seditious and unstamped papers.[1] All these clauses might be fully justified. The part of the Insurrection Act which appears to me objectionable, and which Sir Lawrence Parsons strongly opposed, is that which enabled the magistrates in the proclaimed districts to do by law what had already been done without law and in defiance of law—to send men whom they considered disorderly characters, untried, to the fleet. Under this comprehensive category were comprised all who were out of doors in the prohibited hours and who could not give a satisfactory account of their purpose, all who had taken unlawful oaths, all who could not prove that they had lawful means of livelihood. This treatment of disorderly persons was justified, on the ground that a power to send vagabonds to the fleet or army had been granted to English magistrates. The circumstances of the two countries, however, were very different, and it was only too evident how great were the probabilities in Ireland of scandalous oppression and abuse.

It is worthy of notice that Grattan, though he delivered two or three speeches on the Insurrection Bill, does not appear to have objected to any of its enactments except the last, and with this exception he confined himself to censuring its omissions.[2] As the reader has by this time discovered, he had, at no period of his life, any sympathy with those politicians who look with indifference on outrage and crime, or imagine that ordinary

---

[1] 36 Geo. III. c. 20.
[2] Grattan's *Speeches*, iii. 218-229.

remedies are sufficient to meet extraordinary diseases. He contended, however, with much justice, that the Government showed a scandalous partiality, in directing their measures solely against one class of crime, and keeping a complete and shameful silence about the outrages in Armagh—outrages, the magnitude and atrocity of which had been formally attested by the governor of the county, and by the resolutions of the magistrates—outrages which Government had taken no adequate, stringent, or successful measures to suppress. It was a scandalous thing, he said, that they should have justified this Insurrection Bill, by resolutions specifying the attempts to assassinate magistrates; to murder witnesses; to plunder houses; to seize arms by force; and should have kept an absolute silence about attempts to seize the persons of his Majesty's subjects, and to force them to abandon their lands and habitations, though these crimes were not less great or less notorious, and demanded still more emphatically the interposition of the State, since they had hitherto triumphed over the supineness of the magistracy. He desired to insert among the crimes which the Insurrection Bill was specifically designed to punish, that of forcing his Majesty's subjects to abandon their lands and habitations, and he also wished to make it obligatory upon the county to indemnify fully the sufferer for the injury he received, when beaten, or abused, or driven from his land and habitation. Experience, he argued, had only too clearly shown, that in the state of feeling existing in the North, this compensation should not be left optional with the grand juries, and both in Armagh and elsewhere, the houses of the poorest class of the people had been burned without any redress whatever. The Government, however, refused to accept his proposals, and the Bill was carried in the original form.

'I believe it is not possible,' wrote Camden, 'to explain to others the necessity of certain measures, which a residence in this country forces me to feel.' And he gives, as an example, the Insurrection Bill, 'which seems to alarm the finer feelings of British legislators,' though it had passed ' without a division in an Irish House of Commons, and in the presence of an active and, in some respects, of a spirited and intelligent Opposition, whose chief objection to it was, that it did not meet every possible case of aggression.'[1] 'Of your Insurrection Act,' replied Portland, 'I will only say that, though the necessity of such a measure is but too well established by the facility of its passage through Parliament, my astonishment at the existence of such a necessity in a country enjoying the same form of government as this, is not abated by the event.'[2]

Pelham, whose health was exceedingly bad, hastened, after the adjournment of Parliament, to England, where, indeed, he appears to have spent more time than any other Secretary since the establishment of the Constitution of 1782. Several letters show the anxiety of the Lord Lieutenant for his return, but his absence is not without some compensation for an Irish historian, who has the great advantage of reading the full and confidential reports that were sent to him from Ireland.[3] They show how fast, in spite of a few condemnations at the Armagh Assizes, the Orange movement in its worst form was extending, and how fatally it was inflaming Catholic disaffection. They amply justify Grattan's complaints of the supineness of the magistracy and the inadequacy of the laws, and they are especially significant, as they come chiefly from Cooke, who was himself in sympathy with the strong Protestant and anti-reforming spirit of Clare.

On July 12, a new and irritating Orange commemoration was kept, in a procession to the Diamond. It passed off quietly, but 5,000 Orangemen took part in it, parading without arms, but with banners representing King George on one side, and William III. on the other. 'The Orangemen,' added Cooke, 'are beginning persecution in the county of Down, and the magistrates are not sufficiently active. The effect of this persecution works on the Catholics in other places, and they naturally breathe revenge. The United Irishmen are very active in enlisting and embracing the Catholics. . . . I have just seen Mr. Brownlow. He says, when the Orange boys were passing, a

---

[1] Camden to Portland, March 21.
[2] Portland to Camden, March 24. 'I cannot conceive that any man can doubt the necessity of such a measure [as the Insurrection Act], who had read the accounts which have been transmitted from this country of the machinations and designs of the United Irishmen, the Catholic Committee, the Defenders, Peep of Day Boys, and other disturbers of the public peace.' (Pelham to Portland, March 31, 1796.)
[3] These letters are in the Pelham MSS. in the British Museum.

party of the Queen's County Militia broke away from their officers, and began taking out the Orange cockades. An Orangeman struck one of the soldiers. The soldier bayoneted him. . . . I fear the militia will be tainted from this religious quarrel, and the United Irishmen, in order to seduce the militia and Catholics, promise to join them both against the Orange boys. . . . Nothing can be done till the heads of the United Irishmen can be taken up.' 'The United Irishmen are very active, and uniting with the Defenders daily.' 'The irritating conduct of the Orangemen, in keeping up persecution against the Catholics, does infinite mischief. It has been made the handle for seducing many of the militia, and by information I have just received, I fear apprehensions respecting the militia are too true. Two fellows I employ, and who never deceive me, assure me that there are 700 militia in the garrison, Defenders, and that several of the officers are infected.' 'I own, I see nothing for the safety of this kingdom but an addition of English troops, particularly cavalry, an arming of the gentry, some scheme for reforming the militia, and an effective staff, and I think a bold measure should be struck against the persons and papers of the chief United Irishmen and Defenders.'[1] 'In consequence of the shameful supineness of the magistrates,' wrote another important official from the Castle, 'the Orange boys are still permitted to continue their depredations in the North, with impunity. If this system of spoliation is much longer acquiesced in by the magistrates, the sufferers must be driven to despair, and, considering themselves put out of the protection of the law, they will necessarily associate for their own defence, and will become recruits to the Jacobin Club established at Belfast. It is absolutely necessary that some very vigorous measures should be adopted for the redress of this crying grievance.'[2]

'We are aware, on our part,' wrote Camden himself, 'that the Orangemen in the North, and the Defenders, are only kept down by the force which is stationed there; it is impossible to have much confidence in some of the militia regiments, . . . not much dependence is to be placed upon our generals.'[3]

Crimes, that were manifestly connected with the United

---

[1] Cooke to Pelham, July 14, 19, 27.   [2] William Elliot to Pelham, Aug. 4.
[3] Camden to Pelham, July 30, 1796.

Irish and the Defender movements, were multiplying, and especially murders of informers. Cooke sent to Pelham two long lists of the most recent. Two or three men who had given evidence, had saved their lives by flying from the country, but their relations at home were sometimes pursued. The house of the wife of one of them was nearly destroyed; his brother was obliged to fly from the country; his brother-in-law was fired at. A militia soldier, who was supposed to be an informer, was made drunk in Belfast, flung over the bridge and drowned. A sergeant of the Invalids was waylaid, and shot through the body. A magistrate named Johnson was shot through the body at Lisburn; two men were shot at Newtown Ards, and another in the streets of Belfast. Many persons had been wounded because they had enlisted as yeomen, and one so badly that his life was despaired of. A witness who had been sheltered in the house of Lord Carhampton himself, was imprudent enough to take a short walk with his uncle on Sunday, about midday. They were both murdered in the middle of a field. Two or three other cases had occurred. 'A Derry jury,' adds Cooke in terminating the dismal catalogue, 'acquitted a man clearly proved guilty of administering oaths. The other Crown prosecutions in Derry are put off.'[1]

There were at the same time constant intimations that a French invasion, to be followed by an Irish rebellion, was very near. At the end of May, McNally informed the Government that he had received clear hints that an invasion was meditating,[2] and Cooke wrote two months later: 'All my information coincides in the unceasing activity of the disaffected, and their projects for joining the United Irishmen and Defenders, and of insurrection after harvest, aided by rebellion.'[3] Wickham, the English minister in Switzerland, wrote two letters in July apprising his Government that a formidable French expedition was preparing, and warning them that Ireland was likely to be one of the objects of attack.[4] In September, however, James Tandy received letters, written from America by Rowan and Reynolds, which stated that 'the French resident at Philadelphia had informed his confidential friends of the Irish party there, that France will

[1] Cooke to Pelham, July 27, Aug. 10, 1796.
[2] Ibid. May 31, 1796.
[3] Ibid. July 27, 1796.
[4] Wickham's *Correspondence*, i. 405, 406, 436, 437.

not attempt an invasion of Ireland till after a peace with Germany. This being accomplished, it will be their first, as it is their favourite, object.'¹

The letters of McNally at this time dwell strongly on the rapid spread of disaffection among the Catholics. The original agitators, he said, in the Catholic Committee and Convention, had never aimed, like the Defenders, at 'plunder and massacre.' But many of them, through the rejection of their claims, were now ready to risk the consequences of invasion, and all of them had made 'total separation from Great Britain' their grand object. Of this fact, from an intimate personal acquaintance with them, he was fully convinced. Their immediate aim was to cement the union between Presbyterians and Catholics. Grattan and the parliamentary minority had almost wholly lost their influence. At a recent interview with the parliamentary leaders, 'the Catholics declared, that though there was a time when they looked no further than a reform in Parliament, and a full emancipation of the Catholic body, yet now their interests were general and not confined to themselves; the question to be determined was no longer a Catholic question, but a national question—the freedom of Ireland. They had, in consequence of former disappointments and ill treatment, united with the friends of liberty in the North, with whom they would stand or fall.' They spoke of the abolition of tithes, and the confiscation of the property of absentees; but their language, and their hopes, and their policy, all pointed to separation.²

The organisation, McNally said, was spreading with portentous rapidity. Most of the lower priests, and village schoolmasters, were active agents. Numerous missionaries, supported by subscriptions from their several societies, had gone forth to organise the other provinces. It was reported that 15,000 men had already taken the test in Munster, and several agents had been sent to Connaught to organise the Catholic refugees. Arms were being everywhere collected, and it was believed that not less than 40,000 well-armed men could be counted on in the North. It was determined to wait for the arrival of the French, and it was believed that an invasion would greatly accelerate the revolution; but the conviction was fast spreading

¹ J. W., Sept. 16, 1796. ² Ibid. July 24, Sept. 3, 26, Oct. 1, 1796.

that a general insurrection, even unassisted by the French, must prove successful.¹

Parliament sat again for a few weeks in the October and November of 1796, and its principal measure was a suspension of the Habeas Corpus Act, which was carried through with extraordinary rapidity, and was justified by the danger of permitting treason to spread, when the dangers of invasion were imminent. Grattan was one of the minority of seven who opposed the measure, and his speeches at this time appear to me to have been the most violent he ever delivered. It is evident from them that he considered the country hastening to a catastrophe, and that he felt wholly impotent to avert it. In sentences of condensed power, worthy of Tacitus, he described the triumphs of the French, the military inefficiency of the Ministry, the urgent necessity for peace, the continuous and systematic corruption by which the Irish Parliament was governed, the folly and the perfidy with which the Catholics had been at one time encouraged and at another repelled; and he insisted, in spite of the manifest hopelessness of the attempt, on again introducing the question of Catholic emancipation. The Chief Secretary, he reminded the House, had very recently said that 'the exclusion of Catholics from Parliament and the State, was necessary for the Crown and the connection, . . . that he was ready to support it with life and fortune.' 'What dictation,' asked Grattan, 'could France have suggested more opportune in time, and more pregnant in disaffection,' than such language? 'Eternal and indefeasible proscription denounced by a minister of the Crown, speaking to three-fourths of his Majesty's subjects in Ireland'! 'The Catholic question was made by Government a matter between the people of Ireland and the Crown of England.' 'An English gentleman, on the part of the British Cabinet, comes to this country, to tell us that it is necessary for his country that we should exclude ours, or a principal part of ours.' And this language was used at a time when every effort was being made to seduce the Catholics from their allegiance; at a time when the Government was calling on all denominations of men to make extraordinary exertions for the purpose of securing the Crown and the Constitution; at a time when England was in

¹ J. W., July 24, Sept. 26, Oct. 5, 1796.

the closest alliance with the chief Catholic Powers of the Continent, including the Pope himself. Grattan expressed his deep conviction that, in the present awful crisis, nothing could save Ireland and the Empire from ruin except the unanimity of its people, and that the Government was fast making that unanimity impossible. 'The Minister who separates the Roman Catholics from the Constitution, separates them from the Empire.' 'If they are forced from under the hospitable roof of the Constitution, . . . they will at length repose under the shade of the dreadful tree of liberty.'

The notion that popery, as such, was any longer a danger, he treats with contempt. He who maintains such a position, 'totally mistakes the principles of human action at this day. Controverted points of religion are a principle of human action no longer, and least of all the points which are renounced in the disqualifying oath—the worship of the Virgin Mary and the belief in the Real Presence.' But if religious controversies have ceased to be operative in politics, they have been abundantly replaced. 'A new spirit of reformation has gone forth, and the objects of its wrath are the abuses of the European Governments, abuses in their Churches, and abuses in their States. . . . In other countries it is the despotism, in these the corruption, of monarchical government that is complained of.' Such a spirit, he said, could only be met by an energetic reformation of abuses. In Ireland it was met 'by selling the peerage, creating nameless offices to purchase the Parliament, influencing the corporations, intimidating popular meetings, and making all the constitutional authorities as corrupt as possible, and afterwards by making them proscriptive.'

On the subject of the outrages in the county of Armagh, Grattan dwelt with extreme bitterness, and accused the Government of gross supineness and gross partiality. 'Government had not exerted all the powers which the law gave it. Had Government dismissed any of the magistrates? . . . Will Government say that in a year and a half, with 40,000 soldiers and with summary laws that would have enabled them to pull down the liberties of the whole island, they could not reduce that county to order? I cannot but think, the audacity of the mob arose from a confidence in the connivance of Government. Under an administration sent here to defeat a Catholic Bill, a Protestant mob very naturally conceives itself a part of the State.' Some magistrates, he said, had retired from the scene; others had secretly fomented or openly encouraged the outrages, and when the Government in their recent resolutions classed and recited the different kinds of outrage in the country, they took no notice of those which were perpetrated by the Orangemen, and they defeated a clause for compensating the sufferers.

Such language contained unfortunately much truth, but it was not calculated to pacify the public mind. The resolution in favour of Catholic emancipation, was evidently thought ill timed. George Ponsonby indeed observed that, of all who opposed it, 'only two opposed it on its merits—the rest acknowledged the propriety of the measure, and objected only to the time of bringing it forward.' But on the latter ground, the feeling seems to have been very general. Sir Hercules Langrishe, the oldest, and one of the steadiest, of the friends of the Catholics, spoke in favour of the Government, and tried to calm the troubled waters. 'In the course of the last twenty years,' he said, 'the magnanimity of Parliament has made great concessions to our Catholic brethren; no less than an entirely equal condition of property, and *almost* entirely an equal measure of privilege, and as to the great body of the people, total equality. What little of concession still remains behind (which is little more than pride and punctilio), must be the work of conciliation and not contention, and will not be achieved by carrying on a war of passions and of party. . . . Leave a good cause, for some time, to the operation of reason and retiring passion, and do not by premature efforts unite your opponents by new bonds of confederacy, by the pride of consistency, or the obligation of engagements repeatedly interchanged. . . . Postpone a question of disputation and division, and proceed to the Bill before you, for the defence of the country.' The advice was taken, and Grattan's resolution was defeated by 143 to 19. This was the last occasion on which the question of Catholic emancipation was raised in the Parliament of Ireland.

In addition to the Indemnity Act, the Insurrection Act, and the suspension of the Habeas Corpus Act, a few measures were carried in 1796, which deserve a brief notice. There was an Act which, in my opinion, ought never to have been altered, making conspiracy to murder, a felony of the same nature as murder itself. It might indeed be reasonably contended that this offence, whether measured by its effects upon society, or by the moral guilt it implies, is the more heinous of the two, and in a country like Ireland, where a very large proportion of the worst crimes are prepared in secret societies and committed by deputy, it is especially dangerous. A new Act was passed, preventing the importation, and regulating the sale, of arms and ammunition; the salaries of the judges were again raised; the punishment of hanging was substituted in Ireland, as it had a few years before been in England, in the execution of women, for the much more horrible punishment of burning; and the greater part of the Dublin Police Act, which was still exceedingly unpopular, was repealed, thus restoring to the Corporation the chief control over the maintenance of order.[1]

Whatever may be thought of the coercive legislation of 1796, no one who reads the correspondence of the time can doubt, that remedies of a most exceptional and drastic character were imperatively needed. At the same time, during the whole of this year, the disease appears to have been mainly, though certainly not exclusively, in the North. In August, when a project of raising a yeomanry force was entertained, Toler, the Solicitor-General, wrote: 'I think I can venture to say, from what I know of the South and West of Ireland, that Government may, with safety and effect, appeal to the gentry and farmers in those parts to act under commissions from the Crown, prudently issued. . . . It is evident to demonstration, that the opinion of the multitude, and of all descriptions in the provinces of Munster, Leinster, and Connaught, has grown infinitely more loyal during the war, which evidently saved Ireland, by the exclusion of Jacobins, and by bringing the idle and dangerous under the control of military discipline.'[2] But the state of the North was extremely alarming, and insurrection was constantly expected. Frequent efforts were made to tamper with the loyalty of the soldiers and the militia; several militiamen were found to have taken the

---

[1] 36 Geo. III. c. 26, 27, 30, 31, 42.   [2] Aug. 10, 1796. (I.S.P.O.)

United Irishman's oath, and the dispute between Protestant and Catholic, which originated at Armagh, soon extended to the forces, and showed itself in a violent quarrel between the Mayo and Kilkenny Militia, on the one hand, and the Tyrone Militia on the other.[1]

In August, Camden[2] described the state of the country as growing rapidly worse. Trees of liberty had been planted in Antrim, and bonfires lit in consequence of French victories. Officers of the County Limerick Militia declared that they could place very little dependence on their men. There were great fears about the Queen's County and the West Meath Militia, which were both Catholic, and two men of the latter regiment had been punished for attempting to plant a tree of liberty in the camp. Many of the artillery soldiers quartered at Belfast, were believed to be infected, and four informers had been recently murdered. 'Since Derry Assizes,' wrote a magistrate from Tyrone, 'where all the United Irishmen were tried and acquitted, everyone that will not instantly join that set, is threatened with destruction. . . . God knows how and when this will terminate; no man will pay one penny of debt, so sure are they of an immediate rising.'[3]

'The Protestants about me bordering on the county of Antrim,' wrote another magistrate, from Dromore, 'are in a most horrid panic about those United people rising. They absolutely dare hardly go to bed at night, and never without a watch. . . . They tell me plainly, that they expect every night to be murdered.'[4] Lord Castlereagh, after a journey through Ulster, wrote that it was impossible to doubt the seriousness of the conspiracy in the northern counties. 'Belfast is its centre, it is very general towards Lisburn, the county of Antrim has been largely infected, and the county of Down is by no means exempt. There is sufficient information to ascertain that the societies gain ground rapidly, and that they have formed very sanguine and extensive hopes in consequence of the fatal turn affairs have taken on the Continent. . . . The same infernal system which prevailed in this neighbourhood, of murdering witnesses, is pursued there, with the additional address, which I fear will distinguish any

---

[1] E. Boyle to Cooke, June 21.
[2] Camden to Portland, Aug. 24, 1796.
[3] Andrew Newton, August 15.
[4] Captain Waddell, Aug. 29, 1796.

attempt against the peace of the country which the people of the North may undertake.'[1] Poor men working in the fields in the dusk of the evening, were accosted by armed parties, and compelled, on pain of death, to swear that they would assist the French. Tithes were refused. Tithe receivers, or valuers, were attacked, and threatening notices sent to clergymen who claimed their due. Large subscriptions were raised for prisoners; jurors were carefully marked, and many were challenged in the box because they did not understand certain secret signs.[2]

Several different classes were concerned in the disturbances— a lawless rabble, to whom scenes of confusion and plunder had the same attraction as carrion to the vulture; half-maddened Catholics, infuriated by the proceedings in Armagh, and burning for revenge; adventurers, looking only for excitement or for gain; fanatics, who would be content with nothing short of a purely democratic government; half-educated and unsettled men of all descriptions, who in Ireland so commonly play with treason, though they are seldom prepared to make any real sacrifice for it. It was noticed by an excellent observer, that the ranks of the United Irishmen were largely recruited by men of desperate fortunes, whose small estates were mortgaged beyond their value, and who hoped in a general convulsion to extricate themselves from their debts.[3] With these were mingled some honest and even moderate men, who had been reluctantly driven into rebellion by the conviction, that in no other way could even the most constitutional reform be obtained; and also, as a Derry magistrate remarked, a few able and industrious men, usually of good characters, who had made fortunes of from 1,000*l.* to 6,000*l.*, and who resented the social superiority of the landed gentry. Such men were sedulously cultivated by the United Irishmen, but a little attention might easily conciliate them. The jobs of grand juries about roads, the Church collections imposed upon sturdy Presbyterians, and the manifold oppressions of the agents of great absentee proprietors, all contributed to swell the ranks of the disaffected.[4]

[1] Castlereagh to Pelham, Aug. 23. (I S.P.O.)
[2] H. Alexander, Aug. 1, 1796.
[3] F. H. [Higgins], Jan. 30, 1798.
[4] H. Alexander, Aug. 1, 1796. Emmet stated before the Committee of the House of Lords in 1798, that a great many large middleman tenants had joined the United Irishmen. (McNevin, p. 234.)

Carrickfergus was one of the great centres of disturbance.[1] An active and loyal soldier was fired at and wounded; another loyalist was shot dead in the streets, and it was stated that a regular assassination club had been formed. By the assistance of a very energetic Protestant loyalist named McNevin, the Government obtained the services of a Catholic priest named McCarry, in that town. 'Notwithstanding his priestcraft,' wrote McNevin, 'he would go to hell for money.' 'He knows all the principals except a few great men, who are kept a secret from all but one or two.' 'I am sure he will give such real and useful information as must effectually serve Government; he being at the head of every infamous and rebellious transaction here, and a man of great mischief.' Cooke had an interview with him, and described him to Pelham as 'a cunning, bigoted, low papist,' who was not himself a United Irishman or personally acquainted with the leaders, but who knew well what was going on in the conspiracy, and who, being an artful, inflammatory preacher, had great influence upon the lower Catholics. He became an assiduous correspondent of the Government, and extorted many small sums from them, but it is doubtful whether he ever really wished to serve them, and his letters give the impression of an illiterate, cunning, rapacious man who was deserving of very little credit. The United Irishmen, he reported, believed that the French were about to land 20,000 men in Cushendall Bay, and 20,000 in the West, on condition of obtaining the revenue of Ireland for five years. There was a plot for seizing Dublin Castle, and the castles of Carrickfergus, Down, Athlone, and Limerick. Antrim, Down, and Derry were ripe for revolt. 'Here,' he said, 'we are not certain to live for an hour. Murders are daily committed.' He appears to have pointed out a house in which bullets were cast, and he promised to reveal where cannon were concealed; to procure information against the leading conspirators, and to use his own influence as a preacher to turn the Catholics in favour of the Government. Whether he fulfilled any of these promises, is more than doubtful.'[2]

---

[1] See several letters from Carrickfergus, July 1796. (I.S.P.O.)

[2] McCarry, July 23, Oct. 24; A. NcNevin, Oct. 25, 1796 (IS.P O.); Cooke to Pelham, July 19, 1796. Another ecclesiastic, who is spoken of as 'Friar Philips,' appears to have given the Government some really valuable assistance in detecting Defender leaders. (Cooke to Pelham, Dec. 4, 1795. *Pelham MSS.*)

A much more useful and important correspondent of the Castle, was Francis Higgins, a man who is still vividly remembered in Ireland under the title of the Sham Squire. He obtained this nickname from a discreditable episode of his early life, when he formed a rich marriage by pretending to be a possessor of landed property, and heir to a wealthy lawyer. He was a man of great energy, and of much coarse talent, and had been for some years the proprietor of the 'Freeman's Journal,' which was one of the principal newspapers in Ireland, and which under his influence passed completely into the ranks of the Government. For this service, he had obtained a small annual subsidy some time before the administration of the Duke of Portland, and it was subsequently increased. He was also an attorney and a magistrate; he held two or three small offices from Government, and he took an active part in municipal affairs. Possessing to an eminent degree the peculiar talent of a newspaper editor for forming and maintaining useful connections in many quarters, and hunting out obscure information, his knowledge of Dublin life made him very useful to the Government, and his influence was increased by the fact, that he was owner of some houses inhabited by manufacturers in the Earl of Meath's Liberty in Dublin, and had acquired popularity by acts of kindness to Dublin workmen. His timely warning of an intended attack upon Lord Camden on his first entry into Dublin, has been already mentioned; and at a later period, as we shall see, he was able to render a service to the Government, of transcendent importance.

He appears to have been a warm and steady friend, and liberal in his charities, but his general reputation was not good; he had many enemies, and he was furiously lampooned in prose and verse. His low birth; his imprisonment for fraud when a young man; his alleged connection with a gambling house; his almost deformed person; his coarse, pushing, ostentatious manners, were abundantly commemorated; but, in spite of all opposition, he rose to wealth, and being a man of much humour and of very convivial tastes, he easily gathered men of all parties to his great house in Stephen's Green. In Ireland, even more than in most countries, when the bottle flows freely, information is easily obtained. In enumerating his services to the Government, Higgins especially mentions the expense he had incurred in entertaining priests and other persons of the higher class, for the purpose of obtaining intelligence,[1] and he also adds that he retained and paid weekly from his own means as many as seven persons, 'belonging to and among the different United societies, clubs &c.' His informants were men who could never have been induced to appear in the witness box, but they enabled him to supply the Government with regular accounts of the proceedings of some of the societies in Dublin, and with a great deal of most important information about the aims and conduct of the leaders of the conspiracy. Nearly a hundred and forty letters from his pen are preserved in the Government records, and they furnish valuable materials for the history of the time. Though himself a convert to Protestantism, he had much communication with priests, and singularly full and accurate information about Catholic affairs, and he was on terms of warm friendship with Arthur O'Leary. Among his other intimate friends were, the Chief Justice Lord Clonmell, Lord Carhampton, and John Beresford; and it was mentioned as a proof of the fastidious haughtiness of Lord Clare, that he would never be present at his dinners. Higgins employed many informers, but he was not himself in the ordinary sense of the word an informer, for he professed in the strongest terms his devotion to the Government, his newspaper was a Government organ, and he was accustomed to go openly and frequently to the Castle.[2]

---

[1] There is a series of anonymous reports about the United Irishmen, from an informer in 1796, in the London Record Office. In one of them the informer makes an amusingly candid confession: 'There is one thing wherein they puzzle me, which is, that they seldom say much till they are nearly drunk, and by the time I get them in that plight I am little better myself, and though they were to open their hearts ever so liberally, I stand a fair chance of forgetting it by morning.' McNally, in his requests for money, frequently dwells on the importance of being able to entertain the conspirators. 'Without money,' he says, in one of his letters, 'it is impossible to do what is expected. Those Spartans wish to live like Athenians in matters of eating and drinking. They live so among each other, and without ability to entertain, I cannot live with them, and without living with them I cannot learn from them.'

[2] See, on Higgins, Madden's *United Irishmen*, and especially Mr. Fitz-Patrick's interesting little volumes, *The Sham Squire*, and *Ireland before the Union*. These writers seem to me, however, to exaggerate not a little the turpitude of Higgins, and to attach a great deal too much importance to 'traditional anecdotes' of a very worthless and malevolent gossip. His warning on the occasion of Camden's entry into Dublin, has escaped the notice of his biographers, and rests on his own statement; but as he continually, in his letters to the Castle, puts forward this service as his chief

He informed the Government that the recent French victories had greatly raised the spirits of the seditious; and accounts of them, copied from an English ministerial paper, were circulated widely through the country. Several small seditious clubs, which he pointed out, met in different parts of the city, and there were not fewer than four servants' clubs in Dublin, which might become very dangerous from the peculiar facilities for information possessed by their members. Immediate invasion was expected, and the Catholics, he believed, would be at best neutral. One of them had said in his hearing, that probably the devastations of the French would not be worse than those of the tithe proctor —and some honest men might obtain their own again. At the meetings of the Catholic committees, strong hopes were expressed that there might be at least a change of ministry. It might do the Catholics good, and no Government could be worse than that in which Lord Clare was a leading member. Grattan had promised constantly to urge the Catholic claims. A proposal to petition the King, was abandoned in consequence of the earnest opposition of Keogh. The new yeomanry force was believed to be intended to override the Catholic influence and claims, and the committee determined, by all the agencies at their disposal, to dissuade the Catholics from enlisting in it. Higgins complained that the poor in Dublin were much oppressed by the dearness of bread, in spite of a very good harvest, which he attributed to the combination of the corn merchants, and he predicted that this would one day produce disorder. The Government had not, he thought, been very judicious in their selection of an agent for acting on the Catholics. 'The Roman Catholic body hold a superficial opinion of Dr. Hussey as a courtly priest. If anything was to be effected or wished to be done in the Roman Catholic body, Dr. O'Leary would do more with them in one hour, than Hussey in seven years. Of this, I am perfectly assured—and O'Leary not ten days since wrote me word, he would shortly claim a bed at my house.'[1]

---

claim for favour, and as it never appears to have been disputed, it is no doubt true. He bequeathed a great portion of his property to charities, Catholic as well as Protestant, and O'Leary was one of those to whom he left a legacy. He himself enumerates his services in letters of March 2, June 18, 30, 1798, Dec. 2, 21, 1799, March 18, Nov. 18, 1801. There is also, in the I.S.P.O., an unsigned and undated memorandum about the services and rewards of Higgins and some other persons connected with the press.

[1] F. Higgins, Aug. 1, 15, Sept. 27, 30, Oct. 11, 16, 24, 1796. (I.S.P.O.)

'The suspicions,' wrote Lord Camden, 'which the gentry entertain of the militia, even were an invasion not to take place, have induced great numbers to wish to associate for the preservation of their properties and to form corps of yeomanry cavalry and infantry, for their own, and for the protection of the country, all under commissions from the Crown. I believe your Grace will agree with me, that it is hardly possible to refuse an assent to propositions of this nature.'[1] This was the very plan which Lord Fitzwilliam had proposed, and which the English Government had rejected; but Camden, though he had at first been hostile to it, now recognised its necessity. That there were difficulties and dangers attending it, he clearly saw. It would be very necessary, and at the same time very invidious, to reject the services of many who would gladly obtain arms from the Government. It was possible that the militia might be affronted. It was certain that a project for arming the property of the country might be construed into a project for arming the Protestants against the Catholics. But 'when there is reason to apprehend an attack from the enemy, when a very considerable district is organised in disaffection, as is the case at Belfast and in its vicinity, when there is a *general* disaffection amongst the lower orders, both of Catholics and Dissenters, to English Government,' such a measure was absolutely necessary. The Speaker still doubted its expediency, but the Chancellor, the Attorney-General, and Lord Carhampton, all favoured it.[2]

In the autumn and winter of 1796, great progress was made in enrolling the new force. Charlemont and Conolly, who had much influence in the North, warmly supported it, and a large number of country gentlemen volunteered their services. Considering the strongly anti-Catholic policy of the Government, which presided over the movement, and considering also that the yeomanry were intended chiefly as a protection against the Catholic Defenders, and against the United Irishmen who placed Catholic emancipation in the forefront of their programme, it was inevitable that, in the North at least, it should consist to a large extent of the most violent Protestants—of men who,

---

[1] Camden to Portland, Aug. 24, 1796.
[2] Ibid. Sept. 3, 1796. See, too, Cooke to Pelham, May 31; Camden to Pelham, July 30, Aug. 6, 1796.

by faction fights, or by Defender outrages or menaces, had been inflamed to the highest point of animosity against their Catholic fellow-countrymen. It was equally certain, that a force raised so hastily, under such circumstances, and from such materials, would, in time of trial, prove very undisciplined and prone to unnecessary violence. Lord Downshire, who was actively employed near Newry in enrolling yeomanry cavalry, wrote, 'I am happy to say, that there are some very respectable and loyal papists among them;' but he added, 'the yeomanry infantry are not so liberal as the cavalry; their condition of service is, that no papist should be enrolled with them. . . . They are chiefly Orangemen, and all agree in not admitting a papist, however recommended.'[1] All who were in known sympathy with the United Irishmen and their policy, were of course excluded, and this shut out the great body of those who composed the volunteers of 1782. The Catholic Committee strongly discouraged their co-religionists from enlisting, and the United Irishmen exerted all their influence to paralyse the movement. A powerful address, signed 'Common Sense,' urging the folly of division between Catholics and Protestants, was at this time circulated widely through Ulster. 'Look to America,' said the writer, 'where every persuasion pays its own clergy, and all are in harmony. Let distinctions be forgot, unite with each other, and remember that you have a common interest not to pay useless and oppressive taxes to bribe the men that oppress you all, or tithes to pastors who never instruct you. Try the blessings that will follow union, and trust me, you will in one single session, and that, if you please, the very next, put an end to corrupt taxes, and to tithes under which the Presbyterian and Catholic equally groan.'[2]

The yeomanry movement appears to have been principally in the North, and to have been directed principally against internal enemies, and, as Camden had feared, it was looked upon, or at least represented, as giving a Government organisation and sanction to the Orange movement in the province. In the other provinces, there was as yet much less disturbance and much less enlisting. When, however, at the end of the year, a French descent in the South seemed imminent, a considerable yeomanry

[1] Nov. 25, 1796. (I.S.P.O.)   [2] S. Close to Toler, Oct. 1796. (Ibid.)

force was speedily created in that part of Ireland, and the Catholics showed themselves quite ready to be enrolled in it. Lord Camden at this time wrote to the English Government, that 'offers of more than 20,000 yeomanry corps had been made and accepted, and that on December 7, 9,000 of them were actually armed;'[1] and Lord Clare himself has borne an emphatic testimony to the loyalty then shown by the Catholic peasantry in the southern and midland districts. 'During all the disturbances,' he says, 'which prevailed in other parts of the kingdom, we were in a state of profound tranquillity and contentment there. . . . When the enemy appeared on the coast . . . a general sentiment of loyalty prevailed in all ranks and degrees of the people, who vied with each other in contributing to defend their country against the invaders.'[2]

The letters describing the state of Ulster form a striking contrast to this picture. A new feature, which now came into prominence, was a system of great gatherings of the disaffected, under the pretext of digging potatoes or performing other agricultural operations. A letter from Sir George Hill, an active magistrate in the county of Derry, gives a graphic account of one of these meetings, which he witnessed. The ostensible object was to dig the potatoes of a prisoner, but there were not less than 6,000 men assembled. They were clean, well-appointed men, from many quarters, acting systematically together. They carried their spades like muskets, and marched with an erect and defiant mien; but when ordered by the soldiers to disperse, they at once obeyed, saying with an affected humility, that it was hard to be impeded in their charitable purpose 'of digging a forlorn woman's potatoes,' and asking if they were allowed to dig their own. No other provocation was given. No seditious language or imprecation was used. About 1,500 men had crossed the mountains during the night, to be present at the meeting. 'What alarmed me most completely,' wrote the magistrate, 'was to perceive the calmness observed by the people assembled in such multitudes, from such various quarters, and yet acting with one common system, most evidently by previous arrangement, and under the control of an invisible guidance.' Sir George

[1] Camden to Portland, Dec. 26, 1796.
[2] Speech in the debate of Feb. 19, 1798.

asked some of them, if they would resist the French in case of an invasion. They answered, in a tone that it was impossible either to resent or misunderstand: 'Our arms have been taken away; the volunteers have been put down; we must not talk politics; we pay dearly for the militia: Government has taken everything into its own hand: if the French come, we cannot resist; we are good Christians, resigned to our fate.' The soldiers were out from one in the morning till three in the afternoon; but as soon as they retired, one or two hundred of the neighbours dug the potato field. 'The system of rebellion,' continued the magistrate, 'is planned deeply, and all that is wanting to give it opportunity of breaking forth, is the landing of a few Frenchmen. ... I do believe that more than two-thirds of the country has been sworn.' The main object of the potato digging is probably to enable the leaders to ascertain how their men will act at the word of command.[1]

It is easy to conceive the disquiet which such an incident must have produced, and letters from most parts of Ulster confirmed the impression of imminent danger. From Coleraine a magistrate wrote: 'People assemble in bands of hundreds, and sometimes even thousands, for the ostensible purpose of cutting corn and digging potatoes, but, in my opinion, for the real purpose of settling their plans and accustoming themselves to rise in great bodies at the shortest notice.'[2] 'From what I can collect,' wrote a magistrate from the county of Armagh, 'there is as much a system of terror on foot in this neighbourhood, as ever was in France. No neighbour dare tell his opinion to another, hardly to his wife. There has not been a person here that has not received the most threatening letters—even to the lowest cottager—to force them to unite. ... No man will dare to be out at night, but those that are for bad purposes.' The better class of farmers detested the movement, but they were so terrified, that they had nearly all taken at least the oath of secrecy, after which, if they were known to be resolute and loyal men, they were usually left in peace. A new method had been devised to evade the law against administering unlawful oaths.

[1] Sir G. Hill to Cooke, Nov. 15, 1796. This letter was sent to England, and is in the Record Office. The other magistrates' letters are in the I.S.P.O.
[2] Alexander McNaughten, Oct. 20, 1796.

ANARCHY IN ULSTER.

A man is applied to, and, if he consents to be sworn, he attends a meeting, where he finds a number of men seated round a table drinking, in perfect silence. One of them points to a Bible, and the stranger, acting on instructions he has before received, takes it himself, and swears not to disclose anything that he sees or hears. The silence is then broken, and the others begin to talk, and produce the constitution of the society. If the new comer is prepared to obey, he says so, pointing to the Bible which lies on the table. If not, he has only to keep the oath of secrecy.[1]

All the guns in the neighbourhood, writes a magistrate from Croagh, in the county of Antrim, have been seized by the United Irishmen. Ash trees are everywhere cut down to make pike handles. The magistrates are so unprotected, that they dare not act. There are very few soldiers in the neighbourhood. Many of the militia cannot be depended on, and the post office is no longer safe, on account of the disloyalty of the postmasters.[2] Lord Castlestewart, writing from his house, in the county of Tyrone, reported that numbers of men were accustomed to meet in his district by night, and that smiths were employed in making pike heads. 'They all declare,' he says, 'that though a Frenchman should not land in the kingdom, they will shortly rise in a mass and attempt to execute their designs, that for this purpose they are swearing their different bodies to be ready at an hour's warning to go wherever they are ordered. . . . The impression of terror is so great all over the country, that no one dares give the least degree of information.' A number of ash trees on his own domain had been cut down, probably to form pike handles, and bodies of men were traversing the country in all directions on horseback, plundering arms.[3] About Derry, reported Conolly, the people are as wicked and rebellious as in any part of the North. It was impossible to get them to take the oath of allegiance. A man's ears had been cut off near Garvagh; corn stacks had been stripped, houses attacked, men knocked down and robbed on the highways.[4]

Communications of this kind were pouring incessantly into the Castle, during the last few weeks of 1796. 'Systematic plans of assassination seem to have been established to stop the

[1] N. Alexander (of Boragh), Nov. 15, 1796.
[2] Andrew Newton, Nov. 25, 1796.
[3] Lord Castlestewart, Stewart Hall, undated, but apparently November 1796.
[4] Thos. Conolly, Nov. 19, 1796.

channels of justice.'[1] 'The poor people now dare not put their webs into their looms, lest they should have them cut to pieces. ... There is not a night, almost, passes without racking [wrecking], robbery, burning of houses, sometimes murder, and often very near it.'[2] 'Assassinations are still getting more frequent in this country—a man was shot the day before yesterday, on suspicion of being an informer.'[3] 'Almost the whole country, for many miles round, is disarmed. The disaffected have robbed every one of their guns.'[4] The newly enrolled yeomanry were attacked in the county of Tyrone by a large mob, and several wounded, and 'this disinclination to yeomanry corps manifested by liberty men is not confined to Stewartstown, but may be said to be general in this part of the country.'[5] 'There was not a single individual of a townland of mine, within a quarter of a mile of Garvagh, that was not visited the night before last, and seven stand of arms taken from them, and last night, several more were taken within a mile of this place.' A man is going through that country as an itinerant astronomer, who is known to be a Dissenting minister, and is believed to be a Belfast emissary. 'The cloth merchants in this county are sending off their half-bleached linen to places of safety. ... Everyone is looking forward, with anxiety and dread, to the crisis.'[6]

'The Presbyterian ministers,' said Lord Downshire, 'are unquestionably the great encouragers and promoters of sedition, though, as yet, they have had cunning enough to keep their necks out of the halter.'[7] The degree to which the disloyalty had spread was strongly expressed by a Tyrone gentleman, who declared, though with evident exaggeration, that two years, or even one year, before, he could have enrolled 10,000 men, for the support of the civil power, but that now, 'the bad policy and conduct of gentlemen had united all parties.'[8] The Coleraine magistrates adopted the plan of giving licences only to innkeepers who consented to take the oath of allegiance. Ten of the most respectable took it, but they lost all their custom, and the plan was accordingly abandoned.[9]

---

[1] Geo. Macartney, Antrim, Nov. 12.
[2] R. Waddell, Islanderry, Nov. 8.
[3] Lord Downshire, Hillsborough, Nov. 2.
[4] Alex. Newton, Croagh, Dec. 2.
[5] Hon. Thos. Knox, Nov. 2.
[6] L. Heyland, Borugh, Dec. 8.
[7] Lord Downshire, November 7.
[8] Mr. Welsh, Cookstown, Nov. 3.
[9] N. Alexander, Nov. 15, 1796.

A general disarming had been suggested, but Lord Castlereagh wrote to Pelham, that he did not think such a measure would be expedient, or, perhaps, possible. He added, however, some remarks, to which later events gave a peculiar significance. 'Certainly,' he said, 'since I came to the country, I have had evidence of the extent and danger of the conspiracy, beyond what I was prepared to find, and it is impossible to know that a country is armed in the degree this is, and to have a moral certainty that the people are preparing, and look forward to employ those arms against the State, without entertaining the question whether it is wise to anticipate them, or to wait for their attack in the gross—for in the detail, we are at present suffering from it. The policy entirely depends upon the contingency of their receiving foreign assistance.'[1]

One of the most remarkable facts in this period of Irish history is the tranquillity of the greater part of Catholic Ireland, at the time when both Protestants and Catholics in Ulster were in a condition so nearly approaching anarchy. How far it was loyalty, apathy, or calculation, may be disputed, but the fact cannot be denied. 'I do really believe,' wrote a clergyman, who was accustomed to correspond greatly with the Government, 'that the Catholic priests have more influence than they are willing to acknowledge, and I am fully persuaded, notwithstanding the apparent calm in the southern provinces, that the papists there, many families of whom have lately emigrated from the North, are fully acquainted with the designs of the same party, who have remained behind.'[2] Seditious violence, however, was at this time confined to Ulster, to a very few points in Leinster, and to a somewhat larger area of Connaught. A gentleman from Ballinarobe, in the county of Galway, wrote that he had been trying to get up a district corps of yeomen, and had summoned his tenants, and asked them to take the oath of allegiance, but they all positively refused, and he did not venture to place Government arms in their hands. The hills about were said to be full of arms. Contraband cargoes from France were constantly run into the Killeries, and numerous deserters found a shelter among the mountains. 'The vast numbers of people from the county of Armagh, who have resided for some time

[1] Castlereagh to Pelham Nov. 4.   [2] The Rev. J. Asher, Nov. 22.

among them, may have instilled into the minds of these people some of their own principles.'[1] Sir Edward Newenham stated, in the early part of this year, that a magistrate near Ballintubber, in the county of Roscommon, was accused of having given the Defenders a grove of ash trees, to make pike handles, and that many men in comfortable circumstances had joined them openly. A day or two before the Defenders appear in any district, he said, a man of decent appearance goes through the country, telling the people that the French will soon come to their assistance, that ships have already arrived in the North, that Napper Tandy and Hamilton Rowan will lead them, and that Grattan will defend them in Parliament. When the way is thus prepared, the Defenders appear in small detached bodies, first disarming, and then swearing in the people.

For many miles round Castleblakeney, in the county of Galway, he said, there are very few magistrates, and not more than one or two who have the least idea of their duty. Many are 'trading justices,' 'if not themselves, at least through the means of some ignorant servant or clerk, to whom they often refer the parties for justice. Nothing, I assure you, sir, excites the discontent of the lower classes so much as such conduct; and so accustomed are they to such a traffic, that they make no scruple of offering a bill to any magistrate. It is not taxes that drain the poor. It is their own priests; it is their landlords, changing them from one place to another, and never giving a lease; it is the under agents, or stewards, that fleece them. . . . When their mock patriots cease to inflame the minds of the people with the idea of Catholic emancipation, raising wages, taking off all taxes, and various other ideas, equally absurd, and thereby allow peace and harmony to return to the country, industry will flourish. . . . The innumerable little unlicensed whisky-houses are the destruction of the labourers, and a nest for Defenders and every kind of vagabond.'[2]

The anarchy in Ulster did not extend over the whole province. From some counties the Government seem to have received no communications, and from two or three they received communications differing widely from those I have quoted. Lord Blayney, in sending to the Government a list of the yeomanry

[1] W. Birmingham, December 24.
[2] E. Newenham, Feb. 26, 1796.

cavalry, enlisted near Castleblaney, contrasted the 'shameful state of riot which has so long existed in more northern counties,' with the perfect quiet of his own county of Monaghan. 'There is there,' he says, 'the greatest tranquillity and happiness. No soldier is ever permitted to interfere with the laws; and during three assizes and quarter sessions, there never has been occasion to have an examination returned.' 'In the North,' he adds, 'the inhabitants are generally wealthy and obstinate; therefore, all require a plain and proper explanation of all matters from Government, and to be able to place some degree of confidence in their landlords. I am sorry to observe, that confidence between landlord and tenant throughout Ireland in general, is very much lost from the shameful abuse on the part of the former. It will, therefore, behove Government, this session of Parliament, to adopt some wise and salutary laws which meet the approbation of the people, and whatever the laws are, let them be rigidly enforced.'[1]

From Ballinahinch, Lord Moira wrote in the same spirit. The disaffection, he thought, was much exaggerated, and with large classes, the agitation did not spring from a desire for separation. 'It is not here as in England, where I am sure the notion of a parliamentary reform does not at all awaken the interest of the people. Here the middling and lower orders have had it anxiously in view, and have been encouraged to look to it by distinct avowals in Parliament, of existing abuses. The Association of United Irishmen professed to have no other view than the attainment of that object; and whatever nefarious purposes some of them might have covered under that veil, they have succeeded in persuading the country that such was their sole pursuit.' 'There are persons in this country, who have not adverted to the progress that information has been making, and to the knowledge of their own rights, . . . which individuals draw from it. Those gentlemen have used a tone and manner with the common people which might have answered here twenty years ago, although the peasantry in England would not have borne it within the century. The people here have resisted that domineering pretension; by their resistance have irritated the men of rank, and in some places the quarrel has produced deep

[1] Lord Blayney, Nov. 15, 1796.

animosity.... To my judgment, there is no other policy than conciliation; and from what I have seen of the country, I can have no doubt that such a tone would quiet everything.'[1]

It was, no doubt, true, as Lord Moira thought, that some of the United Irishmen were rebels because they believed that rebellion alone could give them a tolerable system of parliamentary representation. At the same time, the society, as a whole, had now become undoubtedly seditious and undoubtedly republican. Thomas Emmet, in his remarkable sketch of the history of the movement, observes that in the beginning, Catholic emancipation and parliamentary reform were the real and ultimate objects of the leaders; that when the first had been to a great degree acquired, and when the latter appeared desperate, a change of objects took place, and that this change was mainly due to the lower classes, who had become vehement republicans and separatists, and who forced the educated and moderate reformers to adopt their views. Even after the leaders had fully agreed to aim at a republic, Emmet believed that they would have been more ready than their poor associates, to abandon the pursuit if reform had been granted.[2]

The leaders of the party emphatically, and I believe sincerely, disavowed all sympathy with assassination; but there is no doubt that murders, and especially murders of witnesses and informers, were frequent in 1796, and they became still more common in the following year. The crime was one already well known in Ireland,[3] and a clause had been introduced into the Insurrection Act to meet it, by making the information of a murdered witness evidence on a trial. Whether these murders were chiefly due to local exasperation, or to combinations among friends of the accused, or whether they were instigated and authorised by societies of United Irishmen, it is not, I think, now possible to determine. There were at this time, many hundreds of these societies scattered over the country, each of them being a centre of local sedition and agitation, and each of them

---

[1] Lord Moira, Nov. 6, 1796.
[2] McNevin's *Pieces of Irish History*, p. 104.
[3] Several instances (outside Ulster) were given by Sir Lawrence Parsons, in his speech on the Insurrection Bill. Thus, about four years before that Bill was passed, 'three persons were murdered in succession in the county Tipperary. The first was a witness, the second a witness of his murder, and the third a witness of the second murder.' (Seward's *Collectanea Politica*, iii. 168.)

acting very independently of Belfast and Dublin. There was little communication; writing of every kind was discouraged in order to avoid detection, and it is extremely probable that in some of them, murders were discussed and planned. On the other hand, such a condition of society as I have described, would naturally produce murders independently of any regular organisation, and the greater part of the Ulster outrages, which were not due to the Orangemen, appear to have been due to the Defenders, who were, at first, entirely distinct from the United Irishmen.[1]

These two bodies, however, were now steadily gravitating to one another. Defenderism had everywhere become more or less political, and it was especially so in Ulster. The Catholics in this province seem to have been both more political and more anti-English than those of other parts, and the United Irish leaders, who were chiefly Protestant, and whose very slight knowledge of the Catholic mind was chiefly derived from Ulster, appear to me to have, in consequence, greatly exaggerated both the intensity and the amount of Catholic disaffection. With the exception of a few traders in the chief towns, the Catholics in three provinces seem to have cared very little for politics up to the period of Lord Fitzwilliam's administration, and their uniform conduct during many troubled years, certainly betrays nothing of the rooted antipathy to British rule, which Tone and Emmet ascribed to them.[2] A change, however, was now passing over their dispositions, and in 1796 the United Irishmen very generally succeeded in their efforts to incorporate the Defenders into their own body. For some time, the United Irish emissaries had been going among them, endeavouring to learn their views and intentions. They reported that Defenderism was not so much an association, as a mass of

---

[1] The opposite views of Madden and of McSkimmin (the historian of Carrickfergus) on this subject, will be found in Madden's *United Irishmen*, i. 534-536. McSkimmin, who had a very great local knowledge, has collected ten cases of murder, or attempted murder, which took place in Ulster in 1796, and were ascribed to the United Irishmen. Two of the victims were magistrates. Most of the others were informers or soldiers.

[2] Thus Emmet says: 'In Ireland, the Catholics in general, particularly the poor, had long entertained a rooted wish for separation, which they considered as synonymous with national independence.' (McNevin, p. 104.) We have already seen the similar statements of Tone and McNally.

associations, with little or no uniformity of views and action, differing in different counties in its tests and signs, and for the most part wasting its strength in partial and ill-directed insurrections against local grievances. As the Defender organisation owed its origin to religious animosities, and consisted exclusively of the most ignorant Catholics, it was very likely to be turned into a mere engine of bigotry, and very unfit for political enterprise. The United Irishmen now made it their business to impress upon the Defenders the great superiority of the United Irish organisation, the necessity of an alliance with the Protestants, the expediency of pursuing only one thing, 'an equal, full, and adequate representation of the people,' which would put an end to religious distinctions and to most of the grievances of which they complained. They at last succeeded, and the Defenders in great bodies took the oath, and were incorporated into the Union. The most turbulent Catholic element in Ireland thus passed into it, and its introduction into the Catholic militia regiments was greatly facilitated.[1]

It was in the autumn and winter of 1796 that Arthur O'Connor, Thomas Addis Emmet, and Dr. McNevin first formally joined the society, which from this time was to a large extent under their guidance. Tone, Napper Tandy, and Rowan, the most prominent of the original members, had been driven from Ireland, and Rowan appears to have given up all politics. About the same time, the United Irishmen began to give a military organisation to their society. This military organisation was grafted on the civil one, and it was fully elaborated at the close of 1796 and in the beginning of 1797. The secretary of each ordinary committee of twelve was appointed a non-commissioned officer; the delegate of five societies to a lower baronial committee was commonly made a captain, with sixty men under him. The delegate of ten lower baronials to the upper and district committee became a colonel, commanding a battalion of 600 men; the colonels in each county sent in the names of three persons, one of whom was appointed, by the executive Directory, adjutant-general for the county, and it was the duty of these adjutant-generals to communicate directly

---

[1] See Emmet's account of the fusion; McNevin's *Pieces of Irish History*, pp. 117–121.

with the executive. Orders were given that every member of the society should endeavour to procure a gun, bayonet, and ammunition, or, if this was not possible, a pair of pistols, or at least a pike.[1]

In a letter from Arthur O'Connor to C. J. Fox, a copy of which fell into the hands of the Government, the following description is given of the state of public opinion in Ulster. 'The people of the North,' he wrote, 'though perhaps the best educated peasantry of Europe, were violently against any connection with the papists, and the linen manufacture has always been esteemed a peace offering to the Northerners for the injustice our trade and manufactures have suffered, to aggrandise England. This was the state of things before this war, but now it has undergone a total change. The Presbyterians of the North have sought with uncommon zeal an union with the Catholics and Protestants. They have instituted societies in the nature of masons and friendly brothers, which have spread rapidly throughout the whole island; they bind themselves by a voluntary oath to promote brotherly love and affection amongst Irishmen of every religious persuasion, to promote a reform, and never to disclose anything that passes in the society. This, you may rely on it, is the whole of the test which is termed treasonable, and for which so many of the most respectable people in trade and manufacture have been imprisoned. I speak from certainty, having myself taken the test.' The United Irishmen, he says, wait for 'an opportunity to speak their sentiments,' which will only be when they have 'a decided majority of the nation.' 'The Defenders, who were an unthinking, oppressed people, acting without any rational view, have seen their errors, and are mostly become United Irishmen. But their opponents in Armagh are of a new description. They have an oath which binds them to support the Protestant ascendency, and every underhand means have been used by Government to instigate them against the United Irishmen; but they have begun to see their error, and are joining the Union in great numbers.'[2]

Among the Government informers there was an English

---

[1] See the Report of the Committee of Secrecy of the House of Lords (1798), and the evidence of O'Connor, McNevin, and Emmet.

[2] A. O'Connor to C. J. Fox, Dec. 24, 1796. (I.S.P.O.)

Radical, who came over professedly to establish relations between the democrats in the two countries, and who appears to have succeeded in winning the confidence of Neilson, the editor of the 'Northern Star,' as well as of several other members of the party. Neilson, in conversation with him, expressed his belief that in England the Republicans were a minority, but in Ireland a majority, and that the fatal error of the English democratic societies had been their custom of keeping written journals. 'We,' he said, 'commit nothing to paper. We assemble in small numbers, and without any predetermined place, and when our numbers exceed thirty-five we split, and the overplus lays the foundation of a new society.' The independence of Ireland, he thought, must necessarily come, and it ' would be no more injurious to England than the emancipation of America was, which, says Neilson, by increasing her exports, has increased her wealth. . . . What England lost in prerogative, she would gain in commerce.' The informer asked his opinion about the Catholics and the Defenders. 'The Catholics,' Neilson answered, ' have many enlightened men and true patriots among them, but he feared the great mass were bigots to monarchy. Their number,' says Neilson, 'makes them very formidable; their wrongs make them desperate, and though they would most probably render no good by themselves, yet with proper rulers they might be made of very great service to the cause, and so might the Defenders, could they be properly organised; at present they are nothing more than an undisciplined rabble.' According to the information received by this informer, there were nearly forty United Irish societies in Belfast alone. They consisted generally of thirty-five members each, never of more than forty. Belfast and Dungannon were both centres of authority, and each had several hundred clubs depending on it. Neilson was confident that 35,000 men could be brought into the field in Ulster, 'mostly armed and disciplined.' If the clubs were divided into three equal parts, two would be found to consist of Presbyterians and Deists, the third of Catholics and members of the Established Church. When a new society was introduced into any place, printed instructions, copies of the test &c., were sent from Belfast. When the society was full, it gave notice to Belfast, and was empowered to form a new one. No one was permitted to form a club who was not furnished with a certificate from the central committee at Belfast. With this certificate, a man might take tests and create new clubs in any part of Ireland. Any member who completed ten clubs was chosen a member of the chief committee.[1]

Our information about the proceedings of the United Irishmen outside Ulster is less complete, but on the first day of 1797 McNally wrote a very alarming letter on the subject. 'The county of Meath,' he said, 'though everywhere quiet, is not the less resolved upon the principle of separation from England. . . . As I told you before, it pervades, and it rises into, the upper classes everywhere.' It was calculated by the United Irishmen that, irrespectively of the militia and yeomanry, there were at this time only 20,000 soldiers in Ireland, and that a rising might succeed without French assistance. Such a rising, McNally said, was certainly in contemplation, and the first step would be to seize those who were in high Government situations. Very few of the original United Irishmen had fallen away. 'That principle,' he continued, 'I conceive to be now so general and so rooted, that in my opinion no change of administration, no representation of the people with which a House of Lords could possibly exist, would have force or influence to weaken it. The principle springs from republicanism, and demands . . . that all honours, stations, offices &c. shall rise up from the people through the medium of election, and not flow down from the executive power.'[2]

The difference of opinion between the English and the Irish Governments relating to the Insurrection Act still continued. Camden wrote strongly asserting the necessity of putting it into immediate action over a great part of the North. The state of the neighbourhood of Belfast, and of the counties of Down, Antrim, and Armagh, was very bad. There was an organised system of terrorism. Magistrates could get no information. Active magistrates, informers, and even men who had merely

---

[1] Information of Edward Smith, 1796. (I.S.P.O.) The true name of this informer was Bird. He appears to have been a man of very bad character, and the United Irishmen soon found out his true objects. (See J. W., Oct. 9, 1796.) Like some others, he played a double game, and at last quarrelled with the Government. Many particulars about him will be found in Madden.

[2] J. W., Jan. 1, 1797.

taken the oath of allegiance, were threatened with assassination. Within ten days, two magistrates had been fired at; two informers had lately been murdered, as well as a man who insisted on remaining with his troop. 'Immense crowds have assembled, have cut the corn, and dug the potatoes of the persons now confined for high treason in the county gaols, and in Dublin.' Ten barrels of gunpowder had just been stolen from the stores at Belfast.[1] In Down, at least, it was absolutely necessary to issue the proclamation, and twenty-four magistrates of the county asked for it. Portland, on the other hand, expressed his earnest hope that 'the tremendous power of proclaiming districts out of the King's peace, which the law of last session very wisely placed in the hands of Government, may remain suspended, and that the awe of it may be sufficient to restore subordination and tranquillity, without having recourse to more exemplary acts of severity.'[2] He yielded, however, to the representation of the Irish Government; some large districts were put under proclamation, and Lord Carhampton was sent to take the command in the North.

The last confidential reports of the Lord Lieutenant during 1796 seem to indicate some slight improvement in Ulster. The districts round Newry, he said, had been proclaimed with complete success, and were now quiet. Belfast was equally so, probably through fear of the Insurrection Act. In the county of Antrim, the magistrates were disinclined to adopt the Act, and no acts of outrage had lately been committed there, though the dispositions of the people were unchanged. 'I am sorry to add,' writes the Lord Lieutenant, 'that Lord O'Neil and some principal gentlemen of that county seem to have partaken of the frenzy of that neighbourhood [Belfast], so far as to wish to pass some resolutions at a county meeting expressive of their opinion, that a reform of Parliament is necessary to reconcile the minds of the people at this period.' Lord Carhampton is doing his utmost to prevent such resolutions from being brought forward. At Belfast, where Carhampton has been in his magisterial capacity, he believes that he has discovered 'the designs of a set of men called the Assassination Committee, who marked out

---

[1] Camden to Portland, Nov. 1, 1796. [2] Portland to Camden, Nov. 5, 1796.

and actually ordered the assassination of various persons. Four of the principal persons have been taken up upon the charge of conspiring to murder, . . . upon information which I hope will certainly lead to their conviction.'

The terrorism was such, that for some time 'scarcely one of Lord Londonderry's tenants would dare to speak to him, if they met him on the road, or would even show him the slightest mark of respect. . . . In the county of Tyrone, Mr. Stewart, the member of it, has experienced the same sort of treatment,' though 'he has always been the strenuous advocate of parliamentary reform, and has wished to substitute some other mode of paying the clergy, for tithes.' On Lord Londonderry's estate, however, there had been a sudden change, owing in a great degree to the ability of his son, Lord Castlereagh. 1,700 men had come forward to take the oath of allegiance, and he could easily raise a corps of yeomanry, if he could only select those who were to be depended on. On the whole, the state of Ulster seemed better, except the county of Derry, where there was much difficulty to be encountered, 'from the almost total dearth of gentlemen who inhabit that county.'[1]

Still, it seemed impossible to be sure that a spark might not produce explosion, and the condition of Europe was such, that an Irish insurrection would at this time have been peculiarly terrible. On sea, indeed, the flag of England still flew very high, and she had added largely to her colonial possessions. The French had been defeated by Howe in a great battle at Ushant on June 1, 1794; they had been defeated in the following year by Hotham at Savona, and by Bridport at L'Orient and at the Hyères islands. In August 1796, Elphinstone, with a superior force, had surrounded and captured a Dutch squadron of six ships of war in Saldhana Bay. Pondicherry in the East Indies, Tobago, Martinique, Guadaloupe, and San Lucia in the West Indies, had been taken from the French; and when Holland passed under French domination, England, with little difficulty, had seized all her colonies—Ceylon, the Malacca Isles, the Dutch establishments on the Malabar coast; the Cape of Good Hope; Demerara, Essequebo, and the Moluccas. But on the continent of Europe, the star of France seemed now rising rapidly to the

[1] Camden to Portland, Dec. 13, 1796.

ascendant. The coalition against her was shattered and dissolved, and England was entering into one of the darkest periods of her history. Belgium had been annexed to France. Holland was completely subdued, and early in 1795 the newly constructed Batavian Republic concluded an offensive alliance against England, which gave France the command of the navy of a people who had always proved themselves among the best sailors in Europe, and of all the ports and maritime resources of a coast extending from Texel to the Pyrenees. Tuscany about the same time made a separate peace, and a few months later the whole aspect of Europe was changed by the news, that Prussia and the other Northern States of Germany had broken away from the coalition, and had signed a peace at Basle which left France the undisputed mistress of the left bank of the Rhine. The Royalist insurrection which England had supported in Brittany, was crushed. Spain made peace with France in July 1795, and in the October of the following year she declared war against England, bringing a new and considerable fleet to dispute the English empire of the sea. In Germany, it is true, the tide of victory more than once ebbed and flowed, but the great victories of the Archduke Charles in 1796 were much more than counterbalanced by the victories of Buonaparte in Italy. In the course of 1796 and the first months of 1797, almost all its states had been either crushed or intimidated into treaties of submission, and the King of the Two Sicilies and the Republic of Genoa had conspicuously closed their ports against British ships.

At home, meanwhile, discontent, disaffection, and financial embarrassment were steadily increasing, and the English national debt, swollen by enormous subsidies to faithless allies, augmented with appalling rapidity. Pitt anxiously looked forward to peace, but his efforts met with no success. In the February of 1796, Wickham, who was British minister in Switzerland, had been instructed to sound, through Barthélemy, the disposition of the Directory, but his overtures were promptly and scornfully rejected.[1] In the following October, Lord Auckland published, with the sanction of Pitt, a pamphlet which was intended to

---

[1] See Wickham's *Correspondence*, i. 269–274, 312–314; *Annual Register*, 1795, pp. 125, 126.

prepare the public mind for a peace, and at the same time a new English application was made to the Directory. It was most ungraciously received, but they at length agreed to grant passports for an official negotiation, and under these circumstances Lord Malmesbury went to Paris.

The negotiation, however, was almost hopeless. The Directory had no real wish for peace, and they from the beginning declared their belief that England was insincere in her intentions, and only sought, by an apparent desire for peace, to obtain increased supplies, and to quell the murmurs of a discontented nation. Fox and the rest of the separate Whig party took up the same cry, while Burke bitterly denounced the negotiation as a new humiliation to England. When some one said that Lord Malmesbury found the road to Paris a long one, Burke answered that this was not surprising, 'as he went the whole way on his knees.' It was soon evident that England would not make a separate peace, which alone the Directory desired; and when the question of the restoration of Belgium to the Emperor was raised, the negotiations speedily terminated. England, indeed, was ready to purchase that cession by the surrender of all her own conquests from France; but the Directory at once refused, and on December 19 they ordered Lord Malmesbury to leave Paris in forty-eight hours. It was noticed that the funds at this time sank lower than at any period of the American war, and the drain of specie had already begun, which soon after obliged the Bank of England to suspend cash payments. It was under such circumstances, that the news arrived that a great French fleet had reached the coast of Ireland, and had cast its anchors in Bantry Bay.

In order to understand the circumstances under which this fleet was despatched, it will be necessary to recur for a few moments to the proceedings of Wolfe Tone. We have seen that this conspirator had been deeply implicated in the affairs of Jackson, and that after the suicide of Jackson, in the spring of 1795, he had, through the influence of the Beresfords, obtained permission from the Government to emigrate to America. The journey was safely accomplished, though the ship was boarded by an English man-of-war, and Tone was very nearly pressed for the navy. A curious letter, which he wrote to his dear friend

Thomas Russell just after his arrival, was intercepted and seized by the Government, and it gives a graphic picture of his first impressions. Like many later revolutionists, he speedily learnt that it is a profound error to regard the Americans as a revolutionary people, less attached to order and authority, and more prone to political innovation and experiment, than the English; and he frankly confessed that he had seen enough of them, or at least of the Philadelphians, to regard them with 'unqualified dislike.' Public affairs in America, appeared to him nearly as much under the influence of an aristocracy as at home, only it was an aristocracy of merchants and money makers. Washington was 'a very honest man, and a sincere American according to his own theory,' but he was 'a high-flying aristocrat,' and it was a matter of great congratulation that his influence seemed waning. For his own part, Tone said, the subversion of all forms of aristocracy seemed to him the first essential of liberty. 'To borrow Grattan's expression, when he was surprised by his passion into a fit of honesty, "Liberty must extinguish aristocracy, or aristocracy will extinguish her."'[1]

Philadelphia, where Tone now found himself, was at this time a great centre of Irish immigration and influence in America. 'It is a fact,' wrote Franklin in 1784, 'that the Irish emigrants and their children are now in possession of the government of Pennsylvania by their majority in the Assembly, as well as of a great part of the territory; and I remember well the first ship that brought any of them over.'[2] The success, however, of a considerable minority of Irishmen in this colony, must not disguise the fact that the large majority were penniless immigrants, who, at the very moment of landing, fell into the hands of dishonest contractors, and were reduced for long periods to a condition but little removed from slavery. Hamilton Rowan

---

[1] September 1, 1795. (I.S.P.O.) Rowan also greatly disliked America. 'The aristocracy of wealth here,' he wrote, 'is insupportable, for it is mixed with the grossest ignorance. ... The House of Congress is become a boxing school, the Speaker giving challenges from the chair. ... If this is a specimen of a democratic republic, Lord help us, sufferers in the cause! ... The moment I can leave this country without injuring my family, I will do so. ... Over and over again do I say, if I am to live under the lash of arbitrary power, at least let the whip be in the hands of those accustomed to use it, not picked up by a foot passenger, who, unaccustomed to ride, keeps flogging every post and rail he comes near.' (Rowan's *Autobiography*, pp. 300, 321, 323.)

[2] Franklin's *Works*, x. 131.

speaks bitterly of the 'harpies' that awaited them, and added, 'The members of the Society for the Abolition of Slavery have not the least objection to buying an Irishman or a Dutchman, and will chaffer with himself or the captain to get him indented at about the eighth part of the wages they would have to pay a *country born*.'[1]

Although no stipulation appears to have been made with Tone about abstaining from politics, a man of high and delicate honour, who had left his country under such circumstances as I have described, would have considered himself under a tacit obligation. Such feelings, however, are very rarely found among men who have once drunk of the intoxicating cup of political conspiracy, and Wolfe Tone was no exception to the common rule. He found at Philadelphia his old friends and fellow conspirators, Dr. Reynolds, Napper Tandy, and Hamilton Rowan. He immediately entered into close relations with the French minister to the United States, and soon after, in obedience to urgent letters from Ireland, he undertook a mission to France for the purpose of inducing the French Government to invade Ireland.

The missions of Bancroft, Coquebert, Oswald, Jackson, and perhaps other agents, had already shown the interest of the French in Irish affairs, but it was not until the December of 1795 that an invasion of Ireland appears to have been seriously contemplated in Paris. A long report was in that month presented to the Directory by De la Croix, the French Minister of Foreign Affairs, representing the enormous advantages France would derive from a separation of Ireland from England, and informing them that despatches had been received from Adet, the French minister at Philadelphia, announcing the arrival in that city of Wolfe Tone, to ask in the name of his countrymen for the assistance of France. Adet strongly recommended Tone to the consideration of the French Government; reminded them that he had a brother who had recently enlisted in the French service, and inclosed a memoir, written by Tone in the preceding summer, representing insurrection in Ireland as certain if the French would assist. De la Croix considered the

---

[1] Rowan's *Autobiography*, p. 318. In another letter, Rowan writes: 'Swarms of Irish are expected here by the spring vessels, and the brisk trade for *Irish slaves* here is to make up for the low price of flax seed!' (*Ibid.*)

project of invasion worthy of the most serious consideration, and, as it must be prepared in France, he demanded the authorisation of the Directory to invite Tone to Paris.

A French translation of the memoir accompanied the despatch. Ireland, the writer boldly said, was the chief source of the astonishing power which England had hitherto displayed. In the eighteen months of the present war, she had furnished to England 120,000 soldiers; and, according to the most accurate computations, two-thirds of the sailors in the British navy were Irishmen. From Ireland, England derives the whole of the salted provisions required for her fleet and her West Indian colonies; much the largest part of her skins and tallow; a great part of the stuffs with which she clothed her sailors. By separating Ireland from England, France would give a vital blow to her rival, and the time for such an achievement had fully come. Since the Revolution of 1688, the Government of Ireland had been a continued tyranny, and it had been the main object of English statesmen, by corrupting the Legislature and sowing division between the sects, to prevent her from shaking off the yoke. For a time during the American war their policy was baffled, but they succeeded at last in suppressing and disarming the volunteers, and substituting for them a militia, and from that date the eyes of Irish patriots were steadily turned to France. The Irish had taken every means to acquaint France with their anxiety to be helped, and the French Committee of Public Safety had responded by sending Jackson to Ireland. Hamilton Rowan was the chief man in the conspiracy. But the arrest of Jackson had disconcerted the plot; those who were mentioned in his letters were obliged to fly, and they were now at Philadelphia.

A passage follows which is extremely curious as showing the light in which the Fitzwilliam episode was now regarded or represented in Ireland. 'The British Government,' says the writer, 'terrified at the danger their despotism had just incurred in the attempt of the Irish to shake off their yoke, adopted the secret resolution to crush them altogether, by suppressing their Parliament, and bringing them under the laws of the Parliament of England. In order to succeed in this enterprise, it was necessary to gain the Catholics, and to make use of them as an instrument to force the Anglicans and Dissenters to consent to an union. The moment seemed propitious, as the Catholics were at this very time soliciting their emancipation; that is, their restoration to the full rights of citizenship, of which they had for centuries been deprived. The Government did not doubt that the Catholics would gladly accept any condition of which this emancipation was the price. . . . Lord Fitzwilliam was accordingly sent as viceroy to Ireland, to treat with them, and to effect the union as soon as possible.' Fitzwilliam, however, the writer continues, perhaps shocked at the treacherous task imposed on him, suffered the secret to leak out, and the Irish, warned of the danger that menaced them, joined more closely against their oppressor. The Catholics led the way. 'Assembled in the month of April last, to deliberate on the object of their petition,[1] they unanimously determined that no offer on the part of the Government, however advantageous it might be, even though it were complete and absolute emancipation, should separate them from their brethren the Anglicans and Presbyterians, and prevent them from making common cause with them, in opposing with all their force, and to the last drop of their blood, the projected union. Deputations of the Anglicans and Dissenters assisted at this assembly, and from this moment the three parties, so violently opposed, became one.' From this time, the memoir concludes, 'the Irish have in different counties centres of revolution, and their ramifications extend to the principal towns in North America, where there may be found a prodigious number of their fellow-countrymen quite as much interested as themselves, in the happiness and regeneration of their mother country; but it is principally at Philadelphia that the most important meetings are held. It is from there that their arms are constantly stretched towards France, demanding her aid.'[2]

---

[1] *Réclamation.*

[2] French Foreign Office. The only signature to this memoir is that of Madgett, who was employed to make the translation, but it is acknowledged by Tone, who says: 'It was written in the burning summer of Pennsylvania, when my head was extremely deranged by the heat.' (*Memoirs*, ii. 36.) About the same time as this memoir, two other independent memoirs, on the affairs of Ireland, were presented to the French Government by an Irishman named Duckett, who represented himself as having recently travelled through Ireland, and who appears to have been much about the French Government. Tone suspected him of being a spy, but there was no foundation for the suspicion, though

The great improbability of Irish agents being able to go to Paris without being detected by English spies, had induced the Irish seditious party to carry on their negotiations with the French Government mainly through French ministers in neutral countries. Shortly after the negotiation at Philadelphia, another independent and very important one took place at Hamburg. The reader may remember, in the negotiations that preceded the French war, the part which was played by Reinhard, who was then secretary to Chauvelin; he was now French minister plenipotentiary to the Hanseatic Towns, and his letters from Hamburg and from Altona form an important part of the secret history of Ireland, in the period immediately preceding the rebellion.

On May 18, 1796, he wrote to De la Croix that he had received a visit from an Irishman, who was very anxious that his name should be concealed, but whose name Reinhard considered it his duty to disclose in confidence to the French minister. It was Lord Edward Fitzgerald, who had just arrived at Hamburg. Reinhard had already made his acquaintance in London, and Fitzgerald reminded him of certain communications, which some of the Irish deputies sent over to petition the English Government in December 1792, had then had with Chauvelin. Chauvelin had not received them with all the interest the importance of the matter demanded. At that time, too, the Irish did not dare to propose or promise what they had decided to do now; they still hoped for a redress of grievances, and the French Republic was scarcely formed. Now, however, Lord Edward said, the French Republic is consolidated. Ireland is ripe for insurrection. The discontent is no longer confined to a party. The whole nation has been deceived, and since the recall of Lord Fitzwilliam no further reserve is necessary.[1] Lord Edward added, that he had come to Hamburg specially to open a negotiation with Reinhard, and determined to risk the journey to Paris if Reinhard was not accessible, and he begged Reinhard to obtain authority from Paris to conduct it. He talked of 150,000 men rising; of 10,000 Defenders who were armed and ready. Cannon, guns, and gunpowder, however, were urgently

---

Duckett seems to have acted very much for himself, independently of the United Irishmen.

[1] 'Nous n'avons plus rien à ménager depuis le rappel de Lord Fitzwilliam.'

needed, for during the past year the Government had been disarming the Irish. The appearance of a French fleet would be the signal for a general insurrection; but until the French arrived, an unarmed people could do nothing. The Irish priests would not oppose, and would even favour, the movement; and Fitzgerald counted much on Paine to frame a plan of internal organisation.

Reinhard appears to have been a man of much ability and judgment, and he read the character of Fitzgerald very truly. He was a young man, he said, incapable of falsehood or perfidy, frank, energetic, and likely to be a useful and devoted instrument, but with no experience or extraordinary talent, and entirely unfit to be chief of a great party, or leader in a difficult enterprise. At the same time, if an insurrection could be produced in Ireland, it would be of the utmost importance to France.[1]

In the following month, however, Lord Edward reappeared, with a companion who impressed Reinhard as a far abler man. Reinhard thought the matter so important, that he not only wrote the account to his Government in cipher, but added an urgent note, begging that only the most confidential official in the French Foreign Office should be entrusted with the duty of deciphering it. The new arrival was Arthur O'Connor—one of the first orators, Reinhard said, in Ireland, a man of great position and weight. He fully confirmed all that Lord Edward had said about the disposition of the Irish, and the certainty of the success of a French intervention. Representing the Catholics of the South, he had recently travelled among the Dissenters of the North, and found the latter even more determined than the former to rebel. He said that the militia would go with the people; that it would be perfectly easy to seize Cork, Waterford, and even Dublin; that the country was ripe for a general insurrection, and that the manner in which the English Government were seizing, almost without distinction of rank and age, all suspected persons for the navy, had raised the indignation of the people to the highest point. Guns, munitions, artillery officers and a few troops were needed. O'Connor believed that the effective English soldiers in Ireland were not more than

[1] Reinhard to De la Croix, 29 floréal, an iv. (F.F.O.)

10,000 or 12,000, and that an insurrection in Ireland would make it impossible for England to continue the war. 'We only want your help,' he said, 'in the first moment; in two months we should have 100,000 men under arms; we ask your assistance only because we know it is your own clear interest to give it, and only on condition that you leave us absolute masters to frame our government as we please.' O'Connor announced his intention of going secretly with Fitzgerald to Paris. He had told his friends in London that he was going to travel in Switzerland, and he begged to receive, through Barthélemy, who was French minister in that country, a permission from the Directory. Reinhard adds, that O'Connor had dispelled every doubt in his mind about the accuracy of the representations of Fitzgerald, and that he would answer for the sincerity of Fitzgerald with his head.[1]

The French Government were, by this time, very seriously engaged in planning an Irish expedition, and were acting, in a great measure, upon the information they received from Wolfe Tone. He had sailed from Sandy Hook on the first day of 1796, arrived at Havre a month later, and at once proceeded to Paris. He knew no one there. He was almost wholly ignorant of the language, and he had very little money, but the letters of Adet had prepared his way, and by the assistance of Monroe, the American minister at Paris, he at once obtained access to De la Croix, and soon after to Carnot, the great military organiser in the Directory. By Carnot he was put in connection with a French general named Clarke,[2] who, being the son of an Irishman, spoke English perfectly, and who bore a large part in preparing the expedition. The French Ministers were evidently much impressed with the ability, the energy, and the disinterestedness of Tone, and when the project had nearly come to its maturity, they gave him the rank of adjutant-general in the French army. He desired French rank greatly, partly on account of the pay, of which he was in urgent need,[3] and of the recognised place it would give him in the expedition, but partly,

[1] Reinhard to De la Croix, 18 prairial, 1 messidor, an iv. (June 6, 19, 1796. F.F.O.)
[2] Afterwards Duc de Feltre.
[3] 'Here I am with exactly two louis in my exchequer, negotiating with the French Government, and planning revolutions.' (Tone's *Memoirs*, ii. 147.)

also, because he trusted that it would save him, in the event of a capture, from the ignominious death of a traitor—a death from which Tone, though an eminently brave man, shrank with even more than common horror.[1] Many months, however, passed in weary expectations and disappointed hopes, rendered doubly bitter by that intense home sickness, that continual longing for his absent wife and children, and for two or three Irish friends, which was the most amiable feature of his character. 'I will endeavour,' he wrote on his thirty-third birthday, 'to keep myself as pure as I can, as to the means. As to the end, it is sacred—the liberty and independence of my country first, the establishment of my wife and of our darling babies next, and last, I hope, a well-earned reputation.' 'It is now,' he wrote, some time later, 'exactly seven months and five days since I arrived in Paris—a very important era in my life; whether it was for good or evil to my country and to myself, the event must determine; but I can safely say, I have acted all through to the very best of my conscience and judgment, and I think I have not conducted myself ill.'[2]

The journals which he kept during this period, for the sake of his wife and children and of a few intimate friends, are singularly interesting, not only for their bearing on Irish history, but also as furnishing an excellent example of self-portraiture, and an admirably vivid picture of the aspect of Paris in the stirring days of the Directory. It was a time when France had no less than fourteen armies on foot; when Naples and Spain had just detached themselves from the great alliance against her; when Montenotte, and the conquest of Italy which so speedily followed, first revealed to the world the rising genius of Buonaparte. The boundless spirit of adventure, the reckless gaiety, the genuine though theatrical heroism and patriotism, that inspired the nation, filled the young Irishman with astonishment and delight. He was present at the Fête de la Jeunesse, in the church of St. Roch, when the statue of Liberty, surrounded with a blaze of lights, stood before the altar, and the walls were decorated with the national colours, and the municipality were assembled, and all the youth of the district who had attained the age of sixteen were led in procession to receive from veteran soldiers their arms,

[1] Tone's *Memoirs*, p. 71. [2] Ib d. pp. 130, 130.

while the church rang with the thunders of the 'Marseillaise,' and he contrasted the scene with the gangs of wretched recruits he had seen in Ireland, marched handcuffed to the regiments. He described with a few skilful touches the soldiers of the Revolution—ill mounted, slovenly in their march and their manœuvres, each soldier wearing much what he pleased, provided his coat was blue and his hat cocked, the Grenadiers insisting on having their cravats tied in the height of the fashion, and on wearing their hats in whatever shape or form they conceived became them the best; every sentinel with his little bouquet in his hat, or in his breast, or in the barrel of his firelock, but all glowing with high spirits, with sharp, quick, penetrating countenances, and a fire and animation of manner that plainly indicated ardent and impetuous courage; and he remarked with justice the peculiar character of adventure and enthusiasm imparted to a war in which all the leaders were very young men. Pichegru, he said, who was the oldest general, was about thirty-six, Jourdain was thirty-five, Hoche was thirty-two, Moreau was about thirty, Buonaparte was only twenty-nine. He was astonished to find in France a gaiety equal to any in Ireland, without that hard drinking from which in Ireland it was deemed almost inseparable; shocked at a dissoluteness, both in principle and practice, in all matters relating to women, to which he had been wholly unaccustomed at home; perplexed at the strain of sentiment, that could bear without flinching the execution of hundreds on the guillotine, but at the same time made it necessary to rewrite 'Othello,' saving the life of Desdemona, as the catastrophe in Shakespeare would offend 'the humanity of the French nation.' The theatres had never been more brilliant or more popular, and Tone has left admirable descriptions of the acting, and of the military displays which now replaced the ballets of the monarchy upon the stage; and he wandered among the masterpieces in the Louvre, and with true eighteenth-century taste pronounced Guido to be the first of painters, and the Magdalen of Lebrun to be worth all the other pictures in the gallery.

All this time, however, he never for a moment forgot the mission he had undertaken, and in the perfect candour of his journals we can trace most clearly the various motives that actuated him. There was much of the spirit of an ambitious adventurer, who hoped to carve his way, amid the stormy scenes that were opening, to wealth and power and fame. There was much of the spirit of the revolutionist, to whom the democratic ideal of Rousseau had become almost what religion is to a devotee. There was also a true strain of self-sacrificing patriotism; a real sense of the degradation of his country, the corruption of her Government and the poverty of her people, but, like much Irish patriotism, that of Tone was mixed with great levity, and was largely compounded of hatreds. He hated and despised the Parliament of Ireland. He hated the Irish country gentry. He hated the Whig Club, and always remembered with bitterness how Grattan had warned the Catholic Committee against him; but above all things he hated England as the main cause of the evils of Ireland, and looked forward with passionate eagerness to her downfall. Yet not many years had passed since Tone had sent to Pitt and Grenville memorials of a project for establishing a military colony in the South Sea, for the purpose of assisting England in war with Spain, and if these memorials had been acted on, and Pitt had thrown the young adventurer into a career of enterprise under the English flag, he has himself acknowledged that it is extremely improbable that he would have ever been heard of as an Irish rebel.[1] Even after he had been deeply immersed in the conspiracy, even at the time when he was obliged to leave Ireland, he appears to have been perfectly prepared to abandon Irish politics if the Government he deemed so odious would provide for him in the East Indies.[2] He was not a bloodthirsty man, and he was sincerely anxious that rebellion in Ireland should be as little sanguinary as possible, but he distinctly contemplated a massacre of the gentry as a possible consequence of what he was doing, and he became

---

[1] *Memoirs*, i. 26, 27, 36, 37. His friend Russell (who was afterwards hanged for treason) joined him in this overture to Pitt. 'The Minister's refusal,' he says, 'did not sweeten us much towards him. I renewed the vow I had once before made, to make him, if I could, repent of it, in which Russell most heartily concurred.'

[2] His son, speaking of Wolfe Tone's conduct after the arrest of Jackson, says: 'He considered his duty to his country paramount to any personal feeling or consideration.... Even in that extreme peril, he constantly refused to tie his hands by any engagement for the future. He would, however, have accepted the offer which they made at first, to send him to the East Indies, out of the road of European politics; perhaps they feared him even there, when they altered their minds.' (*Memoirs*, i. 120.)

more and more callous about the means that were to be employed. He opposed a French project for landing a devastating force in Ireland to prey upon the property of the country, but he supported, though not without evident qualms of conscience, an atrocious scheme for landing some thousand criminals in England, and commissioning them to burn Bristol, and commit every kind of depredation in their power. 'My heart,' he wrote very candidly, 'is hardening hourly, and I satisfy myself now at once on points which would have staggered me twelve months ago.' 'I do not think my morality or feeling is much improved by my promotion to the rank of adjutant-general. The truth is, I hate the very name of England. I hated her before my exile, and I will hate her always.'[1]

He represented to the French Ministers that it was hopeless to expect a successful, or even a considerable, independent Irish rebellion, but that if a French army effected a lodgment in Ireland, and if they brought with them a large quantity of arms for distribution, they would certainly be joined at once by the great body of the Presbyterians and of the Catholic peasantry, and on the first reasonable prospect of success, by the whole, or the majority, of the Irish militia. If 20,000 French troops were landed, success, he said, would be certain, and almost without resistance. In that case, the landing should be effected near Dublin, which could most easily be captured. The smallest force that could be expected to succeed was 5,000 men, and if the French determined not to exceed this number, they must land as near Belfast as possible, push forward, so as to secure the Mourne Mountains and the Fews, which, with Lough Erne, would enable them to cover the whole province of Ulster, and then endeavour to hold their ground till the country was in arms to support them. The chance of success, in that case, would be greatly increased if a small additional force could be

---

[1] *Memoirs*, ii. 89, 241. The instructions drawn up by Carnot for what he termed the Chouanerie, in England, are printed in full by the Marquis de Grouchy in his little work called, *Le Général de Grouchy et l'Irlande en* 1796, pp. 16–28. A book of much value for this period of Irish history. See also a number of curious despatches from the French archives, in M. Guillon's *La France et l'Irlande pendant la Révolution*. Twelve or fifteen hundred French bandits, under the command of an American adventurer named Tate, were actually landed in Pembrokeshire in Feb. 1797, but the volunteers and militia, assisted by the countrymen, captured them all without the loss of a man. (See Stanhope's *Life of Pitt*, iii. 9; Guillon, pp. 296, 297.)

landed in Galway Bay, could secure a line of defence on the Shannon, and could produce a rising in Connaught. If a smaller force was sent, he begged that he might be allowed to accompany it, but he was of opinion that success would be hopeless, as it would be crushed before a rising could be effected. There were, he believed, exclusive of the militia, nine regiments of dragoons, two regiments of troops of the line, and eighteen of fencibles in Ireland, but the regiments of the line were probably mere skeletons, sent to Ireland to recruit; there were certainly not more than 500 men in each regiment of fencibles, and he doubted whether the whole regular military force exceeded 12,000 men. There were 18,000 militia, but 16,000 of them were Catholics, and a great proportion were sworn Defenders.

He found, among the French Ministers, an extreme ignorance of Irish affairs. He was asked, to his great astonishment, whether some use might not be made in the rebellion of Lord Clare, whether Lord Ormond would not take part in it, whether the aristocracy would not, as in 1782, put themselves at the head of the popular movement, whether Ireland was not still devoted to the Stuarts? He urged upon the French authorities that the reports on Irish affairs, which had been for many years in their archives, could only mislead them, for France, herself, had hardly changed more essentially than Ireland, since 1789. 'As to royalty and aristocracy,' he said, 'they were both odious in Ireland to that degree, that I apprehended much more a general massacre of the gentry, and a distribution of the entire of their property, than the establishment of any form of government that would perpetuate their influence,' and he assured the French that there was no living Irishman the least likely to be raised to the throne, and that the establishment of an Irish republic would be the certain consequence of separation. On the religious aspect of the question, he was equally confident. There was no disposition to set up a Catholic establishment. Tithes would be simply abolished, and each sect would pay its own clergy voluntarily. The priests hated the French Revolution, and they should never be employed, and never trusted; but, with a little tact, no serious opposition from them was to be feared. Their influence, also, had of late years enormously declined. The real leaders of the Catholics were ardent republicans, closely allied with the Presbyterians of the North, and the mass of the Catholic peasantry had enrolled themselves as Defenders, and steadily persisted in the organisation, though all who belonged to it had been excommunicated by the legate of the Pope, and though the priests refused them the Sacraments, even *in articulo mortis*. Few things gave Tone more pleasure than the conquest of the Pope by the armies of the Revolution. 'I am heartily glad,' he wrote, 'that old priest is at last laid under contribution in his turn. Many a long century, he and his predecessors have been fleecing all Europe, but the day of retribution is come at last; and I am strongly tempted to hope that this is but the beginning of his sorrows.' He suggested that pressure might now be put upon him, to make him influence the priests, in favour of the French designs in Ireland. In one of his addresses to the people of Ireland, Tone urged that republicanism must finally subvert monarchy, 'as the Mosaic law subverted idolatry; as Christianity subverted the Jewish dispensation; as the Reformation subverted popery.'[1]

He presented two memorials on the state of Ireland, which appear to have represented his genuine opinions, though the event clearly showed them to be full of the grossest miscalculations of the popular feeling. The population of Ireland, he said in 1796, was, according to the best computations, about 4,500,000. Of these, 450,000 were members of the Established Church, who were still 'a colony of strangers' in the country, possessing, chiefly through confiscation, five-sixths of its landed property, holding in their hands all the force of the Government, all the appointments in the Church, the army, the law, the revenue, and every department of the State, and constantly looking to England for protection and support. From these, nothing could be expected but uncompromising resistance, but they were only a tenth part of the population, and their strength was entirely artificial, composed of the power and influence which the patronage of the Government gave them.

The second division consisted of the Protestant Dissenters,

---

[1] Tone's *Memoirs*, ii. 274. See, too, p. 144, and also his outburst of delight when the Pope was dethroned, and the temporal power destroyed. (Pp. 464 466.)

who numbered 900,000 souls.[1] They were especially powerful in the middle classes; they formed the bulk of the volunteer army of 1782, and they were the most intelligent, the best informed, the most energetic section of the population. 'They are all, to a man, sincere republicans, and devoted, with enthusiasm, to the cause of liberty and France. They would make, perhaps, the best soldiers in Ireland, and are already, in a considerable degree, trained to arms.' Hitherto, 'in all the civil wars of Ireland, they ranged themselves under the standard of England, and were the most formidable enemies of the Catholic natives, whom they detested as papists, and despised as slaves.' In 1790, however, the French Revolution produced a great revulsion of opinion among them. They saw that the danger from popery had disappeared. They caught the contagion of the new spirit of liberty that was abroad. They perceived the fatal consequences of division, and in spite of all the efforts of the English Government and the native aristocracy, they had formed an union with the Catholics, which was the capital fact of the present situation of Ireland.

The Catholics, who form the third class in Ireland, number about 3,150,000. 'These are the *Irish* properly so called, trained from their infancy in an hereditary hatred and abhorrence of the English name, which conveys to them no ideas but those of blood and pillage and persecution.' They have little landed property, but a large share of the commerce of Ireland, and it was Catholic merchants and traders who chiefly composed the Catholic Committee. From his 'personal knowledge' Tone states that a great majority of the members of that committee were 'sincere republicans, warmly attached to the cause of France.' The bulk of the Catholics, however, are 'in the lowest degree of misery and want; hewers of wood and drawers of water. Bread they seldom taste; meat never, save once in the year; . . . their food all the whole year round is potatoes; their drink sometimes milk, more frequently water; . . . in addition to a heavy rent, they pay tithes to the priests of the Protestant religion, which they neither profess nor believe; their own priests fleece them.' These men are prepared for any change, for they feel that no change can make their situation worse. For five

[1] An enormous exaggeration.

years they have looked up to France as the champion of the oppressed, and 'I will stake my head,' writes Tone, 'there are 500,000 men who would fly to the standard of the Republic, if they saw it once displayed in the cause of liberty and their country.' 'The whole Catholic peasantry of Ireland, above 3,000,000 of people, are to a man eager to throw off the English yoke.' The Defender organisation has already prepared the way, and it includes the great body of the Catholic peasantry in Ulster, Leinster, and Connaught, and is spreading through Munster.

The advantages to France of the separation of Ireland from England appear obvious, and Tone especially and most emphatically insisted, that it would inevitably lead to the downfall of the naval ascendency of England. It would place her 'under insuperable difficulties in recruiting her army, and especially in equipping, victualling, and manning her navy, which, unless for the resources she drew from Ireland, she would be absolutely unable to do.' 'From the commencement of the present war to the month of June 1795, not less than 200,000 men were raised in Ireland, of whom 80,000 were for the navy alone. It is a fact undeniable, though carefully concealed in England, that two-thirds of the British navy are manned by Irishmen.' If Lewis XIV. had made it a main object of French policy to separate Ireland from England, he would have for ever sapped that naval ascendency to which England owed her superiority in all succeeding wars.

The assertion that two-thirds of the so-called British seamen were Irishmen, was constantly made by Tone and by other United Irishmen, and it derives some support from a passage in one of the speeches of Grattan.[1] Its extreme improbability will at once strike the reader, who knows how small a proportion of the ships in the British navy sail from or ever touch at an Irish port; how miserably the fisheries, which are one of the

---

[1] In his speech on the Catholic Bill in 1793, Grattan said: 'In the last war, of 80,000 seamen, 50,000 were Irish names; in Chelsea, near one-third of the pensioners were Irish names; in some of the men-of-war, almost the whole complement of men were Irish. . . . The Irish Catholics have supplied his Majesty's fleets and armies so abundantly, and in so great a proportion, that the recruiting service could not well go on without them.' (Grattan's *Speeches*, iii. 46.)

chief natural resources of Ireland, have at all times been neglected, and how little taste or aptitude for maritime life the Irish people have displayed. The military annals of England are crowded with illustrious Irish names, and not a few may be found in those of France and Austria and Spain; but in the roll of distinguished sailors such names are conspicuously rare. Recruiting for the navy, however, in the eighteenth century was largely effected by the press gang or by poverty, and it is probable that the suspected persons who had been recently sent to the fleet from the disturbed districts had increased the proportion of Irish sailors. Tone himself justified his assertion on three grounds. 'First, I have myself heard several British officers, and among them some of very distinguished reputation, say so. Secondly, I know that when the Catholic delegates, whom I had the honour to attend, were at St. James's in January 1793, in the course of the discussion with Henry Dundas, Principal Secretary of State, they asserted the fact to be as I have mentioned, and Mr. Dundas admitted it, which he would most certainly not have done if he could have denied it; and lastly, on my voyage to America, our vessel was boarded by a British frigate, whose crew consisted of 220 men, of whom no less than 210 were Irish.'

The question is sufficiently curious and important to justify a short digression, and there is some evidence on the subject which is more precise and trustworthy than that which was within the knowledge of Tone. Pelham, being convinced of the great exaggeration of the language employed by Grattan caused an exact return to be made 'of the number of men furnished by Ireland for general service, including army and navy, from the commencement of the war in 1793 to November 1, 1796.' It appeared to Pelham, and it appeared to the Commander-in-Chief, the Duke of York, to show that Ireland contributed comparatively little, and it certainly falls far short of the estimate of Tone, but the impression it leaves on my own mind is rather the great military energy which Ireland at this time displayed. Its population in 1796 can hardly at the utmost have exceeded four millions and a half. Including the militia, but exclusive of the yeomanry, rather more than 30,000 men were required for the protection of the country; but over and above this number, Ireland furnished within the period that has been mentioned, 38,653 men for the service of the war. 11,457 of them were for the navy, and 4,058 for the marines.[1]

On the whole, Tone maintained that there could be no reasonable doubt that if France could succeed in landing a considerable force with a large quantity of arms for distribution, Ireland must be lost to England. Catholics and Dissenters, whose mutual animosities had been the radical weakness of the country, were now cordially united, and they constituted nine-tenths of the population. The whole body of the militia would probably go over to the invader, and in such a contest England could not fully rely either on her army or her navy. The French on landing should issue a proclamation disavowing all idea of conquest for themselves, guaranteeing perfect religious freedom, and the abolition of all connection between Church and State, promising, on the one hand, protection to the persons and property of those who supported them, and, on the other, the confiscation of the property both of those who opposed them and of those who did not return to Ireland by a specified date,[2] and inviting the people to take arms and to organise a National Convention. All property belonging to Englishmen in Ireland should be immediately confiscated, and Tone dwelt especially upon the great sums which some Englishmen had invested in mortgages on Irish land.[3]

Such were the schemes, and such the hopes, of the ablest organiser of the United Irishmen. The representation of the state of Ireland which he laid before the French Government,

---

[1] See two valuable reports among the miscellaneous Irish papers in the Pelham MSS. The Duke of York, in acknowledging them, says: 'Many thanks for the papers concerning the number of men furnished by Ireland to Great Britain since the beginning of the war They are exceedingly curious and interesting, and clearly prove what very little assistance, in proportion, Ireland has afforded.' (Duke of York to Pelham, Dec. 3, 1796.) Pelham says he found that 'the men who had enlisted were mechanics, and inhabitants of towns, and that the peasants could seldom be persuaded, under any circumstances, to quit their families and place of nativity. . . . I could hardly believe, until I made a minute inquiry, that even in the militia they were chiefly manufacturers and mechanics. To ascertain the fact, I called for a return from the regiments in garrison who happen to come from the different provinces of the kingdom, and I find that two-thirds or three-fourths of each regiment were of that description.' (Pelham to the Duke of York, Nov. 14, 1796.)

[2] This clause was apparently copied from the Jacobite Parliament of 1689.

[3] See these two memorials in Tone's *Memoirs*, ii. 181–204.

was remarkably confirmed by the independent testimony of Lord Edward Fitzgerald and of Arthur O'Connor. Another memoir, apparently unconnected with them, came nearly at the same time from Ireland, asserting that fourteen counties in the North were already fully organised for revolution, that the organisation was rapidly advancing in the other counties, that the lower orders obeyed those who led them without knowing who they were, and that 17,000 out of the 20,000 militia were secretly sworn to go with the people.[1]

The French Ministers were now fully resolved to attempt the enterprise, but they determined in the first place to send to Ireland a trusted agent to study the situation, and to apprise the revolutionary organisations of their intention. The difficulty of finding such an agent proved very considerable. Tone himself was too well known, and he strongly urged the French not to send a priest, and if possible to choose a military man.[2] A Count Richard O'Shea was at last selected, and he received very elaborate instructions. He was to find out the leaders of the Defenders; to take if necessary the Defender oath; to discover their numbers and their strength; and to ascertain whether they were really allied with the Presbyterians, or led by priests or great landlords. He was also, himself, as an agent of the French Government, to regulate and direct their organisation. A sketch was given of the different districts in Ulster which should be placed under separate commanders. Internal correspondence was to be carried on chiefly through the instrumentality of women and children, and on foot, but never through the Post Office, and it was to be made a special object to seduce Post Office officials in order to become acquainted with the Government correspondence, and to introduce Defenders as servants into the houses of men of position. No member of Parliament was to be admitted into the organisation, and rich proprietors should be in general excluded. O'Shea was authorised to promise that a force of at least 10,000 French soldiers, with arms for 20,000 men, would speedily arrive either in the North in the counties of Derry or Antrim, or else in the West on the coast of Galway. All partial insurrections in Ulster and Connaught,

---

[1] MSS., French Foreign Office. See, too, on this memorial, Tone's *Memoirs*, ii. 137.   [2] Tone's *Memoirs*. ii. 45.

before the arrival of the French, must be avoided, but disturbances might be excited in Munster and Leinster, and especially in Dublin, so as to draw the British forces to the South and to the capital. The best men, however, must not be risked till the French arrived.[1]

Lord Edward Fitzgerald and Arthur O'Connor had by this time gone to Switzerland. At first De la Croix was suspicious of the former, and he expressed his fear lest the husband of Pamela should be an instrument in the hands of the Orleans faction and of Pitt. The assurances of Reinhard, which were strongly confirmed by Barthélemy, appear to have satisfied his mind, but he wrote that the proposed visit to Paris would be dangerous and impolitic, for it would certainly be discovered, and its object guessed by the spies of Pitt. De la Croix mentioned that he had laid the despatches of Reinhard before the Directory, and he now in their name made a proposal which Wolfe Tone had already rejected as impracticable. It was, that an insurrection in Ireland should precede a French expedition. The Directory, he said, authorised him to promise that, 'as soon as the insurrection had broken out,' the Irish should be seconded by 15,000 French soldiers with arms and munitions, and that if, as there seemed every reason to believe, the English were expelled from Ireland, France would exert all her power to secure their independence, and would leave them perfectly free to organise their Government as they pleased.[2]

This plan, however, was decisively rejected by the Irish delegates, and a powerful memorial, probably written by Arthur O'Connor, stated fully their reasons. It might, he admitted, at

---

[1] Secret instructions to Citizen O'Shea. (F.F.O.) Accompanying these instructions there is a paper of comments in French, but evidently written by an Irishman. It states that religion had nothing to say to the Defender movement; that the priests had done all they could to suppress it, but that their influence (to the great regret of the partisans of the Government) was much diminished. The Catholic landlords and noblemen, the writer says, had no influence; their houses were plundered of arms just as much as the houses of Protestants; once the revolutionary movement was en train, the Presbyterians, by virtue of their superior intelligence, would necessarily take the lead, and royalty was out of the question in an independent Ireland. O'Shea appears to have started from Hamburg, and received instructions from Reinhard. Reinhard to De la Croix, 1 messidor, an iv (June 19, 1796). It is, I suppose, this mission which is alluded to in Tone's *Memoirs*, ii. 224.

[2] De la Croix to Barthélemy, 4 messidor, an iv (June 22, 1796). (F.F.O.)

first sight appear reasonable, that in a country where the overwhelming majority of the population were disaffected, an insurrection should precede a foreign expedition, but it must be remembered, that the whole legislative and executive power in Ireland was in the hands of the Protestant aristocracy; that England would support them with all her strength; that the two Governments had been, for many months, fully aware that the Irish people were binding themselves by secret societies and oaths to establish a separate republic, and that they had been taking all the measures in their power to paralyse the scheme. By the Gunpowder Act, the people were prevented from obtaining gunpowder, or transporting arms from place to place. By the Insurrection Act, they were obliged to register all arms in their possession. By the same Act, any four magistrates might seize suspected persons and send them to the fleet. Six magistrates might declare a county in a state of insurrection, and then the Government might do what it pleased, make domiciliary searches, seize all who were out of their houses between 8 P.M. and 4 A.M., and take possession of all arms whether registered or not. The great majority of the militia, it is true, were in the interest of the revolution, but they were scattered; they had no munitions, and all their officers belonged to the anti-revolutionary aristocracy. Under such circumstances, the arrival of a French force must precede the insurrection. The Directory fear the superiority of the English fleet, but they should remember that half its sailors are Irish, and it is hoped that by their means a part of it may be seized. On two points, said O'Connor, the Irish leaders are inexorably resolved. The first is, that they will undertake nothing till the whole scheme of the alliance has been fully arranged. The second is, that the arrival of French aid must be the signal of the insurrection. If the Directory refuse to agree to these points, the Irish will wait till the probable wreck of English finance, or till the moment of peace relaxing the vigilance of the Government, makes it possible for them to supply themselves with arms and ammunition. Oral communication with the French Ministers, O'Connor thought of the highest importance. Fitzgerald was well known in Paris, and it might therefore be wise that he should not go there, but O'Connor was a complete stranger in the French capital, and if the Directory would receive him, he promised not to leave his rooms except at night. He would await their reply in Switzerland.[1]

By this time, however, the preparations for the expedition were nearly ready. The command was entrusted to Hoche, one of the most brilliant and chivalrous of the young generals of France. The recent pacification of La Vendée had given him a reputation which was only surpassed by that which Buonaparte was now gaining in Italy, and he adopted the Irish project with a passionate eagerness. O'Connor did not go to Paris, but he appears to have had an interview with Hoche, near the French frontier.[2] It was hoped that the expedition would be able to sail, by September 1, from Brest,[3] but many delays and disappointments, which it is not here necessary to recount,[4] retarded it till midwinter. Shortly before it started, Tone learnt, with much consternation, that John Keogh, Russell, Neilson, and some others of the United Irishmen, on whose co-operation he had counted, had been arrested for high treason, but there were other rumours, which seemed to confirm his most sanguine hopes. It was reported that, in the North, an explosion was daily expected, that a powder magazine at Belfast had been broken open, that 15,000 arms had just been smuggled successfully into Ireland, that an insurrection had actually broken out, that the arsenal of Dublin had been seized. Tone was commissioned to offer liberty to the prisoners of war, who were imprisoned near Brest, if they would serve on board the French fleet; and while all the Scotch, and nearly all the English, refused, the offer was accepted by fifty out of the sixty Irish. If they were a fair sample of the Irish sailors in the British navy, there was much to be hoped from disaffection in the fleet; but Tone evidently did not count upon it, and he expressed his pri-

---

[1] F.F.O.
[2] *Report* of the Secret Committee in 1798, p. 13. It appears to have been at Basle. (See Guillon, p. 171.)
[3] *Le Général de Grouchy et l'Irlande*, p. 43.
[4] The Marquis de Grouchy has shown, that Hoche himself was so disgusted with the inefficiency and delay of the naval department, that he wrote a letter on December 8, recommending the abandonment of the enterprise; and the Directory at last resolved to act upon his advice; but their letter, ordering that abandonment, only arrived at Brest after the fleet had sailed. (Ibid. pp. 65, 66.) See, too, on the details of this expedition, the recent work of M. Guillon, *La France et l'Irlande pendant la Révolution*.

vate belief, in his journal, that if a superior, or even an equal, English fleet encountered the French, the latter would infallibly be beaten.

In order to lessen the danger of an encounter by sea, the project of an invasion of Ulster was abandoned, but it was hoped that a sufficient force had been collected to make an invasion of Munster decisive.

One of the most remarkable facts in the history of this expedition, is the almost entire absence of those naturalised Irishmen, who had so long and so bravely fought under the French standard. Great numbers of the very flower of the Irish race had, during the past century, taken refuge in France, and the three regiments of Dillon, Berwick, and Walsh, which had been formed in 1689 out of the Jacobite refugees, and replenished by the many Irish Catholics who fled from Ireland during the penal laws, continued to the eve of the Revolution. No regiments in the French army had, for a hundred years, a higher record of honourable service; but since the peace of Aix-la-Chapelle, their character had gradually changed. The severe law passed by the Irish Parliament against those who enlisted under the French flag, coupled with the abolition of the penal laws against the Catholics, and with the great increase of industrial prosperity in Ireland, had checked the tide of emigration to France, and the Irish element among the soldiers had been reduced to small proportions. The officers, however, were still Irish, or of Irish origin, and, to a large extent, representatives of distinguished Catholic families.[1] There was a time when such men would have borne a foremost part in a French expedition for emancipating Ireland from English rule. But the same desperate fidelity with which their fathers had sacrificed home, and country, and fortune, for their faith and for their king, still continued, and the children of the exiles of 1689 were now, themselves, enduring, for the same cause, proscription, confiscation, and exile. With few exceptions, they ranged themselves against

---

[1] See O'Callaghan's *Hist. of the Irish Brigade*, pp. 479, 503, 630. Mr. O'Callaghan attributes more influence than I should do, to the decline of the Stuart cause, in accounting for the diminution of the Irish element in these regiments. Grattan said, in 1793, that the Irish brigade was 'chiefly composed of Dutch, and of the recruits of various nations, of very few Irish,' and that even the officers, though of Irish families, were not generally of Irish birth. (Grattan's *Speeches*, iii. 45, 46.)

the Revolution.[1] Many had gathered round the Prince de Condé, in the first stage of the struggle,[2] and now, by a strange and most pathetic turn, the exiled descendants of the Irish Jacobites found a refuge under the British flag. In September 1794, the Duke of Portland invited the Duke of Fitzjames into the English service, 'with the regiment of the Marshal de Berwick, and with the Irish Brigade, on the same footing as it had been in the service of his Christian Majesty,' and he stated, that it was the intention of the King to add a fourth regiment to the Irish brigade, and to place it under the command of O'Connell—one of the most distinguished officers in the old French army.[3] The offer was gladly accepted, and soon after, some of the officers came to Ireland to recruit.

They found it seething with disaffection and revolutionary ideas. Grattan, it is true, spoke with entire approbation of the enlistment, though he expressed his wonder that the Government should think that the presence of twenty or thirty Irish Catholic gentlemen in the Irish Parliament endangered the throne, while they were prepared to arm a brigade of 6,000 Catholics, under Catholic and French officers.[4] But Grattan's influence was now, for a time, eclipsed. The United Irishmen did all in their power to discredit them, and the Catholic Committee, which was pervaded by the same spirit, utterly repudiated them. The representatives of the old Catholic gentry of Ireland found themselves strangers and aliens among their people, and were exposed to gross insults, which Tone afterwards related, to the keen delight of his French friends.[5] Nor were they well treated by the English Government. It was determined to raise the Irish regiments to six, but it was soon found that recruits did not come in in sufficient numbers to fill them; and an order was given that the regiments which were numerically weakest should be drafted into those that were strongest, and the superfluous officers reduced to half-pay. The regiment of Berwick was one of those which it was proposed to abolish in favour of a new regiment, and Fitzjames complained bitterly that the compact

---

[1] Among these few, the most distinguished was General Clarke, who had served for two years in Berwick's regiment. (Tone's *Memoirs*, ii. 70.)

[2] See v. 575; O'Callaghan, p 633.

[3] He was an uncle of Daniel O'Connell.

[4] Grattan's *Speeches*, iii. 254, 255.

[5] Tone's *Memoirs*, ii. 70, 71.

was violated, under which he and his brother officers had enlisted in the English service.¹ Many officers were reduced to abject poverty; the new regiments were sent to the West Indies and North America, but the brigade was not kept up as a separate body, and it now disappears from history.²

It was on December 15, 1796, that the French expedition at last set sail from Brest. It consisted of seventeen ships of the line, thirteen frigates, and a number of corvettes and transports, making in all forty-three sail, and carrying about 15,000 soldiers, as well as a large supply of arms and ammunition for distribution. Admiral Morard De Galles commanded the fleet, and Hoche the troops. Wolfe Tone, who was now known as Adjutant-General Smith, was on board the 'Indomptable,' which also carried Chérin, the chief of the staff.

As far as the English were concerned, the French had every reason to congratulate themselves, for the bulk of the fleet never appear to have seen an English sail during the expedition; but the profound scepticism which Tone frequently expressed of the capacities of the French sailors, was amply justified by the event. The weather when the fleet set sail was enchanting; the sun was bright as May, and the wind soft and favourable, but some of the vessels speedily came into collision. The 'Séduisant,' a ship of the line carrying seventy-four guns, when endeavouring to thread the dangerous passage called the Raz, ran upon a rock, and sank with almost all the soldiers who were on board her; other ships missed their way, and on the 17th there were but

---

¹ See, in the Pelham MSS., the very interesting memorial of the Duke of Fitzjames, Sept. 1796, and a letter of Pelham to Colonel Brownrigg, May 11, 1797. In an earlier letter, Pelham writes: 'I have never troubled you about the Irish brigade, but it is really a most shocking and disgraceful thing. I have been obliged to advance 1,500l. upon my own credit for the bare subsistence of the officers, who otherwise would have starved, and I very much fear that the opportunity of recruiting is lost, unless some of the rioters in Roscommon should be induced to enlist, to save themselves.' (Pelham to Windham, May 17, 1795.) Something was said in the Irish House of Lords, by Lord Blaney, about the French emigrant officers, which the Duke of Fitzjames considered an insult, and a duel took place in the Phœnix Park, in which the duke was slightly wounded (*Annual Register*, 1797, pp. 9, 10.)

² An 'Irish legion' had been formed by Napoleon in 1804. It continued in the French service till 1814, and served with distinction in many campaigns; but it was mainly formed of revolutionary elements, and was quite different in its spirit and character from the old Irish brigade. Mr. O'Callaghan states (I know not on what authority), that Lord Castlereagh exerted his influence at the time of the Bourbon restoration, to prevent the reconstruction of the old Irish brigade. (*Hist. of the Irish Brigades in the Service of France*, p. 634.)

eighteen sail together, the general and the admiral in command being among the absent. Admiral Bouvet, and General Grouchy who was second to Hoche in the command, were still there. On the 18th there was a dense fog, followed on the 19th by a complete calm. Bouvet opened his instructions in case of separation, and found that they ordered him to cruise for five days off Mizen Head, and at the end of that time to proceed to the mouth of the Shannon, to remain there for three days, and if the fleet did not appear, to return to Brest. As Tone strongly urged, it would be almost a miracle if under such circumstances the English did not attack them, and he hoped that there was still a sufficient force to effect a landing. Some of the missing vessels reappeared, but the 'Fraternité,' which carried Hoche, Morard De Galles, and the whole treasury intended for the expedition, was not among them, and it was not seen again till the fleet returned to France. On the 19th the wind became unfavourable, though the weather was still moderate, and that night there was a new separation, but on the 21st there were once more thirty-five sail in company, only seven or eight, including the 'Fraternité,' being absent. On this day the French saw Mizen Head, which they at first took for Cape Clear. They coasted it with a favourable wind and a smooth sea, sailing at one time so close to land, that it was possible to throw a biscuit on shore; they then stood out to sea, directing their course to Bantry Bay, and on the evening of the 22nd, fifteen vessels, containing between six and seven thousand soldiers, cast anchor off Beer Island, which lies just within its mouth, and about four leagues from the point where the landing was intended. Nineteen or twenty ships lagged behind, and failed to enter the bay, but they were still within sight of the ships that were anchored within.

So far most things had gone favourably for the French, but Tone's experience of the manner in which the expedition was conducted, filled him with apprehension. 'It is scandalous,' he wrote in his journal, 'to part company twice in four days, in such moderate weather as we have had; but sea affairs, I see, are not our forte.' 'I believe this is the first instance of an admiral in a clean frigate, with moderate weather and moonlight nights, parting company with his fleet.' 'All now rests upon Grouchy.' 'I do not at all like the countenance of the Etat-Major in this crisis. When they speak of the expedition, it is in a style of despondency. . . . I see nothing of that spirit of enterprise, combined with strong resolution, which our present situation demands.'[1]

It was on the night of the 22nd that Dalrymple, who commanded the English force at Cork, first learnt the danger that was impending. The news came from several independent quarters. His Majesty's sloop 'Kangaroo,' commanded by the Hon. Captain Boyle, had been driven by stress of weather into Bantry Bay, had left it on the 20th, and had soon after sighted a French fleet, which the captain believed to consist of from nineteen to twenty-two sail. He at once sent Mr. Talbot, his second lieutenant, by land from Crookhaven with the news, and himself set all sail and hastened to England to inform the Admiralty. The news had but just arrived, when Dalrymple received a despatch from Richard White, the chief resident proprietor near Bantry, containing an affidavit sworn by three sailors at Beerhaven, and also a letter written by one of them to a relative at Bantry. They stated that on Wednesday, the 21st, they had seen a fleet between the Dorsays and the Mizen, which they supposed to be English; that a party of them had sailed in a hooker to meet it, but, not liking its appearance, had endeavoured to return to shore, when they were brought to by a cannon shot, and compelled to go on board what proved to be a French man-of-war. Five of the crew were kept on board, and the others detained till nightfall. The French treated them with much civility, and told them the fleet was bound for Bantry, and that it carried 80,000 men. The writer expressed his own belief, that there could not have been half so many. The same night a second courier arrived from Mr. White, with the information of the custom-house officer at Beerhaven, reporting the appearance of a French fleet with many soldiers on board, making for Bantry. Some French sailors, it appears, had gone ashore, and had been detained and examined by a magistrate, and they stated that they had come direct from France, and that it was believed on board that a portion of the fleet had gone to the North of Ireland. An officer was at once sent by Dalrymple to Bantry,

[1] Tone's *Memoirs*, ii. 255-257.

and he met Mrs. White upon the road, and learnt from her that twenty-five French ships were beating to windward in Bantry Bay.[1]

There could be no doubt of the imminence of the danger, but it was completely uncertain what force the French had brought, and whether the expedition to Bantry Bay was isolated, or part of a concerted scheme directed simultaneously to different parts of the island. Every possible measure of defence appears at once to have been taken. The cattle were driven inland, lest they should fall into the hands of the French. Immediate orders were given to concentrate troops, and to make use of every means to retard the advance of the enemy. Mr. White at once called together the yeomanry under his command, organised his tenantry, made arrangements for establishing outposts upon the mountains, and took great pains to obtain and transmit information and to make preparations for the English. The promptitude, energy, and intelligence which he displayed, were repeatedly and warmly recognised by Dalrymple, and they were soon afterwards rewarded by his elevation to the peerage with the title of Lord Bantry. 'I will stand,' he wrote on the 24th, 'with my faithful fellows to the last, certain of your support. All ranks here nobly support me. They [the French] cannot land for some hours—the wind is against them.' Two gentlemen near Bantry, of the name of McCarthy, undertook to supply the expected English force with potatoes, and the best spirit was shown by the surrounding peasantry. But the letters of Dalrymple plainly show how almost desperate the situation would have been if 14,000 or 15,000 good French soldiers had at once landed. 'Our numbers,' he wrote, 'will probably fall so short of those of the enemy, that a diversion is all to be expected. Some artillery are now at Bandon, as well as tents; . . . we will have at or near Bandon towards 2,000 men in some days, if the prospect of affairs does not clear.' With every effort to concentrate the troops, it would be impossible to collect more than 8,000 men near Cork before the enemy had reached it. 'His light troops, at least, may be expected to reach it in four days from the landing of the main body at Bantry. Whatever

[1] Hon. Captain Boyle to Admiral Kingsmill, Dec. 21; Dalrymple to Pelham, Dec. 22, 23, 26, 1796. (*Pelham MSS.*)

can be done by pickaxe and spade upon the three approaches from Bantry, may occasion a further delay of two days, if artillery accompanies the march. In eight days, supposing Cork to be abandoned, by falling back towards the Blackwater with the troops previously advanced, 12,000 infantry may be formed in a strong position near Kilworth and Fermoy, besides a considerable corps of cavalry and artillery.'[1]

It was not the first time that French ships of war had appeared in Bantry Bay. In 1689, Château Renaud had sailed into it with a powerful fleet, had succeeded in landing the money and munitions of war that were necessary for the French army, and had returned triumphantly to Brest, in spite of the opposition of an English fleet. On that occasion, however, the French were favoured both by good seamanship and by propitious winds. Both of these conditions were now wanting, and an obstacle more powerful than any that Dalrymple could oppose to them, baffled their designs.

On the night of the 22nd a strong easterly gale arose, accompanied with snow. It blew directly from the shore, and not only prevented a landing, but threw the whole expedition into confusion. For the fourth time, the fleet was separated. The twenty ships which lay outside the bay, drifting fiercely before the storm, were soon lost to sight, while the remainder tossed in wild confusion and no small danger in the bay. An English fleet, flying before the favouring gale, might appear at any moment, but Tone observed with much bitterness that the French did not even take the common precaution of stationing a frigate at the harbour mouth to give warning. If the enterprise was to be pursued, it must be done with the fifteen or seventeen ships that were stationed near Beer Island, and the responsibility of deciding rested with Grouchy and Bouvet, who commanded respectively the land and sea forces. Grouchy—who was now fully supported by the Etat-Major—was strongly in favour of attempting to land, even with the greatly diminished force. He

[1] White to General Coote, Dec. 24; Dalrymple to Pelham, Dec. 23, 24; Captain Cotter to Dalrymple, Dec. 25, 1796. See, too, the account, derived from many different sources, of the measures taken, and the spirit displayed, in Crofton Croker's admirable history of the Bantry Bay expedition, in his *Popular Songs illustrative of the French Invasions of Ireland*, part iii.

assumed the full responsibility of the step by sending a formal order to Bouvet, and on the 24th he wrote a despatch intended for the Directory, inclosing this order, and stating very clearly the motives that governed him, and the difficulties of his position. He had now only between 6,000 and 7,000 men at his disposal, a force which was less than half of that which had been sent from Brest. In the absence of Hoche, he knew nothing of the military plans which had been adopted in France; nothing of the information which had been so laboriously collected; nothing of the nature and extent of the relations that had been established with discontented Irishmen. Under such circumstances, and after a delay which had given the English time to mass their forces, the landing of so small an army in an unknown country was very perilous, but Grouchy considered it preferable to the alternative of abandoning the enterprise, when they had almost touched the Irish coast, and he believed that he could at least effect a diversion that would be useful to the Republic. Tone described vividly the desperate character of the attempt. The French had not a guinea, not a tent, not a horse to draw the four cannon which were their sole artillery. Their general intended to march on foot. They proposed to leave their baggage behind them, and with nothing but their arms, and the clothes on their backs, to sally forth to encounter an unknown enemy. But the near prospect of adventure filled them with delight, and Tone had never so much admired the invincible buoyancy of the French character as in that hour of peril. They hoped to obtain provisions and means of transport at Bantry; to reach Kinsale and Cork by forced marches, and to receive the support of an armed population.

The anchors were drawn up on the afternoon of the 24th, and the fleet stood for the land. It was at first intended to disembark at Beerhaven, but the Irish sailors, who had been taken on board, pronounced the road thence to Bantry to be impossible for artillery, and it was in consequence resolved to sail to Bantry itself. An hour and a half of good wind would, in the opinion of Tone, have carried them there; but the wind was in their teeth, and in three or four hours they seemed hardly to have gained a hundred yards. In the evening the wind slightly abated, but in the night it rose again into a furious storm, and the waves soon ran so high that no small boat could live.

There could hardly have been a more melancholy Christmas, than that which now dawned upon an expedition which had been so lately flushed with the assurance of success. The hurricane showed no sign of abatement, and its fury was such that the whole squadron was in imminent danger of being dashed in pieces on the rocks. For at least another day a landing was utterly impossible; if it was at length effected, the French had great reason to fear that an English force would by this time have been assembled which would be amply sufficient to annihilate their little army, while a powerful English fleet might at any moment appear at the mouth of the bay. The wind, which was so unfavourable to the French, would have assisted it, and had it arrived, the French would have been caught as in a trap, and not a ship could have escaped. Tone discussed the situation with General Chérin and the rest of the Etat-Major, and acknowledged that it was now all but desperate; but he urged that it was still possible to fly before the gale from Bantry Bay to the mouth of the Shannon, and there to land the troops and march to Limerick, which would probably be undefended, as the garrison would have hastened to Bantry Bay. The proposition was favourably received, but the general and admiral were nearly two leagues away. The storm made all communication or consultation impossible, and the whole day passed in painful suspense. At half-past six, when the dark and stormy winter evening had well closed in, to the extreme astonishment of the Etat-Major, the frigate carrying Bouvet and Grouchy ran swiftly before the wind alongside of the 'Indomptable,' and a voice from on board it, hailed the captain through a speaking trumpet, and ordered him at once to cut his cable and put to sea. No signal of any kind had been seen or heard preparing them for the step, and the first impression was that the ship, which had disappeared so rapidly through the gloom, was an English frigate, which had been concealed in the bay, had availed itself of the storm and darkness to escape, and had adopted this stratagem to separate the fleet. After a hasty consultation, it was resolved at least to wait till the day, and the vessel bearing the admiral and the general was soon alone in the open sea.

This proceeding, which afterwards gave rise to much angry recrimination, was due to Bouvet, and it is easy to explain, if not to justify, it. He was not on cordial terms with Grouchy, and although he had reluctantly acquiesced in the order to disembark the troops, the storm of the 25th had convinced him that the enterprise was now impracticable. In the afternoon one of the cables of his frigate had broken, through the strain, and the ship was for a time in extreme danger. The hour of sunset came, and the storm, instead of diminishing, as had been hoped, rather increased. Bouvet considered that he was responsible for the fleet, and that, even apart from the danger of its being captured by the English, it was not likely, if it remained in a narrow and rock-bound bay, to outlive the night. He therefore resolved at all hazards to gain the open sea, and endeavour to bring his squadron to Brest. Without even informing Grouchy of his intention, he ordered two cannon to be fired as a signal for departure to the fleet; but amid the howling of the tempest, the signal appears to have been unheard in the 'Indomptable,' and no other ship left the bay.

Grouchy angrily but vainly protested, and when the morning broke, and it was found that their vessel was alone on the sea, he vehemently urged Bouvet to return to Bantry Bay to seek the fleet, or else to make for the mouth of the Shannon, where, in obedience to the instructions that had been issued, some of the missing vessels were likely to be found. The first suggestion appeared impracticable, for no vessel could have sailed in the teeth of such a hurricane as was blowing; and Bouvet rejected the second, refusing to run any further unnecessary risk, and alleging that the missing ships, if they had not sunk or been captured, had probably by this time made their way to France. On January 1, 1797, the frigate carrying the admiral and the general, who were now at deadly enmity, arrived safely but alone at Brest.

Contrary to expectation, the ships that remained in Bantry Bay rode out the night, but the next day the gale still continued, and an additional horror was added to the situation by a fog, which was so dense that it was for some time impossible to see more than a ship's length ahead. Several of the ships, including the 'Indomptable,' repeatedly dragged their anchors, and were in the utmost danger. In the afternoon one of the largest could hold out no longer, and sought the only possible safety by putting to sea. At night three others were compelled to take the same course, and on the 27th the remainder of the squadron, availing themselves of a slight improvement in the wind, left Bantry Bay. They sailed through a furious sea towards the mouth of the Shannon, but as none of the missing ships were in sight, they speedily turned their helms towards France, and succeeded in reaching Brest soon after Bouvet and Grouchy.

The danger, which had been so threatening, had passed, but many days elapsed before the English general felt any security. On the 25th, Captain Cotter, who had been sent down to Bantry to reconnoitre, wrote describing the storm, and informed the commander with evident perplexity that not more than seventeen vessels were in sight. As the fleet had been originally reckoned at fifty or sixty sail, he inferred that only a portion was in the bay, and that it was either awaiting a powerful reinforcement, or playing a secondary part to an expedition the nature and object of which were not yet known. 'Whatever troops,' he added, 'may be on board this fleet of seventeen vessels, I presume could never be expected to make much impression on this country, unless they rely upon powerful assistance from the inhabitants, which I am happy to say, for the honour of this part of Ireland, they have not the most distant chance of obtaining.' Dalrymple on the following day wrote to Pelham, that unless the English fleet speedily came and conquered, he had little doubt that on the first fair day the French fleet would be brought together and a landing effected; and although the French would now find many difficulties in their way, he feared there were none which a considerable body of good troops could not surmount. The French fleet disappeared, but on December 30, four large French ships and one or two smaller ones were again seen making for the bay. They entered it, cast anchor, sent out a boat to a small island belonging to Mr. White, and took away some sailors. Next day a second boat was seen to leave one of the ships, and the little garrison which was now posted at Bantry was drawn out on the shore to oppose a landing, but it was not attempted, and in the course of the day all the sailors who had been taken were released except one, who was kept as a pilot. They were examined by an English officer, and they reported that they had been on board two ships, neither of which contained any soldiers, and had been told that these ships had never before been in the bay, and that they would leave it on the first fair day unless the vanguard of the fleet appeared. The officer greatly doubted whether the sailors told the truth, and on the first day of 1797 two more French ships appeared. 'Their size,' wrote Dalrymple, 'I know not; they drop in gradually, and if they sail not to-day, the wind being fair, they certainly mean to remain in the bay, and form a junction with those absent.' It is probable that these vessels were some of those which had formerly failed to enter the bay, and had been driven from its mouth by the storm on the night of December 22. On the 2nd they sailed farther out, and cast anchor off Beer Island near the mouth of the bay, where they were shrouded from view by a thick mist. On the 3rd or 4th they set sail for France.[1]

In the first week of January, most of the ships, which had been so widely and so strangely scattered, had returned to Brest, but the French had some considerable losses to deplore. One transport and one ship of war had been taken by the English, and six other vessels perished in the course of the expedition either from striking against rocks, or from the violence of the waves, or through isolated encounters with English ships. The last ship to return to France was the 'Fraternité,' carrying Hoche and the admiral of the fleet. It had parted from the remainder of the fleet shortly after leaving Brest, and it soon after was descried by a much more powerful English frigate, which chased it for more than twelve hours, far from its intended course. When it endeavoured to regain it, it encountered the great storms of the 27th and 29th, which partially disabled it, and drove it far from the Irish coast. After much hardship and some adventures, which it is not here necessary to relate, the admiral at last succeeded, on January 14, in bringing his shattered frigate to Rochelle.[2]

---

[1] Cotter to Dalrymple, Dec. 25; Dalrymple to Pelham, Dec. 26, 27, 28, 30, 31, Jan. 1, 2, 3, 6, 1797; Col. French to General Coote, Dec. 31, 1796; Jan. 2, 1797; John Brown to Dalrymple, Jan. 3, 1797. (*Pelham MSS.*) See, too, Croker's *Narrative*, pp. 27–29.

[2] Wolfe Tone's *Journal* gives an admirably graphic and, on the whole, an accurate account of this expedition; but Tone naturally saw only

It is not surprising that men who seek to trace in human history the operations of a Divine hand, should have deemed the storm which dispersed the French fleet, when it lay within a cannon shot of the Irish shore, as manifestly providential as that which two centuries before had shattered the proud Armada of Spain. Except perhaps in the beginning of the rebellion of 1641, the connection between England and Ireland had never been in such peril as in the last weeks of 1796. If the expedition had started but a few days earlier, when the weather was still propitious; if it had not encountered a storm of extraordinary violence and duration, at a time when success had almost been attained; if the wind had blown from any other point of the compass, or if the naval part of the expedition had been conducted with common skill, it is certain that an army of some fifteen thousand French soldiers would have been landed without difficulty within forty-five miles of Cork before there was any considerable force to oppose them, and it is scarcely less certain that the second city in Ireland must have fallen into their hands. It is only too probable, that such a success would have been immediately followed by a rebellion in Ulster, if not in the other provinces.

It was a strange and startling thing, that a great French fleet should have been able to sail unmolested to the coast of Ireland, to remain in an Irish bay for five whole days, and then to return to France without encountering an English fleet. In one respect, however, the expedition was very reassuring. It

what took place in the neighbourhood of the vessel in which he sailed. He was not always acquainted with the designs and motives of the commanders, and there are a few slight errors in his narrative. I have compared it carefully with the valuable series of documents published by the Marquis de Grouchy, which include the journals of Grouchy and Chérin, the official despatches and some of the private letters of Grouchy, the reports of the generals of the different divisions of the expedition, and several other documents of great value. The marquis has conclusively disproved the charge which had been brought against his father, of having caused the abandonment of the expedition, and shown a want of zeal or energy in his command; and the Journal of Tone fully supports his view. If any charge, indeed, can be truly brought against Grouchy, it is much more that of rashness than of timidity. The Directory censured the conduct of Bouvet, and M. Guillon, in his recent work, adopts their view; but in the extremely difficult circumstances in which he was placed, it appears to me far from clear that the course which he adopted was not the wisest. The proceedings on land may be best traced in the many letters in the Pelham MSS., and in the various notices brought together in the excellent narrative of Croker. (*Popular Songs, illustrative of the French Invasions of Ireland*, part iii.)

furnished a most valuable, if not decisive, test of the disposition of the Catholics in the South of Ireland, and some test of the disposition of those in the other parts of the kingdom, and their conduct appears to me to show clearly that, although treason had of late years been zealously propagated among them, its influence was as yet very superficial. An invasion had long been expected. Rumours of a coming French army, which was to emancipate the people from tithes and rents, and English rule, had been industriously spread through the Catholic population, and as soon as the fleet appeared in Bantry Bay, the gravity of the crisis was fully understood. If disloyalty had really reached the point which the United Irish leaders imagined, and which some subsequent historians have supposed, it could scarcely have failed under such circumstances to have risen to the surface, and an immediate explosion might have been expected. But all the evidence we possess concurs in showing, that the great body of the Catholics did not at this time show the smallest wish to throw off the English rule, and that their spontaneous and unforced sympathies were with the British flag.

'The people,' wrote Dalrymple from Bandon when the arrival of the French had become known, 'behave most charmingly, and are, I am sure, faithful to their King, and do not aid his enemies.'[1] 'I must,' he wrote a few days later, 'in justice to the inhabitants of the country we have passed through, assure you that their good will, zeal, and activity exceed all description.'[2] The conduct of the people of this country is most meritorious and praiseworthy.'[3] General Smith wrote from Limerick: 'The country is reported to me to be infinitely more attached to Government, than common report ever allowed of. Your yeomanry are guardians, and infuse, by their appearance and indefatigable activity and exertions, the most loyal spirit throughout each barony. The cabins of every town are reported to me to be boiling their potatoes for the soldiers.'[4] Camden, in the middle of the crisis, was able to congratulate Portland on 'the zeal which has been manifested throughout the country in the raising of yeomanry corps, and the temper of those parts of the kingdom which have been made acquainted with the probability of

[1] Dalrymple to Pelham, Dec. 24, 1796.
[2] Ibid. Dec. 27.
[3] Ibid. Dec. 28.
[4] General Smith to Pelham, Dec. 30, 1796.

a descent;' and he adds: 'Lord Shannon informs me, that it is impossible to conceive more loyalty than appears in his part of the county of Cork. The situation and temper of this town is so important, that it must give your Grace satisfaction to be informed of the very general loyalty and spirit which has appeared.'[1]

Dr. Moylan, the Catholic Bishop of Cork, at once issued a useful and very loyal address. Lord Kenmare exerted his great influence in Kerry in favour of the Government, and the chief bankers and traders, both of Cork and Limerick, came forward with offers of money.[2] Lord Donoughmore wrote from Cork that his brother, General Hutchinson, had just been to Galway. The merchants there immediately subscribed 900*l*. which was wanting for military purposes. 'The whole of the yeomanry corps offered to march with him anywhere, even without arms, which they were satisfied with the hope of receiving on their march at Limerick, and he is persuaded that, in the course of two or three days, he would have had it in his power to have marched a thousand men from Galway. All ranks of people were equally zealous and well affected, and, he said, I could not speak too highly to you of the loyalty of all that part of the kingdom. . . . Of the spirit, zeal, and loyalty of the people of this city [Cork] of every description, it is not possible by any words to convey too strong an impression.'[3] From the wilds of Mayo, Denis Browne sent a very similar account. 'This county,' he wrote, 'is perfectly quiet, and the disposition loyal even beyond my expectation. The inhabitants of this part of Mayo have connected the French and the Presbyterians of the North, who, they hear, have invited the French over; consequently they have transferred a *portion* of their hatred to the enemy, who, they are persuaded, are coming with their northern allies to drive them from their habitations and properties; and so strongly does this operate, that I am persuaded they would beat the French out of this country with stones. The unfortunate emigrant Northerners are acting quietly and inoffensively.'[4]

It is a memorable fact that Cork, Galway, and Limerick, the great centres of Irish Catholicism, the cities where at the present

---

[1] Camden to Portland. Dec. 26, 1796. (I.S.P.O.)
[2] Ibid. Jan. 10, 1797; General Smith to Pelham, Dec. 30, 1796.
[3] Lord Donoughmore (Cork), Dec. 29, 1796. (I.S.P.O.)
[4] Denis Browne, Westport, Dec. 30, 1796. (I.S.P.O.)

time the spirit of sedition is probably most formidable, vied with one another in 1796 in proofs of loyalty to the English Government when a French fleet was on the coast. It is a not less memorable fact, that the town which then showed the worst spirit was undoubtedly Belfast, the capital of the most advanced Irish Protestantism, and in the present day one of the most loyal cities of Ireland. Camden described it as the only town where bad dispositions had been shown.[1] A meeting of the principal inhabitants was convened for the purpose of raising a corps for defence against the French, but the only result was the appointment of a committee, which, by a majority of seven to two, passed strong resolutions in favour of parliamentary reform ; and Brown, the Sovereign of Belfast, wrote, that in this moment of danger there was extreme difficulty in enlisting any yeomen, and that the disaffection was grave and general.[2]

'I am not without expectation,' wrote Camden on January 3, 'that a partial landing will be made in order to feel the pulse of the North of Ireland, which I am convinced is ripe for revolt.' On the whole, however, looking back on the anxious period that had passed, he was able to congratulate the English Government very sincerely on the attitude of Ireland. 'Notwithstanding the suspicions I entertain,' he wrote, 'of the North, and notwithstanding the attempts of the disaffected here, I may, without being too sanguine, assure your Grace of the loyalty and spirit of the rest of the kingdom. The towns of Limerick and Galway have vied with each other in expressions of loyalty and attachment, and in actions corresponding with these sentiments. The utmost hospitality has been shown by all descriptions of persons to the troops, and the peasants of the counties of Cork and Limerick have anticipated their wants by preparing potatoes for them on the road.'[3] A few days later, he wrote that 'the best

---

[1] Camden to Portland, Dec. 30.
[2] G. Brown to Pelham, Dec. 28, 1796 ; Jan. 2, 1797 ; *Historical Collections relating to the Town of Belfast*, pp. 450-457. Beresford, in two private letters to Lord Auckland, Dec. 27, 29, 1796, fully corroborates the statements in the text. He says : 'All our accounts bring the most pleasing intelligence of a most universal zeal and ardour; the yeomen are anxious to move against the enemy; they are doing garrison duty everywhere. The farmers of Munster are assisting the military as much as they can.' 'Everything is quiet, and loyalty apparent everywhere, except in the North.' (*Beresford Correspondence*, ii. 142, 145.) I have already quoted the remarkable passage to the same effect, in Lord Clare's speech in the debate of Feb. 19, 1798.
[3] Camden to Portland, Jan. 3, 1797.

spirit' had been manifested both by the regulars and the militia; and he added: 'I have every reason to believe that if a landing had taken place, the latter would have displayed the utmost fidelity.' The Antrim and Down regiments, which had been suspected, seemed unanimously loyal, and the population, wherever the troops passed, showed the best dispositions. 'The roads, which in parts had been rendered impassable by the snow, were cleared by the peasantry. The poor people often shared their potatoes with them [the troops], and dressed their meat without demanding payment, of which there was a very particular instance in the town of Banagher, where no gentleman or principal farmer resides to set them the example. At Carlow a considerable subscription was made for the troops as they passed, and at Limerick and Cork every exertion was used to facilitate the carriage of artillery and baggage by premiums to the carmen; and in the town of Galway, which for a short time was left with a very inadequate garrison, the zeal and ardour of the inhabitants and yeomanry was peculiarly manifested.... In short, the good disposition of the people through the South and West was so prevalent, that I have no doubt, had the enemy landed, their hopes of assistance from the inhabitants would have been totally disappointed. From the armed yeomanry, Government derived the most honourable assistance. Noblemen and gentlemen of the first property vied in exerting themselves at the head of their corps. Much of the express and escort duty was performed by them. In Cork, Limerick, and Galway, they took the duty of the garrisons. Lord Shannon informs me that men of 3,000*l.* to 4,000*l.* a year were employed in escorting baggage and carrying expresses. Mr. John La Touche, who was a private in his son's corps, rode twenty-five miles, in one of the severest nights, with an express.... The merchants of Dublin, many of them of the first eminence, marched sixteen miles with a convoy of arms to the North.... The appearance of this metropolis has been highly meritorious,' and it has been found possible 'greatly to reduce the garrison with perfect safety to the town. The number of yeomanry fully appointed and disciplined in Dublin exceeds 2,000, above 400 of whom are horse. The whole number of corps approved by Government amounts to 440, exclusive of the Dublin corps. The gross number is nearly 25,000.

Of these, 8,359 cavalry have been armed, and 6,046 infantry. . . . In reply to a circular letter written to the commandants of the respective corps, their answer almost universally contained a general offer of service in any part of the kingdom. . . . I am sorry in being obliged to say that in Belfast, and in some parts of the North, a different temper was manifested.'[1]

My task in the present chapter has been to a great extent that of an editor, selecting from the vast mass of Government correspondence such letters as most fully paint the condition of the country. This method of writing history is necessarily wanting in stirring and dramatic interest, but it has the advantage of enabling the reader to form his own judgment of events, very independently of the historian, and it is, I think, peculiarly valuable where the chief facts to be recorded are changes in social conditions, new turns and modifications of popular sympathies and passions. The main problem of Irish history is the fact that Ireland, after a connection with England of no less than 700 years, is as disaffected as a newly conquered province, and that, in spite of a long period of national education, of the labours of many able and upright statesmen, of a vast amount of remedial legislation, and of close contact with the free, healthy, and energetic civilisation of Great Britain, Irish popular sentiment on political subjects is at the present hour perhaps the most degraded and the most demoralised in Europe. The year 1796 contributed largely to this demoralisation. Anarchy and organised crime had greatly extended, and they were steadily taking a more political form, while Grattan and the other really able, honest, moderate, and constitutional reformers, had lost almost all their influence. The discredit which was thrown on the Constitution of 1782, and the utter failure of Grattan to procure either parliamentary reform or Catholic emancipation, had combined with the influences that sprang from the French Revolution to turn many into new and dangerous paths, and to give popularity and power to politicians of another and a baser type. Still the mass of people seem as yet to have been but little touched, and the problem of making Ireland a loyal and constitutional country was certainly not an impossible one. But the men in whose hands the direction of affairs was placed, were de-

[1] Camden to Portland, Jan. 10, 1797.

termined to resist the most moderate and legitimate reforms, and they made the perpetual disqualification of the Catholics, and the unqualified maintenance of all the scandalous and enormous abuses of the representative system, the avowed and foremost objects of their policy. Their parliamentary majority was overwhelming, and with the existing constituencies there seemed no prospect of overthrowing it. Very naturally, then, the reforming energy of the country ebbed more and more away from the constitutional leaders, and began to look to rebellion and foreign assistance for the attainment of its objects. Arthur O'Leary, who was by far the ablest of the Catholic clergy and writers, in a letter to a supporter of the Government, expressed his opinion of the situation and prospects of the country in words which appear to me both weighty and unexaggerated. 'Ireland,' he said, 'owes its present security to the inconstant elements, and to the constant loyalty of the majority of the people, a loyalty which, I am sorry to find, a blind, blundering, and tyrannical policy is constantly endeavouring to shake, if not entirely to annihilate; as is manifestly evident from some late proceedings of the Irish House of Commons, declaring in the face of Europe, and within three days' sailing of a powerful and vigilant enemy, that the emancipation of the Catholics of Ireland is inconsistent with the security of the kingdom and its connection with England. This is as much as to say to the French, "As their emancipation is inconsistent with the security of this kingdom, it is natural to expect that they will fly into your arms from ours, always uplifted to oppress them."'[1]

[1] Arthur O'Leary, Jan. 30, 1797. (I.S.P.O.)

CHAPTER XXVIII.

THE loyalty displayed by the militia and the Catholic peasantry when the French lay in Bantry Bay, made a great impression on all classes of politicians. The United Irishmen, indeed, urged that the French had attempted to land in one of the parts of Ireland where the organisation was least extended; that they had sent no intimation to the leaders of the conspiracy which could render it possible to prepare for their reception, and that if a French fleet had appeared in the North or North-west the result would have been very different. In these statements there was no doubt much truth, but still the attitude of positive and even enthusiastic loyalty exhibited in so many parts of Ireland seemed to show that the seditious spirit was less formidable than might have been imagined, and that a large element of unreality mingled with it. It by no means followed from the fact that the bulk of the peasantry in any district had been sworn in as United Irishmen or as Defenders, that they were prepared to appear in arms for the French, or even seriously desired an invasion. The intimidation exercised by small bands of conspirators induced multitudes to take an oath which they had very little intention of keeping, and even where intimidation did not come into operation, disloyalty was often a fashion, a sentiment, and almost an amusement, which abundantly coloured the popular imagination, but was much too feeble and unsubstantial a thing to induce men to make any genuine sacrifice in its cause. Everyone who has any real knowledge of Irish life, character, and history knows how widely a sentiment of this kind has been diffused, and knows also that districts and classes where it has been most prevalent have again and again remained perfectly passive in times when the prospects of rebellion seemed most favourable, and have furnished thousands of the best and most faithful soldiers to the British army. Genuine enthusiasts, like those who, at the close of the eighteenth century, were sending skilful memoirs to the French Government, representing all Ireland as panting for revolution, or like a few brave men who in later times have sacrificed to their political convictions all that makes life dear, have usually miscalculated its force, and have learnt at last, by bitter experience, that, except when it has been allied with religious or agrarian passions, it usually evaporates in words.

There is indeed, perhaps, only one condition in which its unassisted action can be a serious danger to the State. It is when legislation breaks down the influence of the educated and propertied classes of the community, and then by a democratic suffrage, under the shelter of the ballot, throws the preponderating voting power of the country into the hands of the most ignorant and the most disaffected. A majority of votes represents very imperfectly deliberate opinion. It represents still more imperfectly the course which men desire with real earnestness, and for which they will make real sacrifices; but a languid preference or an idle sentiment may be quite sufficient to place desperate and unscrupulous men in power, and to give them the means of dislocating the whole fabric of the State. It has been reserved for the sagacity of modern English statesmanship to create this danger in Ireland.

But after all that can be said, it is impossible to read this narrative without being impressed with the extremely precarious tenure upon which British dominion in Ireland at this time rested. With a little better weather, and a little better seamanship on the part of the French, the chances were all against it. If an army of 14,000 good French soldiers, under such a commander as Hoche, had succeeded in landing without delay, and if a rebellion had then broken out in any part of the country, Ireland would most probably have been, for a time at least, separated from the British Empire. After the danger was over, Beresford described the situation to Auckland with great candour. 'We had, two days after they [the French] were at anchor in Bantry Bay, from Cork to Bantry less than 3,000 men, two pieces of artillery, and no magazine of any kind, no firing, no hospital, no provisions, &c. &c. No landing was made. Providence prevented it; if there had, where was a stand to be made? It is clear that Cork was gone; who would answer afterwards for the loyalty of the country, then in possession of the French? Would the northern parts of the country have remained quiet? Not an hour.'[1]

The danger, however, was past, and, in the opinion of some of the best judges, the near prospect of the horrors of a foreign invasion and occupation had exercised a sobering effect on popular feeling.[2] A strong reaction of loyalty was unquestionably aroused, and it was felt even in the North, where the disaffection was far deeper and more venomous than in the other provinces. One of the ablest men at this time living in Ulster, appears to me to have been a clergyman named William Hamilton, who was an active magistrate in Donegal, and whose letters to the Government furnish a remarkably vivid picture of the condition of a great portion of the North. Hamilton was a man of some scientific eminence, a former fellow of Dublin University, one of the founders of the Irish Academy, a frequent contributor to its 'Proceedings,' and the author of a singularly interesting little work on the social condition and antiquities of Antrim. He appears from his writings to have been a man of great liberality and humanity; of distinguished talent, and of indomitable courage and energy. In the beginning of 1797, he wrote: 'I have rallied the entire body of Protestants,[3] and detached almost the whole of the Romans from the Dissenters—whom I soon found to be alone the active emissaries of Belfast—from the moment the French appeared on the coast, and in the course of a few days such a tide of loyalty has been raised as bears down all opposition. One hundred and twenty Protestants and a hundred and ten Romans have in two days taken the oath of allegiance before me; and such is the unpopularity of disloyalty at present, that my time is occupied in writing tickets in evidence of individual loyalty. The Dissenting elders and leaders have tried in vain to stem the torrent. Nineteen of the number have been driven in to take the oath under the penalty

---

[1] *Auckland Correspondence*, iii. 376. Beresford erroneously estimated the French army at 25,000 men.
[2] *Beresford Correspondence*, ii. 146; Hardy's *Life of Charlemont*, ii. 379.
[3] The reader will remember that in Ireland the term 'Protestant' was, at this time, always given exclusively to members of the Established Church.

of broken heads or banishment, and by-and-by it is possible I may see the body yield.'[1]

Parliament met on January 16. The speech from the Throne announced the Spanish declaration of war against England, and the failure of Lord Malmesbury's negotiations at Paris; congratulated Ireland on the failure of the expedition to Bantry Bay, and acknowledged in emphatic terms the loyal spirit shown on that occasion, by all classes of the people. As in the two previous sessions, the language of Grattan in dealing with the French war bore a greater resemblance to that of Fox, than at the beginning of the war. He urged the mismanagement of military affairs and the pressing necessity for peace, and he expressed doubts of the sincerity of the recent negotiation, and a strong opinion that it was the democratic character of the French Government that made the English Ministers disinclined to negotiate with it. These two last imputations, which were equally made by the Whig party in England, appear to me to have been essentially unfounded; but Grattan stood on much firmer ground when he denounced the negligence that had been shown in leaving Ireland during twelve critical days unprotected by an English fleet, although the intended expedition to Ireland had been for months foreshadowed by the Paris newspapers. This was the second war, he complained, within fifteen years in which Ireland had been involved by England, and then entirely abandoned. 'In 1779,' he said, 'your army was sent away, and you had no naval protection from England, and yet then, as now, you voted large sums and poured out your population to man the fleets and armies of Great Britain. Your volunteers then, as your yeomen now, were assigned as your sole protectors. Two years back, the British Minister played the same game in Ireland. By a dispensing power he withdrew from the kingdom the troops allotted by law for your defence, and left you but 7,000 men, and that, too, at a time when you had no volunteers.' 'And now, a third time have they left us without the protection of the British fleet, with raw troops, and to the accident of wind and weather for safety.' If the French had reached Cork, even though they had then met with a final defeat, this event would have thrown back beyond calculation

[1] Rev. W. Hamilton, Jan. 14, 1797. (I.S.P.O.)

the prosperity of Ireland. The first Irish interest was now to accelerate the peace, and he therefore strongly censured the position of the Government, that the surrender of Belgium by the French must at all hazards be insisted on. 'It is not that I do not wish to recover Belgium, but I do not wish to hazard Ireland. The Minister is now gambling, not with distant settlements and West India Islands, but with the home part and parcel of the British Empire.' He moved an amendment to the Address, pointing to peace, which only found six supporters, but the proposed intervention of the Irish Parliament in foreign politics was probably not without its effect in deepening Pitt's conviction of the possible dangers which such a Parliament might produce.

It was admitted that the most strenuous and speedy efforts should be made to put the country into a state of defence, and it is remarkable that in this respect the language of the Opposition was much more emphatic than that of the Administration, who appear to have greatly dreaded an increase of any purely Irish force. A motion of Sir Lawrence Parsons for increasing the yeomen by 50,000, was warmly supported by Grattan, but rejected by the Government. A proposal of Sir John Blaquiere authorising the Government to raise 10,000 additional troops, who were to serve only in the British Isles, gave rise to much discussion. Grattan desired that this force should be exclusively devoted to the defence of Ireland, predicting that if this were not done it would be withdrawn in time of danger, to England; but the measure was ultimately carried in its original form, though not yet put in force. On February 21, Pelham, introducing the estimates of the year, stated that the military expenses amounted to a million more than in the preceding year, and he proposed to borrow 2,800,000*l.*, and to raise 305,000*l.* of additional taxes to pay the interest. This sum was to be obtained by increased duties on sugar, tea, wines and salt; by imposing licences on malt-houses, and by some slight changes in the Post Office and in the import duties, and he strongly urged the propriety of making every practicable economy, by suppressing or diminishing bounties. In the course of this session, the bounty on the inland carriage of corn to Dublin, which had continued since 1759, was abandoned after some curious and instructive debates, and in spite of the strenuous opposition of Parsons.

The question which was most debated in the first weeks of the session, was the revived proposal of Vandeleur to impose a tax of two shillings in the pound on the estates of absentees. Camden mentioned in his confidential correspondence, that it gave him great anxiety, as he found that 'there was a general disposition in favour of it among the servants of the Crown.' 'It was not,' he said, 'the mere drain of rents into Great Britain which affected their opinions, but the convulsed state of the lower classes, which they attributed entirely to the want of influence which arises from resident landlords.' Vandeleur urged, in supporting the tax, that the Irish debt would rise in the course of this year to little less than ten millions; that the new taxes on salt and leather would press very heavily on the poor, and that it was unjust that a considerable body of rich men should, in this time of great national difficulty, contribute nothing to the country which defended their property. An Irish landowner who resided in England, paid neither the English land-tax nor the Irish duties on consumption. Vandeleur estimated the number of these proprietors at eighty-three, and he supported his case by citing the law which prevented 'poor artificers' from leaving their country. The proposal was defended, among others, by Grattan and Parsons, and opposed by Castlereagh, who argued against the tax chiefly on the ground that it tended to separate the two countries. Grattan ridiculed this plea, and dwelt especially on the danger and the injustice of exempting a rich class from taxation, when it was found necessary to impose new and severe taxes on the poor; but Camden reported to the Government that he spoke feebly, as if he were half-hearted, and only when the House was exhausted. Forty-nine members supported, and 122 opposed the tax, and this is said to have been the best division obtained by the Opposition during the whole session. 'You can hardly conceive,' wrote Camden, 'how very extensively the determination to impose that tax had spread, and with how much difficulty I was enabled to withstand the torrent of public opinion.'[1]

---

[1] Camden to Portland, Feb. 20, March 1, 2, 1797; *Irish Parl. Deb.* xvii. 378–403; Grattan's *Speeches*, iii. 292–296; Plowden, ii. 598, 599.

On February 26, in accordance with an order of the English Privy Council, the Bank of England suspended cash payments; and on March 2, by the direction of the Lord Lieutenant and Irish Privy Council, a similar course was taken by the Bank of Ireland. The directors, however, in announcing their intention of following the injunctions of the Governments of England and Ireland, added that they were 'happy in being able to inform the public that the situation of the Bank is strong, and its affairs in the most prosperous situation, and that the governors and directors will accommodate the public with the usual discounts, paying the amount in bank notes.' A meeting was at once held of the chief merchants and traders in Dublin, who declared their approval of the measure, their full confidence in the solvency of the Dublin banks, and their readiness to receive their notes.[1]

Much more serious, however, than the shock to public credit, was the anarchy which was now rapidly spreading through the North, and which in a few weeks rose to the point of virtual rebellion. In order to estimate the coercive measures that were taken by the Government, it is necessary to endeavour to obtain a clear notion of the extent, and the kind of the evil. The subject is one which lends itself easily to opposing exaggerations, and it has been chiefly dealt with by historians who are violent partisans. There exists, however, in the confidential letters of magistrates, which are now in Dublin Castle, a large amount of authentic and entirely unused material, and by pursuing the sure, though I fear very tedious, process of bringing together a multitude of detailed contemporary testimonies, it will, I think, be possible to arrive at some just conclusions.

The disturbances were clearly organised, and their centres were innumerable small societies of United Irishmen, which acted very independently of one another, and which were multiplied by incessant propagandism. They consisted of men who, either through French principles, or through disgust at the corrupt and subservient condition of the Government and Parliament in Dublin, now aimed distinctly at a separate

[1] Seward's *Collectanea Politica*, iii. 185-187.

republic, and hoped to attain it by armed rebellion. This rebellion was not to take place till a French army had landed. In the mean time, their business was to prepare for the French by nightly drilling, by the manufacture of pikes, by the plunder of arms, by preventing the farmers from enlisting in the yeomanry, by seducing the soldiers and the militia, by systematically paralysing the law. But with the political movement, there was now combined the whole system of Whiteboyism and Defenderism—all the old grievances about tithes, and taxes, and rent, which had so often stirred the people to outrage—and on the outskirts of the whole movement hung a vast assisting mass of aimless anarchy; of ordinary crime; of the restlessness which is the natural consequence of great poverty.

Donegal and Roscommon appear at first to have been the worst counties. The improvement which Dr. Hamilton noticed in the middle of January soon passed away, and in several graphic letters, he paints the utter anarchy that prevailed near Lough Swilly, where he was magistrate. In one of those letters, written in the beginning of February, he describes how, between his house and Raphoe, houses were everywhere robbed of arms and money, corn destroyed, turf-stacks burnt, windows broken. He succeeded in capturing some of the depredators, and confining them with a guard in his own house, but from 150 to 200 men speedily assembled and attempted a rescue. Hamilton sought for assistance, but found that all the boats on Lough Swilly were destroyed, and that the whole country was watched. He succeeded, however, together with a certain Captain Smyth, in making his way to Derry. Lord Cavan gave him a reinforcement of thirty-two men; he returned with these by a night march to his home, found the prisoners still safe, and began to scour the country. 'The principal offenders,' he wrote, 'who are almost universally Dissenters, have fled.' 'Paine's "Rights of Man," French support, immunity from revenue laws, from tithes, &c., and the overthrow of the King and our form of government in general, seem all to have been resorted to, as principles and topics to influence their party. . . . From common and poor men I have followed up the association to comfortable farmers; from them to Dissenting ministers, not in employment.'[1] 'Not a single night,' wrote another informant, 'has past for this last week in the part of the barony of Raphoe which is near Letterkenny, unmarked by outrage. Every house, with a few exceptions, in the parishes of Ray and Leck, has been plundered of their arms and pewter; and what makes the matter more awful, no argument can induce anyone who has been robbed, to give the slightest hint that may lead to the discovery of the marauders. Nay, their conduct rather argues an easy satisfaction at the loss, than a wish to recover the arms and bring the ruffians to justice.'[2]

From Strabane, which was in the adjoining county of Tyrone, a Scotch colonel writes, 'Unless speedy measures are adopted to separate the soldiery from the inhabitants, the most fatal consequences are to be apprehended, . . . scattered as they are through the houses of the inhabitants, who are completely organised to overthrow the Government of the country.' He states that the most assiduous efforts were being made to seduce the soldiers, that the area of disaffection was increasing with the greatest rapidity, and that, either through fear or through a desire to be on good terms with the people, the magistrates were shamefully supine. Through the system of terror, he says, 'which has in this country unbounded influence,' 'the civil power is becoming totally destitute of energy.' United Irishmen, who demand arms, are never resisted. He had arrested some plunderers wearing, like the old Whiteboys, white shirts over their dress. It is 'most indispensably necessary,' he thinks, 'to proclaim the whole of the North of Ireland without loss of time.'[3]

A melancholy letter soon followed, written from Derry by the Earl of Cavan, describing the murder of the courageous magistrate in Donegal. Dr. Hamilton had been from home for some days on business, and on his return he stopped at the house of a clergyman named Waller, who, like himself, had been a fellow of Trinity College, and who was now the rector of a parish halfway between Derry and Letterkenny, and six miles from Raphoe. In the evening he was sitting playing cards with the family of

---

[1] I.S.P.O. This letter was written on Feb. 1.
[2] Feb. 26, 1797. Paper headed, 'State of the Barony of Raphoe.'
[3] Colonel James Leith, Feb. 7, 1797.

his host, when the house was attacked. Mrs. Waller was shot dead. Hamilton fled to the cellar, but the marauding party declared that they would burn the house, and kill everyone in it, unless he was given up. A man and two women servants dragged him from his place of concealment. He clung desperately to the staple of the hall-door lock, but the application of fire compelled him to loose his hold. He was thrust out, and in a moment murdered, and his body hideously mangled.

Lord Cavan described the situation of the country as getting continually worse, and the few magistrates and resident gentry as so terrified by recent outrages and murders, that they had fled to the towns. There were nightly assemblies of rebels. The stacks and houses of obnoxious persons were burnt within a few miles of Derry. Lord Cavan firmly believed that a rebellion was ready to break out, and that nothing could prevent it except a reinforcement of troops and a proclamation of martial law. He urged also the necessity of 'emptying the gaols of their present crowded numbers, by sending them to the fleet, or disposing of them any way but by trial in this country, where no jury could be found to convict them, and by granting an amnesty to those who come forward and acknowledge their error.'[1] It was stated in Parliament, that 'such was the audacity of the United Irishmen in the neighbourhood of Derry, that Lord Cavan, who commanded there, was obliged to order the garrison men to deposit their arms every night in the courthouse, to prevent them from being taken by force. Above 400 families had been robbed of their arms in that neighbourhood in one night.'[2] This county had, indeed, for some time been perhaps the most disturbed in Ireland, and a letter of Camden

---

[1] Earl of Cavan to Pelham, March 3, 13, 1797. There is also a memorial from the Provost and Fellows of T.C.D. begging the Lord Lieutenant to provide for the family of Dr. Hamilton, and speaking in very warm terms of his character. A few more particulars about this murder will be found in the speech of Lord Clare in the debate in the House of Lords, Feb. 19, 1798, pp. 82, 83; and in a speech of Dr. Browne, the M.P. for Trinity College, *Parl. Deb.* xvii. 411. An Act of Parliament was passed enabling the King to give an annuity of 700*l.* a year to the family of Dr. Hamilton, and another Act authorised a grant of 300*l.* a year to the family of Mr. Knipe, a clergyman who had been murdered on account of his performance of his magisterial duties in the county of Meath, 37 Geo. III. c. 62, 63. A short life of Hamilton is prefixed to an edition of his *Letters concerning the Northern Coast of Antrim*, which was published at Coleraine in 1839.

[2] *Irish Parl. Deb.* xvii. 164.

clearly indicates one cause of the evil. 'Several companies in the City of London own large tracts of ground in it; they have lately refused to renew leases, except at exorbitant fines or great increase of rent. The consequence has been, that the few gentlemen who resided there, and were disposed to improve their estates, have been driven from that county.' The great proprietors, Lord Waterford, Lord Londonderry, and Mr. Conolly, lived in other parts of Ireland, so that over a very large and wild district there was not a resident gentleman of 1,500*l.* a year.[1]

In the county of Armagh similar disturbances were rapidly extending. This county also had, for several months, been in a state of extreme turbulence, and some portions of it had been proclaimed under the Insurrection Act in the preceding December.[2] Large armed parties were going about the country. Detachments of soldiers had been attacked by parties of 200 or 300 men. More soldiers, and a general disarming of the people, it was said, were imperatively required.[3]

The system of carrying away untried men to serve in the fleet, which had been first illegally practised by Lord Carhampton, then indemnified by the Irish Parliament, and then formally sanctioned in proclaimed districts by the Insurrection Act, gave a fiercer tinge to the disaffection of the North. Higgins, who was well informed about the proceedings of the seditious party in Dublin, mentions that many letters had been received from Belfast, and from the county of Down, expressing a belief that this system was about to be again largely practised, and that it would be resisted to the death, and adding that the arrival of a French expedition in the northern province was confidently expected.[4] McNally nearly at the same time warned the Government, that, from daily intercourse with 'the leading men who informed the Catholic Committee in Dublin and the fraternity of reformers in Belfast,' he knew beyond all possibility of doubt that their real object was the establishment of a separate republic. The persecutions of the Catholics in the North were largely made use of. A song

[1] Camden to Portland, April 3, 1797.
[2] Seward's *Collectanea Politica,* iii. 177–179.
[3] W. Sykes, March 3. (Newtown Hamilton.)
[4] F. Higgins, March 14, 1797.

describing them was printed and widely circulated, and Counsellor Sampson was writing a history of the county of Armagh in which he would dilate upon the oppressions of the poor.[1]

The letters of the same correspondent at this time, give several other particulars about the secret history of the conspiracy. I have mentioned the efforts of the leaders in the Catholic Committee, and generally of the United Irishmen, to prevent their followers from enlisting in the regiments which the Government was endeavouring to raise for the purpose of defending the country. This policy, however, was not adopted without much discussion and division. Some even of those who were looking forward most eagerly to a French invasion and an Irish republic, favoured the policy of enlisting. They dwelt on the possibility of the yeomanry force becoming a new volunteer army, and obtaining reform and emancipation by a menace of force; upon the importance of giving their partisans by every means arms and discipline; upon the danger of permitting a new armed Protestant ascendency to grow up. Many Catholics, according to McNally, actually enlisted under these motives, retaining their old aims and sentiments though wearing the British uniform. The majority of the leaders, however, took the other side. Looking forward to invasion and separation, they resolved if possible to paralyse resistance, and those amongst them who best knew their countrymen probably suspected, with good reason, that men who enlisted into a yeomanry regiment with the intention of playing the part of rebels and traitors, would be likely to play a very different part when they found themselves in the battle-field, commanded by loyal officers, with the British flag flying above their heads, and under the spell of military discipline and enthusiasm. Keogh, Braughall, Jackson, and several other leaders very strongly urged that every effort should be made to prevent the Catholics or United Irishmen from enlisting. In September 1796, McCormick went on a mission through Munster for the express purpose of preventing Catholic enlistment. To assist this object, letters were sent through the North

---

[1] J. W., Feb. 4. The writer ends by asking for money. Sampson, who took a prominent part in the defence of the United Irishmen, and who was in a position to know a great deal about what passed in Ulster, afterwards published his memoirs, with accounts of the affairs of 1798, at New York. The book appears to me very mendacious and incredible.

saying, that the Government ·intended to exclude both the Catholics and the Dissenters. Grattan desired above all things that the country should arm to resist invasion, and at his suggestion a paper was placed in a well-known coffee-house, in which those who were prepared to volunteer might write down their names. It was soon, however, found necessary to withdraw it. 'While Grattan's resolution,' wrote McNally, 'lay at the Old Exchange Coffee-house, a number of Catholics and Dissenters attended daily to prevent signatures.'[1]

McNally had specially good opportunities of learning the sentiments of Grattan, for he had himself accompanied his friend James Tandy to Tinnehinch to consult with him about a project of Tandy for raising volunteers. He found Grattan exceedingly alarmed both at the internal condition of the country, and at the prospect of invasion, and exceedingly anxious that a strong volunteer force should be speedily created. In order to set the example, he himself joined a small party of cavalry, which was formed for preserving the peace of his neighbourhood. McNally reported to the Government, that Grattan declared that the only wise and safe policy was to revive the old volunteers of 1778, with their old name, their old principles, and as far as possible their old leaders and organisation. Such a body, he thought, would carry with it a weight and a prestige that might repress disloyalty and anarchy, and it would secure the country against invasion.[2]

It will usually be found that men who have borne a conspicuous part in some great outburst of national enthusiasm, underrate the subsequent changes that pass over public sentiment, and imagine that under wholly different conditions the same enthusiasm may be reproduced. It is difficult to think that Grattan can have failed to see that, in the existing condition of Ireland,

---

[1] J. W., Sept. 3, 28, Oct. 1, Dec. 8, 12, 26, 1796; Jan. 1, 1797.

[2] 'Mr. Grattan is of opinion, that the salvation of the country depends on the *immediately* calling out the old volunteers, to appear under arms on the old establishment and principles. Government, he thinks, will act unwisely in not adopting the measure. The yeomanry will be found inadequate to repel an invasion and keep the country quiet. The old volunteers, he said, would be equal to both. Their appearance would infuse a general spirit, and repress the convulsions of the lower orders. The latter would look on the volunteers as friends; they consider the yeomanry as enemies. If the Dublin volunteers are called out, Mr. Grattan will appear as a private, or in any station his friends may please to call him.' (J. W., Jan. 31, 1797.)

a great loyal, united, constitutional, and national movement, guided by the gentry of the country, like that of 1778 and the four following years, was wholly impossible. It was certain that the Government would not consent to a movement on the lines of the old volunteers, and even if it had been otherwise all the conditions out of which that movement grew had altered. Jacobinism, Defenderism, and Orangism had changed the whole course of Irish sentiments, had left Irish life with rifts and fissures that could never again be filled. It was becoming more and more evident, that while an enrolment of the loyal was absolutely necessary for the safety of the country, such an enrolment would place arms chiefly in the hands of men who were fiercely opposed to a great portion of the citizens.

On the 9th of March, Camden wrote a very important letter to the Government in England, announcing a new and momentous step. He began by describing the alarming condition of the North. 'The most outrageous and systematic murders have been committed in the counties of Down and Donegal.' A farmer had been murdered for having joined the yeomanry, and many others had been obliged by terror to resign their posts in that body. He mentioned the murder of Dr. Hamilton, and added that it was the system of the United Irishmen to prevent the magistrates from acting and the yeomen from assembling. Several districts, on the requisition of the magistrates, had been placed under the Insurrection Act, and there was an almost unanimous voice in the country that no mild measures could eradicate the disease. 'The endeavour to arrest the progress of this system,' he added, 'if it be possible, is the more necessary as infinite pains are taken to spread its influence over other parts of the kingdom. In the counties of Fermanagh, Louth, Kildare, and in the King's County it has appeared, and also in the county of Mayo, and if effectual means are not taken to stop it, I think . . . that the North of Ireland will not be the only part of this kingdom in a state little short of rebellion.' Under these circumstances, General Lake was ordered to disarm the districts in which outrages have taken place. Patrols were to arrest all persons assembling by night, and all assemblies were prohibited. 'If,' he adds, 'the urgency of the case demands a conduct beyond that which can be sanctioned by the law, the

General has orders from me not to suffer the cause of justice to be frustrated by the delicacy which might possibly have actuated the magistracy.'[1]

This letter, as it appears to me, scarcely describes in adequate terms the gravity of the step that had been taken, which was, in effect, to place the whole of Ulster under martial law. On March 3, Pelham had written to General Lake an official letter of instructions, describing at the same time the nature and magnitude of the evil. In the counties of Down, Antrim, Derry and Donegal, secret and treasonable associations still continued to an alarming degree, attempting to defeat by terror the exertions of the well disposed, and threatening the lives of all who gave any evidence against the seditious. There were constant nocturnal assemblings and drillings; peaceful inhabitants were disarmed; the magistrates were openly resisted, and many kinds of outrage were perpetrated. The depredators had collected vast stores of arms in concealed places; cut down innumerable trees on the estates of the gentry to make pike handles; stolen great quantities of lead to cast bullets; prevented numbers by intimidation from joining the yeomanry. 'They refuse,' he continued, 'to employ in manufactures those who enlist in said corps, they not only threaten, but ill-treat the persons of the yeomanry, and even attack their houses by night, and proceed to the barbarous extremity of deliberate and shocking murder: . . . and they profess a resolution to assist the enemies of his Majesty if they should be enabled to land in this kingdom.' The General was accordingly commanded to disarm all persons who did not bear his Majesty's commission; to employ force against all armed assemblages not authorised by law; to disperse all tumultuous assemblages, though they may be unarmed, 'without waiting for the sanction and assistance of the civil authority,' if such a course appeared to him necessary or expedient, and finally to consider those parts of the country where the outrages took place, as requiring all the measures 'which a country depending upon military force alone for its protection would require.' Lake was therefore fully empowered to act as in a country under martial law, and he was authorised to call on all loyal subjects to assist him. On the 13th, Lake accordingly issued a procla-

[1] Camden to Portland, March 9, 1797.

mation at Belfast, ordering all persons in that district who were not peace officers or soldiers, to bring in their arms and ammunition, and inviting information about concealed arms.[1]

This proclamation was made the subject of elaborate debates, in both the Irish and English Houses of Commons; Grattan taking the most conspicuous part in the one, and Fox in the other. In the strange evolutions and transformations of Irish history, it is curious to observe how the active, energetic, dangerous sedition against which the proclamation was directed, was represented as essentially Northern and Protestant. As yet only portions of Ulster had been proclaimed, and they were, for the most part, portions which were emphatically Protestant. 'Who are the people,' said Grattan, 'whom the Ministers attaint of treason, and consign to military execution? They are the men who placed William III. on the throne of this kingdom.' 'The Government have declared they will persist in proscribing the Catholics, and they now consign the Protestants to military execution.' 'The character of the people who inhabit the North of Ireland,' said Fox, 'has been severely stigmatised. . . . It is said that these men are of the old leaven. They are indeed of the old leaven that rescued the country from the tyranny of Charles I. and James II. . . . the leaven which kneaded the British Constitution.'[2]

It was contended that the Proclamation of General Lake was plainly and palpably illegal—as illegal as the recent conduct of Lord Carhampton—so illegal, that Grattan declared that 'any person who broke into a house and took out arms under this order was guilty of felony.' This proposition was not seriously disputed. Something, indeed, was said by a lawyer, of a judgment of Lord Mansfield, during the Gordon riots, to the effect that 'it was perfectly legal for the executive authority to call forth the military power to suppress treason and rebellion, when the civil power was overborne, and the magistrates were either intimidated or unwilling to do their duty,' and something by a member who was not a lawyer, about the prerogative of the Crown 'to act according to discretion for the public good, without the direction of the law, and sometimes even against it.'

[1] Seward, iii. 188–190.   [2] *Parl. Hist.* xxxiii. 151.
[3] *Irish Parl. Deb.* xvii. 133.

But the Government soon abandoned this line of defence. The Attorney-General and the Chief Secretary frankly acknowledged 'that the prerogative was extended beyond the letter of the law,' but they contended that it was justified 'by the most powerful necessity,' 'by that supreme law (*salus populi suprema lex*), that extreme necessity which supersedes every particular obligation.'[1]

Much was said in illustration of this view. Papers had been seized, one Northern member observed, expressing the determination of the rebels 'to abolish all taxes and tithes, and reduce all rents to a certain standard, ten shillings an acre for the best land, and so downwards, and to continue in arms till these things were accomplished.' 'The law in the province of Ulster could not be executed.' 'The United Irishmen, it was notorious, had more influence than the Government,' and Beresford, in some imprudent words which were afterwards much repeated, said, 'They must have recourse to arms, . . . he wished they were in open rebellion—then they might be opposed face to face.'

Similar language was held by at least one other member, and it was severely reprobated by Grattan. 'The French threatening to invade you, the Catholics refused their claims, and the Protestants of the North informed that it is wished they should rise in rebellion that Government itself might act upon them at once!' Such a policy, he maintained, could lead only to ruin, and he strongly urged that the irritation of Ulster would never have risen to its present height, but for the flagrant corruption of the Irish Parliament, and the obstinate resistance of the Government to the most moderate reform. Grattan, as we have seen, more than once supported strenuous measures of exceptional coercive legislation directed against crime, but he now maintained that the whole course of the Government policy relating to Ulster, was essentially wrong. He censured the proclamation of martial law; the suspension of the Habeas Corpus Act; the Convention Act, and the Insurrection Act. He described the Government policy in a skilful phrase as 'law-making in the spirit of law-breaking,' and he formally pledged himself never to connect himself with any Government which did not support 'the total emancipation of the Catholics, and a radical reform of the representatives of the people.'

[1] *Irish Parl. Deb.* 144, 146.

Camden noticed that the tone of Grattan's speech evidently showed that he was acting in conjunction with Fox, and it was clear that he now looked forward eagerly to the downfall of the Ministry. A curious illustration of his changed attitude was the encouragement he gave to Fox to bring forward the discussion of Irish affairs in the British Parliament. No one, it may be boldly said, would a few years before have reprobated such a course more vehemently as, in spirit if not in letter, a plain violation of the Constitution of 1782. But he now spoke with scorn of those who described as unconstitutional 'an inquiry by a British Parliament into a conduct which tends to bring the connection into danger, and which derives its principle of motion from the British Ministry, as if the connection were not a question of empire, or a question of empire were not a question for a British Parliament.' He appears indeed to have been at this time firmly convinced that an invasion accompanied by a rebellion would lead Ireland to absolute ruin; that without a complete reversal of the Government policy, such a catastrophe was extremely probable, and that even if it did not take place, the most intelligent and most energetic portion of the nation was drifting rapidly into Republicanism. The mismanagement of the war, the dissolution of the confederacy against France, the isolation of England, and the overwhelming triumph of French arms, filled him with unfeigned alarm, and he believed that, unless Protestant Ulster could be conciliated, neither Ireland nor the Empire would weather the storm. In the Irish Parliament, he was at last convinced that nothing could be done. The scornful name of 'the seven wise men,' which was now given to the Opposition, sufficiently revealed their impotence, and there was only one division during the session in which a body approaching fifty votes could be rallied against the Government.[1]

In the British Parliament, Fox dilated on the familiar topics of the subservience to which the Irish Parliament had been reduced by the enormous accumulation of Crown influence; the consequent alienation of a Northern population, 'as well informed, as intelligent, as enlightened as the middle classes in Great

[1] This very interesting debate took place in the Irish House of Commons on March 20.

Britain or any other country;' the boast of Fitzgibbon, that half a million had once been expended in defeating an Opposition, and that the same sum might be expended again; the strange vacillation which had been shown on the Catholic question; the exertion of Government influence to exclude Catholics from the corporations which had been formally opened to them; the hopes that had been held out to the Catholics when Lord Fitzwilliam had been sent over, and the fatal consequences of his recall. He concluded by moving an Address to the King, praying him to take into consideration the disturbed state of Ireland, and to endeavour to tranquillise and conciliate it by healing measures.

Such a proposal had no chance of being carried, and Pitt opposed it with great power, as a flagrant violation of the independence of the Irish Parliament. England, he said, had recognised beyond all doubt and cavil the principle that the sole power of legislating for Ireland was in the Parliament of Ireland, 'which is as entirely distinct and incapable of being controlled by us as we are independent of them.' The proposed Address is 'nothing less than an attempt directly to control the legitimate authority of the Parliament of another country; to trespass on the acknowledged rights of another distinct legislative power.' 'Having renounced all power over the Legislature of Ireland, having solemnly divested ourselves of all right to make laws in any respect for Ireland, having given to Ireland a distinct and independent Legislature, and having, with every solid testimony of good faith, laid aside all pretensions to interference in her internal concerns,' can we undertake to prescribe the laws by which she should be governed, or the changes that should be made in her Legislature? The King's good disposition towards Ireland needs no proof. The most minute attention has been paid to her commerce, agriculture, and manufactures. The independence of her Parliament has been recognised beyond a possibility of doubt. The whole reign has been one continued series of concessions, and they have exceeded the sum of all the preceding ones since the Revolution. If something more is required, is not his Majesty bound to act, in what concerns the internal regulation of Ireland, upon the advice of the Legislature of that country? To assent to the

Address would be highly unconstitutional with respect to Ireland, an unwarrantable interference in the duties of the legislative and executive government of that nation.[1]

It was a strange thing to see the founder of the Constitution of 1782 so eager to induce the British Parliament to intervene in Irish legislation, while the men who had originally opposed that Constitution, and the men who at last strangled it by corruption, stood forward as the champions of the parliamentary independence of Ireland. The motives, however, of both parties were obvious, and the two widely opposed policies which were advocated for dealing with disaffection in Ulster might both be defended by plausible arguments. The Irish Government had now firmly resolved to employ to the utmost the resources of military coercion, and at the same time to oppose all constitutional concession, and a large deputation of the most respectable and moderate of the Catholic peers, who went to the Castle to ask for some measure of relief, were curtly and decisively refused.[2]

Portland had just before reported to Camden a saying of Lord Moira, 'that there was not a gentleman in Ireland who did not think it right and necessary, and did not anxiously wish, that the Catholics should be admitted to a full and unreserved participation of every right that was enjoyed by their fellow-subjects of the Established Church,'[3] and in the course of the spring and summer the Irish Ministers received more than one letter from men who were certainly no partisans of the Opposition, urging the supreme necessity of dealing with this question without delay. One of the most remarkable came from the Bishop of Ossory. Whatever evil there might be, he said, in conceding political power to Catholics, had been already incurred when Lord Westmorland gave the suffrage to the lowest and most ignorant among them, and thus 'prepared for himself the absolute and unavoidable necessity of going through with that question, and placed the Government in the situation of one who would still keep a man at enmity after having furnished

---

[1] *Parl. Hist.* xxxiii. 157–165. Another and slightly different version of Pitt's speech will be found in a report of this debate in the British House of Commons, which is bound up with the *Irish Parl. Debates* of the year.

[2] Camden to Portland, March 21, 1797.

[3] Portland to Camden, March 15, 1797. See, too, Camden to Portland, April 3, 1797.

him with arms both of defence and offence.' 'The unfortunate and unlooked-for Revolution which had taken place in Europe, and the insurrection of the lower orders against the higher, and of those who have no property against those who have,' furnish additional and powerful reasons for combining in the general defence all the representatives of property, irrespective of their creed. Those who argue, from the small number of Catholics in the higher ranks, that the boon could have no widespread influence, forget 'the effects of opinion, of pride, of the difference between any great body of men considering themselves as marked by any exclusions, or as admitted into all privileges; as suspected or trusted.' To incorporate the authority and guiding influence of the Catholic gentry in the existing Constitution, was the best means of strengthening it; and while the Constitution lasted, Protestant ascendency was in no serious danger, for it rested on an overwhelming preponderance of property. 'In all the conversations which I have ever had with the Duke of Portland on this subject,' said the Bishop, 'I understood that neither he nor any other person doubted but that some time or other the question must end in gratifying the Roman Catholics,' and every reason of policy points out the danger of delay.[1]

A still more significant letter came from Cork in the June of 1797. Signs of disaffection and disturbance had during the last few weeks been multiplying in the South, and it was plain that the seed which the United Irishmen had scattered was taking root. Among those whom Pelham confidentially consulted about the feelings of the Munster Catholics, was Brigadier-General Loftus. 'I think them,' he replied, 'loyal, and attached to good order and government. I do not believe that parliamentary reform has at all entered into their ideas, or is an object to them, but it is very plain to me that they look to, and expect for a certainty, emancipation *in toto*. I scarcely know an instance of a Catholic of consequence being the agitator of any disturbance here; the promoters of sedition either come from Dublin or the North, some originally from

---

[1] Bishop of Ossory to Pelham, May 30, 1797. The writer of this letter was O'Beirne, who was afterwards Bishop of Meath, and who had been private secretary to Lord Fitzwilliam. See Mant's *Hist. of the Irish Church,* ii. 785

Manchester. . . . The Catholics expect emancipation, and they certainly believe that it is intended to free them. If they did not, I am much inclined to think that they would *risk everything* to attain this object; but give it to them, and they will, in my opinion, be your firm friends.'[1]

Camden, however, was firmly resolved not to concede emancipation; and he clearly told the Government that if they adopted a different course, he would resign.[2] His policy was fully supported in England. Portland wrote to him that the expressions in the letter offering his resignation seemed to imply that, ' the King's servants on this side of the water had it in contemplation to depart from the system for the support of which your Excellency was prevailed on to undertake the administration of the King's Government in Ireland.' He assured him that there was no ground for such a suspicion, and that 'not the least alteration or variation of opinion' on the subject had taken place in the Ministry. He then added these very important words: 'His Majesty, under his own hand, commands me " to express to you most positively his approbation of your conduct, as stated in your private letter on transmitting the memorial from the Roman Catholics, and authorises me to assure you that His sentiments are those of the year 1795, and that you are, therefore, not to give any other answer to that already *judiciously* given by you, of having transmitted the memorial." His Majesty's servants most perfectly concur in the sentiments, the communication of which I have made to you by His particular orders; and as long as the friends and supporters of the Protestant interest and present Establishment, and the connection between the two countries, continue to be of opinion that it is inexpedient and dangerous to give any further indulgences to the Roman Catholics, so long am I convinced, that no reason will be given to your Excellency for renewing the very liberal, but I *trust* not to be accepted offer, which you have made in your letter of the 21st upon this subject.'[3]

The belief of Camden that no policy of conciliation could

---

[1] Loftus to Pelham, June 2, 1797.
[2] Camden to Portland, March 21, 1797.
[3] Portland to Camden (secret), March 27, 1797. A pencil annotation on this letter observes, that the two little words 'I trust' 'seem to let down the force of the sentence.'

now be efficacious, was strengthened by the reports from Ulster. General Lake, who held the chief command in the province, wrote from Belfast at the time of the proclamation, to the effect that all the information he received tended to convince him that matters were rapidly coming to a crisis; that a speedy rising was fully determined on; that, although it would probably not take place till the landing of the French, there could be no certainty, and that every precaution must be taken. Scarcely an hour, he said, passed without accounts of the success of the United Irishmen in swearing in men of the militia. 'The lower order of the people,' he continued, 'and most of the middle class are determined Republicans, have imbibed the French principles, and will not be contented with anything short of a Revolution. My ideas are not taken up hastily, but from conversation with men of all descriptions, many of whom, though strong for Parliamentary Reform, are now frightened, and say we have been the cause of this measure originally, and have now no power over our tenants and labourers.' 'Nothing,' adds Lake, 'but coercive measures in the strongest degree can have any weight in this country.'[1]

The great Irish Rebellion of the eighteenth century is always called the Rebellion of 1798; but the letters from Ulster in the spring and summer of 1797, habitually speak of the province as in a state of real, though smothered rebellion, and the measures superseding civil by military law were justified on that ground.

The first military raid for the purpose of seizing unregistered arms, appears to have come upon the people as a surprise. Between March 10 and 25, more than 5,400 guns, more than 600 bayonets, and about 350 pistols, besides other arms and military accoutrements, were seized;[2] but very soon there was a general concealment of arms which baffled the soldiers, while the condition of the province became continually worse. It is extremely difficult within a short compass to give a vivid and unexaggerated description of it. It varied in different districts, and it is only by the perusal and comparison of great numbers of confidential letters, written by magistrates and military

---

[1] Lake to Pelham, March 13, 1797.
[2] From returns among the *Pelham MSS.*

authorities to the Government in Dublin, that a clear picture is gradually formed. A few pages devoted to extracts from these letters during the three months which followed the proclamation of General Lake, will, I think, enable the reader to form a tolerably distinct conception of a state of society which was as anarchical as any in Europe.

One of the ablest magistrates in the North of Ireland at this time, was Dean Warburton. He had been recommended for a bishopric by Lord Fitzwilliam, but the recommendation was not attended to, and he had a parish at Lough-Gilly, near Newry, in the county of Armagh, where he appears to have discharged his duties as a resident magistrate with the same energy and skill as Butler and Hamilton. When the burning of houses by the yeomen afterwards began, he set himself steadily against it, and he seems to have exercised an extraordinary influence over his parishioners. He wrote in March, that the United Irish movement was being rapidly organised around him, that nearly the whole population were bound by the oath of secrecy, and that murder was the penalty for breaking it. The belief had been widely spread, that the French would arrive on St. Patrick's Day. Not a gun was now to be found in any house in the county. 'From the moment the disarming took place at Newry on Monday last, every gun has been concealed in bogs and other places which we shall not be able to discover, but where the owners can get at them at a moment's warning.' Many of the organisers of treason came from a distance. Two had lately been captured, each carrying a weapon like a scythe fixed on a pole. 'After all,' he said, 'the exertions of Government will signify but little here, unless they are seconded by the immediate presence and personal exertions of all the landed proprietors. I begin to think that experience is of no use to man. We have read an awful lesson in the weak and pusillanimous conduct of the French gentry and clergy in the early stages of that Revolution —and what are we profiting by it? This part of the country is peculiarly unfortunate in the absence of almost all its proprietors.'

He attended the Armagh Assizes, and came back with the most melancholy impressions. 'The game,' he wrote, 'is nearly up in the North.' 'No juries, no prosecutions, no evidences against any person under the denomination of a United Man, the men of property and clergy completely alarmed, and instead of residence all flying away into garrison towns, the mobs plundering every gentleman's house.' 'I am just now sending off every article of value, and I plainly see that I shall not be able to hold my post many days longer. Every young tree has been cut down in this neighbourhood for handles of pikes. They are persuaded the French will land before the first of May, and they are making every preparation by collecting arms. . . . A few of my parishioners, who have been forced to unite in order to save themselves and families from destruction, have been privately with me. . . . From them I have got such information as renders it necessary to take my family into Armagh.' Threatening letters, especially breathing vengeance against any juryman who convicted a United Irishman, were industriously circulated, and they were completely successful. Neither in Monaghan nor in Armagh would any jury in such cases convict. A system of terror was triumphant. 'It is impossible to give you an idea of how ferociously savage the people have become in these parts.'[1]

About Letterkenny in Donegal, where Dr. Hamilton was murdered, there was no improvement. That country was reported to be full of insurgents, but no evidence could be procured, 'the fear of assassination has so thoroughly got possession of the minds of the people.' 'You can have no idea,' wrote a magistrate, 'of the terror that pervades the whole country, . . . entirely by the absence of the great landed gentlemen, for where they are settled on their estates and have been active, the country round them is quiet.' The magistrate who gave this information, though lately one of the most popular men in the country, could now go nowhere without military protection. Loyal people were taking the United Irish oath as the only means of safety. No one would buy from a loyalist, or pay debts to him.[2]

From Tyrone it was reported that the people were daily growing more disloyal. The informant of the Government had tried to discover their objects. They told him they desired a

[1] Dean Warburton, March 13, 16, 17, April 12, 1797. (I.S.P.O.)
[2] John Rae, March 27, 1797; also a paper dated May.

reform of Parliament, and they complained of the salt tax, and the non-taxation of the absentees.[1]

At Ballybay, in the county of Monaghan, a party of militia consisting of a corporal and ten privates had a scuffle with the populace, fired on them and killed several. Their arms were taken from them, on the understanding that the gentlemen would protect them, but a mob of about 1,000 men fell upon them and cut them to pieces. Every man was either killed or wounded.[2]

From Cavan, a magistrate writes that, in the space of a month, a total change had taken place in the dispositions of the people. They formerly enlisted readily in the yeomanry, but now recruits were very rare. The whole population were United. 'I almost doubt whether there is one in forty that is not. They publicly declare themselves, and such people as wish to be well affected are obliged to join them.'[3]

From West Meath, a correspondent writes, that not a night passed without Defender outrages, and that arms were everywhere plundered.[4]

'Almost all the peasantry of every religious description,' writes an informant from Downpatrick, 'are United Irishmen,' and he believed that even many wealthy men sympathised with them, and that nothing but a French invasion was needed to produce a general rising.'[5]

'Several hundreds of men,' wrote a gentleman from Newbliss in the county of Monaghan, 'for this week past have gone about the country under the pretence of setting potatoes, carrying white flags, and singing republican songs.' He had been told that a great assemblage was to be held on the following Friday, and that they intended to cut him and his troop to pieces. He had been living for a month in a state of blockade. The disaffection he believed to be universal, and opposition to it had almost ceased. The few magistrates who tried to do their duty were in hourly danger of assassination. A rumour had been spread, that after a certain date no one would be sworn in as a United Irishman, and that all who by that date had not taken the oath would be put to death, and this rumour had brought great

---

[1] Edward Moore, March 1797.
[2] Ballybay, April 17.
[3] Mr. Clements, April 18.
[4] Edward Purdon, May 14.
[5] John Macartney, April 26, 1797.

multitudes into the conspiracy. 'Were I to presume to offer my opinion to Government,' he continued, 'in a matter of such moment, it would be this, either to propose granting a reform, or to proclaim military law in the North of Ireland.'[1]

The co-operation established between the different marauding parties was now shown by signal fires, that might be seen blazing during the night on every hill.[2] The whole country about Fintona near Omagh, writes a clergyman from that town, is in the hands of the disaffected. 'The insurgents now go about in numerous gangs, swearing, plundering, burning, maiming.' 'No tithes, half rent, and a French constitution, is the favourite toast.' Last week about one hundred men, well armed and officered, paraded the streets of Dromore. 'Yesternight the hills between this and Clogher exhibited a striking scene. The summits topped with bonfires—bugle horns sounding and guns occasionally firing, no doubt as signals to the marauding parties who were employed seeking for weapons in the neighbourhood.' 'The populace are now so powerful and desperate, that for any individual to attempt resistance would be both imprudent and romantic.' There is no legal punishment, for witnesses are completely intimidated. 'Well-meaning people, more especially those of the Established Church, literally dragooned into revolt.' 'The spirit of opposition spreads in all directions. . . . Matters are no longer carried on clandestinely, but with a strong hand. . . . Nor can anyone form an adequate idea of the wanton violence, outrage, and brutality which prevail.' Every morning a fresh list of outrages is reported. A family in which there were three sons stood a siege, and next morning above forty balls were found in a sack of tow with which they had barricaded their window. The more well-to-do inhabitants were defending their houses with gratings and bars of iron; 'but what,' wrote the informant, 'must be the situation of those who inhabit thatched cabins, which a single spark can fire?' The seduction of the military was steadily pursued, and there were great doubts about the loyalty of the yeomanry.[3]

Many lives were lost, and serious skirmishes took place. I

---

[1] Alexander Ker, April 28, May 8, 1797.
[2] See letters from Mr. White (Redhill), and George Lambert (Beau Park, probably in Westmeath).
[3] Letters sent by the Bishop of Clogher, May 9, 14, 1797.

have already mentioned the sanguinary attacks on militiamen at Ballybay. At a place called Cross-Moylan, not far from Dundalk, a few British fencibles with forty yeomen encountered a body of about 250 United Irishmen, killed fourteen, and brought ten prisoners into Dundalk.[1] On several occasions escorts with prisoners were attacked, and on one of them the soldiers killed a prisoner to prevent a rescue.

The military forces in Ireland were at this time very considerable. In February 1797 there was an effective force of about 15,000 regular soldiers, 18,000 militia, and 30,000 yeomanry, of whom 18,000 were cavalry.[2] But an invasion was continually expected, and the country was exposed on all sides. There were scarcely any fortresses in which troops could be concentrated. Soldiers were habitually employed, to a far greater extent than in England, to discharge police functions, such as suppressing riots, and enforcing revenue laws, and they were now called on to put down innumerable concerted outrages, carried on by night over an immense area of wild country, and to disarm a scattered and disloyal population. Lake wrote in the strongest terms about the inadequacy of his force. 'I believe,' he wrote, 'this district requires more than half the troops in Ireland to manage it, as there is no part of it that does not require double the number we have.'[3] A meeting of magistrates and yeomanry officers in the counties of Down and Armagh drew up a remarkable memorial, stating that the late vigorous measure of disarming the people—'which, however,' they added, 'has in many parts disarmed only the well affected, the others hiding their arms'—would be useless without a very large standing force to follow it up by constant piquets and patrols, both of horse and foot, 'and this force,' they said, 'should be the greater, as the yeomanry even in towns are assembled with much difficulty and delay, require so long notice that the design is often foreseen and frustrated, and being scattered in their private houses they may (as is now openly threatened) be either dis-

---

[1] Thomas Gataker, May 14, 1797.
[2] From a memorandum in the Pelham MSS.
[3] Lake to Pelham, March 17, 1797. I may mention, that nearly all the letters of the generals to Pelham will be found in the Pelham MSS. at the British Museum. The letters of the magistrates and informers are, for the most part, in the secret and confidential correspondence at Dublin.

armed or murdered in their houses, or on their way to parade ground.' They added, 'that the daily threats (actually executed in many late instances here) of personal and other injury to those continuing yeomen or supporters of them; and the loss of all trade or employment from the numerous body United, or affecting to be so through fear or interest,' had weakened the yeomanry, and that the protection of the country in a time of extreme danger, and when measures of desperate vigour might be required, could not be safely entrusted to mere volunteers, liable to no coercion except honour and regard to character.[1]

It will be sufficiently evident to anyone who considers the subject with common candour, that under such circumstances numerous military outrages were certain to occur. The only method by which the disarming could be carried out and the men who were engaged in nightly outrages detected, was by nightly raids, in rebellious districts. The Chief Secretary strongly pressed upon the commander in the North, that the soldiers searching for arms should always be accompanied by a superior officer; but Lake answered that, though he would do what he could to prevent abuses, this, at least, was absolutely impossible. Success could only be attained by surprise, by the simultaneous search of innumerable widely scattered cabins. If it was known that a search was proceeding in one place, arms were at once concealed in fifty others. It was impossible that an officer could be present in every cabin which was being searched, and the task had to be largely entrusted to little groups of private soldiers. No one who knows what an army is, and how it is recruited, could expect that this should go on without producing instances of gross violence and outrage, and without seriously imperilling discipline.

This, however, was by no means the worst. The danger of invasion and armed rebellion was so great, and the regular troops in Ireland were so few, that it was necessary to collect them in points of military importance, and to entrust services which did not require a serious display of force to militiamen and yeomen, newly enrolled and most imperfectly disciplined. The yeomen, from their knowledge of the country and its people,

[1] Memorial of magistrates of the counties of Down and Armagh, and officers of the yeomanry, to General Lake, March 18, 1797.

were peculiarly efficient in searching for arms, and they were the force which was naturally and primarily intended for the preservation of internal security, as the regular troops were for the defence of the country against a foreign invasion. The creation of a large yeomanry force for the former purpose had been, as we have seen, one of the projects of Fitzwilliam. It had been strongly and repeatedly urged by Grattan and by Parsons, and, as we shall presently see, the most liberal and enlightened English commander entirely agreed with the most liberal members of the Irish Parliament, that the suppression of outrage which did not rise to the height of actual armed rebellion, ought to be the special province of the yeomanry. But such a force was at this time perfectly certain to be guilty of gross violence. It was recruited chiefly in districts which had been for years the scene of savage faction fights between the Defenders and the Peep of Day Boys; between the United Irishmen and the Orangemen; and it was recruited in the face of the most formidable obstacles. The United Irishmen made it one of their main objects to prevent the formation of this new and powerful force, and they pursued this object with every kind of outrage, intimidation, abuse, and seduction. There had been not a few murders. There were countless instances of attacks on the houses of the yeomen. Their families were exposed to constant insult, and to constant peril. The system had already begun in some disaffected districts of treating the yeomen as if they were lepers, and refusing all dealings with them; while in other districts every art was employed to seduce them from their allegiance.

That a powerful yeomanry force should have been created in spite of all these obstacles, and at a time when Irishmen were pouring into the regular army, the militia, and the navy, appears to me to be a striking proof both of the military spirit and of the sturdy independence and self-reliance which then characterised the loyalists of Ireland. The estimate first laid before Parliament was for 20,000 men, but in six months above 37,000 men were arrayed, and during the rebellion the force exceeded 50,000, and could, if necessary, have been increased.[1]

[1] *Report of the Committee of Secrecy* of 1798, p. 6. Some interesting particulars about the Irish yeomen will be found in a *History of the* *Origin of the Irish Yeomanry*, by W. Richardson, D.D., late Fellow of Trinity College, Dublin, (1801). Dungannon, which was so conspicuous

But although the United Irishmen failed in preventing the formation of this great force, they at least succeeded in profoundly affecting its character. In great districts which were torn by furious factions it consisted exclusively of the partisans of one faction, recruited under circumstances well fitted to raise party animosity to fever heat. Such men, with uniforms on their backs and guns in their hands, and clothed with the authority of the Government, but with scarcely a tinge of discipline and under no strict martial law, were now let loose by night on innumerable cabins.

These circumstances do not excuse, but they explain and largely palliate, their misdeeds, and they do much to divide the blame. Disarming had plainly become a matter of the first necessity at a time when a great portion of the population were organising, at the command of a seditious conspiracy, for the purpose of co-operating with an expected French invasion, and it could hardly be carried out in Ireland without excessive violence. Martial law is always an extreme remedy of the State, but when it is administered by competent officers and supported by an overwhelming and well-disciplined force, its swift stern justice is not always an evil. But few things are more terrible than martial law when the troops are at once undisciplined, inadequate in numbers, and involved in the factions of the country they are intended to subdue.

That many and horrible abuses took place before the outbreak of the Rebellion of 1798 is not open to doubt, but it is very difficult to form a confident opinion of the extent to which they prevailed in Ulster in the spring and summer of 1797. In his earliest letters, after the disarming had begun, Lake wrote, 'I really do not know of any excesses committed by the military since this unpleasant mode of warfare has commenced,' but he acknowledged that 'some irregularities (though I really believe very few) may have been committed . . . chiefly by the yeomanry, . . . whose knowledge of the country gives them an opportunity of gratifying their party spirit and private quarrels;' and he added, 'I fear they will be of very little use if they

---

in the history of the volunteers, appears to have been the cradle of the yeomanry movement, and the first considerable review of yeomanry was held there by General Knox.

are not put under military law, as at present they are under very little control, either officers or men.'[1] Pelham, at first at least, fully accepted this statement, and wrote a few weeks after the disarming, 'I am perfectly convinced that so strong a measure could not have been carried into execution with more temper, mildness, and firmness.'[2] In June, however, he wrote to Lake that he had heard with great regret, that many of the public-houses in Belfast which were centres of the United Irishmen had been wrecked by the Monaghan Militia, and some soldiers of the same regiment attacked and destroyed the offices and types of the 'Northern Star,' which was the chief seditious organ at Belfast.[3]

But in the process of seeking arms in the country districts, far worse acts seem to have been perpetrated. A Welsh regiment of fencible cavalry called the 'Ancient Britons,' stationed at Newry, reduced a country which was probably the most seditious and disorganised in Ulster to complete submission, but it did so by means which left an ineffaceable impression of horror and resentment on the popular mind. In the absence of any searching judicial investigation, it is impossible to say how much of exaggeration there was in the popular reports; but the very absence of such investigation is in itself a condemnation of the Government, and it is but right to say that there is a confidential letter written by an eye-witness, in the Government archives, which sustains the worst charges against it. It was written by a certain John Giffard, who was an officer in the Dublin Militia,[4] engaged in the task of searching for arms. He mentions that he had been present at numerous, but invariably unsuccessful, expeditions for the purpose of discovering and arresting insurgents with arms in their hands, but that another practice was now adopted. The Britons 'burned a great number of houses, and the object of emulation between them and the Orange yeomen seems to be, who shall do most mischief to

---

[1] Lake to Pelham, March 17, 19, 1797.
[2] Pelham to Lake, March 29, 1797.
[3] Pelham to Lake (secret and confidential), June 6, 1797; Madden's *United Irishmen*, iv. 22, 23.
[4] I suppose this to be the John Giffard, a captain in the Dublin Militia, concerning whom the reader may find some particulars in Madden's *United Irishmen*, ii. 291-296. He held several appointments under the Government, edited a newspaper, and is furiously abused by Dr. Madden as a persecuting Orangeman.

wretches who certainly may have seditious minds, but who are at present quiet and incapable of resistance.' He describes an expedition to the mountains to search for arms: His party returned to the main body of the Ancient Britons, 'to which,' he says, 'I was directed by the smoke and flames of burning houses, and by the dead bodies of boys and old men slain by the Britons, though no opposition whatever had been given by them, and, as I shall answer to Almighty God, I believe a single gun was not fired, but by the Britons or yeomanry. I declare there was nothing to fire at, old men, women, and children excepted. From ten to twenty were killed outright; many wounded, and eight houses burned.' Sixteen prisoners were taken, 'poor wretched peasants, whom they marched into Newry, and were asked why they made any prisoners at all, meaning that we should have killed them. The next day they were all proved perfectly innocent. . . . But the worst of the story still remains; two of the Britons desiring to enter a gentleman's house, the yard gate was opened to them by a lad, whom for his civility they shot and cut in pieces. These men had straggled away from their officers.' A scuffle had taken place between two of the Ancient Britons and two members of Giffard's regiment, in which one of the latter was killed and another desperately wounded; a coroner's inquest had brought in a verdict of murder against the Welsh soldiers, and Giffard much feared that it would be impossible to restrain his own soldiers from reprisals.[1]

This letter throws a ghastly light on the condition of Ulster, and the levity with which these things appear to have been regarded is even more horribly significant.[2] There are frequent

[1] John Giffard to Cooke (most private), Dundalk, June 5, 1797, I.S.P.O. The following is Plowden's account of this transaction: 'Information had been lodged that a house near Newry, contained concealed arms; a party of the Ancient Britons repaired to the house, but not finding the object of their search, they set it on fire. The peasantry of the neighbourhood came running from all sides to extinguish the flames, believing the fire to have been accidental. It was the first military conflagration in that part of the country. As they came up, they were attacked in all directions and cut down by the Fencibles. Thirty were killed, among whom were a woman and two children. An old man of seventy, seeing the dreadful slaughter of his neighbours and friends, fled for safety to some adjacent rocks; he was pursued, and though on his knees imploring mercy, his head was cut off at a blow.' (Plowden, ii. 626, 627.)

[2] In a long letter on the accusations brought against soldiers in Ireland, Camden says, 'The Ancient Britons, commanded by Sir W. Wynne, did, on their first landing, act perhaps with too much attachment to

allusions to the multitude of prisoners who thronged the gaols, and many of them were sent, without trial, to the fleet. In one of the proclamations of the United Irishmen, the Government were accused of attempting 'by a premeditated persecution' to drive the people into rebellion; conniving at the persecution of Catholics by Orangemen in Armagh; carrying men on board the fleet illegally; causing women to be dragged from their beds to see their houses burned;[1] and accusations not less serious were made by very responsible politicians in their own names. A meeting of Dublin freeholders, in July 1797, passed a series of resolutions, signed by Valentine Lawless—afterwards the first Lord Cloncurry—in which they asserted that, 'through the recent introduction and violent exercise of military power,' great numbers of persons 'have had their houses burned, or been themselves transported or put to death, without even the form of accusation or trial.'[2] Grattan himself speaks of 'barbarities committed on the habitations, property, and persons of the people, . . . barbarities and murders such as no printer will now dare to publish, lest he should be plundered or murdered for the ordinary exercise of his trade.'[3] In November, Lord Moira, who spoke with the authority of a great Ulster landlord, brought the proceedings in Ulster before the English House of Lords in a remarkable speech, in which he declared that this province was suffering under 'the most absurd as well as the most disgusting tyranny that any nation ever groaned under'—a tyranny which if persevered in must inevitably lead to 'the deepest and most universal discontent, and even hatred of the English name.' He was himself, he said, a witness of much that he described, and he challenged an investigation before the Privy Council.

the sword exercise, which they had recently learnt, but their protection is now anxiously sought by all the gentlemen, and by the various towns and villages in the neighbourhood.' (Camden to Portland, Nov. 3, 1797.) Pelham writes, 'The Ancient Britons from their activity and loyalty, and particularly from the success of one dragoon, who, being attacked by two men with pikes, was enabled by his dexterity in the sword exercise to parry both and kill one, soon became the terror of the disaffected, and might in some instances have pro-ceeded too far, but I have written to General Lake to make particular inquiries.' (Pelham, Nov. 1, 1797.) The address of this letter is not given, nor can I find anything about the result of Lake's inquiries. In the *Charlemont Papers* there is a letter from Robert Livingston to Lord Charlemont, describing the 'wreckings,' and other outrages committed by the Ancient Britons on the Charlemont estates.

[1] I.S.P.O.
[2] Grattan's *Life*, iv. 301.
[3] Ibid. p. 303.

'I know,' he continued, 'instances of men being picketed in Ireland till they fainted; when they recovered, picketed again till they fainted—recovered again, and again picketed till they fainted a third time; and this in order to extort from the tortured sufferers a confession, either of their own guilt or of the guilt of their neighbours. I can even go farther. Men have been half hanged and then brought to life, in order, by the fear of having that punishment repeated, to induce them to confess the crimes with which they have been charged.' The following, he said, is the regular punishment to which every man is subject who refuses to bring in arms under the proclamation of General Lake. 'A party of the military may go and burn his house, and totally destroy his property. I know of instances where this has been practised because the district in which the property has been situated has not brought in such a number of arms as it was conceived were contained in the district.' 'Such outrages,' he declared, 'daily happen,' and he was convinced that, if the present system was not speedily terminated, 'all hope would be lost of seeing Ireland connected five years longer with the British Empire.'[1]

General Lake, when the report of this speech arrived in Ireland, wrote confidentially to Pelham, declaring in the most earnest language that he had never heard of any instance either of picketing or half hanging, and did not believe that anything of the kind had happened in Ulster; that he had endeavoured 'on all occasions to prevent as much as possible any acts of violence on the part of the troops;' and that, 'considering their powers and provocations,' he believed they had acted 'so as to deserve the good opinion of the public, rather than their reproaches.'[2] There is little doubt that enormous falsehoods and exaggerations were scattered through Ulster, but as little that the authorities did all in their power to prevent inquiry and to hush up such abuses as actually occurred. When Lord Moira, in the beginning of 1798, brought the subject before the Irish House of Lords, the charges of picketing and half hanging resolved themselves into a single well-attested instance—that of a blacksmith who had been largely engaged in manufacturing

---

[1] *Parl. Hist.* xxxiii. 1059–1062.
[2] Lake to Pelham (confidential), Nov. 30, 1797.

pikes in Downpatrick, and who was compelled by picketing, by the threat of immediate death, and perhaps by half hanging, to reveal the persons to whom he had given them.[1] We have, however, abundant evidence that great numbers of poor men's houses were at this time burnt on slight reasons,[2] and without a shadow of legal justification; and there is much reason to believe that in the midnight raids many persons were shot by soldiers, or more probably by yeomen, in a manner that differed little, if at all, from simple murder.'[3]

All these things naturally tended to stir up fierce and enduring animosities, and the condition of Ulster at this period was almost as horrible and as critical as can be conceived, except in the case of open war or rebellion. The gaols and guard-houses were thronged with untried prisoners, who were often detained for many months. Many were sent to the fleet, but it was soon found that grave dangers attended this course. The signs of mutiny which this year appeared in the British

---

[1] See the speeches of Lord Clare and Lord Moira in the *Debate in the Irish House of Lords*, Feb. 19, 1798, pp. 97, 98, 154. There was a conflict of testimony about the half hanging, though it was admitted that a rope was put round the culprit's neck.

[2] In the beginning of November, when it was known by the Government that the English Opposition intended to bring forward examples of atrocities in Ireland, Pelham sent over confidentially to England a list of the incidents which might be the subject of attack. He said, 'It cannot be denied that some things have been done which are to be regretted. At the same time, I believe that no army ever behaved better under similar circumstances, and I will venture to say that no army ever was placed in exactly the same situation; and with regard to the British troops, I can assure you that they are not only sought for by those who want protection, but even those who by their conduct expose themselves to any military rigour, acknowledge the humanity of the British soldiers.' He adds, 'Several houses have certainly been burnt in many parts of the country, but in no instance, I believe, excepting where arms and pikes have been concealed, and where the troops have been attacked.' (Nov. 1, 1797.)

[3] Lord Dunsany in the Irish House of Lords said, that if the Government wished for an inquiry, 'he could relate to them, not simply the burning of houses, but the murder in cool blood of their inhabitants. He could give them an account of three men particularly, who, after having had their houses burned to the ground, were shot by the military, whose prisoners they had for some time been; and he could add to these accounts numerous instances of men torn from their family and country, and without the form of a trial transported.' (*Debate*, Feb. 19, 1798, p. 141.) In the House of Commons Dr. Browne, one of the members for Dublin University, asserted that he was prepared to prove that there had been 'numerous instances' of the houses of persons who were not at home by a particular hour of the night being burnt by the military and yeomanry; and of men supposed to be guilty of treasonable offences, but against whom there was no evidence, being shot in cold blood. Some cases of this kind are mentioned with particulars by Plowden, ii. 623, 624.

fleet, and which at last culminated in the mutiny of the Nore, were believed to be not unconnected with the number of seditious Irishmen who had been sent to it. There is even some evidence of a secret correspondence between the Ulster rebels and the mutineers.[1] In more than one letter, Lake complained that he was overburdened with prisoners, whom he could not prosecute with any hope of conviction, but who were notorious villains, quite unfit to be let loose or, through physical defects, to serve in the fleet, and who, if they were sent there, would probably do their utmost to corrupt the sailors. 'These villains,' he wrote, 'pretend to rejoice at going to sea, as they say by that means they will be able to corrupt the sailors, and completely settle the business. . . . I believe the whole country, at least the lower orders of it, are the same in every particular.'[2]

Another fact, which added greatly to the anarchy of the North, and had ultimately a most serious influence on the remainder of Ireland, was the growing importance of the Orange movement, and the alliance which was gradually forming between it and the Government. At first, as we have seen, Orangism was simply a form of outrage—the Protestant side of a faction fight which had long been raging in certain counties of the North among the tenants and labourers of the two religions—and the Protestants in Armagh being considerably stronger than the Catholics, Orangism in that county had assumed the character of a most formidable persecution. Magistrates were frequently accused of being shamefully passive during these outrages; but the movement, in its earlier stages, appears to have been wholly unprompted by and unconnected with the gentry of the country. It was a popular and democratic movement, springing up among the lowest classes of Protestants, and essentially lawless. As, however, it was the main object of the United Irishmen to form an alliance between the Presbyterians and the Catholics; as in pursuance of this policy they constituted themselves the champions of Catholics who had been persecuted by Orangemen; and as the Defenders steadily gravi-

---

[1] See a letter from Lord Westmorland to Cooke, June 16; and also a letter of F. Higgins, May 18, 1797. (I.S.P.O.) It is worthy of notice that a Catholic priest was sent by the Government to appease the mutineers at the Nore. See Hippisley's *Speech*, May 18, 1810, p. 55.

[2] Letter to Pelham, April 23, 1797; see, too, March 25, April 16.

tated to the ranks of the United Irishmen, the Orangemen, by a natural and inevitable process, became a great counterpoise to the United Irishmen, and the civil war which raged between the two sects a great advantage to the Government. The successful efforts of the United Irishmen to prevent their party from enlisting in the yeomanry, resulted in that force being largely composed of men with Orange sympathies; and when the outrages of the Defenders and United Irishmen multiplied, and when the probability of invasion became very great, several considerable country gentlemen in Ulster changed their policy, placed themselves at the head of their Orange tenantry, and began to organise them into societies. The name of Orange was not, even at this time, associated in Ulster, only with the outrages in Armagh. Its primary meaning was simply loyalty to the Revolution settlement, and before the battle of the Diamond it appears to have been sometimes assumed by loyal societies which had no connection whatever with the disputes between the Peep of Day Boys and the Defenders.[1] The country gentlemen who now took the name of Orangemen were mainly, or exclusively, strong opponents of the admission of Catholics to Parliament, though some of them were of the school of Flood, and desired a parliamentary reform upon a Protestant basis. The society as organised by them, emphatically disclaimed all sympathy with outrage and all desire to persecute. It was intended to be a loyal society for the defence of Ulster and the kingdom against the United Irishmen and against the French, and also for maintaining the Constitution on an exclusively Protestant basis, but it included in its ranks all the most intolerant and fanatical Protestantism in the province, and it inherited from its earlier stage, traditions and habits of violence and outrage which its new leaders could not wholly repress,

---

[1] In Bowden's *Tour through Ireland*, which was published in 1791 (four years before the battle of the Diamond), the author says, 'I was introduced [at Belfast] to the Orange Lodge by a Mr. Hyndeman, a merchant of this town. This lodge is composed of about 300 gentlemen, amongst whom are the Hon. Mr. O'Neil, the Marquis of Antrim, the Marquis of Downshire, the Earl of Hillsborough, and many others of the first consequence and property. Mr. Hyndeman informed me this lodge was founded by a Mr. Griffith, who held a lucrative appointment here under Government. At a contested election he supported the popular candidate, contrary to the ministerial interest, which some of his great brethren represented in such colours to Government that he was dismissed.' (Pp. 236, 237.)

and which the anarchy of the time was well fitted to encourage.

A few extracts from the confidential letters of the generals commanding in the North will paint the situation, and show the ideas and tendencies that were prevailing. Lake, who commanded the province, strongly maintained that nothing but the extreme exertion of military law could cope with the evil. 'I much fear,' he wrote, 'these villains will not give us an opportunity of treating them in the summary way we all wish. You may rest assured they will not have much mercy if we can once begin.'[1] 'If we had a large body of troops in this district with martial law proclaimed, I think we should very shortly have all the arms in the country, and put an immediate stop to the rebellion. I see no other way of entirely disarming the province, which certainly should be done instantly, and is not, I fear, practicable without great force and such powers as I mention. The contagion spreads fast, and requires most desperate remedies. I think if they once knew military law was proclaimed, and that one or two of their large towns were threatened to be burnt unless arms of every kind were produced, it would have a great effect; and if they did not bring in their arms, it would be advisable the houses of some of the most disaffected should be set on fire. You may think me too violent, but I am convinced it will be mercy in the end. . . . Surely the "Northern Star" should be stopped. The mischief it does is beyond all imagination. May I be allowed to seize and burn the whole apparatus? Belfast ought to be proclaimed and punished most severely, as it is plain every act of sedition originates in this town. I have patrols going all night, and will do everything I can to thin the country of these rebellious scoundrels by sending them on board the tender.'[2] He laments that complete martial law was not proclaimed. It is, he says, 'very necessary, I assure you, though I believe it will not be long before it is in force here, as, if my information is right, . . . these villains do most undoubtedly meditate a rising, and that very shortly. . . . I cannot help wishing that we had full powers to destroy their houses, or try some of them by our law, if they did not

---

[1] Lake to Pelham, March 25, 1797. [2] Ibid. April 16.

bring in their arms. . . . Nothing but terror will keep them in order.'[1]

A much more instructive correspondence was at this time carried on between the Chief Secretary and Brigadier-General Knox, a man who, in addition to his military talents, had great family influence in the North, and a thorough knowledge of its social and political condition. He commanded at Dungannon, where he seems to have been remarkably successful in pacifying the country. He furnished the Government with elaborate plans for the defence of Ulster against invasion, and he was much consulted on political matters by Pelham. He was evidently a man of a hot temper: quarrelling at one time with Lord Carhampton, and at another with Pelham himself, and he appears to have been of that stern Cromwellian type which flinches from no degree of violence that seems necessary to secure the country. A few extracts from his letters will show the new place which Orangism was beginning to take in Irish politics, and also the judgment of an honest and very able man about the state of feeling in Ulster, and the measures by which Ireland could be pacified.

In March, he wrote strongly objecting to the policy of general and indiscriminate disarming. 'In the counties of Down, Antrim, Derry, and parts of Donegal and Tyrone,' he wrote, 'the whole people are ill disposed; consequently it should be the object of Government to seize all their arms; but in the counties of Armagh, Cavan, Monaghan, Fermanagh, and part of Tyrone, through which my brigade is at present quartered, a proportion of the people are hostile to the United Irishmen—particularly those calling themselves Orangemen.' If, which was not the case, the troops were sufficiently numerous to make a general search, the measure would do more harm than good. 'On the first alarm the United Irishmen would conceal their arms, and the soldiery would find and seize the arms only of those who were well inclined, thereby leaving them to the mercy of their enemies. This actually happened near Omagh.' In one parish the Protestant inhabitants, 'though not embodied in yeomanry corps, associated to defend their property, and to keep the peace

[1] Lake to Pelham, May 18, 1797.

of their neighbourhood. Their arms, and theirs only, were seized by the military.' 'I have arranged,' he says, 'a plan to scour a district full of unregistered arms, or said to be so. . . . And this I do, not so much with a hope to succeed to any extent, as to increase the animosity between the Orangemen and the United Irishmen, or liberty men as they call themselves. Upon that animosity depends the safety of the centre counties of the North. Were the Orangemen disarmed or put down, or were they coalesced with the other party, the whole of Ulster would be as bad as Down and Antrim.' 'In respect to the county of Armagh, I hope no attempt may be made towards a genuine search and seizure of arms. Except in the wild country about the Fews mountains, it might do great mischief.'[1]

'The state of affairs,' he wrote a few weeks later. 'I am sorry to say, has within these few days become very alarming. Disaffection has spread into districts that have hitherto been considered as loyal. The loyalists are under the impression of terror;' the minds of nearly all classes are wavering. Nothing but a large additional supply of English troops can secure the province.[2] 'Mr. Verner informed me that he could enroll a considerable number of men as supplementary yeomen, to be attached to his corps without pay, if Government would give them arms. They would consist of staunch Orangemen, the only description of men in the North of Ireland that can be depended upon. He reckons upon two or three hundred. May I encourage him to proceed?'[3]

Other proposals of the same kind were pressed from other quarters on Pelham, and he wrote to Knox in great perplexity, begging his advice. It was urged that the Armagh Orangemen might be organised into a new fencible corps; that their loyalty was incontestable; that if they were not armed, they would be in much danger in case of an insurrection. 'At the same time,' he continued, 'I am sure that you will see many difficulties in forming them into corps, which have the appearance of establishing religious distinctions.' On the whole, he concluded that the best line of conduct he could follow, was to leave the

---

[1] Knox to Lake, March 18, 1797.
[2] Knox to Pelham, April 11, 1797.   [3] Ibid. April 19.

matter to the discretion of Knox. The object of suppressing the United Irishmen is so great, 'that one can hardly object to any means for gaining it. At the same time, party and religious distinctions have produced such consequences in the county of Armagh, that it will require infinite prudence and dexterity in the management of such an undertaking.'[1]

Knox strongly encouraged the arming of the Orangemen, though he was by no means insensible to the objections to that course. 'If I am permitted,' he wrote, 'as I am inclined, to encourage the Orangemen, I think I shall be able to put down the United Irishmen in Armagh, Monaghan, Cavan, and part of Tyrone.' He sent to Pelham a series of resolutions, which had just been carried at Armagh, by the masters of the different Orange lodges of Ulster, showing that the society had now assumed the character of a legitimate political association. In these resolutions the Orangemen expressed warm loyalty to the Crown, detestation of rebels of all descriptions, and determination to support, at the risk of their lives, the existing constitution of Church and State, dwelling especially on the Protestant ascendency. They recommended the gentlemen of the country to remain on their estates, offered to form themselves into distinct corps under their guidance, and invited subscriptions for the necessary expenses. They also declared that the object of the Orange Association was to defend themselves, their properties, the peace of the country, and the Protestant Constitution, and they solemnly and authoritatively denied that they had sworn to extirpate the Catholics. 'The loyal, well-behaved men,' they said, 'let their religion be what it may, need fear no injury from us.'[2]

It was obvious that a society of this kind was very different from the tumultuous rabble which has been described, and a book of rules and regulations was drawn up and circulated among the Orangemen, which clearly showed the desire of its leaders to give the society a character not only of legality, but of high moral excellence. Every Orangeman, it was said, was expected to have a sincere love and veneration for his Maker, and a firm belief in the sole mediatorship of Christ. He must

---

[1] Pelham to Knox, May 20, 23, 1797.
[2] These resolutions (May 1797) were printed and circulated.

be humane and courteous, an enemy to all brutality and cruelty, zealous to promote the honour of his King and country. He must abstain from cursing, swearing, and intemperance, and he must carefully observe the Sabbath. The society was exclusively Protestant, and it was based upon the idea of Protestant ascendency, but it was intended also to be actively loyal, and to combat the forces of atheism and anarchy. Like the Freemasons, the Orangemen had secret signs and pass-words, but the only object of these was to prevent traitors from mixing with them in order to betray them, and also to recommend each Orangeman to the attention and kindness of his brethren.[1]

'If the Government is resolved,' wrote Knox, 'to resist Catholic emancipation, the measure of adding strength to the Orange party will be of the greatest use. But they are bigots, and will resist Catholic emancipation.' 'The Orangemen,' he says in another letter, 'were originally a bigoted set of men, who were ready to destroy the Roman Catholics. They now form a political party, and are the only barrier we have against the United Irishmen. I do not by any means wish the Government should give them an avowed protection, as it might do mischief in the South, but that protection may be given silently, by permission to enroll themselves in the district corps, and by having it generally understood that their meetings (a sort of freemasonry) shall not be disturbed as long as the Orangemen refrain from outrage.'[2]

This policy appears to have been in fact pursued, and two considerable bodies of avowed Orangemen, raised by Mr. Verner and Mr. Atkinson, were, with the consent of the Lord Lieutenant, now incorporated into the yeomanry.[3] At the same time Knox strongly maintained that Ulster could only be reduced to peace by the most extreme measures, and that an additional force of eight or ten thousand English troops was required for its security. The first step, he urged, was the proclamation of martial law. Pelham answered that this had already in effect been done, for General Lake had been furnished with all the

---

[1] See *The Principles of the Orange Association Vindicated.* By the Rev. S. Cupples, Rector of Lisburn (1799).

[2] Knox to Pelham, May 21, 22, 28, 1797. The Orange resolutions will be found in the I.S.P.O.

[3] Pelham to Knox, May 26, 1797.

powers that martial law could give him, when he was authorised to act without the civil magistrate; but Knox very justly replied that this position was not tenable. 'Two distinct laws of contrary nature cannot exist at the same moment. The judges are now on the circuit. The magistrates are in possession of their powers. There is not an act committed by a soldier for which he is not answerable to civil law. General Lake can have no authority to proclaim martial law. The order must come from the Lord Lieutenant and Council. All civil power then ceases. The military commanding officer has power of life and death, with or without court-martial. He may give his soldiers free quarters. He may lay waste districts, and take such measures of coercion as he may think proper, without being amenable to any tribunal for his conduct. Nothing less than this authority with a powerful British force, will ever disarm and subdue the North of Ireland. . . . The present system is that of irritation, and the rebels are getting confidence, arms, and accession of numbers.' 'Nothing but authority to the military to make war upon property till the arms and ammunition are given up, will answer. It must be resorted to, or the country will remain in a state of smothered war. If the only object of the British Government were to settle Ireland, it might be done in two months.'[1]

This last sentence was somewhat enigmatical, and in reply to an inquiry of Pelham, Knox developed his views in a letter which shows clearly how powerfully the example of the French Revolution was acting on the loyal as well as on the disloyal. 'The country,' he wrote, 'never can be settled until it is disarmed, and that is only to be done by terror . . . authorising the general officers to declare war upon property until the surrender is made. Arms may be hid, ringleaders may conceal themselves, but houses and barns cannot be removed. In every other species of warfare the assailing army has the disadvantage against a hostile people. The bloody scenes of La Vendée would not have happened, had the French Convention adopted immediately that mode of attack. When Hoche did act, the rebellion was at an end.' 'It appears to me,' however, he added, 'that our British Ministers have, at this moment, an

[1] Knox to Pelham, April 19, May 22, 1797.

object more material to the Empire than the immediate settlement of Ireland, viz. a peace, the negotiation of which might be impeded by a public avowal that Ireland was in rebellion, and I do not know how far the Ministers would think it prudent to risk so bold a step, which, perhaps, in the opinion of England, success even could not justify.'[1]

It would, however, be a great injustice to General Knox to suppose that he had no other remedies to suggest, or that he regarded the evil as a mere passing malady which could be easily dispelled. 'The present,' he writes, 'is a contest of the poor against the rich, and of the Irishman against the British Government. Many foolish men of property have joined in the rebellion from the latter motive, but the loyalty of every Irishman who is unconnected with property is artificial.'[2] To deal with this condition of society great organic changes appeared to him necessary, and his views seem to have coincided remarkably with those which were adopted by Pitt. 'As long as there are two distinct Legislatures in England and Ireland, no measures can be adopted to procure a solid peace between them. The great object should therefore be an Union, to obtain which is now within our reach. The first step is by strong military coercion to subdue the people; and while Ireland is yet full of British or foreign troops, to offer the people parliamentary reform; emancipation of Catholics; abolition of sinecure places &c. &c. on condition of their acceding to an Union; thereby subduing the aristocracy with the assistance of the people. One hundred members of Parliament freely chosen by the counties and principal towns of Ireland, would not operate upon the British House of Commons. By reducing the number of both Houses of Parliament, the Minister would be enabled to offer such sacrifices as would be acceptable to the people. The venality of the Irish aristocracy is of more detriment to the British Government here, and of more annoyance to the British Minister, than a few Democrats, chosen perhaps by Belfast and

---

[1] Knox to Pelham, May 28, 1797. This letter, and one of Lake's which I have quoted, will show that there was some colour of plausibility in the reports which were at this time industriously circulated, that persons about the Government were urging that the town of Belfast should be burnt to the ground. See *Historical Collections relating to Belfast*, p. 453.

[2] Knox to Pelham, April 14, 1797.

Newry and two or three other towns, could possibly be in a joint Parliament of the two countries. I shall now point out one popular and just law which, at a future period, it would be desirable to pass—for now all laws of concession would have a bad effect. This law is to oblige all landlords in letting leases to give a preference of ten per cent. to the old tenant. . . . I think the interest of Great Britain, of Ireland, and of the Empire, is first to subdue the people of the North of Ireland; secondly, to subdue the aristocracy of Ireland, and force an Union. Within my memory, the measures of England towards this country have been to remove an existing difficulty without looking forward. It is time to put a stop to the jarring of the two countries; to adopt a plan, and pursue it with perseverance, to obtain an Union of the two Legislatures.'[1]

Pelham, referring to a passing allusion to the Catholic question in one of the letters of Knox, begged the General to write frankly to him on that question, for although, he said, the time was not propitious to any discussion of it in Parliament, yet 'every man who interests himself about the country must look to some permanent settlement beyond the mere suppression of the existing rebellion, and therefore must be discussing, in his own mind at least, the situation of the different religious sects.'[2]

'The mass of the Roman Catholics of Ireland,' answered Knox, 'feel little interest in the question of Catholic emancipation. It is of consequence only to the Catholics of property, of whom there are very few in Ulster. When the question was started, and Catholic emancipation supported by the Presbyterians of the North, it failed of the effect of rousing the lower order of Roman Catholics, and the Republicans were therefore obliged to throw in the bait of abolition of tithes and reduction of rents. This has completely answered the purpose, and the whole mass of the Catholics of Ulster are United Irishmen. The effect of Catholic emancipation unaccompanied by complete parliamentary reform, would be the loss of the whole body of Orangemen, without the acquisition of the Catholics. The Presbyterians would tell them it was a mockery. . . . In my letter written some time ago, I ventured to give an opinion that

[1] Knox to Pelham, April 19, 1797. [2] Pelham to Knox, May 26, 1797.

Catholic emancipation and parliamentary reform should be reserved as *douceurs* to the people of Ireland to agree to an Union of the Legislatures of the two countries. The interest of the aristocracy and of the city of Dublin alone oppose an Union. The former are now of no weight, and the latter deserves punishment. I look upon it that Ireland must soon stand in respect to England in one of these three situations—united with her, the Legislatures being joined; separated from her, and forming a republic, or as a half-subdued province.'[1]

The views which were expressed in these remarkable letters, appear to me to have been very much those which were held in the last years of the eighteenth century by some of the ablest men connected with the Government. In the correspondence of this time, the magistrates and gentry in the North of Ireland are constantly spoken of with great severity. They are represented as flying from their estates to the towns, or as remaining passive in the midst of the popular outrages, and Dean Warburton in more than one letter compares their conduct to that of the French gentry in the earlier stages of the Revolution. There were, indeed, a few conspicuous exceptions. Lord Downshire and Lord Cavan were specially noted for their zeal and courage; Charlemont, though his health was now much broken, hastened, in a manner which the Chief Secretary recognised as extremely honourable to him, to use his influence in the cause of order, even under a Government from which he was wholly separated;[2] and other men in less prominent positions took the same course. But in general, Lake pronounced that 'the system of terror practised by the United Irishmen' had 'completely destroyed all ideas of exertion in most of the magistrates and gentry throughout the country.'[3]

The fact is especially remarkable when it is remembered

---

[1] Knox to Pelham, May 28, 1797. The reader will notice a striking and instructive analogy to contemporary history. In our day it has been found that an agitation, based on purely Nationalist grounds, signally failed to rouse the farming classes; and the Nationalist leaders accordingly adopted with success the plan of connecting with it an attack on rents.

[2] 'Lord Charlemont and Conolly have offered their services in the handsomest manner. The former is going down to Armagh with his son, Lord Caulfield, having accepted a commission of captain, which is a circumstance peculiarly advantageous to Government and honourable to him, as he was a general in the corps of volunteers; and he has been, on this occasion, desired to take the command of two counties.' (Pelham to the Duke of York, Sept. 22, 1796.)

[3] Lake to Pelham, March 21, 1797.

what a prominent part the Ulster gentlemen had taken twenty years before in organising the volunteers, and how admirably they had then secured the province not only from invasion, but also from internal disorder. It is possible that some considerable moral and political decadence may have set in among them, but it is at least certain that the spread of republican idea had enormously aggravated the situation. A country gentleman, in a wild district, who could no longer count upon the support of his tenantry, was almost helpless in the midst of the armed anarchy that was surging around him, and he had the strongest motives to avoid as much as possible a conflict with his people. Every active magistrate was in constant, immediate danger of murder, and in the forecast of events the separation of Ireland from England seemed now extremely probable. The landing of any considerable French force in Ulster would almost certainly have effected it, and it was not, perhaps, astonishing that many men of influence and property should have hesitated under these circumstances to hazard everything they possessed in the defence of a Government which had taken the administration of affairs out of their hands, and which was pursuing a policy that they regarded as absolutely ruinous. Pelham had not only permitted, but expressly directed the military authorities to act without the participation or advice of the civil magistrates,[1] and there are many indications that the resolution of the Government to resist every degree of parliamentary reform was highly displeasing to the Irish gentry, and especially to the Northern gentry, who had so long supported Grattan in the cause. Lord Blayney, who at the head of a regiment of militia or yeomanry was one of the most active men engaged in pacifying Ulster, wrote very earnestly to Pelham disclaiming any wish to oppose or embarrass the Ministry, but at the same time expressing his conviction, that 'some plan might be struck out which would satisfy the moderate party,' and that it would be then possible 'to obtain information against the Jacobins.' Such a reform, he said, might prevent a revolution, not only in the North, but in

---

[1] 'Your instructions about employing the military without the assistance of the civil power, were perfectly explicit. I have ever acted since I received them, without calling upon a magistrate, from being too well acquainted with their indecision and timidity.' (Lake to Pelham, April 16, 1797.)

other parts of the kingdom, and it ought to consist of opening the close boroughs, with compensation to the owners, and of a material reduction in the number of placemen and pensioners.[1] Another informant warned the Government, that multitudes of the rich of the middle classes were avowedly United Irishmen, and that many of the principal gentry inclined that way.[2] 'Men who have hitherto reprobated the conduct of the disaffected,' wrote a very active magistrate, 'have totally changed their sentiments, and now avow that concessions must be made, and that the reasonable requests of the people for the reform of Parliament being refused has been the sole cause of the distracted state we are in.'[3] 'I have good reason to believe,' said another magistrate, 'that many respectable, well-intending people, who are connected with this uniting, would be glad of any good apology to withdraw from it, but they are pledged in such a way that they cannot, unless some reform is proposed by Government.'[4]

There was at the same time an evident desire among many magistrates to mitigate the severity of martial law, and there were complaints of the facility with which they permitted persons under suspicion of disaffection to take the oath of allegiance, and then gave them certificates without exacting a surrender of arms.[5] It is melancholy to observe, Camden wrote, that 'the more respectable part of the inhabitants of the northern counties and the gentlemen are so blind to their own interests . . . that they are beginning to talk the language of encouragement to the pretended principles of the United Irishmen.'[6] In the very Protestant county of Armagh, at a large meeting convened by the High Sheriff and attended by the principal freeholders of the county, an address to the King of the most violent character was carried. It declared that the British Constitution in Ireland was enjoyed only in name; that a system of organised corruption had been established, which made the Irish Parliament a

---

[1] Lord Blayney to Pelham, May 1.
[2] John Macartney, April 26.
[3] Andrew Newton (Croagh), May 3.
[4] Alexander Ker, May 8, 1797. To these testimonies I may add that of MacNally. 'I find many among those who have been long considered aristocrats, decidedly for parliamentary reform. . . . Many, very many, among the yeomanry, and particularly among the attorneys' and lawyers' corps, though they do not hint it in the aggregate, yet individually and in private conversation speak of their arms as a means of obtaining reform.' (J. W., Feb. 9, 1797.)
[5] Knox to Pelham, June 16, 1797.
[6] Camden to Portland (most secret), April 13.

mere passive instrument in the hands of the English Cabinet; that the people were being goaded to madness by accumulated oppressions; that in the richest and most prosperous province of Ireland, military coercion had taken the place of common law, and useful citizens were dragged to the fleet without trial by jury, like the most atrocious felons. Most of these evils, the petitioners said, would have been prevented if the people had been fairly and adequately represented in Parliament; and they added, that the restrictions still maintained upon the Catholics were disgraceful to the age, and that the Government had been deliberately propagating religious animosities and persecutions. Addresses and resolutions of a very similar character came from the freeholders of the great Protestant county of Antrim; from the King's County and the county of Kildare; from the cities of Dublin and Cork; from the Whig Club and from the Bar.[1] The Duke of Leinster protested against the military law in Ulster by giving up his command of the Kildare Militia, and was soon after removed from his post of Clerk of the Hanaper. Lord Bellamont retired from the Cavan Militia, and Grattan resigned his position in the yeomanry.[2]

These signs were very serious, and they appear to me to show clearly that the Government, though supported almost unanimously by the Irish Parliament in their policy, was not carrying with it the genuine sentiments of the Irish gentry. Thomas Emmet, in speaking of this period in his evidence before the Secret Committee in August 1798, most solemnly declared, that if after the Bantry Bay expedition there had been any reasonable hope of reform being adopted, he had determined to propose to the Executive Committee of the United Irishmen, that a messenger should be sent to France to say that the differences between the people and the Government were adjusted, and to ask that no second invasion might be attempted, and he added that he was certain his resolution would have been carried.[3] How far a moderate measure of reform, such as that which was proposed by Ponsonby and Grattan, could still have prevented the rebel-

[1] Grattan's *Life*, iv. 293-301.
[2] Camden to Portland, April 28. 1797. (Grattan's *Life*, iv. 304.) Among the papers of the United Irishmen published by the Secret Committee of 1798 (Appendix, No. II.) there is a list of contributions headed by the curious item, 'Received from the aristocrats of Belfast, 374*l*. 4*s*. 6*d*.'
[3] McNevin's *Pieces of Irish Hist.* p. 215.

lion, it is of course impossible to say. Republicanism and anarchy, and a passion for a pure democracy, which in Ireland would mean a revolution of property, had spread very far. But the policy of Grattan would almost certainly have detached from the United Irishmen a great number of the ablest and most energetic leaders; it would have given many others, who were alarmed at the approach of civil war, and at the prolonged and demoralising anarchy, a pretext to drop away; and it is difficult to believe that some compromise might not have been devised, as long as the chief seat of disaffection was the province in which an intelligent and industrious Protestant population predominated.

The Government, however, thought otherwise. It appears to me very probable that the intention to carry an Union was one of their leading motives, and the ideas of Irish policy which we have seen a few years before, in the letters of Lord Westmorland, were still in the ascendant. 'The severity of the measure which has been pursued in the North,' wrote Camden to Portland, 'is much descanted upon in both Houses of Parliament in England. My doubt is whether, if the measure of severity was right, that which has been adopted is severe enough. The only alternative in the present conjuncture of affairs, therefore, which it appears possible to consider, is whether you shall grant to a disaffected people that boon, the want of which they pretend is the cause of their discontent. In the province of Ulster there are certainly several most respectable persons who look to a change in the representation as an object of just expectation. These would be contented with a moderate reform in Parliament, but that must be upon the narrow scale of excluding all those Catholics who are not by the present law entitled to vote. None of these persons will venture to say that the mass of the Reformists (*sic*) in the North will be satisfied with so limited a change, and no one can say that it will give any relief and satisfaction to the Catholics. I conceive it, therefore, to be necessary to connect together both the questions of Parliamentary Reform and Catholic Emancipation, and to consider if it would be advisable (which must be the case if both measures are adopted) to change the system upon which Ireland has been governed for many years. There are certainly objections to the present Constitution of Ireland. It is a subject of complaint, that individuals have so much influence in the decisions of Parliament; but as long as Ireland remains under circumstances to be useful to England, my opinion is that she must be governed by an English party. There must be such an engine to counteract that jealousy which will always be entertained of the principal seat of empire, and I am convinced that you cannot let the Catholics into a participation of political power without looking to a change in all the establishments of the country. The narrow sphere in which the more enlightened and better educated persons move in this country, and the uninformed state in which many of the lower orders live, render the first not fit to govern, and the last not fit to be trusted with the right to elect; and illiberal as the opinion may be construed to be, I am convinced it would be very dangerous to attempt to govern Ireland in a more popular manner than the present.'[1]

'The change which has taken place within the last fortnight,' he wrote shortly after, 'has, I confess, surprised and alarmed me, and the rather, as impressions appear to have been made upon the minds of the better description of persons, and particularly of some gentlemen of independent principles and conduct.' 'I think that I perceive a different sensation in the country, but I fear it is one even more alarming to Government. A better description of persons, and some gentlemen, have been led into the adoption of the principles of the United Irishmen as far as Reform and Catholic Emancipation. They have also joined in the wish for a change of government. . . . I think it more formidable to good order than the other system, because as long as the gentlemen remained united against these societies, and the military were uncorrupted, the danger was not very formidable; but since an impression appears to have been made upon the better description of persons in some parts of the country, I conceive the points of Reform and Emancipation, which are extremely dangerous, and which they mean to attempt to carry, may more probably be adopted; and I also conceive it to be very questionable, whether, when once the gentry have given themselves up to these associations, they will be able to counteract their more extended and dangerous intentions.'[2]

[1] Camden to Portland (private and secret), April 3, 1797.
[2] Ibid. April 22, 28, 1797.

The policy of the Irish Government was acquiesced in in England, but not without misgiving. Portland again asked confidentially whether something might not be done for the Catholics, which would break their alliance with the Dissenters, secure their 'cordial exertions in support of the present establishment,' or, at least, baffle all attempts to set up a republican government,[1] but Camden gave him no encouragement. 'Whether his Majesty should be advised,' he wrote, 'to accede to, or withhold, any concessions, which are made the excuse for rebellion, or not, that rebellion which it has excited, should be overcome, if possible. It will afterwards be a subject of consideration, in what manner this country is to be governed. As long as it remains upon its present establishment, I fear it will be found a most troublesome appendage to England in times of difficulty.' It appeared to the Lord Lieutenant, that a measure in favour of the Catholics, would be 'merely an expedient to avert a present danger, and that the country should either be governed according to its present system, or that a change more extensive must be adopted.' 'I cannot conceal from your Grace,' he continued, 'with how melancholy a presage I consider the system to which we appear to have been forced, of yielding to the demands of persons who have arms in their hands.'[2]

The question was once more introduced by Ponsonby into the Irish House of Commons, on May 15, in a series of resolutions, asserting that it was necessary 'to a fundamental reform of the representation that all disabilities on account of religion be for ever abolished, and that Catholics shall be admitted into the Legislature and all the great offices of State, in the same extent as Protestants now are,' 'that it is the indispensable right of the people of Ireland to be fully and fairly represented in Parliament,' that 'the privilege of returning members for cities, boroughs &c. in the present form, shall cease; that each county shall be divided into districts, consisting of 6,000 houses each, each district to return two members of Parliament.' He proposed that all persons who possessed freehold property to the amount of 40$l.$ per annum; all who

---

[1] Portland to Camden (secret and confidential), May 19, 1797.

[2] Camden to Portland (private), May 18, 1797.

possessed leasehold interests, or houses, of a value which was to be subsequently determined by Parliament; all freemen of cities, and all who had resided in a city for a certain number of years, following a trade, should be entitled to vote. The duration of Parliament was to be reserved for further consideration.

The Government met these proposals by an adjournment, arguing that a time of war, and tumult, and seditious conspiracy, was very unsuitable for their discussion, and that no constitutional measures could meet the demands of a party which was plainly revolutionary and republican. On the other hand, it was contended that nothing but a measure of reasonable reform, which might satisfy the moderate reformers, could check revolutionary propagandism, and save the country from the horrors of rebellion. In the course of the debate, one member quoted these pregnant lines, from a private letter, which he had received two years before, from Burke. 'Against Jacobinism, this grand and dreadful evil of our times (I do not love to cheat myself or others), I do not know any solid security whatsoever; but I am certain that what will come nearest to it, is to interest as many as you can in the present order of things; to interest them religiously, civilly, politically, by all the ties and principles by which men are held.'

Grattan spoke on this subject with great power and with great bitterness. Most of his speech consisted of a restatement of facts, which, by this time, must have become very familiar to my readers—that in a Parliament of 300 members, more than 200 were returned by venal and close boroughs; that of all the towns and cities of Ireland, not more than twelve were free; that, by means of the nomination boroughs, the Minister, who was himself the representative of the Cabinet of another country, had a permanent and overwhelming ascendency in the Parliament of Ireland; that this borough system was not a part of the ancient Constitution, but had been mainly created by the Stuarts for the express purpose of securing the subserviency of Parliament, and that it was largely responsible for the commercial disabilities, the penal laws, and the long extinction of parliamentary liberties. The plan before the House, he said, goes to the root of the evil, and is no half measure. It would make the House of Commons what it ought to be—a real representation of the people. But if it gave votes to population, it was only to population 'mixed with property and annexed to residence.' If Parliament thought fit to give votes to 40s. freeholders, why should they exclude from the franchise farmers for years, householders and leaseholders of a higher amount, and established and resident tradesmen? There are members, who seem to think 'that the mass of property should be as little represented as the mass of population; that representation should be founded on neither, but should itself be what it is—a property and a commerce.'

Turning to the objections that were drawn from the war and insurrection, he reminded the House that reform had been equally resisted when it was brought forward in time of peace. 'There are two periods, it seems, in which reform should not be agitated; one is the period of war, and the other is that of peace. . . . You will never persuade a borough majority that it is seasonable for them to surrender their borough interest.' 'With respect to insurrection, the original cause of discontent is to be found in the inadequate representation of our people,' and that discontent can only be removed by a removal of the cause. The Ministers argued from the report of the Secret Committee, that the real object of the United Irish leaders was not reform, but separation and a republic, and that reform could, in consequence, have no pacifying effect. Grattan admitted the premise, but denied the conclusion. 'In that report, and from the speeches of gentlemen, we learn that a conspiracy has existed for some years; that it was composed, originally, of persons of no powerful or extensive influence, and yet, these men, under prosecution and discountenance, have been so extended, as to reach every county in the kingdom; to levy a great army; to provide arms and ammunition, and to alarm, as the report states, the existence of the Government with the number of its proselytes procured by these two popular subjects—parliamentary reform and Catholic emancipation. They have recruited by these topics, and have spread their influence, notwithstanding your system of coercion, everywhere. . . . You have loaded Parliament and Government with the odium of an oppressive system, and with the further odium of rejecting these two popular topics, which are the most likely to gain the heart of the nation.' By reversing this policy, Parliament may not reconcile all, but it will reconcile the bulk of the nation, and if the leaders of the conspiracy remain unsatisfied, they will, at least, have lost their proselytes.

It was said that no Reform Bill which was not purely democratic, and founded on the new French model, would now satisfy the people. The answer was, that Ponsonby's plan had been sent to different persons who are much in the confidence of the people, and who have a leading influence among the different sects; and after a full discussion had been approved by them.

'I have in my hand,' said Grattan, 'a paper signed by 900 persons, considerable men of business and northern merchants, containing the following resolutions in substance. "That they conceive the cause of the present discontent to be the miserable state of the representation; that the discontent and suffering will continue until Parliament shall be reformed; and that they will persist in the pursuit of that object, and will not lose sight of it by cavils at the plan, but will expect and be satisfied with such a plan as does substantially restore to the community the right of electing the House of Commons, securing its independence against the influence of the Crown; limiting the duration of Parliament, and extending to his Majesty's subjects the privileges of the Constitution without distinction of religion."'[1]

The concluding passages of Grattan's speech were in a tone of solemn warning, and they appear to me to breathe an accent of the deepest patriotism and sincerity. Recalling the precedent of the American war, he said that there were now also, but two possible policies, a policy of reform and a policy of force. By adopting the latter, Parliament was losing the people while it sought to strengthen the Throne. 'Suppose you succeed, what is your success? A military government! a perfect despotism! ... a Union! But what may be the ultimate consequence of such a victory? A separation! Let us suppose that the war continues, and that your conquest over your own people is inter-

---

[1] See on these discussions Grattan's *Life*, iv. 285-287; *Narrative of the Confinement and Exile of W. S. Dickson, D.D.*, pp. 36, 37.

rupted by a French invasion, what would be your situation then? I do not wish to think of it, but I wish you to think of it. . . . When you consider the state of your arms abroad, and the ill-assured state of your government at home, surely you should pause a little. Even in the event of a peace, you are ill secured against a future war, which the state of Ireland under such a system would be too apt to invite; but in the event of the continuation of the war, your system is perilous indeed. I speak without asperity or resentment. I speak perhaps my delusion, but it is my heartfelt conviction; I speak my apprehension for the immediate state of our liberty, and for the ultimate state of the Empire. I see, or imagine I see, in this system everything which is dangerous to both. I hope I am mistaken; at least, I hope I exaggerate, possibly I may. . . . I cannot, however, banish from my memory the lesson of the American War. . . . If that lesson has no effect on Ministers, surely I can suggest nothing that will. We have offered you our measure. You will reject it. We deprecate yours; you will persevere. Having no hopes left to persuade or dissuade, and having discharged our duty, we shall trouble you no more, and after this day shall not attend the House of Commons.'

The House was deaf to this appeal; the adjournment was carried by 117 to 30,[1] and Grattan fulfilled his promise. Accompanied by Ponsonby, Curran, and a few others, and following the example of Fox and his immediate followers in England, he seceded from parliamentary life, and did not again appear upon the scene till the stirring debates upon the Union. This secession, among other effects, had that of taking away almost all public interest from the proceedings of the Irish House of Commons. From 1781 to the close of the session of 1797 there are excellent reports of its debates, which were evidently revised by the speakers, and which are of the greatest possible value to every serious student of this period of Irish history. They are a source from which I have drawn largely in this work, and there are even now few books on Irish politics which are either so interesting or so instructive. From this period to the period of the Union debates, our knowledge of what passed in the House of Commons is of the vaguest or most fragmentary character, derived

---

[1] *Irish Parl. Debates*, xvii. 551–570; Grattan's *Speeches*, iii. 332–343.

chiefly from short newspaper reports, and we almost wholly lose the invaluable check which parliamentary criticism imposes on the extravagances of partisan statements.

Of the conduct of Grattan himself at this time, there is little more to be said. I have stated that since the recall of Fitzwilliam his speeches had assumed a more violent and more distinctly party character, and that all his hopes were placed in a change of ministry. Peace he believed to be vitally necessary, and he shared the belief which was then very prevalent, though the publication of confidential documents has now shown it to be unfounded, that Pitt did not sincerely desire it. Like Fox, with whom he was in close correspondence, he feared the imminent ruin both of the Empire and of Ireland.[1] No one could doubt that if the war continued, a French invasion of Ireland was in the highest degree probable, and Grattan well knew that it was scarcely possible to exaggerate or to measure the calamities it might produce. But even apart from this, there was the danger of national bankruptcy, the growing probability of a great rebellion, the certainty of a complete and rapid demoralisation of public opinion. The new revolutionary spirit was sweeping over the country like an epidemic, destroying the social and moral conditions on which all sound self-government must rest. In the judgment of Grattan, there was but one policy by which it could be effectually stayed. It was, in his own words, 'to combat the wild spirit of democratic liberty by the regulated spirit of organised liberty'—to carry as speedily as possible through the Irish Parliament measures of parliamentary reform, Catholic emancipation, and a commutation of tithes. It was now evident that the existing Government was inexorably opposed to these measures, and it was dimly seen that if they were ever to be conceded, it was likely to be in connection with or subsequent to a legislative Union. Such an Union, Grattan had foreseen as early as 1785, and he

---

[1] In a curious letter to Grattan (April 7, 1797), Fox speaks of his little hope of either of them 'being able to effect any good, or prevent the absolute ruin of the two countries.' He adds: 'The truth is, that without a change of ministry no good can be done, either with you or with us—without it we cannot have peace; you cannot have reform nor real independence. . . . I really think that the existence of the funded property of England, and the connection between our two countries, depend upon the measures to be taken in a few, in a very few, months.' (Grattan's *Life*, iv. 315, 316.)

regarded it with implacable hostility. But his own ideal was visibly fading, and it was becoming evident that the policy of 1782 was not destined to succeed. In spite of the Place Bill, the Pension Bill, and the Catholic Bill of 1793, the Parliament was sinking in character, influence, and popularity, and the independent minority had greatly diminished. This may be attributed, partly to the more determined attitude of hostility to reform which the Government had assumed, but in part also to a genuine feeling of panic and reaction which the French Revolution had produced in all privileged classes, and which had reduced to insignificant proportions the reform party in the English Legislature.

Outside the House, also, the position of Grattan was no longer what it had been. He was still followed by a large body of the country gentry, and of the more intelligent farmers and tradesmen of the North, but he was no longer sustained by a strong force of national enthusiasm. Another policy, other leaders and other principles, were in the ascendant, and they were hurrying the nation onward to other destinies. In all the utterances of Grattan at this time, private as well as public, a profound discouragement and a deep sense of coming calamities may be traced. In after years he spoke eloquently of the material prosperity that had grown up under the Irish Parliament, and of the many wise, liberal, and healing laws that it had passed, but his language at the time we are considering was in a different strain. He spoke of an experiment which had lasted for fourteen years, and which had failed. He declared that a general election in Ireland meant no more than 'an opportunity to exercise by permission of the army the solitary privilege to return a few representatives of the people to a House occupied by the representatives of boroughs,' and his own secession from that House was the most eloquent confession of defeat.[1]

One of the most alarming signs of the dangerous condition of Ireland was the disaffection which now constantly appeared in the militia, and was not unfrequently discovered or suspected among the yeomanry and the regular troops. The seduction of soldiers was a main object of the United Irishmen, and Lake

[1] See Grattan's *Life*, iv. 302.

and Knox urged in many letters that it had proceeded so far that little or no reliance could be placed upon the militia, and that the introduction of a large additional force from England was imperatively needed. 'It answers no end,' wrote an active magistrate, 'to station small parties of the military in different cantonments, for they are regularly corrupted.'[1] This evil was by no means confined to the North. Infinite pains were taken in Dublin to secure the presence of at least one United Irishman in every company, and sedition spread so fast that one regiment was actually removed, and the Lord Lieutenant doubted whether it would not be necessary to move a second from the capital, for the express purpose of checking the contamination. There were, in May, courts-martial sitting at the same time on disaffected soldiers, in Cork, Limerick, and Belfast. Several militia-men were condemned and shot; no less than seventy men in the Monaghan Militia confessed that they had been seduced into taking the oath of the United Irishmen,[2] and, as might have been expected, the air was charged with vague rumours and suspicions, magnifying and multiplying the real dangers. Lake believed that many United Irishmen had enlisted in the yeomanry for the purpose of obtaining arms.[3] Even the Orangemen were at one time suspected, and apparently not quite without reason, of having been tampered with.[4] At another time, Camden wrote that he had heard, and was inclined to believe, that Archbishop Troy with six other priests had been sworn in.[5] As the Archbishop, during a long, upright, and

---

[1] Alexander Ker, May 8, 1797. This gentleman adds: 'I am assured that the party of Fencibles stationed at Ballibay received pay as regularly from the United Irishmen as from his Majesty.'

[2] Camden to Portland (secret and confidential), April 28, May 6, 1797; see, too, J. W., Oct. 5, 1796.

[3] This is corroborated by a letter of Henry Alexander, Feb. 5, 1797.

[4] 'Even the Orangemen, on whose loyalty and firmness I had the most perfect reliance, are shaken.' (Knox to Pelham, April 1, 1797.) 'The Protestants of the county Armagh, who call themselves Orangemen, and who had for some time been deluded by the United Irishmen, have renounced these societies, and are returning to their loyalty.' (Camden to Portland (secret), May 30, 1797.) Among the papers of the United Irishmen seized at Belfast in April, was one urging them 'to make friends of the Catholics and Orangemen, as that was doing good in Armagh.' (I.S.P.O.)

[5] Camden to Portland (private and confidential), May 6, 1797. Archbishop Troy was a Dominican, and the regular priests were believed to be much more dangerous than the secular priests. (See *Castlereagh Correspondence*, iii. 88, 89.) McNally was questioned about Troy, but could give no information. 'It is very probable,' he wrote, 'he [Troy] may be up, but by whom is, I think, a matter

consistent life, always showed himself one of the steadiest supporters of the law, and one of the strongest opponents of secret societies, this report may, I think, be most confidently discredited; but there is little doubt that many priests were in the conspiracy. Higgins expressed his belief, that there were not twenty loyal priests in Dublin.[1] 'The Catholic clergy,' McNally wrote in April, 'are to a man with the people,' and both he and Higgins warned the Government that the lower clergy were among the most active organisers of sedition, and also that the United Irishmen were taking special pains to enroll domestic servants, and to distribute them as spies through the chief houses in Ireland.[2] Even in the Castle, and in the immediate circle of the Chief Secretary, it was boasted among the United Irishmen that they had sources of information.[3]

Among the numerous arrests that were made in the North, there were several which had great importance. In February, Arthur O'Connor was imprisoned for a seditious libel, as well as two brothers of the name of Simms, who were proprietors of the 'Northern Star.' The paper was, for some months, continued, under the editorship of Neilson; but after its offices had been wrecked, and its types destroyed by the Monaghan Militia, it was not revived. In April, on the information of a miniature painter named Newell, who had been at one time a Defender, and at another an United Irishman, the Government succeeded in arresting, in a single swoop, at Belfast, two whole committees, consisting of about forty persons, and in seizing a number of important papers, disclosing the organisation, objects, and extent of the society. A portion of these papers was soon after published by Parliament. They furnished decisive evidence that separation and a republic were the real ends of the conspiracy, and that a negotiation and correspondence with France

not to be discovered, as a priest most probably was the operator, and you may be assured he attends no organised society.' (J. W., May 22, 1797.)

[1] F. H., May 25, 1797.

[2] J. W., April 28, May 22, 29, Sept. 11, 1797. 'The spirit of disaffection is so great, that no gentleman can trust his Roman Catholic servants. A plot has been discovered (in which several of Mr. Conolly's servants were concerned), to let the Defenders into the house of Castletown in the middle of the night, and some of these servants had been bred in his family from children.... It appears that one of the chief objects of the United Irishmen is to corrupt the servants universally, so as to obtain an avenue to every gentleman whose opposition they may dread.' (Camden to Portland (secret), May 30, 1797.)

[3] F. Higgins, May 30, 1797.

had long been going on, and they also furnished some more or less trustworthy evidence of the extent of its ramifications. It appeared, from the reports of the baronial committees, that rather more than 72,000 men had been enrolled in Ulster, and that the whole province was organised for revolt, by a multitude of small societies, each of which was limited to thirty-five members. The papers that were seized belonged to the eightieth of these societies in Belfast. Outside Ulster, only Dublin, Westmeath, and Kildare appear to have been, at this time, fully organised, though emissaries were busily extending the conspiracy through other parts of Ireland.[1]

Newell told more than was published by Parliament, and he is said to have been taken masked to various places in Belfast, to point out those whom he knew to be connected with the conspiracy. His most startling statement was, that he had himself been one of a secret committee of twelve members, which was formed for the express purpose of assassinating members of the society who were suspected of having betrayed it to the Government. There was a trial, he said, but not in the presence of the accused person, and if that person was found guilty, one or more members of the committee were chosen by lot to murder him. Newell mentioned that he had known of the assassination of several persons, and had himself been present when a soldier was first made drunk, and then flung over a bridge near Belfast, with weights in his pockets.[2]

It is certain that assassinations, and threats of assassination, constantly accompanied the United Irish movement, but it was pretended that these were mere isolated instances of private vengeance, provoked by the severities of the troops and of the Government, and the leading members of the society in Dublin have left on record a solemn protest against the charge of

---

[1] *Report of Secret Committee* (Aug. 1798), Appendix, pp. xii, xxi, xxii.

[2] Several papers relating to Newell will be found in the Irish State Paper Office. He afterwards quarrelled with the Government, and appears then to have pretended that his information had been false. A kind of autobiography, in which he accused himself of all kinds of enormities, and Cooke of having incited him to perjury, was published in his name. It is reprinted by Dr. Madden, who contends that it is genuine. (*United Irishmen,* i. 531-580.) Newell is said to have been ultimately murdered. See, too, on Newell's information and retractation, Lord Clare's speech in the *Debate in the Irish House of Lords, Feb.* 19, 1798, pp. 100, 101

having given any countenance or favour to them. They declared that they entirely disbelieved in the existence of a committee of assassination; that they had heard persons mentioned as being members of it, whom they knew, from 'the most private and confidential conversations, to be utterly abhorrent from that crime;' 'that in no communications from those who were placed at the head of the United Irishmen to the rest of that body, and in *no official* paper, was assassination ever inculcated, but frequently and fervently reprobated;' 'that it was considered by them with horror, on account of its criminality, and with personal dread, because it would render ferocious the minds of men in whose hands their lives were placed.'[1] In the case of Emmet, this statement is corroborated by a document which was found among his papers, strongly censuring any resort to assassination, and it is, I believe, perfectly true, that the leaders of the conspiracy never, as a body, either publicly or secretly, gave any sanction to that crime. They comprised men with very various objects and characters. Some of them aimed only at the avowed and original objects of the society—a reform of Parliament, and an union of friendship and politics between the divided sects, and had become rebels only because they believed that English influence was being steadily employed to prevent both reform and emancipation. But others were passionate disciples of the French Revolution, at a time when tyrannicide was a favourite doctrine in France; they argued that the Insurrection Act, the imprisonments without trial, and the burning of houses, had emancipated them from all restraint, and, if they may be judged by their language, they would gladly, in the event of a successful insurrection, have reproduced in Ireland the French Reign of Terror. Of these men, John Sheares, who was on the Directory of the United Irishmen from March to May 1798, was a typical example. When O'Connell was a young man, he crossed over with him from France, and learnt that he had been present at the execution of Lewis XVI., attracted, as he said, by 'the love of the cause,' and the same spirit continued to animate him in Ireland. He wrote for the

---

[1] See the memorial of Emmet, O'Connor, and McNevin to the Government in 1798 (*Castlereagh Correspondence*, i. 358, 359); and also the evidence of Emmet. (McNevin's *Pieces of Irish History*, p. 219.)

'Press' a letter to Lord Clare, which was a distinct incitement to assassination, and the draft of an unfinished proclamation was found among his papers urging the rebels, when the insurrection began, to give no quarter to any Irishman who persisted in resisting them.[1]

It would perhaps be a mistake to interpret such language too seriously. Irish rebellion has usually been a very rhetorical thing, in which language far outstrips meaning, and it has had neither the genuine fanaticism nor the genuine ferocity of French revolution. Many young enthusiasts, who talked much about Brutus and Cassius, Harmodius and Aristogeiton, would probably have proved in the hour of action neither very heroic nor very ferocious; and Thomas Emmet stated that the plan of the Executive of the United Irishmen, in the event of a successful insurrection, was simply to seize the leading members of the Irish Government, and retain them as hostages till the struggle was over, and then to banish them from the country, confiscating their property, but reserving an allowance for their wives and children.[2] Whether such moderation would have been observed in the hour of triumph, may be much doubted, and it is certain that some of the informers who had best means of knowing, represented the conspirators as looking forward to a proscription and massacre of their most conspicuous enemies. The movement, too, if it comprised at one extremity educated enthusiasts, comprised at the other great numbers of men, of the ordinary Whiteboy type, who pursued their ends by the old Whiteboy methods. Among the innumerable small committees of half-educated men which were acting very independently in every quarter of Ulster, it is in a high degree probable that plans of murder were discussed and organised. Informers, or suspected informers, were frequently murdered, and threats of assassination were habitually employed to deter jurymen, witnesses, and magistrates from discharging their duty. In May, a conspiracy to murder Lord Carhampton was detected, and two of the conspirators were

---

[1] See Madden's *United Irishmen,* iv. 208, 222, 227, 305, 306. The letter to Lord Clare was in print, but not published, when the *Press* was seized. Madden quotes an equally outrageous proclamation of Napper Tandy (iv. 304).

[2] See the statement of Emmet in his examination before the Secret Committee of the House of Lords. (McNevin's *Pieces of Irish History,* p. 219.)

brought to justice.[1] In one of the trials of the United Irishmen, it appeared that at a baronial committee near Carrickfergus, the question of assassination had been formally discussed, that a resolution had been moved and supported, among others by William Orr, demanding that any man who either recommended or practised it should be expelled from the society, but that this resolution had been rejected. In one of the papers seized at Belfast, the following sentence occurs, which is not the less significant because its grammar shows the class of persons from whom it emanated. 'Your county committee thinks that if there is any United Irishman on the jury, that will commit any of the prisoners, that is confined for being United Irishman, ought to lose their existence.'[2]

In the summer of 1797, a secretly printed paper, called the 'Union Star,' appeared in Dublin, openly advocating assassination, and holding up to popular vengeance many particular persons. Its owner, editor, and printer, was a gunsmith named Walter Cox, and it was printed on only one side in order that it might be affixed to the walls. In December, the Government succeeded in suppressing it, the editor having, it appears, voluntarily given himself up, and promising, on condition of pardon, to disclose all that he knew. The terms were accepted, and Cooke had a curious conversation with him, which he reported at length to Pelham. Cox stated that he was the sole author and publisher of the paper, and that he had latterly continued the publication 'more from vanity than mischief.' 'He says,' continues Cooke, 'that he has been for some time against continuing the scheme for making a separation from England, because he thought it would not succeed; thinks it will if there be an invasion. Lord Edward Fitzgerald and O'Connor have been often with him.

[1] Pelham to Colonel Brownrigg, May 20; Camden to Portland, May 30. Pelham, writing to England, says: 'The proneness to murder is sufficiently proved in the trials of the conspirators against Lord Carhampton. The assassination of all informers is part of the system of the United Irishmen, and too many have fallen victims to it. Dunn, who was convicted of having intended to murder Lord Carhampton, acknowledged that he planned . . . the murder of a father and son in one of Lord Carhampton's lodges, and that he actually murdered two other men' (Nov. 1, 1797): Dunn, in his confession, stated that the murder of Lord Carhampton was regularly discussed in a baronial committee. This trial was published. Some particulars relating to it will be found in a pamphlet called *Application of Barruel's Memoirs of Jacobinism to the Secret Societies of Ireland and Great Britain* (London, 1798), pp. 18–21.

[2] Madden, i. 537; *Secret Committee*, Appendix, p. xxvii.

They knew of his writing the "Star." He says Lord Edward is weak and not fit to command a sergeant's guard, but very zealous. O'Connor, he says, has abilities and is an enthusiast, but he thinks they want system. Lord Edward told him . . . that letters had arrived from France giving assurance of invasion. Cox thinks the press is doing much mischief, for he says it is not conceivable with what avidity the lower classes read it. He is a Catholic, says the priests are much concerned, and that the lower Catholics are universally indisposed to the Protestants on account of the oppression they have received, and the insolence they have been treated with for a century. He is angry with the leaders of the United Irishmen. He says they keep themselves behind their curtain, urge on the lower classes to their destruction, and only mean to take the lead and come forward if insurrection should be successful. He is a clever man, and deep.'[1]

The intimacy of Fitzgerald and O'Connor with Cox, is a very suspicious circumstance, though it must be added, that O'Connor stated that 'The Union Star' had been set up during his imprisonment, that on leaving prison he at once remonstrated with Cox upon the evil he was doing, and that it was by his advice that Cox surrendered himself.[2] Emmet, too, as might have been expected from his character, strongly reprobated 'The Union Star,' and did all in his power to suppress it.[3] At the same time, the Government had information which may have been untrue, and which may have been exaggerated, but which cannot be lightly cast aside, that projects of a very sanguinary description were discussed in the inmost circles of the conspiracy, and were supported by some of its principal members. In a confidential letter from Camden to Pelham towards the close of 1797, the following passage occurs. 'J. W. [McNally] informs us that the moderate party have carried their point, and that the intended proscription is given up. O'Connor, Lord E. F. and McNevin are the advocates for assassination, the rest are for moderate measures.'[4]

---

[1] Cooke to Pelham, Dec. 14, 1797. Cox was afterwards accused, but I believe without any just reason, of being concerned in the arrest of Lord Edward Fitzgerald. It appears, however, from a letter of Cooke to Wickham (March 10, 1798), that he gave the Government occasional information, and he ultimately received a small pension. Some particulars about his later life will be found in Madden, ii. 270–288.

[2] Madden, ii. 277.

[3] This is mentioned in an undated letter of McNally.

[4] Camden to Pelham, Dec. 20, 1797.

In the course of the summer, there was some improvement in Ulster. The arrest of so many of the leading conspirators had given a severe blow to the conspiracy; and on May 17, a new proclamation was issued by the Lord Lieutenant and Council, placing the whole country more strictly under martial law. Having asserted that a seditious conspiracy notoriously existed, and that a rebel army was being organised and disciplined for the purpose of subverting the authority of the King, the Parliament, and the Constitution, the proclamation mentioned the assemblage of great bodies under pretext of planting or digging potatoes, or attending funerals; the armed parties, who in different parts of the kingdom were attacking houses and plundering arms; the innumerable trees that had been cut down for the purpose of making handles of pikes; the attempts that had been made to disarm the yeomanry; the frequent forcible resistance offered to the King's troops, and the failure of the civil power to grapple with an evil which was so formidable and so widespread. It had therefore become necessary to employ military force; and all officers commanding his Majesty's troops were accordingly empowered and ordered, 'by the exertion of their utmost force,' to suppress the conspiracy; 'to use their utmost endeavour' to discover concealed arms; to put down all traitorous, tumultuous, and unlawful assemblies, and to bring to punishment all persons disturbing, or attempting to disturb, the public peace. At the same time, while the proclamation foreshadowed a greatly increased severity of repression, it offered a free pardon to all persons who had joined the conspiracy, and had not been guilty of certain specified crimes, provided they went to a magistrate of the county before June 25, took the oath of allegiance, and, if required by the magistrate, gave recognisances for their future good behaviour.[1]

Almost immediately after this proclamation, several members of different inferior committees were captured. Some were sent as vagabonds to the fleet. At Newry a great number of pikes and other arms were discovered; some of the principal traders were apprehended, and many of the country people, terrified by the Ancient Britons, gave up their arms and asked

[1] Seward, *Collectanea Politica*, iii. 196–199.

pardon under the proclamation.¹ Dean Warburton wrote that a very favourable change had appeared, which he ascribed partly to the disappointment of hopes from the French, partly to the proclamation of military law, and perhaps still more to the revival of the Orangemen, 'who,' he said, 'are now beginning to appear in vast numbers.' 'I should earnestly advise,' he continued, ' the return of every gentleman to his home and to his estate, to cherish as well as to *regulate* the rising spirit of loyalty,' and he believed that by such a course the very name of United Irishmen might be extinguished. 'Unless the French appear,' he said, 'I am convinced we shall not only be safe, but triumphant,' and he mentions that in a single day 1,474 of his parishioners came to take the oath of allegiance, and about 400 stand of arms were surrendered.[2]

The military powers which were entrusted to the Commander-in-Chief were at this time very terrible, and it was felt by the Government that they ought to be placed in stronger and more skilful hands than those of Lord Carhampton and Lake. An offer of the command in Ireland was accordingly made, in the May of 1797, to Lord Cornwallis, and Lord Camden very warmly supported it. Camden, indeed, desired to resign into the hands of Cornwallis the Viceroyalty itself, believing that, in the very critical condition of Ireland, all power should, as much as possible, be concentrated in the hands of a competent soldier. If, however, Cornwallis refused to accept the Viceroyalty, Camden implored him to accept the military command, and promised to relinquish into his hands all the military control and power which the Lord Lieutenant possessed.[3] It was extremely unfortunate for Ireland that this negotiation failed. Cornwallis differed radically from the political conduct pursued there, and he believed that

---

[1] Camden to Portland, May 30. There is a curious account of the arrest at Newry of a man named Lawson, in whose house fifty-six pike heads were found. As soon as the arrest was known, a panic spread through the town, and 'an immense number fled.' Lawson was 'marched through the town with the pikes strung round his neck and arms.' It was at first reported that he was about to give information, but 'it was soon known that, in reply to an observation made to him that life was sweet, he said it was, but to him it was not sweet on the terms offered,' and when this saying became known, the fugitives returned. (George Anderson (Newry), June 11, 1797.)

[2] Dean Warburton, May 27, June 1, 1797.

[3] *Cornwallis Correspondence*, ii. 325–327.

it was not possible to dissociate the defence of the country from political measures. As Portland wrote to Camden, he refused to undertake the command in Ireland, 'unless means were taken to separate the Catholics from the Dissenters, and it was evident that the bias of his opinion strongly inclined him to suppose that very great concessions, little, if at all, short of what is termed Catholic emancipation, were necessary for that purpose, and ought not to be withheld.' Cornwallis declared that, in the event of actual or imminent invasion, he was prepared, if necessary, to cross the Channel, but that nothing, in his opinion, could put Ireland in a state of obedience and security, unless strong measures were taken 'to prevent the union between the Catholics and Dissenters, and that he should not act honestly in countenancing a contrary opinion, by undertaking a task which, he believed in his conscience, could never be accomplished.' Portland communicated this answer to Pitt and Dundas, and the proposed appointment was abandoned.[1]

A similar offer was made to Cornwallis on the eve of the outbreak of the rebellion, and was again declined.[2] It is not probable that if it had been accepted on either occasion, the rebellion could have been averted; but if a general of real and commanding ability had at this time presided over the defence of Ireland, the military excesses that took place might at least have been diminished. The almost unlimited discretion that was actually left to subordinate military authorities inevitably led to gross abuses, and it was in the summer of 1797 that the practice of burning houses, as a measure of punishment or police, came into use. Sometimes they were burnt because arms were not surrendered; sometimes because arms had been discovered; sometimes because a great crime had been committed in the district; sometimes because they were found empty at night in proclaimed districts, where the inhabitants were forbidden to leave them after sunset, and because their owners were believed to be absent on marauding expeditions. At the same time, in many quarters, the Orange movement burst out afresh in its old form of outrage and persecution, while the United Irishmen made a skilful use of the

---

[1] Portland to Camden (most secret and confidential), June 10, 1797.
[2] *Cornwallis Correspondence*, ii. 334.

partial alliance of the Government with the more respectable Orangemen, to lash the Catholics into madness and rebellion. The state of Ulster can only be truly realised by collecting much fragmentary information; but if the reader has the patience to follow with me the casual lights furnished by officers and magistrates, it will, I think, gradually dawn upon him, and he will certainly have no difficulty in understanding the dangers and the animosities that were arising.

'I have received information,' wrote Lord Blayney from Castleblaney, in the county of Monaghan, 'of several depredations committed by Orange boys; one man murdered, and two badly wounded. They say they are sanctioned by Government, and I am sorry to say, that formerly sufficient notice was not taken of them. Why sanction a mob of any kind? . . . The report is general through the country, that Government protects them. You should not lose a moment in contradicting the assertion. The United business is fast on the decline, so *don't revive it*, and the scene of civil war and bloodshed which may hereafter ensue by creating distinctions and parties of that nature in the country, may be very dangerous.'[1] 'I am informed,' wrote a brother of the Bishop of Ossory, 'and it is generally understood by everyone, that the depredations committed all round here (which are shocking to humanity), by what they call Orange boys, are done by the sanction of Government. Were I to enumerate the robberies, murders, and shameful outrages committed on the Catholics of this place, by those Orange boys, headed by officers in full yeomanry uniform, it would be an endless business, and if Government has countenanced them, I humbly conceive, and pardon me for the remark, that they ought to act within bounds.'[2] The flight of Catholics from Ulster, which had for a time ceased, began again. Bodies of 100 or 150 men often crossed in a single day from the North of Ireland to Portpatrick, and dispersed in every direction through the country; and the Duke of Portland suggested to the Lord Advocate of Scotland, that those who could not give a good account of themselves should be treated as vagrants and sent back.[3] Lord Altamount and his brother, with whose excellent

[1] Lord Blayney (Castleblayney), June 2, 1797.
[2] Captain O'Beirne, June 3, 1797.
[3] Charles Greville (Secretary of the Duke of Portland) to Pelham, The name of the place is illegible.

letters we are already familiar, wrote that a new stream of Catholics was pouring into Mayo; and although the country about them, they said, was still in a state of 'the most perfect tranquillity,' and although they had no reason to attribute any bad intentions to the immigrants, they feared that these might become highly dangerous, when their means were exhausted, unless some method for giving them employment could be discovered.[1]

Lord Blayney's warnings about the excesses of the Orangemen, and about the reports that the Government were favouring them, were answered by Pelham with the somewhat idle generality, that 'Government did not wish to favour one party more than another, but to do equal justice to all.' Lord Blayney replied, that the management of this matter required the utmost caution. 'Orangemen ought certainly to be shown some countenance, but under that cloke robbers and assassins will shelter themselves, and the most conspicuous who countenance them will be held forward as their leaders.'[2] In the same letter he gives an account of his own conduct in burning houses.

Probably the earliest instance of this practice, and the instance which was accompanied by the most atrocious circumstances, was that of the Ancient Britons near Newry which has been already related. It appears to have taken place in the last days of May. Five days after the letter describing it, Lord Blayney gave the Government an account of his own measures to pacify the county Armagh, and the portion of Monaghan about Castleblayney. He had obtained by surrender or capture a vast quantity of pikes; had disarmed many men by force; had administered the

June 15. Greville does not say that these were Catholics, but the evidence of the flight of the Catholics makes it probable.

[1] Denis Browne, June 17; Lord Altamount (Westport), August 9, 1797. Occasionally disaffected persons were found in this country, and Lord Altamount gives a curious account of a man named McMullet: 'One of the most incorrigible villains I have ever heard of, with extensive abilities such as might most usefully be employed, with a better disposition.' He was imprisoned, and it was soon discovered that 'he had sworn every prisoner in the jail with him, and seduced them all to his own doctrines.' He was, therefore, removed to solitary confinement, and it was found that he 'employed his leisure in designing new improvements for a guillotine.' Another Mayo magistrate, writing from Newport, mentions that emissaries from the North had been discovered trying to swear men in, as United Irishmen. He added that, after the strictest inquiry, this seemed to be the first attempt of the kind in that country, and that 'this part of the country is in the most peaceable condition, and likely to continue so.' (Mr. O'Donnel, May 21, 1797.)

[2] Lord Blayney, June 10, 1797.

oath of allegiance to multitudes, and had on one occasion himself mounted the pulpit in a church, and exhorted the congregation against French principles. In one district, however, which he knew from ample and trustworthy information to be the main source of the disturbances in Louth, Armagh, and the adjacent parts of Monaghan, he admits that he had used very harsh measures. 'I had four people to give information, but no one dare venture to go into the country, for fear of being murdered. I could not go very wrong, so burned several houses, the inhabitants of which were not at home, and I had information of three drills that night which I could not come at.' In one case he burned the house and destroyed the property to the amount of 800*l.* of a noted ringleader whom he was unable to capture. In the other cases he had only set fire to the roofs, and the damage done did not exceed 40*l.* He had taken these extreme measures, he said, in order to stop the intimidation of witnesses, and to show the people what they must expect if they did not surrender their arms. 'Should it prove that any of these persons were innocent, you will have no objection to my making good that loss, it being only for example.'[1]

The outrages had begun to spread into the midland counties,[2] and Westmeath was at this time at least as disturbed as any county in Ulster. Scarcely a night passed without Defender outrages. The plunder of arms was systematically carried on, and the administration of justice was almost paralysed by outrage and intimidation. A gentleman from that county writes a horrible account of the murder of a man named McManus, who had been a witness in a recent trial. He escaped from the place where he was first attacked, and fled for half a mile before his pursuers, who repeatedly fired at him. Being at last wounded, he darted into a cabin and defended himself desperately. The murderers took off the thatch, and the wounded man again tried to run. He caught up a girl, thinking that this would

[1] Lord Blayney, June 10, 1797. There is, in the I.S.P.O., a letter from another magistrate (Norman Steel, Carrickmacross, June 8), protesting strongly against this burning of houses by Lord Blayney.

[2] 'In great parts of the North, the disaffected are so completely organised and arranged under leaders, that the conspiracy is extremely formidable, and might be destructive if assisted by an invading enemy. The Defenders also in the Midland counties of Longford, Westmeath, Leitrim, Cavan, Meath, and Kildare are spreading their outrages, and seizing the arms of the gentry.' (Camden to Portland, May 30, 1797.)

prevent his pursuers from firing, but they shot her through the arm, killed McManus, and then beat his skull into a hundred pieces. 'Surely,' continues the writer, 'there cannot be measures too harsh adopted in respect to this accursed people. I am determined to risk a violent one to-morrow, and burn the whole quarter where the men suspected of this live. It is impossible an innocent person can suffer, for such a person is not to be found. They are all implicated in active or passive guilt.'[1]

From Multifarnham, near Mullingar, an officer reported the proceedings of his soldiers day by day. On Monday two soldiers overheard five persons plotting against the military. Two houses in the town which belonged to them were in consequence immediately burnt. On Wednesday night an avowed leader of the Defenders was taken, and his house burnt. He attempted to escape, and was instantly shot. 'In executing this truly unpleasant business,' the officer adds, 'every humanity consistent with my orders was strictly observed. The beds, furniture, and goods of each house burnt, were previously removed and safely delivered to their unfortunate families. A Mr. Dodd (a person of suspected character and a supposed Committee man) had been pointed out to me at an early stage of the depredations that have disgraced this country. On going to his house in consequence, he was found absent, and as . . . it was thought necessary to make an instant example, his offices were consumed.' On Thursday a notice was posted up that unless the arms that had been plundered were restored, the town would be burnt. Twenty-eight stand of arms were brought in.[2]

An officer sent down by Lord Carhampton to pacify the country round Charleville in the same county, wrote to his commander that for six weeks before his arrival no respectable person there had dared to leave his house after dusk; that loyal

---

[1] Mr. Rochfort (co. Westmeath), June 1797). McNally, who frequently pointed out abuses to the Government, wrote at this time: 'The conduct of Mr. Nugent in the co. Westmeath makes much noise. He hung up a man to make him confess, and has burned eight or ten houses. This terrifies but does not reclaim, and probably will produce retaliation.' (J. W., June 21, 1797.) Mr. Low, the chief constable at Gayville, in this county, wrote that a man named Dunor unguardedly said he knew the Defenders who robbed Charles Rochfort. His body, with his skull broken, was soon after found in a bog hole. 'The Wicklow Militia and Carribineers burned seven houses of the Defenders in this district yesterday. This kind of business, I think, will soon stop the Defenders.' (Mr. Low, June 25, 1797.)

[2] George Bell, June 19, 1797.

subjects were in constant fear of their lives; and that the hopes of the disaffected had been immensely raised by the mutiny in the British fleet. He had gone to the chapel, and after mass addressed a congregation of 800 persons, as he believed with some good results. A robber named Plunket, when on the point of being shot, turned informer. 'The consequent shooting of six of the inhabitants of this neighbourhood the following day, and the burning of a part of Moyvore, upon the information of Plunket, completed the business. . . . Of the thirty-five houses burned, I believe at least thirty of them deserved their fate, and the remainder being the poorest cabins in the place, compensation can easily be made to their owners. . . . I will conclude with giving joy of the restored peace and tranquillity of this part of your district.'[1]

Other letters were in a somewhat different strain. Lord Mountjoy, who was a great proprietor in Tyrone, wrote that his tenants were very prosperous, but exceedingly disaffected owing to a chain of sub-committees extending over the estate. The system of the United Irishmen was to get all the arms on the estate into their hands, returning those of their friends, keeping those of the loyalists. Lord Mountjoy had threatened to bring in the military if the arms that had been taken were not restored. Disaffection, he believed, in his part of the country was at best only smothered, and he had little doubt that if a foreign force landed and gained any success, the people would rise to support it. At present, however, the country was getting quieter. It was reported from Mountjoy that 'the Roman Catholics are all taking measures to leave it; I suppose through apprehensions of the Orange boys.' 'As yet,' he says, 'I have heard no well-founded complaint of the conduct of the military. The Cambridge Fencibles are commanded by officers who are extremely attentive to prevent any outrage. . . . However, the fact is, that the republican spirit of the Presbyterians does not brook well military law, which, however, has been the real cause of the restoration of peace.'[2]

In the neighbourhood of Dungannon the animosities between Protestants and Catholics appear to have run especially high,

---

[1] Charles Sheridan to Lord Carhampton, June 22, 1797.

[2] Lord Mountjoy to Pelham, June 11, 21, 1797.

and there is reason to think that the magistrates there, were far from approving of the proceedings of the military.[1] A letter from one of them gives us a terrible glimpse of the abuses that occurred. 'I will grant you the excursions of the yeomanry at the beginning, when *headed by their officers*, had a happy effect in forcing in the arms and, to appearance at least, turning the country to its duty and allegiance. But for a set of armed men, without any gentlemen at their head, to be permitted at their pleasure day after day, and what is worse, night after night, to scour whole tracts of country, destroy houses, furniture, &c., and stab and cut in a most cruel manner numbers that, from either private resentment or any other cause, they may take a dislike to, will, if permitted to go on, depopulate and destroy the trade of this country. We are beginning anew the county Armagh business, papering and noticing the Romans to fly on or before such a day or night, or if found afterwards in their houses, certain death.'[2]

From Omagh in Tyrone another magistrate wrote that the country around him, and also as he hears the country around Dungannon, was perfectly quiet. More than three weeks had passed without a single attack by United Irishmen on houses. 1,514 persons had come before him to take the oath of allegiance, and to qualify under the proclamation; yet still he had received trustworthy intelligence of the burning of houses. Such unnecessary severity at a time when the country was quiet, he said, could not fail to alienate the King's subjects, and 'if persisted in will, in all probability, insure a rebellion.'[3]

---

[1] 'The return of the people to their allegiance is everywhere fallacious, unless where it is attended by a surrender of arms. Magistrates, as usual, are doing much mischief by administering the oaths of allegiance to the people of districts known to be full of arms, without insisting upon their being given up, and granting certificates which the people consider as a protection to their concealed arms. Generally speaking, I do assert that the people will perjure themselves over and over again, rather than part with a gun. By terror only they can be disarmed.' General Knox (Dungannon) to Pelham, June 16, 1797.

[2] Robert Lowry (Dungannon), June 29, 1797. This account is confirmed by a later letter from Captain Lindsey (near Dungannon), Sept. 14, who says that excesses had been committed on the houses of several Roman Catholics of that neighbourhood; that they were in great distress, and asking for military protection.

[3] Mr. Eccles (Ecclesville, near Omagh), June 30, 1797. There appears to have been a great difference in different localities in the number of people who came in to take the oath of allegiance. From Granard a magistrate wrote, that not more than three persons in that part of the country had yet done so, and he added,

Many incidental signs show clearly how swiftly and how fiercely religious animosities were rising. On one occasion some Orange yeomen were accused of taking part in the destruction of a Catholic chapel. It appeared that they had been purely passive spectators, but the officer, while insisting on this point, very candidly adds, 'I entertain no doubt that almost all the corps of yeomen in this county would look on and possibly encourage such an act, from the great animosity that exists between the Protestants of the Established Church and the Catholics.'[1] Sir George Hill wrote from Derry, that application had been made to him from many quarters to know whether he would 'countenance, or at least wink at, the introduction of the Orange business' into that neighbourhood. He answered, that he would oppose the Orange system as strenuously as that of the United Irishmen. 'The restless disposition and discontented nature of the Presbyterians are such as to impel them to embrace turbulence on any terms. If one could engage them in a good and necessary cause, they are excellent, persevering friends; but as we have nothing in this country to dread from the Catholics, and knowing so well the determined spirit of republicanism which exists, I apprehend by encouraging Orangemen at this period we should only continue treasonable associations under a changed name. The spirit of this country might, at any moment it became necessary, be roused against the Catholics.'[2] Anonymous letters were circulated, accusing the Orangemen of concealing arms in the houses of Catholics, in order to have a pretext for burning them.[3] The report that the Orangemen had sworn an oath to extirpate Catholics was industriously spread, and although it had been explicitly and solemnly denied by the heads of all the Orange lodges, it was persistently repeated and readily believed. There were rumours that the Orangemen were about to massacre the Catholics, and other rumours that not a Protestant would be left alive in Ireland in the following March, and there were

'Never was there a wiser measure adopted in a moment of great peril, than the order of the 20th May, leaving the military to their own discretion, instead of criminal prosecutions, generally the mockery of common sense and justice.' (Alexander Montgomery, June 17, 1797.)

[1] Mr. Verner to Pelham, July 1797.

[2] Sir G. Hill to Cooke, Sept. 23, 1797.

[3] July 14, 1797.

vague, disquieting reports, of great movements of religious fanaticism agitating the Catholic masses.[1] On both sides the habit of wearing distinctive colours had already begun, and it added greatly to the prevailing anarchy. General Knox, whose masculine mind often leant towards stern measures, but never towards trivial ones, mentions that Lord Carhampton himself had taken a green handkerchief 'from the neck of one of the enragés,' and asked what possible good such proceedings could effect.[2] On one occasion a female patriot accosted one of the Ancient Britons who was on guard at Newry, and was very roughly handled. She boasted that, though they might prevent her from wearing a green handkerchief, they could not prevent her from wearing green garters, and the soldiers then tied her petticoats round her neck, and thus sent her home.[3]

Such things naturally produced fierce riots. On one occasion, on a fair day, at Stewartstown, in the county of Tyrone, some yeomen began to tear off promiscuously every green ribbon and handkerchief, from men and women. In a moment, the whole market-place was in a blaze. Swords, bayonets, spades, and every other weapon that could be found, were employed, and a number of men were soon seriously wounded.[4] On the following 12th of July, when the people of the same town were celebrating the usual Protestant anniversary, a large body of the Catholic Kerry Militia attacked them with bayonets in the market-place. The dragoons and yeomen were called out. Seven of the militia were killed, six wounded, and the remainder captured, while five of the dragoons and yeomen, as well as two countrymen, were killed, and many others badly wounded.[5] On the following day, a party of dragoons, under Lord Blayney, who were sent to pacify the country, encountered a party of the North Kerry Militia, and either through resentment, or, as the court-martial decided, through confusion and panic, at once attacked them, and killed three.[6] At Cookstown, the Newry Militia attacked the yeomen, who wore orange ribbons in honour of the Battle

---

[1] Cooke to Pelham, Dec. 23. J. Brownrigg (Edenderry), Aug. 27.
[2] Knox to Pelham, April 19.
[3] See a letter of Pelham to some member of the Government in England, Nov. 1.
[4] Andrew Newton, May 3.
[5] W. Hamilton, July 14; Lord Castlestewart, July 15, 1797.
[6] Camden to Portland, Nov. 3, 1797.

of the Boyne, and a scuffle ensued, in which two lives were lost.[1]

The religious animosity still further increased the prevailing distrust of the militia, who were mainly Catholics. 'Be assured,' wrote Lord Blayney, 'the yeomanry of the North are your sheet anchor. Was it not for the confidence the United Irishmen have in the militia, matters would not have gone the lengths they have. Therefore, beware of the militia. I have strong reasons for saying so. . . . Among the observations I have made, the Roman Catholics alone have universally been guilty of robbery and murder.'[2]

At the same time, during the summer and autumn of 1797, real steps had been made towards the pacification of the North. The process of disarming was steadily carried on, and it met with some considerable success. It appears, from a confidential Government report, that in the first twenty days of July, there were surrendered in the northern district and in Westmeath 8,300 guns, and about 1,100 pikes, besides a large number of swords, pistols, and bayonets, while about 2,500 other guns, and about 550 pikes, were seized by force.[3] Several quarters which, in the spring, had been great centres of disaffection, had become at least passively loyal. From Belfast, Lake wrote, 'The town is more humbled than it has ever been, and many of the villains have quitted it.'[4] Newry, which was only second to Belfast as a centre of disturbance, seems to have been effectually pacified. Dundalk and its surrounding country were pronounced perfectly quiet.[5] The courage and moderation with which Dean Warburton laboured to pacify his district of the county of Armagh received its reward, when he was able to announce to his parishioners in July, that the proclamation was revoked which placed that county under the Insurrection Act.[6] Dungannon also, but not its neighbourhood, had been pacified by General Knox. 'We are under no apprehensions,' wrote a clergyman from that town, 'but to the north of us it is quite lost. Dungannon is frontiered by Stewartstown, an advanced post in the enemies' country, with many royalists in it. Thence,

---

[1] Pelham to one of the officials in England, Nov. 2, 1797.
[2] Lord Blayney, July 21, 1797.
[3] I.S.P.O. More than 4,000 of the guns were said to be unserviceable.
[4] Lake to Pelham, June 4, 1797.
[5] August 1797.
[6] Dean Warburton, July 21, 1797.

to the northern sea, scarce a friend. . . . Be assured Orange is now loyal.'[1] 'In consequence of threats and some rigour,' wrote General Nugent, from Hillsborough, 'the country people are bringing in their arms very fast, and taking the oath of allegiance. . . . Accounts from all parts of the country are very favourable, and agree that the lower orders of people are dropping off rapidly from the cause of the United Irishmen, and we have every reason to think that, with the assistance and continuance of the system which has been lately adopted against them, we shall have nothing to apprehend from their machinations.'[2]

The happiest sign, however, of returning peace, was found in the revived efficiency of the law courts. The prosecutions in the North were judiciously entrusted to Arthur Wolfe, the Attorney-General, a man who was already known in the House of Commons, and at the bar, as a most upright and able lawyer; who afterwards, as Lord Kilwarden, presided over the Court of King's Bench, with conspicuous wisdom and humanity, and who at last closed an honourable life by one of the noblest and most pathetic of deaths.[3] His letters to the Government during the September Assizes, fully confirm the high opinion which was formed of his character. At the Monaghan Assizes, he says,

---

[1] Rev. W. Richardson, Nov. 2, 1797.

[2] Inclosed by Lake to Pelham, June 24, 1797. In another letter Pelham wrote: 'I believe I am not too sanguine when I say, that if there is no invasion, we shall suppress the spirit of insurrection in this country. The troops have universally shown the greatest loyalty and spirit, and there have been fewer excesses than could have been imagined. Sir Watkin Wynne and the Ancient Britons have completely terrified the rebels near Newry, and are the objects of universal admiration amongst the loyal. The firmness and temper of General Lake have been equally successful at Belfast, and that town is now under complete subjection. At a special commission held there by Lord Yelverton and another judge, above 3,000 people came in and took the oath of allegiance in open court. . . . In other parts of the North, there is a great change for the better, and the loyal inhabitants are no longer afraid of avowing their sentiments. . . . Insurrection is becoming every day less likely and less practicable.' (Pelham to the Duke of York, June 15, 1797.)

[3] He was butchered, as is well known, by Robert Emmet's mob in the rising of 1803. Among the Pelham papers will be found a letter, describing his last words, written by Baron Smith to a friend in England. His friends had gathered round, seeing the end to be close at hand. 'Just then a person came in and said to Swan in Lord Kilwarden's hearing, "We have taken four of the villains, what is to be done with them?" Swan, "Executed immediately." Lord Kilwarden (stretching out his hand with effort and difficulty), "Oh, no, Swan, let the poor wretches at least have a fair trial," and almost instantly expired.'

both the juries and witnesses discharged their duty. Ten men were capitally convicted. In one case there was a disagreement, one juror dissenting, 'but,' writes the Attorney-General, 'upon the best inquiry, I am certain he is an honest man, and that he was actuated solely by opinion and conscience, and, indeed, I think that there was room for a juror to hesitate.' Many of the prisoners, 'some of them men of wealth, and, I believe, justly suspected,' were released on bail, as an informer, who was the sole witness against them, did not appear, and Wolfe expressed his opinion that this informer was 'a man of bad character,' who had 'certainly charged men not only innocent, but meritoriously active in resisting and detecting sedition.' At Armagh, there were 151 prisoners. Some who were accused of murder, were acquitted, as Wolfe thought, 'very properly,' the evidence being insufficient, and the juries appear to have discharged their duty with fidelity and discrimination. It was, however, a terrible illustration of the condition of the North, that, in spite of the large amount of undetected crime, Judge Chamberlain was compelled to perform 'the awful and most unexampled duty of pronouncing the sentence of death on twenty men together.' Wolfe took the occasion to address the people on their duty. 'I left Dublin,' he wrote, 'a sort of lawyer; I shall become a preacher. In truth, I have more to enforce of moral duty than to encounter of legal argument.'[1]

In one case, though, apparently, only in one, an officer was at this time prosecuted for illegal conduct. He was a lieutenant of the army, who had acted with great and summary violence in the case of a man who was accused of tampering with the soldiers. The Government appear to have done what they could to discountenance such prosecutions, but Lord Yelverton sentenced the officer to three months' imprisonment.[2]

And yet these assizes, which appeared on the whole to have been so properly and so humanely conducted, are memorable for what a crowd of Irish writers have described as one of the blackest of judicial murders; for a trial which certainly left behind it more bitter and enduring memories than any that had occurred in Ireland since that of Father Sheehy. The cry, 'Remember

[1] Arthur Wolfe, Sept. 1, 4, 10, 12, 13, 17, 1797.
[2] Ibid. Sept. 4, 1797.

Orr,' which was put forward to rally the insurgents of 1798; the noble and pathetic lines of Drennan, called 'The Wake of William Orr;' the great speech of Curran when defending the newspaper which had assailed the execution; the toast given by Fox at an English banquet 'to the memory of the martyred Orr,' and the sentiment which another English politician is said to have proposed at the same banquet, 'that the Irish Cabinet may soon take the place of William Orr,' sufficiently show the violence of the indignation which it aroused. This case is involved in not a little obscurity and contradiction, and it is not without some misgiving that I undertake to place an outline of it before the reader.

William Orr was a young Presbyterian yeoman or farmer of considerable property, high character, and great local popularity and influence. I have already had occasion to mention him as a strong opponent of assassination at a Committee of the United Irishmen, and it appears to be universally admitted, even by those who most strenuously assert his innocence of the offence for which he was executed, that he was an active member of that society.[1] He was indicted for administering the oath to two soldiers named Wheatley and Lindsay. The Insurrection Act had, for the first time, made that offence a capital one, and the trial of Orr was the first instance in which a prisoner was tried for it. In one of the papers of the United Irishmen which had been seized by the Government, the names of these two soldiers were given as 'being up,' which was the usual phrase for being sworn. They were immediately put under arrest, and examined separately. They both agreed in the details of their evidence, and they both swore before a magistrate that the oath had been administered by Orr. The prisoner was left, according to an evil custom which was then but too common in Ireland, for a whole year untried in prison, and he was at last indicted

---

[1] Thus, Dr. Madden, who strongly maintains that the execution of Orr was a judicial murder, says, 'He was a noted, active, and popular country member of the Society of the United Irishmen. He was executed on account of the notoriety of that circumstance, but not on account of the sufficiency of the evidence, or the justice of the conviction that was obtained against him.' (*United Irishmen*, ii. 254.) Orr never appears to have denied that he was a United Irishman. Drennan writes of him:

'Why cut off in palmy youth?
Truth he spoke, and acted truth.
"Countrymen, unite!" he cried,
And died for what his Saviour died.'
The Wake of William Orr.

in September 1797. Both soldiers distinctly swore at the trial to the facts, and they stated that the oath was administered at a baronial committee before several persons whom they mentioned by name. None of these persons appeared to rebut the charge. An attempt was made to shake the credit of Wheatley, but in the opinion of the presiding judge it signally failed. The testimony of Lindsay was unimpeached, but he acknowledged, on cross-examination, that he understood nothing of the nature of the oath which he swore. The prosecution was conducted by Wolfe, the Attorney-General, and the presiding judge was Lord Yelverton, one of the most accomplished and merciful men on the Irish Bench. After his death, Curran finely said of him, that 'he could on his deathbed have had no more selfish wish, than that justice should be administered to him in the world to come, in the same spirit with which he distributed it in this;' and although good critics complained that Yelverton was too rapid in forming his impressions when on the bench, no one ever questioned his uprightness, his ability, and his conspicuous humanity. A few months after the execution, Lord Clare in the Irish House of Lords related the circumstances of Orr's trial as I have told them, in the presence of Yelverton, and he begged that if he fell into any inaccuracy, Yelverton would correct him.'[1]

The jury, at the conclusion of the trial, had not agreed on their verdict. They were locked up, as was the custom, for the night, but early next morning they were summoned into court. Truly or falsely, it was stated, in a contemporary account of the trial which was published, that the foreman twice refused to pronounce the word guilty, saying only, 'We leave him in your Lordship's mercy.' At last, however, he pronounced Orr to be guilty, but accompanied the verdict with a recommendation to mercy, which Yelverton at once transmitted to Dublin.

So far, it appears to me impossible to conceive a trial more perfectly fair or more calculated to inspire confidence, and no two men could be mentioned less likely than Yelverton and Wolfe to be concerned in anything of the nature of a judicial murder. Two days later, when the sentence was to be pronounced, Curran appeared to move an arrest of judgment on some legal points. At the request of Lord Yelverton, Judge Chamber-

[1] *Debate in the Irish House of Peers*, Feb. 19, 1798, pp. 110–117.

lain assisted on this occasion on the bench. The first legal points that were raised, were speedily dismissed, and Curran then produced two most extraordinary affidavits. The first, which was sworn by two of the jurymen, stated that when the jury retired to consider their verdict, two bottles of very strong whisky had been passed in to them through the window; that they had drunk the greater part of them, and that some of them 'became very sick and unwell, which occasioned their vomiting before they gave their verdict,' and one of the two jurymen who signed the affidavit, swore also that by age and infirmity, and the intimidation of another juryman, he had been induced to concur in the verdict contrary to his opinion. A third juryman signed alone another affidavit which was of much less importance. There was nothing in it about drinking or intimidation, nor did the deponent assert that he believed Orr to be innocent of the charge on which he was indicted, but he stated that he had resolved to acquit him, and had only agreed to concur in the verdict of the majority, on the representation of some of his fellow-jurors that a verdict of guilty would not be followed by an execution. It was probably, in accordance with the wishes of this juryman, by a kind of compromise which constantly takes place in jury boxes, that a recommendation to mercy was appended to the verdict. It need hardly be said that the question of punishment is wholly beyond the functions of a jury, and that this last affidavit was not only exceedingly irregular, but was also of a kind to which no weight ought to have been attached.

The two judges pronounced that the affidavits, delivered after the verdict had been duly given and formally received, were no reason for refusing to pass sentence, and Orr was accordingly condemned to death. In this matter there is, I believe, no doubt that the judges acted in strict accordance with the law, but a very grave responsibility now passed to the Executive. Was it right, was it decent, to hang a prisoner when two members of the jury which condemned him, swore that a part at least of the jury were intoxicated when they delivered their verdict, and when one juryman swore that he had been coerced by violence and intimidation into giving a verdict contrary to his belief?

The question was a more difficult one than perhaps might at

first sight appear. One part of it—though not the only one which had to be considered—was, to which of two very different categories the case of Orr belonged. Was it the case of a man who was probably or possibly innocent, and who had been wrongfully convicted on insufficient evidence? Or was it a case, such as frequently occurs in Ireland, of a treasonable conspiracy which had failed to procure an acquittal or a disagreement, and which was now making a last desperate effort to save the life of a popular and important member, and by doing so to inflict a damaging defeat on the administration of justice?

It was the strong opinion of the Government that the case belonged to the second category, and that the affidavits were incredible and procured by undue pressure. Lord Yelverton was consulted about the recommendation of the jury. It was stated that for a hundred years there had been no instance in Ireland of such a recommendation not being attended to if it was supported by the presiding judge.[1] But in this case Yelverton declared that the evidence appeared to him to be so clear, and the guilt of the prisoner so undoubted, that he could not conscientiously support the recommendation.[2] The opinion of Wolfe was only second in importance to that of Yelverton, and it is certain that he also was fully satisfied with the justice of the verdict.[3]

The execution was fixed for October 7. Almost immediately after the condemnation, General Lake discovered that a sum of no less than 900 guineas had been collected, and offered to the gaoler if he would allow Orr to escape.[4] This attempt being frustrated, two other extraordinary efforts were made to save the prisoner. The first was an affidavit which was voluntarily sworn by a Dissenting minister named Elder. He stated that in April 1796, which was the very time when Wheatley laid his first information against Orr, he was sent for to visit a soldier who

[1] This was stated by the Attorney-General in the trial of Finerty. See McNevin's *Lives and Trials of Eminent Irishmen*, p. 504.
[2] Lord Clare's *Speech*, pp. 113, 114.
[3] Immediately after it was given, he wrote a letter to Cooke, in which he said, 'I have nothing to add, except that the defence made upon Orr's trial was, in my judgment, supported by subornation only, and that Mr. Curran is to-morrow to move in arrest of judgment upon two grounds, both of which, I am confident enough to say, will fail him.' (Sept. 19, 1797. I.S.P.O.)
[4] Lake to Pelham, Oct. 3, 1797. The deposition of the gaoler is inclosed.

appeared to be deranged in his mind, and who had attempted to commit suicide. This soldier was Wheatley. Elder found him in a state of extreme excitement and despondency, and he accused himself of a number of grave crimes. He had seduced women in Scotland. In Ireland he had run a man through the body with his bayonet, in an affray which had occurred at the capture of an unlicensed still. In this affray the revenue officer in command was wounded, and afterwards sent to gaol, where he died of his wounds, and the affidavit further states 'that he the said Wheatley was prevailed on to swear against some of the persons who were taken prisoners, a false oath, for which he was afraid they would suffer, which also hung heavy on his mind.' A second affidavit, sworn by a person named Montgomery, who was present at the interview, corroborated the statement of Elder. Nothing in these affidavits had any direct bearing on the case of Orr, but the evidence if it had been produced in court would undoubtedly have done much to shake the credibility of Wheatley; and a third affidavit, sworn by the magistrate who had taken Wheatley's earliest deposition, attempted to carry the defence a step farther. It stated that at the spring assizes of 1797, when there had been a question of bringing Orr to trial, Wheatley had spoken with much alarm about the presence of Elder in Carrickfergus, and had expressed his conviction that 'he was brought there to invalidate his testimony against Orr from a conversation that had passed between him and said Elder' in April 1796.

It is a very common thing after the conclusion of a trial which arouses strong popular passions, to find some piece of evidence stated in public at the last moment in order to invalidate the verdict, which might have been brought, but which was not brought, into court during the trial, and which was, therefore, never submitted to the searching test of cross-examination. Few things in the eyes of a lawyer are more suspicious than such evidence, and it is only in very rare cases, and usually when some grave doubt had already hung over the issue of the trial, that any stress is placed upon it. Nor can it be denied that it would be in the highest degree detrimental to the interests of justice if prisoners were encouraged to hold back a portion of their defence until it could no longer be tested by inquiry, or with the object of obtaining a second trial. In this case it will be observed that the evidence of Lindsay was absolutely unimpeached; that no motive for the pretended perjury of Wheatley was suggested; that the confession of perjury which Wheatley was represented as having made, related solely to another case, in which he was personally implicated, and that he was alleged to have made it when suffering from mental derangement. The execution, however, was respited till the 10th, and afterwards till the 14th of October, in order that further inquiry should be made. 'Orr's respite,' wrote a Government official from Belfast, 'has caused great exultation through every disaffected part of the northern district,' and the same official proceeds to describe the desperate efforts that were made to save the prisoner. Two of the jurymen who condemned him, did not dare to leave their homes after nightfall. Every effort of intimidation as well as of solicitation was employed to procure signatures to a petition to the Lord Lieutenant, and the writer concluded by expressing his own belief that if Orr was pardoned, no jury would convict.[1]

The second step taken to prevent the execution was of a different kind. Orr's brother made an application to the High Sheriff of the county, and to one of the members for Belfast, to sign a memorial for the pardon of the prisoner. These gentlemen adopted a course which was certainly humane, and which under the circumstances appears to me to have been wise. They promised that they would sign such a memorial, but only on the condition that Orr confessed his guilt, and in that case one of them further promised to endeavour to procure the signatures of the other members of the grand jury. A full confession of guilt was accordingly drawn up. It was stated to have been submitted to Orr, and to have been signed by him. It was sent to the Lord Lieutenant, and its substance was published, as 'from the best and most respectable authority,' in the 'Belfast News Letter.'[2] Orr, however, soon after its publication is said to have written to the Lord Lieutenant, thanking him for the respite that had been granted, but at the same time reasserting his innocence and formally denying that he had signed this confession;[3] and

[1] Lucius Barber (Belfast), Oct. 10, 1797.
[2] Sept. 29, 1797.
[3] This letter is dated Oct. 10. It was first printed in the *Press*, and will be also found in McCormick's *Life and Trial of William Orr*. There is no allusion to it, either in the speech of

in the Declaration which was distributed at his execution, but which had been drawn up nearly ten days previously,[1] he reiterated this repudiation with great emphasis. 'A false and ungenerous publication,' he wrote, 'having appeared in a newspaper stating certain alleged confessions of guilt on my part, and thus striking at my reputation, which is dearer to me than life, I take this solemn method of contradicting that calumny. I was applied to by the High Sheriff and the Rev. W. Bristow, Sovereign of Belfast, to make a confession of guilt, who used entreaties to that effect. This I peremptorily refused. Did I think myself guilty, I should be free to confess it; but, on the contrary, I glory in my innocence.'

The truth of this statement is open to very grave doubt. When it was published immediately after the death of Orr, the two gentlemen referred to at once denied it,[2] and they wrote to the 'Belfast News Letter' giving their version of what had occurred. On the 27th of the preceding month they said they had together visited Orr in gaol. 'Mr. Bristow said to him, "Sir, I have seen a paper which your brother and another gentleman brought to the Sheriff on Monday last, with your name annexed to it, in which you acknowledged the justice of your sentence, and cautioned others against being led into bad practices by wicked and designing men." Mr Bristow added that "it was expected, from what your brother and that gentleman told the Sheriff, that it would have been published in last Monday's Belfast paper." "I am confident," said Mr. Bristow to Mr. Orr, "that this acknowledgment, which you had for some time withheld, must now afford you great comfort!" Mr. Orr replied, "Yes, sir, it has relieved my mind very much."' The two gentlemen then proceed to say that Mr. Bristow urged Orr to reveal any further fact that might throw light on the conspiracy, but that Orr said that he could at present remember nothing more. This, the High Sheriff and the Sovereign of Belfast declared, was to the best of their recollection exactly what occurred, and in order to

---

Clare in the House of Lords, or in the speech of Curran in the Finerty trial.

[1] Oct. 5.

[2] Andrew McNevin (Carrickfergus) sent to the Government, Orr's dying declaration; mentioned his emphatic denial of the confession, but added: 'Mr. Skiffington and the Rev. Mr. Bristow can testify on oath, that the declaration or confession forwarded to his Excellency was acknowledged by W. Orr to be his, and that his mind was light after it.' (Oct. 14, 1797.)

give their statement the utmost weight, they attested it on oath before a magistrate.[1] On the other hand, the brother of Orr published a letter, to the truth of which he said he also was prepared to swear, in which he stated that he had tried in vain to induce the condemned man to sign the confession of guilt, and that having failed in all his efforts, and in hopes of saving his brother's life, he had himself signed it in his brother's name, but without his privity or consent.[2]

The reader must form his own estimate of these conflicting statements. Notwithstanding the hopes which had naturally been raised by the repeated respites, the Government ultimately decided that the sentence should be carried out. A paragraph, which was inserted, no doubt, by authority, in the 'Belfast News Letter,' announcing this decision, stated that Pelham had written to the High Sheriff intimating that the respite had been granted for the purpose of enabling the Lord Lieutenant to consult Lord Yelverton and Judge Chamberlain, 'as to certain papers which had been transmitted relative to one of the witnesses on whose testimony Mr. Orr was condemned;' that both judges were of opinion that these papers did not impeach the verdict, and that the law must, therefore, take its course.[3] From the statement of Lord Clare, it would appear that the affidavits which had been made after the verdict had been delivered, were not brought formally before the Lord Lieutenant, and that the decision was taken mainly on the ground that the judge who presided at the trial declared himself fully satisfied with the verdict.[4] Orr met

---

[1] *Belfast News Letter*, Oct. 16, 20, 1797.

[2] Ibid. Oct. 20, 1797; McNevin's *Trials*, p. 493.

[3] *Belfast News Letter*, Oct. 13, 1797.

[4] The following is Lord Clare's own defence of the Government. 'His Excellency, notwithstanding the declaration of the learned Lord [the judge], respited Mr. Orr; to give time for inquiry whether any justifiable ground could be laid for extending mercy to him; and finding that nothing could be substantiated to shake the justice of his conviction, the unhappy man was left for execution. The affidavits which I have stated never were laid before the Lord Lieutenant, but if they had, is there a man with a trace of the principles of justice in his mind, who will say that such affidavits ought to be attended to? Is it to be supposed that a judge would receive a verdict from a jury in a state of intoxication? or was it ever heard that a juryman was received, by voluntary affidavit, to impeach a verdict in which he had concurred? Will any man with a trace of criminal justice in his mind, say that a voluntary affidavit of a person not produced, unexamined at the trial, ought to be received after conviction, to impeach the credit of a witness who was examined and cross-examined, and whose credit stood unimpeached by legal evidence?

his fate with courage and dignity, professed with his last breath that he died in the true faith of a Presbyterian, and distributed as he went to the gallows his dying declaration, in which he asserted his innocence and declared the informer to be forsworn. 'If to have loved my country,' he wrote, 'to have known its wrongs, to have felt the injuries of the persecuted Catholics, and to have united with them and all other religious persuasions in the most orderly and least sanguinary means of procuring redress—if these be felonies, I am a felon, but not otherwise.' It was observed, however, that these declarations were not wholly unequivocal. The prisoner who protested his innocence had always maintained that the oath of the United Irishmen was not only innocent, but laudable, and the witness who was said to be forsworn had sworn an obligation of secrecy.[1]

I have now laid before the reader a very full account of this memorable and most unhappy case. If by a judicial murder be meant the execution of a man who was probably innocent of the charge for which he was condemned, that term does not, in my opinion, apply to the death of Orr. On the other hand, to execute a criminal after two members of the jury which condemned him had sworn that intoxication had prevailed in the jury box when the verdict was considering, and that intimidation had been successfully employed to obtain

'If such an affidavit were to lay the necessary foundation of a pardon after conviction, I will venture to say there is no man who may be convicted hereafter of any crime, however atrocious, that will not be able to obtain a similar affidavit.' (Lord Clare's speech, *Debate in the House of Peers*, Feb. 19, 1798, p. 114.)

[1] A short contemporary account of the trial of William Orr was printed in 1797. Clare spoke of it as 'a partial and garbled report.' It is now very rare, but the substance was reprinted in a little book called McCormick's *Life and Trial of Orr*. The affidavits and other leading documents connected with the case will be found in McNevin's *Lives and Trials of Eminent Irishmen*, in the introduction to the trial of Peter Finerty (the editor of the *Press*). That trial arose out of an attack on Lord Camden's conduct relating to the case. The speech of Curran in defence of Finerty is the best statement of the case for Orr, while the opposite side was fully stated by Lord Clare in his speech in the House of Lords. See, too, Madden's *United Irishmen*, ii. 253–258; and the *Belfast News Letter*, Oct. 1797. Musgrave says that Father Quigly and two Presbyterian ministers, who attended Orr after his condemnation, 'persuaded him that he was not guilty of any crime, and that they could reanimate him;' that his body, after being hung, was brought to a Presbyterian meeting house, where a medical man vainly tried to restore him to life by transfusing the blood of a calf into his veins; and that pieces of his clothing were afterwards preserved as relics in every part of the kingdom. (*Rebellions in Ireland*, p. 178.)

unanimity; to treat such an affidavit, after it had been formally laid before the court, with simple neglect, was a course which appears to me to have been well fitted to shake confidence in the administration of justice. Great as might have been the evils that would have arisen from the escape of Orr, I can hardly think that they would have been so great as those which arose from the feeling of deep, passionate, indignant sympathy which the fate of this young Presbyterian farmer evoked, not only throughout Ulster, but throughout the whole of Catholic Ireland. I have given, in Lord Clare's own words, the defence of the Government. The speech in which Curran defended the writer in the 'Press' who had denounced the execution as a judicial murder, shows how powerfully the other side could be presented by a great advocate. If, he said in effect to the jury, you had known that Orr was apprehended on the charge of abjuring the bigotry which had torn and disgraced his country, pledging himself to restore the people to their place in the Constitution, and binding himself never to betray his fellow-labourers in that enterprise; that he had been left untried in prison for twelve tedious months; that he had been condemned by a drunken and worn-out and terrified jury; that members of this jury, when returning sobriety had brought back their consciences, had implored the humanity of the bench and the mercy of the Crown to save them from eternal self-condemnation, and their souls from the indelible stain of innocent blood; that new and hitherto unheard-of crimes had been discovered against the informer; that a respite had been granted no less than three times, and the hopes of the prisoner and his family thus raised to the highest point, and that, notwithstanding this, he had been brought to the gallows, and had died with a solemn declaration of his innocence, and uttering with his last breath a prayer for the liberty of his country—if you had known all this, and had then been asked to describe it, what language would you have used?

The general judgment which will be formed of the policy and proceedings of the Irish Government at this time, and of the share of responsibility that belongs to them in hastening on the rebellion which was manifestly impending, will vary much according to the character of the reader, and perhaps still more according to the political predisposition with which he reviews the facts that have been related. It is manifestly absurd to describe the severities in Ulster as if they were unprovoked by a savage outburst of anarchy and crime, or to deny that in the midst of a great war, and with the extreme probability of a French invasion of Ireland, the disarming of a disaffected province had become urgently necessary. The rigour and violence of the measures that were adopted were chiefly due to the complete inadequacy of normal means for repressing widespread and organised revolt; to the want of any such body as the modern constabulary; to the military exigency which made it necessary in time of war to entrust semi-police functions to an undisciplined yeomanry. Those measures were judged as might have been expected in a country which, for more than a hundred years, had known nothing of martial law. In countries which were, in this respect at least, less happily situated, they would have excited less astonishment, and they will appear pale and insignificant when compared with the proceedings of those French revolutionists who were extolled by the United Irishmen as ideal champions of Liberty and Progress. The Insurrection Act was an extreme remedy for a desperate disease, limited to a brief period and to the proclaimed districts. Even the burning of houses, though unauthorised by law and eminently fitted to infuriate the people, can hardly be regarded as indefensible as a military measure, if it was found to be the necessary condition of carrying out a necessary disarming.

But although all this may, I think, be truly said, the faults of Irish government during the few years before the rebellion of 1798 appear to me to have been enormously great, and a weight of tremendous responsibility rests upon those who conducted it. By habitual corruption and the steady employment of the system of nomination boroughs, they had reduced the Irish Legislature to a condition of such despicable and almost ludicrous subserviency, that a policy which was probably supported by the great majority of educated Irishmen, could not command more than twenty or thirty votes in the House of Commons. They had done this at a time when the French Revolution had made the public mind in the highest degree sensitive to questions of representation; at a time when the burden of the war was imposing extraordinary hardships on the people. They had resisted the very moderate Reform Bills of Ponsonby and Grattan, which would have left the overwhelming preponderance of political power in the hands of property, loyalty, and intelligence, as strenuously as the wild democratic schemes of the United Irishmen, and they had thus thrown into the path of treason a crowd of able and energetic men, who might have been contented by reform. No one who follows the history of the long succession of dangerous conventions which had existed in Ireland since 1782, can doubt that the Convention Act, making illegal, delegated and representative assemblies other than Parliament, was required; but it could be justified and acquiesced in, only on the condition that the popular branch of the Legislature was in some real sense a representative body; and to this condition the Irish Government was inexorably opposed:

The management of the Catholic question had been still more disastrous—disastrous not only in what was denied, but also in much that was granted. The Relief Act of 1793 had deluged the county constituencies with an overwhelming multitude of illiterate Catholic 40s. freehold voters, who were totally unfit for the exercise of political power; who were certain at some future time to become a great political danger, and whose enfranchisement added enormously to the difficulty and danger of reforming the Parliament, while it still left the Catholics under the brand of inferiority, excluded the Catholic gentry from Parliament, and thus deprived them of political influence at the very period when their services were most needed. At the same time, by the fatal error of not connecting—as might then most easily have been done—the college for the education of the priesthood with the University of the country, they prepared the way for an evil of the most serious kind.

The recall of Lord Fitzwilliam, under circumstances that were calculated to inflame to the utmost, popular passions; the deliberate appeal by the Government to the sectarian spirit among the Protestants, and Pelham's language of eternal proscription against the Catholics, soon completed the work. The loyal and respectable, though unfortunately small and timid, body of Catholic gentry lost all power and influence, and the guidance of the Catholics passed into the hands of seditious demagogues in the towns, who were in close alliance with the United Irishmen. At the same time the transportation by Lord Carhampton of multitudes of suspected persons to the fleet, without a shadow of legal justification; the Act of Indemnity, by which the Irish Parliament closed the doors of the law courts against those who sought for redress, and the shameful apathy shown towards the earliest outrages of the Orange banditti in the North, convinced great masses of the poor, that they were out of the protection of the law. It is not true that the Government inspired or approved of those outrages; but when it was found that a proclamation which specifically condemned the crimes of the Defenders, was silent about those of the Orangemen; that a parliamentary inquiry into these outrages, though repeatedly asked for, was always refused; and that hundreds, and possibly thousands, of Catholics, were obliged by terror to fly from their homes, at a time when Ulster was full of English troops, it cannot be wondered at that the Catholics should have come to look on themselves as completely unprotected, and should have been well prepared to receive the seditious teaching which was so abundantly diffused. In the summer and autumn of 1797 Ulster had grown more quiet, but evidence was almost daily pouring in, that all Catholic Ireland was passing rapidly into active sedition.

It is not surprising that it should have been so. Anarchy is like a cancer, which, once it has effected a lodgment in one portion of the body politic, will inevitably spread. Already, the Catholics of Ulster, as well as of one or two adjoining counties, and the Catholic leaders in Dublin, were thoroughly disaffected, while in many other counties the great mass of the Catholic peasantry were organised as Defenders; and Defenderism, as we have seen, though essentially a Whiteboy movement, and aiming at Whiteboy objects, was now in connection or alliance with the United Irishmen, and hoped to attain its objects by a French invasion and a consequent revolution.

It is important, however, to form a clear idea of the true motives that agitated the great Catholic masses. Catholic emancipation and parliamentary reform, which were the original and ostensible objects of the United Irishmen, had probably no place among them. The refusal of emancipation had been important in decisively turning a number of active Catholics in the towns to rebellion. It had a negative influence in withholding from loyal leaders influence and power, and in maintaining the broad political distinction between the two creeds; but both Lord Clare and the most intelligent leaders of the United Irishmen fully agreed with General Knox, that to the overwhelming majority of the Catholic people of Ireland, it was a matter of utter indifference. At a much later period, the combined influence of O'Connell and the priests made it a really popular question, but this time had not yet come.[1]

A very similar remark may be made about parliamentary reform. To the illiterate Catholic cottiers and small farmers, who covered three out of the four provinces of Ireland, questions of this kind could have but little significance. For itself, they cared nothing, but the United Irishmen, who clearly saw this, tried to persuade them that a reform of Parliament must be followed by the abolition of tithes.

The tithe question, on the other hand, was one of real and passionate popular interest, and it had borne a prominent part in almost every agrarian disturbance of the century. The object of the leaders of the United Irishmen was a complete abolition of religious establishments, as in France; they continually, and,

[1] In the very instructive examinations of Emmet and McNevin by the Secret Committee in 1798, this fact was clearly brought out. 'Lord Chancellor: "Pray do you think Catholic emancipation and parliamentary reform any objects with the common people?" Emmet: "As to Catholic emancipation, I don't think it matters a feather, or that the poor think of it. As to parliamentary reform, I don't think the common people ever thought of it until it was inculcated to them, that a reform would cause a removal of those grievances which they actually do feel. From that time, I believe, they have become very much attached to the measure." McNevin's evidence (which he republished in full, as he thought it unfairly abridged in the parliamentary report), is to the same effect. 'Lord Chancellor: "Do you think the mass of the people in the provinces of Leinster, Munster, and Connaught care the value of this pen, or the drop of ink it contains, for parliamentary reform or Catholic emancipation?" McNevin: "I am sure they do not, if by the mass of the people your Lordship means the common illiterate people; they do not understand it. What they very well understand is, that it would be a very great advantage to them to be relieved from the payment of tithes, and not to be fleeced by their landlords; but there is not a man who can read a newspaper, who has not considered the question of reform. . . . As to Catholic emancipation, the importance of that question has passed away long since; it really is not worth a moment's thought at the present period."' (McNevin's *Pieces of Irish History*, pp. 199, 200, 221; see, too, p. 206.)

no doubt, sincerely, denied that they had the smallest wish to set up a Catholic establishment, or that they believed such an idea to be entertained by the Catholics; and they added, that any such attempt would encounter their strenuous resistance. With the mass of the Catholic peasantry, the question was not, I believe, one of privilege or establishment. It was a desire to be relieved from a heavy and unequal burden, which pressed most severely on the poorest cottiers; which was greatly aggravated by the system of tithe proctors, and by the constant disputes about new and old tithes; which was levied directly on the produce of the soil, and which was levied for the benefit of the clergy of another creed. To abolish this impost was one of their most earnest and unwavering desires, and it is probable that if this had been done they would have cared very little for the existence of the Establishment. We have seen how earnestly, in three successive years, Grattan had pressed upon the Irish Government and Parliament the vital necessity of dealing with this question; how he had proposed schemes for commutation, which would probably have completely allayed the discontent; how Pitt, at a still earlier period, had suggested the same policy; and how the Irish Government had steadily resisted it.[1] The tithe grievance was now the chief political bond between the Presbyterians of the North and the Catholics of the South; and the fact that the French had begun their Revolution by abolishing tithes, was one of the chief motives put forward for welcoming a French invasion.

After the question of tithes, but after it at a considerable distance, came the question of rent. I have described the great and sudden increase of rents which corn bounties and war prices had produced, and the way in which it acted on different classes of the community. The many instances of hardship and distress

---

[1] Vol. vi. pp. 410-412. Both McNevin and Emmet in their examinations strongly expressed their personal desire to abolish all religious establishments in Ireland, but both of them acknowledged that the great mass of the Catholics would have been contented with a much smaller measure. 'Sure I am, sir,' said McNevin, 'that if tithes had been commuted according to Mr. Grattan's plan, a very powerful engine would have been taken out of our hands.' 'If any other way of paying even a Protestant establishment,' said Emmet, 'which did not bear so sensibly on their industry, were to take place, I believe it would go a great way to content them [the Catholics]; though I confess it would not content me.' (McNevin's *Pieces of Irish History*, pp. 212, 228.)

which followed, had an undoubted part in producing Catholic disaffection; and hopes of a lowering of rents, and, still more, of a great agrarian revolution, or confiscation of lands, to be carried out by French assistance, were abroad. At the same time, while the question of tithes appeared habitually, the question of rents only appeared occasionally, in the popular appeals, and it was not, in the main, a question between the owner and the occupier of land. The frequent conduct of landlords in setting up leases to auction, had, no doubt, contributed to the evil, but the great majority of extortionate rents were exacted not by landlords, but by tenants—by the race of middlemen and land-jobbers, who held tracts of land upon lease, subdivided them into small plots, and sublet them, at an enormous profit.

There was another influence, which was not the less serious because it was somewhat more indefinite in its character. It was a vague feeling of separate nationality, which was thrilling powerfully through the Catholic masses. The events of history had divided the inhabitants of Ireland into two distinct and separate nations, divided broadly in creed, and, in some measure, in character and in race, and one of these was an ascendant and governing nation, which had displaced, by conquest, the old rulers and possessors of the soil.[1] A keen sense of the danger of this situation was the keynote of the whole policy of Grattan. In all that he accomplished, and in all that he aimed at, it was his main object to make the Irish one people, instead of two, to soften and efface the old lines of distinction, by blending in the Government and in the Legislature, the representatives of the rival creeds. For some years, this policy seemed destined to succeed. Time had dimmed the memory of old conflicts and confiscations. Religious animosities had subsided. Nearly all the penal code had been abolished. A large share of political power had been conceded to the Catholics. Although the ownership of land was still, almost exclusively, in Protestant hands, there was no longer any law to prevent Catholics from acquiring it, and a great amount of Catholic property, in mortgages and other forms, was now identified with the established

---

[1] See a very remarkable letter of Alexander Knox upon the unexampled clearness with which, owing to their religious difference, the conquering and the conquered race in Ireland have both preserved their separate identities. (*Castlereagh Correspondence*, iv. 221, 222.)

disposition of property. Increasing material prosperity was raising up a wealthy class among them, and their most energetic and ambitious members no longer sought a career in France, or Austria, or Spain. It was the dream of Grattan that a loyal Irish gentry of both denominations could form a governing body who would complete the work, and that, although a Protestant ascendency would continue, it would be the modified and mitigated ascendency which naturally belongs to the most educated section of the community and to the chief owners of property, and not an ascendency defined by creeds, and based on disqualifying laws. But, from the time when the principles of the French Revolution took root in Ireland, and, still more, after the recall of Lord Fitzwilliam, events had taken another turn. The new democratic leaders were chiefly Protestants, and they aimed, like Grattan, though by very different methods, and on a very different basis, at union between Catholics and Protestants, and the abolition of religious disqualifications; but the result of their movement was a furious revival of religious animosities, and a panic among the possessors of property, which greatly deepened the division of classes. At the same time, the extreme probability of a French conquest of Ireland, and the tremendous events on the Continent, which foreshadowed nothing less than a total destruction of the whole political and social order in Europe, and the downfall of the British Empire, aroused hopes in the Catholic population which had slumbered for more than a century. Prophecies, attributed to St. Columkill, pointing to the reinstatement of the old race, and the expulsion of the stranger, had circulated in Ireland during the great troubles of 1641. They were now, once more, passing from lip to lip, and vague, wild hopes, of a great coming change were rapidly spreading.

Another point in which the situation resembled that of 1641, was the belief which was fast growing among the Catholics, that they were marked out for massacre. In the seventeenth century the Catholic population had been driven to madness, by the belief that the English Puritans were about to exterminate their creed. At the end of the eighteenth century a similar fear prevailed, but the object of terror was the Orangeman.[1] It was

[1] The following is part of one of the depositions sworn in 1643 : 'They

asserted by the newspapers of the United Irishmen, and it was taught and believed in every quarter of Ireland, that the secret oath sworn by every Orangeman was, 'I will be true to the King and Government, and I will exterminate, as far as I am able, the Catholics of Ireland.'

Whether such a statement was a pure calumny, or whether any such oath may have been in use among the banditti, who were wrecking by night the homes of Catholic farmers in Armagh and in some adjoining counties, it is impossible to say. The charge was like that which was afterwards brought against the Catholic insurgents, of designing nothing less than a massacre of the whole Protestant population. In both cases it was essentially false, but in both cases it may have derived some colour of plausibility from the frantic utterances and the ferocious actions of excited fanatics. In the Orange Society, as organised by the Ulster gentry, there was no oath even distantly resembling what was alleged, and the masters of all the Orange lodges in Ulster had, as we have seen, most emphatically disclaimed any wish to persecute the Catholics. But the seed had been already scattered among an ignorant, credulous, and suspicious peasantry. The United Irishmen persistently represented the Orange Society as a society created for the extermination of the Catholics, by men high in rank and office, and under the direct patronage of the Government, and they were

---

told this deponent that the Scotch had petitioned the Parliament Houses of England that there should not be a papist left alive in England, Ireland, or Scotland; and that some of the committee employed out of Ireland in England for Irish affairs, having notice thereof, writ over unto them in Ireland to rise in arms and take all the strongholds and forts herein to their hands, or to that effect; and that they commanding the rebels now expected the fulfilling of Columkill's prophecy, which, as they did construe it, was that the Irish should conquer Ireland again, or to that effect.' (Hickson's *Irish Massacres of 1641*, ii. 142, 143.) Compare with this, a letter of Cooke to Pelham (Dec. 23, 1797): 'Reports are propagated among the lower Catholics, that the Orangemen are to rise and murder them. Other reports, that not a Protestant is to be left in Ireland by the 25th of March. Confraternities of Carmelites are establishing near Dublin by the priests, and some old silly prophecy of Columkill is circulated among them, which gives Ireland this year to the Spaniards.' The Committee of Secrecy printed an example of the pretended Orange rules, which were fabricated for the purpose of exciting the passions of the Catholics. (Appendix No. xxvi.) Some curious particulars about the pretended prophecies that were circulated on the eve of the rebellion of 1798, will be found in that interesting book, McSkimin's *History of the Irish Rebellion in Antrim, Down, and Derry*, pp. 48–50. Among them were some attributed to Thomas the Rhymer, and others of the Scotch Covenanter, Alexander Peden.

accustomed to contrast its pretended oath with that of the United Irishman, which bound him only to endeavour to form a brotherhood of affection among Irishmen of every religious persuasion; to labour for the attainment of an equal, full, and adequate representation of all the people of Ireland in Parliament; and never, either directly or indirectly, to inform or give evidence against any member of the society.[1] This was probably their most successful mode of propagandism, and the panic which it created had, as we shall see, a great part in producing the horrors that followed. It is, however, a curious fact, that the fear of the Orangemen appears to have been most operative upon populations who came in no direct contact with them. The worst scenes of the insurrection were in Wexford, where the Society had never penetrated; while in Ulster, and in Connaught, which was full of fugitives from Ulster, the rebellion assumed a far milder form.

In the beginning of 1797, the United Ireland movement was powerful in Dublin, and had overspread all or the greater part of Ulster, but beyond these limits it had probably no considerable influence, except in the counties of Westmeath and Meath, where it entered in the wake of Defenderism. In the first months of the year, there was a sudden and most ferocious and alarming outburst of Defenderism in the King's County. All the houses over a large area were plundered. The depredators 'put several of the honest inhabitants on the fire, to induce them to deliver up their arms and money.' The house of a Mr. Bagenal was set on fire. The owner and his wife were both murdered, and shots were fired at his children. The magistrates, as early as February 17, petitioned the Lord Lieutenant to proclaim certain portions of the county, but more than two months passed before their request was attended to. In the mean time they succeeded in capturing some fifty prisoners, and in obtaining two witnesses; but when the assizes came, these witnesses were so intimidated, that they denied in the witness box everything they had sworn before the magistrate. Confident in impunity, the outrages now burst out with renewed violence. Every night there were robberies; the robbers brought fire to the farmers' houses, and threatened to put it on the thatches,

[1] See e.g. *The Beauties of the Press*, pp. 152, 153.

and to treat the owners 'as they did the Bagenals,' unless they surrendered their money and arms; and they made it a special object to seize the swords and pistols of the yeomanry, who generally lived in small thatched houses. The magistrates wrote, that if this continued, the yeomen would soon be totally disarmed, and therefore useless; that it was hopeless attempting to get evidence; that great numbers of the peasantry were being sworn into the organisation; that nothing short of the proclamation of a portion of the county could stay the evil, and that there were already signs that it was spreading to the adjoining county of Kildare. One serious check was encountered by the Defenders in the King's County. A large party, after midnight, attacked Castle Carberry near Clonard, the house of a gentleman named Sparks, but they found the owner fully prepared, and after a heavy fire, which lasted for more than an hour, they retired, leaving six of their number dead, and several others badly wounded.[1]

The circle of contagion was rapidly expanding. A letter written on May 1 by a magistrate of Enniscorthy, in the county of Wexford—the town which was afterwards the centre of the most horrible scenes of the rebellion—described that county as being still 'perfectly quiet and well disposed,' and the writer said that, although he knew of some turbulent and disaffected characters, and had heard of some attempts to administer oaths, he did not believe that a single person had yet been sworn in, though, he added, 'the neighbouring parts of the counties of Carlow and Kilkenny are by no means so quiet.' Very soon, however, we find seditious papers industriously scattered through this county and through the county of Carlow; and by November, Carlow, Kildare, Kilkenny, Wexford, and Wicklow were all tainted.[2] One Carlow magistrate wrote, that in that county alone there were at least 3,000 United Irishmen, that almost the whole district that lay between the counties of Wicklow, Wexford, and Kilkenny was 'United,' and that additional troops were urgently required.[3] An intercepted letter of a United Irishman

---

[1] John Tyrell (Clonard), April 26; Mr. Everard (near Edenderry), April 26; Mr. Sparks, May 14, 1797. There are several other papers written in May, about the King's County, in the I.S.P.O.

[2] Cæsar Colclough (Enniscorthy), May 1, 29; Edward Croker, May 15; Rev. T. Hardwick, May 18; Hon. B. O. Stratford, June 1797.

[3] Mr. Rochfort, Nov. 2, 1797.

boasted that in a single week 26,741 persons had been 'United' in the counties of Meath, Wicklow, Louth, and Dublin; and predicted that 'in a little time all the people of Ireland would be of one way of thinking.'[1] In Wexford, Wicklow, and for the most part in Carlow, the spread of disaffection appears at this time to have been unaccompanied by crime; but in Kilkenny, Defender outrages were of frequent occurrence, and in the county of Kildare there was a perfect reign of terror. A man named Nicholson, who had assisted in conducting a prisoner to gaol, had his house burnt; he was afterwards dragged out of a farmer's house and pierced by some fifty pikes; the murderers then returned to the farmhouse and deliberately murdered his wife; and such was the terror that reigned, that it is stated that there would have been no inquest or inquiry of any sort, but for the intervention of a party of soldiers from Kildare. Letter after letter came to the Castle describing the growing anarchy, and imploring the Government to send down fresh troops.[2]

In Kildare the situation was much aggravated by the strong political opposition of the chief gentry to the Government. In May, the Duke of Leinster and most of the principal magistrates of the county signed a requisition to the High Sheriff, asking him to call a meeting of the magistrates and freeholders; and on his refusal, they resolved to meet without his consent. The meeting was prohibited by the Government, and they then drew up the petition to the King to which I have already alluded, accusing the Ministry of having, by their corruption and system of irritation, produced the disorders of the country, and predicting that, unless reform and Catholic emancipation were speedily granted, the contest must lead to bloodshed and rebellion, and might terminate in a complete alienation of affection from England, and in the separation of Ireland from the Empire.[3]

---

[1] J. C. Hamilton, May 1797.
[2] Captain Neville (Naas), Nov. 2; Lord Carrick (Kilkenny), Nov. 16; John Wolfe (Balbriggan), Nov. 22, 1797. This last writer, who describes the murder of Nicholson and his wife, adds, that about twenty-seven years before, the great smuggler, Morty Oge O'Sullivan, was much annoyed by a revenue officer named Puxley. O'Sullivan with his brother-in-law Connell, waylaid and killed Puxley, who had his wife with him. Connell wanted to kill the woman also, but O'Sullivan replied, 'What, do you think me so base a scoundrel as to lift my hand to woman!' 'Strange alteration,' adds the writer, 'in the Irish character, long noted for humanity!'
[3] Wogan Brown (high sheriff) to Pelham May 29, 1797.

An attorney of no very high character, named John Pollock, was at this time Crown prosecutor for Leinster, and much in the confidence of the Government, and he has left an interesting, though probably a somewhat partisan, description of the summer assizes in a considerable part of Leinster. In Carlow he found 'no appearance of any political party whatever,' but in Kildare there was 'a most decided and unequivocal determination to subvert the King's Government.' In every case growing out of the disturbances, the prisoner was supported by the countenance of Lord Edward Fitzgerald, Lawless, and every Roman Catholic on the grand jury. The agent and confidential friend of Lord Edward 'challenged the jurors for the prisoners, and appeared the executive officer of sedition and rebellion.' 'A rooted and desperate rebellion' had been planted in the county. There were 'notorious and decided rebels on the grand jury,' who disclosed the evidence of the Crown to the prisoners, and openly encouraged refractory jurymen. In the King's County outrages were numerous and sanguinary, but the adjoining Queen's County was, as usual, perfectly tranquil.[1]

The reports disseminated about the murderous intentions of the Orangemen, played a great part in these disturbances. No other means were so successfully employed to drive the Catholics to desperation. In the county of Carlow, some of the Protestant gentry, combining to maintain the peace of the county in the midst of smothered rebellion, very injudiciously affiliated their association to the Orange organisation in Ulster, and thus gave a pretext to the agitators which was abundantly used.[2] On one occasion two well-dressed men rode in the dead of night through a village about three miles from Carlow, and rapping at every door, warned the inhabitants to fly, as the Orangemen were on the march from Carlow to burn their houses, and slaughter every Catholic they met. The panic was so intense, that the whole population fled for shelter and

---

[1] J. Pollock, Aug. 30, 1797. Pollock was aware of McNally's connection with the Government; he communicated constantly with him, and reports that McNally thought himself cruelly neglected by his friends. An extremely unfavourable account of Pollock, and of the manner in which he conducted himself in dealing with prisoners, will be found in the *Narrative* of the Rev. Dr. Dickson, a Presbyterian minister implicated in the conspiracy. (Pp. 65-75.)

[2] See a letter from W. Elliot to Pelham, Aug. 7, 1798.

protection to a neighbouring magistrate.[1] At Nenagh, in the county of Tipperary, a placard was posted on the chapel door informing the people that every Orangeman was bound by his oath to exterminate the Catholics, and pointing out by name to the popular vengeance a number of persons in the town who were said to be Orangemen.[2] 'The terror,' wrote Lord Camden, 'which was occasioned in a part of the county of Wicklow not seventeen miles from Dublin, from the report which has been sent into that county by the Dublin committees, that the Orangemen were to march into it and murder the Catholics, was such, that those miserable, ignorant, and deluded persons left their houses and lay in the fields, and at last assembled in large numbers for their own protection.' 'This alarm,' the Lord Lieutenant continues, 'of the designs of the Orangemen was really created in some parts; in others it was used as a pretext for mutiny.'[3]

The anarchy and disaffection in Leinster prevailed chiefly in the counties I have mentioned, but even outside this area there were disquieting symptoms. At Clondalkin, within a few miles of Dublin, housebreaking outrages were going on which bore an ominous resemblance to those of the Defenders;[4] and a curious and interesting letter of Sir Edward Newenham, who had been recently staying in the hill country of Tipperary, throws some light on the state of that county. He had been talking, he said, very freely to the farmers, and found that they expected many thousands of French soon to come, and the Protestants of the North to assist the Catholics of the South. A number of pedlars, speaking an accent which was not that of the county, had recently been distributing multitudes of seditious papers, which they carried in secret drawers under their boxes, and there was a widely spread belief that tithes would never again be paid, and that land would be equally divided. 'From the unreserved manner,' concluded Newenham, 'in which these mountaineers spoke to me, I am confident the northern spirit of rebellion has got generally among them, and

---

[1] *Faulkner's Journal*, Jan. 13, 1798.
[2] Camden to Portland, Nov. 15, 1797.
[3] Ibid. See, too, Gordon's *History of Ireland*, ii. 357; Gordon's *History of the Rebellion of* 1798, pp. 30-32.
[4] Mr. Caldbeck (Dublin), Nov. 17, 1797.

if they get any strength, they will endanger the peace of the whole island; for, led by their clergy, they will be more fatal in assassination (*sic*) than those of the North.'[1]

We may now turn to Munster, which had been so signally loyal when a French fleet lay in Bantry Bay, and when the landing of the French army seemed a question of hours. For some weeks after that alarm had passed, all remained quiet in the South, and the most serious incident in General Dalrymple's letters was the flight to France in an American vessel of the military secretary of General Massey, who was well acquainted with military affairs in the South of Ireland.[2] In April, however, the clouds of disaffection were beginning to creep stealthily, but visibly, over the horizon. Dalrymple wrote from Cork, that 'a large proportion of the country people are disaffected, and industrious to render others so;' that Lord Bandon reported signs of perfidy among the yeomen; that a spirit of disorder was increasing, he knew not why, and that some woods had been lately cut down to make pikes. 'The character of the times taken at Cork is indifference; the loss of trade and its advantages seems to have much done away that ardour so much boasted of formerly.'[3] Still, in the beginning of May, Camden wrote: 'The South of Ireland is not in any considerable degree of forwardness in this spirit of disaffection.'[4]

But in a few weeks, the aspect of affairs had become much more serious. In the camp at Bandon, Brigadier-General Coote discovered grave signs of disaffection among the soldiers, while two whole committees of United Irishmen were arrested at Cork. 'The fruits of our investigation,' wrote General Dalrymple, 'are bitter indeed: they only tend to prove the excess of the corruption of the people, civil and military. I should be sorry that lists of persons of this description were given to the world, for it would serve to prove the state of matters being far more dangerous than is at present believed. Our endeavours to counteract this business, however well directed and executed, are but very unavailing when opposed to the torrent of disaffection that is hourly increasing. . . . This is the result of much

---

[1] Sir E. Newenham, May 31, 1797. Higgins notices the great use made of pedlars by the chief conspirators. (F. H., Sept. 27, 1797.)

[2] Dalrymple to Pelham, March 19, 1797.
[3] Ibid. April 15, 20, 22, 1797.
[4] Camden to Portland, May 2, 1797.

inquiry made by myself and others. . . . The evil increases with rapid strides, and is far from being confined to the wretched or needy.' On the 29th of May, two militia soldiers were executed with great solemnity for sedition. Five-thousand men were present under arms, and the culprits, kneeling on their coffins, acknowledged their guilt. But the evil was far from checked, and the investigation a few weeks later at Bandon, showed that an extensive plot had been formed among the inhabitants of that town to seduce the soldiers in the camp, murder General Coote and his officers, and produce a rising. About thirty soldiers and as many civilians were arrested, and Coote considered that many of the soldiers ought to suffer capitally, and that the inhabitants of the town were at the bottom of the business. General Loftus, however, wrote from Cork, 'I scarcely know an instance of a Catholic of consequence being the agitator of any disturbance here; the promoters of sedition either come from Dublin or the North, some originally from Manchester.'[1]

In May, reports were sent to the Castle of the appearance of the United Irish movement at Mallow,[2] and there were also alarming rumours of disloyalty among the Methodists. It appears, however, from an interesting letter of Dr. Croke, who presided over them, that the only foundation for these rumours, was the strong reluctance of some Methodist yeomen to go through military exercises on Sunday. Dr. Croke added, that his co-religionists were now a large body among the middle and poorer ranks of Protestants in Ireland, and that the communicants in the country churches were almost entirely composed of Methodists. They were attached to the Established Church, but thought themselves neglected and despised by it, and something should be done to conciliate them. In England, he said, a small part of the society had broken away from the Establishment, and appeared to have imbibed French principles.[3]

---

[1] Coote to Pelham, May 22, June 25, 27, 29, July 3; Dalrymple to Pelham, May 24; Pelham to Loftus, May 27; Loftus to Pelham, June 3; B. Shaw (Cork), May 29; Col. Massey (Cork), May 31, 1797.
[2] May 25.
[3] Dr. Croke, Limerick, May 23, 1797. The separation of the Wesleyan Methodists in Ireland from the Church did not take place till 1808 or 1809, about fifteen years after a similar separation had taken place in England. See a letter from Alexander Knox to Hannah More, Knox's *Remains*, iv. 231–233, and also Crookshank's *Hist. of Methodism in Ireland*, ii. 110.

As usual, political agitation in Munster was soon followed by its attendant shadow—agrarian crime, organised intimidation, and frequent murder. Tithe grievances and oppression by middlemen were, in this province, especially flagrant, and they prepared the way for the agitators, and determined the character of the movement. The people were told that a successful rebellion would put an end to all such grievances, and that it would be immediately followed by a great confiscation and division of lands, and they pursued their ends by the usual Whiteboy methods.[1] In the September Assizes at Cork, the juries are said to have done their duty, and several persons were convicted, but many undoubted criminals were acquitted because witnesses either refused to appear or grossly prevaricated,[2] and almost immediately after, a large area around Lismore and Boyle became the scene of Defender outrages. There was a general conspiracy to refuse tithes. The houghing of cattle and the burning of corn became common. Every night marauding parties traversed the country, and in a few weeks at least five atrocious murders were committed.[3] Lord Shannon, the chief resident landlord in the county of Cork, wrote to the Government: 'I am persuaded that there are few, if any, of the lower orders in this country who have not taken the United Irish oath, and, though not over-scrupulous about breaking every other solemn tie, they are faithful to that, as the most immediate and barbarous assassination is the certain consequence of even the least suspicion of having violated it; shocking instances of which have happened in parts of the county of Waterford, bordering on the county of Cork. By the prevailing system of terror,

---

[1] Higgins, having gone down to Cork to receive some rents, wrote to the Government describing the war against tithes, the houghing of cattle, and the promises that were held out of a division of land among the rebels. He adds: 'I made the most strict inquiry, if there existed any colourable cause for complaint among the poor as to tithe-gathering, and it appeared that the incumbent or owner of tithes lets them at the highest value to a tithe farmer. The farmer lets to the tithe proctor, and each of them must receive an increased profit. This, with the enormous acreable rent charged for potato ground to the lowest order of the peasantry by the middlemen, is the occasion of great discontent, and renders the peasantry ready instruments in the hands of wicked and designing men.' (F. H., Oct. 15, 1797.)

[2] Robert Day (Cork), Sept. 29, 1797.

[3] Sir R. Musgrave (Lismore), Oct. 6, Nov. 12; General Loftus to Pelham, Oct. 26; Lord Mountcashell (near Boyle), Nov. 11. Several other documents illustrating the outrages will be found in the I.S.P.O., Sept., Oct., Nov. 1797. Among them are many requests for troops.

resident gentlemen of property have lost the influence they formerly had over the lower order of peasantry, and I can say from my own observation, that men who are dependent on me, and frequently had resorted to me for kindnesses, are now visibly terrified at being seen alone with me, lest they may incur suspicion and its consequences. It has been represented to me, that large bodies of horse have been seen parading at night in sequestered parts, well mounted and armed, the main body preceded by an advanced, and followed by a rear guard. . . . I am satisfied the whole country is united in one league, and devoted to the mandates of committees, which I understand sit at Cork and the different baronies of the county. . . . All this seems to me, to lead clearly to rebellion and a general rising on the first opportunity that offers.'[1]

This picture appeared to Camden in no way exaggerated. One of his confidential letters to Portland, written in November, paints in vivid colours the horrors of the scene. 'It is melancholy,' he wrote, 'to observe how much accustomed the mind becomes to histories of outrage and of cruelty, and it is for that reason only that I can account for my despatches to your Grace not being filled with the dreadful information I every day receive of the murders of magistrates, the assassination of informers and yeomen, and the conspiracies against persons of rank, consequence, and station. . . . I have further been informed of a conspiracy to assassinate Lord Shannon and Lord Boyle; and it is a melancholy observation to make to your Grace, that where these noblemen reside, and in a neighbourhood extremely well inhabited by gentlemen, there are and have been more signs of disturbance than in almost any part of the kingdom. The pretence of the county of Cork is the exorbitancy of tithes, and the cattle are houghed and the corn burnt of all those who shall pay them, or who shall draw the corn to the barns of the rector. This pretence is, however, quickly followed by notices to pay no rent. Those persons who have entered into the yeomanry corps are deserted as tradesmen, and there is a combination, which is most alarming, against all those who attempt to support the King and the Constitution. Information was given of some persons in the county of Waterford who were concerned in these trans-

[1] Lord Shannon (Castle Martyr), Nov. 9, 1797.

actions, and those miscreants who suspected the informer, not content with murdering the informer himself, murdered his wife and daughter; and that nothing alive should be left in the house, the dog that belonged to the family was killed also.' 'As long as the war lasts, I fear I cannot promise your Grace any settled tranquillity in Ireland; and even when it shall cease, the seeds of discontent have been so industriously sown, the method of communicating real or supposed grievances is so extensively established, that it will be long before the kingdom regains its former tranquillity; and if the French shall be able to effect a landing, I apprehend much blood will be shed and many atrocities committed.'[1]

Connaught of all the four provinces was by far the most peaceful, but there, too, the traces of the agitators may be found. Around Sligo, the process of swearing in United Irishmen was actively going on, and outrages were beginning, though they appear to have been much less serious and frequent than in the three other provinces.[2] From Ennis, in Clare, a magistrate wrote that he had believed that his county had escaped the contagion, but had just discovered that about 100 persons, chiefly young men, shepherds, and servants, had in June been sworn in by some northern emigrants.[3] From Newport, in the county of Mayo, another magistrate reported that some men from the North had lately appeared in the county trying to swear in United Irishmen, but they had been detected and arrested. 'I am happy,' adds the writer, 'to have it in my power to observe that this part of the country is in the most peaceable condition, and likely to continue so,' and this appeared to him to be the first attempt to seduce the people of that district from their loyalty.[4] Lord Altamount, who watched so wisely and so humanely over the state of his great property around Westport, writes in October: 'All is perfectly quiet here now, but I am sorry to know there is a great deal of bad disposition around me—I know it from those from whom secrets are not concealed—and that those ill intentions are not confined to the lower classes.' At all times, he said, Mayo and Connemara were so wild and

---

[1] Camden to Portland, Nov. 15, 1797.
[2] O. Wynne May 17; T. Soden, May 24, 1797.
[3] H. Sankey, Oct. 5, 1797.
[4] Mr. O'Donnell, May 21, 1797.

uncivilised that they were the asylum of deserters, robbers, and murderers from the whole kingdom; but his special subject of anxiety was the great mass of immigrants from the North, whose state was now almost desperate. Most of them were supported by public or private charity, but he feared they would soon be necessarily driven to plunder.[1]

It would be difficult to conceive a more dreary or a more ignoble picture than Ireland at this time presented. The Parliament had lost almost every quality of a representative body; the Government was at once bigoted and corrupt, and steadily opposed to the most moderate and most legitimate reforms; and in three provinces almost every county was filled with knots of conspirators and incendiaries, who were trying to bring down on their country a foreign invasion, and were stirring up the people to rebellion and to crime. A few of them were men of genuine enthusiasm, and real, though certainly not extraordinary, talent; but the great majority were mere demagogues, adventurers, and criminals—such men as in days of anarchy and revolution ever rise to the surface—and scarcely one of them had the smallest right or title to speak as the representative of the nation. In the mean time, the country as a whole presented the most melancholy of all spectacles, that of general, rapid, and profound demoralisation. Religious animosities were steadily increasing. The old ties of reverence and affection, which, in spite of many unhappy circumstances, had bound the poor to the rich, were giving way. Crimes were multiplying, and they were constantly assuming a character of savage ferocity, while organised outrage was encountered by a military repression which often exceeded the limits of the law, led to horrible abuses, and was fast demoralising the forces that were employed in it. It was evident that there was no sentiment in the great mass of the poorer Catholics that was sufficiently powerful to be turned into a serious political movement, or to bring armed forces into the field, though there was a vague dislike to the English race and name, which was now being steadily fanned. But in 1797, as in later periods, political agitators found it necessary for their purposes to appeal to other than political motives—to agrarian grievances and agrarian cupidity; to religious passions; to the

[1] Lord Altamount, Oct. 1797.

discontent produced by the pressure of poverty in a population which was very poor; to the panic which skilful falsehood could easily create in a population which was very ignorant. All these engines were systematically, unscrupulously, and successfully employed, and what in one sphere was politics, in another soon turned into ordinary crime. Camden noticed in June, that the first leaders of the conspiracy seemed to have in some degree lost their ascendency, and that 'a set of lower mechanics' had 'the greatest sway.' 'The plan of acting under an oath of secrecy,' he added, 'induces in itself such necessary caution, and the regular system of committees is so detailed, that it becomes extremely easy to act upon it,'[1] and the intervention of the leaders was in consequence little needed. McNally noticed that the plan of committees and 'splits'[2] was carrying the wish for French invasion, the military spirit, and the hatred of England through all the common people.[3]

In the first months of 1797, an insurrection in the North of Ireland was frequently expected, and there was a fierce dissension on the subject among the leaders of the conspiracy; but in the summer, the party which desired to postpone the revolt till the arrival of the French, obtained a decisive ascendency, and orders to avoid all provocation to military action were issued, which probably contributed something to the lull in Ulster.[4] New and brilliant hopes of foreign assistance had by this time arisen, and the negotiation with France, which had been for some months suspended, was again active. In April a Catholic attorney named Edward Lewins, who had been originally intended for the priesthood, and educated in a French seminary, and who was therefore a complete master of the French language, was sent, by the executive of the United Irishmen, to Hamburg, to renew with Reinhard the negotiation which in the previous year Lord Edward Fitzgerald and Arthur O'Connor had begun. For greater security he was entrusted with no letter accrediting him to the French Minister, but he brought a letter and a gown from Lady Edward Fitzgerald to a female relation who was

---

[1] Camden to Portland, June 17, 1797.

[2] That is, as I have already explained, dividing every committee into two when it attained the number of thirty-six members.

[3] J. W., Oct. 2, 1797.

[4] See a letter from Reinhard, *Castlereagh Correspondence*, i. 278; also J. W., Jan. 24, June 10, 1797.

living at Hamburg, and having thus established his connection with the family, he authenticated his mission by relating the substance of letters and private conversations that had passed between Reinhard and Lord Edward. He represented Ireland as fully prepared for insurrection, and some parts even of England as pervaded by secret societies, and he was instructed to ask from France armed assistance, and a promise that she would make no peace with England till the 'British troops had been withdrawn from Ireland, and the people left at full liberty to declare whether they wished to continue the connection with England or not;' he was also directed to endeavour to obtain a loan of 500,000*l.* and a supply of arms from Spain, and an alliance with the newly formed Batavian Republic.[1]

Lewins appears from his own letters, and from the testimony of Tone, to have been a man of real capacity, disinterestedness, and sincerity, and to have conducted his mission with skill and with some measure of success. He remained nearly two months at Hamburg, and succeeded, through the medium of a Spanish naval officer, who had been sent on a diplomatic mission to that town, in opening a negotiation with Spain,[2] while communicating frequently with Reinhard, who forwarded copies of his papers to Hoche. When he left Ireland, he hoped to attain his objects by a brief, and not very dangerous, secret negotiation with the French Minister in a neutral town,[3] but he soon found that a longer and more perilous mission was before him. Hoche, who was burning to renew the abortive enterprise of the preceding December, summoned him to the Rhine, and he went there in company with Tone.[4] He learnt that Hoche had already sent one of his adjutant-generals to Paris, to press the Execu-

---

[1] Reinhard to De la Croix, 25, 30 floréal, an 5 (May 14, 19, 1797). (French Foreign Office.) Wolfe Tone's *Memoirs*, ii. 407–409.

[2] Wolfe Tone, ii. 408.

[3] The report of the Committee of Secrecy of the House of Lords in 1879 gives in general a very true account of Lewins' mission, but it is mistaken in supposing that he was originally intended to be a resident Irish Minister at Paris. Lewins himself (under his assumed name of Thompson) wrote a full account of his mission, 13 fructidor, an 6 (Aug. 30, 1797), which is at the French Foreign Office, and which I have followed.

[4] There is here a curious though not important discrepancy of evidence. Wolfe Tone, in his journal, says that they met Hoche on June 21 at Coblentz. He makes no mention of having been at Frankfort, and it is, I think, impossible from his diary that he can have been there. Lewins, in his letter to the French Minister (13 fructidor, an 6), says that he went to Frankfort to meet Hoche, and the same statement is made in the report of the Committee of Secrecy.

tive Directory and Minister of Marine; that he had forwarded to them all the necessary papers, including those which had been drawn up by Lewins; and that he had received from them a very encouraging reply, and a distinct assurance that France 'would make no peace with England, wherein the interests of Ireland should not be fully discussed, agreeably to the wishes of the people of that country.' He learnt also the important fact, that preparations were now making in Holland for a great expedition against England, under the command of General Daendels and Admiral de Winter, and that its destination was likely to be Ireland. Hoche himself, accompanied by the two Irishmen, went in June to the Hague to assist in organising it.

It was intended, at first, to be a joint French and Dutch expedition, but the Dutch Government placed obstacles in the way of French co-operation, and it appears to have been extremely anxious that the new Batavian Republic should by its unassisted efforts strike a blow which would establish its reputation throughout Europe. Hoche with great magnanimity withdrew his claim to participate in the expedition, and it was finally determined that it should be purely Dutch, but that it should be speedily followed and supported by a second expedition, which was preparing at Brest. At the end of June a powerful Dutch fleet of twenty-five ships of the line and frigates, with transports carrying nearly 14,000 soldiers, was collected at the Texel. It was arranged that Tone should accompany it. Hoche promised to send him his instructions for carrying on the war in La Vendée, which appeared to the French general the exact model to be followed in Ireland, and he expressed his belief that a French army would reach the Irish coast in about a fortnight after the arrival of the Dutch. In the first week of July, Tone and Lewins left the Hague, the first proceeding to the Texel and the latter to Paris.[1]

The French Government in the mean time sent a Swede of the name of Jagerhorn to England, with instructions to proceed to Ireland to communicate the intentions of the French Government; to obtain an assurance that Lewins possessed the full

[1] The most detailed account of all this is in Wolfe Tone's *Memoirs*, ii. 409–416.

powers from the United Irishmen which he claimed, and also to form a more sober and unprejudiced estimate of the situation in Ireland, than they were likely to obtain from Irish envoys. Jagerhorn failed in procuring a passport to Ireland, but he succeeded in sending a companion there, and he had himself an interview with Lord Edward Fitzgerald in London. His report to the French Government was very satisfactory as to the disposition of the Irish people in favour of rebellion, but not equally so as to the means at their disposal. About 100,000 persons, he believed, had been enrolled in the conspiracy, and almost the whole nation sympathised with it; but he doubted whether there were more than from 12,000 to 15,000 men who had any arms, and he believed that without artillery and competent officers, and in the presence of a garrison of some 40,000 men, no successful insurrection was possible except by the assistance of the French.[1]

The Irish had meanwhile resolved to send a second messenger to stimulate the efforts of the French. They selected for that purpose McNevin, a Catholic physician, and one of the ablest members of the United Irish Executive. He left Ireland for Hamburg on June 27, and on his arrival drew up for the Directory a very elaborate memoir on the state of Ireland, and on the means of invading it. He recommended Oyster Haven as the best point for a landing in the South, and Lough Swilly in the North, and gave many military and topographical details of much value; but he urged especially, that it was only in the North and North-west of the island that the French could expect really efficacious co-operation from the United Irishmen. In Ulster, he said, not less than 150,000 men were enrolled, and a great part of them were so organised that they could become serious soldiers. Outside Ulster the organisation had spread, and was spreading rapidly; but arms were still greatly wanting. Bandon, however, was now another Belfast; Cork, Tipperary, Limerick, Galway, Roscommon, Meath and Westmeath, Kildare, the King's County, and the city of Dublin were all largely organised. 'Even in those places where the United Irish system is not entirely adopted, the co-operation of the poor and middle classes may be counted on. Their hatred of the English des-

[1] *Castlereagh Correspondence*, i. 277, 286-288.

potism, and the vexations they endure from their lords, cause the most ignorant among them to act in the same sense as the most enlightened republicans. The Catholic priests are no longer alarmed at the calumnies diffused about the irreligion of the French; they have adopted the principles of the people on whom they depend; they are in general good republicans; they have done good service by propagating with a discreet zeal the system of union, and they have persuaded the people to take the oath [of allegiance] imposed on them by force, without in any respect renouncing their principles and their projects.'

The memoir then proceeds to state that very lately the Prince of Wales, who was closely connected with three of the chiefs of the Opposition, sent over a confidential agent in hopes of creating a movement for making him Lord Lieutenant, on the understanding that he would support the emancipation of the Catholics, parliamentary reform, the abolition of the coercive legislation of the last three years, and a complete change of men and things; but the leaders of the Opposition refused to take part in this scheme. McNevin attributes their refusal to their belief that a French invasion was probable, though they had no direct information on the subject. Both the Prince of Wales, he said, and Lord Moira, were moving heaven and earth to change the existing system in Ireland, and to content the people in order to withdraw them from French influence. They had, however, met with no response. The people were resolved to aim at independence and a republican Government, and, in the event of an invasion, the bulk of the militia would undoubtedly join the French. The immediate measure which would act most powerfully on the situation, would be a declaration on the part of France, that she would make no peace with the English Government which did not contain a provision for the independence of Ireland.[1]

---

[1] F.F.O. The greater part of this memoir will be found in the *Castlereagh Correspondence*, i. 295-301, but the passage relating to the Prince of Wales is omitted. It appears to be perfectly true that the Prince of Wales in the beginning of 1797 had wished to be Lord Lieutenant of Ireland, with the object of pacifying Ireland by concessions, and had made a proposition to that effect to the Government. See Lord Colchester's *Diary and Correspondence*, i. 94; Plowden, ii. 589, 590; Buckingham's *Court and Cabinets of Geo. III.* ii. 366.

This last sentence probably refers to the negotiations for peace which had just begun at Lille; and in order to understand the situation, it will be necessary for us again to cast a rapid glance over continental affairs. We have seen that in August 1796, Spain had been forced into an alliance with France, and two months later into a war with England, and French statesmen then imagined that, having command of the Dutch and Spanish navies as well as of their own, they would at last be able to contend on equal if not superior terms with England upon the sea. Wolfe Tone hoped that the Spanish fleet would arrive in time to give an overwhelming strength to the expedition to Bantry Bay; but it was miserably equipped and manned,[1] and it lingered long in the Mediterranean. Its appearance there, in alliance with the French, obliged Admiral Jervis to quit that sea, and led to the recovery of Corsica by the French, and to the establishment of peace between France and Naples. At last, on February 14, 1797, Jervis attacked and totally defeated the Spaniards off Cape St. Vincent. The English were far inferior to the enemy in the number of their ships and guns, but the Spanish crews consisted chiefly of hastily draughted landsmen, who were almost helpless in a naval battle; the victory was won with less loss and less resistance than, perhaps, any other of equal importance during the war, and from this time the Spanish navy ceased to be a serious danger. Cadiz was afterwards bombarded. A few prizes were captured, and the war was carried on with various results against the colonies of Spain. Trinidad, one of the richest of her West Indian isles, was captured in February, but an attack upon Porto Rico in April, and an attack upon Teneriffe in July, were both repelled. The last expedition is memorable as the one great failure of Nelson, and it was on this occasion that he lost his right arm.

The career of victory which Buonaparte had pursued in Italy in 1796 was still unbroken. In February 1797, Mantua, the strongest Austrian fortress, surrendered, and the Pope was compelled to sign a peace, ceding not only Avignon and the Venaisin, but also Bologna, Ferrara, and the Romagna, placing Ancona in French hands till the close of the war, and paying a

---

[1] See James's *Naval History*, ii. 47.

large sum to the conqueror. Buonaparte then turned his undivided forces against the Archduke Charles; he drove him within a few days' march of Vienna, and he extorted in April the preliminaries of a peace at Loeben. The definitive peace of Campo Formio was not signed until October, and it contained some important articles which were not in the preliminaries, but the preliminaries of Loeben put an end to the war and established the complete continental ascendency of France. Austria now formally acquiesced in the incorporation into the French Republic, of Belgium and Savoy. She renounced all her Italian possessions beyond the Oglio, and acknowledged the new Cis-Alpine Republic, but she stipulated that she should be indemnified by the plunder of the neutral Republic of Venice. At the definitive treaty of peace this plunder was consummated by a partition as complete and as iniquitous as that of Poland. The Italian territory of Venice passed to Austria; the Greek islands and the Albanian possessions that had belonged to her passed to France, and thus, after an existence of more than 1,400 years, one of the oldest and most glorious of European States vanished from the world.

The preliminaries of Loeben were signed in opposition to the wishes of the Archduke Charles. They left England without any continental ally except Portugal, but they at the same time took away one of her chief reasons for continuing the war. The negotiations of 1796 had broken off principally on the demand of the English for the restoration of the Austrian Netherlands to the Emperor; but though the expulsion of the French from that territory was of vital importance to England, it had now become plainly impracticable. Pitt, who still ardently desired peace, and who was especially alarmed at the financial aspects of the war, resolved to make another attempt, and, contrary to the wish both of the King and of Lord Grenville, an overture was made to De la Croix, the French Minister of Foreign Affairs. It was accepted, though in very ungracious terms, and three French ministers plenipotentiary were appointed to meet Lord Malmesbury at Lille. They were Le Tourneur, who had recently left the Directory, the Admiral Pléville le Peley, and Maret, whose skill in negotiation, and whose anxiety to avert the war in 1793, we have already seen. The first conference took place on July 6.

It is unnecessary to relate in minute detail the negotiations that followed. On the English side the extreme desire of Pitt to make peace is beyond reasonable doubt. Canning, who was now his closest confidant, wrote a melancholy private letter to Ellis, who was attached to Lord Malmesbury's embassy, in which he disclosed the situation with perfect frankness. 'Were I writing to you,' he said, 'on December 13 last, instead of the present July 13, could I have thought with patience of renunciation and restitution unaccompanied by cessions to balance and compensate them? But we cannot and must not disguise our situation from ourselves. If peace is to be had, we must have it. I firmly believe that we must, and it is a belief that strengthens every day. When Windham says we must not, I ask him, "Can we have war?" It is out of the question, we have not the means; we have not what is of all means the most essential, the *mind*. If we are not at peace, we shall be at nothing. . . . For my part, I adjourn my objects of honour and happiness for this country, beyond the grave of our military and political consequence which you are now digging at Lille. I believe in our resurrection, and find my only comfort in it. . . . We can break off upon nothing but what will rouse us from sleep and stupidity into a new life and action. . . . We are now soulless and spiritless.'[1]

How strangely imperfect is all political prescience! Who could have imagined from such a picture, that England was still destined to struggle on through no less than eighteen years of desperate warfare, to a final triumph? Or, looking backwards, who could have imagined when Pitt reluctantly engaged in 1793, with the support of almost all Europe, in a conflict with a country which seemed utterly disorganised by revolution, that the great and haughty minister of England would be compelled within four years, and in almost absolute isolation, to sue for a peace not less really disadvantageous and scarcely less humiliating to England, than that of 1783? Pitt was prepared to acknowledge Belgium to be a French province, and Holland a French vassal; to acknowledge all the French conquests in

[1] *Malmesbury Correspondence*, iii. 397, 398.

Germany and Italy; to restore to France, without compensation, all the colonial possessions which England had taken from her during the war. He stipulated only that she should retain the Cape of Good Hope and Trinidad; that she should retain Ceylon and Cochin, in exchange for the restoration of Negapatnam on the coast of Tanjore; that the Prince of Orange should be indemnified for his private property; and that Portugal, the last ally of England, should be included in the peace.

If the French Directory had accepted peace on these terms, they would have closed the wars of the Revolution by placing France in a prouder position than she had ever reached during the monarchy. Having baffled and plundered all their enemies on the Continent, they would have compelled their old rival, who was still invincible on the sea, to acknowledge herself vanquished in the struggle of centuries. From generation to generation, it had been a main object of English foreign policy to maintain the balance of power in Europe, and above all to preserve Belgium and Holland—the two countries that were most essential to English security—free from French aggrandisement. It was left to the son of the great Lord Chatham, to the minister whose genius had raised England, after the humiliating peace of 1783, to an almost unexampled height of prosperity and power, to accept and even to solicit a peace, leaving France supreme in Europe, the absolute mistress of Belgium, the virtual mistress of Holland. But Pitt, having taken his resolution, did not flinch, and he assured Lord Malmesbury that 'he would stifle every feeling of pride to the utmost, to produce the desired result.'[1]

It is not difficult to see the overwhelming force of the reasons that impelled him. The enormous increase of expenditure and debt threatened England with ruin, and would certainly, if not speedily checked, cripple her for generations. The Bank of England had been obliged to stop cash payments. The three per cents in May sank to forty-eight, the lowest point they had ever touched. In Ireland, the continuance of the war would almost certainly lead to prolonged and ruinous anarchy, and probably to the dangers and horrors of a great rebellion. Every ally of England, except Portugal, had dropped away, and some

[1] *Malmesbury Correspondence*, iii. 369.

of them were in arms against her. It was impossible, by the most lavish subsidies, any longer to resist France on the Continent, or to drive her within her ancient limits, and the security of England herself from invasion depended on the constant superiority of her navy to the united navies of France, Spain, and Holland. The war was unpopular; the nation was discouraged, and the mutiny of the Nore had disclosed the new and terrible danger of disaffection in the fleet.

It soon, however, appeared that the chances of obtaining peace were very small. Of the five members of the Directory, three were evidently opposed to it, and two at least of the French Commissioners were fully prepared to carry out their views. The French at once demanded the relinquishment by the King of England of his old title of King of France, the restoration of the ships that had been taken at Toulon, and an equivalent for those which had been destroyed; and they raised a question about a mortgage, which they erroneously imagined to be held by England on the Netherlands for money granted to the Emperor. But discussion had not proceeded far on these points, before a new demand was made, which appeared absolutely to close the door to peace. It was, that England should immediately, and as a preliminary to all negotiation, restore everything she had conquered, not only from France, but also from the Batavian Republic and from Spain.

Lord Malmesbury, unwilling at once to break off the conference, asked for further explanations and instructions, and he was confirmed in this course by a very strange and characteristic incident. On July 14, an English gentleman, who had been long residing at Lille, called on the Secretary of the Legation, and showed him a note from M. Pein, who was an intimate friend of his own, and a near relation of Maret. It contained these somewhat enigmatical words: 'It would perhaps be necessary, in order to press on the negotiation, that Lord Malmesbury should have the means of coming to an understanding, and preparing materials with the person who is in truth the only one in a position to conduct the affair. In that case it would be possible to procure for Lord Malmesbury an intermediary who has the entire confidence of the person in question, and who, like that person, has no other end than the interest of all, and an arrangement equally suitable to both parties.' The gentleman then proceeded to explain, that Pein was in the full confidence of Maret, and that this overture was made with the authorisation of Maret. In consequence of this communication, Ellis had a secret interview with Pein, who fully confirmed what had been said, and added that Maret's opinions on all political subjects were very different from those of the other plenipotentiaries; that he had been appointed by his intimate friend Barthélemy, who, with Carnot, was resolved, if possible, to gratify the ardent desire of the French nation for peace; that the other three Directors were of other sentiments, but that if the negotiation was prolonged and prudently conducted, they must in the end give way.

A change of ministers in France, which happened within the next few days, appeared slightly to improve the prospect. De la Croix, who had shown himself violent and impracticable, and personally hostile to Lord Malmesbury, was replaced, as Minister of Foreign Affairs, by Talleyrand; and Pléville le Peley was made Minister of Marine, thus reducing the French plenipotentiaries at Lille to two, one of whom seemed sincerely anxious for peace. It was reported from Paris, that the Government there was extremely unstable, that a large and increasing party in the legislative councils were hostile to the Directory, and that another revolution was very probable, and Malmesbury justly said that the chances of peace depended much more on what took place at Paris, than on what took place at Lille.

A secret understanding between Lord Malmesbury and Maret was speedily formed. It was chiefly arranged between Ellis and Pein, and the latter brought an assurance that Maret utterly disapproved of the recent demands of the Directory. Signs were devised by which Maret could communicate with Malmesbury at the conference, without being suspected by his own colleague. At the request of Maret, the reply of the English Cabinet to the French demand was privately submitted to him, before it was presented, and at his suggestion one of its arguments was strengthened. A confidential letter, in which Barthélemy expressed to Maret his deep sense of the absolute necessity of peace; of the absurdity of the recent demands; of the folly and instability that surrounded him, and of the supreme importance of gaining time, was duly read to the English Minister. The delay now came from the French side, and it was explained that it was owing to the fact that the French were putting pressure on their allies, in order to compel them to acquiesce in cessions to the English. This explanation was given, not by Maret, but by Le Tourneur, who, though he was not in the secret of his colleague, appears at this time, and during the remainder of the negotiation, to have been sincerely desirous of peace. It was added, that on the side of Spain the French found little difficulty, but that the Batavian Republic was obstinately opposed to cessions. In England, only Pitt, Grenville, and Canning were aware of the strange by-play that was going on, and two distinct series of despatches were written by Lord Malmesbury, one of which was intended to be laid before the Cabinet, while the other was intended only for the three Ministers.

The English negotiators doubted the sincerity of the overtures that were made to them, and the reality of the causes of delay that were assigned, but it was plain that the official propositions of the Directory must destroy all hopes of peace. It was probable, or at least possible, that Maret and Talleyrand, and the two members of the Directory, or at least some of them, were sincere in wishing for peace, and if the pressure of French public opinion or of the legislative councils, or the influence of Talleyrand, or any of the numerous political intrigues that were agitating Paris, displaced the majority in the Directory, and gave a casting vote to the peace party, the whole aspect of affairs might change. Pitt desired above all things peace, if it could be accompanied by the retention of such a portion of the many conquests of England as would in some degree save the dignity of a nation which had been everywhere triumphant upon the sea, and in some degree compensate by its commercial advantages for the ruinous sacrifices that had been made. If, however, such a peace could not be obtained, he desired that the French should make requisitions so manifestly unreasonable that the necessity for carrying on the war should be apparent to every Englishman.[1] On the whole, the situation seemed hopeful, though not sufficiently so to inspire confidence. 'Shall we be sent back or not,

---

[1] *Malmesbury Correspondence*, iii. 430.

this time?' wrote Ellis. 'Seriously, the Directory is so strange a body, and this so strange a nation, that I have my doubts, and yet this letter surely contains some reasonable grounds for hope.' 'I am not without my apprehensions,' wrote Malmesbury, 'that you infer too much from what we transmit to you; that you get too sanguine, or at least sanguine too soon. . . . Pray check this too eager hope. It is not to be justified. We may and probably shall have peace, but not soon, not on our own terms (I mean original terms), and it will be a work of labour and altercation to obtain some not very different from them.'[1]

There are few more curious pages in diplomatic history than the account in Lord Malmesbury's papers of these proceedings. Ellis and Pein continued to have frequent conferences, in which the affairs of the two nations seem to have been discussed with complete apparent frankness, and Malmesbury and his French colleagues were soon on the most cordial terms, and had more than one strangely undiplomatic conversation in their boxes in the theatre. But suddenly, like a thunderclap, the news broke upon the English plenipotentiary, that on August 10 the Portuguese Minister at Paris had signed a separate peace for Portugal, and that one of its articles, in direct defiance of the English treaty of 1703, forbade the English fleet to receive supplies in Portugal, and excluded during the war all but a limited number of English vessels from the Portuguese ports. The Court of Lisbon, it is true, ultimately refused to ratify this treaty, but from the time it was signed, the hopes of peace began to dwindle. Combined with the negotiations which were rapidly pressing on for a definitive peace with the Emperor, and with the preparations that were known to be making at the Texel, the Portuguese treaty fully confirmed Lord Grenville in his distrust of French diplomacy. 'The clandestine and precipitate manner,' he wrote, ' in which the business has been conducted, affords indisputable proofs of the total absence of a sincere and candid disposition for peace on the part of his Majesty's enemies;' and he drew up an official note about the proceedings of the Directory, in a strain which was so haughty, and so manifestly calculated to break off the negotiation, that Malmesbury took the very grave step of disobeying his instructions,

[1] *Malmesbury Correspondence*, iii. 434, 464.

and not presenting it.¹ Malmesbury was supported by Pitt, who still wished to negotiate, and still hoped for peace, and who, though startled and irritated by the Portuguese treaty, refused to look upon it as an insuperable obstacle. 'I think it,' he wrote, 'a natural, though an unworthy game, in those we are treating with; but I do not much expect that, if other points could be settled, this would stand in the way of peace.'²

At the beginning of the negotiation, Malmesbury had received a message which purported to come from Barras, one of the majority in the Directory, offering peace in return for a bribe of 500,000*l.*; but Malmesbury, believing the offer to be either unauthorised by Barras, or a trap laid by the Directory, took no notice of it. In the middle of August, a new message was brought to him by an American, who stated that the Portuguese peace had been purchased by a gift of ten or twelve millions of livres to the Directors, and that fifteen millions of livres, distributed between Rewbell and Barras, would secure a similar peace for England. He appears to have had no credentials, and nothing resulted from the overture. Extreme corruption, however, in French Government circles was one of the elements to be calculated on, and the English Ministers had some evidence that Barthélemy, and convincing evidence that Talleyrand, was at this time stockjobbing largely in the English funds.³

The hopes of peace were soon shattered by the *coup d'état* of the 18th fructidor,⁴ when the Triumvirate, who formed the majority of the Directory, brought a great body of troops into Paris, surrounded and dispersed the two legislative councils, and, on the pretext of a royalist plot, arrested a multitude of members who were opposed to them, and ordered the immediate imprisonment of their two colleagues. Carnot succeeded in escaping, and, at last, made his way to Geneva, but Barthélemy was arrested, and, next day, the triumvirs issued a law of proscription, which was sanctioned by the partisan remnant of the

---

¹ *Malmesbury Correspondence*, iii. 489, 490, 497.
² Ibid. p. 491. That Pitt approved of Malmesbury's disobedience, I infer from the full approval of that disobedience expressed by Canning, who was at this time Pitt's mouthpiece. (Ibid. p. 520.)
³ Ibid. pp. 439, 453, 520.
⁴ Sept. 4.

legislative councils, and which condemned Barthélemy and Carnot, forty-two members of one legislative council, and eleven members of the other, to a perpetual banishment to Cayenne, or to the pestilential swamps of Guiana. The proprietors and editors of forty-two journals, and about 180 priests, were, soon after, condemned to the same fate. A few, like Carnot, succeeded in concealing themselves, but in general the savage sentence was savagely executed, and a majority of the prisoners perished by hardship or pestilence. Barthélemy escaped from Guiana, in an American vessel, and took refuge in England.

It was the strong opinion of Malmesbury and Canning, on the one side, and of Maret and Talleyrand, on the other, that if this revolution had not taken place, the majority in the Directory would have been compelled by the legislative councils, and by the pressure of French public opinion, to consent to a peace on the lines which England had proposed. The 18th fructidor, however, at once destroyed the influence of the Moderate party. The French legation at Lille was recalled, and replaced by two violent Jacobins, with peremptory instructions. They arrived at Lille on September 13, and almost immediately after, they demanded whether Malmesbury had power to consent to 'a general restitution of every possession remaining in his Majesty's hands, not only belonging to them, but to their allies,' as a preliminary to any further negotiation; and they added, that when this had been accomplished, there were still many articles to be proposed. The reply being naturally in the negative, Lord Malmesbury was, on September 16, ordered, within twenty-four hours, to quit France.[1]

It is curious to observe, how long it was before the last faint gleam of hope disappeared, and all prospect of negotiation was abandoned. Immediately on hearing of the new revolution, Pitt wrote to Malmesbury, expressing his unaltered determination to continue the negotiation, and his belief that it was still possible to attain a peace;[2] and even after Lord Malmesbury had been ignominiously sent back to London, he exchanged, by the wish of the Government, two or three notes with the French

[1] *Malmesbury Correspondence*, iii. 561-569, 576.
[2] Ibid. p. 554.

plenipotentiaries, who were still at Lille, in hopes of finding some possible basis for resuming the negotiations. Rewbell and Barras, or, perhaps, Barras alone, had made another overture, promising peace, in return for a large bribe. In a letter to the King, dated September 22, Pitt stated that 'he had received communications from a person (who produces as strong proofs as can, in the nature of the case, be given, of the authenticity of his mission), stating that, notwithstanding what had passed at Lille, the Directory will still agree to an immediate peace, giving to this country, both the Cape and Ceylon, on condition of their receiving a large sum of money for their own use. The sum named is 1,200,000*l.* for Ceylon, or 2,000,000*l.* for both,' and Pitt strongly recommended that the proposal should be encouraged, and was even sanguine about its success.[1] Whether it was ever seriously intended, whether Barras found himself unable to carry his colleagues with him, or whether, as Lord Malmesbury believed, the whole proposal was merely a stockjobbing device, must always be doubtful. A French note of September 25, distinctly stated, that a resumption of the negotiations would only be permitted, if the English absolutely submitted to the French demand for the restitution of all the English conquests,[2] and from this time, all hope of peace disappeared.

It was an assertion of Lord Clare, that the 'Irish Directory had three accredited ministers, resident at Lille, during the late negotiations for peace, to counteract the King's minister, Lord Malmesbury.'[3] This statement is unsupported by any evidence, and it is contradicted by Wolfe Tone, but Tone adds that Lewins was actively employed in Luxemburg and elsewhere, with that

---

[1] There appear to have been two distinct negotiations, one coming from Talleyrand, and the other from one or more of the Directors. Compare Stanhope's *Life of Pitt*, iii., Appendix, vii–ix; *Malmesbury Correspondence*, iii. 580–584.

[2] *Malmesbury Correspondence*, iii. 587, 588. There was a later note of Oct. 1, intended to throw the blame of the rupture on the English, but it in no degree modified the French terms. (Pp. 588, 589.)

[3] *Debate in the House of Peers,* Feb. 19, 1798, p. 120. 'Not a word immediately from Napper Tandy as yet, but a person whom J. Tandy will not name, but whom he describes as in the confidence of Government, has assured him, there is an account at the Castle that he is now at Lisle with Tone and others, and that they have been protracting peace between Great Britain and France.' (J. W., Aug. 11, 1797.) Higgins also stated that McNevin, Tone, and Tandy were at Lille during the negotiation. (F. H., Oct. 24, 1797.)

object,[1] and Lewins, himself, has mentioned that, about this time, he received, at Paris, formal assurances from the French Government, that they would make no peace, without stipulating for Irish independence.[2] The conferences at Lille sufficiently show the worthlessness of such assurances. Ireland, as far as is known, was never, from first to last, even mentioned in them, and the lesson derived from this silence is made much stronger, by a document which has not yet passed into history. It will be remembered, that the French demand for the restitution of all English conquests, made during the war, was put forward as a mere preliminary to negotiation, and Maret candidly told Malmesbury, that the original instructions, which were drawn up for the legation, by De la Croix, were so extravagant, that they did not venture to bring them forward.[3] They may be found in the French Foreign Office,[4] and they amply justify the description. In addition to the demands which have been mentioned, the French plenipotentiaries were to insist on the surrender of Jersey and Guernsey; on the restoration of Canada, and the Newfoundland fishery; on the cession of Gibraltar to Spain, and they were even to endeavour to obtain the restoration of those great Indian dominions which had been wrested from France in 1754. But this document, which enumerated, in the most extravagant form, all that France hoped to extort from a humiliated England, keeps an absolute silence about Ireland and Irish independence. What clearer proof could there be that Ireland was, in truth, but a pawn in the game; that in endeavouring to convulse her with civil war, the French Government looked to no other object, than the temporary embarrassment of the enemy; that even if a French invasion had proved successful, Ireland would probably, as Grattan warned his countrymen, have been abandoned at the peace, in compensation for some real object of French ambition?

It would not have been altogether the first experience of the kind. In 1728, Marshal Broglie had obtained permission to recruit for the French service in Ireland, and great numbers of Irishmen had passed under the French flag. A melancholy and

---

[1] *Memoirs*, ii. 469.
[2] Memoir of Thompson [Lewins] to the French Government, 26 primaire, an 8. (F.F.O.)
[3] *Malmesbury Correspondence*, iii. 521, 540, 557.
[4] *Tome Supplémentaire*, xv.

striking memoir, which was presented to D'Argenson in 1757, complains that, 'at the peace of Aix-la-Chapelle, the Irish were abandoned to their evil fortune. No stipulation was made for the revocation of an Act passed by the Irish Parliament during the war, which incapacitated all Irishmen who were then in the French service, or who subsequently entered it, from succeeding to property. The French Government did not even stipulate for an amnesty for those who had already incurred the penalty pronounced by the Act, and yet,' continues the memoir, 'he who will read the second article of the treaty of Utrecht, will find that Holland formally stipulated an amnesty for all the officers, soldiers, and subjects of France, who had served the Republic during the whole course of the war, with permission for them to re-enter into the enjoyment of their goods, privileges, rights, &c.—and it is well known that there were many of those subjects—even entire corps. What Holland then exacted from a king of France, a king of France might assuredly have exacted from a king of England.' He did not do so, and to this conspicuous abandonment and neglect the memorialists ascribed the Act of Parliament of 1757, which condemned to death all English, Irish, and Scotch subjects, who were found in the French service after September 29, 1757, or who should hereafter enter it.[1]

It was in the midst of the conferences of Lille, that the greatest Irishman of the eighteenth century—one of the greatest and best men who have ever appeared in English politics—vanished from the scene. The last days of Edmund Burke, though soothed by that deep, passionate, and devoted friendship, which he had pre-eminently the gift of inspiring, were very sad. The death of his only son had broken his heart; and in the triumph of the Revolution, he saw the eclipse of all that he valued the most in public life. 'If I shall live much longer,' he wrote shortly before his death, 'I shall see an end of all that is worth living for in this world.' Among the subjects that occupied his thoughts during the last months of his life, Irish affairs took a prominent place, and he watched them with the gloomiest forebodings. 'The Government,' he wrote, 'is losing the hearts of the people, if it has not quite lost them. . . . The Opposition in that country, as well as in this, is running the

[1] French Foreign Office.

whole course of Jacobinism, and losing credit amongst the sober people, as the other loses credit with the people at large.'[1] The United Ireland movement he regarded as one of the greatest calamities that could have befallen the country, and he predicted utter ruin if it succeeded. 'Great Britain,' he wrote, 'would be ruined by the separation of Ireland; but as there are degrees even in ruin, it would fall the most heavily on Ireland. By such a separation, Ireland would be the most completely undone country in the world; the most wretched, the most distracted, and in the end, the most desolate part of the habitable globe. Little do many people in Ireland consider how much of its prosperity has been owing to, and still depends upon, its intimate connection with this kingdom.'[2] Burke died on July 9, and at his own urgent request he was buried, without pageantry or ostentation, in the quiet churchyard of Beaconsfield, and in the same grave as his son and brother. 'There is but one event,' wrote Canning to Malmesbury, 'but that is an event for the world. Burke is dead. . . . He had among all his great qualities, that for which the world did not give him sufficient credit, of creating in those about him, very strong attachments and affection, as well as the unbounded admiration, which I every day am more and more convinced was his due. . . . He is the man that will mark this age, marked as it is itself by events, to all time.'[3]

The intrigues of the French Revolutionists with the United Irishmen, which had been in some degree suspended by the probability of peace, received a new stimulus from the rupture of the negotiations, but only a small part of them escaped the notice of the English Ministers. Their channels of information were numerous and very good. In the middle of May, they received from McNally an account of the mission of Lewins,[4] and

---

[1] Burke's *Correspondence*, iv. 433.
[2] Prior's *Life of Burke*, ii. 393.
[3] *Malmesbury Correspondence*, iii. 398, 399.
[4] J. W., May 16, 1797. On June 20 the Prince de Bouillon, who appears to have frequently given valuable information, wrote to Dundas, on the authority of one of the members of the Council or Committee at Paris, that a 'project against Ireland, digested by Buonaparte, and intended to be committed to his direction and execution in the event of a separate peace being signed with the Emperor, had been under consideration and accepted.' This letter was at once forwarded to Camden, and it was corroborated in July by a letter from Wickham, who stated that an expedition to Ireland had been finally determined on; that the command had

they learnt from the same informant in July, that McNevin had disappeared, and was believed by James Tandy to have gone to France. Later letters informed them, that a man named Chambers had brought from France assurances, that the French Government would make no peace which did not include the independence of Ireland; that an invasion was promised when the first fair winds blew after the equinoctial gales; that Tone and Napper Tandy were to take part in it, and that the French Government had agreed to give Ireland complete independence. 'All mouths,' said McNally, 'were spreading this news through every village in the kingdom,' and preparations were busily making to receive the invaders.[1] Higgins furnished an independent corroboration of these statements, and he mentions a meeting in Dame Street, in which, in the presence of Emmet, Arthur O'Connor, and other leaders, letters were read from McNevin, and from Browne of Antrim, giving the most absolute and unequivocal assurance of the French Directory having agreed to an invasion of Ireland, 'for the purpose of assisting the natives to rise in arms, and throw off the English yoke.'[2]

The Government were perfectly aware that Hamburg was the great centre of Irish diplomacy; they discovered the part which Lady Edward Fitzgerald took in the correspondence, and the lady to whom her letters were addressed; and they even derived some of their best information about the conspiracy in Dublin, from Hamburg letters. Lord Grenville had a correspondent in that town, from whom he obtained much information in the August of 1797, and a still more important channel of information was soon afterwards opened by Lord Downshire. The new informer was Samuel Turner, who was the son of a person of some property near Newry, and who had taken a conspicuous part in a committee of Ulster United Irishmen, formed in the spring of 1797 for the purpose of baffling Government prosecutions. He fled from Ireland, went to Hamburg in

---

been offered to Buonaparte, who (on the advice of Barras) declined it; that it was then assigned to Hoche, and that the chiefs of the conspiracy in Ireland had received directions to remain quiet till the beginning of August.' (Wickham's *Correspondence*, ii. 41, 42.) Other letters of the Prince de Bouillon, about the intended invasion of Ireland, had been written Oct. 4, 1796, Feb. 14, 1797.

[1] J. W., July 28, Sept. 11, 25, Dec. 8, 1797.

[2] F. H., Oct. 17, 20, 1797.

June, lived there under the name of Furnes, and seems to have obtained the confidence of Reinhard, who gave him a passport, with which he went to Paris at the end of July. It appears to have been in the winter of 1797, that he first undertook, through the medium of Lord Downshire, to give information to the English Government, and he gave them full and valuable details, not only about the proceedings of the conspirators on the Continent, but also about the names, characters, and objects of the leading United Irishmen in Ireland. From no other source, indeed, does the Government appear, at this time, to have received accounts which were at once so ample and so accurate, for Turner was quite free from the anxiety to screen individuals, which was manifest in the letters of McNally.[1]

After the illustrations that have been given, of the characters of the men who held the first positions in Paris, it will not appear surprising that there also the English Government were able to obtain abundant information. The names of the informers were carefully concealed by the few persons who were in the secret, even in their confidential correspondence, but they will probably, some day, be found among their unpublished papers, and the mystery might perhaps be even now unravelled from accessible documents, if something of the patience and ingenuity that have been applied to the authorship of Junius, were devoted to the task. Most of this information was probably ultimately due to William Wickham, who had been sent to Switzerland on a special mission in October 1794, and had been appointed, about nine months later, minister in that country. It was his special task to assist, with money and with advice, the French emigrants, and the conspirators and insurgents against the Revolutionary Government in the interior of France, and he succeeded in opening communications with great numbers of Frenchmen, in confidential and important positions.[2] Among

---

[1] Turner's letters to Lord Downshire and to the Ministers were signed 'Richardson,' but his true name was sent by Camden to Portland, Dec. 9, 1797. His full and interesting revelations are at the Record Office. See especially Dec. 9, 19, 1797, and also a letter from 'Richardson' to Lord Downshire, dated Nov. 19, 1797, sent by Camden to Portland, Jan. 5, 1798. See, too, the *Castlereagh Correspondence*, i. 277–288.

[2] See that curious and very instructive book, the *Correspondence of William Wickham*; and also *Malmesbury Correspondence*, iii. 454, 531. A quantity of letters, addressed in cipher and under false names, fell into the hands of Moreau, who, however, for a long time thought fit to conceal the

them, was Pichegru,[1] one of the ablest of the French generals, who, as early as 1795, appears to have meditated a Royalist restoration, and to have looked forward to playing the part which Monk played in England; which Benedict Arnold wished to play in America, and Dumouriez in France. Pichegru's negotiations with the Royalists were in part discovered, and he was removed from his military command, but he was speedily elected a member of the Council of the Five Hundred, which was strongly opposed to Jacobin violence, and he was president of that body when the Revolution of the 18th fructidor ruined his prospects, and condemned him to transportation to Guiana. Barthélemy had been French minister in Switzerland, when Wickham was in that country. Wickham describes him as very hostile,[2] but the English minister succeeded in opening some channel of information which enabled him to see the most confidential correspondence and instructions of his rival.[3] Whether this source of information was still available when Barthélemy became one of the Directors, I am not able to say; but there is at least good reason for believing, that men in very confidential positions, both in the French Foreign Office and about the Directors, were in English pay. The *arrêté* of the French Directory, ordering the expulsion of Malmesbury from French soil, was communicated at once by a secret channel to London, and was known to Pitt even before it was known to Malmesbury,[4] and two important letters from Reinhard to De la Croix, relating to the mission of Lewins, and also a French translation of McNevin's memorial to the Directory, speedily found their way into the English archives.[5]

---

fact, probably because he had himself been mixed up with Royalist conspiracies. Wickham's *Correspondence*, i. 416; ii. 28. Lacretelle, *Précis Historique de la Révolution. Directoire*, ii. 49–57, 109.

[1] Wickham's *Correspondence*, i. 184, 274, 275, 282, 283, 326, 327, 356, 357, 369, 374–378, 472, 492–495; ii. 40.

[2] Ibid. i. 65–67.

[3] Ibid. i. 31, 155, 339, 356, 462, 463.

[4] *Malmesbury Correspondence*, iii. 580, 581. It is said to have been communicated to Pitt by a banker named Boyd. In the Irish State Paper Office there is a letter (Sept. 9, 1796), signed N. Madgett, containing some (not very important) information from Paris. The writer seems to have been a relation of the Madgett often mentioned by Tone, who was very confidentially employed in the French Foreign Office.

[5] See *Castlereagh Correspondence*, i. 272–310. Compare *Malmesbury Correspondence*, iii. 520, 580. In a letter written as early as Aug. 30, 1797, Camden comments upon McNevin's plan for a descent on Ireland, which, he says, 'is conceived very ably, and shows a thorough knowledge of the dispositions of the country.' (Camden to Portland, Aug. 30, 1797.)

The hopes of the conspirators were now principally directed to the spread of disaffection in the English navy, and to the Dutch expedition for the invasion of Ireland which was preparing at the Texel. The first evil had attained its climax before the conferences of Lille, and had probably been one of the reasons which made the English Ministers so anxious to negotiate. Some serious signs of mutiny, which had appeared in the fleet before Cadiz, had been repressed with great courage and energy, and five of the mutineers had been hanged;[1] but in the April of 1797, a mutiny broke out in the Channel fleet at Spithead, which in its magnitude and success had no precedent in English history. The grievances alleged by the seamen were serious, and for the most part only too well founded. Their pay had been unchanged since the reign of Charles II., though the price of provisions had greatly, and, since the outbreak of the war, enormously risen, and though the allowances both of the army and the militia had been recently increased. The Greenwich pensions for sailors were still but 7*l*. a year, while the Chelsea pensions for soldiers were 13*l*. Unfair and unequal distribution of prize money; defects, both in quality and quantity, in the allowance of food; the excessive severity of some of the rules of the service, and the harsh and tyrannical conduct of many officers, were also alleged. Reports of spreading discontent came to the Admiralty, and orders were given to send the fleet to sea, but an immediate revolt was the result. It was so perfectly concerted, that the whole Channel fleet, on which the security of the English coast mainly depended, passed without a blow into the hands of the mutineers, and it remained in them from the fifteenth to the twenty-third of April. The Admiralty were obliged to negotiate, and the offer of a general pardon, and the concession of all the chief demands, induced the sailors to return to their allegiance. Doubts, however, soon spread, and false reports were circulated, and on May 7, when a rumour had arrived, that a French fleet had left Brest harbour, and when orders were given to the British fleet to set sail, the mutiny broke out again. After a slight resistance, it was perfectly successful; the unpopular officers were sent on shore, and for several days the situation seemed desperate. On the 14th, however, Admiral

[1] James's *Naval History*, ii. 60, 61.

Howe, who was very popular with the sailors, went down to the fleet, and succeeded in bringing it back, but only on condition that a large number of the officers were superseded. The fleet then sailed for the coast of Brittany.

A precedent so fatal to all discipline threatened an utter disorganisation of the British navy, at a time when the very salvation of the Empire depended upon its efficiency. The contagion of successful insubordination naturally spread. On May 10, while Howe was quelling the mutiny at St. Helen's, another broke out in the ships at Sheerness, and it was soon evident that, unlike the former mutiny, a strong political element mingled with it. Revolutionary handbills had been industriously circulated, and active agitators appeared among the sailors. The mutineers chose a bold, ambitious, and educated sailor named Parker for their admiral. Under his orders the revolted fleet sailed to the Nore, and partly by persuasion, and partly by force, all the ships of war in the Nore and in the Medway were brought into the conspiracy. The news spread to the northern fleet, which was blockading the Dutch near Texel; the red flag of revolt was speedily hoisted, and the greater part of the fleet abandoned Admiral Duncan in the face of the enemy, and sailed for the Nore. The Board of Admiralty went to Spithead, and tried to negotiate with the mutineers, but without success. The revolted squadron was raised by the ships from the North to twenty-four sail. It proceeded to blockade the mouth of the Thames and seize merchant vessels, and the inhabitants of the towns along the coast began moving their families and their goods, in hourly expectation of a bombardment, not by a foreign, but by an English fleet.

Never, perhaps, in the long history of England, had there been a period when the peril was so great. Happily, both the French and the Dutch were unprepared, ill informed, and perfectly passive, for if an invasion of the North of Ireland had been undertaken in these critical weeks, it could not possibly have been prevented. The Government and country met the danger with courage and determination. A flotilla of gunboats was fitted out. Volunteers were raised. The buoys and beacons at the mouth of the Thames were removed. Soldiers were massed along the threatened parts of the coast; batteries were constructed, and furnaces for heating shot red hot prepared. In response to a King's message, the Parliament hastily passed a stringent law for repressing treason in the army and navy, and a royal proclamation forbade, under pain of death, all intercourse, either personal or by letter, with the ships that were in rebellion.

These methods gradually succeeded. The difficulties of obtaining water and provisions; the divisions and insubordination that soon broke out in the revolted fleet; the feeling of loyalty and patriotism, which was by no means extinct among the sailors, and the clear signs that the nation repudiated and reprobated their conduct, had soon their effect. Parker speedily lost his authority, and every ship was left to its own guidance. In each of them there was a loyal element, and in most of them there was soon one of those strong reactions of feeling to which impulsive sailors are peculiarly liable. It was a strange and touching fact that, on June 4, the King's birthday, the red flag was hauled down on every ship except that of Parker, and a royal salute was fired, and the royal colours were hoisted. Soon ship after ship began to drop away. Lord Northesk, the captain of one of them, who had been detained as prisoner, was sent on shore to carry a letter to the King. The sailors in the fleet at Plymouth, and the sailors in the fleet at Spithead, exhorted their revolted comrades to make their submission. The ships from the northern fleet went back to Admiral Duncan, and the whole fleet at last returned to its allegiance. On June 14, the mutiny of the Nore was terminated by the arrest of Parker, and a few days later he was tried and hanged. Some of the other ringleaders were either executed or flogged.

It is not surprising that, after such an episode, all the enemies of England should have entertained sanguine hopes that the invincible fleet would soon perish by internal decay. Few persons could have expected that its tone and discipline and efficiency could be speedily restored, and some months elapsed before all dangerous symptoms had passed. In September, the crew of a frigate called the 'Hermione,' which was quartered in the West Indies, being exasperated by the gross tyranny of their captain, rose in mutiny, murdered their officers and carried the ship into a Spanish port, and in the following month serious signs of insubordination appeared in the ships at the Cape of Good Hope.[1] The reputation of British sailors had never sunk so low as in the spring and summer of 1797. But the grievances that were felt, were much more professional than political; the evil was much more riotous insubordination than deliberate disaffection; and good administration, the redress of grievances, and perhaps, still more, active service under commanders in whom the sailors had unbounded confidence, soon effected a cure. It is a memorable fact, that the few years that immediately followed the mutiny of the Nore, form one of the most glorious periods in the whole history of the British navy.

That history is, indeed, a very singular one, when we consider at once the elements of which the British navy was composed, the treatment it underwent, and the services it rendered. Criminals whose offences were not very great, or against whom the legal evidence was not perfectly conclusive, were at this time constantly permitted to escape trial, by enlisting in it, and, as we have already seen, the press-gangs hung specially around the prison doors, to seize upon discharged prisoners when their sentences had expired. The navy, too, was usually the last resort of tainted reputations and broken careers. Scapegraces in respectable families, disqualified attorneys, cashiered excisemen, dismissed clerks, labourers who through idleness or drunkenness had lost their employments, men from every walk of life, who, through want of capacity or want of character had found other careers closed to them, poured steadily into it.[2] With these were mixed multitudes of United Irishmen, and of other Irish peasants, who had been torn from their cabins by the illegal violence of Lord Carhampton, or under the provisions of the Insurrection Act;[3]

[1] James's *Naval History*, ii. 102–104.
[2] See the *Annual Register*, 1797, p. 208; James's *Naval History*, ii. 65.
[3] 'I have already noticed the large proportion of Irish sailors in the British navy in some periods of the war. I may add a passage from the very interesting speech on the Catholic question by Sir J. Hippisley, published in 1810. 'Sir J. H. held in his hand a list of forty-six ships of the line, which at two different periods had belonged to the Plymouth division, and in the majority of which the Catholics greatly exceeded the Protestants; in some of the first and second rates amounting even to two-thirds; in one or two first-rates nearly the whole; and in the naval hospital, about four years since, of 470 sick, 303 were Catholics.' (Substance of the speech of Sir J. Hippisley, May 18, 1810, p. 53.)

and multitudes of merchant seamen who were victims of the press-gangs. The ships were often hells upon earth. The pay was miserable. The allowances were inadequate. The lash was in constant use, and in no other English profession were acts of brutal violence and tyranny so common. Yet it was out of these elements, and under these circumstances, that a navy was formed, which under Duncan, and Collingwood, and Nelson, covered England with undying glory, carried her triumphantly through the struggle with the united navies of the Continent, swept every sea, and defeated every rival. Reckless courage and contempt for death, a boundless spirit of adventure, complete devotion to every chief who was fully trusted, discipline and fertility of resource in the hour of battle, kindliness and chivalry in the hour of victory, were seldom wanting, and the careless, dauntless, generous, childlike sailor type, which shines so brightly in the life of Nelson, and in the songs of Dibdin, is perhaps more popular than any other with the English people.

All the qualities of the British navy were now needed to guard against the storm which was brewing in the North. Wolfe Tone arrived at the Texel on July 8, and his journals furnish a vivid and authentic picture of the expedition.[1] The admiral, De Winter, and still more, General Daendels—a man who, in after years, played a great part as Governor of Java—at once impressed him by their manifest resolution and ability, and he was no less struck by the enormous superiority of the Dutch fleet at the Texel to the French fleet at Brest. The Dutch expedition for the invasion of Ireland, now consisted of fifteen ships of the line, besides ten frigates and sloops, and 13,544 soldiers, a force, in the opinion of Tone, amply sufficient to accomplish the task; and a French expedition, in which Hoche was to take part, was intended to follow it. The number of the ships with Duncan varied greatly, and the intelligence relating to them was very scanty. At the period of the mutiny of the Nore, the desertion of many ships appears to have reduced the fleet almost to a skeleton,[2] but at that time the

---

[1] Tone's *Memoirs*, ii. 419-441.
[2] James states that Admiral Duncan then found himself with only one ship besides his own, but that he concealed the desertion from the Dutch by making signals, 'as if to the main body of his fleet in the offing.' (*Naval History*, ii. 66.) In the very elabo-

Dutch expedition was still unprepared. On July 9, all was ready at the Texel, and at this date the Dutch admiral estimated that the ships of the line in the English fleet were at the utmost not more than thirteen, and he believed that they could make no effectual opposition.[1] This forecast may have been too confident, but English sailors, who knew how immeasurably superior the Dutch navy still was to the navies of France and Spain, in seamen, ships, and discipline, and how stubbornly it had always contended with England for the empire of the sea, would hardly think lightly of a combat with a superior Dutch fleet, commanded by a very competent admiral, and in the immediate neighbourhood of the enemies' coast.

But the winds, which had so signally defeated the French expedition to Bantry Bay, when success seemed almost within its grasp, once more assisted the English, in a way which, in another age, would have been deemed manifestly providential. Day after day, week after week, with a monotony which rather resembled the trade winds of the tropics, than the inconstant climate of the North, the wind blew steadily against the Dutch, making it impossible for their fleet to sail out of the Texel. A concurrence of wind and tide was necessary for it to do so, and for more than six weeks, this concurrence never once occurred. In the mean time, Duncan received reinforcements, and the favourable season was fast passing away. The diary of Tone describes graphically the rage of disappointed hope that was gnawing at his heart. 'At Brest, we had, against all probability, a fair wind for five days successively, during all which time we were not ready, and at last, when we did arrive at our destination, the wind changed, and we missed our blow. Here all is ready, and nothing is wanting, but a fair wind. . . . Everything now depends upon the wind, and we are totally helpless. . . . I am, to-day, eighteen days aboard, and we have not had eighteen minutes of fair wind. . . . I am, to-day, twenty-five days aboard, and at a time when twenty-five hours are of importance. There seems to be a fate in this business. Five weeks, I believe six weeks, the English fleet was paralysed

---

rate account, however, of the mutiny in the *Annual Register*, it is said that Duncan was deserted by only four men-of-war and one sloop, and that the other ships remained with him. (*Annual Register*, 1797, pp. 214, 215.)

[1] Tone's *Memoirs*, ii. 433.

by the mutinies at Portsmouth, Plymouth, and the Nore. The sea was open, and nothing to prevent both the Dutch and French fleets to put to sea. Nothing was ready; that precious opportunity, which we can never expect to return, was lost; and now that we are ready here, the wind is against us, the mutiny is quelled, and we are sure to be attacked by a superior force. . . . Had we been in Ireland, at the moment of the insurrection of the Nore, we should, beyond a doubt, have had, at least, that fleet. . . . The wind is as foul as ever, viz. south-west, in or near which point it has now continued thirty-six days that I am aboard.'[1]

Two United Irishmen, fresh from Ireland, arrived at the beleaguered fleet, and their news was not encouraging. The people, they said, were losing confidence in the organisation, and in French assistance, especially since the French Government had suffered the great crisis of the mutiny to pass, without making the smallest attempt to profit by it. They waited, in general, till the last day allowed by the proclamation, and then made their submission, took the oath of allegiance, received their pardon, and surrendered their arms. There were fewer guns than was supposed, among the United Irishmen, and their leaders seemed wanting in promptitude and courage. Three months ago, the United Irishmen said, an expedition to Ulster with only 500 men would have succeeded, but 'public spirit was exceedingly gone back in that time, and a great number of the most active and useful chiefs were either in prison or exile.' Still, Down and Antrim were ready to rise, and it was reported that there were, last June, in the former county, 'twenty-four regiments of 1,000 men each, ready organised, with all their officers and sub-officers.' Tone himself believed, that if either the Dutch or the French effected a landing, the submissive attitude of the people would speedily cease. 'If no landing can be effected, no part remains for the people to adopt but submission or flight.'[2]

One other judgment of the probable effects of an invasion, given about the same time, by a man who was very competent to estimate them, may here be cited. McNally reported a con-

[1] Tone's *Memoirs*, ii. 421, 424, 427, 435.   [2] Ibid. ii. 428, 436.

versation between Keogh, Braughall, and himself, in which Keogh said, 'that an invasion some time since would have settled the government of the country without bloodshed, for men of influence would have stood forward between the adherents of Government and the enemy; but now, who could venture to say, he could control the resentment of a people, whose injuries accumulate every day?' 'He thought,' continues McNally, 'an invasion would be attended with great bloodshed. I think so, too. I have no doubt, but every man who has taken an active part against the Northern insurgents, and the Catholic claims, stands proscribed.'[1]

In the middle of August, Tone learnt, what he had long feared, that the expedition to Ireland, at least on its original scale, was, for the present, abandoned. The Dutch admiral represented that, owing to the long enforced delay, the provisions of the fleet were falling short; that the favourable season had almost passed; that the English fleet was now stronger than the Dutch one, and that, under these circumstances, an expedition encumbered with the great number of slowly sailing transports, that was required for an army of 14,000 men, would be exceedingly rash, if not absolutely impracticable. Various alternative plans were proposed. One was to place two or three thousand soldiers on board the frigates, and with them to endeavour to reach the Irish coast. Another was, that the fleet, alone, should, on a favourable opportunity, sail out, and encounter that of Duncan, and that if it won the day, and the English fleet was seriously weakened, the enterprise should be resumed, but the troops, in the first place, at any rate, landed on the nearer coast of Scotland. A third was to land the troops where they might be collected in forty-eight hours; to give out that the expedition was abandoned, and then, when the vigilance of the English was relaxed, and the equinoctial gales obliged them to seek a port, to seize a favourable opportunity to reach the coast of Scotland. It was proposed that a French expedition should be directed to the same point, and it was hoped that a powerful army might be assembled in Scotland, part of which might menace England with invasion, while the remainder was despatched to Ulster. In the beginning of September, Tone

[1] J. W., Sept. 19, 1797.

was sent by the Dutch general, to communicate this plan to Hoche.[1]

Little more than a month later, all such schemes were crushed by the great battle of Camperdown. On October 8, the Dutch fleet sailed out with a favourable wind, and on the 11th, it encountered Duncan, nine leagues from Scheveningen. In ships, the fleets were about equal, but the English were superior in the number of men, and in the weight of metal. The battle was a very obstinate one. It was afterwards noticed, that whereas in most battles with the French and Spaniards, the English masts and riggings were shattered and torn, in this action, nearly every shot from the enemies' guns struck the opposing hulls, and the great and almost equal bloodshed on each side[2] showed how stubbornly the day was fought. It ended, however, in a complete English victory. The sailors, who had so lately been in open mutiny, fought with all the valour of their forefathers. The flagship of Duncan and the flagship of De Winter, which were equal in size, lay for three hours alongside of each other, within the distance of a pistol shot, and when at last the Dutch admiral struck his flag, he is said to have been the only man on board unwounded. Nine Dutch ships of the line, and two Dutch frigates, were captured. The shattered remnant of the fleet took refuge in the Texel, and another of the great dangers that had menaced England passed away.[3]

A new and not less serious stroke had just fallen on the United Irishmen and on their cause. Two Frenchmen, who had seemed destined to play foremost parts in Revolutionary France, had thrown themselves heartily into the scheme for the invasion of Ireland. One of them was Carnot, who had fallen in the

---

[1] Tone's *Memoirs*. On Aug. 30, Camden wrote that Cooke had heard from 'a clever man, high in confidence among many of the leaders of the United Irishmen, that a French invasion was definitely determined on; that it was to take place in the first fine weather after the storms of the autumn equinox; that Tandy, Tone, and Lewins were the principal agents, but that there were other subordinate ones employed in carrying intelligence; that Tandy was to have a military command, and Tone to be secretary to the commander of the land forces; and finally, that all intelligence from France had come through London and by parole. 'All mouths,' he added, 'are at work whispering the intelligence from France, and thereby spreading it through the country.' 'Peaceable conduct is the order of the day.' (Camden to Portland, Aug. 30, 1797.) For the sources of this information, see p. 400.

[2] The Dutch lost more than 1,100, the English more than 1,000.

[3] See James's *Naval History*; Stanhope's *Life of Pitt*, iii. 69-71.

Revolution of the 18th fructidor. The other was Hoche, who was looked upon as the most serious probable rival of Buonaparte, and in whom Tone placed his highest hopes. Tone now found the young general so weak, that he had to be assisted from room to room by his grenadiers, and with that dry, hollow cough, which indicates the final stage of rapid consumption. He died on the morning of September 19, and with him perished the last serious hope of French assistance. French statesmen still, as we shall see, endeavoured to raise embarrassments to England in Ireland; but Buonaparte was completely sceptical about Irish revolution, and no extended scheme for the separation of Ireland from Great Britain was again undertaken. At the end of 1799, Lewins presented a remarkable memoir to the French Government, on the effects of the legislative Union which was then impending. 'After the formal and reiterated assurances,' he said, 'given me from the moment when, on the invitation of General Hoche, I went from Frankfort to Paris, I cannot doubt, that it is the fixed resolution of France in all ways to assist the Irish in shaking off the English yoke, and to make no peace in which this great object was not accomplished,' and 'yet,' he continued, 'when I think of the little attention paid by the French to Irish affairs, since the death of Hoche, in spite of my pressing requests, and the indifference with which the Union seems regarded, it needs my unlimited faith in the promises of the French Government to sustain my hope.'[1]

We must now return to the course of events in Ireland itself. The Irish Parliament was prorogued on July 3, and shortly after dissolved. This was the last dissolution before its final abolition, and it was not due to any signs of opposition. Camden wrote, that the House of Commons had shown, during a critical period, 'the most marked firmness and spirit, and the most unbounded liberality;' a determination 'to stake their existence with that of the sister kingdom.'[2] For a time he was inclined to think that it would be better that the House should meet once more; but it was ultimately decided, that the present moment was very propitious for a dissolution. As usual, one of the first tasks

---

[1] Memoir of Thompson (Lewins) on the effects of the Union, 26 primaire, an 8. (F.F.O.)

[2] Camden to Portland, June 17, 1797.

of the Ministers was to provide for a long list of parliamentary supporters, in order ' to carry into execution those promises which Government was under the necessity of contracting in the course of that Parliament.' Camden accordingly recommended that three viscounts should be made earls, and three barons, viscounts. Lady O'Neil was made a viscountess, and Mrs. Toler, the wife of the Solicitor-General, a baroness; and six new peers, as well as five baronets, were created. To the great displeasure of the Lord Lieutenant, two of the new peers were Englishmen, who were apparently unconnected with Ireland, and who were rewarded for English services with Irish peerages.[1]

Another peerage shortly after followed, which gave rise to some curious letters, and which has real interest and importance. Few names appear more frequently in the Irish history and Government correspondence of the eighteenth century, than that of Lord Kenmare, but the person so designated had in reality no right to the title which he assumed, and which by social usage was invariably given to him. His ancestor, Sir Valentine Browne, had been made Viscount Kenmare and Baron Castlerosse by James II. immediately after his abdication, and these titles had never been recognised or ratified by the new Government. The present head of the family had eminent claims upon the Government, from his services in maintaining order and loyalty in Kerry, and perhaps still more from his conduct as the leader of the moderate party in the Catholic Committee, and he had long been extremely anxious to obtain a legal right to the titles which he bore. He had petitioned for this under Lord Westmorland; but though supported by the Lord Lieutenant, no answer appears to have been returned. In 1795, Camden made an application in his favour, but Portland answered that the King had said, 'Lord Kenmare certainly deserves attention, but has any Roman Catholic in this country been created a peer?' and Portland himself believed the request to be impracticable. Camden, however, now again urgently pressed the claim of Kenmare; and in a letter to Pitt himself, he suggested the possibility of 'some management which should make the peerage devolve upon him.'

The meaning of this last suggestion will be explained by the

[1] Camden to Portland, July 8, Aug. 7, Oct. 1797.

sequel. Portland wrote, that there were two serious objections to the proposal. In the first place, an arrangement was contemplated, which would have the effect of giving a peerage to another Catholic. Under Lord Westmorland's Government, a Galway Catholic gentleman, named Sir Thomas French, had been asked to make use of his influence upon certain members of his persuasion in the Catholic Committee, and he had done so in a way which the Government deemed so valuable, that Lord Westmorland promised to recommend him for a peerage. This peerage, however, was not to be given personally to himself, but to his mother, Lady French, who was a Protestant, and from whom it would in due course descend to him. The peerage had not yet been conferred, but Portland wrote, that 'Pitt considers Government to have been so pledged, as not to make it possible to deny or resist Lady French's claim.'

Portland added, however, that there was another and still graver obstacle to the proposal of Camden. 'Such I know to be the King's opinion with regard to the admission of Roman Catholics to seats in the Legislature, that I am sure I do not say too much, in declaring it to be my belief that there is not any measure whatever, from which he would so determinately withhold his sanction, as that by which he would give *directly*, and by his own act, to a Roman Catholic the right of sitting and voting in Parliament, and I do not believe that he could reconcile himself to it, except in a circuitous way, even for the sake of Lord Kenmare, whose merits are most certainly as highly appreciated by his Majesty as by your Excellency, or by any person whatever. But when your Excellency recollects, that his Majesty's objections to granting the privilege to which Lord Kenmare would be entitled by the grant of a peerage, are founded not on principles of policy only, but of conscience, it must be unnecessary for me to insist.'

Camden was exceedingly disconcerted by this letter. All additions to the Irish peerage were made on the formal recommendation of the Lord Lieutenant, and he therefore spoke on the subject with authority. He answered, that the claims of Lord Kenmare were greatly and manifestly superior to those of Sir Thomas French, and that there was no difference in principle between giving a Catholic a peerage on account of his services on the Catholic question, and giving a peerage to the Protestant mother of a Catholic, on account of the services of her son on the same question, and in order that the peerage should devolve on him. There was no question of asking the King to give Lord Kenmare a right of sitting or voting in the House of Lords. He was excluded from the Legislature by oaths, which could only be repealed by Act of Parliament. Neither the King nor the English Government could suspect the Administration of Camden of any partiality towards Catholics, or of any wish to increase their political importance. He had more than once refused to recommend Lady French for a peerage, but as a distinct pledge appeared to have been given to her, he would submit; but he could not too strongly express his opinion, that if this peerage was granted, the other could not with any propriety be withheld. If directly or indirectly any Catholic was made a peer, Kenmare had indisputably the first claim. Camden did not now press for either peerage, but he said, he must decline to recommend that for Lady French, 'unless the creation is accompanied by that of Lord Kenmare, or unless some means are found which may cause the title to devolve upon him.'

The King yielded to the desire of Camden. In the February of 1798, both Kenmare and Lady French were, on the same day, raised to the peerage, and the title of baron, which the King was at first disposed to give to Lord Kenmare, was, at the request of Camden, exchanged for a viscountcy.[1] The correspondence is especially important, as furnishing clear and unequivocal evidence, that if the King only hesitated about conferring merely honorary distinctions upon Catholics, he had, at least, to the full knowledge of his English Ministers, formed a fixed resolution, grounded upon religious scruples, that he would never consent to their admission into the Legislature. This fact had a fatal influence on the future history of the Catholic question, and it appears to me to make the conduct of the Ministers inexcusable in having, at the time of the Union, endeavoured to win Catholic support by holding out hopes of emancipation, without taking any step to shake the resolution

[1] Camden to Pitt, Sept. 23; to Portland, Oct. 26; Portland to Camden, Oct. 19, 1797; Camden to Portland, Jan. 12, 22, 1798. The earlier applications appear from some letters of June 1795.

of the King; without the knowledge of the King; without communicating the royal sentiments to the Catholic leaders.

The election for the last Irish Parliament passed off quietly, and the influx of a great multitude of Catholic voters into the county constituencies appeared, for the present at least, to have made very little difference, and to have excited very little attention. Grattan refused to stand for this Parliament, and he gave his reasons in a long 'Letter to the Citizens of Dublin,' which was published as a pamphlet. It is a curious and most characteristic performance; eloquent, ingenious, full of sentences of condensed wisdom and beauty; but full also of overstrained metaphor and antithesis, of exaggerated and unexpected turns of phrase, of passages which were very little fitted to accomplish any useful and healing end. He mentions that, at the close of the American War, it had been a common saying in Tory circles, that Lord North ought to have admitted the claims of the Colonial Legislatures, and then to have endeavoured to re-establish British dominion by building up a dominant influence within them. This, Grattan said, had been the precise policy which had been pursued in Ireland since the declaration of independence. It had been the deliberate object of the Government, by systematic corruption, ' to give the monarch a power which the Constitution never intended; to make the King in Parliament everything, and the people nothing,' and thus to render absolutely abortive the parliamentary rights that had been nominally conceded. This attempt to regain by corruption what had been lost in prerogative, was the true cause of the disaffection which had now become so formidable. There had been concessions, it is true, but they had been of little avail, on account of the spirit in which the Ministers had made them. 'In every Bill of a popular tendency, they resisted at first; they yielded at last, reluctantly and imperfectly, and then opposed, condemned, and betrayed the principle of their own acquiescence.' They agreed to the independence of the Irish Parliament, and then created a multitude of offices to make that independence an idle name. They agreed to a place Bill, and yet contrived, after it was passed, to add largely to their patronage. They agreed, with extreme reluctance and after extreme vacillation, to a Bill giving the franchise to the Catholics, and they at the same time maintained their exclusion from Parliament, and used their influence to prevent their election to the corporations. 'It is an observation of Lord Bacon, that the fall of one of the Roman emperors was due, not to his tyranny nor his relaxation, but to both; and that the fluctuating system is ever fatal. . . . Unhappily, our Ministers differed from Bacon; their system was faithful to no one principle, either of violence or concession.' 'Had the Government, instead of aggravating, restrained abuses, they would have put the State at the head of a spirit of reform which they could no longer resist, and could only hope to moderate. It was to such a policy, adopted by Queen Elizabeth, that the Church of England owes principally what it retains of power and splendour, preserved by the Government of the country, who took the lead in the Reformation.'

These words appear to me profoundly true. I shall not follow the Address through its summary of past Irish history, and through its well-worn arguments in favour of Catholic emancipation and parliamentary reform. Grattan seemed blind to the strength of the religious animosities that were rising, and still clung to the illusion, which he shared with so many leading statesmen and thinkers, that Catholicism, or at least 'Popery,' had for ever passed away as a distinct and dangerous political force, and that 'priestcraft' was a mere 'superannuated folly.'

'The only impediment to the Catholic claim as the law now stands, is the oath requiring the abjuration of the worship of the Virgin Mary, and of the doctrine of the Real Presence. To make these points at such a time as this, matter of alarm to the safety of the King, is . . . a mockery of the situation.' 'The Irish Catholic of 1792 does not bear the smallest resemblance to the Irish Catholic of 1692. The influence of Pope, priest, and Pretender are at an end. Other dangers and other influences might have arisen, . . . but those new dangers were to be provided against in a manner very different from the provisions made against the old.' 'The Ministry, however, thought proper to persist in hostility to the Catholic body, on a false supposition of its bigotry. The consequence was that . . . the most popular and energetic [Catholics], disappointed, suspected, reviled and wearied, united with that other great body of the reformers and formed a Catholic, Presbyterian, and Protestant league, for the freedom of the religion, and the free and full representation of the people. Out of this league a new political religion arose, superseding in political matter all influence of priest and parson, and burying for ever theological discord in the love of civil and political liberty. This is at present in all political matters the Irish religion.' 'The progress of the human mind in the course of the last twenty-five years has been prodigious in Ireland. I remember when there scarcely appeared a publication in a newspaper of any degree of merit, which was not traced to some person of note on the part of Government or the Opposition; but now a multitude of very powerful publications appear from authors entirely unknown; . . . and when once the powers of intellect are possessed by the great body of the nation, it is madness to hope to impose on that nation civil or religious oppression.'

But the danger did not spring simply from the conditions of Irish life. The 'democratic principle' was now sweeping over Europe, and, 'like the Government, we wished to provide against the storm.' 'Democracy, a gigantic form, walks the earth, smiting crowns with a hundred hands, and opening for the seduction of their subjects a hundred arms.' 'We implored Ministers against such an enemy to ally and identify the King with all his people, without distinction of religion.'

There were some things in the letter much more questionable than these. No candid man can, I think, deny that acts of illegal, criminal, shameful, and exasperating violence, were, at this time, committed in Ireland with the full sanction of the Government; but it seems to me equally impossible to deny that a conspiracy existed, with which ordinary law was utterly unable to cope, that the prompt disarming of a large section of the people had become imperatively necessary, and that, at a time when a French invasion might at any moment take place, it would have been suicidal madness to permit an unlimited sale of arms. Grattan, however, made no allowance for the enormous difficulties of this situation, and massed together the whole system of 'coercion' in an equal and undiscriminating condemnation. He was not content with denouncing 'the imprisonment of the middle orders without law; the detaining them in prison without bringing them to trial; the transporting them without law, burning their houses, burning their villages, murdering them, . . . preventing the legal meetings of counties to petition his Majesty, . . . and finally, the introduction of practices not only unknown to law, but unknown to civilised and Christian countries.' The Convention Act, the Gunpowder Act, the Insurrection Act, the suspension of the Habeas Corpus, the proclamation of General Lake, for disarming the people, were all equally condemned. Many magistrates and officers had, no doubt, acted with excessive violence; but it was absurd and mischievous rant, to accuse the Government of endeavouring 'to blood the magistracy with the poor man's liberty, and employ the rich, like a pack of Government bloodhounds, to hunt down the poor;' it was uncandid and untrue to deny that 'a spirit of plunder,' as well as of 'politics,' was abroad, and that a great portion of the outrages that were taking place, were utterly unconnected with any desire for mere 'political reformation;' it was very useless to inveigh against the war at a time when there was no power, either in England or Ireland, that could have stopped it.

A few more sentences will show Grattan's view at its strongest. 'The trade of Parliament ruins everything; your Ministers rested their authority entirely on that trade, till now they call in the aid of military power, to enforce corruption by the sword. The laws did, in my judgment, afford the Crown sufficient power to administer the country, and preserve the connection with Great Britain, but our Ministers have despised the ordinary tract.' 'The historian of these melancholy and alarming times . . . will, if a candid man, close the sad account by observing that, on the whole, the cause of the Irish distraction of 1797 was the conduct of the servants of Government endeavouring to establish, by unlimited bribery, absolute power; that the system of coercion was a necessary consequence and part of the system of corruption; and that the two systems, in their success, would have established a ruthless and horrid tyranny, tremendous and intolerable, imposed on the Senate by influence, and the people by arms.'

This remarkable paper closed with a series of eloquent aspirations. 'May the kingly power, that forms one estate in our Constitution, continue for ever; but let it be, as it professes to be, and as, by the principles and laws of these countries, it should be, one estate only; and not a power constituting one estate, creating another, and influencing a third.

'May the parliamentary Constitution prosper; but let it be an operative, independent, and integral part of the Constitution, advising, confining, and sometimes directing the kingly power.

'May the House of Commons flourish; but let the people be the sole author of its existence, as they should be the great object of its care.

'May the connection with Great Britain continue; but let the result of that connection be the perfect freedom, in the fairest and fullest sense, of all descriptions of men, without distinction of religion.

'To this purpose we spoke; and speaking this to no purpose, withdrew. It now remains to add this supplication, However it may please the Almighty to dispose of princes or of parliaments, may the liberties of the people be immortal.'[1]

These words were well fitted to sink deeply into the popular mind. Whether, amid the fever and distraction of the times, they were likely to fulfil any good purpose, is another question. Grattan himself, in after years, reviewed this portion of his career with the transparent candour which was one of his most beautiful qualities. The secession from Parliament appeared to him to have been a simple duty. He and his friends could not approve of the conduct of the United Irishmen nor of that of the Government, and they feared to encourage the former by making speeches against the latter. From the summer of 1795, when the old rulers and the old system came back; when military law was virtually established, and when poor men were transported without trial, the state of Ireland was, in truth, a state of war; the people looked to France, and the Government to arms; rebellion had become almost inevitable; its success would consign Ireland to French despotism and revolution, and its failure would probably be followed by the extinction of all popular influence and control. 'Our error,' he said, 'was in

[1] Grattan's *Miscellaneous Works*, pp. 40–64.

not having seceded sooner, for the Opposition, I fear, encouraged the United men by their speeches against the Government.... There was high treason, certainly, but the measures of the Government were so violent, that no man would sanction them. Nothing could excuse the torture, the whippings, the half hanging. It was impossible to act with them, and in such cases it is always better that a neutral party should retire. We could do no good. We could not join the disaffected party, and we could not support the Government.'

Coming to his letter to the citizens of Dublin, he says that it was considered, at the time, imprudent, and he acknowledged that the charge was a just one. 'It was true; it was well written, but it tended to inflame. I had also written strongly to the Catholics. I had just returned from England, and we smarted under the disappointment of Lord Fitzwilliam's recall. ... We were angry. It was not wise, but there is no man, who, in a long public life, will not be guilty of some political errors.'[1]

Except perhaps in Ulster, where matters had been for some time subsiding, the last months of 1797 produced no alleviation in the state of Ireland, and Grattan and the Government differed little about its gravity, though they differed much about its causes and its remedies. Pelham, in a desponding private letter to Portland, complained that the language of the Opposition tended to alienate the people from England, and that absenteeism had a similar effect, but he laid special stress upon 'the religious distinctions, which will always make the lower class of the people more open to seduction than the same class of men in other countries, and will make it impossible to expect any permanent security, either in peace or war, without a great military force.' Nothing, he thought, short of an establishment of the Catholic religion, would satisfy them; and he added with more truth, 'As long as the poor and the rich are of different persuasions in religious matters, there will always be a jealousy between the democratic and aristocratic parts of the Constitution.'[2]

Clare, who knew the country much better, expressed the Government view with force and candour. 'Emancipation and

[1] Grattan's *Life*, iv. 345-347.
[2] Pelham to Portland, Sept. 29, 1797.

reform,' he said, ' were far short of the designs of the disaffected ; the separation of the country from her Imperial connection with Great Britain, and a fraternal alliance with the French Republic, were the obvious purposes of the insurgents. The Government of Ireland had, by measures necessarily strong, at length quieted that part of the country in which the conspiracy originated. *These measures were, to his knowledge, extorted from the nobleman who governed this country*; they had been successful, and the state of the North at that day, was a proof of their wisdom. The county from which he had lately returned [Limerick], and which had formerly been a loyal and industrious county, was infested by emissaries from the North, exciting the peasantry to insurrection. Emancipation and reform were not the means which they employed for the seduction of the peasant. The suppression of tithes, the abolition of taxes, and exemption from the payment of rent, were the rewards they promised. Emancipation and reform were only used to delude the better classes.'[1]

'It is one great misfortune of this country,' he said in another speech, ' that the people of England know less of it than they know perhaps of any other nation in Europe. Their impressions I do verily believe to be received from newspapers, published for the sole purpose of deceiving them. There is not so volatile or so credulous a nation in Europe as the Irish; the people are naturally well disposed, but are more open to seduction than any man would credit who had not lived among them ; . . . and therefore the kingdom of Ireland is, of all the nations of Europe, the most dangerous to tamper with or to make experiments upon. Her present disturbed and distracted state has certainly been the consequence of a series of experiments, practised upon her for a course of years.'[2]

In spite of the battle of Camperdown, the expectation of invasion was very constant. The rupture of the negotiations at Lille, and the definitive peace between France and the Emperor, had reduced the war, for the present, to a duel between France and England. Buonaparte himself was at Paris, organising an 'English army,' which, it was thought, might be directed wholly or partly to Ireland. He had interviews both with Lewins and

[1] Plowden, ii. 652.
[2] *Debate in the Irish House of Peers, Feb.* 19, 1798, pp. 132, 133.

Tone, and more than one assurance was sent to Ireland, that French soldiers would speedily arrive.[1] Dean Warburton discovered that in his district, which had a few weeks before become quite peaceful, men were going from house to house whispering the news, and telling the people that tithes and taxes would soon be abolished; and although he had reason to believe that he was himself personally popular, he feared that the people welcomed 'every circumstance that afforded the smallest hope of an invasion.'[2] McNally assured the Government that, at a party at Grattan's house, the opinion was unanimously expressed that an invasion would be attempted, and that if it succeeded, the only course would be to form a convention, exclusive of Parliament, to treat for the country with the French.[3] There were rumours of plots to seize Dublin Castle and barracks; confident assertions that, in a few weeks, all Ireland would be in a blaze; reports that a French expedition was about to start for Lough Swilly; that Lawless, Lord Cloncurry's son, had gone over to London to confer with a French agent; that Lord Edward Fitzgerald and Arthur O'Connor desired an immediate outbreak.[4]

Pelham was at this time in England, but Cooke sent to him, near the end of the year, a most circumstantial and alarming story which had come from McNally. It was, 'that Lord Edward received, some days since, orders from Paris to urge an insurrection here with all speed, in order to draw troops from England. In consequence of it, there was a meeting of the head committee, where he and O'Connor urged immediate measures of vigour. They proposed arming a body of 500 with short swords; that this body should repair to all the mass-houses at midnight mass on Christmas morning; that by false attacks they should persuade the people to raise a cry that the Orangemen were murdering the Catholics; that, having raised the uproar, they should begin their attack on the Castle, &c. Many priests were anxious for this plan, but Emmet, Chambers &c. opposed, and in consequence, the bishops, who were against outrage, put off mass till seven o'clock in the morning. The moderate party are against

---

[1] J. W., Sept. 11, Oct. 2; Tone's *Memoirs*, ii. 454–456.
[2] Dean Warburton, Nov. 12, 1797; Jan. 29, 1798.
[3] J. W., Nov. 19.
[4] Pelham to King, Nov. 7; F (Higgins), Dec. 9, 29; J. W., Nov Dec. 26, 1797.

insurrection till the French land. . . . Our friend received his intelligence from James Tandy, son of Napper; who was alarmed beyond expression at the scheme, and, being consulted, had opposed it.'[1] Next day, however, the Lord Lieutenant himself wrote that, 'the account which J. W. gave in writing, fell far short of the verbal communication made to me by Pollock.' He added, however, that he was glad that he had at once summoned the Speaker and Attorney-General to Dublin, to consult about the measures to be taken, as the intention to produce an insurrection on Christmas Eve was undoubted. The propriety of arresting at once Lord Edward Fitzgerald and Arthur O'Connor was seriously discussed; but Camden reported that, 'under all the circumstances of our chance of further information, and under the impression of the disadvantage of taking up persons without bringing them to trial,' the idea was, for the present, relinquished.[2] It was observed, that there was, about this time, a strangely sudden diminution in the number of outrages; but it was doubtful whether this was due to the Government measures, or to the orders that came from the chiefs of the rebellion to avoid all provocation on the eve of the rising.[3]

Two other facts may be noticed, before drawing our account of the year to its close. Since the violent suppression of the 'Northern Star,' in May 1797, the United Irishmen had no recognised organ till the end of September, when a newspaper called 'The Press' was established, which for the next six months represented their aims with conspicuous ability. Its registered proprietor was an obscure printer named Finnerty, but it belonged in reality to a group of shareholders, among whom Lawless had the chief part, but which included also, Arthur O'Connor, Lord Edward Fitzgerald, Bond, Chambers, and Jackson. Among the shareholders and occasional contributors, was

---

[1] Cooke to Pelham (*Pelham MSS.*), Dec. 26, 1797.
[2] Camden to Pelham, Dec. 27. See, too, J. W., Dec. 26, 1797. By 'our friend,' McNally always means himself. In the *Memoirs of Miles Byrne* there is a case of United Irishmen acting for their own purposes the part of Orangemen, and thus producing a panic (i. 14, 15.).
[3] 'Except the robbing of arms, no serious outrage has lately taken place in any part of the kingdom; but I believe this apparent calm is the consequence of very strict orders, which have been issued to the United Irishmen not to be guilty of any excess. These orders are accompanied with the assurance of assistance from France.' (Camden to Portland, Jan. 22, 1798.)

Leonard McNally, whose share was probably paid by the Government, and who was thus able to obtain much additional information for his employers.[1]

The other fact was the arrival of a new Commander-in-Chief in Ireland. For some time Camden had felt that Lord Carhampton, though a man of undoubted zeal and courage, had neither the ability nor the tact required for his very difficult position, and he was much disappointed that Lord Cornwallis could not be induced to accept the military government of Ireland. A new overture, however, was more successful, and in November, Carhampton was removed to the post of Master of the Ordnance, and replaced by Sir Ralph Abercromby. This distinguished soldier had just returned from the West Indies. He knew Ireland well, having been quartered there before the outbreak of the war of the American Revolution, and having remained there during the whole period of its continuance. He was a man of a very independent and honourable character, and of liberal opinions, and he had the reputation of a commander who was not only skilful in the field, but also eminently successful in maintaining a high standard of discipline among his soldiers.

Such an officer was peculiarly wanted in Ireland, but such an officer was very unlikely to find his task a smooth one. Dalrymple, who commanded in the South of Ireland, showed himself profoundly disappointed at not being promoted to the first place. Knox informed Pelham that Lake, who commanded in the North, was not on good terms with Abercromby; and almost immediately after the arrival of the new Commander-in-Chief, signs of friction began. Abercromby wrote to England, that he had accepted the command with great reluctance, owing to the nature of the Government; that he understood that, with the exception of the patronage, the army was to be totally under his command; and that he must come to a clear understanding on this point, as a command divided between himself and the Lord Lieutenant was entirely incompatible with good military administration; while Camden wrote confidentially that Aber-

---

[1] J. W., Oct. 17, 31, Nov. 19, 28, Dec. 15, 1797; Madden's *United Irishmen*, ii. 241–246. McNally positively states that it was Lawless, not Arthur O'Connor, who advanced most of the capital for the undertaking, but he says that O'Connor acted as editor.

cromby was not easy to get on with, and very peremptory about managing military matters himself.[1]

All these signs were ominous, and the more Abercromby studied the state of affairs in Ireland, the less he was satisfied with them. The first thing which appeared to him absolutely necessary for the defence of the country in case of invasion, and for the enforcement of military discipline, was a concentration of the troops on a few points. Like Fitzwilliam, and Ponsonby, and Grattan, he believed that the suppression of riot and outrage, and the maintenance of internal tranquillity, must necessarily be entrusted chiefly to the yeomanry, and that the regular troops ought only to be employed on rare and serious occasions. Almost immediately after his arrival he went on a tour of inspection through the South of Ireland, and in that part of the country, at least, the danger from disaffection appeared to him to be exaggerated. A few extracts from his letters will give a clear view of his judgment of the situation, and of the course which he determined to adopt.

'The disturbances which have arisen in the South,' he wrote, 'are exactly similar to those which have always prevailed in that part of the country, and they hold out the old grievances of tithes and oppressive rents. The country gentlemen and magistrates do not do their duty; they are timid and distrustful, and ruin the troops by calling on them upon every occasion to execute the law, and to afford them personal protection.' 'With an army composed of so various a description of troops, and in a country so unprepared for war, it requires all the authority that the Lord Lieutenant can give me, to enable me to carry on the King's service.' 'As far as my information goes, the country through which I have passed [the neighbourhood of Cork] is in a state of tranquillity. . . . It would now be very desirable if the troops could, without alarming the gentlemen, be collected, and their discipline restored, which suffers exceedingly from their dispersed state. I am morally certain that many of the regiments could not at present take the field, from their various wants, which cannot be known or supplied till more brought together. The yeomanry appear to advantage; they are well

---

[1] Dalrymple to Pelham, Nov. 19; Knox to Pelham, Nov. 29; Abercromby to Elliot, Dec. 25; Camden to Pelham, Dec. 26, 1797.

clothed and mounted, and express great willingness and zeal. I am, however, nearly convinced that to bring them together, and to appoint officers to command them, must not be attempted. They must be left at home, and appointed to the defence of the interior.' 'The dispersed state of the troops is really ruinous to the service. The best regiments in Europe could not long stand such usage. . . . If I could be informed what number of regiments in aid of the yeomanry would be wanted in each province for the preservation of the peace of the country, I would willingly abandon a certain proportion for that peculiar purpose, provided the remainder were to be kept together, and in a situation to move if a foreign enemy should appear. I have found the cavalry in general unfit for service, and more than one-half of the infantry dispersed over the face of the country, in general under officers very little able to command them. At Fermoy more than three-fourths of the light infantry are "on command."'[1]

Although a great part of the country was apparently in a state of tranquillity, there was, he said, reason to believe that the minds of the people were neither softened nor subdued, and there was a serious possibility of a French invasion. 'On the yeomanry and the exertions of the gentlemen, and of the well-disposed inhabitants of the country, its internal security must principally depend;' and he mentioned the great good which had been done in Scotland by loyalist associations, that had been formed in each county in 1792 and 1793.[2]

Abercromby might have found quite as good an example in the Irish volunteers during the period of the American War; and if Ireland in the last years had been governed on the principles of Grattan instead of on the principles of Clare, the gentry of all creeds might have still been able and willing to maintain the order of the country. Camden expressed his perfect agreement with this portion of Abercromby's recommendations. He mentions that he had communicated them to several gentlemen connected with different parts of the country, and found them very ready to adopt the suggestions; and he expressed, on his own part, his appreciation of the great good sense and knowledge

---

[1] Dunfermline's *Life of Abercromby*, pp. 81-86.
[2] Abercromby to Pelham, Feb. 21, 1798.

of the world that were combined with the military talents of Abercromby.[1] But no one, who has perused the letters which were pouring in from most parts of the country asking for military protection, can doubt that Abercromby's policy was likely to be far from popular, and in some of the worst districts the scattered yeomanry appear to have been almost disarmed by nocturnal parties.

Abercromby had another object before him, which brought him speedily into conflict with the men who had the leading influence in the Government of Ireland. It was to bring back the army into the limits of legality, and to put a stop to the scandalous outrages which were constantly occurring, if not under the direct prompting, at least with the tacit connivance, of Government officials. Almost immediately after his arrival in Dublin, he issued an order reminding the officers that, though they might sometimes be called upon to aid the magistrates, 'they must not forget that they are only called upon to support the laws of the land, and not to step beyond the bounds of them. Any outrage or excess, therefore, on their part is highly culpable, and they are strictly enjoined to observe the greatest moderation and the strictest discipline when they are called upon to execute this part of their duty.'[2]

The outrages which took place were of different kinds. Many were mere isolated acts of drunken or half-disciplined soldiers, scattered in small parties among the peasantry, and had little or no relation to politics. But a large class, of which the burning of houses formed the most conspicuous example, were illegal acts of violence deliberately carried out in places where murders had been committed or where arms had been concealed, and deliberately screened by men in authority from the intervention of the law courts. Against the whole of this system, Abercromby resolutely set his face. In one case, when the sergeant of a fencible regiment had been murdered, and when the usual military excesses had followed, he wrote to Pelham: 'It is much to be regretted that the civil magistrate has not hitherto discovered the murderer of the sergeant, and I still more lament that no evidence has been brought forward sufficient to convict the authors of the notorious acts of violence which have been in

---

[1] Dunfermline's *Abercromby*, pp. 95, 96.   [2] Ibid. p. 77.

some measure the consequence of the murder. It is to be hoped, sir, that the magistrates of the county of Kildare will be instructed to prosecute still further the investigation of this business. Although they may not discover the murderer of the sergeant, they cannot fail to discover the soldiers who first set fire to the houses and committed several acts of violence at noonday, and in face of all the inhabitants of Newbridge. The soldiers are all at Kildare, and every assistance shall be afforded in the further prosecution of the inquiry. The future discipline of the army may depend on the conduct observed in this affair. If the civil power should decline taking any further steps, it must be taken up in a different point of view.'

On another occasion, writing to General Johnston, who commanded at Fermoy, he fully approved of the assistance that general had given to the civil magistrates in their attempts to seize the perpetrators of two horrible murders which had just taken place, but added, 'I have always wished that the law should be supported by the troops when called on properly, but I have as strongly wished that they should not take any part that was not strictly legal. . . . I hope the magistrates have not put their intention of burning houses in force. I hope the soldiers have taken no part in it.' 'I have endeavoured,' he wrote to the Duke of York, 'as far as possible to resist the interference of the troops in all matters where the civil magistrate ought alone to have interfered. I clearly saw that the discipline of the troops would be completely ruined, and that they would be led into a thousand irregularities contrary to law, which would bring disgrace upon themselves, and in which they ought not to be supported by the Government of the country.'[1]

Charlemont wrote about this time to Halliday, that Sir Ralph was acting 'with the strictest propriety in his most difficult situation, and has the happiness of being cordially disliked and abused.'[2] It is evident, indeed, how offensive his conduct must have been to men like Lake and Knox, who had steadily advocated the policy of burning houses; to Clare and Foster, who supported every measure of rigour in the Council; and to the many magistrates whose proceedings, frankly communicated to the Government in Dublin, have been already related.

[1] Dunfermline's *Abercromby*, pp. 90-93. [2] Ibid. p. 90

These differences culminated in the famous general orders issued on February 26, 1798, from the Adjutant-General's Office. 'The very disgraceful frequency of courts-martial, and the many complaints of irregularities in the conduct of the troops in this kingdom,' they said, 'having too unfortunately proved the army to be in a state of licentiousness which must render it formidable to everyone but the enemy,' it had become necessary to enjoin all commanding officers ' to compel from all officers under their command the strictest and most unremitting attention to the discipline, good order, and conduct of their men, such as may restore the high and distinguished reputation the British troops have been accustomed to enjoy in every part of the world.' ' It becomes necessary,' the writer added, ' to recur and most pointedly to attend to the standing orders of the kingdom, which, at the same time that they direct military assistance to be given at the requisition of the civil magistrate, positively forbid the troops to act (but in case of attack) without his presence and authority, and the most clear and precise orders are to be given to the officer commanding the party for the purpose.'[1]

These orders, though certainly not uncalled for by the circumstances of the case, produced a feeling approaching to consternation in Government circles both in England and in Ireland. They were issued without consultation with either Camden or Pelham, and at a time when Lord Moira had just brought forward his motion deploring the violent, tyrannical, and illegal proceedings in Ireland. They supplied the most decisive confirmation of his charges, and it is impossible to deny that they were in direct conflict with the proclamation of May 18, by which the military were instructed to act without waiting for the civil magistrate. The storm, however, did not immediately burst. In Parliament, Pelham defended the document as 'a military order called for by the relaxation of discipline in the army, composed as it is of very bad militia and fencible officers;'[2] and Abercromby himself repeatedly and earnestly disclaimed any political object, declaring that he had no sympathy with Lord

---

[1] Seward's *Collectanea Politica*, iii. 214, 215. These orders have been often reprinted.

[2] Camden to Portland, March 15, 1798.

Moira's politics, and had not even read his speech or the Chancellor's reply.

Abercromby immediately after issuing his orders went on a tour of inspection in Ulster; and during his absence a cabal of the most formidable kind was instigated against him, which was greatly assisted by the serious illness of Pelham. Among the Pelham Papers there is the draft of a curious letter, written but not sent by Pelham to the Duke of Portland, detailing what occurred. Pelham asserts that he had himself much reason to complain. His health in the beginning of 1798 was so broken, that he had begged to be relieved of his post; but he received no answer till the eve of the meeting of Parliament, when he was entreated to continue in office, and was obliged to undertake the management of the session, and among other things to give the official view of Abercromby's orders. In his own opinion, the description Abercromby gave of the state of the army was perfectly true, although the word 'licentiousness' was an injudicious one to use, and although part of the orders could not be reconciled with the proclamation of May 18. Pelham, by travelling through Ireland, had painfully convinced himself that the discipline of the army had been steadily declining up to the period of the arrival of Abercromby. He had, therefore, no hesitation in justifying Abercromby completely in Parliament, and his 'open and explicit justification' there, was at the time unanswered and uncensured. But no sooner had his illness become so serious that he was confined to his bed, than the Chancellor, the Speaker, and many others talked openly of impeaching Abercromby, and employing every means to punish and degrade him. Dinners were got up to bring together politicians of different types with this object, and a fixed resolve was expressed 'to get rid of him.' The Speaker, standing at the bar of the House of Lords to deliver the money Bills, took occasion, in the course of his address to the Lord Lieutenant, to commit the House of Commons against Abercromby by expressing the full confidence of the House in 'the high discipline' of the army. The measure, however, Pelham wrote, was not full till 'Your Grace thought fit, in declaring the sentiments of the British Cabinet, to give countenance to the cabal here, . . . to condemn without hearing, not only Sir Ralph Abercromby, but Lord Camden.' It was evident, Pelham added, that Portland received private reports from members of the Irish Cabinet.[1]

'The hue and cry has been raised in London,' wrote Abercromby, 'by letters from hence, and has been carried on, as I hear, principally by that immaculate character, Lord Auckland.'[2] This information seems to have been quite true, and the part which Auckland played at this time was an extremely mischievous one. Having been, when Mr. Eden, Chief Secretary, under Lord Carlisle, he had formed Irish connections, and was in close correspondence with Clare, Beresford, and Cooke, the men who had taken the chief part in producing the recall of Lord Fitzwilliam, and who were the centre of nearly everything that was reactionary and tyrannical in Irish government. Auckland was intimate with Pitt, and through his intervention these men had a constant channel of communication with Pitt, independently of the Lord Lieutenant and Chief Secretary. They were at this time busily intriguing against Abercromby. Clare especially wrote furiously about 'the peevish indiscretion of Sir Ralph Abercromby's orders,' declared that 'he must have lost his senses,' and that it was 'provoking that the critical situation in which we stand made it ineligible to resent his intemperance as it merited,' and he added, in characteristic phraseology, that 'if Lord Moira had not retracted his charges against the Irish army, . . . this Scotch beast certainly would have given him strong grounds to stand upon.'[3]

The letter of the Duke of Portland to which Pelham refers, was written on March 11. In it Portland expresses his astonishment at the general order ascribed to Abercromby, about the conduct of the army; asks whether it is genuine, and declares that it is considered a great triumph for Lord Moira's party over that of the Chancellor, and that the Irish in London inferred from it that the loyalists were abandoned to ruin.[4]

Camden was evidently perplexed. He thought it right to communicate the substance of Portland's despatch to Abercromby, and he was himself exceedingly annoyed at the publication of the orders, but he was also extremely anxious that

[1] April 1799.
[2] Dunfermline's *Abercromby*, p. 126.
[3] *Auckland Correspondence*, iii. 393–397. See, too, p. 411.
[4] Portland to Camden, March 11, 1798.

Abercromby should not resign his command. Such a resignation, he said, would deprive him in a very dangerous moment of a commander of tried military capacity, and would also add the weight of a most respectable opinion 'to the representations of those who are endeavouring to attack the system which has been pursued in Ireland.' He urged the English Ministers to be as conciliatory as possible towards Abercromby; and he wrote to Abercromby declaring his full confidence in him, absolving him from all imputation of having been actuated by a political motive, expressing a most earnest wish that he should continue at his post, but at the same time clearly stating his dissent from one portion of the orders. 'You have had the candour,' he wrote, 'to acknowledge that you did not consider the proclamation of May 18 as then in force. There is no doubt that until such a proclamation is recalled, or until the state of the country is so altered that it is a dead letter, the proclamation exists. Under that proclamation the military received orders to act without waiting for the civil magistrate. . . . That necessity exists, and since it does exist, it appears to me that the proclamation must be acted on.'[1]

If it was, as Pelham stated, the object of Clare and Foster to 'get rid of Abercromby,' that object was most easily attained. He had accepted the command with great reluctance, and he was not a man who would acquiesce with the smallest patience in the censure of his superiors or the restriction of his powers. On the very day on which he received the letter from Camden he sent in his resignation, and all the efforts of Camden and Dundas were unable to induce him to withdraw it. 'I feel the most perfect conviction,' he wrote to Dundas, 'that the principal members of Lord Camden's Cabinet have lost their confidence, if they ever had any, in me; that they did during my absence attempt my ruin by machinations here and in England, is a matter beyond all doubt.'[2] In two private letters to relations he threw off the reticence required in official correspondence, and stated his case with a clearness that leaves nothing to be desired. 'The struggle,' he said, 'has been, in the first place, whether I was to have the command of the army really or nominally, and

[1] Camden to Portland, March 15, 1798. Dunfermline's *Abercromby*, p. 101.
[2] Dunfermline's *Abercromby*, 106.

then whether the character and discipline of it were to be degraded and ruined in the mode of using it, either from the facility of one man, or from the violence and oppression of a set of men who have for more than twelve months employed it in measures which they durst not avow or sanction. . . . Within these twelve months every crime, every cruelty that could be committed by Cossacks or Calmucks, has been transacted here. The words of the order of February 26 were strong; the circumstances required it. It has not abated the commission of enormities, and I will venture to predict that when the moment for calling forth the Irish army arrives, one-half of it will dissolve in a month. . . . Within less than two months since the issuing of my orders, a private man has thrown a chair at the colonel of his regiment, when sent for to be reprimanded. Houses have been burned, men murdered, others half hanged. A young lady has been carried off by a detachment of dragoons, and in the room where she was, an officer was shot through the thigh, and a blunderbuss snapped at another gentleman's head. These are but a few of the enormities which have disgraced us of late; were the whole to be collected, what a picture would it present! Such a degree of insubordination has been allowed, that the general officers write directly to the Castle, overlooking every decency and order. Almost all those who were here before me have a plot and a conspiracy which they cherish, and which is the subject of their correspondence and consequence; and instead of attending to their duty and to the discipline of their troops, they are either acting as politicians or as justices of the peace. . . . There must be some change, or the country will be lost. The late ridiculous farce acted by Lord Camden and his Cabinet must strike everyone. They have declared the kingdom in rebellion, when the orders of his Excellency might be carried over the whole kingdom by an orderly dragoon, or a writ executed without any difficulty, a few places in the mountains excepted.' 'Since my arrival here, I have been under the necessity of supporting myself by great exertions and strong representations, otherwise I should have been a mere cipher, or, what is worse, a tool in the hands of a party who govern this country. Their dislike to me has, of course, been visible, and in my absence they took the opportunity of attempting to crush me. The Speaker, at the head of a junto, met in his chamber, canvassed and censured my order, and, interfering with a matter which did not belong to him, sent a deputation to Mr. Pelham to convey to him their opinion, and their determination to bring it before Parliament. This was only part of their plan; they wrote the most furious representations against me to the Duke of Portland, and to others of high rank in England. . . . After this there can be no mutual confidence. In times so difficult it is next to impossible to separate the civil and military business of the country; and with all the wisdom, all the vigour, that can be shown, it is impossible for any general to answer for success. Should, therefore, any one thing go wrong, I could expect nothing but the fullest effects of their resentment. . . . The abuses of all kinds I found here can scarcely be believed or enumerated. I tried various means with little success; it was necessary to speak out; the order is strong, but be assured it was necessary. The way in which the troops have been employed, would ruin the best in Europe. Here are 35,000 yeomanry, raised for the express purpose of protecting the country. . . . I therefore restricted the troops to the standing orders of the kingdom, that their discipline might be pursued if possible, and that the gentlemen might be obliged to trust to the yeomanry, on whom they must ultimately depend in case the troops should be called away to oppose a foreign enemy.'[1]

I have quoted these passages at much length, as they have a great historical importance. The resignation of Abercromby completed the fatal policy which the recall of Lord Fitzwilliam had begun, and it took away the last faint chance of averting a rebellion. If the French had arrived, no human power could have prevented a rising; but in the absence of French assistance, it was perhaps still just possible that it might have been avoided. Many and various influences concurred to produce, accelerate, or extend it; but among them, the burning of houses, and other lawless acts of military violence, which were countenanced by the Government, had an undoubted part. The resignation of a Commander-in-Chief, mainly because he endeavoured to repress them, and because he had been censured for that

[1] Dunfermline's *Abercromby*, pp. 108–110, 112–114.

endeavour, was one of the most calamitous events that could at this time have happened. Lord Camden was not blind to its probable effects. Scarcely any other event, he wrote to Portland, could have been so calculated 'to shake his Majesty's interest in Ireland,' and he strongly urged that, as Abercromby could not be induced to withdraw his resignation, he should be at once replaced by a very good general, as 'the nature of the government is now become so military, that it is absolutely essential that an officer of the most approved ability and experience should be sent to this kingdom.'[1]

Abercromby, though he refused to withdraw his resignation, spoke with great personal warmth and respect of Lord Camden, and consented, before leaving the country, to revoke the chief part of his general orders, and himself to go, armed with the full powers of martial law, to quell certain disturbances which had broken out in some counties of Leinster and Munster. The little town of Cahir, in Tipperary, had been occupied at noonday by a party of armed and mounted rebels, numbering, according to the Lord Lieutenant, 1,000,[2] and, according to the lowest estimate, at least 300 men, and they had proceeded systematically to disarm the inhabitants, and had carried away more than 100 stand of arms. Great robberies of arms were taking place in the county Kildare. Lord Clare, in a letter burning with hatred of Abercromby, declared that the whole province of Munster, and many of the counties of Leinster, were in a complete state of anarchy, if not of open rebellion; that the system of robbery was rapidly extending, and that the gentry over large districts had universally fled for refuge to the towns. 'Under these circumstances,' he said, 'Lord Camden was obliged to issue a peremptory command to Sir Ralph, to revoke his general order, and to give immediate directions to the troops to reduce the rebels, for which desirable purpose he has been invested with full discretionary powers.' Abercromby had undertaken to put down the disturbances in a fortnight, and Clare wrote that if he did not do so, the King should disgrace him.[3]

[1] Camden to Portland, March 26, 1798. Cornwallis wrote two days later: 'For your private ear, Abercromby is coming from Ireland. He has been exceedingly wrong-headed.' (*Cornwallis Correspondence*, ii. 333.)

[2] Camden to Portland, March 30, 1798.

[3] *Auckland Correspondence*, iii. 395–397. Cooke wrote very significantly: 'Sir Ralph . . . is gone into Munster with full martial law powers

The military were now ordered to act without waiting for directions from the civil magistrates, in dispersing tumultuous assemblies. Abercromby received express orders to disarm the rebels, to recover the arms that had been taken, and to crush rebellion, in whatever shape it might show itself, and wherever it might appear, by the most summary military measures; and a proclamation issued on March 30, established the most stringent martial law.[1] Of this proclamation, and of the measures that resulted from it, we shall learn more in the following chapter.

Abercromby agreed to act as the Government desired, but he at the same time, instead of waiting, as he ought to have done, till his resignation had been accepted by the King, at once informed his brother officers that he expected soon to be relieved. It became, therefore, well known that the military command was about to be changed, and that the Commander-in-Chief disapproved of the measures he was obliged to enforce. In the mean time, he issued instructions to the generals, directing them to disarm the people; authorising free quarters in disaffected districts, but also limiting and defining these measures, and taking every precaution that martial law should be exercised with leniency and moderation.[2]

In the opinion of Camden, he did not always execute his task judiciously. He was accused of refusing to consult with the country gentry, and treating those whom he met with marked coldness, and he appears to have greatly affronted Sir Lawrence Parsons, by his strictures on the King's County Militia.[3] He went through Kildare, the Queen's County, the King's County, Tipperary, and a considerable part of Munster, encountering little or no open opposition. The word had evidently gone forth that all should be quiet, and although Abercromby was not blind to the existence of deep-seated disaffection, he found the actual disturbances much exaggerated, and was more and more convinced of the impolicy of the steps which had been taken. There is, I think, little doubt that he greatly underrated the extent of the conspiracy, and the real imminence of the

to quell the rebellion there, which is more dangerous to individuals than the State, for I think its breaking out will do good.' (Ibid. p. 400.)

[1] *Castlereagh Correspondence*, i. 164, 168, 169.

[2] Dunfermline's *Life of Abercromby*, pp. 116–121.

[3] Camden to Portland, April 23, 1798; *Auckland Correspondence*, iii. 401.

danger. 'I had reason,' he wrote, 'from the proclamation and instructions I received, to believe that an insurrection had taken place in the province of Munster. I have been through all the disaffected districts, and found nothing but tranquillity, the people employed in cultivating their lands, and following their usual avocations. They were civil and submissive, and although I never took any escort, or anything more than one servant, I was under no apprehension, even the most distant, of any danger. Several robberies have been committed, as has been, at all times, the custom in this country; some private quarrels have been avenged, and arms have been taken from the Protestants. The people, however, are induced to give them up partly through fear, partly through persuasion. I do not, however, doubt, that if an enemy should land, the Roman Catholics will rise, and cut the throats of the Protestants. I really think Lord Camden is ill advised to declare the kingdom in rebellion, and to establish something more than martial law over the whole kingdom. It was, perhaps, right to do something in that way, in some particular districts where the greatest outrages had been committed, and where the magistrates had fled from their duty. I am now convinced that a writ may be executed in any part of Ireland. Do not, therefore, be under any immediate apprehension about this country.'[1]

Abercromby is nearly the last figure of any real interest that, in the eighteenth century, flitted across the troubled scene of Irish politics. He left Ireland towards the end of April, just a month before the rebellion broke out, and he was replaced by Lake, who, more, perhaps, than any other military man, was associated with the abuses which Abercromby had tried to check. The reign of simple force was established beyond dispute, and the men whose policy had driven Lord Fitzwilliam from Ireland, and Grattan from Parliament, were now omnipotent.

Abercromby himself in after years looked back on his brief Irish command as the most meritorious page of his long and brilliant career. After the scene of blood that was opening in Ireland had closed, and when the measure of a legislative Union was in contemplation, he wrote some melancholy lines, giving his impressions of Irish life. To the illiberal, the unjust, and

[1] Dunfermline's *Abercromby*, pp. 127, 128.

the unwise conduct of England during the long period of her government, he mainly attributed the profoundly diseased character of Irish life. The Legislature and the Executive had become corrupt; the upper classes dissipated, neglectful of duty, and too often oppressive to the poor; the peasantry cunning, deceitful, lazy, and vindictive. 'Although,' he said, 'the French Revolution and Jacobin principles may be the immediate cause of the events which have lately taken place in Ireland, yet the remote and ultimate cause must be derived from its true origin, the oppression of centuries.' It will need a long period, and the wisest system of government that can be devised, to cure the evil. 'In the mean time you must trust to the due execution of the law, and to a powerful and well-disciplined army, for your protection. . . . Till a new system has begun to take effect, the Irish people will remain the tools of a foreign enemy or of domestic agitators and demagogues. God grant that the measures on the affairs of Ireland, which they say are now under consideration, may be well weighed, and that the spirit of party may give way to true wisdom!'[1]

It will not be surprising to the reader, that everything of the nature of political concession was at this time obstinately refused, though representations often came to the Government, pointing out its importance and its necessity. Pelham wrote from London, in the last days of 1797, that he found a strong disposition in English ministerial circles, to endeavour to alienate the Catholics from the conspiracy by some measures of concession, if the Irish Government would consent; and he begged Camden to consult with the Chancellor on the subject; but the answer was an absolute refusal.[2] Francis Higgins, the shrewd proprietor of the 'Freeman's Journal,' was at this time much about the Government, and gave them very valuable information. No one who was not himself a United Irishman knew better the movements and changes of popular Irish feeling, and he strongly urged the importance of doing something to conciliate the Catholics. He told them that there had been a meeting of United Irishmen, in which Emmet, Sampson, Lord Edward Fitzgerald, and others, had expressed extreme alarm lest the speech from

[1] Dunfermline's *Abercromby*, pp. 127, 129, 130, 216.
[2] Pelham to Camden, Dec. 21; Camden to Pelham, Dec. 26, 1797.

the Throne should give hopes of a measure of Catholic emancipation, declaring that in that case 'there would be an end to freedom and their design.' In the opinion of Higgins, the wisest thing the Government could do, would be to enter on such a course, and especially to make use of the services of his illustrious friend Arthur O'Leary. 'I know,' he said, 'O'Leary would be a tower of strength among them. He was their first champion, and is most highly respected by the multitude. His writings and preaching prevented the White Boys and insurgents of the South from joining the rabble of Cork, and rising *en masse* at the period when the combined fleets of Spain, France &c. were in the English Channel.'[1]

Another letter arrived, to which no great weight can have been attached, but which may be noticed in passing, as it is, I believe, with one exception, the last appearance in Irish politics of a strange, wild figure, which fills a considerable space in an earlier portion of this narrative. Lord Bristol, the Bishop of Derry, now lived entirely in Italy, from whence accounts of his mad pranks were from time to time brought back by travellers.[2] In the spring of 1797, his palace at Derry had been occupied by soldiers under Lord Cavan, and he wrote a furious letter, ordering that legal proceedings should be immediately taken against that officer.[3] In the beginning of 1798, Pelham received a long letter from him, dated from Venice, and giving his views of the state of Ireland. It is full of poetical quotations, and very extravagant in form, but not in substance. The diocese of Derry, he said, was the real centre of rebellion in Ireland, and the present was the third paroxysm which had taken place in the last thirty years. The Hearts of Oak, the Hearts of Steel, and the Defenders were all symptoms of the same deep-seated discontent and disease; and as he had gained the confidence of his turbulent people more completely than any other member of his cloth, he could tell the Ministers confidently, that there were only two measures which could ever effect a real and radical cure.

---

[1] See the letters of F. H., Dec. 9, 22, 29, 1797; Jan. 2, 12, 16, 1798. The *Freeman's Journal* wrote, on the whole, favourably towards the Catholics. See Madden's *History of Irish Periodical Literature*, ii. 480-482.

[2] See vol. vi. p. 387. Some curious additional anecdotes of the Bishop's proceedings in Italy, will be found in the *Personal Memoirs of Pryce Lockhart Gordon*, i. 172-177.

[3] Lord Cavan to Pelham, May 27, 1797.

The first was, a complete change in the law of tithes. He described at length the hardship and irritation the existing system produced in Ulster, and continued: 'My remedy for all this evil is simple. I proposed it in 1774, and it was accepted by the Bench of Bishops assembled at the late Primate's, but—by way of experiment—confined to the diocese of Derry; but my illness and other circumstances made me drop it. This was the remedy, grounded on the English statute for inclosing parishes, ... an Act to enable every rector and vicar, with consent of the patron of the parish and the bishop of the diocese, to exchange his tithe, or any portion of his tithe, for land of the same value, so that the exchange will only be gradual in the parish.'

He explained the process by which such a measure could be made to work, but added that it must be accompanied by another great change, the payment of the priests and Dissenting ministers. The Presbyterians, who had a few years before, so enthusiastically supported the Bishop as the great champion of religious liberty, would have been somewhat startled had they seen the very plain language in which he now expressed his views on this subject. 'Is it not a shame that in any civilised country, and where there is an established religion as well as a Government, there should be teachers professedly paid by their hearers for preaching against both the one and the other? Neither popish nor Presbyterian parson should, in my opinion, be permitted by law to preach or pray indoors but under the Great Seal of Ireland. The Crown should be the patron of all Dissenters, seceders, and schismatics whatever, and the Crown should either pay them, or be the cause of their being paid, and then Government would be certain of the people they appoint, and the doctrines they would teach.' The payment might be made either by a direct grant, or by a county or baronial rate, or by dividing the Church funds as livings became vacant. 'This would effectually tear up rebellion by the roots. ... Where the treasure is, there would be the heart likewise. ... Anything so anomalous as a man in a civilised state paid for preaching anarchy, confusion, and rebellion, I do not conceive.' Unless 'some radical antidote' is very speedily applied to the diseased body politic, that body will infallibly burst.[1]

[1] Lord Bristol to Pelham, Jan. 16, 1798.

In the new Parliament also, which met on January 9, voices of protest and remonstrance were not wanting. I have already spoken of Lord Moira's motion in the House of Lords; and in the same House, Lord Bective, in a maiden speech, on the motion for the Address, strongly urged the necessity of conceding both parliamentary reform and Catholic emancipation.[1] In the House of Commons, Sir Lawrence Parsons moved for a Committee of the House to inquire into the discontent of the nation, and he prefaced his motion by an elaborate and very powerful speech. He reminded the House that, at the time of Lord Fitzwilliam's recall, he had predicted, amid a storm of derision and dissent, that the effect of that fatal measure would be, that each gentleman's house would soon have to be protected by four or five soldiers, and he asked whether in very many cases this prediction had not proved literally true. To that recall; to the obstinate refusal of the Government to concede Catholic emancipation and parliamentary reform; and to the settled design to divide and corrupt the country, he attributed, not indeed the existence of the United Irish conspiracy, but the immense success which had attended it. There were, however, other reasons: 'To make the people respect the laws, the Government should itself obey them. Such had not been the conduct of Government, and to that misconduct were the outrages and the assassinations which had disgraced the country to be traced. A general officer had in a western district taken out of the gaols a number of prisoners, whom the law would perhaps have pronounced innocent, and by his own authority transported them. A Bill of Indemnity was passed to protect this violation of law, and upon that Bill being debated, he well recollected an honourable gentleman [Mr. G. Ponsonby] observing, that by thus proving to the common people, that the law might be broken with impunity, by taking from them the resource of its protection, the practice of assassination would become as common in Ireland as it was in modern Rome; and that prediction had been unhappily fulfilled. Parliament went farther. In the Insurrection Bill, the conduct which had been thus indemnified, was made the law of the land, and it was notorious that almost every assassination which had taken place, had occurred in the districts in which that law had

[1] Camden to Portland, Jan. 16, 1798.

been enforced.' But Castlereagh, on the part of the Government, absolutely opposed all inquiry and all concession, and the House supported him by 156 to 19, and then carried an address to the Lord Lieutenant praising, in unqualified terms, the measures that had been pursued in Ulster, and asserting that they had been attended with complete success.[1]

Equally unsuccessful were the attempts of the Opposition to impose some restraint on military violence. Dr. Browne, one of the members for the University, asked 'by what authority, Act of Parliament, or proclamation, the house of every person was burned who was not at home at a particular hour at night;' and he asserted that there were many instances of persons who were supposed to be guilty of treasonable offences, but against whom there was no evidence, having been deliberately shot in cold blood. But the only answer he received was, that 'if some of the irregularities complained of had been committed, they were without the sanction and approbation of the Government. The military had been moderate, and so had the Administration.'[2]

It is no doubt true that such acts of illegal military violence were usually provoked by great crimes, or by serious dangers, and that their number has been much exaggerated; but it is also true that the power of the Government was constantly employed to shelter them. In one case, a certain Colonel Sparrow, who was found guilty of having, without sufficient reason, killed a prisoner whose rescue he feared, and committed other acts of violence, produced the King's pardon immediately after the sentence was pronounced.[3] In the county of Kildare, there was a case, which is apparently well attested, of a respectable old man,

---

[1] Seward's *Collectanea Politica*, iii. 215–220; Camden to Portland, March 6, 1798.

[2] Grattan's *Life*, iv. 340, 341. One of the members for the county of Westmeath refused to attend the debate in which the military violence was discussed, and he gave Pelham an account of the state of his county, which seems to me very impartial. 'Great enormities, I do confess, were practised by the soldiery at the other side of this county, which I can by no means defend. Were I, therefore, in my place, my silence would be a sanction to the Opposition. . . . It may, perhaps, be some extenuation of these facts to state, that the most horrid barbarities had been previously practised by the insurgents, that witnesses had been cruelly murdered (one of them in open daylight), and that the minds of the soldiery had been exasperated by the recent fact of attacking twenty-four houses in one night, and almost in the same hour, which seemed to indicate a general rising. Other cruelties might be cited, such as the roasting of three women in one parish, to force them to confess where their money was deposited.' (Mr. Smyth, March 4, 1798.)

[3] Plowden, ii. 623.

who, intending to go on the morrow to Dublin, was mending his cart after sunset, in a district which was perfectly peaceful, and not included in the proclamation, when an officer of a Scotch fencible regiment, who had drunk too freely, mistaking either the district or the law, arrested him on the supposition that he was out of doors after the legal hour. At the first turnpike, the officer got into an altercation with the turnpike keeper. While it was continuing, the prisoner endeavoured to return to his own home, but was at once cut down, killed and mangled with no less than sixteen wounds, nine of which were pronounced to be mortal. The coroner's inquest returned a verdict of wilful murder, but the military authorities refused to give up the culprit. The magistrate was driven back by force, and the Government refused to interfere. At last, when the scandal became very grave, the officer marched into Athy with a band playing before him, and gave himself up for trial. Toler, the Solicitor-General, was then acting as Judge of Assize, and in a charge, which appears to have been abundantly garnished with the judicial buffoonery for which, as Lord Norbury, he was afterwards so notorious, he directed the jury to acquit the prisoner, on the ground that 'he was a gallant officer, who had only made a mistake.'[1]

On a third occasion, twelve persons were released by the Court of King's Bench from an imprisonment which the judges pronounced entirely illegal.[2] Some persons, whose property had been destroyed in the search for arms, applied to the King's Bench for redress, and legal proceedings were instituted against some magistrates and yeomen.[3] But the Government interfered to obstruct the action of the law courts, and a new Act of Indemnity was carried, which sheltered all magistrates, and other persons employed to preserve the peace, from the consequences of every illegal act they had committed since the beginning of

---

[1] See the account of this trial in Lord Cloncurry's *Personal Recollections*, pp. 49-51. Lord Cloncurry, then Mr. Lawless, was present at the trial, and the murdered man was a tenant of his father. McNally, referring to this case, wrote: 'The refusal of Mr. Pelham to give the aid of Government towards apprehending Lieutenant Fraser, of the Scotch Fencibles, is considered, or at least represented, as a gross instance of partiality and injustice, particularly as the inquest brought in a verdict of wilful murder.' 'The conduct of Toler on circuit,' he says in another letter, 'is the principal topic.' (J. W., July 24, Sept. 19, 1797.)

[2] Plowden, ii. 639, 640.

[3] Knox to Pelham, Nov. 29, 1797.

the year 1797, with the object of suppressing insurrection, preserving peace, or securing the safety of the State.[1] The Opposition endeavoured to add a clause granting compensation to honest injured men whose property had been destroyed by such illegal violence, but this clause, though inspired by the most obvious and indisputable justice, was opposed and rejected.[2]

Such a policy could hardly fail to drive the country into rebellion, and to plant in it savage animosities and a distrust of law more dangerous, because more enduring, than rebellion. The efforts of the Opposition were hopeless, but not inglorious. The eloquent voices of Grattan, Ponsonby, and Curran were indeed no longer heard; but Parsons, Browne, and Knox maintained their cause with eminent ability, and they were reinforced by Lord Caulfield, the son of Charlemont; by Charles Kendall Bushe, one of the most graceful and attractive of speakers; and by another young lawyer of still higher powers, who was now brought into Parliament by Lord Charlemont, and who at once took his natural place among the very greatest of debaters. William Conyngham Plunket, the last of that remarkable group of statesmen and orators produced by the Irish Protestants in the closing half of the eighteenth century, can perhaps hardly be called a great man. He had neither the glow of imagination, nor the warmth and disinterestedness of character, that kindle the enthusiasm of nations. He has left no serious contribution to human thought or knowledge; and devoting himself mainly to professional ends, he neither sought nor won the fame of a party leader or of a great legislator. Even as an orator—though his place is in the foremost rank—his popularity was somewhat limited by the extreme severity of a taste which rarely stooped to ornament, or indulged in anything that was merely rhetorical or declamatory. But in the power of rapid, lucid, and most cogent extemporaneous argument; in the grave, dignified, reasoned, and persuasive eloquence, which is most fitted to charm and subjugate an educated audience, he has very seldom had an equal, scarcely ever a superior.

As a politician, he belonged essentially to the school of Grattan, with whom he was linked in the closest friendship, whom he succeeded in the conduct of the Catholic question in

[1] 37 Geo. III. cap. 39.   [2] Grattan's *Life*, iv. 343.

the Imperial Parliament, and of whom he was accustomed to speak to the end of his long life as the greatest and best man he had ever known. He agreed with Grattan in his hostility to the Union and in his views on the Catholic question, and he equally agreed with him in his detestation of the United Irish conspiracy; in his dislike and distrust of the democratic character which O'Connell afterwards gave to Irish politics; in his freedom from all French sympathies; in his genuine hatred of anarchy and disorder. In the Imperial Parliament he was at once recognised as one of the very greatest of orators and debaters,[1] but he confined himself to a few questions, and was never a keen party politician. The affinity of his intellect and character drew him naturally to the moderate Whigs who followed Lord Grenville, and like most of Lord Grenville's followers he joined the Government of Lord Liverpool in 1821, and supported the liberalised Toryism of Canning. On two memorable occasions, he separated himself from the bulk of those with whom he usually acted. In 1815, when the great body of the Whig party were prepared to sacrifice the fruits of twenty years' war by acquiescing in the restoration of Napoleon, Plunket, with Grattan and with Lord Grenville, strenuously advocated the renewal of the war, and in 1819 he surprised many of his friends by maintaining the necessity of the six Acts of Castlereagh. In the session of 1798, his main object seems to have been to restrain illegal violence, and he was the proposer of the clause for granting compensation to the innocent victims of military violence.

The discontent produced by the refusal of the Irish Parliament to grant any measure of redress or of reform, was seriously increased by the renewed rejection of the absentee tax. The arguments, both of principle and policy, which Burke had urged against this tax, were very powerful, and in ordinary times they might have been accepted as conclusive, but Ireland was now struggling with no ordinary difficulties. It was scarcely pos-

---

[1] I may here mention, that Lord Russell once told me that, looking back on his long life, he considered that there were two men in his early days, who excelled as orators any in the generation that succeeded them. They were Canning and Plunket; and of these two, he considered Plunket the greater. There is an admirable description of Plunket's speaking in Bulwer's *St. Stephen's*, part 3. See, too, much on the subject which is collected in Plunket's *Life*, by his distinguished grandson, the member for Dublin University.

sible that any small and poor country could bear, for many successive years, the financial strain of such a war as that which was now raging. England herself staggered under the burden, and seemed to many good judges on the verge of bankruptcy; and in Ireland the situation was aggravated by the necessity of immense military preparations to maintain the Government at home, and by the collapse of credit and paralysis of industry that always follow extreme anarchy and imminent danger of invasion and rebellion. I have described the excellent financial condition of Ireland when the war began, and the very moderate and equitable taxation imposed by the Irish Parliament. But in 1797, the fifth year of the war, the condition of affairs had become very serious.

The Government deemed it necessary to raise nearly four millions by loan, and they found the operation exceedingly difficult. They were obliged to issue five per cent. 100*l*. debentures at 63, and they obtained with some difficulty a loan of a million and a half from England.[1] It was no longer possible to exempt the poor from taxation, and the salt tax and the leather tax fell upon them with great severity. Some of the principal articles of Irish manufacture, it is true, still showed a surprising vitality, and high prices gave prosperity to agriculture, but those prices greatly aggravated the distress of large classes, and it was stated that in 1797 there were no less than 37,000 persons in Dublin alone, in a state of extreme destitution.[2]

Under these circumstances, and at a time when the poor were suffering so severely, the exemption of the great absentee proprietors from all taxation for Irish purposes seemed peculiarly unjust. Another year of war was now opening; there was no prospect of returning peace, and it was certain that new sacrifices would be required. The tax was proposed by Latouche, the principal banker, and one of the most respected characters in Dublin, but he desisted, when he found the Government inflexibly opposed to it. It was then taken up again by Vandeleur, and it was defeated by 104 to 40. In this case, the real opposition came not from Ireland, but from England, and

[1] See the financial debates in *Irish Parl. Deb.* xvii. part 2. Adolphus' *History of England*, vi. 547, 548.
[2] Plowden, ii. 644.

Portland gave the Lord Lieutenant peremptory orders that the tax must be rejected. 'It is impossible,' writes Camden, 'to describe the ill humour which pervades all descriptions of persons, from finding Government determined to oppose this measure. It will, however, I trust, be defeated by a larger majority than your Grace might have supposed; but I must repeat the great disgust with which most of the friends of Government support it upon the present occasion.'[1]

This session of Parliament did nothing to quiet the country, and nothing to regain the affections of the people, and the shadow of great coming calamity fell darkly on the land. In Ulster, it is true, there was a sudden, mysterious, perplexing calm. Cooke wrote to England in March, that, although the leading agitators were still busy there, the lower classes were at work, and peaceable and industrious, and he added, 'I believe no part of the King's dominions more apparently quiet, or more evidently flourishing, than the North of Ireland.'[2] Clare, as we have seen, boasted of it in the House of Lords, as a clear proof of the success of martial law. Lake wrote from Belfast, 'The natives continue quiet, waiting with anxious expectation for the arrival of the French, which, they are taught to believe, will happen very shortly; their dispositions remain precisely the same. The flame is smothered, but not extinguished.'[3] Others believed that the very calm of Ulster was an evil sign, for it only showed how perfectly the people were organised, how fully they obeyed the order to remain passive till the French invasion, which was confidently expected in the early spring.[4] But over

---

[1] Portland to Camden, Jan. 29; Camden to Portland, Feb. 5, 15, 23, 1798.
[2] *Auckland Correspondence*, iii. 392.
[3] Lake to Pelham, Jan. 27, 1798.
[4] Among the papers in Ireland there is an information endorsed, 'V. (secret), March 27, 1798,' from some one who professes that 'all the plans, resolutions, and correspondence of the United Irishmen' were communicated to him. He says that the North seems quiet, but it is only because it is awaiting orders from France, and adds: 'It was in the North that the spirit of rebellion took its birth. It is in the North it is fostered. It is there that it is brought to maturity. It is there, in fine, lie the hopes, the spring, the wealth, the force of the United Irishmen.' Another very important informer, who can be shown to be Magan. wrote: 'The North is now, more than at any former period, held out as an example to the other provinces. To their perfect state of organisation there, is their apparent tranquillity owing.' (April 22, 1798; Anon., but dated from Stephen's Green and endorsed 'Mag. [secret.']) We have already seen that orders had been issued in France, that Ulster was to remain quiet till the rebellion, but that efforts were to be made, by exciting disturbances in other quarters.

a great part of Leinster and Munster, horrible murders were of almost daily occurrence,[1] and an extreme terror prevailed. Lord Longueville, writing from the county Cork, to report the murder of Sir Henry Merrick, said that Abercromby's order forbidding the military to act without the presence of a magistrate, would be fatal, as the magistrates would not dare to expose themselves to the lasting vengeance that would pursue them, and he mentioned that, in a single week, three men had been shot in clear daylight, within eight miles of his own house.[2] Even the sentinels on guard in Dublin were frequently fired at.[3] Dr. Lanigan, the Catholic Bishop of Ossory, wrote in March to Archbishop Troy, describing the condition of the Queen's County, and some charges that had been brought against the priests, and his letter contains this very significant sentence: 'The priests told me, and I believe them, that the fear of assassination prevents them from speaking as much as they wished against United Irishmen.'[4]

In the towns, the United Irish ranks were rapidly recruiting. McNally writes that men in respectable and independent positions, and even 'of considerable property,' were 'daily Uniting;' that the conspiracy was making rapid progress in the public offices, and among the yeomen; that nearly all the clerks in banks and great merchant and trading houses were involved in it; that there was hardly a house with three men servants which had not a domiciliary committee; that the United Irishmen had already their agents and their spies in the most confidential departments of the Castle and the law courts, and that they were actively introducing them into the post offices.[5] In Trinity College, seditious sentiments were spreading among the young men, and a visitation was held by the Vice-Chancellor Lord Clare, and by Dr. Duigenan, who was deputed to act in the place of the Archbishop of Dublin. Several

---

to draw the troops from the quarter which was intended to be the chief scene of the rebellion.

[1] *Beresford's Correspondence*, ii. 154; Musgrave's *Rebellions in Ireland*, pp. 196, 197, 203.
[2] Lord Longueville, March 8, 1798.
[3] Musgrave, p. 203.
[4] *Castlereagh Correspondence*, i. 160–162.
[5] See the letters of J. W. for Feb.

and March 1798. An Athlone magistrate, named Parker, wrote that he had been sending a confidential agent to attend a mendicant friar in his annual circuit through a great part of the co. Roscommon, and that he found that nearly all the servants in gentlemen's houses were disaffected, and acquainted with the Defenders' signs. (T. Parker, April 6, 1798.)

students were expelled, and among those who were examined was young Thomas Moore, who has left a graphic description of the scene.[1] An informer wrote, that the leaders of the conspiracy believed that the expulsions from Trinity College would have the happiest effect on their cause, and that it was 'a master stroke to have thus committed the Government with the youth of the country.'[2]

Printed papers were now widely circulating, warning the people to be prepared, and telling them that the moment of deliverance was at hand, when all their troubles would be over. Itinerant pedlars were going to and fro, busily spreading the contagion. A translation of a tract by Volney, called 'The Torch,' was widely distributed. Women, paid by the United Irishmen, went through every town and village, singing seditious songs. There were handbills, exhorting the people to abstain from spirituous liquors, partly in order to starve the revenue but chiefly in order to diminish the danger of the betrayal of secret designs, and a marked diminution of drunkenness is said to have followed. Other handbills forbade the people to purchase the quit rents of the Crown, which were being sold to raise supplies, and recommended them to refuse all paper money in their commercial dealings. There were, at the same time, incessant efforts to seduce the soldiers, the militiamen, and the yeomen.[3]

It was a state of society in which no man knew whom he could trust, or what was the true extent of the danger, and panic and passion were steadily increasing. Camden was honest and humane, but weak, incapable, bewildered, and utterly desponding. 'Your Grace can hardly conceive,' he wrote, 'the timidity which prevails in many parts of the country, and the intemperance which is felt and expressed by the friends of Government in Dublin. It is as difficult to repress the zealous, as to give courage to the timid.' 'A jealousy of

[1] See the preface to the Irish Melodies in the Collected Edition of *Moore's Works*; and also Camden to Portland, March 6, 1798. Many particulars about this visitation, and about the spread of disaffection in Trinity College, will be found in the recently published *History of the University of Dublin*, by Dr. Stubbs, pp. 294–299.

[2] Mag. [Magan], April 22, 1798.

[3] February, March, and April letters, I.S.P.O.; *Memoirs of Miles Byrne*, i. 13, 14; *Report of the Secret Committee*, Appendix, No. xxviii.

English influence; a nonsensical and short-sighted pride of independence; religious differences; carelessness towards their inferiors, which, in the higher classes, is general; cruelty towards them, which is too frequent amongst some of them; the want of parochial communication; the non-residence of the clergy of the Established Church, and the influence acquired by a discontented and, frequently, a seditious priest, render this kingdom peculiarly adapted to receive the impressions it has done,' and the success of the French Revolution had kindled the discontent into a flame. The kingdom was becoming more and more disturbed. In Kildare, very lately, two magistrates were shot in broad daylight, and not one of the labourers who were standing near made a single effort to arrest the murderers. In the Queen's County, which had lately been very peaceful and prosperous, and which contained a large resident gentry, houses were now being continually broken open and plundered, and outrages and murders were multiplying. 'Add to this, most extravagant party prejudices. The eager Protestants, calling the present conspiracy a popish plot, and indulging in language and in conduct revolting to the Catholics, are encouraging the Orangemen, avowing themselves of their society, and averring that until the penal laws against the Catholics are again enacted, the country cannot be safe.' Grants of 25*l*. a year to 200 students at Maynooth, had lately been carried by the Government, against the opinion of the Speaker and of several other of their usual supporters; yet it was noticed, with some bitterness, that when, soon after, there was a proposal before the Bank of Ireland, for granting a sum of money for the prosecution of the war, not one Roman Catholic among the Bank proprietors voted for it, and that the minority who opposed it consisted almost entirely of Roman Catholics.[1] In a letter written a few weeks later, to announce and justify the proclamation of military law, Camden speaks of innumerable houses plundered of arms; attacks on villages in noonday; yeomen disarmed by night; loyalists driven in multitudes from their homes.[2]

We have seen that Abercromby, while acting in obedience to the Government, believed that there was no small measure of

[1] Camden to Portland, March 6, 1798.
[2] Ibid. March 30, 1798.

exaggeration in such descriptions of the country. Other accounts, however, which were even more highly coloured, came to England from the great placemen and borough owners, who were the real governors of Ireland, and they were no doubt intended to be laid before Pitt, if not before the King. Of these men, Beresford was perhaps the most powerful, and also the most violent. 'The country,' he wrote to Auckland, 'is in a desperate state; the seeds of rebellion are sown far and wide, and the Irish Directory have now so organised every part of the kingdom, that they can make them rise when they please. In Munster, Leinster, and Connaught, it is a popish plot; in Ulster, a Presbyterian plot; but in each case the end is the same—a separation from Great Britain, and a republican government. The popish and Presbyterian clergy are deep in the business, and the former have actually persuaded the people in Munster, that their salvation depends upon murdering and massacring every person who stands in their way; and they have established such a system of terror, that it is with the greatest difficulty any magistrate can be got to act, or any witness to come forward. They murder every man whom they suspect, in the slightest manner, to be inclined to give evidence against them.'

To such a state of society, Beresford contended that Lord Moira's system of conciliation, and Sir Ralph Abercromby's system of leniency, were utterly unsuited. The rebels 'show us how they think they can carry their point, viz. by terror; and that points out to us how to counteract them, and experience in the North confirms the fact. The people are persuaded that everything they have obtained has been given them through fear, and that it is fear of them alone, which prevents us from taking the same measures in the other three provinces which were taken in Ulster—that was forcing them to give up the arms they had plundered . . . by threatening to throw down or burn their houses and destroy their property; that stopped them at once, without the necessity of destroying more than a dozen houses. They had destroyed ten times as many, and had plundered innumerable others, and murdered many persons, and continued to do so until they found retaliation begin, when they stopped directly. They are now in Leinster, Munster, and Connaught, plundering and burning houses, murdering witnesses and magistrates ... and in the middle of the noonday, in the streets of towns, obliging, by force and threats, men to take their oaths and pay contributions for their plans. ... They murder people merely for the purpose of keeping up their system of terror. We are thus deprived of witnesses; we see and know everything that is doing, but cannot bring legal evidence to convict these people. ... If in such circumstances we should use the power which the law gives us to counteract such outrages by the military—even if we did in some instances exceed the law—it is probable that a dozen acts of severity may have happened on our side—how many hundreds have been performed by the rebels? ... How many of the military have been shot within six months, and not one of their murderers brought to punishment?'[1]

We have had much evidence, in the course of the present work, that the political sentiments of the main body of the Irish gentry differed widely from those of the great borough owners who controlled the Parliament; that they viewed with impatience and disgust the prevailing system of corrupt monopoly, and that up to the date of the outbreak of the war, and even up to the recall of Lord Fitzwilliam, they would have gladly accepted Grattan's policy of a moderate reform, and an abolition of the chief remaining religious disqualifications. Their sentiments, however, were now materially changed. A considerable but much diminished body still followed Grattan. Some were in sympathy with the United Irishmen, and looked forward either with hope or with acquiescence to a separate republic; others, panic-stricken by the turn which events had taken, both in France and Ireland, had lost all faith in reform, and had convinced themselves that there was no longer any prospect of a popular Government in Ireland, consistently with the maintenance of order and the security of property, while a few had begun to look forward to a legislative Union as the only possible solution. A curious incident, which has never been related, but which at this time greatly occupied the Government, throws some light upon this subject, and at the same time brings into

---

[1] *Auckland Correspondence*, iii. 401-405. This letter was written April 10. In a letter written a month later, he says: 'At present the quiet which appears in certain parts is deceptive. Where the country is organised, quiet appears. Where the organisation is going on, there is disturbance. It appears in Kildare there are complete regiments.' (*Auckland Correspondence*, iii. 412.)

clearer relief the character and opinions of a remarkable man, with whom we have been already concerned.

Among the suspected persons in England was a gentleman named Bell, who was known to be on intimate terms with Arthur O'Connor. His letters were seized or intercepted, and the Duke of Portland was startled to find among them a correspondence from General Knox. The letters are not disclosed, but they showed that Knox was a warm friend both of Bell and of Arthur O'Connor; and it is evident from the description of them that he had written with perfect candour, and had expressed very fully his contempt for the men and the system of government that prevailed in Ireland. Knox, from his connections, his abilities, and his military command, was one of the most important persons in Ulster. He had been largely employed by the Government in drawing up plans for the defence of the province, and we have seen, from his letters to Pelham, how intimate he at one time was with the Chief Secretary, and how ready he was to counsel the most drastic measures of repression. Portland asked with dismay, whether this distinguished general was among the traitors?[1]

Camden wrote two letters on the subject, which appear to me very interesting and significant, and quite consistent with the letters of Knox, which the reader has already perused. He in the first place expressed, in the strongest terms, his perfect confidence in the integrity of Knox, and he desired that the discovery of the correspondence should be most carefully concealed, lest any breath of suspicion should attach to him. Knox, he said, was a very able and honest officer, of great influence in the North, and of the highest personal honour; but he was 'a man of speculative and capricious independency;' of 'a busy speculative mind;' indiscreet, and apt to communicate his ideas much too freely. Camden then adds some general remarks, which, when due allowance is made for the point of view from which he naturally wrote, are not a little instructive. 'I know that at the beginning of the French Revolution there was much free and theoretic speculation here, not only on general political topics, but particularly on the state and relative situation of Ireland, and I am confident

[1] Portland to Camden, March 7, 1798.

that if the French Revolution had taken a humane and genial turn, and had not degenerated into such a rapid succession of tyranny upon tyranny, the speculative minds among the educated and superior classes of this kingdom would have hearkened eagerly to democratic novelties. It is the failure of the French Revolution to produce happiness which has generated opposition to it here.' There was, however, another cause which had been lately changing the sentiments of the educated and propertied classes in Ireland. 'The great point which General Knox broadly states, that a revolution here would give the power of the country to the descendants of the ancient Irish, and destroy every vestige of British settlement, begins to open itself to all of English origin.' The opinions expressed by Knox, were not new or surprising to the Lord Lieutenant. 'He has often mentioned the decidedly mean opinion he has of the aristocracy of this country, and the necessity of such an Union of the two kingdoms, as would correct the flightiness of Ireland by the introduction of English sobriety.'[1]

Amid the blinding mists of passion, prejudice, and exaggeration that sweep over this dismal period of Irish history, one great change may be distinctly discerned. The movement which owed its origin in a great measure to the decline of theological fanaticism, which was chiefly originated by Protestants and freethinkers, and which aimed at the political union of Irishmen of all religious denominations, was gradually turning into a religious war; reviving fierce religious passions which had been for generations subsiding, and which had at last become almost dormant. Beresford spoke of Ireland as suffering from a Presbyterian plot, and also from a popish plot, but it was not possible that two such plots could co-exist in alliance, though it was quite possible that members of the two denominations might be blended in one political conspiracy. I have traced the beginning of the change which was taking place—the rise and rapid extension of the Orange movement; the attempts of some conspicuous loyalists to organise it for the defence of the country; the partial alliance between it and the Government;

[1] Camden to Portland (private), March 10, 19, 1798. There is also a letter on this subject from Wickham to Cooke, March 26, 1798. The reader may find some additional particulars about General Knox in Richardson's *History of the Irish Yeomanry* (1806).

the persistent efforts of the United Irishmen to goad the Catholic masses into rebellion, by representing the Orange society as a conspiracy to massacre them, and by representing the English Government as supporting it. The United Irish conspiracy when it passed into a perfectly ignorant Catholic population at once changed its character, and its original political objects almost disappeared. 'The popish spirit,' wrote Cooke, 'has been set up against the Protestants, by reporting every Protestant to be an Orangeman, and by inculcating that every Orangeman has sworn to exterminate the papists; to these fictions are added the real pressure of high rents from the undertakers of land, and high tithes from tithe proctors.'[1] Fanaticism was rapidly rising, and it was rising on both sides. 'The most alarming feature of the movement,' Camden wrote in April, is 'the appearance of the present contest becoming a religious one.'[2] Loyalty in Ireland was beginning more and more to rally round the Orange standard, and to derive a new energy and courage from religious passion. At the same time, the essentially popish character which the revolution was assuming in Leinster and Munster, had begun to shake the confidence of the conspirators in Ulster.

In a letter written a few weeks before the proclamation of martial law, Camden described the terror which the frequent murders were producing among the loyal classes, and expressed great fear that the juries in the approaching assizes would not have the courage to do their duty.[3] It is possible that the proclamation may have done something to check the panic, but it is at least certain that this foreboding was somewhat signally falsified. The spring assizes, which immediately preceded the outbreak of the rebellion, were, on the whole, very satisfactory, and their character was scarcely consistent with the representations that had been made of the state of the country. Camden at this time summed up in a few lines the condition of a great part of Ireland. In the King's County there were more signs of repentance than anywhere else in the South. One hundred pikes had been given up, and there were many convictions at the assizes. In Tipperary there was more open rebellion than

---

[1] *Auckland Correspondence*, iii. 392.
[2] Camden to Portland, April 23, 1798. [3] Ibid. March 11, 1798.

in other counties, but the outrages were now somewhat checked, though the progress towards quiet was slow. 'At the assizes which were held in Kildare, the juries in general did their duty; but there appeared no good disposition among the Catholics, as I am informed, during the trials, and it was reported to me that those juries who did not act with propriety were of that persuasion.' The Queen's County had been 'harassed with constant nocturnal pillage and many murders.' 'The assizes in this county were remarkably well attended, and if any fault is to be found in the administration of justice there, it is that the juries were almost too anxious to convict. Many very desperate villains were condemned and executed.' 'From the counties of Waterford, Cork, Limerick, Carlow, Kilkenny, Meath and Westmeath, all of which have been disturbed, I hear the most satisfactory accounts from the judges, of the behaviour of the juries.' The accounts from the North were also good, but Camden was not sanguine that there was a real political improvement, and he knew from secret intelligence that many and dangerous agitators were abroad. At the same time, he wrote, 'Your Grace ought to be informed that the general observation of those who have gone that circuit [Ulster], as well as other well-informed men, is, that a much better spirit pervades it. Industry is restored; trade is flourishing; there are great quantities of linen on their bleach greens, which was not the case last year, no outrages, and apparent content, and the judges and bar all declare that they never remember so much civil and so little criminal business upon that circuit.' In Connaught there were some disquieting signs. 'Very suspicious appearances were observed in the county of Galway, and I cannot do the gentlemen of that county too much justice. Upon the first rumour of the possibility of disturbance, they repaired to their houses. All sects and all religions united themselves, and have checked completely the system. . . . Mayo has been disturbed only in a trifling degree, and the rest of Connaught is yet quiet.'[1]

Other letters from different sources corroborate the statement, that the juries over a great part of Ireland no longer feared to convict, and that many of the worst criminals were detected

---

[1] Camden to Portland, April 23, 1798.

and punished.[1] I must not, however, omit to mention, that there is painful evidence that in at least one county, Orange fanaticism, and the blind passion and resentment produced by a long course of outrages, had begun to invade the law courts. The reader will have noticed a significant sentence in the letter of Lord Camden, which has been just quoted, relating to the Queen's County. This county had usually been one of the most prosperous, peaceful, and apparently best administered in Ireland, and it contained a large resident gentry, but for several weeks parties of savage banditti had been ranging through it by night, attacking and plundering houses, and committing many murders. McNally, though secretly in the pay of the Government, was the favourite advocate of the prisoners, and he wrote from Maryborough an earnest remonstrance to Cooke about the manner in which the trials in this county were conducted.

He wrote, he said, in court, with the shrieks of men, women, and children sounding in his ears. 'Thirteen men have received sentence of death—a sight most piteous, however just, and two of them are to die on Monday. . . . In my opinion, many of the convictions were not so much owing to conclusive evidence, as promptitude of juries, determined on making examples; for the defences set up by the prisoners were treated too often with inattention, laughter, and contempt; everything against them received as truth. In some cases the judge's authority could scarcely preserve the decorum necessary to a court of justice, and this conduct was severely felt, and bitterly complained of by the lower people to those in whom they could confide. I apprehend it has instilled more resentment than terror, and that they consider the sufferers under sentence, objects of vengeance rather than of justice.' In the Queen's County, McNally says, 'the plan of insurrection' was rather of the Defender than of the United Irishman type, though the latter—which was politically by far the more dangerous—would probably follow; and the fact that there was no subscription for

---

[1] See the statements of Cooke and Beresford (*Auckland Correspondence*, iii. 392, 401). Beresford says: 'Our gentry have acted well this assizes, . . . and I must say the Roman Catholics of property who have been on the juries have done their duty. There was but one man escaped as yet, who, in my opinion, ought not, and that by direction of the judge.'

lawyers to defend the prisoners, proved to him that the northern organisation did not yet exist. He added, 'The landed men in this county are strongly connected. In my judgment, they have strength and influence sufficient to quiet the people. Yet I never knew a peasantry bear a more inveterate antipathy to their superiors, owing, as I understand, to great oppressions under which many of them suffer; but I do not say this is general. I observe that in this county, the distinction between Protestant and papist is more inveterately and invidiously kept up than in any other place. Some gentlemen of fortune wore orange ribands, and some barristers sported orange rings with emblems. Such ensigns of enmity, I assure you, are not conducive to conciliation. Are they necessary to any good purpose ? On several of the trials the witnesses were Roman Catholics, and a family of that persuasion beat and apprehended the leader of a most dangerous gang.'[1]

I will conclude this chapter by a few remarks illustrating the designs and the secret dispositions of the English Government towards Ireland at the eve of the rebellion. There is, I believe, no evidence that they at this time contemplated a legislative Union as likely to be introduced in the immediate future, or even that they had formed any fixed determination that the existing Parliament was to be the last in Ireland. It is indeed abundantly evident, that they looked forward to an Union as the ultimate solution of the Irish question ; that with that view they were determined, in accordance with the Irish Government, to maintain unaltered the borough system, which made the Irish Legislature completely subservient to the Executive; and that they wished Catholic emancipation, as well as parliamentary reform, to be adjourned till an Union had been carried. But in none of the confidential correspondence which took place at the time of the election for the Parliament which met at the beginning of 1798, is there, as far as I am aware, any mention of a legislative Union ; no opinion appears to have been as yet formed about the time or circumstances of introducing it, and beyond the lines that I have indicated, it is not, I think, true, that English Ministers were directing Irish policy with that object. In general, they allowed the administration of Ireland to be

[1] J. W. (Maryborough), April 8, 1798.

almost wholly shaped by the Irish Government; and even when they interfered with advice, they did so with little energy or persistence. When Fox and Lord Moira introduced into the British Parliament a discussion upon the military outrages, the Ministers replied that those matters were within the sole competence of the Irish Parliament and Government. If they resented Sir Ralph Abercromby's order, it was because it was certain to furnish a formidable weapon to the English Opposition; if they opposed an absentee tax, it was chiefly because it would affect men who had great political influence in England. They assisted the Irish Government, by intercepting the correspondence of suspected rebels, and by collecting evidence through confidential agents on the Continent, and they more than once assisted them by loans in the great financial crisis of the war. On the other hand, they insisted that a considerable though much diminished number of lucrative Irish posts should be bestowed on Englishmen, and they wished to make the Irish peerage in some measure a reward for English services. For the rest, they only asked that Ireland should not be an embarrassment; that England should derive trade advantages from her connection with her, and that Ireland should contribute larger forces to carry on the war, than were needed for keeping her in her allegiance.

The advice of the English Government was usually in the direction of moderation, and especially in the sense of conciliating the Catholics. To separate as much as possible the Catholics from the Dissenters, and the Catholic question from the question of reform, was for some considerable time the keynote of the Irish policy of Portland. He was much struck with the fact that Protestant Ulster was the most disaffected of the four provinces; that at least five-sixths of the leaders of the United Irishmen were Protestants; that Munster, though now profoundly disturbed, had shown itself perfectly loyal during the French expedition at the end of 1796; that Connaught, the most purely Catholic province in Ireland, was the one province which was still almost untainted. He believed with good reason that the genius of the Catholic Church was essentially opposed to the revolutionary spirit, and that the higher clergy, at least, were sincere in their hostility to it, and he probably hoped that the influence of the papacy might contribute something to the peace of Ireland.

The great French war which was raging, had among its other consequences produced, for the first time since the Revolution of 1688, a close and friendly communication between the English Government and the Vatican. In 1794 the 12th Lancers had gone from Corsica to Civita Vecchia, where they remained for three months, mounted guard, and discharged other garrison duty. Their officers were presented to Pius VI., who took one of their helmets in his hands and blessed it, and who on the departure of the regiment gave each commissioned officer a gold medal, and each non-commissioned officer a silver one, as an expression of his gratitude for the excellent behaviour of the English troops.[1] Lord Hood's fleet, when excluded from the other ports in the Mediterranean, was, with the approval of the Pope, provisioned in the papal dominions.[2] Burke at this time strongly urged the policy of establishing a formal diplomatic connection with Rome. 'I would,' he wrote, 'if the matter rested with me, enter into much more distinct and avowed political connections with the Court of Rome, than hitherto we have held. If we decline them, the bigotry will be on our part, and not on that of his Holiness. Some mischief has happened, and much good has, I am convinced, been prevented, by our unnatural alienation.'[3]

The English Ministers were not prepared to face the outcry which might have followed such a step, and it was still forbidden under an unrepealed statute of Elizabeth; but it is a remarkable and little known fact, that in the reign of George III. a real though unofficial diplomatic connection subsisted for some years between London and the Vatican. The English representative was Mr.—afterwards Sir John—Hippisley, who had been at-

---

[1] See Cannon's *Historical Records of the British Army*, 12th Royal Lancers, p. 19. Sir J. Hippisley, *Substance of Additional Observations intended to have been delivered in the House of Commons on May* 13 *or* 14, 1805, pp. 93, 94; Hippisley's *Statement of Facts presented to Pius VII.* pp. 73, 74; Bullen's *Historical Outlines of Political Catholicism*, pp 92, 93. In 1799 British sailors cleared the papal dominions of their enemies the French, and British marines were sentries at Rome till the evacuation by the French.

[2] Sir J. Hippisley, *Substance of a Speech on the Motion of the Right Hon. H. Grattan*, April 24, 1812 (with Appendix), pp. 102–104.

[3] This letter was written Oct. 10, 1793, to Hippisley. See his *Substance of Additional Observations*, pp. 94, 95.

tached to the embassy at Naples, and who negotiated at Rome, not only on the common interests of the two Powers in their struggle with France, but also on various matters connected with the interests of the Catholic subjects of the King. The regulation of the Catholic churches in Corsica and Minorca; the appointment of a bishop in St. Domingo, and the nomination of the superiors of the British and Irish seminaries at Rome, were all made matters of very amicable arrangement, and Hippisley succeeded in obtaining from Cardinal Antonelli an assurance, that no friar should in future be appointed to the Irish episcopacy.[1] His position was clearly recognised in letters of the Congregation de Propaganda Fide, and of the Congregation of State;[2] and on his recommendation, the Pope in 1793 sent over to London, Monsignor Erskine, a member of the great Scotch family of Mar, and the grandson of an Earl of Kellie, as resident at the Court of England. Erskine was not of course officially recognised, and his mission was not generally known, but he appears to have been received unofficially at Court, and he resided in London for several years.[3] Bishop Douglas, the Catholic prelate who presided over the London district, had previously held confidential communications with Lord Grenville;[4] and Hippisley, after his return to England, was much employed in negotiating with the Irish prelates. Catholic chaplains were appointed, under the royal sign-manual, for the new Franco-Irish brigade in the English service.[5] At

[1] *Castlereagh Correspondence*, iii. 82, 83, 89, 92, 117; Hippisley's *Substance of a Speech*, May 18, 1810, pp. 24, 25; Hippisley's *Letters to Lord Fingall*, pp. 68, 69; *Statement of Facts presented to Pius VII.* (1818), pp. 66, 67.

[2] Hippisley's *Statement of Facts presented to Pius VII.* (1818), p. 68. Hippisley adds: 'After two centuries and a half, during which no political or ecclesiastical intercourse between the two Courts was permitted, or at least avowed, with an exception to a few letters which had passed between the Cardinals de la Lanze and Buoncompagni, and the late Mr. Dutens, at that time appointed Secretary of Embassy to the Court of Spain, Sir J. H. had the gratification of finding that, through his own instrumentality, this state of estrangement was interrupted and an intercourse revived.

. . . He had also the gratification of having his conduct on that occasion distinctly approved, both by the Government of his own country and that of his Holiness.' The earlier communications referred to in this passage, were in 1777 and 1786. Hippisley's pamphlets, and his letters in the third volume of the *Castlereagh Correspondence*, throw much light on this curious page of eighteenth-century history.

[3] Several interesting particulars about Monsignor Erskine and his mission will be found in Moroni, *Dizionario Ecclesiastico*, tome xxii. (Erskine). See, too, *Castlereagh Correspondence*, iii. 87, 88.

[4] *Castlereagh Correspondence*, iii. 88.

[5] Hippisley's *Statement*, p. 126; *Supplementary Note*, p. 66.

the suggestion of Hippisley, the Irish prelates introduced into the ordinary catechism employed in Ireland, some additional clauses, enforcing the duty of obedience to the civil power.¹ In the Canadian Catholic Church, the King seems to have virtually possessed the nomination of the bishops;² and when the Cardinal of York, the last direct heir of the Stuarts, was plundered by the French, he was relieved by a liberal pension from George III.³

All these things show the very friendly relations that subsisted between the Vatican and the Court of St. James, in spite of the strong sentiments of George III. about Catholic emancipation. The English Ministers saw in this good understanding, a powerful instrument for one day pacifying Ireland. Archbishop Troy appears at this time to have been much suspected by the Irish Government, and his letters were opened at the Post Office. Among them was found one from Monsignor Erskine, urging the Archbishop 'to prevail on his brethren and his flock, to exert themselves on behalf of the law and Government.' Camden communicated this gratifying fact to Portland, but he found that Portland was already aware of it, for Monsignor Erskine had been in communication with the Ministers, and had informed them of what he had written.⁴ In reply to one of the letters that have been quoted, Portland wrote that, 'notwithstanding the very unpromising return which was made by the Catholic proprietors of the Bank to the liberality which the Parliament has manifested in the course of the session to the Seminary of Maynooth, the meritorious and exemplary conduct of the whole province of Connaught' induced him to recur to a suggestion which he had before made, that it would be in a high degree useful to the State, to make a provision for the Catholic clergy.⁵ In another letter he wrote, that he had been informed of 'the spoliation and sacrilege which had been committed in several of the Roman Catholic chapels, for the express purpose,' as he believed, 'of exasperating the lower orders of these people against the present Establishment of Government;' and he suggested that the Irish Government should offer

---

¹ *Castlereagh Correspondence*, iii 134–136.
² Hippisley's *Letters to Lord Fingall*, p. 68.
³ *Castlereagh Correspondence*, ii.
332; iii. 14–16, 385, 386.
⁴ Portland to Camden, April 20, 1798. Camden called Erskine the Pope's Nuncio.
⁵ Ibid. March 20, 1798.

rewards for the discovery of the perpetrators of such outrages.[1] At the same time, he desired to encourage, as much as possible, all voluntary loyalist efforts in Ireland, even when they assumed an ultra-Protestant character. From two quarters, he said, he had heard 'that an association is formed by the Orangemen of Ulster, which consists already of 170,000 persons, and has been joined by all the principal gentry and well-affected persons of property in that province, for the purpose of protecting themselves against the combinations which have been formed by the United Irishmen;' and he added, 'It seems to me, that such a proof of energy on the part of the country, would be likely to do more than all the military force you could apply.'[2]

There is nothing said in the replies of Lord Camden, about the spoliation of Catholic chapels, and the letter of the Duke of Portland is, as far as I know, the earliest allusion to the revival of a form of outrage which, a few weeks later, became common.[3] The policy of paying the priests, though a profoundly wise one,[4] was naturally not acceptable to such men as Clare, Foster, and Beresford; and Camden, while stating that 'the servants of the Crown' were wholly opposed to it, added, 'I am indeed convinced that the strong prejudices now entertained by the House of Commons against the Catholics, would prevent Government from carrying the measure were it thought expedient to introduce it. Indeed, there seems much reason to think the Catholics in general are not hostile to these commotions, and that even some of the most loyal of them wait with some hope that a revolution in Ireland will restore them to those possessions, and that consequence, they have lost.' The strength of the Orange Society, also, was much less than Portland had been told. There were perhaps 40,000 men enrolled in it, and Camden thought that much caution must be used in dealing with

---

[1] Portland to Camden, April 2, 1798.

[2] Ibid. March 24, 1798.

[3] I have already mentioned that it was one of the Peep of Day Boy outrages.

[4] McNally, in a letter dated Sept. 22, 1802, gives the outline of a very elaborate and skilfully devised plan for paying the priests, which he had drawn up and submitted to the Government several years before the rebellion. He says that at that time he took great pains to ascertain the sentiments of the priests, and that he found the secular clergy favourable, but the regulars strongly opposed to a Government endowment; and he adds, the latter description of clergy were, in general, active fomenters of the rebellion. (I.S.P.O.)

them, for it was very dangerous for a Government to employ one party in the kingdom to put down another. 'I think them likely to increase,' he wrote; 'and although it is possible they may be useful, if the disorders in this country should take a still more serious turn, at present any encouragement of them much increases the jealousy of the Catholics, and I should therefore think it unwise to give an open encouragement to this party, although it is certainly not expedient to suppress them.'[1]

I must now draw this long and melancholy chapter to a close. Like that which preceded it, it is a record of steadily growing disorganisation; of many distinct forms of anarchy and discontent, combined and directed by one seditious conspiracy. Much of the evil had long existed in Ireland, though it had for some generations been steadily diminishing. It was quickened into a new vitality by the French Revolution, and by the near prospect of invasion, but it also owed a great part of its energy to enormous political faults, and to many acts of illegal and oppressive violence. We have now arrived at the brink of the catastrophe. A scene of blood was about to open, which not only left an indelible stain on the page of history, but also gave a fatal and enduring bias to the future of the nation.

[1] Camden to Portland, March 29, 1798

www.ingramcontent.com/pod-product-compliance
Lightning Source LLC
Chambersburg PA
CBHW051851300426
44117CB00006B/352